PRAJÑĀ-PĀRAMITĀ-RATNA-GUṆA-

(Sanskrit Recension A)

MS. K

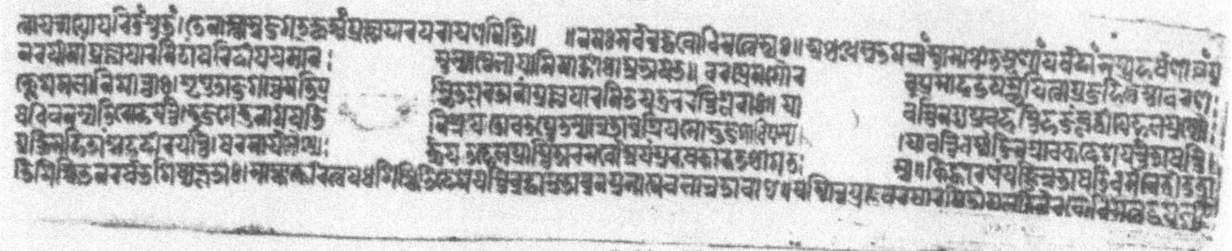

Folio 2B

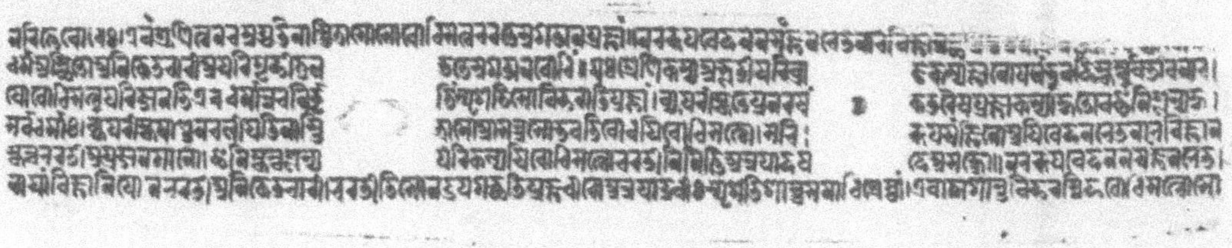

Folio 3A

*Note*:- As a whole MS. K has been preserved in a good condition (cf. 'Bibl. Notes' IA1: pp. xxiii-xxv). Fol. 2B begins with the final verse 21 of Rāhulabhadra's *Prajñā-pāramitā-stotra*, which runs from fols. 1B1 to 2B1 (cf. 'Bibl. Notes' IA1 N.B. 5): ... *stu*(2B1)*tvā yan mayopacitaṃ* ... *iti* // Then follow the homage to all the Buddhas and Bodhisattvas and the introductory passage (2B1-2)(cf. Skt. text p. 7). Verse I.1 starts in the middle of fol. 2B2: *vara-prema-gauravu-prasādu* ... (cf. Skt. text p. 8). Fol.3A begins with *na citte bodheḥ* (emend to *na citta bodhe*) ... (verse I.5b)(cf. Skt. text p. 9), and ends with ... *bodhisatvo so* (verse I.11b)(cf. Skt. text p. 11).

# *Prajñā-pāramitā-ratna-guṇa-saṃcaya-gāthā*

(Sanskrit Recension A)

Edited

With an Introduction, Bibliographical Notes and a Tibetan Version from Tunhuang

*by*

Akira Yuyama

CAMBRIDGE UNIVERSITY PRESS
CAMBRIDGE
LONDON · NEW YORK · MELBOURNE

CAMBRIDGE UNIVERSITY PRESS
Cambridge, New York, Melbourne, Madrid, Cape Town, Singapore,
São Paulo, Delhi, Dubai, Tokyo, Mexico City

Cambridge University Press
The Edinburgh Building, Cambridge CB2 8RU, UK

Published in the United States of America by Cambridge University Press, New York

www.cambridge.org
Information on this title: www.cambridge.org/9780521143202



First published 1976
First paperback printing 2010

*A catalogue record for this publication is available from the British Library*

*Library of Congress Cataloguing in Publication data*

Prajñāpāramitās. Ratnaguṇasañcayagāthā.
Prajñā–pāramitā–ratna–guṇa–saṃcaya–gāthā.

Revision of the author's thesis, Australian National
University at Canberra, 1970, with title: A study of
the Prajñā–pāramitā–ratna–guṇa–saṃcaya–gāthā.
Bibliography:
I. Yuyama, Akira.
BQ1920.Y86 1976 294.3'8 75–32910

ISBN 978-0-521-21081-2 Hardback
ISBN 978-0-521-14320-2 Paperback

*To the Memory of the late*
*Professor Dr. Franz Bernhard*

CONTENTS

T A B L E S

# PREFACE

The present work is a revised version of a thesis 'A Study of the *Prajñā-pāramitā-ratna-guṇa-saṃcaya-gāthā*' (3 parts) submitted for the degree of Doctor of Philosophy in the Australian National University at Canberra in 1970.

The principal aim of my thesis was to present a critical edition of the *Prajñā-pāramitā-ratna-guṇa-saṃcaya-gāthā,* using the best available manuscript, which is in the possession of the Asiatic Society at Calcutta (Inventory No. 10736: palmleaf MS. dated 1174 A.D.). I call this version Sanskrit Recension A. This text forms the main part of my book. It appears to preserve more original readings than the other MSS. and blockprint text (= Sanskrit Recension B). It is almost impossible to edit such a difficult text by listing only variant readings. I have therefore added somewhat detailed footnotes explaining the readings adopted in my edition.

In my thesis I have then added an edition of the hitherto unknown Tibetan version from Tunhuang (= Tibetan Recension A), which offers better readings in many verses. This text is to be found as a supplement to the present book. The critical apparatus had to be omitted. However, I have underlined the words which are different in the hitherto known version (= Tibetan Recension B). Variant readings in Recension A are recorded at the end of the supplement.

A preliminary edition of the Chinese version was also added in my thesis. In this book, however, it has been omitted for technical reasons. I have instead noted some critical remarks on the readings found in the Taishō edition (see 'Bibliographical Notes' III N.B. 11).

A descriptive grammar of the Sanskrit text, which formed Part II of my thesis, has been published by the Australian National University Press (1973). The *Prajñā-pāramitā-ratna-guṇa-saṃcaya-gāthā* is a fine example of Buddhist Sanskrit literature at its earliest stage. It appears to be the only known text among the *Prajñāpāramitā* literature that is written in the so-called Buddhist Sanskrit.

In the course of translating the text I have met quite a few verses where I should review my grammatical analyses. I plan later to publish a supplementary note on my grammar and an annotated translation of the text. An exhaustive index will be ready by then.

It was originally intended to give in this book a straightforward translation of the Sanskrit text. I have now abandoned this plan for three reasons. In the first place, a translation of such a complicated text with few notes makes little sense. Secondly, it is hoped that my textual notes would explain how I have adopted the readings. Thirdly, it seems somewhat superfluous to present another straightforward translation, as Professor Edward Conze's English translation has recently been published in book form, although it is true that the text on which his translation is based is different from mine.

There are a number of problems concerning the status of this literature, which will be discussed in the Introduction. There is no doubt that the *Prajñā-pāramitā-ratna-guṇa-saṃcaya-gāthā* is philologically and linguistically a very interesting and important text. The prime necessity is to have critically edited texts of the different recensions made available to specialists in the fields concerned.

On publishing a portion of the thesis, my thanks are above all due to my supervisor, Professor J. W. de Jong, on whose suggestions and with whose advice I undertook this work as a staff candidate for the degree within the Department of South Asian and Buddhist Studies at the Australian National University. I am grateful to Professor A. L. Basham of the Department of Asian Civilizations of the same university, who kindly acted as my supervisor for one year during Professor de Jong's leave in 1968-1969. I am also indebted to Mrs. Luise Hercus(-Schwarzschild), who went to great trouble to check my unidiomatic English text.

To Professor John Brough of Cambridge I owe a deep debt of gratitude for all the suggestions and advice he has given to me. Without his generous help this book would never have been published.

A study such as this necessarily owes much to the work of previous scholars, which has served as the basis for further insights. In particular, I am under a heavy debt to Professor Edward Conze through his pioneering works on the *Prajñāpāramitā* literature, and to the late Professor Franklin Edgerton through his monumental works on the Buddhist Sanskrit language.

To Professor Miyoko Nakano of Hokkaidō University at Sapporo, a former colleague of mine at Canberra, I have seldom turned in vain with regard to Sinological topics.

The Chinese and Japanese characters in the text were typewritten in Japan through the kind arrangements of Professor Nakano. Some old characters are difficult to find their way into print. In this book they appear in the abbreviated forms currently used in Japan. A comparative table of new and old characters is to be found on page lxxii.

On this occasion I would like to tender my sincere gratitude to Professor Heinz Bechert, who has kindly arranged for me to work as a Humboldt Fellow within his Department of Indian and Buddhist Studies at the University of Göttingen. It is thus my pleasant duty to express my gratitude to the Alexander von Humboldt Foundation of Bonn for having given me the opportunity to continue with my research work here in Göttingen.

Finally, I wish also to extend my cordial thanks to my teachers in Ōsaka, Tōkyō and Leiden, who have always watched over my work with their advice and encouragement.

For any errors of fact or heresies of opinion, needless to say, I am alone responsible.

There remains a pleasant task of thanking the Cambridge University Press for its generous support. The publication of this book has been made possible only by the fact that the Syndics of the Press offered to meet the whole cost of its publication. In this regard I owe a debt of gratitude to Mr. M. H. Black, Publisher to the University of Cambridge on the Executive Board of the Press. My thanks are also due to the Editor, Mr. Robert Seal of the Publishing Division of the Cambridge University Press, for the help he has given to me while the work was going through the press.

A word of gratitude is herewith recorded for my wife Hiroko, whose constant encouragement has enabled me to accomplish this book.

*Göttingen, August 1975* *Akira Yuyama*

# A C K N O W L E D G M E N T S

I am very grateful to those who have kindly enabled me to consult the Sanskrit and Tibetan materials in their possession. My sincere thanks are due to:

Asiatic Society (Calcutta) for having given me permission to publish the text found in the MS. in their possession (see 'Bibl. Notes' IA1: MS. K). I have used a microfilm of MS. K, which Professor de Jong of Canberra kindly lent to me (see below).

Bibliothèque Nationale (Paris) for sending me microfilms of the Tibetan MSS from Tunhuang (see 'Bibl. Notes' IIA2: Th, Ti, Tj).

British Museum (London) for sending me a microfilm of the Tibetan text of the manuscript Kanjur (see 'Bibl. Notes' IIB1b: E).

Deutsche Staatsbibliothek (Berlin and Marburg-Lahn) for sending me microfilms of the Tibetan texts (see 'Bibl. Notes' IIB2b: Ga, Gb, Gc; and IIB1b: M).

Historisches Staatsarchiv (Altenburg) for sending me a microfilm of the Tibetan blockprint text (see 'Bibl. Notes' IIB2b: W).

India Office Library, Commonwealth Relations Office (London) for sending me microfilms of the Tibetan MSS from Tunhuang (see 'Bibl. Notes' IIA1: Tb, Tc; and IIB3b: Ta, Td, Te, Tf, Tg).

International Academy of Indian Culture (New Delhi) for sending me a microfilm of the Tibetan text from the Urga edition through the kind arrangements of Professor Lokesh Chandra (see 'Bibl. Notes' IIB1a: U).

Professor J. W. de Jong of the Australian National University (Canberra) for letting me use the microfilm, in his possession, of the Sanskrit MS kept in the Asiatic Society at Calcutta (see 'Bibl. Notes' IA1: MS. K).

Kōyasan University Library (Kōyasan) for sending me photocopies of the Tibetan texts from the Sde-dge edition through the kind arrangements of Professor Shinten Sakai (see 'Bibl. Notes' IIB1a: D; IIB4: D'; and VIII 1-b1, 2-1, 3-1).

Sächsische Landesbibliothek (Dresden) for sending me microfilms of the Tibetan MSS (see 'Bibl. Notes' IIB3a: Sa, Sb; and IX 2a, 2b).

Seminar of Indian Philosophy and Sanskrit Philology, University of Tōkyō (Tōkyō) for letting me have microfilms of the Tibetan texts from the Lhasa edition through the kind arrangements of Dr. Shin-ichi Tsuda (see 'Bibl. Notes' IIB1a: L; and IIB4: L').

Tōyō Bunko (Tōkyō) for letting me have microfilms of the Tibetan texts from the Co-ne and Snar-thaṅ editions through the kind arrangements of Professor Zuihō Yamaguchi and Dr. Shin-ichi Tsuda (see 'Bibl. Notes' IIB1a: C, N; and IIB4: C', N').

University of Cambridge Library (Cambridge) for sending me a microfilm of the Sanskrit MS (see 'Bibl. Notes' IB1: MS. C).

University of Tōkyō Library (Tōkyō) for letting me have photocopies of the Sanskrit MSS (see 'Bibl. Notes' IB1: MSS. Ta, Tb, Tc).

# INTRODUCTION

## Prefatory

1. The *Prajñā-pāramitā-ratna-guṇa-saṃcaya-gāthā* (abbr. *Rgs* hereafter) has been somewhat neglected despite its philological and linguistic importance. One of the reasons for this was probably the unavailability of a critically edited Sanskrit text. The *editio princeps* by E. Obermiller was practically unobtainable until 1960 when it was photomechanically reprinted (cf. 'Bibl. Notes' IC1). Moreover, those scholars who were more interested in the Chinese sources overlooked the importance of the Sanskrit text. The Chinese version is very corrupt.

## Title

2. E. Conze has translated the title of the *Rgs* as 'Verses on the Accumulation of the Precious Qualities of the Perfection of Wisdom' (cf. para. 11 below). He understands the word *saṃcaya-* as meaning 'accumulation (of qualities)'.

3. The *Rgs* seems to have been widespread with a simplified title *Saṃcaya-gāthā / Sdud-pa tshigs-su bcad-pa*. In his *Prasannapadā* Candrakīrti has adduced one and a half verses from the *Rgs* under this title (cf. 'Bibl. Notes' VII, also para. 20-21 below). J. May renders it as 'Stances colligées' in his *Candrakīrti: Prasannapadā Madhyamakavṛtti* (1959), p. 130. May must have understood the word *saṃcaya-* as meaning 'collection (of verses)'. In his review of May's book J. W. de Jong has proposed a translation 'Stances sur l'accumulation' (*IIJ*, V, 1961, p. 164), which seems to correspond to Conze's rendering.

4. J. Brough has suggested to me that the original intention of the title should be 'Verses Summarizing the Precious Merits of the Prajñāpāramitā'. The meaning of the word *saṃcaya-* is taken as 'summary' secondarily through 'collecting (the essentials)'. This is probably much the same as May (cf. para. 3 above). He does not think it inconsistent with the Tibetan translation of the title. It appears to be common to Obermiller's inference of the 'Prajñāpāramitā in verse' (cf. para. 12 below). Taking the status of this text into consideration (cf. para. 8-24 below), I am more inclined toward Brough's understanding of the title.

5. The Tibetan word *sdud-pa* (for Skt. *saṃcaya-*) in its title *Śes-rab-kyi pha-rol-tu phyin-pa yon-tan rin-po-che sdud-pa tshigs-su bcad-pa* means both 'summary' and 'collection, compilation'. It is therefore not very helpful to understand the original meaning. In fact, L. Feer has trans-

lated the Tibetan title *Śer-phyin sdud-pa tshigs-su bcad-pa* as 'Vers où sont resumées les matières de la Prajñâ-pâramitâ' in his 'Analyse du Kandjour' (1881), p. 201, while A. Csoma has originally given its English title as 'Verses collecting the contents of the Prajná-páramitá' in his 'Analysis of the Sher-Chin, etc.' (1836), p. 395.

6. To the Chinese version Fa-hsien has given a title *Fo-shuo Fo-mu pao-tê-tsang pan-jo po-lo-mi-ching* in full and *Fo-mu pao-tê-tsang pan-jo chia-t'o* in brief (cf. 'Bibl. Notes' III). One may take the meaning of the word *tsang* (for Skt. *saṃcaya-*) as a 'collection, storage (of qualities)', like Skt. *kośa-*, and pregnantly a 'womb', like Skt. *garbha-*, in which the 'embryo, foetus (of wisdom)' is brought up to perfection. As a matter of fact, in reconstructing the original title in his *Catalogue*, B. Nanjio has used the Sanskrit word *garbha-* for *tsang* (cf. 'Bibl.Notes' III N.B. 5, below).

7. The adherents of this sūtra are after all guided to reach the goal by means of 'accumulating' the qualities of the Prajñāpāramitā, which have been 'collected/compiled' and 'summarized/recapitulated' in the *Rgs*. It looks as though the interpretation of the title depends upon how to grasp the meaning of the word *saṃcaya-*. We shall find it more complicated, if we look into the problems concerning the canonical status of the *Rgs* within the *Prajñāpāramitā* literature.

Status

8. The status of the *Rgs* has not attracted much attention of specialists in Japan. In his article 'Yo ni Shiraretaru Bongo Butten' (1914) [= *Bunshū*, p. 460a], Unrai Wogihara has identified the Sanskrit text with the Chinese, but has classified it under the 'Miscellaneous works'. Ryūjō Yamada has noted the *Rgs* as a collection of the Prajñā-pāramitā-gāthā in a list of the extant Buddhist Sanskrit texts: 'Genson Bonbun Butten Mokuroku' (1929), p. *20*. The *Rgs* is considered to be a 'summary based upon the *Aṣṭasāhasrikā*' by Hajime Nakamura, 'A Critical Survey of Mahāyāna and Esoteric Buddhism' (1964), p. 66. In his *Bongo Butten no Shobunken* (1959), p. 85, Yamada briefly describes it as one of many versified summaries of the *Aṣṭasāhasrikā-Prajñāpāramitā* (abbr. *AsP* hereafter). Chizen Akanuma simply lists the title of the Chinese version with its Sanskrit and Tibetan titles in his book *Bukkyō Kyōtenshiron* (1932), p. 272. One finds similar enumerations by Tokumyō Matsumoto, *Die Prajñāpāramitā-Literatur* (1932), p. 8, and Ryūshō Hikata, *Suvikrāntavikrāmi-Paripṛcchā Prajñāpāramitā* (1958), p. XIX.

9. In his *Genshi Hannyagyō no Kenkyū* (1944), pp. 102-103, Kōun Kajiyoshi, quoting the Chinese version, states that the *Rgs* is a versified summary of the contents of the *AsP* and that it is to be considered as an 'interpretation', although it has the word *ching* ('*sūtra*') in its title (cf. para. 6 above). Therefore it has no canonical status in the *AsP*-group; cf. also K. Kajiyoshi, 'Butsumo Hōtokuzō Hannya Haramitsukyō' (1935), p. 344a-b. This may explain the reason why the Japanese translation, made by S. Taki, of the Chinese version is included not in the section of the canonical texts of the *Prajñāpāramitā* literature but in the commentary section of the *Kokuyaku Issaikyō* (see 'Bibl. Notes' VI 2).

10. For a brief description of the textual studies see Shōyū Hanayama, 'A Summary of Various Research on the Prajñāpāramitā Literature by Japanese Scholars' (1966), esp. p. 22 n. 28 and p. 26.

11. Edward Conze puts forward the points at issue in his book entitled *The Prajñāpāramitā Literature* (1960), pp. 16-17:

"A verse summary of this text [= *AsP*], or at least of its first 28 chapters, is called *Verses on the Accumulation of the Precious Qualities of the Perfection of Wisdom,* in 302 verses in irregular Vasantatilaka metre. Many of the early Mahāyāna Sūtras exist in two forms, in verse and in prose. Usually the verse form is the earlier of the two. The original *Ratnaguṇasaṃcayagāthā* is now lost. All we possess is Haribhadra's revision, which to some extent brings the text in line with the chapter divisions of the *Aṣṭasāhasrikā,* as they existed in the 8th century.

"The status of this work is not quite clear. There are three possibilities: 1) The verses formed originally part of the *Aṣṭa,* and were later on separated. 2) The verses are the original form of the *Aṣṭa.* 3) The verses have been made up afterwards. It is very difficult to come to a decision on this, because, whereas in some instances the correspondence between *Rgs* and *A* is nearly literal, in others where the text of *A* is summed up or rewritten, it sometimes appears that the text of *A* is prior to *Rgs*, because *Rgs* is elliptic and unintelligible without reference to *A*.

"In chapters 1 to 28, the *Rgs* follows the text of *A* fairly closely. There are, however, even in that section a number of verses, i.e. 31, or 36, one seventh of the total, which have no counterpart in our text of *A*. These are iii 8, v 2(?), 5-8, vii 7, ix 1, xii 6-9, xiv 1 (?), xix 3-5, xx 5-7, 11, 12(?), 13, 14(?), 15, 16(?), 17-20, xxi 8, xxii 6, xxiii 1, 3, xxiv 2, 6, xxvi 2, 3, xxvii 8. On the other hand, the following passages of *A* are unrepresented in our text of *Rgs*: ii 33-4, 41; iii 50-57, 10; 75-80, 82-92; v 102-112, 114-122; vi 138, 12-142, 12; 143, 3-150, 11; 161-169; vii 170-1; viii 196-9; ix 200, 201-211, 5; x 221-230; xi 235-238, 240-242, 244-248; xii 257, 20-281, 8; xiii 281-283, xvi 312-321, xix 357-360, 365-369, xxii 405-409, xxiii 410-413, 414-415, xxiv 417-420, 421-423, xxv 428-430, xxvi 434-435, xxvii 444-446, 449, 19-452, 9; xxviii 457-458, 459-466, 471-474, xxix 475-xxxii 529. There are roughly 240 out of 529 pages, or

> between one half and one third of the total.
> "The verses which are given under chapters 29 to 32 of *Rgs* do not at all correspond to the text of *A*. Chapters 29 to 31 describe the five *pāramitās*, beginning with the *dhyānapāramitā* and ending with the *dānapāramitā*, while chapter 32 first of all explains in 5 verses the rewards of practising the six perfections, with verse 6 forming the conclusion of the whole work and giving its title."

Conze has also discussed the points briefly in his *Selected Sayings from the Perfections of Wisdom* (1954, 2nd ed. 1968), p. 12.

12. E. Obermiller suggests, however, that the *Rgs* in question represents a summary of the 'Prajñāpāramitā in verse', its *gāthā* portion, similar to the *gāthās* of the *Laṅkāvatārasūtra* and those of the *Daśabhūmikasūtra* (see 'Introduction' to his edition, p. 3). He believes that the text revised by Haribhadra, as is stated at the end of some of the texts representing Recension B, has most probably been arranged in accordance with the chapters of the *AsP* (see *ibid.*, p. 4). In favour of Obermiller's view, one can draw attention to the fact that no Tibetan text, except the one found in the Chinese blockprint at his disposal, is divided into chapters.

13. According to the final colophon of the Sanskrit Recension A, i.e. MS. K (see 'Bibl. Notes' IA1), the text is the 84th chapter of the *Śatasāhasrikā-Prajñāpāramitā* (abbr. *ŚsP* hereafter), of which the Sanskrit text has only 72 chapters (cf. 'Bibl. Notes' IA1 N.B. 9-11). Moreover, four out of the five MSS of the Tibetan Recension A (or Tunhuang Recension) state that the text is a chapter of the *ŚsP*, and one of them clearly states that it is chapter 84 of the *ŚsP*.

14. The number '84' reminds us of the fact that chapter 84 of the Tibetan version of the *Aṣṭādaśasāhasrikā-Prajñāpāramitā* (abbr. *AdP* hereafter) is exactly identical with Recension B of the Tibetan version of the *Rgs* (cf. 'Bibl. Notes' IIB4).

15. At a very early stage in its history the *Rgs* must already have been possessed of canonical characteristics, but may not have been regarded as a text of great importance for a long period. It obtained definite canonical status at some later stage, by the time the *AsP*, *AdP* and *ŚsP* had all established their firm status within the *Prajñāpāramitā* literature. It was at this stage that the tradition split into factions —— as to which group the *Rgs* should belong to. The

adherents of the *AsP* have then applied the chapter-divisions of the *AsP* to the *Rgs*. It is to be noted that the contents of the two texts do not entirely correspond to each other (cf. para. 11 above). The *Rgs* is no summary of the *AsP*, and has no commentarial feature whatsoever.

16. So far, chapter 84 of the Tibetan *AdP* is a clear evidence of this development (cf. 'Bibl. Notes' IIB4 N.B. 3). The devotees of the *AdP* have interpolated the *Rgs* into the *AdP*. A rapid development must have taken place within the sphere of Tibetan Buddhism. It is perhaps worthwhile noting that the *Rgs* has been the most important canonical text for the Źi-byed-pa School which was established in Tibet by a Southern Indian, Pha-dam-pa saṅs-rgyas by name, in the twelfth century A.D.; see Kōhō Hashimoto, *Mōko no Ramakyō* (1942), p. 65. For the Źi-byed-pa School see further H. Hoffmann, *Die Religionen Tibets* (1956), pp. 129-130 (with reference).

17. The compilers of the Ōtani Kanjur Catalogue (1930-1932), however assume (p. 219 n. 1) that chapter 84 of the Tibetan *AdP* (Peking No. 732) has been separated and become an independent text as the *Rgs* (Peking No. 735). Cf. also E. Obermiller, *History of Buddhism by Bu-ston*, II (1932), p. 49 n. 330.

*Rgs* revised by Haribhadra?

18. All the Sanskrit MSS which belong to Recension B (see 'Bibl. Notes' IB), the hitherto known text, as edited by E. Obermiller and P. L. Vaidya, contain two verses attributed to Haribhadra. The verses are written in the metre called *śārdūlavikrīḍita* (ed. Obermiller, pp. 123-125; ed. Vaidya, p. 397; Taki's Japanese translation of the Chinese version, pp. 27/373-28/374). However, the Tibetan version of the two verses is to be found only in the bilingual blockprint text X (see 'Bibl. Notes' IB2). It is stated in the second verse that the corrupt text has now been revised by Haribhadra himself.

19. It is to be noted that the name Haribhadra (Seṅge bzaṅ-po) is mentioned only in the final colophons of the Chinese blockprint texts of the Tibetan version (see 'Bibl. Notes' IIB2b), and in those of the two Tibetan MSS (see 'Bibl. Notes' IIB3a).

20. Also to be noted is the fact that in his *Prasannapadā* (ed. L. de La Vallée Poussin, pp. 166.11-167.2 and 167.4) Candrakīrti (see para. 21 below), quotes one verse (*Rgs* XX 5) and one pāda (*Rgs* II 3d)(cf. 'Bibl. Notes' VII).

21. Candrakīrti is generally believed to have lived at the beginning of the seventh century A.D.; see M. Winternitz, *Geschichte der indischen Litteratur*, II (1920), p. 251 (English edition, p. 363; Nariman's English version, p. 90; Japanese edition, p. 323); E. Frauwallner, *Die Philosophie des Buddhismus* (1956), p. 241; Mochizuki's *Bukkyō Daijiten*, VIII (1958), p. 87a, 'Gesshō', s.v. Candrakīrti is dated about 600-650 A.D. by S. Yamaguchi in his *"Jōmyōkuron" to Nazukuru Gesshō-zō: Chūronshaku*, I (1947), p. IV. His date is put as far as the sixth century A.D. by C. Regamey, *Buddhistische Philosophie* (1950), p. 57, by E. Lamotte, *Histoire du bouddhisme indien* (1958), p. 657, and by R. H. Robinson, *Early Madhyamika in India and China* (1967), p. 27. In his *Studies in the Buddhistic Culture of India* (1967), p. 163, L. Joshi says: 'As Bhāvaviveka lived about the second half of the sixth century A.D. and was a contemporary of Dharmapāla, the immediate predecessor of Śīlabhadra (cir. 640 A.D.) at Nālandā, Candrakīrti, who criticises Bhāvaviveka, may be placed between 560-620 A.D.' Candrakīrti is roughly dated 600-700 A.D. by L. Joshi in the same book on p. 443. According to J. May, *Candrakīrti: Prasannapadā Madhyamakavṛtti* (1959), p. 5, Candrakīrti composed his *Prasannapadā* about 600 A.D.; see also J. Filliozat, *L'Inde classique*, II (1953), para. 2021 (p. 379). Cf. also E. Obermiller, *History of Buddhism by Bu-ston*, II (1932), pp. 134-136.

22. There are two main theories concerning the date of Haribhadra. He is considered to belong to the tenth century A.D. by C. Regamey, *Buddhistische Philosophie* (1950), p. 65, and J. Filliozat, *L'Inde classique*, II (1953), para. 2019 (p. 377). According to Bu-ston's *History of Buddhism*, translated by E. Obermiller, II (1932), pp. 156-159, Haribhadra should have lived in the ninth to tenth centuries A.D. This does not seem to be acceptable, because one of his works was translated into Tibetan by Dpal-brtsegs who played an active role in compiling the Ldan-dkar-ma Catalogue at the beginning of the ninth century (cf. 'Bibl. Notes' IIB1 N.B. 3). In fact, Haribhadra lived in the latter half of the eighth century A.D., according to Tāranātha's *History of Buddhist Doctrine*, ed. by A. Schiefner (1868), pp. 166.22-167.10 and translated by A. Schiefner (1869), pp. 219-220, Japanese translation made by E. Teramoto (1928), p. 296, English translation made by Chimpa and A. Chattopadhyaya and edited by D. Chattopadhyaya (1970), p. 277, and also according to Sum-pa mkhan-po's *History of Buddhism*, ed. by S. C. Das, Part I (1908), p. 113.16-19 (text), also p. cxix (index under 'Seṅ-bzaṅ'); cf. Mochizuki's *Bukkyō Daijiten*, X (1963), pp. 824b-825a, and L. Joshi, *Studies in the Buddhistic Culture in India* (1967), pp. 203-204. Haribhadra is dated about 770 A.D. by E. Conze, *The Prajñāpāramitā Literature* (1960), p. 120. For the date of Buddhaśrījñāna, a pupil of Haribhadra, see 'Bibl. Notes' VIII 2 N.B. 1. Both Haribhadra and Buddhaśrījñāna wrote commentaries on the *Rgs* (cf. 'Bibl. Notes' VIII 1 and 2).

23. We have five recensions of the *Rgs* at our disposal: two Sanskrit (A and B), two Tibetan (A and B), and one Chinese. Recension A (both Sanskrit and Tibetan) contains more original forms than Recension B (both Sanskrit and Tibetan). The latter is more corrupt. The Chinese version represents a quite different recension, or rather the most corrupt text (cf. 'Bibl. Notes' III N.B. 2-3). It is, however, note-

worthy that the different recensions offer many variant readings, and yet every recension contains almost exactly the same number and order of verses.

N.B. It may be somewhat misleading to use the term recension in such a case, and confusing to use the signs A and B for both the Sanskrit and Tibetan versions. I should also have adopted the word Indian or Indic instead of Sanskrit. I have left them unchanged for technical reasons.

24. Here arises the question whether it is true that all we possess now is Haribhadra's revision (see para. 11 above). How could the text revised by Haribhadra have obtained its canonical status in the *AdP* or *ŚsP*? Did the celebrated Ācārya not know of the existence of the better recension? Has the revised text simply become corrupt in the course of tradition? I would suggest that Recension B has been ascribed to Haribhadra, and that the two verses were interpolated in order to authenticate his authorship.

Chronology

25. E. Conze compares in detail the contents of the *AsP* with those of the *Rgs* in his article 'The Composition of the Aṣṭasāhasrikā Prajñāpāramitā' (1952). He believes that the first two chapters of the *Rgs* represent the initial stage of the *Prajñāpāramitā* thought, and may well go back to 100 B.C.; cf. his 'The Development of the Prajñāpāramitā Thought' (1960). From this point of view, E. Conze has published his English translation of the two chapters, entitled 'The Oldest *Prajñāpāramitā*' (1958).

26. I am not yet able to make a genealogical 'stemma' of the recensions of the *Rgs*. A very careful comparative study of the recensions is needed (cf. 'Bibl. Notes' II N.B. 3 for some examples of confusions among the recensions).

Reference to *AsP*

27. Reference for each verse to the *AsP* (ed. R. Mitra, 1888) was first made by E. Obermiller in his edition of the *Rgs*. In his English translation of the *Rgs* (pp. 173-178), E. Conze has also given references to the contents of his English translation of the *AsP*. P. L. Vaidya has appended to his edition of the *Rgs*, pp. 399-404, a table of verses corresponding to his edition of the *AsP*.

Place of origin

28. As to the question of the place of origin of the *Prajñāpāramitā* literature, see R. Yamada, 'Hannya Kyōtenrui no Keiseisareta Jidai no Haikei' (1951); cf. J. W. de Jong's review in the *T'oung Pao,* XLII (1953), pp. 345-347. R. Yamada has reproduced this article in his book *Daijō Bukkyō Seiritsuron Josetsu* (1959), pp. 523-532. He makes a thorough study of the traditions, found in Buddhist literature, which place the origin of the *Prajñāpāramitā* literature in Southern India. The theory has been rejected after a detailed examination by E. Lamotte, *Le traité de la Grande Vertu de Sagesse,* I (1944), pp. 25-26 (note 1). It has also been rejected on account of lack of evidence by A. Hirakawa, *Shoki Daijō Bukkyō no Kenkyū* (1968), p. 105.

Language

29. E. Obermiller attaches much importance to the statement made by Haribhadra at the beginning of his commentary (see 'Bibl. Notes' VIII 1b) that the *Rgs* had first been preached in the dialect of Central India, or in the dialect of Magadha as described by Bu-ston; cf. E. Obermiller, *History of Buddhism by Bu-ston,* II (1932), p. 51. According to Obermiller, this could perhaps be taken as an indication that there must have existed a Prakritic *Prajñāpāramitā* in verse (see 'Introduction' to his edition of the *Rgs,* p. 5).

30. The *Rgs* composed in verse is a fine example of Buddhist Sanskrit literature at its earliest stage. It appears to be the only known text among the earlier *Prajñāpāramitā* literature that is written in the so-called Buddhist Sanskrit, or Buddhist Hybrid Sanskrit as F. Edgerton calls it; cf. also E. Lamotte, *Histoire du bouddhisme indien* (1958), p. 636. The language of the *Rgs* is perhaps even more corrupt and difficult than that of the *Mahāvastu-avadāna* (cf. Edgerton 1.73). It contains a great many forms and constructions peculiar to the *Rgs* --- prosodically, phonologically, morphologically, syntactically, stylistically, and lexically.

31. Morphologically, Middle Indic noun and verb forms are prevalent. Phonologically, the metre proves Middle Indic pronunciation of the text. It is written exclusively in the metrical scheme called *Vasantatilakā̆* in Sanskrit literature; cf. A. Yuyama, 'Remarks on the Metre of the *Rgs*' (1973).

32. Many forms have been Sanskritized orthographically in the course of transmission. It is, however, unnecessary (or rather incorrect) to edit the text in the expected Middle Indic spellings. In the *Rgs* are found a number of lexically or lexicographically interesting words, some of which are to be treated phonologically or morphologically; cf. A. Yuyama, 'Some Glossarial Notes on the *Rgs*' (1972).

33. In my *A Grammar of the Rgs* (1973) is given a brief description of every phenomenon of non-Sanskritic phonology and morphology found in the language of the Sanskrit text (Recension A). These linguistic features are important in regard to the formation of the text, and of the *Prajñāpāramitā* literature as a whole. It is to be noted, however, that they do not necessarily lay down a definite criterion to determine the date of this literature.

## B I B L I O G R A P H I C A L   N O T E S

For a short bibliographical description see Yuyama, *Indic Manuscripts and Chinese Blockprints* (1967), pp. 26-32, 110-111, and 118-119.

### I. Sanskrit Texts

Title in full: *Prajñā-pāramitā-ratna-guṇa-saṃcaya-gāthā.*

Title in brief: *Saṃcaya-gāthā.*

A. Recension A:

The recension represented by MS. K mostly offers better readings. Recension A has 303 verses, while Recension B has 302 (see Sanskrit text, chapter XII, verse 5 fn.).

1. Manuscript:

MS. K = No. 10736, Asiatic Society (of Bengal), Calcutta.

Palmleaf MS., 29 folios, 6 lines.

Size: 25·4 x 5·1 cm.

Date: Sunday, the full-moon day of the Month Agrahaṇa (Āgrahāyaṇa) of N.S. 295, under the régime of King Rudradeva (folio 29B5).

This date has been verified for 10 November 1174 A.D. by L. Petech, *Mediaeval History of Nepal (c. 750-1480)* (1958), p. 68; cf. also D. R. Regmi, *Medieval Nepal*, I (1965), p. 183.

Reference: H. P. Śāstrī, *A Descriptive Catalogue of Sanskrit Manuscripts in the Government Collection under the Care of the Asiatic Society of Bengal*, I (1917), pp. 26-27: No. 28; cf. also C. Chakravarti, 'Sanskrit Manuscripts in the Asiatic Society' (1959-1960), p. 666.

Studies: E. Conze, 'The Calcutta Manuscript of the *Ratnaguṇasaṃcayagāthā*', *IIJ*, IV (1960), pp. 37-58; F. Edgerton, 'The *Prajñā-Pāramitā-Ratna-Guṇa-Saṃcaya-Gāthā*', *IIJ*, V (1961), pp. 1-18.

N.B. 1) E. Conze has often misread MS. K and has omitted many important readings from it. F. Edgerton has relied entirely on Conze's readings.

2) MS. K is without doubt the best available one and appears to preserve more original readings than the other MSS. In some cases, however, MS. K shows more Sanskritized forms orthographically.

3) Folio 1 is a restoration by another (very bad) hand (= verses 1-10 of Rāhulabhadra's *Prajñāpāramitāstotra* or *°stuti*; cf. N.B. 5, below.

4) Folio 29B6 is also written by a different hand (pro-

bably a bookseller's?) stating the price of the MS. It is written in Newārī: *thva puṣṭakayā mula 18 rūpaiā,* 'The price of this book is 18 rupees'.

5) This is the only *Rgs* MS. that contains Rāhulabhadra's *Prajñāpāramitāstotra* (folios 1B1-2B1). I do not intend to give another edition of the *Stotra* in the present work, and I refer to E. Lamotte, *Le traité de la Grande Vertu de Sagesse de Nāgārjuna,* tome II (1949), pp. 1060-1065 (an extensive bibliography is to be found on page 1060 n. 2); cf. also W. Baruch, 'Compte rendu de Lamotte, *Le traité ... de Nāgārjuna,* I-II (1944-1949)', *Asia Major,* III, 1 (1953), p. 112. One can add some later references: E. Conze, 'Hymn to Perfect Wisdom', *The Middle Way,* XXV, 1 (1951), pp. 24-25 [= E. Conze, *Buddhist Texts through the Ages* (1954), pp. 147-149 (Text No. 142); also his *Buddhist Scriptures* (1959), pp. 168-171]; R. Hikata (ed.), *Suvikrāntavikrāmi-Paripṛcchā* (1958), pp. 1-2; P. L. Vaidya (ed.), *Aṣṭasāhasrikā-Prajñāpāramitā* (1960), pp. 1-2 fn. (Vaidya attributes it to Nāgārjuna!).

6) Only MS. K pays homage to all the Buddhas and Bodhisattvas (see my edition, p. 7 n. 2).

7) At the end of each colophon the number of verses in the chapter is given (e.g. '*gāthā 10*' at the end of chapter XII). This is not found in any other MS.

8) Each colophon of the first ten chapters enumerates 10 *bhūmis* (cf. Mvy 886-895) and 10 *pāramitās* (cf. Mvy 914-923) in the same order of the *Mahāvyutpatti.* In the Chinese version this enumeration is also found. It is certainly a later interpolation.

9) The final colophon states that the text is chapter 84 of the *ŚsP.* Conze assumes that the scribe has made a mistake (see his 'The Calcutta MS. of the *Rgs*', pp. 37-38). It seems to me that this is a much more complicated problem as mentioned above (see my 'Introduction', para. 13-17 above).

10) The final colophon reads as follows:

*śata-sāhasrikāyā bhagavatyā⟨h⟩ prajñā-pāramitāyāḥ sañcaya-gāthā-parivartaś caturaśītitamaḥ* (29B3) *samāptaḥ* // //

*ye dharmā hetu-prabhavā*
*[hetuṃ teṣ]āṅ tathāgato hy avadat* ⟨/⟩
*teṣāñ ca yo nirodha*
*evaṃ-vādī mahā-śramaṇaḥ** /

*deya-dharmo yaṃ (= 'yaṃ) pravara-mahā-yāna-*(29B4)*yāyinaḥ śākya-bhikṣu-sthavira-śrījñānasya yad atra puṇyaṃ tad bhavatv ācāryopādhyāya-mātā-pitṛ-pūrvaṅgamaṃ kṛtvā sakala-sattva-rāśer* (MS. *°-rāser*) *anuttara-jñā*(29B5)*na-phalāvāptaya iti* //

*mahā-rājādhirāja-śrī-rudradevasya rājye saṃvat 295 agrahaṇa-pūrṇa-māsyāṃ* (so MS. with anusvāra) *āditya-dine likhāpitam idaṃ pustakam iti* //

* MS. *°-śravaṇaḥ* (cf. BHSD p. 534b, s.v.). This verse is

also found in the MSS. belonging to Recension B (except X); for the so-called *Pratītya-samutpāda-gāthā* see A. Yuyama, '"Jūni Innenju" Oboegaki', *IBK*, XX, 1 (1971), pp. 448(48)-444(52).

11) Herewith I give a translation of the final colophon:

'Here ends the "Verses in Summary", the 84th chapter of the "Lord-Mother Perfection of Wisdom in 10000 (Lines)".

"Things which arise from causes ——
The Tathāgata has expounded the cause of them;
(That) which is the cessation of them ——
The thus-speaking Great Ascetic (has) also (expounded)

'This is the donation by Śrījñāna, the Elder Monk of the Śākyas (i.e. Buddhists), practising the best Great Vehicle. Whatever virtue (there may arise) here —— may it be for attaining the results of the supreme knowledge of a mass of all living beings beginning with (his) teacher, preceptor, mother and father.

'This book was made to be written on Sunday, the full moon day (i.e. 15th day) of the Month Agrahaṇa (Āgrahāyaṇa) of N.S. 295 (i.e. Sunday, 10 November 1174 A.D. as verified by Petech), under the reign of His Majesty King Rudradeva the Great King'.

12) In the edition some graphic characteristics are neglected (e.g. *sattva* for MS. *satva*). With regard to the script a more careful study is needed.

B. Recension B:

1. Manuscripts:

MS. Baroda = Serial No. 68, Accession No. 13278, Oriental Institute, Baroda.

Paper MS., 24 folios (600 granthas).

Reference: *An Alphabetical List of Manuscripts in the Oriental Institute, Baroda*, Vol. II (1950), XXXIV 'Bauddha-śāstram', pp. 1064-1065; cf. also P. L. Vaidya, *Mahāyāna-Sūtra-Saṃgraha*, Part I (1961), pp. X-XI (pp. XX-XXI in Hindī).

N.B. 1) To my regret I have not been able to consult this MS.

2) It was used by P. L. Vaidya as basic MS. for his edition of the *Rgs* (see 'Bibl. Notes' IC2).

3) As far as I can judge from Vaidya's edition, the MS. cannot be used as a basic text for a critical edition. It is very similar to MS. Tc. In some instances the two MSS. show the same corruptions. Both of them must have been copied from a common source.

4) There is a postscript by a scribe (see Vaidya's edition, p. 397). It is not a '*Lekhaka-praśasti*' as Vaidya calls it.

MS. C = No. Add. 1596, University of Cambridge Library, Cambridge.

Paper MS., 26 folios, 6 lines.

Size: 34·3 x 7·6 cm.

Date: N.S. 950 (= 1829/1830 A.D.).

Reference: C. Bendall, *Catalogue of the Buddhist Sanskrit Manuscripts in the University Library of Cambridge* (1883), pp. 133-134.

N.B. 1) Bendall, p. 133: 'The leaves have the double numberings, 1-26, and (more conspicuously) 71-96, so that the present MS. would have belonged to a series'.

2) This very bad MS. can be disregarded as we have more reliable MSS. at our disposal.

3) R. O. Meisezahl gives variant readings from MS. C in his review of the reprint of Obermiller's edition (see 'Bibl. Notes' IC1).

MS. Ta = No. 246 (old No. 32), Kawaguchi Collection, University of Tōkyō Library, Tōkyō.

Paper MS., 30 folios, 5 lines.

Size: 37·3 x 6.2 cm.

Date: not recorded (but modern).

Reference: S. Matsunami, *A Catalogue of the Sanskrit Manuscripts in the Tokyo University Library* (1965), pp. 93 and 202-203. I have not been able to see Matsunami's notebooks 'Catalogue of the Kawaguchi-Takakusu Collection of Sanskrit Manuscripts' kept in the University of Tōkyō Library.

N.B. 1) MS. Ta is used for my edition.

2) MS. Ta preserves the readings of Recension B fairly well.

MS. Tb = No. 247 (old No. 48), Kawaguchi Collection, University of Tōkyō Library.

Paper MS., 25 folios, 7 lines.

Size: 34·5 x 11·3 cm.

Date: not recorded (but modern).

Reference: Matsunami's Catalogue, pp. 93-94 and 202-203.

N.B. MS. Tb is another example of barbarously corrupt MSS. It can be disregarded.

MS. Tc = No. 248 (old No. 402), Takakusu Collection, University of Tōkyō Library.

Paper MS., 40 folios, 6 lines.

Size: 33·0 x 7·3 cm.

Date: not recorded (but modern).

Reference: Matsunami's Catalogue, pp. 94 and 202-203.

N.B. Though this MS. is beautifully written, there are many mistakes. As mentioned under the Baroda MS., some confusions and omissions are common to the two MSS. I have, however, consulted this MS. for my edition.

2. Chinese Blockprint Text (aabr. X hereafter):

Sanskrit text in Lañ-tsha (or Rañja) script with Tibetan transliteration and Tibetan translation in Dbu-can script in three lines alternately.

Paper, 109 folios, 3 lines (folios 1B-2A), 2 x 3 lines (folios 2B-109A).

Size (A.N.U. copy): 40·5 x 10·8 cm.

Copies are kept in the following places:

1) Leningrad (?).

Discovered by M. Tubiansky in the Monastery of Mañjuśrī (Mandzuśriin kiit), Mongolia.

Used by E. Obermiller for his edition of the *Rgs* as its basic text (cf. 'Bibl. Notes' IC1).

Reference: Obermiller's 'Introduction' to his edition, p. 3.

N.B. 1) From the fact that this copy was obtained by Tubiansky (1893-1943 A.D.), it is certain that it is not the only copy in Leningrad; cf. (a) *Katalog' knigam', rukopisjam' i kartam', na kitajskom', man'čžurskom', mongol'skom', tibetskom' i sanskritskom' jazykax', naxodjaščimsja v' Biblioteke Aziatskago Departamenta* (1843), p. 96: No. 577; (b) O. Böhtlingk, 'Über einige Sanskrit-Werke in der Bibliothek des Asiatischen Departements' (1845), Sp. 348-349: No. 577; (c) - - , 'Verzeichniss der auf Indien bezüglichen Handschriften und Holzdrucke im Asiatischen Museum der Kaiserlichen Akademie der Wissenschaften' (1846), p. 731: No. 120; (d) A. Schiefner, 'Bericht über die neueste Büchersendung aus Peking', *Bulletin*, IX (1852), Sp. 11: No. 120*apl*/*Mélanges*, I (1851), p. 406: No. 120*apl*.

2) See item 6 (New Delhi) below.

2) Berlin: Deutsche Staatsbibliothek.

Inventory No. Tib.Bl. 1.

Bought in Peking by E. Haenisch in 1929.

Reference: M. Taube, *Tibetische Handschriften und Blockdrucke*, Teil I (1966), p. 8: No. 14.

3) Canberra: Asian Studies Division, Australian National University Library.

Inventory No. (OS) BL1410.P7T5.

Reference: A. Yuyama, *Indic Manuscripts and Chinese Blockprints of the Oriental Collection of the Australian National University Library* (1967), pp. 19-25: Case No. I-1.

N.B. I have used this copy for my edition.

4) Kyōto: Ōtani University Library (?).

Reference: Ōtani Daigaku Toshokan, *Chibetto Daizōkyō Kanjūru Kandō Mokuroku* (1930-1932), pp. 219-221 (esp. p. 219 n. 5).

N.B. 1) The copy was not registered in the Library at the time of my visit in January 1966.

2) In the above Ōtani Kanjur Catalogue, p. 219 n. 5, is mentioned a K'ang-hsi edition of the *Rgs* which is not divided into chapters. To my regret, I have not been able to learn more about it.

5) London: Library of the School of Oriental and African Studies, University of London.

Inventory No. 82 825.

Reference: E. Conze, *The Prajñāpāramitā Literature* (1960), p. 57.

6) New Delhi: International Academy of Indian Culture.

Donated to Raghu Vira by the U.S.S.R. Academy of Sciences.

Reference: Sushama Devi, *Samantabhadracaryāpraṇidhānarāja* (1958), p. 9.

N.B. It is probably one of the copies kept in Leningrad (see item 1 'Leningrad' above).

7) Sendai: Tōhoku University Library.

Tōhoku No. 6774.

Reference: Y. Kanakura, R. Yamada, T. Tada and H. Hadano, *Chibetto Senjutsu Butten Mokuroku* (1953), pp. 465b-466a.

C. Critical editions:

1. Obermiller, E. (ed.), *Prajñā-Pāramitā-Ratna-Guṇa-Saṃcaya-Gāthā. Sanscrit and Tibetan Text (= Bibliotheca Buddhica,* XXIX)(Moscow-Leningrad: U.S.S.R. Academy of Sciences, 1937), 125 pp.

   Photomechanic reprint (Osnabrück: Biblio Verlag, 1970).

   N.B. 1) This *editio princeps* is based solely on the Chinese block-print X. After each verse of the Sanskrit text is given its Tibetan version. Reference for each verse to the *AsP* (ed. R. Mitra, 1888) has been made by Obermiller in this edition.

   2) Photomechanically reprinted with a Sanskrit-Tibetan-English Index by E. Conze (= *Indo-Iranian Reprints,* Vol. V)(The Hague: Mouton & Co., 1960), V, 157 pp. I have used this reprint for my edition. It is noted, however, by the editors of this series that the reproduction had to be made from a microfilm and has not come out as clearly as in the other volumes of the series (p. V); cf. F. Edgerton, 'The *Prajñā-Pāramitā-Ratna-Guṇa-Saṃcaya-Gāthā*', *IIJ,* V, 1 (1961), para. 1 (p. 1).

   3) Review of the reprint (1960): R. O. Meisezahl, *Oriens,* XVII (1964), pp. 289-301.

   4) E. Conze's Sanskrit-Tibetan-English index in the 1960 reprint edition has been incorporated in his *Materials for a Dictionary of the Prajñāpāramitā Literature* (Tōkyō, 1967).

   5) I have not been able to see E. Conze, *Dictionary to the Prajñāpāramitā Texts* (typescript, 1954), kept in the Library of the

School of Oriental and African Studies, London.
Reference: *Library Catalogue* (School of Oriental and African Studies), Vol. XXII, p. 55c: No. 96340.

6) The 1970 reprint appeared, to my regret, too late to be used in my edition.

2. Vaidya, P. L. (ed.), *Mahāyāna-Sūtra-Saṃgraha*, Part I (= *Buddhist Sanskrit Texts*, No. 17)(Darbhanga: Mithila Institute of Post-Graduate Studies and Research in Sanskrit Learning, 1961), pp. 352-404: Text No. 22 '*Ratnaguṇasaṃcayagāthā*', with critical notes.

N.B. 1) Based on the Baroda MS. (see 'Bibl. Notes' IB1) in comparison with Obermiller's edition. The Tibetan version is not given.

2) It is often very doubtful if the Baroda MS. has the readings which are found in this edition (cf. 'Bibl. Notes' IB1 N.B. 3). Many are apparently taken from Obermiller's edition or from the readings suggested by Conze and Edgerton without reference to the readings of the Baroda MS.

3) Vaidya has appended to this edition, pp. 399-404, a table of verses corresponding to the texts of the *AsP* edited by him.

3. Conze, E. (ed.), *A Collection of Prajñā-pāramitā Texts*, I: 'Ratna-guṇa-saṃcaya-gāthā in Sanskrit and Tibetan' (typescript, 1952), kept in the Library of the School of Oriental and African Studies, University of London, London.

Reference: *Library Catalogue* (School of Oriental and African Studies), Vol. XXII, p. 57c: No. 96341.

N.B. Towards the end of 1973 Professor Conze kindly sent me a xerox copy of a typescript of his tentative edition of the *Rgs*. It appears to be the one mentioned above. Parallel passages from MS. K and variant readings from various sources are given in the footnotes. To my great regret, however, it arrived at my hand too late to have it incorporated in my present book. (This xerox copy numbers 71 pages. It does not contain the Tibetan text edited by him.)

# II. Tibetan Texts

Title in full: *Śes-rab-kyi pha-rol-tu phyin-pa yon-tan rin-po-che sdud-pa tshigs-su bcad-pa.*

Title in brief: *Sdud-pa tshigs-su bcad-pa.*

N.B. 1) There are two recensions: Recension A (or Tunhuang Recension), and the hitherto known Recension B.

2) The recension represented by several MSS. from Tunhuang offers in most cases better readings (cf. 'Bibl. Notes' IIA1 N.B. 3 under MS. Tb). It often supports the better readings found in the Sanskrit Recension A (cf. 'Bibl. Notes' IA1 above). The Tunhuang Recension is very important for the textual history of the *Rgs* (cf. also 'Introduction' para. 13-15).

3) We must, however, note that the Sanskrit Recension A is not always confirmed by the Tibetan Recension A, and likewise the Sanskrit Recension B by the Tibetan Recension B, Some examples:

(a) Skt. A = Tib. B ≠ Skt. B = Tib. A:

XX 4d: Skt.A *agre samādhi sthiti*, 'abiding in the supreme concentration'<br>
= Tib.B *tiṅ-'dzin mchog-la gnas-śiṅ*<br>
[= Chin. 安住第一三摩地]<br>
≠ Skt.B *asmiṃ samādhi sthitu* (so V; O wrongly)<br>
= Tib.A *tiṅ-'dzin 'di-la gnas-śiṅ*

(b) Skt. AB = Tib. B ≠ Tib. A:

II 13b: Skt.AB *imāya vara-pāramitāya* (loc.)<br>
= Tib.B *pha-rol phyin-pa mchog 'di*<br>
≠ Tib.A *śes-rab pha-rol phyin 'di*

(c) Skt. A ≠ Skt. B = Tib. AB:

XXIX 12b: Skt.A *ākruṣṭu cāpy atihatāpy atha tāḍitā vā*<br>
≠ Skt.B *ākruṣṭu cāpi athavā eada tāḍitā vā*<br>
= Tib.AB *spyo-ba byas-sam 'on-te rtag-tu brdegs-kyaṅ-ruṅ*

(d) Tib. B gives a better interpretation:

XXXI 3b: Skt.AB *so śīla-artha guṇa-dharma-samanvitānāṃ*<br>
Tib.B *de-ni* (vv.ll. *'di-ni, de-yi*) *yon-tan chos ldan-rnams-kyi tshul-khrims don*<br>
but Tib.A *de-ni yon-tan chos don ldan-pa'i tshul-khrims yin*

(e) Skt. A supported only by Chin.:

XXIX 4b: Skt.A *deva-uttara-kurū* (acc.)<br>
= Chin. 北洲 (but cf. Skt. text XXIX 4b, fn.)<br>
but Skt.B *deva-uttama-purā* (acc.)<br>
Tib.A *lha-yi khaṅ-pa dam-pa*<br>
Tib.B *lha-yi groṅ-khyer mchog-tu*

4) The Tibetan texts (both Recensions A and B) have the same metrical scheme: 1 stanza consists of 4 pādas, each of which has 11 syllables; cf. J. Vekerdi, 'Some Remarks on Tibetan Poetry' (1952), p. 225.

5) No Tibetan text is divided into chapters with the exception of the bilingual Chinese blockprint text X (cf. 'Introduction', para. 12 above).

A. Recension A (or Tunhuang Recension):

N.B. 1) There are at our disposal five Tunhuang MSS. belonging to the Tibetan Recension A: MSS. Tb, Tc, Th, Ti and Tj. The other MSS. from Tunhuang belong to Recension B (cf. 'Bibl. Notes' IIB3b).

2) In the present book I have included as a supplement the text of Recension A. The critical apparatus had to be omitted, but I have underlined the words which are different in Recension B. Variant readings in Recension A are recorded as Appendix 5 at the end of the Supplement.

3) MSS. Tc, Th, Ti and Tj state that the text is a chapter from the *ŚsP*, and Tc clearly states that it is chapter 84 of the *ŚsP* (cf. 'Introduction', para. 13-17 above).

4) No MS. of Recension A records the name of its translator or a revisor. At this stage I am not able to give the date of this version (cf. 'Bibl. Notes' IIB1 N.B. 1-5).

1. Tunhuang MSS. kept in the India Office Library, Commonwealth Relations Office, London:

Tb = Ch.2.A, folios KA 1A-78B, 23·5 x 5·0 cm., 4 lines.

Reference: L. de La Vallée Poussin, *Catalogue of the Tibetan Manuscripts from Tun-Huang in the India Office Library* (1962), p. 43a: No. 111.

N.B. 1) MS. Tb is the only complete text of Recension A.

2) The title and the colophon give only the title of the text (cf. Appendices 1-2 to the Supplement).

3) De La Vallée Poussin thinks (p. 43b) that the translation in this MS. is worse than Ta (cf. 'Bibl. Notes' IIB3b). My view is quite to the contrary.

Tc = Ch.0066, etc., folios KA 2-3, 6-8, 11, 13, 15, 18, 20-22, 24, 26-34, 37-39 (25 folios), 41·0 x 8·0 cm., 5 or 6 lines.

Reference: De La Vallée Poussin's Catalogue, p. 43a-b: No. 112-1.

N.B. 1) Folios 2-3 (*Rgs* I 6b-22a), 6-8 (II 10b-V 3c), 11 (VII 2a-VIII 3c), 13 (X 5d-XI 4d), 15 (XII 4a-XIII 2d), 18 (XV 8b-XVII 2a), 20-22 (XVIII 2d-XX 11b), 24 (XX 20a-XXI 3c), 26-34 (XXII 3a-XXX 7a), 37-39 (XXXI 8b-final colophon).

2) The colophon (folio 39A4) states that the text is chapter 84 of the *ŚsP* (not *AdP*!)(cf. Appendix 2 to the Supplement).

2. Tunhuang MSS. kept in the Bibliothèque Nationale (Fonds Pelliot tibétain), Paris:

Th = No. 1442, folio ṄA 565A-B, 20·0 x 70·0 cm., 12 lines.

Reference: M. Lalou, *Inventaire des manuscrits tibétains de Touen-houang conservés à la Bibliothèque Nationale (Fonds Pelliot tibétain)*, III (1961), p. 58.

N.B. 1) MS. Th contains the beginning of the text up to I 25a.

2) The title (folio 565A1-2) state that the text is a chapter from the *ŚsP* (cf. Appendix 1 to the Supplement).

Ti = No. 1474, one large damaged folio bearing no pagination.

Reference: Lalou's Inventaire, III, p. 66.

N.B. 1) MS. Ti gives the text from XXXI 11c to the final colophon. The last part of the colophon is missing.

2) The colophon (verso, lines 1-2) states that the text is a chapter from the *ŚsP* (cf. Appendix 2 to the Supplement).

Tj = No. 1475, a very damaged fragment without pagination.

Reference: Lalou's Inventaire, III, p. 66.

N.B. MS. Tj gives only two lines on the verso (?). It reads the very beginning of the title, from which we learn that the text is a chapter from the *ŚsP* (cf. Appendix 1 to the Supplement).

B. Recension B:

1. Kanjur texts:

Translators: Vidyākarasiṃha, Dpal-brtsegs (Śrīkūṭa).

Date of translation: probably early ninth century A.D.

N.B. 1) After the title of the *Rgs* in Tibetan in the final colophon the Kanjur texts N and E do not give the name of translators, while the others mention thus: (C 21B4-5, D 19B7, L 215A3-4, P 22A8, U 19B7, M 29A2-3) *rgya-gar-gyi mkhan-po vidyākarasiṅha* (CL *vidyak°*, P *vadhik°*, M *vidhyakarsiṅha*) *daṅ / źu-chen-gyi* (L *bod-kyi*) *lo-tsā-ba* (M *lo-tsa-ba*) *bande* (LM *bandhe*) *dpal-brtsegs-*(P *-rtsegs-*)*kyis bsgyur-*(PM *rgyur-*)*ciṅ źus-te gtan-*(PM *btan-*)*la phab-pa'o* (D *-pa*) // 'Ācārya Vidyākarasiṃha of India and the Great Revisor (L: Tibetan) Lo-tsā-ba, the Reverend Dpal-brtsegs have translated, corrected and edited [this text]'; cf. F. A. Bischoff, *Der Kanjur und seine Kolophone,* II (1968), p. 328 (ad Mongolian Kanjur No. 767).

2) Vidyākarasiṃha translated more than twenty texts into Tibetan with the Tibetan translators who played an active role from the end of the eighth to the beginning of the ninth centuries A.D. Among them are famous translators, such as Ye-śes sde (Jñānasena) and Mañjuśrīvarman, who took part in compiling the *Mahāvyutpatti*; cf. E. Obermiller, *History of Buddhism by Bu-ston,* II (1932), p. 197. The *Mahāvyutpatti* is believed to have been written at the beginning of the ninth century A.D., probably two years after [not 'before' as mentioned in my bibliography of the Lotus Sūtra (1970), p. 88 n. 24] the compilation of the *Ldan-dkar-ma Catalogue* (cf. N.B. 3 below). For the chronology of the *Mahāvyutpatti* see T. Kagawa, '*Mahāvyutpatti* no Hensan Nendai ni tsuite' (1956); - - , '*Mahāvyutpatti* no Hensan Nendaikō' (1958); S. Sakai, 'Honyaku Myōgi Taishū no Nango-shaku *Pañjikā-Madhyavyutpatti* ni tsuite' (1955); W. Simon, 'Tibetan Lexicography and Etymological Research' (1965), pp. 93-95; G. Tucci, *The Tombs of the Tibetan Kings* (1950), p. 18; S. Yoshimura, 'Shoki Chibetto Bukkyō ni okeru Honyaku Keisei' (1958). For the names of Vidyākarasiṃha's Tibetan collaborators see, besides the indices to the catalogues of the Tibetan Tripiṭakas, S. Yoshimura, 'Tibetan Translators of the Tri-Pitaka' (1955/repr. 1974), p. 1b/63b (Klu'i dbaṅ-po), 14b/76b (Dpal-gyi lhun-po'i sde), 15a/77a (Dpal-brtsegs), 26a/88a (Ye-śes sñiṅ-po), 26b/88b (Ye-śes sde), 36a/98a (Kha rin-po-che).

3) Vidyākarasiṃha translated and revised some other texts with Dpal-brtsegs, and one text with Klu'i dbaṅ-po (Nāgendra)(cf. N.B. 2 end, above). These two Tibetan translators are well known because they compiled the *Dkar-chag Ldan-dkar-ma*, the oldest catalogue of the Tibetan Tripiṭaka; cf. E. Obermiller, *History of Buddhism by Bu-ston*, II (1932), p. 191; S. C. Das ed.), *Pag Sam Jon Zang* (of Sum-pa mkhan-po), II (1908), p. 173.5-9. This catalogue is said to have been compiled about the time when the *Mahāvyutpatti* was written (cf. N.B. 2 above). There are several theories concerning the date of this catalogue:
(a) 788 A.D.: H. Satō, *Kodai Chibettoshi Kenkyū*, II (1959), p. 772.
(b) 800 A.D.: E. Frauwallner, 'Zu den buddhistischen Texten in der Zeit Khri-Sron-Lde-Btsan's' (1957), p. 103.
(c) 812 A.D.: G. Tucci, *Minor Buddhist Texts*, I (1958), p. 48; H. Hadano, 'Chibetto Daizōkyō Engi' (1966), p. 78b. Cf. also Hadano, 'Himitsushū Tantora ni okeru Jinyānapāda-ryū ni tsuite' (1950), p. 22(162)a.
(d) 824 A.D.: S. Yoshimura, *The Denkar-Ma* (1950), pp. xi-xvi(?) [= repr. 1974, pp. *109*-*114*]; M. Takahashi, 'Kengugyō to Zan-run' (1963), p. 53. Takahashi seems to think that the present catalogue was revised in 824 A.D.
(e) 848 A.D.: S. Sakai, *Ramakyō no Tenseki* (1944), p. 68; S. Yazaki, 'Hokekyō Denyaku to sono Keitai' (1965), p. 240. I have not been able to see S. Tachibana, 'Chibetto Bukkyōshi Josetsu' (1934)[cf. Mochizuki's *Bukkyō Daijiten*, X (1963), pp. 692c-693c].

4) In fact, in the *Dkar-chag Ldan-dkar-ma* the abridged title of the *Rgs* is found in the section on the *Prajñāpāramitā* literature: Peking edition, No. 5851, CHO 353A7 (reprint edition, Vol. 145, p. 143): *'phags-pa sdus-pa* (so Peking) *tshigs-su bcad-pa / śloka sum-brgya-ste / bam-po gcig*,'"Ārya-saṃcaya-gāthā", 300 ślokas, 1 bam-po'. Cf. S. Yoshimura, *The Denkar-Ma* (1950), p. 3 [= repr. 1974, p.*119](Text No. 10); M. Lalou, 'Les textes bouddhiques au temps du Roi Khri-sroṅ-lde-bcan' (1953), p. 319 (section I, item No. 10). This must be the text which belongs to Recension B.

5) As regards the textual history of the Tibetan versions, I would like to pay attention to the fact that all the *Prajñāpāramitā* canonical texts were translated into Tibetan in its 'ancient' period (before King Glaṅ-dar-ma), and no single text is known to have been translated in the 'mediaeval' period; cf. S. Inaba, 'Chibetto Chūsei Shoki ni okeru Hannya-Chūgan Ronjo no Yakushutsu (I)' (1966), p. 17. King Glaṅ-dar-ma seems to have reigned in the early forties of the ninth century A.D. There are, however, some theories on the dates in connection with the King. As for the Tibetan and Chinese historical materials, see G. Roerich, *Izbrannye Trudy* (1967), p. 274f. ('Introduction' to his *The Blue Annals*). A comprehensive 'Comparative Table of Dates of King Glañ-Dar-ma' is to be found in B. Aoki, *Study on Early Tibetan Chronicles* (1955), p. 62 (see also Table B, sheet No. 3 between pp. 25-26); for the Tibetan materials see further A. I. Vostrikov, *Tibetan Historical Literature* (1970). A critical survey of the modern studies on the dates of King Glaṅ-dar-ma is given by H. Satō, 'Rendaruma-ō no Zaii Nenji ni tsuite' (1963), pp. 32-57 (the king's reign is dated 841-846 A.D. by Satō); cf. also Aoki, *op.cit.*, p. 61.

6) One can also draw attention to the fact that the Kanjur and the Tunhuang texts of the Lotus Sūtra represent different recensions, and both of them seem to have been revised from the older Tibetan version through a certain intermediate text; cf. N. Simonsson, *Indo-tibetische Studien*, I (1957), p. 176. I am inclined to apply this theory to our texts.

7) I have been able to consult the following Kanjur texts:

a) Editions:

C = Co-ne edition, No. 1002, KA 1B1-21B5.

Reference: T. Mibu, 'A Comparative List of the Bkaḥ-ḥgyur Division in the Co-ne, Peking, Sde-dge and Snar-thaṅ Editions with an Introduction to the Bkaḥ-ḥgyur Division of the Co-ne Edition' (1959), p. 30.

D = Sde-dge edition, No. 13, KA 1B1-19B7.

Reference: H. Ui, M. Suzuki, Y. Kanakura and T. Tada, *Chibetto Daizōkyō Sōmokuroku*, Vol. I (1934), p. 5a; cf. E. Haarh, 'A Comparative List of the Derge and Lhasa Editions of the Kanjur' (1963), p. 181.

L = Lhasa edition, No. 17 KA 189A2-215A4.

Reference: J. Takasaki, *Tōkyō Daigaku Shozō Rasa-ban Chibetto Daizōkyō Mokuroku* (1965), p. 6.

N = Snar-thaṅ edition, No. 17, KA 196B6-222A5.

Reference: A. Csoma, 'Analysis of the Sher-Chin__P'hal-Ch'hen__ Dkon-Séks__Do-Dé__Nyáng-Dás__and Gyut' (1836), p. 395: II 'Sher-Chin', No. 6 'Sna-tshogs' iv; L. Feer, 'Analyse du Kandjour' (1881), p. 201.

N.B. This edition does not give the names of translators in the final colophon.

P = Peking edition, No. 735, TSI 1A1-22A8.

Reference: Ōtani Daigaku Toshokan, *Chibetto Daizōkyō Kanjūru Kandō Mokuroku* (1930-1932), pp. 219-221; *Eiin Pekin-ban Chibetto Daizōkyō Sōmokuroku* (1961), pp. 92-93.

U = Urga edition, 'Śes-rab [Śer-phyin] sna-tshogs', KA 1B1-19B7.

Reference: Lokesh Chandra, 'A Newly Discovered Urga Edition of the Tibetan Kanjur' (1959), p. 178.

N.B. 1B - 5 lines; 2A - 6 lines; 2B-8A, 9A-19B - 7 lines; 8B - 8 lines.

b) Manuscripts:

E = Or. 9724, British Library (British Museum), London: Folios 181A5-205B4.

Reference: E. D. Grinstead, 'The Manuscript Kanjur in the British Museum' (1967), p. 50.

N.B. This text does not give the names of translators in the final colophon.

M = Orientalische Abteilung, Deutsche Staatsbibliothek, Berlin (once in Marburg-Lahn, and now back in Berlin again).

Folios KA 1A1-29A3.

Reference: H. Beckh, *Verzeichnis der tibetischen Handschriften der Königlichen Bibliothek zu Berlin*, I (1914), p. 10: Nr. 40 (II. Śer-phyin, Band 24-1).

2. Chinese blockprint texts:

a) Bilingual text (abbr. X):

For details see 'Bibliogeaphical Notes' IB2 above).

N.B. This text states in the colophon that it belongs to the *AsP* (folio 109A3/6), but it does not give the names of translators.

b) Other blockprint texts:

N.B. 1) The following four blockprints state in the colophons that the text belongs to the *AdP*, and that Dharmapālabhadra has collated it with the Sanskrit text revised by Haribhadra (cf. also 'Bibl. Notes' IIB3a, below).

2) I have no information about the date of the lo-tsā-ba Dharmapālabhadra, who did not translate any Kanjur text. He translated several Tanjur texts.

3) The Tibetan *AdP* does not record the names of translators.

Ga = Tib.bl. 347(134), Deutsche Staatsbibliothek, Berlin.

Gzuṅs-bsdud edition (1691 A.D.): folios 1B1-19B1.

Reference: M. Taube, *Tibetische Handschriften und Blockdrucke*, I (1966), p. 6: No. 8.

Gb = Tib.Bl. 198(111), Deutsche Staatsbibliothek, Berlin.

Gzuṅs-bsdus edition (1731 A.D.): folios 411A(B?)1-446B2 (numbered in Chinese).

Reference: M. Taube's Catalogue, I, p. 7: No. 10.

Gc = Tib.Bl. 9, Deutsche Staatsbibliothek, Berlin.

Bought by E. Haenisch in Peking in 1929.

Gzuṅs-bsdus edition (?): folios 1A1-108B1, with a postscript (folios 108B1-109B3) by Lcaṅ-skya Rol-pa'i rdo-rje (1717-1786 A.D.), and its colophon (folios 109B3-110A2).

Reference: M. Taube's Catalogue, I, pp. 7-8: No. 13.

W = Tib. 134, Historisches Staatsarchiv, Altenburg.

Gzuṅs-bsdus edition (1729 A.D.): folios 190B6-207B4.

Reference: M. Taube's Catalogue, I, p. 6: No. 9.

3. Tibetan manuscripts:

a) Manuscripts kept in the Sächsische Landesbibliothek, Dresden:

N.B. The following two MSS. state in the colophons that the text belongs to the *AdP*, and that Dharmapālabhadra has collated it with the Sanskrit text revised by Haribhadra (cf. also 'Bibl. Notes' IIB2b N.B. 1-3, above).

Sa = E471/2, folios 1B1-31B2.

Reference: B. Laufer, 'Verzeichnis der tibetischen Handschriften der Königlichen Bibliothek zu Dresden' (1901), p. 102: No. 8; also M. Taube, *Tibetische Handschriften und Blockdrucke*, I (1966), p. 7: No. 11.

N.B. 1) MS. Sa seems to be written by the same hand as Sb.

2) Someone has marked dubious readings.

Sb = E470/3, folios KHA 1B1-28B5.

Reference: Laufer's Catalogue, p. 102: No. 7; also Taube's Catalogue, I, p. 7: No. 12.

N.B. 1) MS. Sb seems to be written by the same hand as Sa.

2) Wrong readings are mostly marked on the MS. as in Sa.

b) Tunhuang MSS. kept in the India Office Library, London:

N.B. 1) Among the following Tunhuang MSS. Ta is the only complete text belonging to the Tibetan Recension B.

2) In the final colophon Ta mentions the names of the translators Vidyākarasiṃha and Dpal-brtsegs (cf. 'Bibl. Notes' IIB1 N.B. 1-3, above), but does not state anything as to which *Prajñāpāramitā* text it belongs.

Ta = Ch.9.1.43, folios KA 1A1-60B1.

Reference: L. de La Vallée Poussin, *Catalogue of the Tibetan Manuscripts from Tun-Huang in the India Office Library* (1962), pp. 42b-43a: No. 110.

Td = Ch.0024, folio KHA 94.

Reference: De La Vallée Poussin's Catalogue, p. 44b: No. 113.

N.B. This fragment which reads only 8 lines in all gives the text from *Rgs* IV 3a-V4b. It lacks IV 4d-6c.

Te = Ch.51.I.54 and 77.XV.6, folios KA 16, 18, 22, 30, 36, 44, 46.

Reference: De La Vallée Poussin's Catalogue, pp. 44b-45a: No.114.

N.B. 1) De La Vallée Poussin wrongly numbers 24 for 44.

2) Folios KA 16 (*Rgs* X 7c-XI 4b), 18 (XII 1b-7b), 22 (XV 6c-XVI 4d), 30 (XX 20b-XXI 3a), 36 (XXV 1c-XXVI 1a), 44 (XXX 8c-13d), 46 (XXXI 5a-10b).

3) Te sometimes adds *d* after the liquid *r* (e.g. *'gyurd-, gyurd-*); cf. J. Bacot, *Grammaire du tibêtain littéraire*, I (1946), p. 54 cum n. 2; S. Inaba, *Chibetto Koten Bunpōgaku* (1954), pp. 75-76 (para. 65-68). Cf. Tf: N.B. 2, below.

Tf = Ch.85.IX.9; 0062; 77.X.11 and 87.v, folios KA 3, 10, 18, 21, 32, 33.

Reference: De La Vallée Poussin's Catalogue, pp.45a-46a: No.115.

N.B. 1) Folios KA 3 (*Rgs* I 11c-18a), 10 (IV 5a-V 3d), 18 (XI 3b-9b), 21 (XIII 1b-XIV 5b), 32-33 (XX 18b-XXI 5b).

2) Tf sometimes adds *d* after the liquids *r* and *l* (e.g. *gyurd-, rold-, btuld-, spruld-*); cf. Te: N.B. 3, above.

Tg = Ch.2.C, folios KA 3 and 10.

Reference: De La Vallée Poussin's Catalogue, p. 46a: No. 116-1.

N.B. 1) Folios KA 3 (*Rgs* I 24c-II 9b) and 10 (XII 5c-XIV 8b).

2) At the bottom of folio 3A are written in *dbu-med* two pādas which are missing in the main part. Some missing letters are added in *dbu-med*.

3) Three pādas XIX (not XIV!) 1c-2a are written in *dbu-med* at the top of folio 10B (cf. Table VIIa, below). It is absolutely out of place.

4. Chapter 84 of the Tibetan *Aṣṭādaśasāhasrikā-Prajñāpāramitā*:

C' = Co-ne edition, No. 1027, GA 193B7-214B4.

D' = Sde-dge edition, No. 10, GA 163A5-181A7.

L' = Lhasa edition, No. 12, GA 253B2-280B4.

N' = Snar-thaṅ edition, No. 11, GA 147A6-175A4.

P' = Peking edition, No. 732, PHI 180A4-199A5.

N.B. 1) In his *The Prajñāpāramitā Literature* (1960), p. 46 (and p. 58) E. Conze assumes that the Tibetan *AdP* was probably translated by Ye-śes sde (without reference to his sources).

2) Chapter 84 of the Tibetan *AdP* offers exactly the same text as others belonging to Recension B; cf. E. Conze, *The Prajñāpāramitā Literature*, p. 58; also R. Hikata, *Suvikrānta-vikrāmi-Paripṛcchā* (1958), Table III (with n. 2).

3) No fragment of the Sanskrit *AdP* relating to this chapter has yet been found. The Chinese *AdP* does not contain this chapter.

4) For the problems concerning this text see further 'Introduction', para. 13-17, above).

5) Catalogue references are omitted (cf. 'Bibl. Notes' IIB1a, above).

5. I have not been able to consult the following texts:

a) *Mdo-maṅ*, No. 108: folios 345B-379A.

Reference: M. Lalou, *Catalogue du fonds tibétain de la Bibliothèque Nationale*, IV, 1 (1931), pp. 42-43.

N.B. According to M. Lalou, the text was translated by Siṃhabhadra and Dharmapālabhadra (cf. 'Bibl. Notes' IIB2b N.B. 1-2, also IIB3a N.B.). For the problem concerning the name of Siṃhabhadra see E. Conze, *The Prajñāpāramitā Literature* (1960), p. 58.

b) A blockprint text of the Sera edition (Tantra College of the Sera Monastery):

Reference: S. Devi, *Samantabhadracaryāpraṇidhānarāja* (1958), p. 9.

c) A blockprint text kept in the Schilling von Canstadt Collection, Bibliothèque de l'Institut de France, Paris:

Reference: J. Bacot, 'La collection tibétaine Schilling von Canstadt à la Bibliothèque de l'Institut' (1924), p. 337: No. 3547.

d) Three fragmentary blockprint texts kept in the Linden-Museum für Länder- und Völkerkunde, Stuttgart:

(1) Sammlung Hans Leder: No. 23 944: No. 3a (23 folios), and No. 3b (8 folios).

Reference: R. O. Meisezahl, 'Die tibetischen Handschriften und Drucke des Linden-Museums in Stuttgart' (1957), p. 10.

(2) Sammlung Firma J. F. G. Umlauf: No. 72 194 (1 final folio).

Reference: Meisezahl's Catalogue, p. 140.

e) A blockprint text published in Leh in 1968 A.D. (94 folios):

Reprinted from the blocks carved at the beginning of the 18th century and preserved at the Royal Palace of Leh.

Translator: Chos-skyoṅ-bzaṅ-po (Dharmapālabhadra).

f) *Mdo-maṅ*, No. 85: folios GI 1-48A(missing folios 10, 12, 13).

Reference: P. Aalto, 'Le mdo-maṅ conservé à la Bibliothèque Universitaire de Helsinki' (1952), p. 41.

Translators: Padhikarasiṅha (cf. 'Bibl. Notes' IIB1 N.B. 1, above) and Dpal-brtsegs.

g) Lhasa edition kept in the Tōhoku University Collection, Sendai:

Tōhoku No. 6764: folios 1-86, 5 lines.

Reference: Y. Kanakura, R. Yamada, T. Tada and H. Hadano, *Chibetto Senjutsu Butten Mokuroku* (1953), p. 464a.

h) A Tibetan MS. kept in the Chester Beatty Library, Dublin:

Tib. No. 1704: 90 folios.

Reference: D. L. Snellgrove, *A Catalogue of the Tibetan Collection* (1969), p. 12, with illustr. facing p. 12.

i) Two MSS. kept in the Victoria and Albert Museum, London:

(1) No. I.S.48A - 1965: 51 folios, numbering KA 1-3, 6, 8-34, 40-43, 45-49, 51-60.

Reference: R. O. Meisezahl, 'Zwei alttibetische Ratnaguṇasaṃcayagāthā-Handschriften und andere Prajñāpāramitā-Texte im Victoria and Albert Museum, London' (1973), pp. 209-232.

(2) No. I.S.48B - 1965: 60 folios, numbering KA 4-6, 8-64.

Reference: Meisezahl's Catalogue, pp. 233-236.

## III. Chinese Texts

Title in full: *Fo-shuo Fo-mu pao-tê-tsang pan-jo po-lo-mi-ching* 仏説仏母宝徳蔵般若波羅蜜経

Note that this full title is given only at the beginning and the end of each fascicle. The text is divided in 3 fascicles and 32 chapters (cf. N.B. 10, below): fasc. I (chap. I-XI), fasc. II (chap. XII-XXII), fasc. III (chap. XXIII-XXXII).

Title in brief: *Fo-mu pao-tê-tsang pan-jo chia-t'o* 仏母宝徳蔵般若伽陀

(Sanskrit: *Bhagavatī-prajñā-⟨pāramitā-⟩ratna-guṇa-saṃcaya-gāthā, Bhagavatī-ratna-guṇa-saṃcaya-prajñā-⟨pāramitā-⟩gāthā*?; cf. N.B. 5, below).

Note that this short title is given only before the title of each chapter. Chapters I and XXIII, however, give no title of the text. Only *Pan-jo chia-t'o* is given before the title of chapter XII. These three chapters appear as the first chapters of the three fascicles respectively.

Translator: Fa-hsien 法賢 (= T'ien-hsi-tsai 天息災 ; cf. N.B. 6-7)

Date of translation: 991 A.D. (cf. N.B. 8-9, below).

I have consulted the following four editions of the Tripiṭakas:

a) *Taishō Shinshū Daizōkyō* 大正新修大蔵経 , No. 229, Vol. VIII (Tōkyō, 1924), pp. 679c16-684b27.

Reference: *Shōwa Hōbō Sōmokuroku*, I (1929), No. 3: 'Taishō Shinshū Daizōkyō Kandō Mokuroku', pp. 212b-213a; *Taishō Shinshū Daizōkyō Mokuroku* (rev.ed. 1969), p. 25; *Hôbôgirin*, fascicule annexe: *Tables du Taishô Issaikyô* (1931), p. 13; *Fo-tsang tzu-mu yin-te* (1933), I p. 155b, II p. 383b.

Note: I have consulted this edition, because it is most widely used by scholars.

b) *Dainippon Kōtei (Shukusatsu) Daizōkyō* 大日本校訂(縮刷)大蔵経, Tsuki-8 月八 (Tōkyō, June 1882), pp. 1A-9A.

Reference: *Dainippon Kōtei Daizōkyō Mokuroku* (Dec. 1885), p. 18b.

Note: I have consulted this edition, because it is well-known for the reliability of its collations and its freedom from textual errors; cf. A. Hirakawa and E. B. Ceadel, 'Japanese Research on Buddhism since the Meiji Period' (1955), p. 225.

c) Chi-sha 磧砂 (or Sha 沙 ) edition, 3 fascicles.

Photomechanically reprinted by Ying-yin Sung-pan tsang-ching-hui 影印宋版蔵経会 (Shanghai, 1935): No. 505, Kao 高 (Fasc. DV)(No. 6), pp. 39A-50A. Again reprinted by Hsiu-ting Chung-hua Ta-tsang-ching-hui 修訂中華大蔵経会 : *Chung-hua Ta-tsang-ching*, First Series, No. 9, Vol. XXXIII (Taipei, 1963)[= Fasc. LXV (Taipei, 1965)], pp. 28481b-28488c.

Reference: *P'ing-chiang-fu Chi-sha-pan Yen-shêng-yüan hsin-tiao-tsang ching-lü-lun-têng mu-lu* 平江府磧砂版延聖院新雕蔵経律論等目録 No. 1214 (= *Shōwa Hōbō Sōmokuroku*, I, No. 12, p. 942a1); cf. also *Ying-yin Sung Chi-sha tsang-ching*, Shou-t'sê, Part I (Shanghai, 1936), p. 48b; *Chung-hua Ta-tsang-ching*, First Series (Chi-sha edition), Pamphlet 'List of titles, etc.' (Taipei, 1965), p. 24b17; *Chung-hua Ta-tsang-ching*, Shou-pien (Taipei, 1968), p. 151: No. 1226.

Note 1: The pagination of the original text runs from 39 to 42 (Yung-lo-pan 永楽版 kept at Sung-p'o T'u-shu-kuan in Peking); cf. *Ying-yin Sung Chi-sha tsang-ching*, Shou-t'sê, Part II, p. 59B (= *Chung-hua Ta-tsang-ching*, First Series, Pamphlet List, 1965, p. 71).

Note 2: I have consulted this edition, because it was discovered after the publication of the Taishō edition. Moreover, the text is carefully collated. On the Chi-sha edition see J. W. de Jong, *Buddha's Word in China* (1968), p. 17 and pp. 25-26 n. 57 (with an extensive bibliography).

d) Korean edition [高麗大蔵経], 3 fascicles.

Hsüan 縣 : fasc. I (chap. I-XI), 11 chang; II (chap. XII-XXII), 10 chang; III (chap. XXIII-XXXII), 9 chang.

Note 1: I have used this edition reprinted from the original blocks and kept in the Orientalia Section of the National Library of Australia, Canberra.

Note 2: I have consulted this edition, because it has been made the basis of modern editions of the Chinese Tripiṭaka. On the Korean edition see further J. W. de Jong, *op.cit.*, p. 17 and p. 26 n. 58; - - , 'Korea's Edition of the Chinese Buddhist Canon' (1969).

N.B. 1) For the modern translation of the Chinese version see 'Bibl. Notes' VI 2, below.

2) The Chinese version of the *Rgs* is probably the recension which is most corrupt. It is quite different from the Sanskrit and Tibetan recensions. Yet, the number and order of verses almost always agree with the other recensions. The translator must have followed a Sanskrit original. One may safely say that the Chinese version is closer to Sanskrit Recension A than to any other.

3) The fact that the Chinese version is a very different recension may well be due to the translator's free (or perhaps bad) rendering. I wonder whether Fa-hsien is a faithful translator. Has he in translating other texts closely followed the original Sanskrit texts? For instance, is the *Ta-ch'êng wu-liang-shou chuang-yen-ching* (Taishō No. 363) strictly based upon the Sanskrit original?; cf. T. Shibata, 'Muryōjushōgongyō Honganbu ni tsuite' (1963); - - , 'Muryōjushōgongyō ni tsuite' (1964); - -, 'Hōken Yakushutsu Kyōten ni tsuite' (1966). [I have not been able to see J. Ikemoto, 'Muryōjukyō Shohon no Seiritsu Katei' (1961).] I do not think that Fa-hsien has made his translations without consulting the original Indic texts, although he seems not to have brought any Sanskrit manuscript to China; cf. P. Demiéville, *L'Inde classique*, II (1953), para. 2097 (p. 426). A more careful study is needed in connection with Fa-hsien's translations.

4) One can prepare a critically edited text of this recension only after a careful comparison with the Sanskrit and Tibetan versions. In his Japanese translation of the Chinese version, S. Taki has numbered the verses (cf. 'Bibl. Notes' VI, 2). I have also tried to number the verses corresponding to those of the Sanskrit version. My numbering is only slightly different from that of Taki. The Chinese verses, which do not correspond to the verse numbers of the Sanskrit version, are herewith recorded, although I had to omit my tentative edition of the Chinese text:

| Chinese version | Sanskrit version |
|---|---|
| I 29 | II 1 |
| II 1 | II 2 |
| (One verse corresponding to Skt. II 3 is missing in Chin.) | |
| II 2 | II 4 |
| 3 | 5 |
| 4 (prose!) | 6 |
| 5 | 7 |
| 6 | 8 |
| 7 | 9 |
| 8 | 10 |
| 9 | 11 |
| 10 | 12 |
| 11 | 13 |
| IX 1a-2a | IX 1 |
| 2b-d | 2 |
| XI 1 | Missing in Skt. |
| 2a-f [= Taki 2a-d/3a-d] | Missing in Skt. |
| 3 [= Taki 4] | XI 1 |
| 4 [= Taki 5] | 2 |
| 5 [= Taki 6] | 3 |
| 6 [= Taki 7] | 4 |
| 7 [= Taki 8] | 5 |
| 8 [= Taki 9] | 6 |
| 9 [= Taki 10] | 7 |
| 10a-c [= Taki 11a-c] | 8 |
| 10d-11a [= Taki 11d-12a] | 9 |
| 11b-d [= Taki 12b-d] | 10 |

5) With reference to the Tibetan version Nanjio restores the Sanskrit title of the Chinese version as *Buddhamātrika-ratna-guṇagarbha-prajñāpāramitā-sūtra: Prajñāpāramitā-saṃcayagāthā* (Nanjio Catalogue, col. 197: No. 864).

6) Fa-hsien has long been identified with Fa-t'ien 法天 as has been done in the first place by Chih-p'an in his *Fo-tsu-t'ung-chi* (1258-1269 A.D.)(Taishō No. 2035, Vol. XLIX, p. 399c) under the year 985 A.D. (cf. *Hôbôgirin,* fasc. annexe, p. 138b, 'Hôken'; *Fo-tsang tzu-mu yin-te,* I, p. 155b, 'Fa-t'ien'; P. C. Bagchi, *Le canon bouddhique en Chine,* II, p. 585 'Dharmadeva', p. 595 'T'ien si tsai', ss.vv.). This mis-identification of Fa-hsien with Fa-t'ien was for the first time pointed out by Z. Tsukamoto, and Fa-hsien was rightly identified with T'ien-hsi-tsai in his article 'Bukkyō Shiryō to shite no Kinkoku Daizōkyō' (1934)[unseen]; cf. *Sōdai Kenkyū Bunken Teiyō,* ed. by Aoyama (1961), p. 359b (item 4).

7) In 980 A.D. T'ien-hsi-tsai (Devaśānti?) came from Kashmir to China, where he died in 1001 A.D. [His death is dated back to 1000 A.D. by H. Durt, 'Chōmyōtō' (1967), p. 360a. It should be a misprint.] He was renamed as Fa-hsien (Dharmabhadra) in 987

A.D.; cf. S. Mochizuki, *Bukkyō Kyōtenshiron* (1946), pp. 206-207. Mochizuki has made a comprehensive list of the texts translated by Fa-t'ien from Central India and Fa-hsien (alias T'ien-hsi-tsai) from Kashmir with catalogue references (see Mochizuki, *op. cit.*, pp. 168-170 and 170-176 respectively). It now admits of no doubt that Fa-hsien should not be identified with Fa-t'ien; see for example G. Ono, 'Bukkyō Kyōten Sōron' (1936), pp. 182-183; T. Shibata, 'Hōten Kaimei Hōken-setsu ni tsuite' (1965), pp. 80-81. In regard to this mis-identification R. Yamada does not yet see an established theory in his book *Bongo Butten no Shobunken* (1959), p. 43 (with n. 4). For the problem of the identification of Fa-hsien see further Jan Yün-hua, 'Buddhist Relations between India and Sung China' (1966), pp. 34-37 (with an extensive bibliography).

8) B. Nanjio has put the date of the translation of the Chinese version of the *Rgs* in 982-1001 A.D. (see Nanjio Catalogue, col. 197 ad No. 862 *in fine*, also col. 451 No. 864). I do not see from where Nanjio has taken the year 982 A.D. (cf. Nanjio Catalogue, col. 450-452 article 159 for Fa-t'ien/Fa-hsien, and col. 452-453 article 160 for T'ien-hsi-tsai). In the *Shōwa Hōbō Sōmokuroku*, I (1929), p. 212b, the translation is dated in 1001 A.D., the year in which Fa-hsien died. This is followed by D. Tokiwa and U. Wogihara, who have published a supplement to Nanjio Catalogue: *Japanese Alphabetical Index* (1930), p. 117b. This date has also been given by T. Matsumoto, *Die Prajñāpāramitā-Literatur* (1932), pp. 8 and 25; R. Hikata, *Suvikrāntavikrāmi-Paripṛcchā* (1958), p. XIX; R. Yamada, *Daijō Bukkyō Seiritsuron Josetsu* (1959), p. 201. In his review of R. Hikata, *op.cit.* (*IIJ*, III, 1959, p. 233) E. Conze adopts the year 1001 A.D. without any reference, but in his later publications Conze dates it in 980 A.D., the year of T'ien-hsi-tsai's arrival in China. The latter is endorsed by S. Hanayama, 'A Summary of Various Research on the Prajñāpāramitā Literature' (1966), p. 26.

9) We have, however, at our disposal the catalogue entitled *Ta-chung Hsiang-fu fa-pao-lu* (1011-1015 A.D.) which was compiled by Yang I and others just after the death of Fa-hsien (1001 A.D.). If the description of this catalogue is to be relied upon, the translation of the *Rgs* was completed in the 10th month of the second year of Ch'ung-hua 淳化 era, i.e. 991 A.D.; see *Sung-tsang i-chen*, Box XI, Text No. 41 'Ta-chung Hsiang-fu fa-pao-lu', fasc. II, p. 9 = *Chung-hua Ta-tsang-ching*, First Series, Vol. X, fasc. LXXX, p. 34589c. This is in fact accepted by H. Ōno, *Daijō Kaikyō no Kenkyū* (1954, repr. 1963), pp. 73 and 84. Incidentally, in the same month Fa-hsien completed his translation of the *Ta-ch'êng wu-liang-shou chuang-yen-ching* (Taishō No. 363). With regard to the translator and the date of translation, much confidence has been placed in the description of this catalogue by K. Fujita in his *Genshi Jōdokyō no Kenkyū* (1970), p. 29.

10) It is to be noted that the following catalogues state that the text is in 33 chapters:
(a) *Ta-chung Hsiang-fu fa-pao-lu*, Fasc. VIII; see *Sung-tsang i-chen*, Box XI, Text No. 41, fasc. II, p. 9 = *Chung-hua Ta-tsang-ching*, First Series, Vol. X, fasc. LXXX, p. 34589c.
(b) *Ta-yüan Chih-yüan fa-pao k'an-t'ung tsung-lu*, by Ch'ing Chi-hsiang and others, Fasc. I; see *Shōwa Hōbō Sōmokuroku*, II (1929), p. 183b28-29: No. 27; *Chung-hua Ta-tsang-ching*, First Series (Chi-sha edition), Vol. X, fasc. LXXIII, p. 31811c.

11) A preliminary edition of the Chinese version has been omitted in this book. I would like to make brief notes on the following readings adopted in the Taishō edition:

II 11c: T. 受記 (so Li, Sha, Shuku, Taki) for 授記 (cf. T. VIII 677 fn. 7); cf. also 授記 I 11b, X 6c, XX 21d, 22d, 23d, 24d, XXI 1ac, XXIV 5a.

Fasc. I col.: T. 仏母宝徳蔵般若伽陀巻上 (so Li, Shuku) for ... 般若波羅蜜経巻上 (so Sha; cf. Shuku p. 4B note).

XII 2b: T. 遍 (wt.n.; so Taki) for 徧 (so Li, Sha, Shuku).

XVI 5a: T. 難 (cf. T. VIII 680 fn. 8) for 雖 (so Li, Sha, Shuku, Taki: Skt. *yady āpi*); cf. also X 6c 雖 : Skt. *yady āpi*).

XVII 6b: T. 更互相 (so Li, Shuku; cf. T. VIII 680 fn. 12) for 男女互 (so Sha, Taki: Skt. *puruṣestri*).

XIX 3bc: T. 華菓 (so Li, Shuku, Taki) for 菓果 (so Sha); cf. also XXVIII 3a, below.

XX 5b: T. 火地 (so Li, Shuku, Taki; cf. T. VIII 681 fn. 6) for 大地 (so Sha: Skt. *mahā-pṛthivī*).

XX 12d: T. 子退倦 is undoubtedly a misprint for 不退倦 (so Li, Sha, Shuku, Taki).

Fasc. II col.: T. 仏母宝徳蔵般若経伽陀巻中 (so Li, Shuku) for ... 般若波羅蜜経巻中 (so Sha; cf. also Shuku p. 6B note).

XXVII 5d: T. 菓樹 (so Shuku; but Sha 果樹 ; cf. also Shuku p. 7B note) is probably to be emended to 華樹 : Skt. *su-phulla druma*.

XXVIII 3a: T. 華菓 (so Li, Shuku, Taki) for 菓果 (so Sha; cf. Shuku p. 7B note); cf. also XIX 3bc, above).

## IV. Mongolian Texts

I have been unable to consult the Mongolian version of the *Rgs*: *Qutuɣ-tu bilig-ün činadu kiǰaɣar-a kürügsen quriyangɣui silüg* (Sanskrit: *Ārya-prajñā-pāramitā-ratna-guṇa-saṃcaya-gāthā*):

1. Kanjur text:

   Kanjur text No. 767, Vol. XLVII, *Eldeb bilig baramid*, VI-1, folios 1-27B.

   Reference: L. Ligeti, *Catalogue du Kanǰur mongol imprimé*, Vol. I (1942-1944), pp. 184-185; cf. also F. A. Bischoff, *Der Kanjur und seine Kolophone*, II (1968), p. 328.

2. Chinese blockprint texts:

   (a) No. 3589, Schilling von Canstadt Collection, Bibliothèque de l'Institut de France, Paris.

   Reference: L. Ligeti, 'La collection mongole Schilling von Canstadt à la Bibliothèque de l'Institut' (1930), p. 159: No. LVI (J̌u: folios 14B-42A).

   (b) Libr. Mongol. 150 (314 folios), Deutsche Staatsbibliothek, Marburg-Lahn (now in Berlin).

   Reference: W. Heissig, 'Die Libri Mongolici der westdeutschen Bibliothek Marburg' (1953), p. 421; - - , *Die Pekinger lamaistischen Blockdrucke in mongolischer Sprache* (1954), p. 35: No. 34 (with p. 35 n. 4).

   (c) No. 17, Manchu-Mongol Section, Tōyō Bunko, Tōkyō.

   Reference: N. Poppe, L. Hurvitz and H. Okada, *Catalogue of the Manchu-Mongol Section of the Toyo Bunko* (1964), pp. 21-22 [same as (b) above].

3. Text No. 106 of the dhāraṇī-sūtra collection: *Qutuɣ-tu taranis-un (tarnis-un) quriyangɣui zungdui kemegdekü yeke kölgen sudur*, folios 287A-320B.

   Reference: W. Heissig, *Die Pekinger lamaistischen Blockdrucke in mongolischer Sprache* (1954), pp. 44-47: No. 49 (esp. p. 46: Text No. 106 'Qutugtu sanjiya gata').

   N.B. This Mongolian version must be a different text from the *Prajñā-pāramitā-ratna-guṇa-saṃcaya-gāthā-mantra-dhāraṇī* (cf. 'Bibl. Notes' IX 1 N.B. 1, below).

   (a) M 205, Division of Orientalia, Library of Congress, Washington, D.C.

Reference: D. Farquhar, 'A Description of the Mongolian Manuscripts and Xylographs in Washington D.C.' (1955), p. 180: No. 23.

(b) No. 63, Manchu-Mongol Section, Tōyō Bunko, Tōkyō.
Reference: N. Poppe, L. Hurvitz and H. Okada, *Catalogue of the Manchu-Mongol Section of the Toyo Bunko* (1964), pp. 53-55.

(c) Libr. Mongol. 72, Deutsche Staatsbibliothek, Marburg-Lahn (now in Berlin).
Reference: W. Heissig, 'Die Libri Mongolici der westdeutschen Bibliothek Marburg' (1953), p. 408.

(d) H.3511, Sven Hedin Collection, Ethnographical Museum, Stockholm.
Reference: P. Aalto, 'Notes on the Collection of Mongolian Books in the Ethnographical Museum in Sweden, Stockholm' (1950), p. 6; also his 'A Catalogue of the Hedin Collection of Mongolian Literature' (1953), pp. 84-85.

(e) L-318, Berthold Laufer Collection, Far Eastern Institute, University of Chicago, Chicago.
Reference: J. R. Krueger, 'Catalogue of the Laufer Mongolian Collection in Chicago' (1966), pp. 167a-168a (esp. p. 168a: Text No. 106).

(f) No. 81 175, Library of the School of Oriental and African Studies, University of London, London.
Reference: W. Heissig, *Die Pekinger lamaistischen Blockdrucke in mongolischer Sprache* (1954), p. 44 n. 7; also his *Mongolische Handschriften - Blockdrucke - Landkarten* (1961), p. 199: No. 347.

(g) No. 02.05, Raghu Vira Collection, International Academy of Indian Culture, New Delhi.
Reference: W. Heissig, *Mongolische Handschriften - Blockdrucke - Landkarten* (1961), p. 199: No. 347.

(h) E 43, Walther Heissig Collection, Bonn.
Reference: W. Heissig, *Die Pekinger lamaistische Blockdrucke in mongolischer Sprache* (1954), p. 44 n. 7.

## V. Hsi-hsia Texts

I have been unable to consult the Hsi-hsia version of the *Rgs*. The texts listed below are all kept in the Leningrad Branch of the Institute of Oriental Studies (Institut Vostokovedenija)[formerly: Institute of the Peoples of Asia/Institut Narodov Azii], U.S.S.R. Academy of Sciences:

1. Inventory No. 806: 聖勝慧彼岸到集頌
   [Sanskrit: *Ārya-prajñā-pāramitā-saṃcaya-gāthā*]
   Reference: Z. I. Gorbačeva i E. I. Kyčanov, *Tangutskie rukopisi i Ksilografy* (1963), p. 94: No. 65.
   N.B. A list of Hsi-hsia characters is given in this catalogue.
2. Inventory Nos. 595-598, 602-605, 687, 2727, 3705, 5711, 6888, 7440: 聖勝慧彼岸到德用宝集頌
   [Sanskrit: *Ārya-prajñā-pāramitā-ratna-guṇa-saṃcaya-gāthā*]
   Reference: Gorbačeva and Kyčanov, *op.cit.*, p. 94: No. 66.
3. Inventory No. 4087: 集頌般若波羅蜜多経 (?)
   [Sanskrit: *Prajñā-pāramitā-saṃcaya-gāthā*]
   Reference: Gorbačeva and Kyčanov, *op.cit.*, p. 97: No. 93.
4. Inventory No. 5564: 番言聖慧彼岸到方用宝集頌唱
   [Sanskrit: *Ārya-prajñā-pāramitā-ratna-guṇa-saṃcaya-gāthā*]
   Reference: Gorbačeva and Kyčanov, *op.cit.*, p. 113: No. 294.

N.B. No text of the Hsi-hsia version of the *Rgs* is contained in *The Tangut Tripiṭaka*, 9 parts, edited by E. Grinstead (New Delhi, 1971). I have not been able to see E. Grinstead, *Tangut Studies* (Leiden, 1967), which includes 'Indexes to Buddhist and Taoist Literature'. No *Rgs* text is mentioned in the list of extant Hsi-hsia literature by T. Nishida in his book *Seikago no Kenkyū*, II (Tōkyō, 1966), pp. 301-302.

## VI. Modern Translations

1. From the Sanskrit:

a) Conze, Edward, 'Verses on the Accumulation of Precious Qualities (*Ratnaguṇasaṃcayagāthā*)', *Indo-Asian Studies*, Part I (= *Śatapiṭaka Series*, No. 31)(New Delhi: International Academy of Indian Culture, 1962), pp. 126-178.

N.B. 1) Chapters 1 and 2 were first published by E. Conze, 'The Oldest *Prajñāpāramitā*', *The Middle Way*, XXXII, 4 (London, 1958), pp. 136-141. Cf. my 'Introduction', para. 25, above.

2) E. Conze's prefatory note: 'This translation is based on E. Obermiller's text of the *Ratnaguṇa* (*Bibliotheca Buddhica*, XXIX, 1937), as corrected by me in *Indo-Iranian Reprints* (V, 1960), and in the *Indo-Iranian Journal*, IV, 1960, pp. 37-58, and by Prof. F. Edgerton in *Indo-Iranian Journal*, V, 1961, pp. 1-18. I have added headlines throughout, ...'. In a number of cases, however, Conze's translation appears to be based on the Tibetan version (Recension B). There are few textual notes.

3) Conze gives a table of contents (pp. 173-178) with the references to the parallel passages of his English translation of the *AsP*: E. Conze (trsl.), *Aṣṭasāhasrikā-Prajñāpāramitā* (Calcutta, 1958); cf. b, N.B. 2, below.

4) I have not been able to see E. Conze, *A Collection of Prajñāpāramitā Texts* (typescript, 1952), No. 7 'English translation of the *Ratnaguṇasaṃcayagāthā*', kept in the Library of the School of Oriental and African Studies, University of London, London. Reference: *Library Catalogue* (School of Oriental and African Studies), Vol. XXII, p. 57c: No. 96341.

b) Conze, Edward, *The Perfection of Wisdom in Eight Thousand Lines & its Verse Summary (= Wheel Series,* 1)(Bolinas: Four Seasons Foundation, 1973), xxii, 327 pp.

N.B. 1) 'Preface', pp. ix-xxii; 'Contents (of the translation of the *Rgs*)', pp. 3-7; 'Verses on the Perfection of Wisdom', pp. 9-73.

2) Reference is made to the corresponding pages of R. Mitra's edition of the *AsP* (Calcutta, 1888), of which Conze's translation is to be found in this book, pp. 75-300 (page references to Mitra's edition are also marked in the text); cf. also a, N.B. 3, above.

3) The main text of Conze's translation published in 1962 has not been radically changed in this book. It is to be noted, however, that the title of Conze's translation now expressly shows his view on the status of the *Rgs* in relation to the *AsP* (cf. my 'Introduction', para. 8-17).

4) This book appeared, to my regret, too late to be used in my present work.

2. From the Chinese:

Shiio, Benkyō 椎尾辨匡 and Taki, Shōdō 滝照道, 'Bussetsu Butsumo Hōtokuzō Hannya Haramitsukyō 仏説仏母宝徳蔵般若波羅蜜経', *Kokuyaku Issaikyō* 国訳一切経, *Indo Senjutsu-bu* 印度撰述部, *Shaku-kyōron-bu* 釈経論部, V-b (Tōkyō: Daitō Shuppansha, 1936), pp. 339-374 (8 plus 26 pages).

N.B. 1) This translation is based on the text in the Taishō edition: No. 229, Vol. VIII, pp. 679c16-684b27 (cf. 'Bibl. Notes' IIIa, above). In a few cases, however, readings in other editions are adopted without giving reference.

2) The translation was made by Taki under the supervision of Shiio.

3) The verses are numbered in the Japanese translation (though it is in prose). The numbering refers to the Sanskrit text: MSS. Ta, Tb, Tc, and X; cf. 'Bibl. Notes' III N.B. 4, above.

4) As for the status of this literature see my 'Introduction', para. 8-17, esp. para. 9, above.

5) I have not been able to see the reprint edition of this Japanese translation with a new introduction by Gadjin M. Nagao (Tōkyō: Daitō Shuppansha, 1974?).

VII. *Rgs* quoted by Candrakīrti in his *Prasannapadā*

a) *Rgs* II 3d = *Prasannapadā* (ed. L. de La Vallée Poussin. 1903-1913), p. 167 line 4.

b) *Rgs* XX 5 = *Prasannapadā*, pp. 166.11-167.2.

N.B. 1) The fact that Candrakīrti has quoted the *Rgs* at the beginning of the seventh century A.D. is very important (see my 'Introduction', para. 20-21). Thanks to the Sanskrit texts of the *Rgs* at our disposal, we can now emend the passages from the *Rgs* which have been corruptly transmitted in the MSS. of the *Prasannapadā* of Candrakīrti.

2) Puzzled by the *Prasannapadā* MSS. reading *uktaṃ cārya-sacarya-gāthāsu* (ed. La Vallée Poussin, p. 166.10), which is simply a mistake for *uktaṃ cārya-saṃcaya-gāthāsu*, the editor has conjectured the reading *°-saṃgīti-gāthāsu* (p. 166 n. 5) on the basis of the Tibetan translation *'phags-pa sdud-pa tshigs-su bcad-pa-las*, and has given a wrong reference to A. Csoma, 'Analysis of the Sher-Chin ...' (1836), p. 462 'Yaṅ-dag-par sdud-pa = Saṃgīti' (V. Mdo, No. 1); cf. 'Bibl. Notes' IIB1a, under N = Snar-thaṅ edition.

3) J. May has rightly emended the wrong title *sacarya-gāthā-* to *saṃcaya-gāthā-* in his book *Candrakīrti: Prasannapadā Madhyamaka-vṛtti* (1959), p. 130 n. 349. In his review of J. May, *op.cit.* (*IIJ*, V, 1961, p. 164) J. W. de Jong (ad May p. 166.10) has proposed to correct May's translation of the title 'Stances colligées' to 'Stances sur l'accumulation', and identified the two verses quoted by Candrakīrti in his *Prasannapadā* with the *Rgs* (cf. also my 'Introduction', para. 2-7, above). I am indebted to the reviewer, who has pointed out this reference to me. It had escaped my attention, when I wrote an article mentioned below (see N.B. 6).

4) Translating the *Prasannapadā* into Japanese, S. Yamaguchi has identified *Prasannapadā* 166.11-167.2 (chapter VII, verse 25) with the Chinese version of the *Rgs* (Taishō No. 229, Vol. VIII, p. 681b1-2); see Yamaguchi, *"Jōmyōkuron" to Nazukuru Gesshō-zō: Chūronshaku*, II (1949), p. 102 (cf. also p. 103 n. 15). He does not refer to the Sanskrit texts of the *Rgs*. This is followed by T. Mitsukawa, 'Shōben, Gesshō no Chūronshaku ni Mirareru Hannya-gyō' (1968), pp. 16, 18 and 23.

5) *Prasannapadā* 167.4 is the *Rgs* II 3d. In the Chinese version of the *Rgs* this verse is missing. This explains probably why Yamaguchi and Mitsukawa have failed to identify the quotation.

6) For further details see A. Yuyama, '*Candrakīrti* no *Prasannapadā* ni Inyōsareta *Prajñāpāramitā-Ratnaguṇasaṃcayagāthā*' (1970); and as for the title see Yuyama, 'Hōtokuzō Hannya ni Kansuru Jakkan no Mondai' (1973), pp. 271-272. See also my 'Introduction' para. 2-7 above.

## VIII. Commentaries

1. Haribhadra's commentary:

a) Sanskrit text: *Ratna-guṇa-saṃcaya-gāthā-vyākhyā.*

Vol. XI, 4 (serial number 42), Spos-khaṅ Monastery near Gyangtse.

Palmleaf MS., 52·5 x 5·9 cm. (incomplete).

Reference: R. Sāṅkṛtyāyana, 'Sanskrit Palm-leaf MSS. in Tibet' (1935), p. 30.

N.B. 1) I have not been able to consult this MS. which was discovered by R. Sāṅkṛtyāyana during his first expedition (1929-1930).

2) Sāṅkṛtyāyana must have seen this MS., but apparently has made no copy of it. It is not mentioned in a list of the Rāhula Sāṅkṛtyāyana Collection kept in the K. P. Jayaswal Research Institute at Patna: 'List of Sanskrit Manuscripts in the Tibetan Collection Arranged Alphabetically' (mimeographed). This list is reproduced by A. Hirakawa in his article 'Yōroppa no Chūō Ajiya Bukkyō Shahon' (1962), pp. 322-323.

b) Tibetan text: *Bcom-ldan-'das yon-tan rin-po-che sdud-pa'i tshigs-su bcad-pa'i dka'-'grel* (Sanskrit title: *Bhagavad-ratna-guṇa-saṃcaya-gāthā nāma Pañjikā*).

Author: Seṅge bzaṅ-po (Haribhadra).

Translators: Jetahadu Śāntibhadra, Śākya'i 'od.

(1) Sde-dge edition, No. 3792, JA 1B1-78A8.

Reference: H. Ui, M. Suzuki, Y. Kanakura and T. Tada, *Chibetto Daizōkyō Sōmokuroku,* I (1934), p. 570b; cf. A. Fonahn, 'Notes on the Tanjur in Oslo' (1936), p. 171a.

(2) Peking edition, No. 5190, JA 1A1-93A5.

Reference: P. Cordier, *Catalogue du fonds tibêtain de la Bibliothèque Nationale,* III (1915), pp. 277-278: 'Mdo-'grel' VII (Tibêtain 202)-1 [cf. M. Lalou, *Rêpertoire du Tanjur d'après le Catalogue de P. Cordier* (1933), p. 32b (Skt. title), p. 77a (Tib. title), p. 216a (author's name in Tib.); also A. Chattopadhyaya, *Catalogue of Indian (Buddhist) Texts in Tibetan Translation,* I: 'Texts (Indian titles) in Tanjur' (1972), p. 270]; *Eiin Pekin-ban Chibetto Daizōkyō Sōmokuroku* (1961), pp. 591-593.

N.B. 1) On the authorship of this commentary see E. Obermiller, 'The Doctrine of the Prajñā-pāramitā as exposed in the Abhisamayālaṃkāra of Maitreya' (1933), p. 10 n.5: 'Acc. to Gser [-phreṅ of Tsoṅ-kha-pa] I.8b.6-9a.1 the Paṇḍit Sthirapāla or Trilakṣa (Ḫbum-phrag-gsum-pa) and the Great Translator Ṅog Lo-dan Śei-rab deny the authorship of Haribhadra. However, as Abhayākaragupta in his Marmakaumudī directly quotes it as the work of Haribhadra, it will be correct to consider it as such'. For the date of Haribhadra see my 'Introduction', para. 22, above.

3) The citations of the *Rgs* are from the Tibetan Recension B. I have not fully used this commentary, because in most cases it offers little help for the textual study of the original Sanskrit versions of the *Rgs*.

4) The Tibetan title *'Phags-pa sdud-pa'i tshigs-su bcad-pa'i 'grel-pa* (1800 śloka, 6 bam-po) is mentioned in the section of the commentaries on Mahāyāna-sūtras in the so-called Denkarma Catalogue; cf. S. Yoshimura, *The Denkar-Ma* (1950), p. 49 [= repr. 1974, p. *165*](Section XVII, Text No. 518); M. Lalou, 'Les textes bouddhiques au temps du Roi Khri-sroṅ-lde-bcan' (1953), p. 331 (Section XX, Text No. 518). This must be Haribhadra's commentary.

2. Buddhaśrījñāna's commentary:

Tibetan text: *Sdud-pa tshigs-su bcad-pa'i dka'-'grel* (Sanskrit title: *Saṃcaya-gāthā-pañjikā*).

Author: Buddhaśrījñāna, a pupil of Haribhadra.

Translators: Vidyākarasiṃha, Dpal-brtsegs (Śrīkūṭa).

(1) Sde-dge edition, No. 3798, ÑA 116A7-189B1.

Reference: Tōhoku Catalogue, p. 572a; cf. A. Fonahn, *op.cit.*, p. 172a.

(2) Peking edition, No. 5196, ÑA 135B5-223A8.

Reference: P. Cordier, *op.cit.*, p. 280: 'Mdo-'grel' VIII (Tibétain 203)-3 [cf. M. Lalou, *op.cit.*, p. 53b (Skt. title), p. 99b (Tib. title), p. 156a (author's name in Skt.); also A. Chattopadhyaya, *op.cit.*, pp. 234 and 462]; *Eiin Pekin-ban Sō-mokuroku*, pp. 595-596.

N.B. 1) This commentary was written at Nālandā in response to an earnest request from a Brahman called Guṇamitra; see H. Hadano, 'Himitsushū Tantora ni okeru Jinyānapāda-ryū ni tsuite' (1950), p. 15(155)a. Buddhaśrījñāna (or Jñānapāda) is dated about 750-800 A.D. by Hadano, *op.cit.*, p. 22(162)a. For the date of Haribhadra see my 'Introduction', para. 22, above; as for the translators see 'Bibl. Notes' IIB1 N.B. 2-3, above.

2) I have very seldom consulted this commentary, which gives almost no help for the textual study of the original Sanskrit versions of the *Rgs*.

3. A commentary ascribed to Dharmaśrī:

Tibetan text: *Śes-rab-kyi pha-rol-tu phyin-pa'i mdzod-kyi lde-mig* (Sanskrit title: *Prajñā-pāramitā-kośa-tāla*).

Author: Dharmaśrī (?).

Translators: Dharmaśrī, Ba-reg maha lo-tsā-ba.

(1) Sde-dge edition, No. 3806, DA 228A4-235A7.

Reference: Tōhoku Catalogue, p. 573b; cf. A. Fonahn, *op.cit.*, pp. 173b-174a.

(2) Peking edition, No. 5204, DA 331B1-340A8.

Reference: P. Cordier, *op.cit.*, p. 283: 'Mdo-'grel' XI (Tibétain 206)-3 [cf. M. Lalou, *op.cit.*, p. 28b (Skt. title), p. 126b (Tib. title), p. 150b (author's name in Skt.); also A. Chattopadhyaya, *op.cit.*, p. 232.

N.B. 1) I have not used this commentary at all. It has been 'considered to have been composed by a translator or some other Tibetan author' (E. Obermiller, 'The Doctrine of Prajñā-pāramitā etc.', 1933, p. 10 n. 7). Moreover, it 'is not held in esteem by the Tibetan scholars. Its authorship is dubious and it is characterized by Tsoṅ-kha-pa as "a feeble work of some unknown Tibetan author"' (E. Obermiller's 'Introduction' to his edition of the *Rgs*, p. 5).

2) A more careful study of this commentary is needed.

## IX. *Prajñā-pāramitā-ratna-guṇa-saṃcaya-gāthā-mantra-dhāraṇī*

1. Sanskrit manuscript:

Dhāraṇī No. 371 of the *Bṛhad-dhāraṇī-saṃgraha*, kept in the Durbar Library, Katmandu.

Reference: Haraprasād Śāstrī, *A Catalogue of Palm-leaf and Selected MSS. belonging to the Durbar Library*, Vol. II (1915), p. 244 (description of the MS.), and p. 262 (contents of the collection).

N.B. 1) To my regret, I have not been able to consult this MS. I imagine, however, that the text is simply a *dhāraṇī* and not the whole text of the *Rgs* (cf. Tibetan MSS. mentioned below). It must be different from a Mongolian version of the *Rgs* found in the dhāraṇī-collection (cf. 'Bibl. Notes' IV 3, above).

2) According to Śāstrī's Catalogue, p. 244, this undated MS. has been copied about 1850 A.D. from an MS. which was then in Japan. I do not know the whereabouts of the original MS.

3) It is not known if this *dhāraṇī* is also included in other collections, for example in the *Bṛhad-dhāraṇī-saṃgraha* kept in the Bir Library at Katmandu: see Sanskrit Seminar of Taisho University, 'Buddhist Manuscripts of the Bir Library' (1956), p. 61b, No. 71d: MS. No. *te* 641/1.

2. Tibetan manuscripts:

a) E 493(6), Sächsische Landesbibliothek, Dresden.

Folio 4A4-B1 (6th text of the collection).

Reference: M. Taube, *Tibetische Handschriften und Blockdrucke*, I (1966), p. 8: No. 15.

Text: (4A4) *rgya-gar-skad-du / arya-pra-dzña-pra-*(so MS.)*ra-mi-da / san-tsa-ya-ga-*(so MS.)*thā / bod-skad-du /* (title written at the bottom of the leaf) *'phags-pa śes-rab-kyi pha-rol-tu phyin-pa sdud-pa tshigsu* (so MS.) *bcad-pa'o / 'phags-pa* (4A5) *'jam-pa-la* (so MS.) *phyag-'tshal-lo // ta-dya-thā / oṃ gha-de gha-de pā-ra-gha-de pā-ra-saṃ-gha-de bho-dha-ye* (r. *oṃ gate gate pāra-gate pāra-saṃgate bodhaye*)(4B1) *svā-hā / śag 'di brjod-pa'i sdud-pa sdon-par* (r. *ston-par*; but MS. seems to be amended to *stoṅ-°*; Taube r. *stoṅ-par*!) *gyuro* (so MS.).

b) E 514a(6), Sächsische Landesbibliothek, Dresden.

Folio 5A3-B4 (6th text of nine dhāraṇī).

Reference: Taube's Catalogue, I, p. 9: No. 16.

Text: (5A3) *rgya-gar-skad-du / arya-pra-*(5A4)*dzña-pā-ri-*(so MS.)*mi-ta-santsa-ya-ga-ta* ⸰ *bod-skad-du / 'phags-pa śes-rab-kyi pha-rol-tu* (5B1) *phyin-pa bsdud-pa tshigs-su bcad-pa* ⸰ *'phags-pa 'jam-dpal-la phyag-'tshal-*(5B2)*lo // ta-dya-thā* ⸰ *ga-te ga-te pā-ra-ga-te pā-ra-saṃ-ga-te bo-dhi-ye* (so MS.) *svā-hā / 'phags-pa* (5B3) *bsdud-pa bton-pa* (Taube wrongly repeats *bton-pa*) *daṅ mñam-mo // źes bcom-ldan-'das-kyi gsuṅs-pa-la* (5B4) *mṅon-par bstod-do // bkra-śis /* ⸰ */*

# A B B R E V I A T I O N S

1. Sanskrit texts of the *Rgs:*

K = MS. No. 10736, Asiatic Society of Bengal (cf. 'Bibl. Notes' IA1).
O = Obermiller's edition (cf. 'Bibl. Notes' IC1).
Ta = MS. No. 246, University of Tōkyō Library (cf. 'Bibl. Notes' IB1).
Tc = MS. No. 248, University of Tōkyō Library (cf. 'Bibl. Notes' IB1).
V = Vaidya's edition (cf. 'Bibl. Notes' IC2).
X = The bilingual Chinese blockprint (cf. 'Bibl. Notes' IB2).

2. Tibetan texts of the *Rgs:*

C = Co-ne edition, No. 1002 (cf. 'Bibl. Notes' IIB1a).
C' = Co-ne edition, No. 1027 (cf. 'Bibl. Notes' IIB4).
D = Sde-dge edition, No. 13 (cf. 'Bibl. Notes' IIB1a).
D' = Sde-dge edition, No. 10 (cf. 'Bibl. Notes' IIB4).
L = Lhasa edition, No. 17 (cf. 'Bibl. Notes' IIB1a).
L' = Lhasa edition, No. 12 (cf. 'Bibl. Notes' IIB4).
M = Manuscript Kanjur kept in the Westdeutsche Staatsbibliothek, Marburg-Lahn (cf. 'Bibl. Notes' IIB1b).
N = Snar-thaṅ edition, No. 17 (cf. 'Bibl. Notes' IIB1a).
N' = Snar-thaṅ edition, No. 11 (cf. 'Bibl. Notes' IIB4).
O = Obermiller's edition (cf. 'Bibl. Notes' IC1).
P = Peking edition, No. 735 (cf. 'Bibl. Notes' IIB1a).
P' = Peking edition, No. 732 (cf. 'Bibl. Notes' IIB4).
Tb = Tunhuang MS. Ch.2.A, India Office Library (cf. 'Bibl. Notes' IIA1).
Tc = Tunhuang MS. Ch.0066 etc., India Office Library (cf. 'Bibl. Notes' IIA1).
Th = Tunhuang MS. No. 1442, Bibliothèque Nationale, Paris (cf. 'Bibl. Notes' IIA2).
Ti = Tunhuang MS. No. 1474, Bibliothèque Nationale, Paris (cf. 'Bibl. Notes' IIA2).
Tj = Tunhuang MS. No. 1475, Bibliothèque Nationale, Paris (cf. 'Bibl. Notes' IIA2).
U = Urga edition (cf. 'Bibl. Notes' IIB1a).
X = The bilingual Chinese blockprint (cf. 'Bibl. Notes' IB2 and IIB2a).

3. Miscellaneous:

A = Recension A; recto of a folio.
a = the first column of a page; pāda *a*.
abbr. = abbreviated, abbreviation.
acc. = according; accusative.
AdP = *Aṣṭādaśasāhasrikā-Prajñāpāramitā*.
adv. = adverb, adverbial(ly).
aor. = aorist.
AsP = *Aṣṭasāhasrikā-Prajñāpāramitā*. Cited from Vaidya's edition by pages and lines (cf. 'Bibliography', VAIDYA, s.v.).
B = Recension B; verso of a folio.
b = the second column of a page; pāda *b*.
beg. = at the beginning of a pāda or of a line.
BHSD = Edgerton, *Buddhist Hybrid Sanskrit Dictionary* (cf. 'Bibliography', EDGERTON, s.v.).
Bibl. Notes = my 'Bibliographical Notes', above.
Bibliography = my 'Bibliography' at the end of this work.
Br. = (in a language of) the Brāhmaṇa literature.
BSkt. = Buddhist Sanskrit.
c = the third column of a page; pāda *c*.
caus. = causative.
cf. = refer(ence) to.
chap. = chapter(s).
Chin. = Chinese.
Chos-grags = *Dge-bśes Chos-kyi grags-pas brtsams-pa'i brda-dag miṅ tshig gsal-ba* (cf. 'Bibliography', CHOS-GRAGS, s.v.).
Cl.Skt. = Classical Sanskrit.
col. = colophon; column.
coll. = collective(ly).
Conze Dict. = Conze, *Materials for a Dictionary of the Prajñāpāramitā Literature*, 1967 (cf. 'Bibliography', CONZE, s.v.).

Conze Index = Conze's Index to Obermiller's edition (cf. 'Bibliography', OBERMILLER, s.v.).
Conze Rgs. = Conze, 'The Calcutta Manuscript of the *Rgs*' (cf. 'Bibliography', CONZE, s.v.). --- Quoted by the number of pages.
Conze Trsl. = Conze, 'Verses on the Accumulation of the Precious Qualities' (cf. 'Bibliography', CONZE, s.v.).
correl. = correlative(ly).
corresp. = corresponding.
CPD = *A Critical Pāli Dictionary*, begun by V. Trenckner (cf. 'Bibliography', TRENCKNER, s.v.).
cpd(s). = compound(s).
d = the fourth column of a page; pāda *d*.
dat. = dative.
denom. = denominative.
du. = dual.
ed. = editor, edited, edition.
eds. = editors.
Edgerton = Edgerton, *Buddhist Hybrid Sanskrit Grammar* (cf. 'Bibliography', EDGERTON, s.v.). —— Quoted by the numbers of sections.
Edgerton Meter = Edgerton, 'Meter, Phonology, and Orthography in Buddhist Hybrid Sanskrit' (cf. 'Bibliography', EDGERTON, s.v.). —— Quoted by the numbers of sections.
Edg.Rgs. = Edgerton, 'The Prajñā-Pāramitā-Ratna-Guṇa-Saṃcaya-Gāthā' (cf. 'Bibliography', EDGERTON, s.v.). —— Quoted by the numbers of sections.
e.l. = at the end of the line.
em. = emend(s), emended, emendation.
encl. = enclitic.
e.p. = at the end of the pāda.
esp. = especially.
f., fem. = feminine.
f., ff. = following.
fn. = footnote(s).
fut. = future.
gdve. = gerundive.
Geiger = Geiger, *Pāli Literatur und Sprache* (cf. 'Bibliography', GEIGER, s.v.). —— Quoted by the numbers of sections.
gen. = genitive.
ger. = gerund.
Gr. = Yuyama, *A Grammar of the Rgs* (cf. 'Bibliography', YUYAMA, s.v.) —— Quoted by the numbers of sections.
IBK = *Indogaku Bukkyōgaku Kenkyū.*
IIJ = *Indo-Iranian Journal.*
impv. = imperative.
indecl. = indeclinable.
inf. = infinitive.
instr. = instrumental.
Jäschke = Jäschke, *A Tibetan-English Dictionary* (cf. 'Bibliography', JÄSCHKE, s.v.).
KTRS = Semičov-Parfionovič-Dandaron, *Kratkij tibetsko-russkij slovar'* (cf. 'Bibliography', SEMIČOV-PARFIONOVIČ-DANDARON, s.v.)
l. = line.
Laṅk. = *Laṅkāvatāra*. Cited from Nanjio's edition by pages and lines (cf. 'Bibliography', NANJIO, s.v.).
Lex. = Yuyama, 'Some Glossarial Notes on the *Rgs*' (cf. 'Bibliography', YUYAMA, s.v.).
lex. = lexical(ly), lexicographical(ly).
Li = Korean edition of the Chinese Tripiṭaka (cf. 'Bibl. Notes' IIId, 'KOREAN EDITION', s.v.).
lit. = literal(ly).
loc. = locative.
m., masc. = masculine.
Mayrhofer = Mayrhofer, *Kurzgefasstes etymologisches Wörterbuch des Altindischen* (cf. 'Bibliography', MAYRHOFER, s.v.).
m.c. = metri causa.
Mehendale = Mehendale, *Historical Grammar of Inscriptional Prakrits* (cf. 'Bibliography', MEHENDALE, s.v.).
metr. = metrical(ly).

mg. = meaning.
MInd. = Middle Indic.
mispr. = misprint(s), misprinted.
misr. = misread(s), misreading.
MS., MSS. = manuscript(s).
Mvy = *Mahāvyutpatti*. Cited by the serial numbers of Sakaki's edition (cf. 'Bibliography', SAKAKI, s.v.).
MWD = Monier-Williams, *A Sanskṛit-English Dictionary*, 2nd rev. ed. (cf. 'Bibliography', MONIER-WILLIAMS, s.v.).
hypermetr. = hypermetrical(ly).
n. = neuter; nominative.
N.B. = note well.
neg. = negative.
Nobel Suv. Index = Nobel, *Suvarṇaprabhāsottamasūtra: Wörterbuch Tibetisch-Deutsch-Sanskrit* (cf. 'Bibliography', NOBEL, s.v.).
nom. = nominative.
nt. = neuter.
num. = numeral.
om. = omit(s), omitted.
op.cit. = (in) the work cited.
opt. = optative.
orig. = original(ly).
para. = paragraph(s).
pass. = passive.
pcle. = particle.
perf. = perfect.
perh. = perhaps.
Pischel = Pischel, *Grammatik der Prākrit-Sprachen* (cf. 'Bibliography', PISCHEL, s.v.). —— Quoted by the numbers of sections.
Pkt. = Prākrit.
pl. = plural.
p.m. = prior member of the compound.
poss. = possible, possibly.
pple. = participle.
ppp. = past passive participle.
pres. = present.
pret. = preterite.
prob. = probable, probably.
PTSD = *Pāli Text Society's Pāli-English Dictionary* (cf. 'Bibliography', RHYS DAVIDS, s.v.).
q.v. = which see.
r. = read(s), reading.
rec. = recension.
rev. = revised.
Rgs = *Prajñāpāramitā-Ratnaguṇasaṃcayagāthā*. Cited by the numbers of chapters and verses.
Schmidt = Schmidt, *Nachträge zum Sanskrit-Wörterbuch in kürzerer Fassung von O. Böhtlingk* (cf. 'Bibliography', SCHMIDT, s.v.).
sec. = secondary, secondarily.
Sen = Sen, 'An Outline Syntax of Buddhistic Sanskrit' (cf. 'Bibliography', SEN, s.v.).
Seṭh = Seṭh, *Pāia-sadda-mahaṇṇavo* (cf. 'Bibliography', SEṬH, s.v.).
sg. = singular.
Sha = Chi-sha edition of the Chinese Tripiṭaka (cf. 'Bibl. Notes' IIIc 'CHI-SHA EDITION', s.v.).
Shuku = *Dainippon Kōtei Daizōkyō* (cf. 'Bibliography', FUKUDA-SHIMADA-SHIKIGAWA, s.v.).
Skt. = Sanskrit.
Speijer = Speijer, *Sanskrit-Syntax* (cf. 'Bibliography', SPEIJER, s.v.). —— Quoted by the number of sections.
Speyer = Speyer, *Vedische und Sanskrit-Syntax* (cf. 'Bibliography', SPEYER, s.v.). —— Quoted by the numbers of sections.
ŚsP = *Śatasāhasrikā-Prajñāpāramitā*.
Sūtrāl. = Asaṅga's *Mahāyāna-Sūtrālaṃkāra* (cf. 'Bibliography', LÉVI, s.v.).
Suv. = *Suvarṇaprabhāsottamasūtra*.
s.v., ss.vv. = under the word(s).
T., Taishō = *Taishō Shinshū Daizōkyō* (cf. 'Bibliography', TAKAKUSU, s.v.).
Tagare = Tagare, *Historical Grammar of Apabhraṃśa* (cf. 'Bibliography', TAGARE, s.v.). —— Quoted by the number of sections.

Taki = Taki's Japanese translation of the Chinese version of the *Rgs* (cf. 'Bibl. Notes', VI 2; 'Bibliography', TAKI, s.v.).
Thumb-Hauschild = Thumb, *Handbuch des Sanskrit*. 3. Auflage von Hauschild (cf. 'Bibliography', THUMB, s.v.). —— Quoted by the numbers of sections.
Tib. = Tibetan.
trsl. = translate(s), translated, translator(s), translation.
trslit. = transliterate(s), transliterated, transliteration.
unmetr. = unmetrical(ly).
Ved. = Vedic.
v.l., vv.ll. = variant reading(s).
voc. = vocative.
vs., vss. = verse(s).
w. = with.
Wackernagel(-Debrunner) = Wackernagel(-Debrunner), *Altindische Grammatik* (cf. 'Bibliography', WACKERNAGEL, s.v.). —— Quoted by the numbers of volumes and sections.
Whitney = Whitney, *A Sanskrit Grammar* (cf. 'Bibliography', WHITNEY, s.v.). —— Quoted by the numbers of sections.
Whitney Roots = Whitney, *The Roots, Verb-Forms, and Primary Derivatives of the Sanskrit Language* (cf. 'Bibliography', WHITNEY, s.v.).
w.n. = with note(s).
Wogihara Mvy = Wogihara, *Bon-Kan Taiyaku Bukkyō Jiten* (cf. 'Bibliography', WOGIHARA, s.v.). —— Quoted by the numbers of sections.
w.r. = wrong reading.
WSJD = *Kanyaku Taishō Bon-Wa Daijiten*, begun by U. Wogihara (cf. 'Bibliography', WOGIHARA, s.v.).
wt.n. = without note.

## Symbols used for textual readings

[ ] indicates that this part is damaged in the manuscript.
< > indicates that this part is missing in the manuscript.
: indicates that the reading agrees with another version, e.g. Skt. *tathatā* : Tib.A *de-bẑin-ñid*.
= indicates that the reading is adopted by Obermiller (abbr. O) or by Vaidya (abbr. V), e.g. KX *tathatā* (= O), Tac *oa tathā* (= V).

## Underlines used in the Tibetan text

——— indicates that this part of Recension A differs from Recension B.
~~~~~ indicates that there are two variant readings in Recension B, and one of them is identical with that of Recension A.
===== indicates that there are two variant readings in Recension B, and both of them are entirely different from that of Recension A.
~~~~~

Table I

Explanations as to which Prajñāpāramitā text each recension belongs

| Recensions | Texts | Reference to 'Bibl. Notes' | Has Haribhadra revised text? | AsP | AdP | ŚsP | No statement | Title/colophon missing |
|---|---|---|---|---|---|---|---|---|
| Skt.A | K | IA1 | No statement | | | x | | |
| Skt.B | Baroda | IB1 | Yes | x | | | | |
| ,, | C | ,, | Yes | x | | | | |
| ,, | Ta | ,, | Yes | x | | | | |
| ,, | Tb | ,, | Yes | x | | | | |
| ,, | Tc | ,, | Yes | x | | | | |
| ,, | X | IB2 | Yes | x | | | | |
| Tib.B | C | IIB1a | No statement | | | | x | |
| ,, | D | ,, | ,, | | | | x | |
| ,, | L | ,, | ,, | | | | x | |
| ,, | N | ,, | ,, | | | | x | |
| ,, | P | ,, | ,, | | | | x | |
| ,, | U | ,, | ,, | | | | x | |
| Tib.B | C' | IIB4 | No statement | | x | | | |
| ,, | D' | ,, | ,, | | x | | | |
| ,, | L' | ,, | ,, | | x | | | |
| ,, | N' | ,, | ,, | | x | | | |
| ,, | P' | ,, | ,, | | x | | | |
| Tib.B | E | IIB1b | No statement | | | | x | |
| ,, | M | ,, | ,, | | | | x | |
| Tib.B | X | IIB2a | Yes | x | | | | |
| Tib.B | Ga | IIB2b | Yes | | x | | | |
| ,, | Gb | ,, | Yes | | x | | | |
| ,, | Gc | ,, | Yes | | x | | | |
| ,, | W | ,, | Yes | | x | | | |
| Tib.B | Sa | IIB3a | Yes | | x | | | |
| ,, | Sb | ,, | Yes | | x | | | |
| Tib.B | Ta | IIB3b | No statement | | | | x | |
| Tib.A | Tb | IIA1 | ,, | | | | x | |
| ,, | Tc | ,, | ,, | | | x | | |
| Tib.B | Td | IIB3b | ,, | | | | | x |
| ,, | Te | ,, | ,, | | | | | x |
| ,, | Tf | ,, | ,, | | | | | x |
| ,, | Tg | ,, | ,, | | | | | x |
| Tib.A | Th | IIA2 | ,, | | | x | | |
| ,, | Ti | ,, | ,, | | | x | | |
| ,, | Tj | ,, | ,, | | | x | | |
| Chin. | | III | No statement | | | | x | |

Table II

Contents of the Sanskrit Manuscripts
(Cf. 'Bibliographical Notes' IA1, IB1-2)

| Chap. | Baroda | C | K | Ta | Tb | Tc | X |
|---|---|---|---|---|---|---|---|
| title | * | 71A* | * | 1A | 1A | 1A | 1A1* |
| preface | 1B | 71B1-2 | 2B1-2 | 1B1-2 | 1B1-2 | 1B1-3 | 1B1-2B1 |
| I | 1B-3B | 71B2-74A4 | 2B2-5A1 | 1B2-4A3 | 1B2-3B7 | 1B2-4B5 | 2B1-11B4 |
| II | 3B-4A | 74A4-75A5 | 5A1-6A2 | 4A3-5A5 | 3B7-4B7 | 4B5-6B2 | 11B4-16A1 |
| III | 4B-5A | 75A5-76A1 | 6A2-6B6 | 5A5-6A3 | 4B7-5B3 | 6B2-7B2 | 16A4-19A1 |
| IV | 5A-B | 76A1-76B2 | 6B6-7B1 | 6A3-B5 | 5B3-6A4 | 7B2-8B1 | 19A1-21B1 |
| V | 5B-6A | 76B2-77A5 | 7B1-8A5 | 6B5-7B4 | 6A4-B7 | 8B1-9B2 | 21B1-24B4 |
| VI | 6A-B | 77A5-78A2 | 8A5-9A3 | 7B4-8B2 | 6B7-7B3 | 9B2-10B4 | 24B4-27B4 |
| VII | 6B-? | 78A2-B3 | 9A3-B5 | 8B2-9A4 | 7B4-8A5 | 10B4-11B2 | 28A1-30A4 |
| VIII | ? - ? | 78B3-79A1 | 9B5-10A3 | 9A4-B3 | 8A5-B2 | 11B2-12A2 | 30A4-31B4 |
| IX | ? -7B | 79A1-4 | 10A3-6 | 9B3-5 | 8B3-5 | 12A2-6 | 31B4-32B1 |
| X | 7B-8B | 79A4-80A1 | 10A6-11A4 | 9B5-10B5 | 8B5-9B3 | 12A6-13B2 | 32B1-36A1 |
| XI | 8B- ? | 80A1-B5 | 11A4-12A2 | 10B5-11B4 | 9B3-10A7 | 13B2-15A6 | 36A1-39A4 |
| XII | ? -10A | 80B5-81B1 | 12A3-13A1 | 11B4-12B2 | 10A7-11A3 | 15A6-16B1 | 39A4-42A1 |
| XIII | 10A-B | 81B2-4 | 13A1-4 | 12B3-5 | 11A3-6 | 16B1-5 | 42A1-43A4 |
| XIV | 10B-11A | 81B4-82B2 | 13A4-14A3 | 12B5-13B3 | 11A6-B6* | 16B5-18A1 | 43A4-46B4 |
| XV | 11A-B | 82B2-83A4 | 14A3-B5 | 13B3-14B1 | 11B6-12A5 | 18A1-19A1 | 47A1-49B4 |
| XVI | 11B-12A | 83A4-B4 | 14B5-15A6 | 14B1-15A1 | 12A6-13A1 | 19A1-B5 | 49B4-51B4 |
| XVII | 12A-B | 83B5-84A6 | 15A6-16A2 | 15A1-B2 | 13A1-B5 | 19B5-20B4 | 52A1-54B1 |
| XVIII | 12B-13A | 84A6-85A1 | 16A2-B4 | 15B2-16B2 | 13B6-14A7 | 20B4-21B4 | 54B4-57A4 |
| XIX | 13A-14A | 85A2-B3 | 16B5-17B1 | 16B2-17B1 | 14A7-15A2 | 21B4-22B5 | 57B1-60A4 |
| XX | 14A-15B | 85B3-87B3 | 17B1-19B1 | 17B2-19B3 | 15A2-17A1 | 22B5-25B3 | 60A4-68A4 |
| XXI | 15B-16A | 87B4-88A5 | 19B1-20A4 | 19B3-20A5 | 17A1-B3 | 25B3-26B2 | 68A4-71A1 |
| XXII | 16A-17A | 88A5-89A5 | 20A4-21A5 | 20A5-21B1 | 17B3-18B3 | 26B2-28A4 | 71A1-75A4 |
| XXIII | 17A-B | 89A5-B3 | 21A5-B4 | 21B2-5 | 18B3-19A1 | 28A4-B5 | 75A4-76B4 |
| XXIV | 17B-18A | 89B3-90A4 | 21B4-22A5 | 22A1-B1 | 19A1-B1 | 28B5-29B3 | 76B4-79A1 |
| XXV | 18A-B | 90A4-B4 | 22A5-B5 | 22B1-23A2 | 19B1-20A1 | 29B3-30A6 | 79A1-81A4 |
| XXVI | 18B-19A | 90B4-91A6 | 22B5-23B2 | 23A2-B5 | 20A2-B3 | 30A6-31B1 | 81A4-84A1 |
| XXVII | 19A-B | 91A6-92A3 | 23B2-24A5 | 23B5-24B3 | 20B3-21A6 | 31B1-32B3 | 84A1-87A1 |
| XXVIII | 19B-20A | 92A3-B3 | 24A6-25A1 | 24B3-25A5 | 21A6-B7 | 32B3-33B2 | 87A4-89B1 |
| XXIX | 20A-21A | 92B4-93B4 | 25A1-26A3 | 25A5-26B3 | 21B7-23A2 | 33B2-35A6 | 89B4-94B1 |
| XXX | 21A-22A | 93B5-94B6 | 26A4-27B1 | 26B3-28A1 | 23A2-24A3 | 35A6-36B5 | 94B1-99B1 |
| XXXI | 22A-23B | 94B6-98A6 | 27B1-29A1 | 28A1-29B2 | 24A3-25B1 | 36B6-39A2 | 99B1-105B4 |
| XXXII | 23B-24A | 98B1-99A1 | 29A1-B2 | 29B2-30A3 | 25B1-7 | 39A2-B6 | 105B4-107B4 |
| 2 vss | 24A | 99A1-3 | missing | 30A3-5 | missing | 39B6-40A4 | 108A1-B4 |
| col. | 24A-B | 99A4-6 | 29B2-6 | 30B1-2 | | 40A4-5 | 109A1-4 |

Notes: Baroda * The pagination is taken from Vaidya's edition.
C * Another pagination runs from 1 to 19.
K * Rāhulabhadra's *Prajñāpāramitāstotra* (folios 1B1-2B1).
Tb * MS. gives a figure *15* for this chapter.
X * The text is written in both Lañtsha and Dbu-can scripts: 1 = 1/2, 4 = 4/5.

Table III

Contents of the Tibetan Texts in the Kanjur Editions
(Cf. 'Bibliographical Notes' IIB1a)

| Chap. | C | D | L | N | P | U |
|---|---|---|---|---|---|---|
| title | 1B1-2 | 1B1 | 189A2-3 | 196B6 | 1B1-2 | 1B1 |
| homage | 1B2-3 | 1B1-2 | 189A3 | 196B6-7 | 1B2 | 1B1-2 |
| preface | 1B3-5 | 1B2-3 | 189A3-4 | 196B7-197A1 | 1B2-4 | 1B2-3 |
| I | 1B5-4A1 | 1B3-3B2 | 189A4-191B3 | 197A1-199B1 | 1B4-3B1 | 1B3-3B2 |
| II | 4A1-B6 | 3B2-4A6 | 191B3-192B4 | 199B1-200B4 | 3B1-4A7 | 3B2-4A7 |
| III | 4B6-5A6 | 4A6-B5 | 192B4-193A7 | 200B4-201A7 | 4A7-B8 | 4A7-B5 |
| IV | 5A6-B5 | 4B5-5A4 | 193A7-194A1 | 201A7-202A2 | 4B8-5A7 | 4B5-5A4 |
| V | 5B5-6A7 | 5A4-B4 | 194A1-B5 | 202A2-B6 | 5A7-6A1 | 5A4-B4 |
| VI | 6A7-7A1 | 5B4-6A4 | 194B5-195B2 | 202B6-203B3 | 6A1-B3 | 5B4-6A4 |
| VII | 7A1-B1 | 6A5-B3 | 195B2-196A3 | 203B3-204A4 | 6B3-7A3 | 6A5-B3 |
| VIII | 7B1-6 | 6B3-7 | 196A3-B1 | 204A4-B2 | 7A3-7 | 6B3-7 |
| IX | 7B6-8 | 6B7-7A1 | 196B1-4 | 204B2-5 | 7A7-B2 | 6B7-7A1 |
| X | 7B8-8B3 | 7A1-B2 | 196B4-197B1 | 204B5-205B2 | 7B2-8A5 | 7A1-B2 |
| XI | 8B3-9A5 | 7B2-8A3 | 197B1-198A6 | 205B2-206A5 | 8A5-B7 | 7B2-8A3 |
| XII | 9A5-B6 | 8A3-B4 | 198A6-199A3 | 206A5-207A2 | 8B7-9B1 | 8A3-B4 |
| XIII | 9B6-8 | 8B4-6 | 199A3-5 | 207A2-4 | 9B1-4 | 8B4-5 |
| XIV | 9B8-10B1 | 8B6-9A6 | 199A5-200A2 | 207A4-B7 | 9B4-10A5 | 8B6-9A6 |
| XV | 10B1-11A1 | 9A6-B5 | 200A2-B5 | 207B7-208B2 | 10A5-B6 | 9A6-B5 |
| XVI | 11A1-7 | 9B5-10A3 | 200B5-201A5 | 208B2-209A2 | 10B6-11A6 | 9B5-10A3 |
| XVII | 11A7-B6 | 10A3-B2 | 201A5-B7 | 209A2-B3 | 11A6-B5 | 10A3-B2 |
| XVIII | 11B6-12A6 | 10B2-11A2 | 201B7-202B2 | 209B3-210A6 | 11B5-12A6 | 10B2-11A2 |
| XIX | 12A6-B5 | 11A2-B1 | 202B3-203A4 | 210A6-B7 | 12A6-B6 | 11A2-B1 |
| XX | 12B5-14A4 | 11B1-12B7 | 203A4-205A4 | 210B7-212B5 | 12B6-14B1 | 11B1-12B7 |
| XXI | 14A4-B4 | 12B7-13A7 | 205A4-B7 | 212B5-213A7 | 14B1-15A3 | 12B7-13A7 |
| XXII | 14B4-15B1 | 13A7-14A4 | 205B7-207A1 | 213A7-214B1 | 15A3-16A2 | 13A7-14A4 |
| XXIII | 15B1-5 | 14A4-B1 | 207A1-6 | 214B1-6 | 16A2-7 | 14A4-B1 |
| XXIV | 15B6-16A4 | 14B1-6 | 207A6-B6 | 214B6-215A6 | 16A7-B6 | 14B1-6 |
| XXV | 16A4-B2 | 14B6-15A4 | 207B6-208A7 | 215A6-B6 | 16B6-17A5 | 14B6-15A4 |
| XXVI | 16B2-17A2 | 15A4-B3 | 208A7-209A2 | 215B6-216A7 | 17A5-B5 | 15A4-B3 |
| XXVII | 17A2-B4 | 15B3-16A4 | 209A2-B7 | 216A7-217A4 | 17B5-18A7 | 15B3-16A4 |
| XXVIII | 17B4-18A4 | 16A4-B3 | 209B7-210B1 | 217A4-B5 | 18A7-B7 | 16A4-B3 |
| XXIX | 18A4-19A2 | 16B3-17B1 | 210B1-211B5 | 217B5-219A1 | 18B7-19B6 | 16B3-17B1 |
| XXX | 19A2-20A2 | 17B1-18A6 | 211B5-213A1 | 219A1-220A4 | 19B6-20B6 | 17B1-18A6 |
| XXXI | 20A2-21A5 | 18A6-19A7 | 213A1-214B2 | 220A4-221B4 | 20B6-22A1 | 18A6-19A7 |
| XXXII | 21A5-B4 | 19B1-6 | 214B2-215A3 | 221B4-222A5 | 22A1-8 | 19A7-B6 |
| 2 vss | missing | missing | missing | missing | missing | missing |
| col. | 21B4-5 | 19B6-7 | 215A3-4 | 222A5 | 22A8 | 19B6-7 |

Table IV

Contents of the Tibetan Texts from the *AdP*, Chapter 84
(Cf. 'Bibliographical Notes' IIB4)

| Chap. | C' | D' | L' | N' | P' |
|---|---|---|---|---|---|
| title | 193B7 | 163A5 | 253B2-3 | 147A6 | 180A4 |
| homage | missing | missing | missing | missing | missing |
| preface | 193B7-8 | 163A5-6 | 253B3-4 | 147A6-B1 | 180A4-5 |
| I | 193B8-195B7 | 163A6-165A1 | 253B4-256A2 | 147B1-149B7 | 180A5-182A1 |
| II | 195B7-196B5 | 165A1-B5 | 256A2-257A4 | 149B7-151A2 | 182A1-183B6 |
| III | 196B5-197A6 | 165B5-166A4 | 257A4-B6 | 151A2-B5 | 182B6-183A6 |
| IV | 197A6-B5 | 166A4-B3 | 257B6-258B1 | 151B6-152A7 | 183A6-B5 |
| V | 197B6-198A7 | 166B3-167A4 | 258B1-259A5 | 152A7-153A4 | 183B5-184A7 |
| VI | 198A7-199A1 | 167A4-B5 | 259A5-260A2 | 153A4-154A1 | 184A7-B8 |
| VII | 199A1-B1 | 167B5-168A4 | 260A2-B3 | 154A1-B3 | 184B8-185A7 |
| VIII | 199B1-5 | 168A4-7 | 260B3-261A1 | ;54B3-155A1 | 185A7-B3 |
| IX | 199B5-7 | 168A7-B2 | 261A1-4 | 155A1-4 | 185B3-5 |
| X | 199B8-200B2 | 168B2-169A3 | 261A4-262A2 | 155A4-156A2 | 185B5-186A7 |
| XI | 200B2-201A4 | 169A3-B4 | 262A2-263A1 | 156A2-B7 | 186A7-187A1 |
| XII | 201A4-B6 | 169B4-170A5 | 263A1-B5 | 156B7-157B5 | 187A1-B2 |
| XIII | 201B6-8 | 170A5-7 | 263B5-264A1 | 157B5-158A1 | 187B2-4 |
| XIV | 201B8-202B2 | 170A7-171A1 | 264A1-B5 | 158A1-B5 | 187B4-188A5 |
| XV | 202B2-203A2 | 171A1-B1 | 264B5-265B1 | 158B5-159B1 | 188A5-B5 |
| XVI | 203A2-B1 | 171B1-6 | 265B1-266A2 | 159B1-160A2 | 188B5-189A4 |
| XVII | 203B1-204A1 | 171B6-172A5 | 266A2-B4 | 160A2-B4 | 189A4-B3 |
| XVIII | 204A1-B2 | 172A5-B5 | 266B4-267B1 | 160B4-161B1 | 189B3-190A4 |
| XIX | 204B2-205A1 | 172B5-173A3 | 267B1-268A3 | 161B1-162A3 | 190A4-B3 |
| XX | 205A1-206B4 | 173A3-174B2 | 268A3-270A5 | 162A3-164A5 | 190B3-192A4 |
| XXI | 206B4-207A5 | 174B2-175A2 | 270A5-271A2 | 164A5-165A1 | 192A4-B4 |
| XXII | 207A5-208A3 | 175A2-B5 | 271A2-272A4 | 165A1-166A5 | 192B4-193B1 |
| XXIII | 208A3-8 | 175B5-176A2 | 272A4-B2 | 166A5-B3 | 193B1-5 |
| XXIV | 208A8-B7 | 176A2-7 | 272B3-273A3 | 166B3-167A4 | 193B5-194A3 |
| XXV | 208B7-209A6 | 176A7-B5 | 273A3-B4 | 167A4-B5 | 194A4-B1 |
| XXVI | 209A6-B6 | 176B5-177A5 | 273B4-274A6 | 167B5-168B1 | 194B1-195A1 |
| XXVII | 209B6-210B1 | 177A5-B5 | 274A6-275A4 | 168B1-169A6 | 195A1-B2 |
| XXVIII | 210B1-211A1 | 177B5-178A4 | 275A4-B6 | 169A6-170A2 | 195B2-196A1 |
| XXIX | 211A1-B8 | 178A4-179A2 | 275B6-277A3 | 170A2-171A7 | 196A1-B7 |
| XXX | 211B8-212B8 | 179A2-B7 | 277A3-278A7 | 171A7-172B5 | 196B7-197B5 |
| XXXI | 212B8-214A4 | 179B7-181A1 | 278A7-280A2 | 172B5-174B2 | 197B5-198B6 |
| XXXII | 214A4-B3 | 181A1-6 | 280A2-B3 | 174B2-175A3 | 198B6-199A4 |
| 2 vss | missing | missing | missing | missing | missing |
| col. | 214B3-4 | 181A6-7 | 280B3-4 | 175A3-4 | 199A4-5 |

Table V

Contents of the Tibetan Texts of the Blockprints
(Cf. 'Bibliographical Notes' IIB2a-b)

| Chapters | X | Ga | Gb | Gc | W |
|---|---|---|---|---|---|
| title | 1A3/1B3 | 1B1 | 411B1-2* | 1A1-3 | 190B6 |
| homage | 1B3-2A3 | 1B2 | 411B2* | 1A3-B1 | 190B6-7 |
| preface | 2A3-B3 | 1B2-3 | 411B2-4* | 1B2-2B2 | 190B7-8 |
| I | 2B3-11B6 | 1B3-3A7 | 411B4*-415A2 | 2B2-12A4 | 190B8-192A8 |
| II | 11B6-16A3 | 3A7-4A3 | 415A3-416B1 | 12A4-17A1 | 192A8-193A2 |
| III | 16A6-19A3 | 4A3-B2 | 416B1-417A7 | 17A1-19B3 | 193A2-B1 |
| IV | 19A3-21B3 | 4B2-8 | 417A7-418A4 | 19B3-22A2 | 193B1-8 |
| V | 21B3-24B6 | 4B8-5B1 | 418A4-419A5 | 22A2-25A3 | 193B8-194A8 |
| VI | 24B6-27B6 | 5B1-6A1 | 419A5-420A5 | 25A3-28B1 | 194A8-B9 |
| VII | 28A3-30A6 | 6A1-8 | 420A5-421A1 | 28B1-30B3 | 194B9-195A6 |
| VIII | 30A6-31A6 | 6A8-B4 | 421A2-B1 | 30B3-32A3 | 195A6-B1 |
| IX | 31A6-32B3 | 6B4-5 | 421B1-5 | 32A3-33A1 | 195B1-3 |
| X | 32B3-36A3 | 6B6-7A7 | 421B5-422B6 | 33A2-36A4 | 195B3-196A4 |
| XI | 36A3-39A6 | 7A7-B8 | 422B6-423B7 | 36A4-39B3 | 196A4-B4 |
| XII | 39A6-42B3 | 7B8-8B1 | 423B7-425A1 | 39B3-42B4 | 196B4-197A4 |
| XIII | 42B3-43A6 | 8B1-3 | 425A1-4 | 43A1-B2 | 197A4-6 |
| XIV | 43A6-46B6 | 8B3-9A4 | 425A4-426A5 | 43B2-47A2 | 197A7-B7 |
| XV | 47A3-49B6 | 9A4-B4 | 426A5-427A4 | 47A2-49B4 | 197B7-198A6 |
| XVI | 49B6-51B6 | 9B4-10A1 | 427A4-B7 | 49B4-52A1 | 198A6-B3 |
| XVII | 52A3-54B3 | 10A1-8 | 427B7-428B4 | 52A1-54B1 | 198B3-199A1 |
| XVIII | 54B6-57A6 | 10A8-B8 | 428B4-429B3 | 54B1-57A4 | 199A1-10 |
| XIX | 57B3-60A6 | 10B8-11A7 | 429B3-430B1 | 57A4-59B4 | 199A10-B9 |
| XX | 60A6-68A6 | 11A7-12B6 | 430B1-433A3 | 60A1-68A1 | 199B9-201A5 |
| XXI | 68A6-71A3 | 12B6-13A6 | 433A3-434A1 | 68A1-70B2 | 201A5-B4 |
| XXII | 71A3-75A6 | 13A6-14A2 | 434A1-435B1 | 70B2-74A2 | 201B4-202A9 |
| XXIII | 75A6-76B6 | 14A2-6 | 435B1-7 | 74A2-76A4 | 202A9-B3 |
| XXIV | 76B6-79A3 | 14A6-B4 | 435B7-436B2 | 76B1-78B1 | 202B3-10 |
| XXV | 79A3-81A6 | 14B4-15A1 | 436B2-437A5 | 78B1-80B1 | 202B10-203A6 |
| XXVI | 81A6-84A3 | 15A2-B1 | 437A5-438A4 | 80B2-83A4 | 203A6-B5 |
| XXVII | 84A3-87A3 | 15B1-16A1 | 438A4-439A5 | 83A4-86B2* | 203B5-204A5 |
| XXVIII | 87A6-89A3 | 16A1-8 | 439A5-440A3 | 86B2*-89A2 | 204A5-B3 |
| XXIX | 89A3-94B3 | 16A8-17A5 | 440A3-441B5 | 89A2-94A2 | 204B3-205A8 |
| XXX | 94B3-99B3 | 17A5-18A2 | 441B5-443A7 | 94A2-99A2 | 205A8-206A4 |
| XXXI | 99B3-105B6 | 18A2-19A2 | 443A7-445B2 | 99A2-105B1 | 206A4-207A4 |
| XXXII | 105B6-107B6 | 19A2-8 | 445B2-446A6 | 105B1-107B3 | 207A4-B2 |
| 2 vss | 108A3-109A3 | missing | missing | missing | missing |
| colophon | 109A3-6 | 19B1 | 446A7-B2 | 107B4-108B1 | 207B2-4 |

Notes: Gb * Gb numbers 411A twice: title page and beginning of the text. The latter page should be 411B.
Gc * I have not received microfilms of folios 85B, 86B and 87B. The figure 86B2 is therefore calculated from the previous and following pages.

Table VI

Contents of the Tibetan Manuscripts
(Cf. 'Bibliographical Notes' IIB1b, 3a)

| Chapters | E | M | Sa | Sb |
|---|---|---|---|---|
| title | 181A5-6 | 1A1-2A2 | 1B1-2 | 1B1-2 |
| homage | 181A6 | 2A2 | 1B2 | 1B2 |
| preface | 181A6-8 | 2A2-B1 | 1B2-3 | 1B2-3 |
| I | 181A8-183B4 | 2B1-5B3 | 1B3-4B2 | 1B4-4A4 |
| II | 183B4-184B6 | 5B3-6B6 | 4B2-5B7 | 4A4-5A7 |
| III | 184B6-185A8 | 6B6-7B2 | 5B7-6B3 | 5A7-6A4 |
| IV | 185A8-186A1 | 7B2-8A4 | 6B3-7A6 | 6A4-B6 |
| V | 186A1-B5 | 8A4-B8 | 7A6-8A5 | 6B6-7B3 |
| VI | 186B5-187A8 | 8B8-9B5 | 8A5-9A3 | 7B3-8A7 |
| VII | 187A8-B8 | 9B5-10A6 | 9A3-B6 | 8B1-9A2 |
| VIII | 187B8-188A5 | 10A7-B4 | 9B6-10A5 | 9A2-7 |
| IX | 188A5-7 | 10B4-7 | 10A5-7 | 9B1-3 |
| X | 188A7-189A3 | 10B7-11B4 | 10B1-11A7 | 9B3-10B2 |
| XI | 189A3-B7 | 11B4-12B1 | 11A7-12A5 | 10B2-11A7 |
| XII | 189B7-190B2 | 12B1-13A5 | 12A5-13A3* | 11A7-12A4 |
| XIII | 190B2-5 | 13A5-8 | 13A3-5 | 12A4-6 |
| XIV | 190B5-191A7 | 13A8-14A4 | 13A5-14A4 | 12A6-13A5 |
| XV | 191A7-192A1 | 14A4-B7 | 14A4-B7 | 13A6-14A1 |
| XVI | 192A1-192B1 | 14B7-15A7 | 14B7-15B2 | 14A2-B2 |
| XVII | 192B1-193A2 | 15A7-16A1 | 15B2-16A5 | 14B2-15A4 |
| XVIII | 193A2-B4 | 16A1-B4 | 16A5-17A2 | 15A4-B7 |
| XIX | 193B4-194A5 | 16B4-17A5 | 17A2-B5 | 15B7-16B3 |
| XX | 194A5-196A3 | 17A5-19A5 | 17B6-20A3 | 16B3-18B2 |
| XXI | 196A3-B6 | 19A5-B8 | 20A3-B7 | 18B2-19A5 |
| XXII | 196B6-197B7 | 19B8-21A2 | 20B7-22A4 | 19A5-20A6 |
| XXIII | 197B7-198A5 | 21A2-7 | 22A4-B2 | 20A7-B3 |
| XXIV | 198A5-B5 | 21A8-B8 | 22B2-23A3 | 20B3-21A5 |
| XXV | 198B5-199A5 | 21B8-22A8 | 23A3-B4 | 21A5-B5 |
| XXVI | 199A5-B7 | 22A8-23A3 | 23B4-24A7 | 21B5-22A7 |
| XXVII | 199B7-200B3 | 23A3-B8 | 24A7-25A6 | 22A7-23A5 |
| XXVIII | 200B3-201A5 | 23B8-24B1 | 25A6-26A2 | 23A5-B7 |
| XXIX | 201A5-202A8 | 24B1-25B4 | 26A2-27B1 | 23B7-25A3 |
| XXX | 202A8-203B3 | 25B4-26B8 | 27B1-28B6 | 25A3-26A6 |
| XXXI | 203B3-205A4 | 26B8-28B1 | 28B6-30B3 | 26A6-28A1 |
| XXXII | 205A4-B4 | 28B1-29A1 | 30B3-31A6 | 28A1-B2 |
| 2 vss | missing | missing | missing | missing |
| colophon | 205B4 | 29A1-3 | 31A6-B2 | 28B3-5 |

Note: Sa * This final pāda is however written at the bottom of the page.

### Table VIIa

### Contents of the Tibetan Manuscripts from Tunhuang*
[India Office Library]

(Cf. 'Bibliographical Notes' IIA1, IIB3b)

| Chapters | Ta | Tb | Tc | Td | Te | Tf | Tg |
|---|---|---|---|---|---|---|---|
| title | 1A1-2 | 1A1-2 | | | | | |
| homage | 1A2 | 1A2-3 | | | | | |
| preface | 1A2-4 | 1A3-B1 | | | | | |
| I | 1A4-6B2 | 1B1-9A1 | (2A1-3B6) | | | (3A1-B5) | (3A1)-5 |
| II | 6B2-9A1 | 9A1-12B1 | (6A1)-B1 | | | | 3A5-(B6) |
| III | 9A1-10B2 | 12B2-14B3 | 6B1-7B3 | | | | |
| IV | 10B2-11B5 | 14B3-16B2 | 7B3-8B2 | (94A1)-4 | | (10A1)-5 | |
| V | 11B5-13B2 | 16B2-19A1 | 8B2-(5) | 94A4-(B4) | | 10A5-(B5) | |
| VI | 13B2-15A4 | 19A1-21B1 | | | | | |
| VII | 15A4-16B2 | 21B1-23A4 | (11A1)-B2 | | | | |
| VIII | 16B2-17A5 | 23A4-24A4 | 11B2-(6) | | | | |
| IX | 17B1-4 | 24A4-B4 | | | | | |
| X | 17B4-19B4 | 24B4-27A4 | (13A1)-B2 | | (16A1)-B1 | | |
| XI | 19B4-21B2 | 27A4-29B1 | 13B2-(6) | | 16B1-(5) | (18A1-B5) | |
| XII | 21B2-23A5 | 29B2-31B3 | (15A1)-B3 | | | | (10A1)-4 |
| XIII | 23A5-B4 | 31B3-32A3 | 15B3-(5) | | | (21A1)-3 | 10A5-6 |
| XIV | 23B4-25B1 | 32A3-34B1 | | | | 21A3-(B5) | 10A6-B6 |
| XV | 25B2-27A2 | 34B1-36A4 | (18A1) | | (22A1)-4 | | |
| XVI | 27A2-28A4 | 36A4-37B4 | 18A1-B4 | | 22A5-(B5) | | |
| XVII | 28A4-29B4 | 37B4-39B2 | 18B4-(5) | | | | |
| XVIII | 29B4-31A4 | 39B2-41B2 | (20A1)-B4 | | | | |
| XIX | 31A5-32B3 | 41B2-43A4 | 20B4-21B2 | | | | (10B top)* |
| XX | 32B3-37A3 | 43A4-49A3 | 21B2-24B2 | | (30A1)-B2 | (32A1)-33A3 | |
| XXI | 37A3-38B4 | 49A3-51A3 | 24B2-(5) | | 30B2-(5) | 33A3-(B5) | |
| XXII | 38B4-41A4 | 51A3-54A4 | (26A1)-27A3 | | | | |
| XXIII | 41A4-42A2 | 54A4-55A4 | 27A3-B3 | | | | |
| XXIV | 42A2-43A4 | 55A4-56B4 | 27B4-28B1 | | | | |
| XXV | 43A4-44A5 | 56B4-58A4 | 28B1-29A4 | | (36A1)-B5 | | |
| XXVI | 44A5-46A1 | 58A4-60A4 | 29A4-30A5 | | 36B5(-36B5) | | |
| XXVII | 46A1-47B4 | 60A4-62B2 | 30A5-31B2 | | | | |
| XXVIII | 47B4-49A3 | 62B2-64A4 | 31B2-32A5 | | | | |
| XXIX | 49A4-52A3 | 64A4-67A2 | 32A5-34A2 | | | | |
| XXX | 52A3-55A2 | 67A2-71B4 | 34A2-(B5) | | (44A1-B5) | | |
| XXXI | 55A2-58B5 | 71B4-76B2 | (37A1)-38A4 | | (46A1-B5) | | |
| XXXII | 59A1-60A4 | 76B2-78A4 | 38A4-39A3 | | | | |
| 2 vss | missing | missing | missing | | | | |
| colophon | 60A4-B1 | 78B1 | 39A4(bottom) | | | | |

Notes: * ( ) indicates that the text is incomplete in the chapter.

Tg * XIX 1c-2a (3 pādas) are written in *dbu-med*.

Table VIIb

Contents of the Tibetan Manuscripts from Tunhuang*
[Fonds Pelliot, Bibliothèque Nationale, Paris]

(Cf. 'Bibliographical Notes' IIA2)

| Chapters | Th | Ti* | Tj* |
|---|---|---|---|
| title | 565A1-2 | | (B1-2) |
| homage | 565A2 | | (B2) |
| preface | 565A2 | | |
| I | 565A3-(B12) | | |
| II | | | |
| III | | | |
| IV | | | |
| V | | | |
| VI | | | |
| VII | | | |
| VIII | | | |
| IX | | | |
| X | | | |
| XI | | | |
| XII | | | |
| XIII | | | |
| XIV | | | |
| XV | | | |
| XVI | | | |
| XVII | | | |
| XVIII | | | |
| XIX | | | |
| XX | | | |
| XXI | | | |
| XXII | | | |
| XXIII | | | |
| XXIV | | | |
| XXV | | | |
| XXVI | | | |
| XXVII | | | |
| XXVIII | | | |
| XXIX | | | |
| XXX | | | |
| XXXI | | (A1-7) | |
| XXXII | | (A7-12) | |
| 2 vss | | missing | |
| colophon | | (B1-2) | |

Notes: * ( ) indicates that the text is incomplete.
Ti, Tj * No pagination is available.

Table VIII

Contents of Haribhadra's Commentary
[Sde-dge and Pekings editions]

(Cf. 'Bibliographical Notes' VIII 1b)

| Chapters | Sde-dge | Peking |
|---|---|---|
| title | 1B1 | 1A1-3 |
| homage | 1B1-2 | 1A3-4 |
| preface | 1B2-4B7 | 1A4-6A8 |
| I | 4B7-20A4 | 6A8-24B2 |
| II | 20A4-25A1 | 24B2-30A5 |
| III | 25A1-27A5 | 30A5-32B5 |
| IV | 27A5-28B4 | 32B5-34A8 |
| V | 28B4-30A5 | 34A8-36A7 |
| VI | 30A5-32A7 | 36A8-38B8 |
| VII | 32A7-33B6 | 38B8-40B3 |
| VIII | 33B6-35B1 | 40B3-42B4 |
| IX | 35B1-36A3 | 42B4-43A8 |
| X | 36A3-37B7 | 43A8-45B3 |
| XI | 37B7-39A4 | 45B3-47A5 |
| XII | 39A4-40B7 | 47A5-49B5 |
| XIII | 41A1-7 | 49B5-50A7 |
| XIV | 41A7-43A2 | 50A7-52A6 |
| XV | 43A2-45A3 | 52A6-54B5 |
| XVI | 45A3-46B2 | 54B5-56B1 |
| XVII | 46B2-48A5 | 56B1-58B1 |
| XVIII | 48A5-50A5 | 58B1-60B8 |
| XIX | 50A5-52A5 | 60B8-63A2 |
| XX | 52A5-56A2 | 63A2-67A4 |
| XXI | 56A2-57A7 | 67A4-68B3 |
| XXII | 57A7-59B3 | 68B3-71A2 |
| XXIII | 59B3-60A5 | 71A2-B6 |
| XXIV | 60A5-61A4 | 71B6-72B7 |
| XXV | 61A5-62A5 | 72B7-74A2 |
| XXVI | 62A6-63B6 | 74A2-75B7 |
| XXVII | 63B6-65B1 | 75B7-77B5 |
| XXVIII | 65B1-67A1 | 77B5-79B1 |
| XXIX | 67A2-70B1 | 79B1-83B1 |
| XXX | 70B1-73A2 | 83B1-86A7 |
| XXXI | 73A2-76A1 | 86A7-89B7 |
| XXXII | 76A1-78A4 | 89B7-92B3 |
| postscript | 78A4-7 | 92B3-93A6 |

Table IX

Contents of Buddhaśrījñāna's Commentary
[Sde-dge and Peking editions]
(Cf. 'Bibliographical Notes' VIII 2)

| | | Sde-dge | Peking |
|---|---|---|---|
| title | | 116A7 | 135B5-6 |
| homage | | 116A7 | 135B6 |
| bam-po | I | 116A7-126B5 | 135B6-148A8 |
| | II | 126B5-138B1 | 148A8-162B5 |
| | III | 138B1-150A5 | 162B5-176B5 |
| | IV | 150A6-162B6 | 176B5-191B5 |
| | V | 162B6-174B5 | 191B5-206A2 |
| | VI | 174B5-189B1 | 206A2-223A8 |
| Chapter | I | 116A7-135B5 | 135B6-159B2 |
| | II | 135B5-144A5 | 159B2-169B2 |
| | III | 144A5-145B3 | 169B2-171A4 |
| | IV | 145B3-158B7 | 171A4-187A1 |
| | V | 158B7-185B2 | 187A2-218B4 |
| | VI | 185B2-187B1 | 218B4-221A2 |
| | VII | 187B1-188A1 | 221A2-B3 |
| | VIII | 188A1-B2 | 221B3-222A6 |
| piṇḍārtha | | 188B2-189A7 | 222A6-223A7 |
| colophon | | 189A7-B1 | 223A7-8 |

* * *

Chapter I: *Rnam-pa thams-cad mkhyen-pa-ñid*

II: *Lam-gyi rnam-par śes-pa-ñid-kyi mtshan-ñid*

III: *Thams-cad śes-pa-ñid-kyis mtshan-ñid*

IV: *Rnam-pa thams-cad mṅon-par rtogs-pa*

V: *Rtse-mo'i mṅon-par rtogs-pa'i rab-tu dbye-ba*

VI: *Mthar-gyis-pa'i mṅon-par rtogs-pa*

VII: *Skad-cig-ma gcig-gis mṅon-par rdzogs-par byaṅ-chub-pa*

VIII: *Chos-kyi sku*

Table X

Contents of the Commentary ascribed to Dharmaśrī
[Sde-dge and Peking editions]
(Cf. 'Bibliographical Notes' VIII 3)

| Chapters | Sde-dge | Peking |
|---|---|---|
| title | 228A4-5 | 331B2 |
| homage | 228A5 | 331B2 |
| I | 228A5-B6 | 331B2-332A5 |
| II | 228B6-230A1 | 332A6-333B5 |
| III | 230A1-233B3 | 333B5-338A7 |
| IV | 233B3-235A5 | 338A7-340A4 |
| colophon | 235A5-7 | 340A4-8 |

* * *

Chapter I: *Śes-rab-kyi pha-rol-tu phyin-pa spyi'i rnam-par bźag-* (D *gźag-*)*pa dgos-pa daṅ bcas-pa 'byed-pa'i lde-mig*

II: *Brjod-par bya-ba'i don gtan-la 'debs-*(so DP)*pa'i lde-mig*

III: *Mtshon-pa dpe'i lde-mig*

IV: *Rjod-par byed-pa'i tshig phul gdab-pa'i lde-mig*

Table XI

Comparative Table of Chapters in the Sanskrit, Tibetan and Chinese Versions with reference to Haribhadra's Commentary and *AsP* (Sanskrit and Tibetan)*

* For a detailed table of chapters of other texts in this group see further K. Kajiyoshi, *Genshi Hannyagyō no Kenkyū* (1944), pp. 981-984 (Table I); R. Yamada, *Daijō Bukkyō Seiritsuron Josetsu* (1959), pp. 206-208; R. Hikata, *Suvikrantavikrāmi-Paripṛcchā* (1958), Table I at the end of his work.

| Chap. | Sanskrit A | Sanskrit B (if different from A) | *AsP* (Sanskrit) | Tibetan (found only in X) | Haribhadra's Commentary (if different from X) | *AsP* (Tibetan) | Chinese *Rgs* |
|---|---|---|---|---|---|---|---|
| I | Sarvākārajñatā-caryā | | | Rnam-pa thams-cad mkhyen-pa-ñid-la spyod-pa | Rnam-pa thams-cad mkhyen-pa-ñid-la 'jug-pa | Rnam-pa thams-cad mkhyen-pa-ñid-kyi spyod-pa | 行 |
| II | Śakra | | | Brgya-byin | | | 帝釈 |
| III | Aprameya-guṇa-dhāraṇa-pāramitā-stūpa-satkāra | | | Gźal-du med-pa'i yon-tan yoṅs-su gzuṅ-ba daṅ sku-gluṅ-la ri-mor bya-ba | Pha-rol-tu phyin-pas dpag-tu med-pa'i phan-yan 'dzin-pa daṅ mchod-rten-la bkur-sti byed-pa | Pha-rol-tu phyin-pa daṅ mchod-rten-la bkur-stir byed-pa gźal-du med-pa'i yon-tan 'dzin-pa | 持無量功徳建塔 |
| IV | Guṇa-parikīrtana | | | Yon-tan yoṅs-su brjod-pa | | | 功徳 |
| V | Puṇya-paryāya | | | Bsod-nams-kyi rnam-graṅs | | | 福量 |
| VI | Anumodanā-pariṇāmanā | Anumodana | Anumodanā-pariṇāmanā | Rjes-su yi-raṅ-ba | Yoṅs-su bsṅo-ba | Rjes-su yi-raṅ-ba daṅ yoṅs-su bsṅo-ba | 随喜功徳 |
| VII | Niraya | | | Dmyal-ba | | | 地獄 |
| VIII | Viśuddhi | | | Rnam-par dag-pa | | | 清浄 |
| IX | Stuti | | | Bstod-pa | | | 〈歎〉 |
| X | Dhāraṇa-guṇa | Dhāraṇī-guṇa | Dhāraṇa-guṇa-kīrtana | 'Dzin-pa'i yon-tan | Yon-tan gzuṅ-bar yoṅs-su brjod-pa | 'Dzin-pa'i yon-tan yoṅs-su brjod-pa | 称讃功徳 |

| | | | | | | |
|---|---|---|---|---|---|---|
| XI Māra-karman | | | Bdud-kyi las | D: Bdud-kyi las; P: Bdud | Bdud-kyi las | 魔 |
| XII Loka-saṃdarśana | | | 'Jig-rten ston-pa | 'Jig-rten bstan-pa | 'Jig-rten yaṅ-dag-par ston-pa | 現世 |
| XIII Acintya | | | Bsam-gyis mi khyab-pa | | | 不思議 |
| XIV Aupamya | | | Dpe | | | 譬喩 |
| XV Deva-putra | Deva | Deva | Lha'i bu | Lha | Lha | 天 |
| XVI Tathatā | | | De-bźin-ñid | | | 如実 |
| XVII Avinivartanīyākāra-liṅga-nimitta | Avinivartanīya-liṅgākāra | Avinivartanīyākāra-liṅga-nimitta | Phyir mi ldog-pa'i rtags-kyi rnam-pa | Phyir mi ldog-pa'i rnam-pa | Phyir mi ldog-pa'i rnam-pa daṅ rtags daṅ mtshan-ma | 不退地祥瑞 |
| XVIII Śūnyatā | | | Stoṅ-pa-ñid | | | 空 |
| XIX Gaṅga-devā-bhaginī | | Gaṅga-devī-bhaginī | Sriṅ-mo gaṅga'i lha-mo | Gaṅgā'i lha-mo | Sriṅ-mo gaṅgā'i lha-mo | 昻誐天姉 |
| XX Upāya-kauśalya-mīmāṃsā | | | Thabs-la mkhas-pa | | Thabs mkhas-pa-la spyod-pa | 善解方便 |
| XXI Māra-karman | | | Bdud-kyi las | | | 魔業 |
| XXII Kalyāṇa-mitra | | | Dge-ba'i bśes-gñen | | | 善友 |
| XXIII Śakra | | | Brgya-byin | | | 法王 |
| XXIV Abhimāna | | | Mṅon-pa'i ṅa-rgyal | | | 我 |
| XXV Śikṣā | | | Yoṅs-su bslab-pa | Bslab-pa | Bslab-pa | 戒 |
| XXVI Māyopama | | | Sgyu-ma'i dpe | Sgyu-ma lta-bu | Sgyu-ma lta-bu | 幻化 |
| XXVII Sāra | | | Sñiṅ-po | | | 妙義 |
| XVIII Avakīrṇa-kusuma | | | Me-tog bkram-pa | | | 散華 |
| XXIX Anugama | | | Rjes-su 'gro-ba | Rjes-su rig-pa | Rjes-su rig-pa | 聚集 |
| XXX Sadā-prarudita | | | Rtag-par rab-tu ṅu-ba | Rtag-tu ṅu-ba | Rtag-tu ṅu | 常歓喜 |
| XXXI Dharmodgata | | | Chos 'phags | | | 出法 |
| XXXII Parīndanā | | | Yoṅs-su gtaṅ-ba | | | 善護 |

## Comparative Table of New and Old Sino-Japanese Characters

*It is difficult to put some old Chinese characters into print. In this book they are typewritten in the abbreviated forms currently used in Japan. The following list of abbreviated characters is arranged in the order of numbers of strokes with their corresponding old characters. In this table are omitted some abbreviated forms easily identifiable with the old ones and some of those used for Japanese titles of works and names of authors.*

| Numbers of strokes | New characters : | Old characters | Numbers of strokes | New characters : | Old characters |
|---|---|---|---|---|---|
| 4 | 仏 | 佛 | 8 | 担 | 擔 |
| 5 | 処 | 處 | | 変 | 變 |
| 6 | 会 | 會 | | 学 | 學 |
| | 当 | 當 | 9 | 発 | 發 |
| | 両 | 兩 | 10 | 称 | 稱 |
| 7 | 図 | 圖 | | 帰 | 歸 |
| | 囲 | 圍 | 11 | 釈 | 釋 |
| | 応 | 應 | | 訳 | 譯 |
| | 寿 | 壽 | 12 | 証 | 證 |
| | 来 | 來 | | 覚 | 覺 |
| | 声 | 聲 | 13 | 随 | 隨 |
| | 医 | 醫 | 15 | 蔵 | 藏 |
| | 麦 | 麥 | | 歓 | 歡 |
| 8 | 宝 | 寶 | 17 | 繊 | 纖 |
| | 実 | 實 | 18 | 観 | 觀 |

# S A N S K R I T   T E X T

(Recension A)

# ĀRYA-PRAJÑĀ-PĀRAMITĀ-RATNA-GUṆA-SAṂCAYA-GĀTHĀ

## TABLE OF CHAPTERS

ārya-prajñā-pāramitā-ratna-guṇa-saṃcaya-gāthā [1]

*

namaḥ sarva-buddha-bodhisattvebhyaḥ [2] /

atha khalu bhagavāṃs tāsāṃ catasṛṇāṃ parṣadāṃ sampraharṣaṇārthaṃ punar apīmāṃ prajñā-pāramitāṃ paridīpayamānas tasyāṃ velāyām imā [3] gāthā abhāṣata [4] //

---

[1] Only X gives this title at the beginning of the text. X also reads on the title page: Skt. *°-gāthā-nāma viharati sma*, Tib. *'phags-pa śes-rab-kyi pha-rol-tu phyin-pa yon-tan rin-po-che sdud-pa* [X om. *tshigs-su bcad-pa*] *źes bya-ba bźugso* [r. *bźugs-so*].

[2] Only in K: Tib. LNTb *saṅs-rgyas daṅ byaṅ-chub-sems-dpa' thams-cad-la phyag 'tshal-lo*. But X *namo 'rya-mañjuśriye* (O em. *nama ārya-°*), Ta *namo ārya-°*, Tb *oṃ namaḥ mañjuśriyaiḥ (!)*, C *oṃ namaḥ śri-mañjaiśriyaiḥ* (!), Tc *oṃ namo bhagavatyai ārya-prajñā-pāramitā-ratna-guṇa-saṃcaya-gāthāyai namo ārya-mañjuśriye (=* V, w. daṇḍas after *-gāthāyai* and *-mañjuśriye):* Tib. XCDPTa *'phags-pa 'jam-dpal-la phyag 'tshal-lo*.

[3] K *imāṅ*.

[4] XTac *abhāṣataḥ* (for *°ta*, K = OV).

## <I. SARVĀKĀRAJÑATĀ-CARYĀ>

vara-prema-gauravu-prasādu upasthayitvā
     prajahitva āvaraṇa-kleśa-malāni śāntāḥ /
śṛṇutā jagārtham abhiprasthita-sūratānām
     prajñāya pāramita yatra caranti śūrāḥ // 1 //

yāvanti nadya pra(X3A)vahant' iha jambudvīpe
     phala-puṣpa-auṣadhi-vanaspati rohayanti /
bhujagendra-nāgapati niśray' anovatapte
     tasyānubhāva-śriyaso bhujagādhipasya // 2 //

yāvanti dharma jina-śrāvaka deśayanti
     bhāṣanti yukti-sahitāṃś ca udīrayanti /
paramārya-saukhya-kriya tat-phala-prāptitā ca
     sarvo ayaṃ puruṣa-kāru tathāgatasya // 3 //

---

1a Tac *para-* (= OV wt.n.)(for *vara-*, KX); Tac *-gaurava-* (= V)(for °*vu-*, KX = O); Tc *-prasāda* (= V)(for °*du*, KXTa = O); X *upasthapitvā* (= OV) (for °*yitvā*, KTac; cf. Edg.Rgs. 40).

1b XTa *malātikrāntāḥ* (= OV), Tc °*tā* (for *-malāni śāntāḥ*, K: Tib.A *dri-ma bstsal-nas rab ži-bas*, Chin. 住寂静); OV *prajahitva āvaraṇa kleśa malāti°* (V *kleśa-m°*, cpd.): Tib.B *sgrib-pa ñon-moṅs bsal-nas dri-ma-las 'das-pa*.

1c K *-śūratānāṃ* (for *sūr°*, XTac = O: Tib. *des-pa*), V *su(vra?)tānāṃ* (Vaidya however says on p. 399 that his em. is superfluous); cf. XXXI 3a *sūratānāṃ* (= OV).

1d K *-prajñā-*, unmetr. (for *prajñāya*, XTac = OV); cf. III 1b *prajñāya pāramita yatra caranti nāthāḥ*, VIII 2d *prajñāya pāramita yatra caranti dhīrāḥ*.

2 Cf. V 7.

2a KX *pravahantiha* (so prints V), O *pravahanti ha*, Ta *pravahanti*, Tc *pravahatī* (Tac om. *ha*)(for *pravahant' iha*: Tib. *'dzam-bu'i gliṅ 'dir*).

2b K *-puṣpauṣadhi-*, Ta *-puṣpa-auṣadhī-*, Tc *-puṣpa-auṣadha-*, O *-puṣpa-auṣādha-* (? mispr. for *-auṣadhi-*), V sep. *phala puṣpa auṣadhā(dhi)-*; only X *-puṣpa-auṣadhi-* or Tc°*dha* is metr. poss.

2c Tac *bhūjagendra-*, V *bhūja(ta)gajendra-* (for *bhujagendra-*, KX = O: Tib. *klu-dbaṅ klu-bdag*, Chin. 龍王主); K *niśrayatovatapte*, XTac *niśrayanov°*, O *-niśraya nopatapte*, V *niśrayanovata(na)sya* (for *niśray' anovatapte*); *niśray'* is 3 sg.opt. for *niśraye*, *niśrayi*, m.c., and *anovatapte* (not *anop°*) is simply m.c. for *anavatapte* (Tib. *ma dros*, Chin. 無熱池); but Edg.Rgs. 18, 'The word in Rgs. should be spelled *Anopatapta*'; this is not acceptable.

2d X *-śriyāsā*, O *-śriyasā* (wt.n.; instr. = Tc *-śriyā*; cf. Edg.Rgs. 17) (for *-śriyaso*, KTa; abl.); V *-śriya sābhu jagādhipasya* (!); K *bhujagădhipasya*, Ta *bhūjagādh°* (for *bhujagādh°*, XTc = O: Tib.A *klu-bdag de-yi*, B *klu-yi bdag-po de-yi*, Chin. 彼龍).

3a Tc *deśanti* (for *deśayanti*, KXTa = OV).

3b Tc *yuśmi-sahitāṃś codīr°* (for *yukti-sahitāṃś ca udīr°*, KXTa = OV).

3c V *paramārtha-* (for *paramārya-*, MSS. = O: Tib.B *mchog 'phags*, but A *mchog*; Chin. 最聖); O *-kriya-tat-*, cpd.; Tc *va* (for *ca*, KXTa = OV).

kiṃ (Tc2A) kāraṇaṃ ya jinu bhāṣati dharma-netrī
tatrābhiśikṣita nara-ṛṣabha-śiṣya-bhūtāḥ /
sākṣāt-karitva yatha-śikṣita deśayanti
bu(Ta2A)ddhānubhāvu na punātma-balānubhāvā // 4 //

yasmin na (X4A) prajña-vara-pāramitopalabdhi
na ca bodhisattva-upalabdhi (K3A) na citta bodhe /
evaṃ śruṇitva na ca muhyati nāsti trāso
so bodhisattva carate sugatāna prajñāṃ // 5 //

na ca rūpa-vedana na saṃjña na cetanā ca
vijñāna-sthānu aṇu-mātra na bhonti tasya /
so sarva-dharma a-sthito a-ni(X4B)keta-cārī
a-pariggṛhītu labhate sugatāna bodhiṃ // 6 //

yatha śreṇikasya abhutī parivrājakasya
jñānopalambhana hi skandhu-vibhāvanā ca /

---

4a KXTa *yaj* (= O), Tc *yarj* (for *ya* = V; cf. Edg.Rgs. 39); V *jina*(for *jinu*, MSS. = O).

4c K *-śikṣiti* (for °*ita*, XTac = OV, but V sep. *yatha śikṣita)*.

4d XTac *buddhānubhāva* (= OV)(for °*bhāvu*, K); Ta om. *na* (= V!); V *puna ātma-balānubhāvā* wt.n.(for *punātma-*°,MSS. = O); at the end of the verse K reads one akṣara which appears to be a letter numeral 4(?).

5a XTa *prajñā-* (= O)(for *prajña-*, KTc = V; cf. Edg.Rgs. 32); X (Tib. trslit.) *-para-* (for *-vara-*, KXTac = OV); K °*labdhir*, V *labdhiḥ* (for *labdhi*, XTac = O).

5b Tc °*sattve* (for °*sattva-*, KXTa = OV); K *citte* (for *citta*, XTac = O); K *bodheḥ* (so em. O)(for *bodhe*, XTac; cf. Edgerton 10.72); V °*-bodhe(ḥ)*, cpd.!

5c Tc *mucyati* (for *muhyati*, KXTa = OV: Tib. *rmoṅs-pa*).

5d Tc om. *so;* V *prajñām* (w. *-m*).

6a Tc *na va rūpa-vedana-saṃjñe* (for *na ca rūpa-vedana na saṃjña*, KXTa = OV; but V sep. *rūpa vedana)*.

6b K *-sthā*[.....]; Ta *amātralabhonti*, XTc *anumātralabh*°, O em. *aṇu-mātra labhonti* [O *lambhonti* seems to be a fault in the photomechanical reprint]; but Edg.Rgs. 34 '*anumātra* [w. dental -*n*-] *laṃbhonti* (! so printed; ignored in [Conze's] Index) *tasya*, read *anumātr'* [dental -*n*-] *ala* (m.c. for *alaṃ*) *bhonti tasya (alaṃ-bhavati* 'is a match for', with gen.)'; V em. *aṇu-mātra na bhonti* is more acceptable: Tib.B *rdul tsam yod ma yin* (v.l. *yod-pa min*), Chin. 不著纖塵無処所; Tib.A *rdul tsam mi rñed-pa*suggests *aṇu-mātr' a-labhonti* (or prob. *a-labhanti)*.

6c K [*so sarva-*]; Tc *-dharmāsthito* (for *dharma a-sthito*, KXTa = OV; but V *-dharma-asthito*, cpd., which may be better).

6d KX *aparigṛhītu*, Ta *aparigṛhīta* (= O wt.n.), Tc *aparīṃgṛhīta*, V *aparī(ri)gṛhīta*(for *apariggṛhītu;* cf. Edg.Rgs. 37); V *bodhim* (w. *-m*).

7a XTa *atha* (= OV: Tib.A *de-nas*), Tc *a*<*tha*> (for *yatha*, K: Tib.B *ji-ltar*); Ta *śrenikasya* (dental *-n-*) *abhūtī*; K *śreṇikasya abhūtī*, unmetr.!; Tc *śreṇi-kasyābhuti* (for *śreṇikasya abhutī*, X = OV); Edg.Rgs. 40 analyzes *abhutī* as *a-bhūtī* (Skt., Pāli *a-bhūti-*, 'calamity' with Tib.B *dmigs med*, 'no support'); *abhutī* should be analyzed as a root aorist *a-bhu* with 3 sg. ending in *-tī* (m.c. for *-ti*; cf. Gr. 37.3); *abhutī* agrees w. Tib.A *gyur*, B *'byuṅ-ba*.

7b KX *jñānopalambhu na* (= OV), Ta °*lambhū na*,Tc °*lasnū na* (r. perh. °*lambhū na*)(Tib.B *śes-pa-yis / dmigs med*?)(for °*lambhana:*Tib.A *śes-pa dmigs-pa*); Tc *skandha-* (= OV)(for °*dhu-*, KXTa); cf. Chin. 照見五蘊無実相 (? Skt. *pañca-skandha-vibhāvanām upalabdhvā / upalabhya)*; cf. VII 3b.

yo bodhisattvu parijānati eva dharmān

na ca nirvṛtiṃ spṛśati so viharāti prajñāṃ // 7 //

vyuparīkṣate punar ayaṃ katar' eṣa prajñā

kasyā (X5A) kuto va imi śūnyaku sarva-dharmāḥ /

vyuparīkṣamā(Tc2B)ṇu na ca līyati nāsti trāso

āsannu so bhavati bodhayi bodhisattvo // 8 //

saci rūpa saṃjña api vedana cetanā ca

vijñāna-skandha caratī a-prajānamāno /

imi skandha śūnya parikalpayi bodhisattvo

(X5B) caratī nimitti an-upāda-pade a-sakto // 9 //

na ca rūpa-vedana na saṃjña na cetanāyā

vijñāni yo na caratī a-niketa-(Ta2B)cārī /

caratīti so na upagacchati prajña-dhīro

an-upādu-dhīḥ spṛśati śānta-samādhi śreṣṭhāṃ // 10 //

---

7c Tac *bodhisattva* (= OV)(for °*vu*, KX); XTac *dharmā*, O *dharma* (wt.n.), V *dharmāṃ* (for *dharmān*, K).

7d XTa *spṛṣati*, Tc *spṛṣaṃti* (for *spṛśati*, K = OV); V *prajñām* (w. -*m*).

8a Ta *vyuparīkṣata* (for °*ate*, KXTc = OV; cf. Edg.Rgs. 40 on haplology for *vyupapar*°); K *katareṣa*, XTa *katareṣu* (= OV), Tc *karateṣu* (for *katar' eṣa*: Tib. *'di-ni gaṅ yin)*.

8b XTac *kasmāt* (= OV: Tib.A *gaṅ-gi phyir*)(for *kasyā*, K: Tib.B *su-yi yin);* Tc *kuṭo* (for *kuto*, KXTa = OV: Tib. *gaṅ-las*); XTac *śūnyaka* (= OV)(for °*ku*, K); V sep. *sarva dharmāḥ*.

8c Tc *vyūparīkṣamānu* (for *vyuparīkṣamāṇu*, KXTa = OV).

8d XTa *āsantu*, Tc *āsanu* (for *āsannu*, K = OV); Tc *bodhisattvaḥ* (for °*sattvo*, KXTa = OV).

9a O always sep. *sa ci* (for *saci* = V; cf. Edgerton 3.48, BHSD p. 549b, q.v.); K *saṃjñino*, XTa *saṃjñā* (= O!), Tc *saṃjñā* (*'pi*)(for *saṃjña*= V; cf. Edg.Rgs. 32); O *rūpa-saṃjñā*, cpd. (cf. Speijer 423, 437).

9b V sep. *vijñāna skandha;* Tc *carati* (for *caratī*, KXTa = OV); Tc *aprajānamono* (for °*māno*, KXTa = OV).

9c Tc *bodhisattva* (for °*sattvo*, KXTa = OV).

9d XTac *nimitta* (= OV; but V °*tta-*, cpd.)(for *nimitti*, K); Tc *a-śakto* (for *a-sakto*, KXTa = OV: Tib.A *reg ma yin*; but B *dad ma yin* = ?Skt. *a-śraddho / a-saddho*; Conze trsl. 'not attentative'?).

10a Tc *rūpaṃ vedana* (for *rūpa-*°, KXTa = OV; but V sep. *rūpa vedana*); Tc *saṃjñe* (for *saṃjña*, KXTa = OV); K *cetanāyaṃ*, Skt. (for °*āyā*, XTac = OV).

10c XTac *nu upagacchati* (for *na upag*°, K = OV: Tib.A *khas-len mi byed-de*, B *mi dmigs*); Tc *prajña-dhāro*, V °*-dhārī* (for °*-dhīro*, KXTa = OV: Tib.A *śes-rab brtan-te*, B *śes-rab brtan*); cf. AsP ... *sa caraṃś caramīti nopaiti*.

10d XTa *anupāda-dhī* (= OV), Tc *'nupāda-dhī* (for *anupādu-dhīḥ*, K, Bhvr.; Conze Rgs. 56 misr. K as °*pāda-*°); O *spuśati* (for *spṛśati*, MSS. = V) seems to be a misprint (cf. also VII 1d, fn.), although Edg.Rgs. 1 pays much atten tion to this form; XTac *śānti-* (= OV)(for *śānta-*, K; cf. *śānta-samādhi*, XXVI 7b); Tc *sama dhi* ; Tc *śreṣṭhā* (for *śreṣṭhāṃ*, KXTa = OV; but O *śānti-samādhi-śreṣṭhaṃ*, cpd., V sep. *śānti samādhi śreṣṭhāṃ!*); cf. *imaṃ pravara-śūnya-samādhi śāntaṃ* XX 7b; *samādhi śāntaṃ* XXIX 8a; *samādhi catasra śreṣṭhā* XXIX 2 and perh. *śūnyānimitt'-apraṇidhīṃ samādhīṃ* XX 19b.

evātma-śānta viharann iha bodhisattvo
    (X6A) so (K3B) vyākṛto purimakehi tathāgatehi /
na ca manyate ahu samāhitu vyutthito vā
    kasmārtha dharma-prakṛtiṃ parijānayitvā // 11 //

evaṃ carantu caratī sugatāna prajñāṃ
    no cāpi so labhati yatra carāti dharme /
caraṇaṃ ca so a-caraṇaṃ ca prajānayi(X6B)tvā
    eṣā sa prajña-vara-pāramitāya (Tc3A) caryā // 12 //

yo 'sau na vidyati sa eṣa a-vidya-nāmā
    taṃ bālu kalpayi a-vidya karāti vidyāṃ /
vidyā-a-vidya ubhi eti a-santa dharmā
    niryāti yo imi prajānati bodhisattvo // 13 //

māyopamān ya iha jānati pañca skandhān
    na ca (X7A) māya anya na ca skandha karoti anyān /
nānātva-saṃjña-vigato upaśānta-cārī
    eṣā sa prajña-vara-pāramitāya caryā // 14 //

---

11a Ta *śā‹nta›*, Tc *-śānti* (= V!)(for *-śānta*, KX = O); XTa *viharaṇtiha*, Tc *va harantiha* (for *viharann iha*, K = OV); Tc *bodhisattvā* (for °*sattvo*, KXTa = OV).

11b XTac *puramakehi* (= OV)(for *purim*°, K: Tib. *sṅon-gyi*, Chin. 過去 ); K *tathāgatehiḥ* (for °*ehi*, XTac = OV).

11c Tc *aha* (for *ahu*, KXTa = OV); Tc *samāhita*, V *samādhitu*(for *samāhitu*, KXTa = O); X *vyusthito* (= O), Tc *vyutito* (for *vyutthito*, KTa = V; cf. Edg.Rgs. 24).

11d K *karmānta*, Tc *kasmārthaṃ* (for *kasmārtha*, XTa = OV: Tib.A *ci-phyir-źe-na don*, B *ci-phyir-źe-na*, Chin. 因果 ); XTac *-prakṛti*, O em. °*tī* (for °*tiṃ*, K = V; Conze Rgs. 57 misr. K as °*tīṃ*).

12a Tc *eva* (for *evaṃ*, KXTa = OV: Tib. *de-ltar*); K *prajñān* (for *prajñāṃ*, XTac = OV).

12b Tc *dharmaṃ* (= V w. *-m*), XTa *dharmā* (= O)(for *dharme*, K).

12c KX *aca‹ra›ṇañ* (for *acaraṇaṃ*, Tac = OV: Tib.A *mi spyod*, B *spyod med*); K *prajāniyitvā*(for °*nayitvā*, XTac = OV).

13a MSS. *yo sau* (= O)(for *yo 'sau* = V); Tc *nara* (for *na*, KXTa = OV: Tib. *ma*); Tc *saiṣu* (for *sa eṣa*, KXTa = OV); XTac *a-vidyamāno* (= OV)(for *a-vidya-nāma*, K: Tib. *med ces bya*); r. poss. *a-vidya nāmā*.

13b XTa *tāṃ* (= V), Tc *tā* (= O; mispr. for *tāṃ*?)(for *taṃ*, K); XTac *karoti* (= OV)(for *karāti*, K); Tc *vidyā* (for *vidyāṃ*, KXTa = OV; but V w. *-m*).

13c OV sep. *vidyā avidya*.

13d K [*yo*]; Tc *yā ini* ... *bodhisattvaḥ*, V *yo iti* ... °*sattvo* (for *yo imi* ... °*sattvo*, KXTa = O).

14a XTac *māyopamā* (= O), K °*māṃ* (= V)(for °*mān*); XTa *skandhāṃ* (= V), Tc *skandhā* (for *skandhān*, K = O wt.n.).

14b MSS. *anyāṃ* (for *anyān*, so em. O = V).

14c XTac *-vikato* (for *-vigato*, K = OV wt.n.: Tib. *bral-źiṅ*).

14d Vaidya (p. 354 n. 1) wrongly notes that O reads *na* (for *sa*, MSS.).

kalyāṇa-mitra-sahitasya vipaśyakasya
    trāso na bheṣyati śruṇitva jināna mātāṃ /
yo pāpa-mitra-sahito ca para-praṇeyo
    so (X7B) āma-bhājana ya(Ta3A)thodaka-spṛṣṭa bhinno // 15 //

kiṃ kāraṇaṃ ayu pravucyati bodhisattvo
    sarvatra saṅga-kṣaya icchati saṅga-chedī /
bodhiṃ spṛśiṣyati jināna a-saṅga-bhūtāṃ
    tasmā hu nāma labhate ayu bodhisattvo // 16 //

maha-sattva so atha kinocyati kāra(Tc3B)ṇena
    mahatāya agru ayu bheṣyati (K4A) sattva-rāśe /

---

15a Tc *kalyāṇaṃ* (for *kalyāṇa-*, KXTa = OV); MSS. *vipasyakasya* (for *vipaśy°* = OV wt.n.).

15b Ta *trāso . na* (wrong division of pādas); Tc *bhaviṣyati* (for *bheṣyati*, KXTa = OV); Tc *māṃtrā*, V *mātrām* (for *mātāṃ*, KXTa = O: Tib. *yum*).

15c XTac *-sahitā* (for *-sahito*, K = OV wt.n.); XTa *-praṇeyoḥ* (for *°eyo*, KTc = OV wt.n.); em. *para-praṇeyo* perh. to *parā-praṇeyo* (cf. Edgerton 3.7, 8.15) or to *paro-°* (cf. Edgerton 3.84, 8.12), but it cannot be em. to *parāpraṇeyo* or to *(c') a-parǎ-°/a-paro-°* (Tib. *gźan-gyi driṅ 'jog-pa*, but v.l. *gźan-gyi driṅ mi 'jog*; Chin. 化他 ); cf. XV 6d *a-para-praṇeya*: Tib. *gźan-gyi driṅ mi 'jog-ciṅ* (no v.l.), but Chin. 化他 (? Skt. *apara-°*); XVII 4c *a-para-praṇeyāś*: Tib. *gźan-gyi driṅ mi 'jog*, but Chin. 化他 ; cf. also Conze Dict. p. 49 *a-para-praṇeya-*, *°-praṇeyatā*, ss.vv., p. 240 *para-praṇeya*, s.v.; Suzuki Index Laṅk. p. 20b *a-para-praṇeya*: Tib. *gźan-gyi driṅ mi 'jog-pa*, p. 103a *para-°*; cf. also VII 1b, fn.

15d Ta *-spṛṣṭha* (for *-spṛṣṭa*, KXTc = OV: Tib. *reg*).

16a K *kāraṇam*, Tac *°ṇa*, X *°ṇā* (Tib.trslit. *°ṇa*)(for *kāraṇaṃ* = OV wt.n.).

16b This pāda seems to be rather corrupt; X *saṅga-kriya* (= V; cf. V p. 354 n. 3), Tac *saṅgā-kriya* (for *saṅga-kṣaya*, K = O; cf. O p. 13 n. 1); Ta *saṅgā-cchedī* (for *saṅga-°*, KXTc = OV); cf. Tib.A *chags-pa'i byed-pa kun-la*, v.l. *-las*) *chags-pa gcod 'dod-pas*, B *chags-pa gcod* (v.l. *spyod*) *byed kun-la chags-pa zad-par 'dod*, Chin. 一切楽行皆無著 .

16c KTac *bodhi* (for *bodhiṃ*, X = OV); Tc *jinānā* (for *jināna*, KXTa = OV); K *asaṅga-bhūtāt*, Ta *asaṅgā-bhūtāṃ*, Tc *'saṃgā-bhūtāṃ* (for *asaṅga-bhūtāṃ*, X = OV): Tib. *rgyal-ba-rnams-kyi byaṅ-chub chags med gyur-la*, Chin. 仏菩提無所著

16d XTac *tasmādvi*, O em. *tasmād dhi* (= V)(for *tasmā hu*, K: Tib. *des-na*); Tac *aya* (for *ayu*, KX = OV).

17a Tac *mahā-* (for *maha-*, KX = OV); MSS. *so tha*, OV *so 'tha*(wt.n.)(for *so atha*); *so atha* must be the true r., as it satisfies the metre; in our text the nom.sg.m. ending in *-o* very frequently stands w. hiatus before the following initial *a-* (cf. *sarvo ayaṃ* I 3d; *-sthito aniketa-* I 6c, II 3b; *so acaraṇaṃ* I 12c; *so anabhisaṃskṛtu* I 23c; *-sthito arahanta-*II 2c; *nāyako asthitu* II 3a; *yo adhigato* II 5c; *-kuśalo avivartiyaś* II 6b; *vyākṛto ahu* II 13c; *-vigato adhiṣṭhāna-* X 10c; *dharmo anālayu* XV 8c; *-gato aniketa-* XX 12b; *-sthito ayu* XXI 1d; *upagato ahu-* XXII 6c; *so anu* XXIX 12d; *gurutaro ayu* XXXI 5d; *kathito ayu* XXXII 6b); K *keno*[...(b)...] *sattva-rāśeḥ*; XTac *kenocyati* (= OV wt.n.)(for *kinocyati*); Edgerton thinks that *ke* (of *kenocyati*) takes the place of two short syllables, i.e. *kĕĕ* (cf. Edg.Rgs. 12: p. 4 n. 1); this is not acceptable; there is no such a case in our text; it can hardly be *kĕnǎ* (cf. Edgerton 3.64-65 for a metr. short *e*); *kinā*, instr.sg.nt. (= Pkt. *kiṇā*; cf. Pischel 428) must have been changed into *kena* in the course of transmission, although *kinā* has not been found in BSkt. before (cf. Edgerton 21.14).

17b K [.....]*sattva-rāśeḥ*; Ta *agra* (= O wt.n.), Tc *agu*, V *atra!* (for *agru*, X: Tib.A *mchog*, B *mchog-tu*); K *-rāśeḥ* (= V), Tc *-rāśre* (for *-rāśe*, XTa = O).

dṛṣṭī-gatān mahati chindati sattva-dhāto
    maha-sattva tena hi pravucyati kāraṇena // 17 //

maha-dāyako mahata-buddhi mahānubhāvo
    maha-yāna uttamu jināna samābhirūḍho /
mahatā-sanaddhu namuciṃ śaṭhu dharṣayiṣye
    maha-sattva tena hi pravucyati kāraṇe(X8B)na // 18 //

māyā-karo yatha catuṣ-pathi nirmiṇitvā
    mahato janasya bahu chindati śīrṣa-koṭī /
yatha te 'hatāyu tatha jānati bodhisattvo
    nirmāṇu sarva jagato na ca tasya trāso // 19 //

rūpaṃ ca saṃjña api vedana cetanā ca
    vijñānu-bandhu na ca mukta a-santa-bhūto /

---

17c XTac *dṛṣṭī-gatām*, OV *°-gatāṃ* (for *°-gatān*, K; cf. BHSD p. 269b, q. v.); Conze Rgs. 41 misr. K as *mahate* (for *mahati*, MSS. = OV); Tc *-dhā<to>*, V *-dhātoḥ* (for *-dhāto*, KXTa = O).

17d Tc *<maha-sa>tva tena hi pravucyati kāraṇena*//(3B2) *dya*(?) *mahāsattva tena hi pravucyati kāraṇena* //

18a Tc *mahatāyako*, V *maha-nāyako* (for *°-dāyako*, KXTa = O: Tib. *gtoṅ-ba che*); Tc *muhata-buddhi* (for *mahata-°*, KXTa = OV: Tib. *blo che-ba*); K *mahā-prabhāvo*, Tc *masanubhāvo* (for *mahānubhāvo*, XTa = OV: Tib. *mthu che*).

18b Tc *mahedyayānu* (for *maha-yāna*, KXTa = OV: Tib. *theg chen*); XTac *uttama* (= OV; but V *uttama-*, cpd.)(for *uttamu*, K); K *ji*[.....]*mābhirūḍho*; Ta *samādhiruḍho*, V *samādhirūḍho* (for *samābhirūḍho*, XTc = O: Tib. *źugs-pa*).

18c K *sannaddhu* (for *-sanaddhu*, XTac = OV; but OV sep. *mahatā sanaddhu*; cf. Edg.Rgs. 29, Edgerton 2.89); Tc *ramuviṃ* (for *namuciṃ*, KXTa = OV: Tib. *bdud*); XTac *śaṭha* (= OV)(for *śaṭhu*, K); K *varṣayiṣye* (for *dhar°*, XTac = OV: Tib.A *gdul* [*phyir*], B *'dul-ba*).

18d Tc *mahā-* (for *maha-*, KXTa = OV); XTac *prabuddhati* (for *pravucyati*, K = OV: Tib.A *brjod-pa yin*, B *rab-tu brjod*).

19a XTc *niminitvā*, Ta *nirminitvā* (= O)(for *nirmiṇitvā*, K = V).

19b K *ma*[*hato ja*]*nasya* ... *cchindat*[*i*]; Tc *chidati* (for *chindati*, KXTa = OV); KXTa *śīrṣa-koṭīḥ*, Tc *śirṣa-koṭīṃ* (for *śīrṣa-koṭī* = OV wt.n.).

19c This pāda seems to be corrupt; K *tehatāyu* [Conze Rgs. 39 misr. K as *te hatāgu* (?)](for *te 'hatāyu*); but cf. Tib.B *bsad-bya de-dag* (?? = Skt. *te hatāyu* or *te* [*a-*]*hatya*); K *prajānati*, hypermetr. (for *jānati*,Tib.A *śes*, but B *rab śes*); OV (w. XTac) *yatha te ca māya* (Tc *gāya*) *tatha jānati sarva-sattvān* (O *-sattvān* wt.n.; V *-sattvaṃ* w. XTa; Tc *-sattvā*): Tib.A *sgyu-ma ji-'dra de-'drar sems-can de kun śes*, but B *bsad-bya de-dag ci-'dra de-ltar byaṅ-chub-sems*.

Cf. AsP 10.31-32 *tat kiṃ manyase subhūte api nu tatra kena cit kaś cid dhato vā mṛto vā nāśito vā antar-hito vā? subhūtir āha — no hīdaṃ bhagavan.*

But cf. Buddhaśrījñāna ad Rgs.: *"gsad-bya de-dag ci-'dra" źes bya-ba-ni "sgyu-ma byas-pa'i gsad-par bya-ba de-dag ji-ltar" źes bya-ba'i tha-tshig-go* (Peking ÑA 155B8, Derge ÑA 132B6), also Haribhadra ad Rgs.: *sgyu-ma mkhan-gyi sprul-pa "bsad-pa de-dag ci-'dra-bar de-ltar" gñen-po'i sgyu-ma byed-pa'i "byaṅ-chub-sems-dpas" lha'i bu'i bdud-la sog-pa'i sprul-pa 'joms-pa-na* (Peking JA 212A4, Derge JA 17B2).

20a K *saṃjñi api*, Tc *saṃjñāpi* (for *saṃjña api*, XTa = OV).

20b XTac *vijñāna-* (= OV; but OV sep. *vijñāna bandhu*)(for *vijñānu-*, K); but cf. Tib. *rnam-par śes-pa ma bciṅs* (? = Skt. *vijñān' a=bandhu*); K *a-sanna-*, X *a-saṅga-* (= OV), Ta *a-saṃgā-*, Tc *a-saṃgo-* (for *a-santa-*: Tib. *yod-pa min*); cf. I 16c *a-saṅga-bhūtaṃ*: Tib. *chags med gyur-la*.

evaṃ ca bodhi kramate na ca (X9A) līna-citto

    saṃnāha eṣa vara puḍgala-uttamānāṃ // 20 //

kiṃ kāraṇaṃ ayu pravucyati bodhi-yāno

    yatrāruhi(Tc4A)tva sa nivāpayi sarva-sa(Ta3B)ttvān /

ākāśa-tulya ayu yānu mahā-vimāno

    sukha-saukhya-kṣemam abhiprāpuṇi yāna-śreṣṭho // 21 //

na ca labhyate ya vrajate (X9B) diśa āruhitvā

    nirvāṇu ukta gamanaṃ gati nopalabdhiḥ /

yatha agni nirvṛtu na tasya gati-pracāro

    sā tena nirvṛti pravucyati kāraṇena // 22 //

pūrvāntato na upalabhyati bodhisattvo

    aparāntato pra(K4B)tiūpanna triy-adhva-śuddho /

yo śuddha so an-abhisaṃskṛtu niṣpra(X10A)pañco

    eṣā sa prajña-vara-pāramitāya caryā // 23 //

yasmiṃś ca kāli samaye vidu bodhisattvo

    evaṃ carantu an-upādu vicintayitvā /

---

20d MSS. *puṅgala-* (for *pudgala-*, OV: Tib. *gaṅ-zag*; V *vara-°*, cpd.; cf. Lex. *puṅgala-*, s.v.): Tib. *gaṅ-zag dam-pa-rnams-kyi go-cha mchog*; V *-uttamānam* (w. *-m*).

21a K *kāraṇam*, unmetr. (for *°ṇaṃ*, XTac = OV).

21b Tc *yatrānuhitva*, O *yatrā ruhitva* (= Conze Index)(for *yatrāruhitva*, KXTa = V, so Conze Dict.; cf. Edg.Rgs. 40); MSS. *nirvāpayi* (= OV)(for *nivāp°*; cf. Esg.Rgs. 36).

21c X *-tulyu* (= O)(for *-tulya*, KTac = V); Tac *aya* (for *ayu*, KX = OV); XTac *yāna* (= OV)(for *yānu*, K).

21d Tac *-kṣemabhi-* (= V!)(for *-kṣemam abhi-*, KX = O); Tc *abhiprāpraṇi*, V *abhiprāpaṇu* (for *abhiprāpuṇi*, KX = O: Tib. *mṅon-par thob byed)*; K *-śreṣṭhaṃ* (for *-śreṣṭho*, XTac = OV, w. *ayu yānu* in *c*).

22a Tc *diśāruhitvā* (for *diśa āruhitvā*, KXTa = OV).

22b XTac *nirvāṇa* (= O), V *nirvāṇa-*, cpd. (for *nirvāṇu*, K); Tc *ukamamaṃ*, V *-oka-gamanaṃ* (for *ukta gamanaṃ*, KXTa = O; but O *ukta-°*, cpd.): Tib. *mya-ṅan 'das-par 'gro-bar gsuṅs-na* (B *-pa*).

22c Tc *yathāgni* (for *yatha agni*, KXTa = OV; but O *agni-*, cpd.); Tc *nirvūtu*(for *nirvṛtu*, KXTa = OV); XTa *ratasya*, Tc ⟨*na*⟩*tasya* (for *na tasya*, K = OV wt.n.: Tib.A *de-yi ... mi*, B *de-yis ... med-pa* ); *gatī-* (for *gati-*, no v.l.; cf. Edgerton 10.11) is prob. the true reading (not *gatiṃ-*) in our text (cf. also footnotes to I 15c and VII 1b).

22d XTac *so* (= OV)(for *sā* K); Tc *tana* (for *tena*, KXTa = OV).

23a Tc *pūrvātato* (for *pūrvāntato*, KXTa = OV: Tib. *sṅon-gyi mtha')*.

23b MSS. *pi* (so OV *'pi!*), hypermetric after *aparāntato*, should be omitted (cf. Edg.Rgs. 40); K *pra*[(4B1).....(pāda *c*)...]*ñco*; Tc *pratyutpanna* (for *pratiūpanna*, XTa = OV; cf. Edg.Rgs. 9 end).

23c K [.....]*ñco*; Tc *anabhisaskṛta niṣprapaṃcā* (for *°saṃskṛtu °pañco*, XTa = OV).

24a X *bodhisattvā* (= O)(for *°sattvo*, KTac = V, w. sg. *carantu* and *janeti*).

24b K *carantu a*[.....]; Tc *anurpādu* (for *anupādu*, XTa = OV: Tib.A *skye-ba med-par*, B *skye med)*.

mahatiṃ janeti karuṇāṃ na ca sattva-saṃjñā
eṣā sa prajña-vara-pāramitāya caryā // 24 //

saci sattva-saṃjña dukha-saṃjña upāda(X10B)yātī
cariṣyāmi duḥkha jagatī kariṣyāmi a(Tc4B)rthaṃ /
so ātma-sattva-parikalpaku bodhisattvo
na ca eṣa prajña-vara-pāramitāya caryā // 25 //

yatha ātmanaṃ tatha prajānati sarva-sattvān
yatha sarva-sattva tatha jānati sarva-dharmān./
an-upād'-upādu ubhaye a-vikalpamāno
eṣā sa prajña-va(X11A)ra-pāramitāya caryā // 26 //

yāvanti loki pari(Ta4A)kīrtita dharma-nāmu
sarveṣ' upādu-samatikramu nirgamitvā /

---

24c K somewhat damaged at *mahatiñ janeti;* X *mahatīñ* (= OV: *°tīṃ*), Ta *°ti,* Tc *°tī* (for *°tiṃ;* cf. Edgerton 10.44); K *janeti karuṇān,* X *janeti karuṇā,* Ta *jñaneti karuṇā,* Tc *raṇāneti karuṇā,* O *jane 'tikaruṇā* (wt.n.; Conze ad O p. 127 em. O to *janeti* ...)(for *janeti karuṇāṃ* = V); KTa *-sajñā* (for *-saṃjñā,* XTc = OV: Tib. *'du-śes).*

25a Tc *savi,* O sep. *sa ci* (for *saci,* KXTa = V: Tib. *gal-te*); XTc *sattva-saṃjñā* (= O), Ta *-sajñā* (for *-saṃjña,* K = V; cf. Edg.Rgs. 32; K *saṃjña* has escaped Conze's notice); K *dukhaṃ-,* XTac *duḥkha-* (= O)(for *dukha-* = V; cf. Edg.Rgs. 35, also Edgerton 2.85; K *dukha-,* m.c. for *duḥkha-,* has always escaped Conze's attention); cf. Edg.Rgs. 13 for the lengthening of short vowels at the ends of pādas.

25b XTac *kariṣyāmi,* OV em. *har°* w. Tib.B *spaṅ* (Conze Rgs. 39 reports O and Tib. as *kar°,* which seems to be a misprint for *har°*)(for *cariṣyāmi,* K: Tib.A *spyad-par bya-źiṅ*; cf. Chin. 修諸苦行); K *duḥ[kha ... arthaṃ]*; OV *jagatīṃ* (wt.n.)(for *jagatī,* XTac; loc.sg. *jagatī,* so VIII 3c, IX 1b, XI 2d, XV 4b, XVI 6b, XX 6b, 19a, XXII 10c, XXIII 2c, XXVI 2d, 6b, XXVIII 2b, 4b, XXIX 13b, XXX 6b, 10d, 12d, 14c, XXXI 16d, 17c, XXXII 4d); Tc *artha*(for *arthaṃ,* XTa = OV; but V w. *-m*).

25c K somewhat damaged at *so* [...]*tva-parikalpa*[...] *bo* [...]; XTac *ātma-saparikalpaku,* O em. *ātma-sattva-parik°* [= V *ātma-sa(ttva)-°*], which is supported by K [...]*tva,* and Tib. *bdag daṅ sems-can yoṅs rtog.*

26a Tc [*yatha ... prajānati* ]; Conze Rgs. 42 misr. O as *atha* (for *yatha,* KXTa = OV: Tib. *ci-'dra-ba);* K *ātmanan,* XTa *ātman* (for *ātmanaṃ* = OV wt. n.); O *prajñānati* (? mispr.), Ta *pujānati* (for *prajānati,* KX = V); K [*sa*]*rva-;* XTa *-sattvāṃ* (= V), Tc *-sattvānāṃ* (for *-sattvān,* K = O wt.n.).

26b K *yatha* [...](4B4) *jānati sarva*[...]; Tc *yathā* (for *yatha,* KXTa = OV); X *prajānati* (= V, hypermetr.), Ta *pujānati,* Tc *pūjānati* (for *jānati* = O wt.n.: Tib. *śes*); XTa *-dharmaṃ,* Tc *-dharmā* (for *-dharmān,* OV wt.n.).

26c Tc *ubhaya* (for *ubhaye,* KXTa = OV)

27a XTac *dharma-nāmā,* OV *°-nāma* (wt.n.)(for *°-nāmu,* K).

27b K [*sarveṣupādu sa*](4B5)*mati°;* XTac *sarveṣupādu,* O *sarveṣu pādu,* V *sarveṣupādu-,* cpd. (for *sarveṣ' upādu*); XTac *samutikramu* (for *samati°* = OV wt.n.): Tib.A *skye-ba kun-las yaṅ-dag 'das-śiṅ,* B *kun-la skye-ba daṅ-ni yaṅ-dag 'das;* Ta *nirggayitvā* (for *°amitvā,* KXTc = OV: Tib.A *thal byas-nas,* B *spaṅs-nas).*

a-mṛtaṃ ti jñānu paramaṃ na tu yo pareṇa
    etārthu prajña ayu pāramiteti nāmā // 27 //

evaṃ carantu na ya kāṅkṣati bodhisattvo
    jñātavya so viharate sa-upāya-prajño /
prakṛ(X11B)tī-a=santa parijānayamāna dharmān
    eṣā sa prajña-vara-pāramitāya caryā // 28 //

bhagavatyāṃ ratna-guṇa-saṃcaya-gāthāyāṃ sarvākārajñatā-caryā-parivarto nāma prathamaḥ (K5A) // 1 //

---

27c KXTa *amṛtan* (for *amṛtaṃ*, Tc = OV); X *paraman* (for °*maṃ*, KTac = OV); Tc *ra* (for *na*, KXTa = OV); Conze Rgs. 42 misr. K as *va ju*(?) *yo pareṇa*: Tib. *de-las (= tatu?) gźal med thob;* syntacitically *pareṇa* is construed w. the prec. acc. (cf. Speijer 173, Speyer 88.4, 90.13); in this case one would expect *yaṃ* for *yo*, which seems to be correl. used w. *ayu* in *d*; but most Tib. texts (*de-las gźan med-de / med thob*) suggest *na tato pareṇa* (not *tatu yo pareṇa* as suggested by Conze); it appears less poss. to em. *na tuyo* (m.c. for **tuyyo*: Skt. *tulya-*: Tib. v.l. *de-las gźal med-de / med thob;* cf. Chin. 最上無比甘露智, as this phonetic change in MIndic is not common (cf. Pischel 286, Geiger 54.5, Mehendale I 44.3).

27d K *etrārthu*, XTac *ekārtha* (= OV!)(for *etārthu*, so Conze ad O p. 127: Tib. *de-phyir*); Ta *prajña aya*, Tc*prajñāya* (for *prajña ayu*, KX = OV); Tc *pāramita ti nāso* (for *pāramiteti nāmā*, KXTa = OV): Tib. *'di-ni śes-rab pha-rol phyin ces bya*.

28a K *cara*[*ntu* ... *kāṅkṣati*] *bo*[*dhisattvo*]; Tc *ra* (for *na*, XTa = OV); V *ca* (wt.n.)(for *ya*, XTa = O); Tc *kākṣati* (for *kāṅkṣati*, XTa = OV).

28b K almost illegible; this line seems corrupt; XTac *ya*, OV *yo* (wt.n.) (for *so*: Tib.A *de-ni*, B v.l. *de*); Tc *viharite* (for *viharate*, XTa = OV); Tc *so ya pāya-prajño* (for *sa-upāya-*°, XTa = OV; but OV sep. *sa upāya-*°; this should be a cpd., as O p. 10 n. 2 expects Tib. to read *thabs daṅ śes-rab ldan de*...:Tib.A *de-ni thabs daṅ śes-rab gnas-par śes-par bya*, cf. B *śes-rab ldan te* [v.l. *de* = O] *mñam-ñid gnas-par śes-par bya);* it seems less possible to em. *ya* in *a* to *ca* (so V) and *yo* in *b* remains as OV emend it.

28d XTa *dharmāṃ* (= V), Tc *dharmām* (for *dharmān*, K = O wt.n.).

I col. K [*gāthāyāṃ* ... *prathamaḥ*]; only the word *parivarta-* is used to denote 'chapter' in this text (cf. Renou, 'Les divisions dans les textes sanskrits', 1957, p. 31); Tc adds num. 1 at the end of the colophon.
Only K (5A1) reads after the col.: *atra pramuditā-bhūmi-m* (r. prob. *-bhūmir) anugantvayā dāna-pāramitā ca paripurṇā gāthā 9*; this corresponds to the Chin.Rgs., which reads it after the title of the next chapter: 歓喜地攝布施波羅蜜伽陀; in the first ten chapters ten *bhūmi*s (Mvy 886-895) and ten *paramitās* (Mvy 914-923) are enumerated in the order of the *Mahāvyutpatti*; they must have been interpolated later in the course of tradition. Number 29 agrees with the Chin.Rgs., which r. 29 verses in chap. I. Chin. I 29 corresponds to Skt. II 1, which is missing from MS.K (although number 13 is given at the end of the col. of chap. II). The ancestor of MS.K must have had I 29 which has been kept in other MSS. as II 1, and therefore had 12 verses in chap. II (so Chin.). There would have been after all no division of chapters in the original Rgs (cf. 'Introduction' para. 6 end).

## ⟨II. ŚAKRA⟩

rū(Tc5A)pasmi yo na sthihate na ca vedanāyāṃ
    saṃjñāya yo na sthihate na ca cetanāyāṃ /
vijñāni yo na sthihate sthitu (X 12A) dharmatāyāṃ
    eṣā sa prajña-vara-pāramitāya caryā // 1 //

nityaṃ-a=nitya-sukha-duḥkha-śubhâ=śubhaṃ ti
    ātmany an-ātmi tathatā tatha śūnyatāyāṃ /
phala-prāptitāya a-sthito arahanta-bhūmau
    pratyeka-bhūmi a-sthito tatha buddha-bhūmau // 2 //

yatha nāyako a-sthitu dhātu (X12B) a-saṃskṛtāye
    tatha saṃskṛtāya a-sthito a-niketa-cārī /
evaṃ ca sthānu-a=sthito sthitu bodhisattvo
    a-sthānu sthānu ayu sthānu jinena ukto // 3 //

---

1 K om. the whole verse; this is a mistake made by the scribe, for K gives number 13 at the end of the colophon, and there are 13 verses in this chapter of all the other recensions (see also footnotes to the colophons of chapters I and II).

1a Ta *rupasmi* (for *rūp°*, XTc = OV); Tc *sthitate* (for *sthihate*, XTa = OV).

1b V *cetanāyām* (w. *-m*).

1c Tc *vijñāna* (= O wt.n.!)(for *vijñāni*, XTa = V); *vijñāni* is wt. doubt the true r., although *vijñāna* (O) is noted by Edg.Rgs. 16 as 'a particularly clear case of a loc. (endingless stem-forms; Edgerton 8.11)'.

2a K *nitya-anitya-*, XTac *nitya-m-°* (= OV, unmetr.!), Edg.Rgs. 33-34 em. *nityā-m-°* (for *nityaṃ-°*); Tc *duḥ⟨kha⟩*;K *subhāśubhanti*, XTa *śubh°* (= O; for *-aśubh'-anti*, loc.?, so Tib.?)(for *-śubhāśubhaṃ ti*, Tc = V; cf. AsP p. 18 passim: ... *iti na sthātavyam*).

2b Tc *ātmany anāt // mi*; K [*ś*]*ūnyatāyāṃ*, Ta *śūnyat°* (for *śūnyatāyāṃ*, XTc = OV: Tib.A *stoṅ-ñid*, B *stoṅ*).

2c K [*phala-*]*prā*[*p*]*ti*(5A2)*tāya*; XTac *athito* (= OV), X (Tib.trslit. *athite*) (for *asthito*, K, Sktized); K *a⟨ra⟩hanta-*, Tc *'rahaṃta* (for *arahanta-*, XTa = OV: Tib. *dgra-bcom*).

2d XTac *athito* (= OV)(for *asthito*, K, Sktized); V *-bhūmi-athito*, cpd.; *-bhūmi* is a loc., cf. *arahanta-bhūmau* in *c* and *buddha-bhūmau* in *d*: Tib. *dgra-bcom sa-la ... raṅ-rgyal sa daṅ saṅs-rgyas sa-la*.

3a XTac *sthitaku*, OV *'sthitaku* (for *a-sthitu*, K); K *asaṃskṛto ye*, XTa *asaṃskṛtāyā* (= OV; but V *dhātu-°*, cpd.); Tc *asaskṛtāyātaḥ*, Taki pp. 3-4 n. 3 *asaṃskṛtāyāṃ* (for *asaṃskṛtāye*).

3b Tc om. *tatha*; XTac *athito* (= OV)(for *asthito*, K); Taki pp. 3-4 n. 3 *saṃskṛtāyām*, unmetr. (for *saṃskṛtāya*, MSS. = OV); Tc *anikete* (for *aniketa-*, KXTa = OV).

3c X *sthānu-athito* (= OV; but V sep. *sthānu athito*)(for *sthānu-asthito*, KTac: Tib. *gnas-la gnas med*); XTac *sthita* (= OV)(for *sthitu*, K); Taki pp. 3-4 n. 3 *sthita-bodhisattvo*, cpd.

3d This pāda is quoted by Candrakīrti in his *Prasannapadā* (ed. L. de La Vallée Poussin, p. 167.4); cf. Yuyama, '*Candrakīrti* no *Prasannapadā* ni Inyōsareta *Prajñāpāramitā-Ratnaguṇasaṃcayagāthā*' (1970); XTac *āsthānu*, Taki pp. 3-4 n. 3 *asthāna-*, cpd. (for *asthānu*, K = OV wt.n.: Tib. *gnas med*); Tac *aya* (for *ayu*, KX = OV); Tc *uktaḥ* (for *ukto*, KXTa = OV).

yo icchatī su(Ta4B)gata-śrāvaka haṃ bhaveyaṃ
    pratyeka-buddha bhaviyāṃ tatha dharma-rājo /
imu kṣānty an-āgami na śakya(X13A)ti prāpuṇetuṃ
    yatha āra-pāra-gamanāya a-tīra-darśī // 4 //

māyā-ja dharmata ya śroṣyati bhāṣyamāṇāṃ
    phala-prāpta pratyaya-jino tatha loka-nātho /
nirvāṇu yo adhigato vidu-paṇḍitehi
    sarve ta māya-ja nidiṣṭu tathāgatena // 5 //

catvāri (X13B) pudgala ime iha nā trasanti
    jina-putra satya-kuśalo a-vivartiyaś ca /

---

4a Tc *icchati* (for °*atī*, KXTa = OV); K *suga⟨ta⟩-śrāvakāham* (for *sugata-śrāvaka haṃ*, XTac = OV).

4b K *bhaviyās* (for °*iyāṃ*, XTac = OV); Tc *dharma-rājaḥ* (for °-*rājo*, KXTa = OV).

4c K *anāga*[*mi*], Tc *anāgammi* (for *anāgami*, XTa = OV); K *sakyati* (for *śak*°, XTac = OV); cf. AsP 20.2 *imāṃ kṣāntim anāgamya* ...

4d Conze Rgs. 42 misr. K as *āra-pāra-*; Ta *-gamanāya atīda-darśī*, Tc *gamanāyātī-darśī*, V *-gamanāya atīta-darśī* (for *-gamanāya atīra-darśī*, KX = O: Tib. *ṅogs mi mthoṅ*, Chin. 不見岸

5 This verse is different in all the recensions (two Sanskrit, two Tibetan, and of course Chinese).

5a K *māyāya* should have intended *māyā-ja* 'illusive'; cf. *māya-ja* in *d*: Tib.B *sgyu-ma lta-bur*, also Laṅk. 305.17 (verse) *māyā-jāti-kṛta-*: Tib. *sgyu-ma'i rnam byas*, Chin. 幻生作，幻所起色 (Suzuki Laṅk. Index p. 138b, WSJD p. 1034a, ss.vv.); *maya-ja* is however not supported by the other recensions; K *yā*, unmetr. (for *ya*); Conze Rgs. 39 misr. K as *yo?ti* (for *śroṣyati*, so written clearly!); K *bhāṣyamāṇā* (for °*māṇāṃ*).
   Recension B is different: XTac *yo* (Tac *yā*) *dharma bhāṣyati ya śroṣyati bhāṣyamāṇāṃ* (Ta °*māṇā*, Tc °*mānā*); O misr. X *śroṣyati* as *bhāṣyati* (= V!), and Conze Rgs. 39 em. O *bhāṣyati* to *śṛṇoti* (unmetr.!) w. Tib.B *ñan* (A *thos-pa*); moreover, Edg.Rgs. 40 suggests em. *śṛṇvati* (3 sg.) as 'a good BHS form (Edgerton 28.6)'(!); MSS. *śroṣyati* is without doubt the true reading.
   Cf. Tib.A *gaṅ-źig chos-ñid 'gro daṅ gaṅ bśad thos-pa daṅ*, B *chos 'chod-pa daṅ ñan daṅ bśad-bya gaṅ yin daṅ* (v.l. *yin-pa*).

5b K *-prāpti* (for *-prāpta*, XTac = OV): Tc *pra⟨tya⟩ya-*.

5c XTac *nirvāṇato* (= OV), Edg.Rgs. 40 analyzes *nirvāṇato* as *nirvāṇ'* (nom.sg.) plus *ato* 'thence, therefore' (for *nirvāṇu yo*, K; Conze Rgs. 42 r. K as *nirvāṇuyo*); K *-paṇḍitehiḥ* (for °*ehi*, XTac = OV).

5d XTac *ātma-ja* (= OV: Tib.A *sras-su*)(for *māya-ja*, K: Tib.B *sgyu-ma lta-bur*; cf. V p. 356 n. 2); X *nidṛṣṭu*(= OV: Tib.A *gzigs*), Ta *nidṛṣṭā*, Tc *nidṛṣṭvā*, K *nirdiṣṭu* (for *nidiṣṭu*: Tib.B *bstan*; cf. XII 9d, 10c *nidiṣṭu tathagatena*: Tib. *de-bźin-gśegs-pas bstan;* cf. Edg.Rgs. 10).
   Recension A seems to agree w. Tib.B *de kun sgyu-ma lta-bur de-bźin-gśegs-pas bstan;* but Rec. B (OV = XTac) w. Tib.A: *sarve ta ātma-ja ni-dṛṣṭu tathāgatena: de-dag thams-cad de-bźin-gśegs-pas sras-su gzigs.*

6a Taki p. 4 n. 5 *catvāru* (for *catvāri*, MSS. = OV); Tc *puṃgala* (for *pudgala*, KXTa = OV); cf. Lex. *puṅgala-*, s.v.; K *iha nāsti santi* (Conze Rgs. 42 misr. K as *nātrisanti*), XTac *na trasanti ye smi* (= V, but *ye 'smin*), O em. *na trasanti tasmi* (= Taki, but *tasmin*: Tib. *de-la mi skrag-ste*)(for *iha nā trasanti*); as far as Rec. B is concerned, V is the true reading; cf. Bernhard, 'Gab es einen Lokatif auf *-esmiṃ* im buddhistischen Sanskrit?' (1964).

arhan vidhūta-mala-kleśa prahīṇa-kāṅkṣo
    kalyāṇa-mitra-parivārita yaś caturthaḥ // 6 //

evaṃ cara(K5B)ntu vidu-paṇḍitu bodhisattvo
    nārhatva śikṣati na pratyaya-buddha-bhūmau /
sarva-jñatāya (X14A) anuśikṣati buddha-dharme
    śikṣā-a-śikṣa-naya śikṣati eṣa śikṣā // 7 //

na ca rūpa-vṛddhi-parihāṇi-parigrahāye
    na ca śikṣate vividha-dharma-parigrahāye /
sarva-jñatāṃ ca parigṛhṇati śikṣamāṇo
    niryāti yo 'ya iha śikṣa guṇe ratānāṃ // 8 //

rū(X14B)paṃ na prajña iti rūpi na a(Tc6A)sti prajñā
    vijñāna saṃjña api vedana cetanā ca /

---

6c XTc *arham*(O p. 19 n. 2 misr. X as *aham*), V and Taki p. 4 n. 5 *arhaṃ* (for *arhan*, KTa, so em. O); Tc *vidhuta-* (for *vidhūta-*, KXTa = OV).

6d XTa *-paripācita* (= OV), Tc *-paripǎrita* (for *-parivārita*, K; but cf. Tib.A *yoṅs-su smin byas*, B *yoṅs-su zin-pa*); KXTa *yañ*, Tc *yaṃ*, Taki p. 4 n. 5 *sañ* (for *yaś* = OV wt.n.); cf. I 15a-b *kalyāṇa-mitra-sahitasya ... trāso na bheṣyati:* Tib. *dge-ba'i bśes daṅ ldan-źiṅ ... skrag-par yoṅ mi 'gyur*.

7a Tc *caratu*, O *caranta* (wt.n.)(for *carantu*, KXTa = V); Tc *-paṇḍitra* (for *-paṇḍitu*, KXTa = OV; but V sep. *vidu paṇḍitu)*.

7b X *nārhamvi*, Ta *nārhaṃvi*, Tc *nārhaviṃ*, O em. *nārhammi*, V *nārhaṃmi* (for *nārhatva*, K; cf. AsP 21.26-27 *nārhatve śikṣate na pratyeka-buddhatve śikṣate na buddhatve śikṣate);* Edg.Rgs. 40 however believes that *arhammi* is a misprint or misreading for *arhasmi* (Edgerton 8.64), for he has not found the Pkt. loc. ending *-ammi* in BSkt.

7c Tc *sarvajñatāyā* (for °*tāya*, KXTa = OV).

7d Tc *śikṣādu aśikṣaṇa ya*, OV *śikṣā aśikṣa* (V *śikṣā-*°,cpd.) *na ya*(: Tib. B *gaṅ-źig slob mi slob-la mi slob*)(for *śikṣā-aśikṣa-naya*, KXTa: Tib.A *bslab-pa mi slob tshul-gyis bslob-pa)*; cf. XXV 1c-d *śikṣā-aśikṣa ubhaye a-vikalpamāno yo śikṣate sa iha śikṣati buddha-dharme*.

8a Ta *rǔpa-* (for *rūpa-*, KXTc = OV).

8b XTac *śikṣati* (= V!), O em. *śikṣatī* (for *śikṣate*, K; Conze Rgs. 42 misr. K as *śikṣatu*); XTac *vicidha-* (for *vividha-*, K, so em. O = V: Tib. *sna-tshogs)*.

8c K *sarvajñatānupari*° (for °*jñatāṃ ca pari*°, XTac = OV); Tc *parigṛhṇāti* (for °*ṇati*, KXTa = OV); Tac *śikṣamāno* (for °*māṇo*, KX = OV).

8d XTac *niryāyatī* (Tc *niy*°) *ya iya* (= OV)(for *niryāti yo 'ya* [K *ya*] *iha*, K); cf. Tib.A *ṅes-'byuṅ 'di-ni*, B *ṅes-'byuṅ gaṅ yin 'di-ni;* V *ratānam* (w. *-m*); cf. XXVII 6d *śāntaiṣiṇām ayu vihāra guṇe ratānaṃ*.

9a KXTc *rūpeṇa* (Conze Rgs. 57 misr. K as *rǔpeṇa*), O em. *rūpe na* (= V) (for *rūpaṃ na*: Tib. *gzugs-ni ... ma yin*, Chin. 色非 ...); Ta *rǔpi* (for *rūpi*, KXTc = OV); Tc *nāsti* (for *na asti*, KXTa = OV; poss. r. *na cāsti* as in *c* and *d*); X *prajñāḥ*, Tac *prajñaḥ* (for *prajñā*, K, so em. O = V); cf. AsP 22.27-29 *tathā hi na rūpaṃ prajñā-pāramitā, nāpy anyatra rūpāt prajñā-pāramitā / evaṃ na vedanā na saṃjñā na saṃskārāḥ / na vijñānaṃ prajñā-pāramitā, nāpy anyatra vijñānāt prajñā-pāramitā*.

9b K *vijñāne* (for °*na*, XTac = OV).

na ca eti prajña iti teṣu na cāsti prajñā
    ākāśa-dhātu-(Ta5A)sama tasya na cāsti bhedaḥ // 9 //

ārambaṇāna prakṛtī sa an-anta-pārā
    sattvāna yā ca prakṛtī sa an-anta-pārā /
ākāśa-dhātu-prakṛtī (X15A) sa an-anta-pārā
    prajñāpi loka-vidunāṃ sa an-anta-pārā // 10 //

saṃjñeti nāma parikīrtitu nāyakena
    saṃjñā vibhāviya prahāṇa vrajanti' pāraṃ /
ye etu saṃjña-vigamaṃ anuprāpuṇanti
    te pāra-prāpta sthita pāramite ti bhonti // 11 //

---

9c Ta *eca eti*, Tc *na vaiti* (for *na ca eti*, KX = OV: Tib.A *'di-dag ... ma yin*, but Tib.B omits a word corresponding to *eti*); XTac *teṣa* (= V) (for *teṣu*, K, so em. O: Tib.A *de-la*, B *'di-dag-la-yaṅ*); Tc *ṇa* (for *na*, KXTa = OV: Tib. *med*); XTac *asti* (= OV)(for *cāsti*, K).

9d K *tāsya* (intending *°-samatāsya*?; cf. VIII 1d *°-samatāya*)(for *tasya*, XTac = OV).

10a Tc *ārambanāna* (w. dental *-n-*)(for *°ṇāna*, KXTa = OV); Tc *prakṛti* (for *°tī*, KXTa = OV); Tc om. *sa*; XTa *ananta-pārāḥ*, Tc *aṃta-pārāḥ*, V *a(na)nta-pārā* (for *ananta-pārā*, K, so em. O: Tib. *pha mtha' med*).

10b Tc *prakṛti* (for *°tī*, KXTa = OV); Tc *ananta-pārāḥ* (for *°-pārā*, KXTa = OV).

10c Tc *-prakṛti* (for *°tī*, KXTa = OV); Tc *ananta-pārāḥ* (for *°-pārā*, KXTa = OV).

10d V sep. *prajñā pi* (for *prajñāpi* = O); K *loka-vidunā*, Tc *°-vidurā* (for *°-vidunāṃ*, XTa = OV: Tib. *'jig-rten mkhyen-pa'i)*; Tc *śa* (for *sa*, KXTa = OV: Tib. *de-yaṅ)*.

11 The Sanskrit text represents a different recension:
Cf. Tib. / *'du-śes tshu -rol yin źes 'dren-pas yoṅs-su bsgrags* /
/ *'du-śes rnam-par bśigs-nas spoṅ-ba pha-rol 'gro* /
/ *gaṅ-dag de-la 'du-śes bral-ba rjes thob-pa* /
(B: *gaṅ-dag 'du-śes bral-ba 'di-ni rjes thob-pa)*
/ *de-dag pha-rol phyin-nas ston-pa'i bka'-la gnas // 11 //*
Chin. 智慧無色仏所説 離一切想到彼岸
若人得離諸想已 是人語意住真如 (9)

11a K *saṃjñoti* (for *°jñeti*, XTac=OV); Tib. *tshu-rol* (Skt. *āra* for *nāma*?).

11b XTac *saṃjño*, O *saṃjña* (wt.n.), V *saṃjñāṃ* (for *saṃjñā*, K, so em. Edg.Rgs. 40); *prahāṇa* 'strenuously' (cf. BHSD p. 389b, *prahāṇa*, s.v. 1; but Tib. *spoṅ-ba)*.

11c XTa *atra*, Tc *ava* (for *etu*, K, '*atra*'); KTc *-vigamam* (for *°maṃ*, XTa = OV); K *anuprāpuṇāti*(3 sg.!; this seems to be simply a mistake made by the scribe, for this kind of confusion hardly occurs in our text), XTa *anuprāptavanti* (= O), Tc *anuprāpnuvanti* (= V)(for *anuprāpuṇanti*; cf. XI 10b *parāpuṇanti)*.

11d K *sāra-prāpta* (for *pāra-°*, XTac = OV); XTac *sthitu* (= O)(for *sthita*, K = V); XTac *paramitehu* (= OV; but V sep. *°te hu*)(for *°te ti*, K; Conze Rgs. 42 misr. K as *°tehi*, w. which Edg.Rgs. 40 suggests em. of *°tehu* to *°tehi*'instr. in sense of loc., Edgerton 9.105, 7.30ff.'(!); K *bhoti*, Ta *bhontī* (for *bhonti*, XTc = OV; cf. 11c, footnote, above).

saci gaṅga-vālika-samāni sthihitva (X15B) kalpān
sattveti śabda parikīrtayi nāyako 'pi /
sattvasy' upādu kutu bheṣyati ādi-śuddho
eṣā (K6A) sa prajña-vara-pāramitāya caryā // 12 //

evaṃ jino bhaṇati a-pratikūla-bhāṇī
yada haṃ imāya (Tc6B) vara-pāramitāya āsī /
tada vyākṛto ahu purā puruṣottamena
(X16A) buddho bhaviṣyasi an-āgata adhvakasmin // 13 //

bhagavatyāṃ ratna-guṇa-saṃcaya-gāthāyāṃ śakra-parivarto nāma dvitīyaḥ // 2 //

---

12a O sep. *sa ci* (for *saci*: Tib. *gal-te*); XTac *-vāluka-* (= OV)(for *-vālika-*, K; cf. BHSD p. 478a, 1 *vālikā-*, s.v.); Tc *-samāri* (for °*āni*, KXTa = OV); XTac *kalpā* (= O), V *kalpām* (wt.n.)(for *kalpān*, K): Tib.A *gaṅgā'i bye-ma sñed-kyi bskal*, B *gaṅgā'i bye bskal-par;* cf. AsP 24.8 *gaṅgā-nadī-vālukopamān kalpān.*

12b Tc *parikīrtapi* (for °*ayi*, KXTa = OV); K *pi*, XTac *yaṃ*, O *'yaṃ*, V *'yam* (for *'pi*: Tib.B *kyaṅ*, but A *'di-yis ... kyaṅ).*

12c MSS. *sattvasyupādu* (so print OV)(for *sattvasy' upādu*: Tib. *sems-can skye-ba);* Tc *bheṣyati . ādi-śuddhoḥ* (for °*ti ādi-śuddho*, KXTa = OV).

12d Tc *prajñā-* (for *prajña-*, KXTa = OV).

13 Cf. Tib. / *gaṅ-tshe ṅa-ni śes-rab pha-rol phyin 'di daṅ* /
(B: *gaṅ-tshe ṅa-ni pha-rol phyin-pa mchog 'di daṅ)*
/ *mthun-par smra gyur de-tshe sṅon-gyi skyes mchog-gis* /
/ *ma-'oṅs-pa-yi dus-na saṅs-rgyas 'gyur-ro źes* /
/ *ṅa-la luṅ-bstan gyur ces rgyal-bas de-skad gsuṅs // 13 //*
(B: *ṅa luṅ-bstan-par gyur ces rgyal-bas de-skad gsuṅs)*
Chin. 仏説種種之語言　　　皆具最上般若義
過去仏為我授（T．受）記　　　於未来世証菩提　　　(11)
AsP 24.20-25 *yadāhaṃ ... dīpaṃkarasya ... antike ... (a)nayā prajñā-pāramitayā a-virahito 'bhūvam, tadāhaṃ dīpaṃkarasya bhaviṣyasi tvaṃ ... anāgate 'dhvani ... śākyamunir nāma tathāgato ... iti.*

13a Tc *eva* (for *evaṃ*, KXTa = OV); Ta *bhavati*, Tc *bhagavaty* (for *bhaṇati*, KX = OV): Tib. *de-skad gsuṅs;* X *apratikūla-bhānī* (w. dental *-n-*), Tc *apratikūla-bhātī* (for *apratikūla-bhāṇī*, KTa = OV wt.n.: Tib. *mthun-par smra).*

13b K *yada ham*, XTac *yada ha*, OV *yadahaṃ* (wt.n.)(for *yada haṃ*: Tib. *gaṅ-tshe ṅa-ni*); K *āsīn*, Tc *āsīda* (for *āsī*, XTa = OV). .

13c K *tadu*, Tc *ta* (for *tada*, XTa = OV: Tib. *de-tshe*); Tc *aha* (for *ahu*, KXTa = OV: Tib.A *ṅa-la*, B *ṅa*); XTac *parā-puruṣottamena* (= OV!)(for *purā pur*°, K: Tib. *sṅon-gyi skyes mchog-gis*, Chin. 過去仏

13d XTac *anāgatu* (= O)(for *anāgata*, K = V; but V *anāgata-*,cpd.; K °*gata* has escaped Conze's notice, and Edg.Rgs. 40 suggests em. of O °*gatu* to °*gati* or °*gata*, loc., cf. Edgerton 8.11); XTa *adhvanasmin*(= OV), Tc *adhvonasmin* (for *adhvakasmin*, K).

II col. Tc *catna-* (for *ratna-*, KXTa = OV); Tc adds num. 2 at the end of the colophon.
Only K (6A2) reads after the colophon: *bhūmir vimalā śīla-pāramitā ca gāthā / 13 // //* Cf. Chin. (T. VIII, 677c24) 無垢地摂持戒波羅蜜伽陀 (after the title of chapter III), cf. Mvy 887, 915.

## ⟨III. APRAMEYA-GUṆA-DHĀRAṆA-PĀRAMITĀ-STŪPA-SATKĀRA⟩

ya imāṃ gṛhīṣyati paryāpuṇatī ca nityaṃ
    prajñāya pāramita yatra caranti nāthāḥ /
viṣa-vahni-śastra-udakaṃ na kramāti (X16B) tasyo
    otāru māru na ca vinda(Ta5B)ti māra-pakṣo // 1 //

parinirvṛtasya sugatasya kareya stūpaṃ
    pūjeya sapta-ratanā-mayu kaś cid eva /
tehī prapūrṇa siya kṣetra-sahasra-koṭyo
    yatha gaṅga-vālika-samaiḥ sugatasya stūpaiḥ // 2 //

yāvanta sattva pun' an-anta-sahasra-koṭyo
    te (X17A) sarvi pūjana kareyu an-anya-karmāḥ /

---

1a XTa *grahīṣyati* (= OV)(for *gṛh°*, KTc); XTa *paryāpunatī* (w. dental *-n-*; = O), Tc *°purati* (for *°puṇatī*, K = V); Edg.Rgs. 12 (p. 4 n. 1) tries to read *grahīṣi pariyāpunati* (w. dental *-n-*), but this is not plausible; XTac *sa nityaṃ* (= OV)(for *ca nityaṃ*, K: Tib.A *rtag*, but B *gus byas* = ? Skt. *sa[t-]kṛtya*, cf. Conze Rgs. 39).

1b Ta *prajñā-pāramita*, Tc *prajñā-pāramitā* (for *prajñāya pāramitā*, KX = OV; but O *prajñāya-°*, cpd.!); Tc *yatraṃ* ... *nāthā* (for *yatra* ... *nāthāḥ*, KXTa = OV: Tib.A *gaṅ mgon-rnams*, B *gaṅ-la mgon)*.

1c Tc *viṣā-vahni-śakrodakaṃ* (for *viṣa-vahni-śastra-udakaṃ*, KXTa = OV; but O sep. *udakaṃ*, and V sep. all: Tib.A *dug daṅ me daṅ mtshon daṅ chus*, B *dug daṅ mtshon daṅ me daṅ chus)*; Tc *ta* (for *na*, KXTa = OV: Tib. *mi*); Tc *tayyo* (for *tasyo*, KXTa = OV: Tib. *de-la)*.

1d Tc *otārū* (for *otāru*, KXTa = OV: Tib. *glags* 'chance, opportunity, possibility'); KXTa *pāru*, Tc *pānu* (for *māru* = OV wt.n.: Tib. *bdud*); Tc *ra* (for *na*, KXTa = OV: Tib. *mi*); K *vivandati* (for *vindati*, XTac = OV: Tib. *rñed* ... *'gyur)*.

2a XTac *stūpāṃ* (= V), O em. *stūpān* (O p. 23 n. 1 misr. X as *stūpā*)(for *stūpaṃ*, K).

2b X *pūjoya*, Tc *pūjāya* (for *pūjeya*, KTa, so em. O = V).

2c Ta *tahi* (later amended *tahī*), Tc *tehi* (for *tehī*, KX = OV; but O sep. *te hī*: Tib. *de-dag-rnams-kyis*); Tc *prapurṇa* (for *prapūrṇa*, KXTa); O *prapūrṇasi ya* (= Conze Index p. 147: *bkaṅ* 'would fill')(for *prapūrṇa siya*, so Conze Dict. p. 283 = V: Tib.A *gaṅ-ste*, B *bkaṅ-ste*); cf. Edg. Rgs. 40 'No em. is necessary; only correction of false division. Read *tehī* (instr., Edgerton 21.37) *prapūrṇa* (n.pl. of ppp.) *siya* (= *syāt*, Edgerton 29.41)'; Tc *kṣatra-* (for *kṣetra-*, KXTa = OV: Tib. *źiṅ)*.

3a XTa *yavanta* (for *yāvanta*, KTc, so em. O = V); K *punar ananta-*, hypermetr., XTac *puna* (Tc *pura*) *tāntaka* (= V), O em. *puna nāntaka-* (for *pun' ananta-*); Rec. B appears to intend *tāntaka-*, which must be a variant of *tātaka-*, etc. (cf. BHSD p. 251a, q.v.); cf. XXVII 2c K *tātuka*, XTac *tāntaka* (= OV); XTac *kṣetra-koṭyo* (= OV: Tib. *źiṅ-rnams bye-ba mtha'-yas-na*!)(for *-sahasra-koṭyo*, K: Chin. 衆生無辺千倶胝)

3b XTac *kareyur* (= V), O *kareya-r-* (? mispr.; cf. Edg.Rgs. 40)(for *kareyu*, K); K *ananya-karmān*, XTa *aṇanta-kalpāṃ*, Tc *aṇanta-kalpā*, OV em. *ananta-kalpān* (but V p. 358 n. 2 suggests *ananya-karmā* w. Tib. *las gźan mi byed*)(for *ananya-karmāḥ*).

divyehi puṣpa-vara-gandha-vilepanehī
    kalpāṃs triy-adhva parikalpya tato ca bhūyaḥ // 3 //

yaś co imāṃ suga(Tc7A)ta-māta likhitva puste
    yata utpatī daśa-balāna vināyakānāṃ /
dhāreya sat-karayi puṣpa-vilepanehī
    kala-(X17B)puṇyu bhoti na sa stūpi kari(K6B)tva pūjāṃ // 4 //

maha-vidya prajña ayu pāramitā jinānāṃ
    dukha-dharma-śoka-śamanī pṛthu-sattva-dhāto /
ye 'tīta-'n=āgata-daśa-d-diśi loka-nāthā
    ima-vidya-śikṣita an-uttaru-vaidya-rājā // 5 //

ye vā caranti cari(X18A)yāṃ hita sānukampā
    iha vidya-śikṣita vidū spṛśiṣyanti bodhiṃ /

---

3c XTac *divyahi* (for *divyehi*, K, so em. O = V); XTac *-gandhi-* (= O)(for *-gandha-*, K = V); XTac *-vilepanehi*(= OV)(for °*ehī*, K; cf. III 4c end).

3d Tc *parikalpāṃ*, V °*-parikalpa* (for *parikalpya*, KXTa = O; cf. XXVII 2b *parikalpya)*; Tc *ra*, V *'pi* (for *ca*, KXTa = O).

4a Ta *-mā⟨ta⟩* (for *-māta*, KXTc = OV: Tib. *yum*); Tc *likhittva* (for °*itva*, KXTa = OV: Tib.A *bris byas-te*, v.l. °*-nas*, B *bris-te)*.

4b Tc *yatobhpatī* (for *yata utpatī*, KXTa = OV: Tib. *gaṅ-las ... 'byuṅ)*; V *vināyakānām* (w. *-m*).

4c Tc *dhāraya*, V *dhāreyi* (wt.n.)(for *dhāreya*, KXTa = O: Tib. *'chaṅ-źiṅ)*; XTac *-vilepanehi* (= OV), Tc *-vilehi* (for *-vilepanehī*, K; cf. III 3c end).

4d XTa *kala-puṇya* (= OV; but V sep. *kala puṇya*), Tc *karu-puṇya* (for *kala-puṇyu*, K); XTa *bhonti* (= OV)(for *bhoti*, KTc); Tc *stūyi* (for *stūpi*, KXTa = OV: Tib. *mchod-rten)*; cf. AsP 36.11-15.

5a Tc *-vijña* (for *-vidya*, KXTa = OV: Tib. *rig-sṅags*); Tac *aya* (for *ayu*, KX = OV).

5b MSS. *duḥkha-* (= O!)(for *dukha-* = V: cf. Edg.Rgs.35,Edgerton 2.85,BHSD p. 266a, q.v.); K *-dharme* (for *-dharma-*, XTac = OV); K *-śoka-* (for-*soka-*, XTac = OV: Tib. *mya-ṅan*); K *-dhātoḥ* (= V wt.n.)(for *-dhāto*, XTac = O).

5c XTac *ye tīta ye pi ca* (= OV: *ye 'tīta ye 'pi ca:* Tib. *gaṅ-dag 'das daṅ gaṅ-dag)*(for *ye 'tīta-'nāgata-*, K wt. avagrahas; Conze Rgs. 39 misr. K as *ye 'tītānāgata-*); K *daśa-diśi*, unmetr., XTa *daśa-d-diśa* (= OV; but O °*-diśa-*°, cpd.), Tc *daśa-diśa* (for *daśa-d-diśi*: Tib. *phyogs bcu*; cf. Edg.Rgs. 7); cf. *daśa-d-diśi* XI 10d, XII 1c, 2a, XVI 1c, XXVII 1c,XXVIII 2c (cf. Edgerton 2.79); cf. XII 2a *ye 'tīta ye 'pi ca daśa-d-diśi loka-nāthā:* Tib. *gaṅ-dag 'das daṅ phyogs bcu'i 'jig-rten mgon gaṅ-dag*.

5d Tc *ima-vidya-śikṣitānut*° (for *ima-vidya-śikṣita anut*°, KXTa = OV; but OV sep. all); XTac °*uttara-* (= OV)(for °*uttaru-*, K); V *-rājāḥ* (wt.n.) (for *-rājā*, MSS. = O): Tib. *rig-sṅags 'di bslabs sman-pa'i rgyal-po bla med 'gyur*, Chin. 学此明得無上師; cf. III 6b *iha vidya-śikṣita vidū*, Tib. *rig-sṅags 'di-la bslabs-nas mkhas-pa*.

6a K *cariyān*, X (Tib.trslit.) *cariyā* (for *cariyāṃ*, XTac = OV); XTa *-sānukampaṃ* (= O), Tc °*kampām* (= V)(for °*kampā*, K); OV *hita-*°, cpd. (for *hita sān*°, cf. XV 7c, XX 24b *hitânukampī)*: Tib. *gaṅ-dag phan daṅ sñiṅ-brtser* (v.l. °*-rjer)* *bcas-par* (vv.ll. *bcas-pa* = O, *bcas-pas)*, Chin. 行般若行利有情.

6b O sep. *vidya śikṣita* (for *vidya-*°, cpd. = V; cf. III 5d *ima-vidya-śikṣita)*; Tc *vidu* (= V)(for *vidū*, KXTa = O); O *spaśiṣyanti* (? mispr. for *spṛśiṣyanti*, MSS. = V: Tib. *reg;* °*iṣyanti*may have been pronounced as °*iṣanti*(cf. Edg.Rgs. 38); V *bodhim* (w. *-m*).

ye saukhya saṃskṛta a-saṃskṛta ye ca saukhyāḥ
sarvaṃ ti saukhya prasutā itu veditavyāḥ // 6 //

bījāḥ prakīrṇa pṛthivī-sthita saṃbha(Ta6A)vanti
sāmagri-labdha viruhanti aneka-rūpāḥ /
(X18B) yāvanti bodhi-guṇa pāramitāś ca pañca
prajñāya pāramita te viruhanti sarve // 7 //

yenaiva rāja vrajate sada cakra-vartī
tenaiva sapta-ratanā bala-kāyu sarvo /
(Tc7B) yenaiva prajña ima pāramitā jinānāṃ
tenaiva sarva-guṇa-dharma samācaranti // 8 //

bhagavatyāṃ ratna-(X19A)guṇa-saṃcaya-gāthāyām aprameya-guṇa-dhāraṇa-pāramitā-stūpa-satkāra-parivarto nāma tṛtīyaḥ // 3 //

---

6c V *saukhyā* (wt.n.)(for °*āḥ*, MSS. = O).

6d XTac *sarve ca* (= OV), K *sarvaṃ ni* (for *sarvaṃ ti*: Tib. *de kun*; poss. r. *sarve ti*); Tc *prasūtā* (for *prasutā*, KXTa = OV; cf. Edg.Rgs. 40).

7a Tac *bījā* (for *bījāḥ*, KX = OV); K *prakīrṇṇaḥ* (Conze Rgs. 42 misr. K as °*kīrṇuḥ*)(for °*kīrṇa*, XTac = OV); K *-sthit[a]*(slightly damaged).

7b XTa *sāmagri-labdhu* (= O), V *sāmagri labdhvā* (? w. Tib. *tshogs-pa rñed-nas*, Chin. 得和合 )(for *sāmagri-labdha*, KTc); Ta *viru⟨ha⟩nti*; Tc *viciṃtyāneka-* (for *viruhanti aneka-*, KX = OV: Tib.A *rnam-par skyed*, B *rnam-par skye*, Chin. 生).

7c Tc *-gaṇa* (for *-guṇa*, KXTa = OV: Tib. *yon-tan*); Tc *pāramitā re* (for *pāramitāś ca*, KXTa = OV).

7d O *prajñāya-pāramita*, cpd.; cf. AsP 40.31-41.4.

8a Tc *⟨vraja⟩te*; Tc *saha* (= V; but V sep. *sa ha*; V p. 359 n. 1 misr. O as *bhaṭa*!)(for *sada*, KXTa = O: Tib. *rtag*); Tc *cakravarti* (for °*vartī*, KXTa = OV).

8b Tc *ra⟨ta⟩nā*; OV sep. *sapta ratanā*, which is not impossible; Tac *bala-kāya* (= V)(for °*-kāyu*, KX = O); Tc *sarve* (= V)(for *sarvo*, KXTa = O): Tib. *rin-chen bdun daṅ dpuṅ-tshogs kun*, Chin. 七宝四兵

8c Tc *prajñe* (for *prajña*, KXTa = OV); XTac *iya* (= OV)(for *ima*, K); K *jinānan* (for °*nāṃ*, XTac = OV).

8d O sep. *sarva guṇa-*; XTac *samāgamanti* (= OV: Tib. *'gro-bar 'gyur*) (for *samācaranti*, K).

III col. K *-gāthāyāṃ* (for °*yām*, XTac = OV); XTa *nāmas* (for *nāma*, KTc, so em. O = V); Tc adds num. 3 at the end of the colophon.

Only K (6B5-6) reads after the colophon: *prabhākarī-bhūmi⟨ḥ⟩ kṣānti-pāramitā ca gāthā 8 //* Cf. Chin. (T. VIII, 678a13) 発光地摂忍辱波羅蜜伽陀 (after the title of chapter IV); cf. Mvy 888, 916.

## ⟨IV. GUṆA-PARIKĪRTANA⟩

śakro jinena paripṛcchitu praśnam āhu
    saci gaṅga-vālika-samā siya buddha-kṣetrāḥ /
jina-dhātu sarvi paripūrita cūḍi-baddhā
    ima(X19B)m eva prajña-vara-pāra(K7A)mitāhu gṛhṇe // 1 //

kiṃ kāraṇaṃ na mi śarīri a-gauravatvaṃ
    api tū khu prajña-paribhāvita pūjayanti /
yatha rāja-niśritu naro labhi sarvi pūjāṃ
    tatha prajña-pāramita-niśritu buddha-dhātuḥ // 2 //

maṇi-ratna sarva-guṇa-yuktu an-argha-prāpto
    yasmin ka(X20A)raṇḍaki bhave sa namasyanīyaḥ /
tasyāpi uddhṛta spṛhāti karaṇḍakasmiṃs
    tasyaiva te guṇa-mayā ratanasya bhon(Ta6B)ti // 3 //

---

1b O sep. *sa ci*; Tc *gaṃgā-* (for *gaṅgā-*, KXTa = OV); K *-samān* (cf. Edgerton 8.85, 102)(for *-samā*, XTac = OV).

1c Cf. AsP 48.2-3, 5 *ayaṃ jambudvīpaḥ paripūrṇaś cūlikā-baddhas tathāgata-śarīrāṇāṃ* ...

1d Cf. AsP 48.7 *imām evāhaṃ bhagavan prajñā-pāramitāṃ parigṛhṇīyām.*

2a K *a-gauravatvam*(Conze Rgs. 57 misr. K as *a-gauratvam*[mispr.?]), O °*tva* (wt.n.)(for °*tvaṃ*, XTac = V).

2b K *tu*, Tc *ta* (for *tū*, XTa = OV); O sep. *prajña par*°; OV *pūjayanti*?, so Tib.?: A *śes-rab yoṅs-su bsgoms-pas mchod-par 'gyur*, B ... *mchod-par bgyid* (v.l. *mchod bgyid-de*); cf. *śraddha-paribhāvitu bodhisattvo*, *prajña-vihīnu* XIV 8a-b; but r. poss. *pūjayan*, n.sg.m.pres.pple. (w. expected *aham*), plus *ti* (= *iti*); then *-paribhāvita*, acc.sg.nt. (w. expected *śarīram*); cf. AsP 48.12-13 *api tu khalu punar* ... *prajñā-pāramitāto nirjātāni tathāgata-śarīrāṇi prajñā-pāramitā-paribhāvitatvāt pūjāṃ labhante* (also 50.24-25).

2c XTa *-niśrita* (= OV; but O *-niśrita-*, cpd.), Tc *-niścita* (for *-niśritu*, K: Tib. *brten*).

2d XTa *-niśrita* (= OV; but O *-niśrita-*, cpd.), Tc *-niścita* (for *-niśritu*, K); cf. Tib. *saṅs-rgyas riṅ-bsrel śes-rab pha-rol phyin-la brten.*

3a Tac *sarvi* (= V)(for *sarva-*, KX = O: Tib. *yon-tan kun ldan*); XTa *-yukta anargha-* (= OV), Tc *-yurktānargha-* (for *-yuktu anargha-*, K).

3b XTac *yasmi* (= O), V *yasmiṃ* (for *yasmin*, K, so r. Edg.Rgs. 40); K *bhavet* (for *bhave*, XTac=OV); XTac *namasyanīya* (= O)(for °*īyaḥ*, K = V).

3c XTac *spṛhanti* (= OV)(for *spṛhāti*, K: Tib. *dga' bgyid-de*; Conze Rgs. 42 misr. K as *spṛhānti*, but Conze Dict. p. 435 *spṛhati* 'emit radiance'!); however, Edg.Rgs. 29 analyzes *spṛhānti* as *spṛhā* plus *ante* for *antaḥ* 'there is an end of desire' (and *karaṇḍakasmiṃ* as meaning 'for the box'); Edgerton's analysis of *spṛhānti* is not acceptable; *spṛhāti* (3 sg.pres.ind.) is used for Skt. *spṛhayati*, cf. *spṛhate* XX 22b, but *spṛheti* XXV 6c; XTac *karaṇḍakasmiṃ*(=OV)(for °*asmiṃs*, K); cf. AsP 50.8-10 *yatra ca karaṇḍake tan maṇi-ratnaṃ prakṣiptaṃ bhavati utkṣiptaṃ vā, tata uddhṛte 'pi tasmin maṇi-ratne karaṇḍakāt spṛhaṇīya eva sa karaṇḍako bhavati / tair maṇi-ratna-guṇaiḥ para tatra karaṇḍake spṛhotpadyate.*

3d V em. *guṇa mahā-ratanasya*, Tc *guṇa-mayā ratarasya* (for *guṇa-mayā ratanasya*, KXTa = O); poss. r. *guṇa maṇī-ratanasya*: Tib. *yon-tan de-dag nor-bu rin-chen de-yi lags.*

e(Tc8A)m eva prajña-vara-pāramitā-guṇāni
    yan-nirvṛte 'pi jina-dhātu labhanti pūjāṃ /
tasmā hu yo jina-guṇān parighetu-kāmo
    so prajña-pāra(X20B)mita gṛhṇatu eṣa mokṣo // 4 //

pūrvaṃ-gamā bhavati dānu dadanti prajñā
    śīle ca kṣānti viriye tatha dhyāyamāne /
parigrāhikā kuśala-dharma-a-vipraṇāśe
    ekā ca sā api nidarśayi sarva-dharmān // 5 //

yatha jambudvīpi bahu-vṛkṣa-sahasra-koṭyo
    nānā-prakāra vividhāś ca aneka-rūpāḥ /
(X21A) na pi chāya nānatu bhaven na viśeṣatāpi
    anyatra chāya-gata-saṃkhya-prabhāṣamāṇe // 6 //

---

[4a] Tc *evam eva* (for *em eva*, KXTa = OV).

[4b] Tc *ya-nirvṛta* (for *yan-nirvṛte*, KXTa = OV: Tib. *rgyal-ba mya-ṅan 'das-pa'i* [B *'das-kyaṅ*] *riṅ-bsrel*); cf. AsP 50.17 *evaṃ tāni tathāgata-śarīrāṇi pūjāṃ labhante*.

[4c] Tc *bhasmā hu* (for *tasmā hu*, KXTa = OV; but O *tasmāhu*: Tib.A *de-ltar*, B *de-ltas*); XTc *yā*, V *tān* (for *yo*, KTa, so em. O: Tib. *gaṅ-žig*, X *-guṇāṃ*, Tc *-guṇā* (for *-guṇān*, KTa, so em. O = V).

[4d] KTc *prajña-vara-pāramita*, hypermetr. w. *-vara-* (for *prajña-pāramita*, XTa = OV); K *gṛhṇantu* (for *gṛhṇatu*, XTac = OV); Tc *eva mokṣaḥ* (for *eṣa mokṣo*, KXTa = OV: Tib. *'di-ni thar-pa lags*).

[5a] XTac *bhavatu* (= OV)(for *bhavati*, K); X *dadantu* (= OV), Tac *dadaṃta* (for *dadanti*, K); Edg.Rgs. 40 explains that *dadantu* agrees w. *prajña* as subject of *bhavati* (or *bhavatu*), but this is not acceptable; K *dadanti* (loc., cf. Edgerton 18.16) is better: Tib. *sbyin-pa sbyin-pa'i sṅon-du 'gro-ba śes-rab-ste*; cf. also AsP 51.14-17 *prajñā-pāramitā ... pūrvaṃ-gamā bodhisattvasya dānaṃ vā dadataḥ, śīlaṃ vā rakṣataḥ, kṣāntyā vā saṃpādayamānasya, vīryaṃ vā ārabhamāṇasya, dhyānaṃ vā samāpadyamānasya, dharmān vā vipaśyataḥ bodhisattvasya mahā-sattvasya prajñā-pāramitaivātra pūrvaṃ-gamā*.

[5b] Tc *śāle* <*ca*>(for *śīle ca*, KXTa = OV: Tib. *tshul-khrims*); XTac *tatha vīrya tathaiva dhyāne* (= OV)(for *viriye tatha dhyāyamāne*, K).

[5c] K *parigrāhikān* (Conze Rgs. 42 misr. K as *parigrāhikān*)(for °*ikā*,XTac = OV); XTac *-avipranāśe*(w. dental *-n-*)(for °*ṇāśe*, K, so em. O = V: Tib. *chud mi gzan-phyir*).

[5d] Tc *nidarśayī* (for °*ayi*, KXTa = OV); XTa *-dharmāṃ*, Tc *-dharmā* (for *-dharmān*, K, so em. O = V).

[6a] XTac *jambudvīpa*(= O)(for °*dvīpi*, K = V: Tib. *'dzam-bu'i gliṅ-na*); XTac *-koṭī* (= OV)(for *-koṭyo*, K).

[6b] Tc *cāreka-* (for *ca aneka-*, KXTa = OV: Tib. *maṅ-ba*).

[6c] Tc *na vi* (= V!)(for *na pi*, KXTa = O); MSS. *cchāyanānatu* (so prints V!), O *cchāyanā na tu*; Edg.Rgs. 40 explains, '"*chāyana*", a new word; not in [Conze's] Index. Did Conze mean to read *chāya-ta*? That would seem to me a good emendation: "shade-condition" (like *viśeṣa-tā*, same line, "differentiation")', but this is not at all acceptable; *chāyanānatu* should be divided as *chāya nānatu* : Tib. *grib-ma sna-tshogs*; cf. also AsP 51.20-21 *na ca teṣāṃ vṛkṣāṇāṃ chāyāyā viśeṣo vā nānā-karaṇaṃ vā prajnayate, api tu chāyā chāyety evaṃ saṃkhyāṃ gacchati*; XTac *bhavetu* (= O), V *bhaveta* (for *bhaven na*, K: Tib. *yod ma yin*).

[6d] V *-saṃkhya prabhāṣamāṇā* (for *-saṃkhya-prabhāṣamāṇe* = O); *anyatra*

em eva pañca ima pāramitā jinānāṃ
    prajñāya pāramita-nāmita yā bhavanti /
sarva-jñatāya pariṇāmayamāna sarve
    ṣaḍ apīha eka-naya gacchati bodhi-nāmā // 7 //

bhagavatyāṃ ratna-gu(K7B)ṇa-saṃcaya-gāthāyāṃ guṇa-parikī(Tc8B)rtana-parivarto nāma caturthaḥ // 4 //

---

'except', which is normally construed w. abl. in a neg. sentence (cf. Speijer 183), is here used w. loc.: Tib. *brjod-pa ma gtogs-par*, 'except speaking of ...'; but Edg.Rgs. 40 takes this *anyatra* as meaning 'on the contrary' (cf. BHSD p. 41a, *anyatra* 1, s.v.); cf. XXI 5a, XXIX 6a *anyatra*, 'on the contrary'.

7a K *im eva*, Tc *evaṃm eva* (for *em eva*, XTa = OV: Tib. *de-bźin)*; XTac *imi* (= OV)(for *ima*, K).

7b O *prajñāya-*, cpd.; Tc *pāramitā-* (for °*tă-*, KXTa = OV); XTac *-nāmatayā* (= OV; Conze Dict. p. 219 'have their name from': Tib.B *śes-rab pha-rol phyin-pa'i miṅ-ñid thob-par 'gyur*)(for *-nāmita yā*, K: Tib.A ... *phyin-pas yoṅs-su bsṅos gyur-te)*; cf. AsP 51.22-23 *evam eva .. āsaṃ ṣaṇṇaṃ pāramitānām ... prajñā-pāramitā-pariṇāmitānāṃ sarvajñatā-pariṇāmitānāṃ na viśeṣaḥ, na ca nānā-karaṇam upalabhyate.*

7c XTa *pariṇāmayamāṇa* (= OV), Tc °*māṇā* (for °*māna*,K).

7d XTac *-nayam archati*(= OV)(for *-naya gacchati*, K: Tib.A *tshul gcig 'gyur*, B *ro gcig 'gyur)*; cf. Tib.A *byaṅ-chub bsṅos-pas drug kun 'dir-ni tshul gcig 'gyur*, B *byaṅ-chub ces bya* (v.l. *byar) drug-po 'di kun ro gcig 'gyur*, and Chin. 一味同帰菩提名.

IV col. Tc *-gāthāyā* (for *-gāthāyāṃ*, KXTa = OV); Tc *-pariparikīrtana-* (for *-parikīrtana-*, KXTa = OV); K *-parivartaś caturthaḥ*, XTac *-parivarto nāmaś caturthaḥ* (for *-parivarto nāma caturthaḥ*, so em. O = V); Tc adds num. 4 at the end of the colophon.

Only K (7B1) reads after the colophon: *arciṣmatī-*(MSS.*arccismatī-) bhūmi<r> vīrya-pāramitā ca gāthā // 7 //* Cf. Chin. (T. VIII, 678a29) 焰慧地摂精進波羅蜜伽陀 (after the title of chapter V), cf. Mvy 889, 917.

## ⟨V. PUṆYA-PARYĀYA⟩

saci rūpa saṃjña api vedana cetanā ca
    cittaṃ a-nitya paridīpayi bodhisattvo /
prativarṇikāya carate a-prajānamāno
    na hi (Ta7A) dharma paṇḍitu vināśa karoti jātu // 1 //

(X22A) yasmin na rūpa na ca vedana nāpi saṃjñā
    vijñāna naiva na pi cetanayopalabdhiḥ /
an-upādu-śūnya-naya jānati sarva-dharmān
    eṣā sa prajña-vara-pāramitāya caryā // 2 //

yāvanti gaṅga-nadi-vālika-tulya-kṣetre
    sattvāni sarvi arahatvi vineya kaś cit /
yaś cai(X22B)va prajña ima pāramitāṃ likhitvā
    para-sattva pustaku dadeyu viśiṣṭa puṇyaṃ // 3 //

kiṃ kāraṇaṃ ta iha śikṣita vādi-śreṣṭhā
    jānanti dharma nikhilān iha śūnyatāyāṃ /

---

[1a] Tc *savi* (for *saci*, KXTa = OV; but O sep. *sa ci*: Tib. *gal-te*); Ta *rūpa*, Tc *bhūpa* (for *rūpa*, KX = OV; but O *rūpa-*, cpd.: Tib. *gzugs*); Tc *saṃjñāpi* (for *saṃjña api*, KXTa = OV); XTac *cetanāyāṃ* (= OV)(for *cetanā ca*, K; cf. I 9a *cetanā ca*).

[1b] KTc *cittam* (for *cittaṃ*, XTa = OV); Tc *avityaṃ* (for *anitya*, KXTa = OV: Tib. *mi rtag*); XTac *pariṇāmayi* (= OV)(for *paridīpayi*, K, so em. Conze ad O p. 127; cf. V p. 360 n. 1: Tib.A *yoṅs-su brjod-pa*, B *yoṅs-su ston-pa*).

[1d] XTac *paṇḍita* (= OV)(for *paṇḍitu*, K); XTa *vināya*, Tc *vanāya* (for *vināśa*, K, so em. OV: Tib.A *chud-gzon*, B *'jig-par*).

[2a] Ta [*rūpa*]; XTac *api* (= OV)(for *na ca*, K); XTa *cāpi* (= OV), Tc *vā // pi* (for *nāpi* K); cf. Tib.A *gaṅ-la gzugs daṅ tshor-ba 'du-śes mi dmigs-śiṅ*, B *gaṅ-la gzugs min tshor min 'du-śes* ...

[2b] K *vijñānu*, Tc *vijñānaṃ* (for *vijñāna*, XTa = OV); Tc *cetanayo⟨pa⟩labdhiḥ*.

[2c] V sep. *na ya* (for *-naya* = O: Tib. *tshul-du*); XTac *-dharmā* (for *-dharmān*, K = OV wt.n.).

[3a] Tac *gaṅgā-* (for *gaṅgă-*, KX = OV); Tc *-nadī-* (for *-nadi-*, KXTa = OV).

[3b] XTac *tāvanti sattva arhanti* (Tc *sattvārh°*), OV *tāvanti sattva arahanti* (wt.n.), K *śattvāni sarvi arhatvi* (Conze Rgs. 43 misr. K as ... *arhanti*)(for *sattvāni sarvi arahatvi*); cf. Tib.A *gaṅgā'i kluṅ-gi bye sñed źiṅ-rnams ji-sñed-pa, de-sñed sems-can la-las dgra-bcom-ñid btul-bas*, B *la-las gaṅgā'i kluṅ-gi bye sñed źiṅ-rnams-na, sems-can ji-sñed 'khod kun dgra-bcom-ñid btul-bas*.

[3c] Tc *yathaiva* (for *yaś caiva*, KXTa = OV: Tib. *gaṅ-gis*); K *iva* (for *ima*, XTac = OV: Tib. *'di*, Chin. 此 ); XTac *pāramitā* (= OV)(for *°itāṃ*, K).

[3d] XTac *para-sattvi* (= OV)(for *°-sattva*, K); cf. Tib.A *sems-can gźan-la*, Chin. 他 , and Tib.B *sems-can mchog-la;* Tac *dadeya* (= V)(for *dadeyu*, KX = O); XTac *viśiṣṭa-puṇyaḥ* (= OV)(for *viśiṣṭa puṇyaṃ*, K: Tib. *bsod-nams khyad-par 'phags*, Chin. 功德勝

[4a] *śikṣiti* (for *°ita*, KXTc = OV: Tib. *bslabs-nas*); Tc *-śreṣṭā* (for *śreṣṭhā*, KXTa = OV: Tib. *mchog*).

[4b] XTac *gamayanti* (= V), O *gamayānti* (? mispr.)(= Conze Dict. p. 164) (for *jānanti*, K; cf. Tib. *ston byed!*); V *śūnyatāyām* (w. *-m*).

yaṃ śrutva śrāvaka spṛśanti vimukti śīghraṃ
    pratyeka-bodhi spṛśayanti ca buddha-bodhiṃ // 4 //

a-sa(X23A)to 'ṅkurasya (Tc9A) druma-saṃbhavu nāsti loke
    kutu śākha-pattra-phala-puṣpa-upādu tatra /
vina bodhi-citta jina-saṃbhavu nāsti loke
    kutu śakra-brahma-phala-śrāvaka-prādu-bhāvā // 5 //

āditya-maṇḍalu ya(K8A)dā prabha-jāla-muñcī
    karma-kriyāsu tada sattva parākra(X23B)manti /
tatha bodhi-citta sada loka vidusya jñāto
    jñānena sarva-guṇa-dharma samāgamanti // 6 //

yath' anovatapta a-sato bhujagādhipa(Ta7B)sya
    kutu nadya prasravu bhaved iha jambudvīpe /
a-satā nadīya phala-puṣpa na saṃbhaveyu
    na ca sāgarāṇa ratanā bhavi 'neka-rūpāḥ // 7 //

---

4c XTac *yā* (= O), *yāṃ* (for *yaṃ*, K; but Tib. *de*, v.l. *de-dag*); Tc *spaśaṃti* (for *spṛśanti*, KXTa = OV: Tib. *reg*)[O p. 29 n. 1 seems to have misr. X as *arhanti*]; XTac *vimukta* (for °*kti*, K, so em. O = V: Tib. *rnam-par grol-la*).

4d Tc *spṛśaṃti* (for *spṛśayanti*, KXTa = OV); V *-bodhim* (w. *-m*).

5a X *asato ṅkurusya* (O misr. X as *asato ṅkarusya*, and em. °*to 'karusya*!), Tac *asatv aṅkurusya* (for *asato 'ṅkurasya*, K = V: Tib.A *lcug-ma med-par*, B *myu-gu med-par*).

5b XTac *kuta* (= OV)(for *kutu*, K: Tib. *ga-la*).

5d XTac *kuta* (= OV)(for *kutu*, K: Tib. *ga-la*); V sep. *-phala śrāvaka-*; K *-prādurbhāvā*, XTa *-prādubhāvaḥ* (= OV; Conze Rgs. 43 misr. O as *prādurbhāvaḥ*), Tc *-prādurbhavā* (for *prādubhāvā*).

6a Tc *-muṃcā* (for *-muñcī*, KXTa = OV; but V sep. *-jāla muñcī*: Tib. *'od-kyi dra-ba 'gyed*, Chin. 如日舒光照諸天

6b Tc *dana* (for *tada*, KXTa = OV: Tib. *de-tshe*).

6c Ta [*sa*]*da*; OV *loka-vidusya*, cpd. (*loka*, loc.; cf. V 5c).

6c-d 'Thus [if] the thought of enlightenment (*bodhi-citta*) is always cognized (nt. subject w. masc. predicate) to the wise in the world, by this cognition all the laws of qualities would meet'. (But see Conze Trsl., p. 136 n. 22). Cf. Tib. *mkhas-pa śes-phyir 'jig-rten byaṅ-chub sems byuṅ-na, ye-śes-kyis-ni sems-can* (Skt. *sattva-*!) *yon-tan chos daṅ ldan*.

7 Cf. Rgs. I 2.

7a Tc *anocatapta*, OV *(yatha) nopatapta* (wt.n.; cf. Edg.Rgs. 18)(for *anovatapta*, KXTa: Tib. *ma-dros mtho-la*, v.l. *ma-dros-pa-yi*, Chin.無熱池 cf. I 2c, fn.); Tac *bhūjagādhipasya* (for *bhuj*°, KX = OV: Tib. *klu bdag*, Chin. 龍主 , v.l. 龍王).

7b XTac *kuta* (= OV)(for *kutu*, K; cf. V 5bd); Tc *prasnavu* (for °*sravu*, KXTa = OV: Tib. *'bab-par*); V *nadya-prasravu*, cpd.; K *jaṃbūdvīpe* (for *jambū*°, XTac = OV).

7c K *saṃbhaveyur* (for °*eyu*, XTac = OV).

7d K *neka-rūpāḥ*, XTac *naika-*° (= OV!)(for *'neka-*°: Tib. *gzugs maṅ*, Chin. 種種 ).

tatha (X24A) bodhi-citta a-satīha tathāgatasya
    kutu jñāna-prasravu bhaved iha sarva-loke /
jñānasya co a-sati nāsti guṇāna vṛddhir
    na ca bodhi sāgara-samā na ca buddha-dharmāḥ // 8 //

yāvanti loki krimi dyotaka-prāṇi-bhūtā
    obhāsanārtha prabha osara(Tc9B)yanti sarve /
yada (X24B) sūrya-maṇḍalu-pramuktita eka-raśmī
    na kalāpi jyotika-gaṇe siya sarvi ābhā // 9 //

bhagavatyāṃ ratna-guṇa-saṃcaya-gāthāyāṃ puṇya-paryāya-parivarto nāma pañcamaḥ // 5 //

---

8a XTa *-cita* (for *-citta*, KTc = OV wt.n.: Tib. *byaṅ-chub sems*).

8b XTac *kuta* (= OV)(for *kutu*, K); Tc *-prasravra* (for *-prasravu*, KXTa = OV: Tib. *ye-śes ... 'byuṅ*; cf. V 7b *nadya prasravu*).

8c K *vo* (for *co*, XTac = OV); Tc *asita* (for *asati*, KXTa = OV: Tib. *med-na*); XTac *guṇāna* (cf. Edgerton 8.125), O *guṇânu°* (Conze Rgs. 43 misr. O as *guṇānu vṛddhiḥ*)(for *guṇāna*, K = V); XTa *vṛddhiḥ* (= OV; but O *guṇânu-vṛddhiḥ*)(for *vṛddhir*, KTc).

8d K *-same* (for *-samā*, XTac); O *na ca bodhi-sāgara-samāna ca buddha-dharmāḥ* (for *na ca bodhi sāgara-samā na ca* ... = V: Tib. *byaṅ-chub med, rgya-mtsho 'dra-ba'i saṅs-rgyas chos-kyaṅ med-par 'gyur*).

9 Cf. Rgs. XXIII 1.

9a XTac *kva ci* (= OV)(for *krimi*, K); XTac *jotika-* (= OV)(for *dyotaka-*, K); V *-prāṇa-* (for *-prāṇi-*, MSS. = O); cf. XXIII 1c *sarva-krimi jyotika-prāṇa-bhūtān*.

9b Tc (*-bhūtâ*)*vabhāsanārtha* (for *obhās°*, KXTa = OV); Tc *osara*⟨*yan*⟩*ti*.

9c XTac *vara* (= V; but V *vara-*, cpd.), O *para-* (wt.n.)(: Tib. *ches mchog-ste* (for *yada*, K); XTac *-maṇḍala-* (= OV)(for *-maṇḍalu-*, K); XTa *-vinisṛta* (= O), Tc *-vinisṛtaika-* (w. *eka-*), V *-viniḥsṛta* (so Edg.Rgs. 40)(for *-pramuktita*,K: Tib. *phyuṅ*); Tc *-raśmi* (for *-raśmī*, KXTa = OV).

9d O om. *na* (wt.n.; ? mispr.); O *-gaṇesiya* (for *-gaṇe siya* = V; cf. Edg.Rgs. 40: Tib.A *me-khyer tshogs-kyi ...*, B *snaṅ byed tshogs-kyi ...*); XTac *sarva ābhāḥ* (= O), V *sarva-ābhāḥ*, cpd. (for *sarvi ābhā*, K).

V col. K om. *bhagavatyāṃ ratna-guṇa-saṃcaya-gāthāyāṃ*; Tc adds num. 5 at the end of the colophon.

Only K (8A5) reads after the colophon: *sudurjayā-bhūmi*<*r*> *dhyāna-pāramitā ca gāthā 9 //*    Cf. Chin. (T. VIII, 678b20) 難勝地攝定波羅蜜伽陀 (after the title of chapter VI), cf. Mvy 890, 918.

## ⟨VI. ANUMODANĀ-PARIṆĀMANĀ⟩

yāvanti śrāvaka-gaṇāḥ prasavanti puṇyaṃ
     dānaṃ ca śīlam api bhāvana-saṃ(X25A)prayuktaṃ
sa hi bodhisattva anumodati eka-citte
     na ca sarva-śrāvaka-gaṇe siya puṇya-skandho // 1 //

ye buddha-koṭi-niyutāḥ purimādhv'-atītāḥ
     ye vā an-anta-bahu-(K8B)kṣetra-sahasra-koṭyo /
tiṣṭhanti ye 'pi parinirvṛta loka-nāthā
     deśanti dharma-ratanaṃ dukha-saṃkṣayāye // 2 //

(X25B) prathamaṃ upādu (Ta8A) vara-bodhayi citt'-upādo
     yāvat sa-dharma-kṣaya-kālu vināyakānāṃ /

---

1a Tc *-yāṇā* (for *-gaṇāḥ*, KXTa = OV: Tib. *ñan-thos-tshogs-rnams*); Tc *'prasavaṃti* (for *prasavanti*, KXTa = OV: Tib.A *skyed-pa-yaṅ*, B *(b)skyed-pa'aṅ)*.

1b Tc *śālam* (for *śīlam*, KXTa = OV: Tib. *tshul-khrims*); K *saṃprayuktāḥ*, *saṃvāprayukta* (for *saṃprayuktaṃ*, XTa = OV): Tib. *(b)sgom daṅ rab-tu ldan-pa'i bsod-nams (B -nams-tshogs)*; cf. AsP 69.4-5 *sarva-sattvānāṃ dāna-mayaṃ puṇya-kriyā-vastu, śīla-mayaṃ puṇya-kriyā-vastu, bhāvanā-mayaṃ puṇya-kriyā-vastu, ...*: also Chin. Rgs. (T. VIII, 678b21) 所有声聞衆功徳布施持戒観照行.

1c XTa *anumodana* (= OV), Tc *anumodateka*(w. *eka-*)(for *anumodati*, K); K *-citto* (for *-citte*, XTac = OV): Tib. *byaṅ-chub-sems-dpa' rjes-su yi raṅ sems gcig-la*, Chin. 菩薩発一心随喜.

1d Tc *-skandhā* (for *-skandho*, KXTa = OV); O *sarva-śrāvaka-gaṇesiya-puṇya-skandho*, cpd. (for°*-gaṇe siya puṇya-*° = V; cf. V 9d).

2a Tc *ya* (for *ye*, KXTa = OV); XTc *-niyutā* (= OV), Ta *-niyutā[ḥ]*(for *-niyutāḥ*, K); K *parimādhvatītāḥ*, XTc *purimādhvatītā*(= O; V misr. O as *purimādhat*°), V *purimā vyatītā*!(for *purimādhv'-atītāḥ*: Tib. *'das dus sṅon-gyi)*.

2b Tc om. *vā*; Tc *anaṃtā-* (for *anantă-*, KXTa = OV); K [*-kṣetra-saha*]*sra-*; XTac *-koṭyaḥ* (= OV)(for *-koṭyo*, K).

2c XTa *niṣṭhanti* (for *tiṣṭhanti*, KTc, so em. O = V: Tib. *bźugs*); Tc *parinīrvṛta* (for °*nirvṛta*,KXTa = OV; but O °*nirvṛta-*, cpd.).

2d XTac *duḥkha-saṃkṣayāya* (= O), V *dukha-saṃkṣayāya* (for *dukha-saṃkṣayāye*, K: Tib. *sdug-bsṅal zad-par bya-phyir*; cf. XXVI 2d *dukha-saṃkhayāye*: Tib. *sdug-bsṅal zad-par bya-phyir)*.

3a KTc *prathamam* (for °*maṃ*, XTa = OV); K *cintupādo*,XTac *cittapādo* (= O), V *cittupādo* (for *citt'-upādo*: Tib. *sems bskyed*, v.l. *thugs bskyed*;cf. Chin. 先発最上菩提心); cf. also AsP 69.17 *yāvat prathama-cittot-pādam upādāya* ... ; cf. Rgs. XXVI 1b, XXX 3a, 12b *citt'-upādu* (MSS. *cittapādu* = O; V *cittupādu*, wt.n.), XXXI 5d *citt'-upādo* (K *cintupādo*, XTac *cittapādo* = O; V *cittupādo*, wt.n.); cf. XXX 3a-b *prathamaṃ upādu vara-bodhayi citt'-upādo, yāvann* ...: Tib.A *byaṅ-chub mchog-tu sems bskyed thog-mar bskyed byas-nas*, B ...*bskyed daṅ-pos-nas bzuṅ-ste*, ... *bar*: Chin. 従初発心為菩提，乃至...

3b Tc *su-dharma-* (= V; but V sep. *su dharma-*!)(for *sa-dharma-*, KXTa = O: Tib. *dam chos* = Skt. *sad-dharma-*); Tc *-kālū* (for *-kālu*, KXTa = OV: Tib. *dus*); V *vināyakānām* (w. *-m*); cf. AsP 69.18 *yāvac ca saddharmo nāntar-hitaḥ*.

etasmin antari ya teṣa jināna puṇyaṃ
    sa hi yukta-pāramita ye 'pi ca buddha-dharmāḥ // 3 //

yaṃ caiva buddhu-tana(Tc10A)yasya ya śrāvakāṇāṃ
    śaikṣā a-śaikṣa kuśalāśrava 'n-āśravāś ca /
paripiṇḍayitva (X26A) anumodayi bodhisattvo
    sarvaṃ ca nāmayi jagārtha nidāna bodhau // 4 //

pariṇāmayantu yadi vartati citta-saṃjñā
    tatha bodhi-saṃjña-pariṇāmana sattva-saṃjñā /
saṃjñāya dṛṣṭi-sthitu citta ti-saṅga-sakto
    pariṇāmitaṃ na bhavatī upalabhyamānaṃ // 5 //

saci (X26B) eva jānati nirudhy' imi kṣīṇa dharmāḥ
    taṃ caiva kṣīṇu pariṇāmayiṣyāmi yatra /

---

3c X *ekasmin antari ya* (= O), Ta *ekasmin atnari ya*, Tc *ekasminn anta jita*, V *ekasmi tatra ciya* (?)(for *etasmin antari ya*, K: Tib. *de-bar ... gaṅ yin-pa*); Tc *yeṣa* (for *teṣa*, KXTa = OV: Tib. *de-dag*); K *puṇyan* (Conze Rgs. 57 misr. K as *puṇya*[*ṃ*])(for *puṇyaṃ*, XTac = OV).

3d XTac *saha-* (= OV; but V sep. *sa ha*)(for *sa hi*, K); Tc *yukṣma* (for *yukta-*, KXTa = OV; but V sep. *yukta pāramita*: Tib. *pha-rol phyin daṅ ldan*); cf. AsP 69.20 *ṣaṭ-pāramitā-pratisaṃyuktāni kuśala-mūlāni*.

4a XTac *yaś* (= OV)(for *yaṃ*, K; cf. VI 3c *puṇyaṃ*); XTac *buddha-tanayāna* (= OV)(for *buddhu-tanayasya*,K; cf. Tib. *saṅs-rgyas sras-rnams*); XTa *ca* (= O), Tc om. *ca*(= Baroda MS.; V adds *ca*: Tib. *daṅ-ni*)(for *ya*, K).

4b XTac *śaikṣa* (= OV)(for *śaikṣā*, K, so em. Edg.Rgs. 32); K *kuśalāsrava* (= OV wt.n.)(for °*āśrava*, XTac; cf. BHSD p. 110a, *āśrava-*, s.v.); K *nāśravāṃś*(Conze Rgs. 57 misr. K as *nāsra*°), X *ṇāsravāś*, Ta *nāsravāś* (= OV wt.n.), Tc *nāśravāś* (for *'nāśravāś*): Tib. *slob daṅ mi slob dge-ba zag bcas med-pa*.

4d XTac *bodhi* (= OV)(for *bodhau*, K); V *jagārtha-nidāna*, cpd.!

5a Tc *parināmayaṃtu* (for *pariṇ*°, KXTa = OV); XTac *yadhi* (for *yadi*,K, so em. O = V: Tib. *gal-te*); cf. Tib. *yoṅs bsṅo gal-te sems daṅ* (B *sems-su*) *'du-śes gnas byed-ciṅ* (B *'byuṅ 'gyur-źiṅ*); also AsP 72.17-20 *bodhisattvo mahā-sattvo yena cittena yat pariṇāmayati, tasmiṃś citte na citta-saṃjñī bhavati ... evaṃ bodhisattvasya mahā-sattvasya na saṃjñā-viparyāso na citta-viparyāso na dṛṣṭi-viparyāso bhavati ...*

5b XTac *bodhisattva-* (= OV)(for *bodhi-saṃjña-*, K: Tib. *byaṅ-chub 'du-śes*; cf. Conze ad O p. 127, also V p. 362 n. 4).

5c Tc *saṃjñāpa* (for °*āya*, KXTa = OV); K *cinta* (Conze Rgs. 43 misr. K as *citta*), Tc *citiṃ* (for *citta*, XTa = OV: Tib. *sems*); K *ti-saṅga-śakto*, XTa *ti-saṃga-yukto* (= O), Tc *ta-saṃga-yukto*, V *tri-saṅga-yukto* (for *ti-saṅga-sakto*: Tib.A *gsum ldan-par gnas*, B *gsum-la chags*)[*tri-saṅga = saṃjñā-saṅga/viparyāsa, dṛṣṭi-*°, *citta-*°].

5d Tc *bhavati* (for °*atī*, KXTa = OV).

6a Conze Rgs. 43 misr. K as *jānatī* (for *jānati*, so MSS. = OV); K *virudhy-imi*, XTac *nirudhyati* (= OV; r. perh. *nirudhya ti*)(for *nirudhy' imi*: Tib. A *chos-rnams 'gags-śiṅ*, B *chos 'di 'gags-śiṅ*); cf. AsP 72.24 *niruddhaṃ* (ed. Wogihara: *vir*°!); OV *kṣīṇa-dharmāḥ*, cpd.!

6b XTa *tac caita kṣīṇa pariṇāmayiṣyanti* (= OV), Tc *tc caitac caita kṣīṇa pariṇāmayiṣyāmi* (for *taṃ caiva kṣīṇu pariṇāmayiṣyāmi*, K; Conze Rgs. 43 misr. K as *tathaiva kṣīṇu-!*); Tc *ya ca* (for *yatra*, KXTa = OV: Tib. *gaṅ-du*): Tib. *gal-te 'di-ltar chos-rnams* (B *chos 'di*) *'gags-śiṅ zad-pa daṅ, gaṅ-du yoṅs-su bsṅo-ba de-yaṅ zad-pa daṅ, chos-kyis chos-la nam-yaṅ mi bsṅo śes gyur-na*.

na ca dharmu dharmi pariṇāmayate kadā cit
    pariṇāmitaṃ bhavati eva prajānamāne // 6 //

saci so nimitta kurute na sa nāmayāti
    atha ānimitta pariṇāmita bhoti bodhau /
viṣa-(X27A)sṛṣṭa bhojanu yathaiva kriyā-praṇīto
    tatha śukla-dharmu-upalambhu jinena ukto // 7 //

tasmā hu nāma pariṇāmana (K9A) śikṣitavyā
    yatha (Tc10B) te jinā kuśala eva prajānayanti /
yaj-jātiyaṃ ya-prabhavaṃ ca ya-lakṣaṇaṃ ca
    anumodamī tatha ta(Ta8B)thā pariṇāmayāmi // 8 //

e(X27B)vaṃ ca puṇya pariṇāmayamāna bodhau
    api so na buddhu kṣipate jina-ukta-vādī /

---

6c XTac *dharma-*(= OV; but O *dharma-*, cpd.!)(for *dharmu*, K).

7a O sep. *sa ci*; XTac *na ca mānayātī* (= O), V *na ca mānayātī* (for *na sa nāmayāti*, K; Conze Rgs. 39 misr. K as *na manyamayāti* and suggests em. to *na sa nāmayāti* w. Tib. *de-ni bsho ma yin*: Chin. 作有相施非真施); cf. AsP 76.16-17 *saced evaṃ nimittī-karoti ... na pariṇāmayaty anuttarāyāṃ samyak-saṃbodhau.*

7b XTac *pariṇāmitu* (= O)(for °*ita*, K = V); XTa *bhonti* (= OV)(for *bhoti*, KTc); cf. AsP 76.19 *atha ... na ca nimittī-karoti, evaṃ pariṇāmitaṃ bhavati.*

7c Tac *bhojana* (for °*anu*, KX = OV; but O *-sṛṣṭa-bhojanu*, cpd.); Tc *yartheva* (for *yathaiva*, KXTa = OV: Tib. *ji-ltar*); Tc *kiya* (for *kriyā-* KXTa = OV); Conze (Index p. 138a, Dict. p. 157) suggests em. to *siyā*: cf. AsP 77.3-4 *tad-yathāpi nāma praṇītaṃ bhojanaṃ sa-viṣaṃ bhavet.*

7d XTac *-dharma-upalambha* (= OV)(for *-dha⟨r⟩mu-upalambhu*, K).

8a KXTa *tasmāhu* (so prints O), Tc *tasmāha* (this corresponds to Tib.A *de-ltar bdag-gis*)(for *tasmā hu*, so divides V: Tib.B *de-ltas 'di-ltar*); cf. *tasmā hu* (v.l. *tasmād dhi* = V) I 16d, IV 4c, VII 7a, X 6d (but Tib.B *bdag*), XII 4d, XXII 1a; Tc *pariṇāmana* (for °*mana*, KXTa = OV); V *nāma-pariṇāmana*, cpd.!(*nāma*, indecl., is used w. *tasmā hu*).

8b Cf. AsP 77.31-78.1 *yathā te tathāgatā ... jānanti ... tat-kuśala-mūlaṃ ...*: Tib. (Peking MI 92B2-3) *ci-ltar de-bźin-gśegs-pa ... mkhyen-ciṅ ... dge-ba'i rtsa-ba de ...*

8c Ta *yarj-* (for *yaj-*, KXTa = OV); XTa *-jātiyo* (= OV), Tc *-jitiyo* (for *jātiyaṃ*, K); K *yat-*, XTac *yaṃ-*, O sep. *yaṃ*, V *'yaṃ* (for *ya-*; cf. Edg.Rgs. 34); K *-prabhavāñ* (Conze Rgs. 43 misr. K as °*vāś*, which is adopted by Edg.Rgs. 34!), XTa *-prabhavo* (= OV; but OV sep. *ya prabhavo*), Tc *-prabhavā* (for *-prabhavaṃ*: Tib. *'byuṅ*, Chin. 威力; but cf. AsP *yat-svabhāvaṃ*!); K *ca yal-lakṣaṇāñ* (Conze Rgs. 43 misr. K as °*ṇāś*, which is adopted by Edg.Rgs. 34!), XTac *yad-alakṣaṇaṃ* (= OV)(for *ca ya-lakṣaṇaṃ*; cf. Edg.Rgs. 34); cf. Tib. *rnam-pa gaṅ-dag* (B *gaṅ yin*) *'byuṅ gaṅ mtshan-ñid gaṅ yin-la*; also AsP 78.2 *yaj-jātikaṃ ... yat-svabhāvaṃ yal-lakṣaṇam*: Tib. (Peking MI 92B3) *rigs gaṅ yin-pa daṅ ... raṅ-bźin gaṅ yin-pa daṅ mtshan-ñid gaṅ yin-pa daṅ ...*

8d Tc *anumodanāmi* (for *anumodamī*, KXTa = OV).

9b XTac *na ca so hi* (= OV)(for *api so na*, K): cf. Tib. *dug med* (no v.l.; ? Skt. *a-viṣo*, and then *a-viso*, *avi so*, MIndic to *api so*?; cf. Pischel 143); XTa *buddha* (= OV), Tc *buddhā* (for *buddhu*, K); Tac *kṣiyate* (for *kṣipate*, KX = OV: Tib. *spoṅ*); Tc *jinokta-* (for *jina-ukta-*, KXTa = OV; but V sep. *jina ukta-*!: Tib. *rgyal-bas gsuṅs-pa smra*).

yāvanti loki upalambhika bodhisattvā
    abhibhoti sarva pariṇāmayamāna śūro // 9 //

bhagavatyāṃ ratna-guṇa-saṃcaya-gāthāyām anumodanā-pariṇāmanā-parivarto nāma ṣaṣṭhaḥ // 6 //

---

9c XTac *bodhisattvo* (for °*sattvā*, K, so em. O = V).

9d XTac *abhibhonti* (= OV)(for °*bhoti*, K); XTac *sarvi* (= OV)(for *sarva*, K); Tc *śūroḥ* (for *śūro*, KXTa = OV); cf. Tib. *de-ltar yoṅs bsṅo dpa'-bo* (v.l. °*-bos*) *'jig-rten dmigs-can-gyi* (v.l. °*-gyis* =O), *byaṅ-chub-sems-dpa' ji-sñed thams-cad zil-gyis non.*

VI col. XTac *anumodana-* (= O), V *anumodanā-* (for *anumodanā-pariṇāmanā-*, K, so AsP); K *-parivarta* (for *-parivarto*, XTac = OV); K om. *nāma*; XTac *ṣaṣṭhamaḥ* (= V)(for *ṣaṣṭhaḥ*, K, so em. O); Tc adds num. 6 at the end of the colophon.

Only K (9A3) reads after the colophon: *abhimukhī-bhūmi⟨h⟩ prajñā-pāramitā ca gāthā // 9 //* Cf. Chin. (T. VIII, 678c11) 現前地攝智慧波羅蜜伽陀 (after the title of chapter VII), cf. Mvy 891, 919.

## 〈VII. NIRAYA〉

(X28A) jāty-andha-koṭi-niyutāny a-vināyakānāṃ
    mārge a-kovidu kuto nagara-praveśe /
vina prajña pañca imi pāramitā a-cakṣū
    a-vināyakā na prabhavanti spṛśetu bodhiṃ // 1 //

yatrāntare 'smi bhavate pragrahīta prajñā
    tatu labdhu cakṣu bhavatī imu nāma-dheyaṃ /
(X28B) yatha citra-karma pariniṣṭhitu cakṣu-hīno
    na ca tāva puṇyu labhate a-kari(Tc11A)tva cakṣuḥ // 2 //

yada dharma saṃskṛta-a-saṃskṛta-kṛṣṇa-śuklā
    aṇu-mātru no labhati prajña vibhāvamānaḥ /

---

1b Tc *kuto vidu kuto* (for *a-kovidu kuto*, KXTa = OV): Tib. *lam-yaṅ mi śes groṅ-khyer 'jug-par ga-la 'gyur*; *nagarā-°* (for *nagara-°*, no v.l.; cf. Edgerton 8.15-17) or poss. *nagaraṃ-°* (cf. Edgerton 8.14) seems to be the true reading (rather than *nagara-*, followed by a double consonantal initial); cf. *para-praṇeya-* (r. prob. *parā-°*, or *paro-°*) I 15c, XV 6d, XVII 4c, *gati-pracāro* (r. prob. *gatī-°*) I 22c, but *a-prameyaṃ*(prob. pronounced *appam°*) XVIII 6d, XXXI 14d; in all its other occurences in our text the initial *pr-* is treated prosodically as a single consonant.

1c Tc *vira* (for *vina*, KXTa = OV: Tib. *med-na*); Tc *pāramitā-r-* (for *°itā*, KXTa = OV); XTac *a-cakṣuḥ* (= OV)(for *°kṣū*, K; Conze Rgs. 57 misr. K as *acakṣŭ*).

1d Tc *āvināyakā* (for *avi°*, KXTa = OV: Tib. *dmigs-bu med-pas*); V (p. 363 n. 1) r. O as *spaśetu* and Edg.Rgs. 1 as *spuśetu*; O *spaśetu/spuśetu*seems to be a reprinting fault for *spṛśetu*, MSS.: Tib. *reg-par*.

2a K *yatrāntaresmin* (Conze Rgs. 57 misr. K as *°asmin*), XTac *yatrāntaraśmi* (O p. 35 n. 2 misr. X as *yattant°*), O em. *yatrāntarasmi* (= V)(for *yatrāntare 'smi*, 'when ... in the meantime/in this respect'; cf. Tib. *gaṅ-tshe*); XTa *pragṛhīta* (= OV), unmetr., Tc *pragṛhita* (for *pragrahīta*, K, hyper-Skt. for MInd. **(p)pa(g)gahīta-*; cf. Edgerton 43 p. 211a, *grah-* 3, Edg.Rgs. 37); Tc *prajā* (for *prajñā*, KXTa = OV: Tib. *śes-rab-kyis-ni*).

2b V *labdha-cakṣu*(for *labdhu cakṣu*, MSS. = O); Tc *nāma-dhyeyaṃ* (for *°-dheyaṃ*, KXTa = OV; but V w. *-m*: Tib. *miṅ*); cf. AsP 87.9 *pāramitā-nāma-dheyaṃ pāramitā-śabdaṃ labhate*.

2c Tc *yathā* (for *yatha*, KXTa = OV); X *pariniṣṭita*, O em. *pariniṣṭhita* (= V; but V *-karma-parin°*, cpd.), Ta *pariniṣṭina*, Tc 〈pa〉*riniṣṭhit* (for *pariniṣṭhitu*, K: Tib. *yoṅs zin*).

2d Tc *tāvat punyu* (dental *-n-*) *ya labhate* (for *tāva puṇyu labhate*, KXTa = OV: Tib.A *de-tshe rhan-pa ... thob*, B *ji-srid ... rhan-pa ... thob*).

3a Tc *saṃskṛtāsaṃskṛta-* (for *saṃskṛta-asaṃsk°*, KXTa; but Ta *°-asa〈ṃ〉sk°*); XTac *-śuklo* (for *-śuklā*, K): O sep. *saṃskṛta asaṃskṛta kṛṣṇa śuklo*, V *saṃskṛta asaṃskṛta kṛṣṇa-śuklo* (for *saṃskṛta-asaṃskṛta-kṛṣṇa-śuklā*, K); em. poss. to *°-śuklān*.

3b Tac *anu-* (for *aṇu-*, KX = OV: Tib. *rdul*; cf. Edgerton 2.39, BHSD p. 26a, *anu-* 2, s.v.); *aṇu-* seems to be the true reading in our text; cf. I 6b (MSS. corrupt, but at least XTc *anu-*), X 1c (XTac *anu-*), XIX 8d (MSS. *anu-* = OV!), XXX 1c (XTac *anu-*); K *labhate*, unmetr. (for *labhati*, XTac = OV); K *vibhāvamātaḥ* (for *°mānaḥ*, XTac = OV); O *prajña-vibhāv°*, cpd.! (cf. Edg.Rgs. 21): cf. Tib. *gaṅ-tshe 'dus byas ma 'dus byas daṅ dkar nag chos, śes-rab rnam-par bśigs-nas* (v.l. *bśig-nas* = O) *rdul tsam mi dmigs tshe*; cf. also I 7b.

tada prajña-pāramita gacchati saṃkhya loke
 ākāśu yatra na pratiṣṭhitu kiṃ ci tatra // 3 //

saci manyate ahu ca(X29A)rāmi jināna prajñāṃ
 mociṣyi sattva-niyutān ba(K9B)hu duḥkha-spṛṣṭān /
ayu sattva-saṃjña-parikalpaku bodhisattvo
 (Tc9A) na ca eṣa prajña-vara-pāramitāya caryā // 4 //

yo bodhisattva iha pāramite ti cīrṇo
 puri cārikāya na sa kāṅkṣati paṇḍitena /
sa hi śrutva tasya puna bheṣya(X29B)ti śāstra-saṃjñā
 sau vā laghuṃ anubudhiṣyati bodhi śāntā // 5 //

---

3c XTac *yada* (= OV)(for *tada*, K; cf. Tib. *tshe*); Tc *gacchāti* (for °*ati*, KXTa = OV); cf. AsP 87.19-20 *tadā prajñā-pāramiteti saṃkhyāṃ gacchati*.

3d K *ăkāśu*, XTac *ākāśa* (= OV)(for *ākāśu*: Tib. *nam-mkha'*); O em. *tatra* (so KTc = V; XTa *tattra*) to *tad-vat* (? w. Tib.A *bźin*, B *de daṅ. 'dra*); cf. Tib.A *nam-mkha' gar mi* (!) *gnas-pa ji-yaṅ med-pa bźin*, B *nam-mkha' gaṅ-la'aṅ cuṅ-zad mi gnas de daṅ 'dra*.

4a O sep. *sa ci* (Conze Rgs. 44 misr. O as *na ca*, and V p. 363 n. 3 misr. O as *na ci*), Tc *savi* (for *saci*, KXTa = V: Tib. *gal-te*); Tc *'hu* (for *ahu*, KXTa = OV); Tc *prajñā* (for *prajñāṃ*, KXTa = OV).

4b XTa *mociṣya*(=OV),Tc *moviṣya*(for *mociṣyi*, K: Tib. *bdag-ni ... dgrol)*; XTac *-niyutāṃ* (= V)(for *-niyutān*, K, so em. O; cf. VII 6a *buddha-*°); K *dukha-* (Conze Rgs. 39 misr. K as *duḥkha-*), XTac *roga-* (= OV)(for *duḥkha-*: Tib. *sdug-bsṅal*); K *-spṛṣṭāḥ*, XTa *-spṛṣṭāṃ* (for *-spṛṣṭān*, so em. O = V); cf. Tib. *sems-can sdug-bsṅal reg-pa khrag-khrig maṅ dgrol*.

4d Tc *vaiṣa* (for *caiṣa*, KXTa = OV).

5a Tc om. *yo;* Tc *bodhisattvo* (for °*sattva*, KXTa = V); XTac *vara-pāramite ti* (= V; but V *-pāramiteti*!): O *bodhi sattva-vara-pāramiteha* (!); Edg. Rgs. 40 em. O to *bodhisattva vara-*° (for *bodhisattva iha pāramite ti);* *pāramite*, loc. w. *car-*: Tib. *pha-rol phyin 'dir spyad-pa* (v.l. *spyod-pa)*, but cf. Chin. 菩薩若行最上行 (!); Tc *vīrṇo* (for *cīrṇo*, KXTa = OV).

5b XTac *paricārikāya* (so r. Edg.Rgs. 29, taking it as a dat. w. *kāṅkṣ-)*, OV sep. *paricārikā ya*!; *paricārikāya* is corrupt for K *puri* (m.c. for *pure*, cf. BHSD p. 348b, q.v.) plus *cārikāya* (loc.; cf. VII 6a *puri cārikāyaṃ); kāṅkṣati* is to be construed w. *paṇḍitena* (instr. for loc.; cf. Edgerton 7.30-34; for an example of *kāṅkṣati* used w. loc. see BHSD p. 175a, q.v.): Tib. *sṅon-chad spyod-pa'i tshe ... mkhas-pa som-ñi med;* but cf. AsP 88.25-26 *yo ... iha gambhīrāyāṃ prajñā-pāramitāyāṃ ... na kāṅkṣiṣyati ...*; XTac *ca* (= OV)(for *sa*, K); XTac *paṇḍitehi* (= OV)(for °*ena*, K); Conze Rgs. 44 misr. K as *praricārikāya ... paṇḍiteva*!

5c XTac *saha* (= OV; r. perh. *sa ha*)(for *sa hi*, K: Tib. *de-ni*, v.l. *des-ni*); Tc *bhaṣyati* (for *bheṣyati*, KXTa = OV); OV em. *śāstṛ-* (so AsP 89.2; cf. Tib.Rgs. *ston-pa'i 'du-śes*, Chin. 仏想 )(for *śāstra-*, MSS.; cf. Edgerton 13.14).

5d XTc *so* (= OV), Ta *yo* (for *sau*, K: = *asau "bodhisattvaḥ"*: Tib. *de-ni* v.l. *des-ni* = O; cf. Edgerton 4.12, also Speijer 271); K *laghum* (Conze Rgs. 44 analyzes K as *laghu-m-* [? w. a hiatus-bridger *-m-*]), X *laghū* (= OV, metr.), Ta *laghu*, Tc *laghv* (for *laghuṃ*, m.c.: Tib. *myur-du*, Chin. 速 ); K *anubudhyiṣyati*, unmetr. (for *anubudhi*°, XTac = OV; cf. Edg.Rgs. 29); O *bodhi-śānta*, cpd., V sep. *bodhi śāntām* (for *bodhi śāntā*, MSS.: Tib. *byaṅ-chub źi-ba*, Chin. 寂静仏菩提 ); cf. Haribhadra ad Rgs. VII 5 (Peking JA 40A1-2) *byaṅ-chub-sems-dpa' gaṅ-źig-gis de-bźin-gśegs-pa mñes-pa sṅon-du bsṅo-bas śes-rab-kyi pha-rol-tu phyin-pa-la mṅon-du phyogs-pas yun riṅ-por spyad-pa-ni sṅon spyad-de / thabs-la mkhas-pa'i stobs-kyis mkhas-pa-yaṅ yin-te /* (!) *thos ma thag-tu de-ni ston-pa'i 'du-śes bskyed-pa 'gyur-ro //*

sat-kṛtva buddha-niyutān puri cārikāyāṃ
    na ca prajña-pāramita śrad-dadhitā jinānāṃ /
śrutvā ca yo imu kṣipiṣyati alpa-buddhiḥ
    sa kṣipitva yāsyati avīci a-trāṇa-bhūto // 6 //

tasmā hu śrad-dadhata eta jināna mātāṃ
    ya(Tc11B)di icchatā spṛ(X30A)śitu uttama-buddha-jñānaṃ /
so vāṇijo yatha vrajitvana ratna-dvīpaṃ
    mūlātu chedana karitva punāgameyā // 7 //

bhagavatyāṃ ratna-guṇa-saṃcaya-gāthāyāṃ niraya-parivarto nāma saptamaḥ // 7 //

---

6 MS. K places VII 7 (folio 9B2-3) before VII 6 (folio 9B3-4); Tib.A interposes VII 6cd and 7cd; but the context is in favour of Recension B (both Sanskrit and Tibetan) and the Chinese version.

6a XTac *sat-kṛtya* (= OV)(for °*-kṛtva*, K); K *-niyutām* (= V), XTa *-niyutām*, Tc *-riyutām* (for *-niyutān*, so em. O; cf. VII 4b *sattva-niyutān*); K *puri cārikāyān*, XTac *paricārikāyāṃ* (= OV; cf. Edg.Rgs. 29) (for *puri cārikāyāṃ*: Tib. *sñon spyod tshe-na*, v.l. *sñon-chad tshe-na*; cf. VII 5b *puri cārikāya*, w.n.).

6b Tc *-pāramite* (for °*ita*, KXTa = OV; but O °*ita-*, cpd.); XTac *śrad-dhadhitā* (for *śradda*°, K, so em. O = V); cf. Tib. *rgyal-ba'i śes-rab pha-rol phyin-la ma dad-na*, also AsP 89.23-31 *imāṃ prajñā-pāramitāṃ na śraddadhyur ... evaṃ te prajñā-pāramitāṃ na śraddadhati*; V *jinānām* (w. *-m*).

6c XTac *so* (= OV: Tib.B *de-yis*)(for *yo*, K: Tib.A *gaṅ-źig*); XTa *kṣip-īṣyati* (= O; cf. Edg.Rgs. 29), Tc *kṣiyiṣyati* (for *kṣipiṣyati*, K = V: Tib. *spoṅ byed-pa*); XTac *solpa-*, OV *so 'lpa-* (for *alpa-*, K).

6d XTa *khipitva* (= O; cf. Edg.Rgs. 8), Tc *khiyitva* (for *kṣipitva*, K = V: Tib.A *spaṅs-pas-na*, B *spaṅs-nas*); Tc *yāsyaty* (for *yāsyati*, KXTa = OV); XTa *avīcim* (= OV), Tc *avicīm* (for *avīci*, K); K *atrānubhūto* (for *atrāṇa-bhūto*, XTac = OV: Tib.A *skyabs med 'gyur*, B *skyabs med gyur-pa*).

7 Cf. VII 6, footnote.

7a MSS. *tasmāhu* (so prints O)(for *tasmā hu* = V: Tib. *de-lta-bas-na*); XTa *śraddhadhata*, Tc *śraddhadhana* (for *śraddadhata*, K, so em. O = V: Tib. *dad-par gyis*); XTac *eva* (= OV)(for *eta*, K: Tib. *'dir*).

7b XTa *icchathā* (= OV), Tc *yadīcchathā* (w. *yadi*)(for *icchatā*, K; cf. Edgerton 26.11-12); V *-jñānam* (w. *-m*).

7c K *sā* (K must not be **sāvāṇijo*)(for *so*, XTac = OV: Tib.A *de-ni ... tshoṅ-pa*, B *tshoṅ-pa*); K *vrajitva<na>*, O *vrajitva na* (!)(for *vrajitvana*, XTac = V; cf. Edg.Rgs. 40: Tib.A *soṅ-la*, B *soṅ-nas-ni*; cf. XX 15a, 16a *vrajitvana ratna-dvīpaṃ*).

7d Tc *mulātu* (for *mūlātu*, KXTa = OV: Tib.A *zoṅ-rnams*, B *zoṅ*); K *punar āgameyā*, Tc *pranāgameyā*, V *puna āgameyā* (for *punāgameyā*, XTa = O).

VII col. K om. *bhagavatyāṃ ratna-guṇa-saṃcaya-gāthāyāṃ*; Tc adds num. 7 at the end of the colophon.

Only K (9B4-5) reads after the colophon: *dūraṅgamā-bhūmi<r> upāya-pāramitā ca gāthā // 7 //* // Cf. Chin. (T. VIII, 678c27) 遠行地攝方便波羅蜜伽陀 (after the title of chapters VIII/IX), cf. Mvy 892,920.

## ⟨ VIII. VIŚUDDHI ⟩

rūpasya śuddhi phala-śuddhita veditavyā
    phala-rūpa-śuddhita (X30B) sarva-jñata-śuddhim āhuḥ /
sarva-jñatā-phala-viśuddhita rūpa-śuddhī
    ākāśa-dhātu-samatāya a-bhinn'-a-chinnā // 1 //

trai-dhātukaṃ samatikrānta na bodhisattvāḥ
    kleśāpanīta upapatti nidarśayanti /
jara-vyādhi-mṛtyu-vigatāś cyuti (Ta9B) darśayanti
    prajñāya pāramita yatra caranti dhīrāḥ // 2 //

kā(X31A)me ca rūpi jagatī a(K10A)yu paṅka-saktā
    saṃsāra-cakri bhramate 'nila-cakra-tulye /
jānitva bhrānti jagatī mṛga-vāgure vā
    ākāśa-pakṣi-sadṛśā vicaranti prajñāḥ // 3 //

---

[1a] Ta *rŭpasya* (for *rūpasya*, KXTc = OV: Tib. *gzugs-kyi*); Tc om. *śuddhi phala-*; Tc *-śraddhita* (for *-śuddhita*, KXTa = OV: Tib. *dag-par*); cf. AsP 93.25 *phala-viśuddhito rūpa-viśuddhī rūpa-viśuddhitaḥ phala-viśuddhiḥ*.

[1b] Ta *-rŭpa-*, Tc *-bhūpa-* (for *-rūpa-*, KX = OV: Tib. *gzugs*); MSS. *sărva-jñata-* (= OV; cf. Edg.Rgs. 39); MSS. *-śuddhim* (= OV), nom.sg.f. (cf. Edgerton 10.23), could be *-śuddhi-m-* w. a hiatus-bridger *-m-* (cf. Edgerton 4. 59).

[1c] MSS. *sravajñatāya phala-* (for *sarvajñatā-phala-*, dvandva-cpd.: Conze 'the purity of all-knowledge and of the fruit': Tib.A *thams-cad mkhyen-ñid 'bras-bu dag-nas*, B ... *dag daṅ)*; XTa *-śuddhita* (= OV)(for *viśud°*, K); Tc om. *(-vi)śuddhita rūpa-;* Ta *rŭpa-* (for *rūpa-*, KX = OV: Tib.*gzugs*); cf. AsP 93.31 *sarvajñatā-viśuddhito rūpa-viśuddhiḥ rūpa-viśuddhitaḥ sarvajñatā-viśuddhiḥ*.

[1d] Tc *'bhinna-* (for *a-bhinna*, KXTa = OV); XTac *-cchinnāḥ* (= OV)(for *-cchinnā*, K): Tib.A *gcad med dbye-ba med*, B *dbyer med gcad-du med;* cf. AsP 93.30-31 *a-dvayam etad a-dvaidhī-kāram a-bhinnam a-cchinnam*.

[2a] Tib.A om. a word corresp. to Skt. *na* (so trsl. Conze?), and Tib.B is somewhat confused; but cf. AsP 94.10-11 *atyantānupapattir bhagavan prajñā-pāramitā kāma-dhātu-rūpa-dhātv-ārūpya-dhātuṣu;* XTac *bodhisattvā* (= OV)(for *°sattvāḥ*, K).

[2c] Tc *jaraṃ* (for *jara-*, KXTa = OV); O sep. *jaravyā dhimṛtyu vigatāś*(? mispr.); O *darśayānti* (for *°yanti*, MSS. = V: Tib. *ston)*.

[2d] Tc *dhāḥ* (for *dhīrāḥ*, KXTa = OV: Tib. *dpa'-bo)*.

[3a] XTac *nāmeva* (= OV; r. perh. *nāme va*: Tib.B *miṅ*)(for *kāme ca*, K: Tib. A *'dod*, Chin. 欲 ; Conze Rgs. 39 misr. K as *kāmeva*); Ta *rŭpi* (for *rūpi*, KXTc = OV: Tib. *gzugs-kyi*); O *yagatī* (!)(for *jagatī*, MSS. = V: Tib.*'gro-ba*); XTa *-sakto*, Tc *-śakto* (for *-saktā*, K = OV wt.n.: Tib.*'dam-la chags)*.

[3b] Tc *-cakra* (for *-cakri*, KXTa = OV: Tib.A *'khor-lo*, B *'khor-lor*); XTac *nila-*, K *'nila-* (= OV: Tib.B *rluṅ-gi*, Chin. 風 , but Tib.A *til-gyi* 'sesame'!); K *-tulyo* (for *-tulye*, XTac = OV).

[3c] Tc *jātitva* (for *jānitva*, KXTa = OV; Edg.Rgs. 25 misr. O as *jāniva* : Tib. *śes-nas* 'having known, knowing'); *jānitva* could be a ger. to 'to beget, to be born', *jānayati* (cf. Edgerton 38.15, 43 p. 213a, 3, also 2, BHSD p. 241b, *jānayati*, ss.vv.); XTa *bhrāntu* (= OV), Tc *bhāṃtu* (for *bhrānti*, K: Tib. *'khrul-pa*); OV *mṛga-vāgurevă* (for *mṛga-vāgure vā*: Tib. *ri-dvags rgyar chud 'drar)*; cf. Mvy 5895 *śaśa-vāgurah* (masc.!): *(ri-)boṅ rgya* (cf. Wogihara Mvy Note p. 43 ad 233.9); for *vā* = *iva*, cf. Edgerton 4.6, 3.6, BHSD p. 475b, *vā*, s.v.

rūpasmi yo na carate pariśu(Tc12A)ddha-cārī
    vijñāni saṃjñi api vedani cetanāyāṃ /
(X31B) evaṃ carantu parivarjayi sarva-saṅgā
    saṅgād vimuktu caratī sugatāna prajñāṃ // 4 //

bhagavatyāṃ ratna-guṇa-saṃcaya-gāthāyāṃ viśuddhiparivarto nāma aṣṭamaḥ // 8 //

---

3d OV sep. *ākāśa* (O mispr. *ǎkāśa* for MSS. *ākāśa*) *pakṣi-sadṛśā*: Tib. *mkha'-la bya bźin;* cf. XXIV 2c *khaga-pakṣi-tulyaṃ*.

4a Tac *rūpasmi* (for *rūpasmi*, KX = OV: Tib. *gzugs-la)*.

4b X *vijñāna saṃjña api vedana* (= OV), Tac *vijñāna saṃjñā* (Ta *saṃjñāṃ*) *na saṃjña api vedana* (for *vijñāni saṃjñi api vedani*, K); V *cetanayām* (w. *-m*).

4c V *-saṅgāṃ* (for *-saṅgā*, MSS. = O).

4d XTa *vimukta* (= O), Tc *vimuhya*, V *vimucya* (for *vimuktu*, K: Tib.A *rnam-par grol-ba*, B *rnam grol*); XTac *carate* (= OV)(for *caratī*, K); Tc *sūgatāna* (for *sug°*, KXTa = OV: Tib.A *bde-gśegs*, B *bde-gśegs-rnams-kyi*); XTa *prajñāḥ*, Tc *prajñā* (for *prajñāṃ*, K, so em. O; V *prajñām* w. *-m*).

VIII col. XTc *viśuddha-* (for *viśuddhi-*, KTa, so em. O = V); K *-parivarto 'ṣṭamaḥ*, Tc *-parivarto nāmāṣṭamaḥ* (= V)(for *°rto nāma aṣṭamaḥ*, XTa = O); Tc adds num. 8 at the end of the colophon.

Only K (10A2-3) reads after the colophon: *bhūmir acalā praṇidhāna-pāramitā ca gāthā 4 // //* Cf. Chin. (T. VIII, 679a12) 不動地攝波羅蜜 (after the title of chapter X, with the names of the next *bhūmi* and *pāramitā;* Chapter IX of the Chinese text is included in chapter VIII without colophon), cf. Mvy 893, 921.

## ⟨ IX. STUTI ⟩

evaṃ carantu vidu-paṇḍitu bodhisattvo
    saṅgātu chintu vrajate jagatī a-sakto /
(X32A) sūryeva rāhu-graha-mukta virocamāno
    agnīva muktu tṛṇa-kāṣṭha-vanaṃ dahāti // 1 //

prakṛtīya śuddhi pariśuddh' imi sarva-dharmāḥ
    prajñāya pāramita paśyati bodhisattvo /
na ca paśyakaṃ labhati no 'pi ca sarva-dharmān
    eṣā sa prajña-vara-(X32B)pāramitāya caryā // 2 //

bhagavatyāṃ ratna-guṇa-saṃcaya-gāthāyāṃ stuti-parivarto nāma navamaḥ // 9 //

---

1a Tac *-paṇḍita* (for °*itu*, KX = OV; but V sep. *vidu paṇḍitu*).

1b XTa *saṅgātra* (= O!), Tc *sagādu* (for *saṅgātu*, K); K *cchitum* (? scribal mistake for *chiṃtu*; less poss. *chetuṃ* / *chetu*), Tac *cchinna* (for *chintu*, X; O p. 39 n. 3 misr. X as *cchinta* and em. to *cchinnu*!); V *saṅgā uchinnu* (? w. Baroda MS.); cf. Tib. *chags-pa bcad-pa;* Tc ⟨*ja*⟩*gatī;* K *aśakto*, XTac *asaktoḥ*, O em. *asaktaḥ* (for *asakto*, so V).

1c X *sūryopa*, O em. *sūryo 'vi* (!), Ta *sūryo va* (= V, perh. better), Tc *sūrya va* (for *sūryeva*, K: Tib. *ñi-ma ... bźin);* Conze Rgs. 44 misr. O as *'viṇhu* (for O *'vi rāhu-;* MSS. *rāhu-* = OV: Tib. *sgra-gcan).*

1d K *yuktu*, XTac *yukta* (= OV)(for *muktu*, so Conze ad O p. 127: Tib. *btaṅ);* Tc *-gāṣṭha-* (for *-kāṣṭha-*, KXTa = OV: Tib. *śiṅ).*

2a XTac *śuddha* (= OV)(for *śuddhi*, K); MSS. *paribuddhimi* (Conze Rgs. 57 thinks it a probable mistake), O em. *pariśuddhimi* (= V; r. perh. *pariśuddh' imi*: Tib.B *yoṅs dag-par;* cf. AsP 100.13-21 passim *pariśuddhā prajñā-pāramitā*); *paribuddh(i)* is also construed w. *imi sarva-dharmāḥ* as *śuddhi* (nom.pl.m., cf. Edgerton 8.81): Tib.A *yoṅs rtogs-śiṅ;* XTac *-dharmāṃ* (= V), O *-dharmān* (wt.n.)(for *-dharmāḥ*, K).

2c K *labhitai* (for *labhati*, XTac = OV: Tib. *dmigs ... dmigs-te);* K *nopi*, XTac *nāpi* (= OV)(for *no 'pi);* XTa *-dharmāṃ*, Tc *-dharmām* (for *-dharmān*, K = OV wt.n.).

IX col. K om. *nāma* ; Tc adds num. 9 at the end of the colophon.
Only K (10A5-6) reads after the colophon: *sādhu-matī-bhūmi(r) bala-pāramitāś* (r. °*itā*) *ca gāthā // 2 // //* Cf. Chin. (T. VIII 679a 12-13) 善慧地摂力波羅蜜伽陀 (after the title of chapter X, with the preceding *bhūmi* and *pāramitā*), cf. Mvy 894, 922.

## ⟨ X. DHĀRAṆA-GUṆA ⟩

śakro jinasya (Ta10A) paripṛcchati deva-rājo
    caramāṇu prajna katha yujyati bodhisattvo /
aṇu-(Tc12B)matru yo khalu na yujyati skandha-dhātau
    na ca dharmi yujyati (X33A) sa yujyati bodhisattvaḥ // 1 //

ci(K10B)ra-yāna-prasthitu sa vedayitavyu sattvo
    bahu-buddha-koṭi-niyutehi kṛtādhikāro /
yo śrutva dharma imi nirmita māya-kalpān
    na ca kāṅkṣate bhuyu prayujyati śikṣamāṇo // 2 //

kāntāra-mārga puruṣo bahu-yojanehi
    gopālu-sīmu-va(X33B)na-sampadu paśyayeyā /
āśvāsa-prāptu bhavatī na ca caura-trāso
    abhyása grâma-nagarāṇa ime nimiitāḥ // 3 //

---

1a K *jitasya* (for *jinasya*,XTac = OV: Tib. *rgya-ba-la-ni*).

1b XTac *caramāna*,O em. °*māṇa* (= V)(for °*māṇu*, K); Tc *yuhyati* (for *yujyati*, KXTa = OV: Tib. *brtson*); cf. AsP 105.14-15 *kathaṃ prajñā-pāramitāyāṃ caran prajñāpāramitāyāṃ yogam āpadyate?*

1c XTac *anu-mātra*, OV *aṇu-mātra* (wt.n.)(for *aṇu-mātru*, K: Tib. *rdul tsam*; cf. VII 3b, fn.); XTac *yo na khalu* (= OV)(for *yo khalu na*, K); Tc *yuhyati* (for *yujyati*, KXTa = OV).

1d XTac *yo eva* (= OV)(for *na ca dharmi*, K, so Edg.Rgs. 40); K offers a better reading, but it is supported neither by Tib. *phuṅ-por mi brtson* (? Skt. *na ca skandhi yujyati*; cf. AsP 105.17-25) nor by Chin. 無此蘊界之菩薩 ; Tc ⟨*yu*⟩*hyati* ⟨*sa yujyati*⟩ *bodhisattvaḥ*.

2a Ta *vira-* (for *cira-*, KXTc = OV: Tib. *riṅ-nas*); XTac *vedayitavya* (= OV)(for °*itavyu*, K); Tc *sattvā* (for *sattvo*, KXTa = OV).

2b V *-nayutehi*(for *-niyu*°,MSS. = O).

2c XTac *dharmi* (= OV)(for *dharma*, K); Ta *nimita*, Tc *nimitta* (for *nirmita*, KX = OV; but V *nirmita-*, cpd.; cf. Tib. *sprul daṅ sgyu-ma 'drar*); XTac *-kalpāṃ* (= V)(for *-kalpān*, K, so em. O).

2d KTc *kā*⟨*ṃ*⟩*kṣate*; XTa *ayu* (= OV), Tc *trāyu* [? *(a)trâyu*](for *bhuyu* K: Tib. *phyir-źiṅ*; cf. Mvy 5423; Edgerton 3.46, BHSD p. 410a, *bhuyo*, s.v.); XTac *śikṣamāṇaḥ* (= OV)(for °*māṇo*, K).

3a XTac *-mārgi* (= OV)(for *-mārga*, K: cf. Tib.A *dgon-pa'i lam-du*, B ... *lam-ni*; cf. XIX 8a *kāntāra*, but B *kāntāra-mārgi*; XX 3b *kāntāra-*[K °*ri-*] *mārgi*); Tac ⟨*bahu-yo*⟩*janehi*, V *bahu(bhī) janehi* (!)(for *bahu-yojanehi*, KX = O: Tib. *dpag-tshad maṅ-por*); cf. AsP 107.16 *puruṣo yojana-śatikād aṭavī-kāntārād* ...

3b XTac *gopāla-sīma-vana-sampada*, O *gopāla sīma-*°, V *gopāla sīma vana-*° (for *gopālu-sīmu-vana-sampadu*, K); XTac *paśyayeyoḥ* (= O), V *paśyate yo* (wt.n.)(for *paśyayeyā*, K; cf. Edg.Rgs. 40): Tib. *gnag-rdzi mtshams daṅ* (B *mtshams-kyi*) *nags-tshal phun-sum-tshogs mthoṅ-na*; cf. AsP 107.18-19 *paśyet ... gopālakān vā ... sīmā vā ... vana-sampado vā* ...

3c Tc *āśvāsu-* (for °*āsa-*, KXTa = OV); K *-prāpnu*, XTac *-prāpta* (= OV)(for *-prāptu*): Tib. *dbugs-'phyin* (B *-phyin*) *rñed-par gyur-ciṅ*; cf. AsP 107.21 *sa āśvāsa-prāpto bhavati*; Tc *bhavati* (for °*atī*, KXTa = OV); XTac *tasya* (= OV)(for *caura-*, K; cf. Conze ad O p. 127, V p. 365 n. 1: Tib. *chom-rkun*); cf. AsP 107.21-22 *nāsya bhūyaś cora-*(r. *caura-*)*manasi-kāro bhavati*.

3d V *abhyāśa* (for °*āsa*, MSS. = O: Tib. *ñe-ba'i*, v.l. *ñe-bar*) could be the true r.; but cf. MWD p. 76c, *abhy-āśa-*, s.v.; also Yuyama, 'The Bodhi Tree in the *Mahāvastu-Avadāna*' (1968), p. 489 n. 8; XTac *-nagarāṇi* (= O)(for °*āṇa*, K = V); Tc *ma nimittā* (for *ime nimittāḥ*, KXTa = OV: Tib. *'di-dag ... rtags*).

em eva prajña-vara-pāramitā jinānāṃ
     śruṇanāya yo labhati bodhi gaveṣamāṇo /
āśvāsa-prāptu bhavate na ca tasya trāso
     nārhatva-bhūmi na pi pratyaya-buddha-(X34A)bhūmī // 4 //

puruṣo hi sāgara-jalaṃ vraji paśyanāya
     saci paśyate druma-vanaspati-śaila-rājaṃ /
athavā na paśyati nimitta nikāṅkṣa bhotī
     abhyāsito maha-samudra na so 'tidū(Tc13A)re // 5 //

em eva bodhi-vara-prasthitu veditavyo
     śruṇamāna prajña ima pāra(X34B)mitā jinānāṃ /
yady āpi saṃmukha na vyākṛtu nāya(Ta10B)keno
     tatha pī spṛśiṣyi na-cireṇa hu buddha-bodhiṃ // 6 //

---

4a Tc *evam eva* (for *em eva*, KXTa = OV); Tc *jinānā* (for °*nānāṃ*, KXTa = OV).

4b K *śruṇanāpa* (Conze Rgs. 44 misr. K as °*āya*), XTac *śṛṇutāya* (= O), V *śṛṇu tāta* (!)(for *śruṇanāya*, inf. to *śruṇati*, cf. Edg.Rgs. 40, Edgerton 36.15, 43 p. 234b, *śru-* 3, s.v.); K *gaveśamāṇo*, XTac *gaveṣamāṇaḥ* (= OV; but O *bodhi-*°, cpd.!)(for *gaveṣamāṇo*); cf. Tib. *de-bžin byaṅ-chub yoṅs-su tshol tshe rgyal-rnams-kyi śes-rab pha-rol phyin 'di* (? Skt. *prajña ayu/ima pāramitā*) *mñam-pa gaṅ thob-pa*; also AsP 107.26 *imāṃ gambhīrāṃ prajñā-pāramitāṃ labhate ... śravaṇāya*.

4c K *-prāpnu*, XTa *-prāpta* (= OV), Tc *-prāpna*(?)(for *-prāptu*; cf. X 3c *-prāptu*); XTa *bhavatī* (= OV), Tc *bhavati* (for *bhavate*, K; Conze Rgs. 45 misr. K as *bhavatu*).

4d XTac *nārhanta-* (= OV)(for *nārhatva-*, K); XTac *tvayi* (for *na pi*, K = OV wt.n.): Tib. *dgra-bcom sa-la ma yin rkyen* (no v.l.) *rtogs sa-la min*.

5a XTac *-jala* (= O!)(for *-jalaṃ*, K = V; cf. Edg.Rgs. 40; Conze Rgs. 45 misr. K as *sāgarajasaṃvraji*): Tib. *rgya-mtsho'i chu-ni ...'gro-ba-yis*.

5b Tc *savi* (for *saci*, KXTa = OV; but O sep. *sa ci*: Tib. *gal-te*); Tc *-vanaspatiṃ* (for °*pati-*, KXTa = OV); V *-rājam* (w. *-m*).

5c Tc *anavā* (for *athavā*, KXTa = OV: Tib.A *ji-ste*, B *ci-ste*); XTa *bhonti* (= O), Tc *bhoti* (= V)(for *bhotī*, K).

5d Edg.Rgs. 40 *abhyās'* (for *abhyāse*) *ito* 'near from this place', V *a(bhyāśa)to* (for *abhyāsito*, MSS. = O; *abhy-ās-ita-*, synonymous to *abhy-ā-san-na-*); cf. Tib.A *rgya-mtsho che de mi riṅ-ste ñe-bar gyur-pa'i ...*, B *rgya-mtsho chen-po-ni ñe-bar gyur-to ...* (so Haribhadra ad Rgs. X 5: Peking JA 44A6-7); also AsP 108.2-5 *abhyāsanna ito mahā-samudra iti ... abhyāsanno 'smi mahā-samudrasya, neto bhūyo dūre mahā-samudra iti*: Tib. (Peking MI 129B8-129A2) *'di-nas-ni rgya-mtsho chen-po daṅ ñe'o sñam-du ... rgya-mtsho chen-po-ni bdag-gis bsñen-te 'di phan-chad rgya-mtsho chen-po ma riṅ-ṅo sñam-mo*.

6a Cf.Tib.A *de-ltar byaṅ-chub dam-par rab žugs rig bya-ste, rgyal-ba'i śes-rab pha-rol phyin-na 'di ñan-pa*, B ... *rab žugs rgyal-ba-yi śes-rab pha-rol phyin-pa 'di ñan rig-par bya*; also AsP 108.5-6 *evam eva bhagavan bodhisattvena mahā-sattvenemāṃ gambhīrāṃ prajñā-pāramitāṃ śṇvatā veditavyam*.

6b XTa *śruṇamāṇa* (= OV), Tc *śruṇāmāna* (for *śruṇamāna*, K); X *prajña imi* (= OV), Ta ⟨*prajña*⟩ *imi*, Tc *prajñemi* (for *prajña ima*, K); V *jinānām* (w. *-m*).

6c Tc *saṃsamukha* (for *saṃmukha*, KXTa = OV: Tib. *mṅon-sum*); Tc *vyākṛtuṃ* (for °*tu*, KXTa = OV).

6d MSS. *tathapī* (so prints O, r. *tath' apī*?), V *tathapī* (for *tatha pī* cf. Edgerton 4.11); XTac *spṛśiṣyati* (= OV, hypermetr.!)(for *spṛśiṣyi*, K):

su-vasanti kāli patite tṛṇa-pattra-śākhā
    na-cireṇa pattra-phala-puṣpa samānayanti /
prajñāya pāramita yasy' imu hasta prāptā
    na-cireṇa bodhi-vara prāpsyati nāyakānāṃ // 7 //

(X35A) yatha istri gurviṇi (K11A) ya ceṣṭati vedanābhir
    jñātavyu kālu ayu-m-asya prajāyanāya /
tatha bodhisattva śruṇamāna jināna prajñāṃ
    chandaṃ ca vīkṣati spṛśiṣyati bodhi śīghraṃ // 8 //

caramāṇu prajña-vara-pāramitāya yogī
    na ca rūpa-vṛddhi na ca paśyati pārihāṇiṃ /
dharmā (X35B) a-dharma ima paśyati dharma-dhātuṃ
    na ca nirvṛtiṃ spṛśati so viharāti prajñāṃ // 9 //

---

cf. Tib.A *rnam-par 'dren-pas mṅon-sum luṅ-bstan ma gyur kyaṅ, riṅ-por mi thogs saṅs-rgyas byaṅ-chub reg-par 'gyur*, B ... *kyaṅ, saṅs-rgyas byaṅ-chub riṅ-por mi thogs bdag (hu = ahaṃ!) reg 'gyur*, also AsP 108.6-8 *kiṃ cāpy ahaṃ tais tathāgatair ... na saṃmukhaṃ vyākṛtaḥ, atha ca punar abhyāsanno 'smy anuttarāyāḥ samyak-saṃbodher vyākaraṇasya; spṛśiṣyi* should be 3 sg.fut. as usggested by B *spṛśiṣyati*, and *hu* is most prob. MIndic for Skt. *khalu* (thru *kho*, *khu*) in our text; O sep. *na cireṇa* (for *na-c°* = V; cf. Speijer 403 Rem.: Tib. *riṅ-por mi thogs*); V *-bodhim*(w.*-m*).

7b Tc *ra-cireṇa* (for *na-°*, KXTa = OV; but O sep. *na c°*: Tib.B *riṅ-por mi thogs*; cf. X 6d, fn.); XTac *samāgamanti* (= V), O *samāgamānti* (? mispr.) (for *samānayanti*, K: Tib.A *yaṅ-dag skyed-par byed*, B *lhags gyur-na ... (b)skrun*).

7c K *yasyimu*, XTa *paśyimu* (= O!), Tc *paśyamu* (for *yasy' imu*, so Conze ad O p. 127 = V: Tib. *śes-rab pha-rol phyin 'di su-yi lag thob-pa*); Tc *hastasya* (for *hasta*, KXTa = OV; but OV *hasta-*, cpd.!).

7d O sep. *na cireṇa* (cf. X 6d, 7b, fn.); XTa *prāpsati* (for *prāpsyati*, KTc, so em. O = V: Tib.A *thob 'gyur*, B *thob*); Ta *nāyakā⟨nā⟩ṃ*, V *nāyakānām* (w. *-m*).

8a Tc *yathaṃ* (for *yatha*, KXTa = OV: Tib. *dper-na*); Tc *isti* (for *istri*, KXTa = OV: Tib. *bud-med*); X *vedanābhiḥ* (= O), Ta *°ātiḥ*, Tc *°āti*, V *°ābhi* (for *°ābhir*, K).

8b XTa *ayam asya* (= OV), Tc *ayasasya* (? scribal mistake for *ayamasya*) (for *ayu-m-asya*, K, with a hiatus-bridger *-m-*).

8c XTa *śruṇamānu* (= O), Tc *śruṇamāṇū*, V *°māṇu* (for *°māna*, K).

8d X *rati cchinda vīkṣati*, O em. *rati cchanda vīkṣati* (= V: Tib.B *dga' daṅ 'dun-pa skyed-pa*), Ta *rabhi cchinda vīkṣati*, Tc *rabhi cchiṃda vījāti* (for *chandaṃ ca vīkṣati*, K: Tib.A *'dun-pa rtog-ciṅ*); V *śīghram* (w. *-m*).

9a Tc *caramāṇū* (for *°māṇu*, KXTa = OV; O *°māṇa* seems to be a reprinting fault); Ta *-pāramitā⟨ya⟩*.

9b O *-vaddhi* seems to be a reprinting fault (for *-vṛddhi*, MSS. = V); Tc *na va* (for *na ca*, KXTa = OV); V *pārihāṇim* (w. *-m*).

9c Tc *dharmā 'dharma* (for *dharmā adharma*, KXTa = OV); XTac *imu* (= OV) (for *ima*, K); O *paśyayi* (wt.n.)(for *paśyati*, MSS. = V); K *dharmādhātun* (for *dharma-dhātuṃ*, XTac = OV): Tib.A *chos dbyiṅs chos daṅ chos min-rnams su mi mthoṅ-ste*, B *gaṅ-źig chos daṅ chos min chos dbyiṅs mi mthoṅ-źiṅ*, but Chin. 見法非法如法界 ; cf. AsP 109.10 *dharmaṃ na samanupaśyati ... a-dharmaṃ na samanupaśyati ...*

9d X *nirvṛti* (= O), Tac *nivṛti* (for *nirvṛtiṃ*, K = V; Edg.Rgs. 32 em. *nirvṛtī*; K *nirvṛtiṃ* has escaped Conze's attention); XTac *viharātri* (for *°āti*, K, so em. O = V: Tib. *gnas*); Tc *prajñā* (for *prajñāṃ*, KXTa = OV; but V *prajñām* w. *-m*).

caramāṇu yo iha na kalpa(Tc13B)yi buddha-dharmān
bala-ṛddhi-pāda na ca kalpayi bodhi śāntāṃ /
a-vikalpa-kalpa-vigato adhiṣṭhāna-cārī
eṣā sa prajña-vara-pāramitāya caryā // 10 //

bhagavatyāṃ ratna-guṇa-saṃcaya-(X36A)gāthāyāṃ dhāraṇa-guṇa-parivarto nāma daśamaḥ // 10 //

---

10a Tc *caramāṇū* (for °*māṇu*, KXTa = OV); XTa *na iha* (= OV), Tc *naiha* (for *iha na*, K); XTa *buddha-dharmāṃ* (= V; O misr. X as *buddhardharmāṃ*), Tc °*-dharmā* (for °*-dharmān*, K, so em. O after having misr. X).

10b V sep. *bala ṛddhi-*!; Tc *na va* (for *na ca*, KXTa = OV); O *kalpati* (wt.n.)(for *kalpayi*, MSS. = V);O *bodhi-*°,cpd.!); V *śāntām* (w. *-m*).

10c Tc *adhiṣṭhā-cārī* (for *adhiṣṭhāna-cārī*, KXTa = OV).

10d Tc *sū* (for *sa*, KXTa = OV).

X col. X *dhāraṇī-guṇa-* (= OV), Ta *dhāraṇī-⟨guṇa-⟩*, Tc *dhāraṇīm-⟨guṇa-⟩* (for *dhāraṇa-guṇa-*, K; cf. AsP *dhāraṇa-guṇa-kīrtana-*: Tib. *'dzin-pa'i yon-tan yoṅs-su brjod-pa;* also Haribhadra ad Rgs. X *yon-tan gzuṅ-bar yoṅs-su brjod-pa);* Tc adds num. 10 at the end of the colophon.

Only K (11A4) reads after the colophon: *dharma-meghā-bhūmiḥ* (read °*-bhūmir) jñāna-pāramitā ca gāthā 10 //  //* Cf. Chin. (T. VIII, 679b6) 法雲地摂智慧彼岸伽陀 (after the title of chapter XI), cf. Mvy 895, 923.

## ⟨XI. MĀRA-KARMAN⟩

buddhaṃ subhūti paripṛcchati vādi-candraṃ
    kiyu antar-āyu bhaviṣyan(TallA)ti guṇe ratānāṃ /
bahu antar-āyu bhaviṣyanti bhaṇāti śāstā
    tatu alpa-mātra parikīrtayiṣyāmi tāvat // 1 //

pratibhāna 'neka-vivi(X36B)dhāny upapadyiṣyanti
    likhamāna prajña ima pāramitā jinānāṃ /
puna śīghra vidyuta yathā parihāyiṣyantī
    a-karitva arthu jagatī imu māra-karma // 2 //

(Tc14A6-B2) kāṅkṣāpi keṣa ci bhaviṣyati bhāṣyamāṇe
    na ma(K11B, Tc14B)mātra nāma parikīrtitu nāyakena /

---

1a Tc *subhūtiḥ* (for °*ti*, KXTa = OV).

1b X *kiṃ antar-āyu* (= O), Ta *ki ant°*, Tc *kāṃtār°*, V *kyantantarāyu* [? *kyant' ant°* (*kiyanto 'nt°*)](for *kiyu ant°*, K); cf. Tib. *gaṅ*, also AsP 115.2-5 *ke cit ... teṣām antarāyā utpatsyante, ... kiyad-rūpāṇi ... teṣāṃ bahūni antar-āyakāṇy utpatasyante;* MSS. *bhaviṣyanti* may have been pronounced as °*iṣanti*, m.c. (cf. Edg.Rgs. 38); K *ratanān* (for *ratanāṃ*, XTac = OV; but V w. *-m*).

1c Ta *antar-āyū* (for °*-āyu*, KXTc = OV); MSS. *bhaviṣyanti* may have been pronounced as °*iṣanti*, m.c. (cf. Edg.Rgs. 38); K *vibhaṇāti*, Ta *bhanāti* (for *bhaṇāti*, XTc = OV: Tib.A *gsuṅs-na*, B *bka' stsal*); K *śantā* (for *śāstā*, XTac = OV: Tib. *ston-pas*).

1d Ta *parikīrttayiṣyati* (for °*iṣyāmi*, KXTc = OV; °*iṣyāmi* may have been pronounced as °*iṣāmi*, m.c., cf. Edg.Rgs. 38).

2a Tc *pratibhāṇa* (for °*āna*, KXTa = OV: Tib. *spobs-pa;* cf. BHSD p. 366b, *pratibhāna-*, s.v.); Tc *teka-*, KXTa *neka-*(= OV; but OV sep. *neka vi°*!) (for *'neka-°*, cpd.); V *vividhāni* (!)(for °*āny*, MSS. = O): Tib. *tha-dad rnam-pa du-ma* (= Skt. *aneka-vividha-*); Ta *apapadyiṣyanti*, Tc *aparpay-iṣyanti* (for *upapadyiṣyanti*, KX = OV: Tib. *'byuṅ 'gyur-źiṅ*); °*iṣyanti* may have been pronounced as °*iṣanti*, m.c. (cf. Edg.Rgs. 38).

2b XTac *prajñā* (= OV!)(for *prajña*, K); XTc *imu*, Ta *imū* (for *ima*, K); V *jinānām* (w. *-m*).

2c XTa *yuna*, Tc *punaḥ*, V *yuta* (wt.n.!)(for *puna*, K = O wt.n.: Tib. *yaṅ*); O *śīghra-*, cpd.!; XTac *parihāyiṣyanti* (= OV)(for °*iṣyantī*, K); °*iṣyantī* may have been pronounced as °*iṣantī*, m.c. (cf. Edg.Rgs. 38); Tc (folio 14A5-15A2) repeats *vidyuta* (XI 2c) to *kena* (for *'neka-*, XI 8b); variant readings in this repeated part are recorded in (   ) in my footnotes; the Baroda MS. is also confused in the same part (cf. V p. 366 n. 2).

2d Tc(c) *akaritvārtha*, XTa *akaritva artha* (= OV)(for °*itva arthu*, K); Ta *imū* (for *imu*, KXTc(c) = OV); XTac(c) *-karmaḥ* (for *-karma*, K, so em. O = V); cf. AsP 155.7 *idaṃ ... prathamaṃ māra-karma veditavyam.*

3 Tc first omits this verse entirely, but later reads in the wrongly repeated place (folio 14A6-B2).

3a X *kāṃkṣā ca* (= OV), Ta(c) *kāṃkṣā va* (for *kāṃkṣāpi*, K; Conze Rgs. 45 misr. K as *kāmkṣāyi*); K *keśavi* (for *keṣa ci*, XTa(c) = OV; but OV print *keṣaci*: Tib. *kha-cig*); Ta *bhaviṣyanti* (for °*iṣyati*, KXT(c) = OV; Conze Rgs. 45 misr. O as °*anti*).

3b K *ma[m]ātra*, Ta *mama atra* (for *mamātra*, XT(c) = OV).

na ca jāti-bhūmi pari(X37A)kīrtitu nāpi gotraṃ
    na ca so śruṇiṣyati kṣipiṣyati māra-karma // 3 //

evaṃ tu mūla apahāya a-jānamānāḥ
    śākhā-palāśa pariyeṣayiṣyanti mūḍhāḥ /
hastiṃ labhitva yatha hasti-padaṃ gaveṣet
    tatha prajña-pāramita śru(Tc14A)tva sūtrānta eṣet // 4 //

yatha bhojanaṃ śata-rasaṃ la(X37B)bhiyāna kaś cit
    mārgeyu ṣaṣṭiku labhitva sa bhojanāgryaṃ /
tatha bodhisattva imu pāramitāṃ labhitvā
    arhanta-bhūmiya gaveṣayiṣyanti bodhiṃ // 5 //

sat-kāra-kāma bhaviṣyanti ca lābha-kāmāḥ
    sāpekṣa-citta kula-saṃstava-saṃprayuktāḥ /

---

3c V sep. *jāti bhūmi;* cf. Tib. *rigs daṅ sa daṅ rus-kyaṅ yoṅs-su ma brjod;* T(c) *nāyi* (for *nāpi*, KXTa = OV).

3d K *śrūṇivyati* (for *śruṇiṣyati*, XTa(c) = OV: Tib. *ñan-par ... 'gyur);* XTa *kṣipisyati* (for °*iṣyati*, KT(c), so em. O = V: Tib. *spoṅ 'gyur;* Conze Rgs. 45 misr. K as *kṣepeṣyati*); cf. AsP 115.23 *idam api ... teṣāṃ māra-karma veditavyam.*

4a XTac(c) *ta* (= OV: Tib. *de-dag*)(for *tu*, K); V *mūlam* (for *mūla*, MSS. = O); XTc(c) *ajānamāno* (= V!), Ta *ajāyamāno* (for *ajānamānāḥ*, K, so em. O: Tib.A *yoṅs-su mi śes-pas*, B *mi śes).*

4b K *-palāsa* (for °*āśa*, XTac(c) = OV; but O sep. *śākhā palāśa*); XTa(c) *parieṣayiṣyanti* (= OV), Tc *pari⟨eṣa⟩yiṣyanti* (for *pariyeṣayiṣyanti*,K); °*iṣyanti* may have been pronounced as °*iṣanti*, m.c. (cf. Edg.Rgs. 38); KTc *mūḍhāḥ* (for *mūḍhāḥ*, XTa(c) = OV: Tib.A *blun-po*, B *rmoṅs-pas).*

4c Tac *hasti* (for *hastiṃ*, KXT(c) = OV); XTac(c) *gaveṣe* (= V)(for *gaveṣet*, K, so em. O).

4d Tc *-pāramitā* (for °*ita*, KXTa(c) = OV); Ta *śrutya* (for *śrutva*, KXTc(c) = OV); K *sūtrānya* (for *sūtrānta*, XTac(c): Tib. *mdo*); *sūtrānta* may have been pronounced as *sutanta*, m.c. for *suttanta-* (cf. Edg.Rgs. 33 and 39).

5a K *sata-* (for *śata-*, XTac(c) = OV: Tib. *brgya).*

5b K *mārgepu* (or perh. °*eyu*; Conze ad O p. 127 misr. K as °*eṣu* and suggests em. to *bhogeṣu* w. a question mark), XTac(c) *mārgeṣu* (= OV!)(for *mārgeyu*, 3 sg.opt.: Tib. *tshol-bar byed-pa*, v.l. *'tshol-*[c] = O); X *ṣaṣṭhiku* (for *ṣaṣṭiku*, KTac(c), so em. O = V: Tib.A *drug-cu-pa-dag*, B *zas ṅan*); Ta *tojanāgryaṃ*, Tc(c) *tojanāgpraṃ* (for *bhojanāgryaṃ*, KX = OV; but V w. *-m*: Tib. *zas mchog).*

5c T(c) *bodhisattvaṃ* (for °*sattva*, KXTac = OV); XTc(c) *ima* (= OV)(for *imu*, KTa).

5d Tc *⟨ar⟩hanta-*, T(c) *⟨a⟩rhanta-*, V *(a)rhanta-* (for *arhanta-*, KXTa = O: Tib. *dgra-bcom*); XTac(c) *-bhūmi*, O em. *-bhūmita*, V *-bhūmi(ta)*(for *-bhūmiya*, K: Tib.A *sa-las*, B *sa-yis*, v.l. *sa-yi* = O); MSS.*gaveṣayiṣyanti* (= OV) may have been pronounced as °*iṣanti*, m.c. (cf. Edg.Rgs. 38); V *bodhim* (w. *-m*).

6a Tc *bhaviṣyati* (for °*iṣyanti*, KXTa(c) = OV); °*iṣyanti* may have been pronounced as °*iṣanti*, m.c. (cf. Edg.Rgs. 38).

6b Ta *sopekṣa-citta*, Tc *sāyekṣa-cittaṃ* (for *sāpekṣa-citta*, KXT(c) = OV: Tib.A *lta-ba'i sems daṅ bcas-te*, B *lta daṅ bcas-pa'i sems-kyis);* K *kuśala-saṃstava-*, XTac *kula-sambhava-* (= O), T(c) *kulaṃ sambhava-* (for *kula-saṃstava-*, so em. Conze ad O p. 127 = V); XTac(c) *-saṃprayuktā* (for °*tāḥ*, K, so em. C = V): Tib. *khyim 'dris byed ldan-źiṅ;* cf. Haribhadra ad Rgs. XI 6 (Peking JA 46A8) *khyim bsten-pa daṅ ldan-par 'gyur-źiṅ-ṅo.*

choritva dharma ka(T a11B)riṣyanti a-dharma-kāryaṃ
    patha hitva utpatha-(X38A)gatā imu māra-karma // 6 //

ye cāpi tasmi samaye imu dharma-śreṣṭhaṃ
    śruṇanāya chandika upādayi(T(c)15A)ṣyanti śraddhāṃ /
te dharma-bhāṇaku viditva na-kārya-yuktaṃ
    premāpanīta gamiṣyanti su-durmanāś ca // 7 //

imi māra-karma bhaviṣyanti ya tasmi kāle
    anye c' aneka vividhā ba(X38B)hu antar-āyāḥ /
yehī samākuli-kṛtā bahu bhikṣu tatra
    prajñāya pāramita etu na dhārayanti // 8 //

ye te bhavanti ratanā hi an-argha-prāptā
    durlābhu te bahu-pratyarthika nitya-kā(K12A)laṃ /

---

6c MSS. *kariṣyanti* (= OV) may have been pronounced as *°iṣanti*, m.c. (cf. Edg.Rgs. 38); T(c) *-kārya* (for *-kāryaṃ*, KXTac = OV).

6d MSS. *yatha* (for *patha*, so em. O = V; cf. Conze ad O p. 127: Tib.*lam*); XTac(c) *ima* (for *imu*, K; cf. XI 2d *imu māra-karma*); XTac(c) *-karmaḥ* (for *-karma*, K, so em. O = V).

7a Tac *tasmin* (for *tasmi*, KXT(c) = OV); XTa *-śreṣṭhāṃ* (= O), Tc *°ṣṭāṃ*, T(c) *°ṣṭhā*(for *°ṣṭhaṃ*, K=V; but V sep. *dharma śre°*:Tib.*chos-kyi dam-pa*).

7b Tc *śrananāya* (for *śruṇ°*, KXTa(c) = OV); XTa *chandika utpādayiṣyanti* (= OV), Tċ(c) *chandikotpād°* (for *chandika upād°*, K); *upādayiṣyanti* may have been pronounced as *°iṣanti*, m.c.(cf.Edg.Rgs.38); V *śraddhām* (w.-*m*).

7c XTac(c) *-bhāṇaka* (= OV)(for *°aku*, K); MSS. *viditvana* (so print OV) (for *viditva na*; or perh. *viditva 'n-a-°* or *viditv' an-a-°* w. an emphasizing *an-* plus neg. *a-*; cf. Thumb-Hauschild, para. 669 Anm. 2 w. bibl. notes); cf. Tib.A *de-dag chos smra bya-ba min daṅ ldan rig-nas*, B *de-dag-gis-ni chos smra bya-ba ldan rig-nas* (!), but Haribhadra ad Rgs. XI 7c (Peking JA 46B2-3) *de-dag-gis-ni chos smra-ba rig-pa-ni bya-ba ma yin-pa'i bsam-pa daṅ ldan-pa rtogs-pa'o.*

7d Ta *premāpraṇīta*, Tc *premāpanita* (for *premāpanīta*, KXT(c) = OV: Tib.A *dga'-ba med-par (gyur-ciṅ)*, B *dga'-ba med-ciṅ*); Tc *gāmiṣyanti* (for *gam°*, KXTa(c) = OV); *gamiṣyanti* may have been pronounced as *°iṣanti*, m.c. (cf. Edg.Rgs. 38); XTa *sa-durmaṇāś*, Tc(c) *sa-durmanāś* (so em. O)(for *su-durmanāś*, K = V wt.n.); cf. Tib.A *yid-kyaṅ mi bde-ba*, B *yid mi bde-bar gyur-nas.*

8a Ta *imu*, Tc *iti* (for *imi*, KXT(c) = OV); Ta *māla-* (for *māra-*, KXTc(c) = OV: Tib. *bdud-kyi*); MSS. *bhaviṣyanti* (= OV) may have been pronounced as *°iṣanti*, m.c.(cf.Edg.Rgs.38); Tc(c) *tasmiṃ*(for *tasmi*, KXTa = OV).

8b T(c) *ane* (for *anye*, KXTac = OV: Tib. *gźan*); K *ca aneka*, XTa *caneka* (= OV; but OV sep. *ca neka*), Tc(c) *ca kena* (for *c' aneka-*: Tib.A *rnam-pa du-ma-ste*, B *rnam maṅ*); XTac *antarāyā* (= OV)(for *°āyāḥ*, K).

8c O sep. *ye hī* (for *yehī*,= V: Tib. *gaṅ-dag-gis-ni)*; K *samākula-kṛtā*, Tc *samākuli-kṛpā* (for *samākuli-kṛtā*, XTa = OV: Tib. *dkrugs-nas; cf.dūri-bhaviṣyanti* XXIV 3d, 4a); O *bahu-*, cpd.; Tc *taṃtu* (for *tatra*, KXTa = OV: Tib. *de-tshe)*.

8d Conze Rgs. 57 misr. K as *prajñā⟨ya⟩ pāramitā.*

9a Ta *ratāna* (for *ratanā*, KXTc = OV: Tib. *rin-chen*); Tc *jy*, V *ya* (for *hi*, KXTa = O); Conze Rgs. 45 misr. K as *anarghā-* (for *anargha-*, MSS. = OV); KTc *-prāptāḥ* (for *°tā*, XTa = OV); cf. AsP 123.27-29 *yāni tāni ... mahāratnāni, tāni bahu-pratyarthikāni bhavanti / ... durlabhatvān mahārghatvā ca / ... tasmāt tāni ca bahu-pratyarthikāni bhavanti* [OV give no reference to the AsP].

9b Ta *durlābhū*, Tc *durlābha*, X *durlābha te* (= O), V *te durlabhā* (!)(for

em eva prajña-vara-pāramitā jinānāṃ
    durlābhu dharma-ratanaṃ bah'-upadravaṃ ca // 9 //

nava-yāna-prasthitu ta sattva parītta-buddhī
    (X39A) ya imaṃ dulābhu ratanaṃ na parāpuṇanti /
māro 'tra utsuku bhaviṣyati antar-āye
    buddhā daśa-d-diśi parigraha-saṃprayuktāḥ // 10 //

bhagavatyāṃ ratna-guṇa-saṃcaya-gāthāyāṃ māra-karma-parivarto nāmaikādaśamaḥ // 11 //

---

*durlābhu te*, K); Ta om. *te bahu-* (XI 9b) to *ya imaṃ* (XI 10B); *-praty-arthika* must have been pronounced as *-păcatthika*, m.c. for *paccatthika-* (cf. Edg.Rgs. 39); V *-kālam* (w. *-m*).

9c Tc *evam eva* (for *em eva*, KX = OV: Tib. *de-bźin)*.

9d Tc *durlābhū* (for °*bhu*, KX = OV); MSS. *bahupadravaṃ* (so prints O), V *baddup*° (? mispr.)(for *bah'-upadravaṃ*: Tib.A *gnod-pa byed-pa maṅ*, B *'tshe-ba'aṅ maṅ)*.

10a XTc *-prasthita* (= OV)(for °*itu*, K); XTc *sa* (= OV)(for *ta*, K); XTc *sarva-* (for *sattva*, K, so em. O = V: Tib. *sems-can*); K *parītu-* (or perh. r. *parītta-*), XTc *parīta-* (for *parītta-*, so OV wt.n.); XTc *-buddhi* (=O), V *-buddhiḥ* (wt.n.)(for *-buddhī*, K): Tib. *blo chuṅ-ba;* cf. AsP 123.31-124.1, 124.7-9 *nava-yāna-saṃprasthitāś ca te ... bhaviṣyanti, alpa-buddhayaś ca te ... bhaviṣyanti, parītta-buddhayaś ca te ... bhaviṣyanti.*

10b X *imāṃ* (= O!), Tc *imā* (for *imaṃ*, K = V wt.n.); KX *durlābhu* (= OV), Tc *durlābhū* (for *dulābhu*: Tib. *dkon-pa'i;* cf. Edg.Rgs. 39); MSS. *dharma-ratanaṃ* (= V, hypermetr.!)(for *ratanaṃ*, so em. O: Tib. *rin-chen*); V om. *na* (? mispr.); cf. Tib. *gaṅ-źig dkon-pa'i rin-chen 'di-ni ma rñed-pa* (v.l. °*-na)*.

10c Tc *mātro tra*, KXTa *māro tra* (for *māro 'tra* = OV: Tib. *de-la ... bdud-ni)*; XTa *utsaku* (for *utsuku*, KTc, so em. O = V: Tib. *spro-bar*); Ta *antar-āya*, Tc *atar-āya* (for *antar-āye*, KX = OV: Tib. *bar-chad bya-phyir)*.

XI col. XTa *nāma ekā*°, Tc *nāmekā*° (for *nāmaikā*°, K, so OV wt.n.); K reads *gāthā 10* at the end of the colophon; Tc adds num. 11 at the end of the colophon.

## ⟨XII. LOKA-SAṂDARŚANA⟩

mâtâya putra bahu santi gilāni(X39B)kā(Tc15B)ya
te sarvi durmanasa tatra prayujyayeyuḥ /
em eva buddha pi daśa-d-diśi loka-dhātau
imu prajña-pāramita mātu samanvāharanti // 1 //

ye 'tīta ye 'pi ca daśa-d-diśi loka-nāthā
itu te prasūta bhaviṣyanti an-āgatāś ca /
lokasya darśika janetri (Ta12A) jināna mātā
para-sattva-citta-ca(X40A)ritāni nidarśikā ca // 2 //

lokasya yā tathatā yā tathatārahāṇāṃ
pratyeka-buddha-tathatā tathatā jinānāṃ /

---

1a Tc *mātrāya* (= V)(for *mātāya*, KXTa = O); K *gilānikārya*, X *gilānikāyes* (= O), Ta *girānikāyes*, Tc *śinānikāyes*, V *gilāni kāye* (!)(for *gilānikāya* w. *mātāya*: Tib. *ma źig na-bar gyur-la;* but cf. Chin. 子疾病 w. *putra*!); cf. AsP 125.2-4 *striya bahavaḥ putrā bhaveyuḥ ... sarve te mātur glānāya udyogam āpadyeran;* also Haribhadra ad XII 1 (Peking JA 47A6) *ma źig bu maṅ-po yod-pa nam na-bar gyur-na ...*

1b K *ayujjayeyuḥ*, XTa *prayujyayeyu* (= O), Tc *prayujyayepu* (for *prayujyayeyuḥ* = V; but cf. Tib. *rim-gro byed* [? Skt. *prapūjayeyuḥ*]).

1c MSS. om. *pi; O buddhapi* (? *buddh' api*), V *buddha pi*: Tib. *saṅs-rgyas-kyaṅ;* Tc *daśa-diśi* (for *daśa-d-diśi*, KXTa = OV; cf. Edg.Rgs. 7 and 9).

1d X *ima* (= OV)(for *imu*, KTac); XTa *mātra* (= OV), Tc *māṃtra* (for *mātu*, K, so r. Conze Rgs. 45, Edg.Rgs. 29); K *samancāharanti*, X *samandhāhar°*, Ta *samaddhāranti*, Tc *samaṃddhāharati* (for *samanvāharanti*, so em. O = V); this hypermetric form is very corrupt (cf. O p. 48 n. 2); Edg.Rgs. 29 (end) suggests that the original *samarcayanti* might have been replaced by the common form *samanvāharanti*; but cf. AsP 125.15-16 *evam eva ... tathāgatā ... imāṃ prajñā-pāramitāṃ samanvāharanti*: Tib. (Peking MI 149 B4-5) *de-bźin-gśegs-pa ... śes-rab-kyi pha-rol-du* (r. *°-tu*) *phyin-pa 'di-la dgoṅs-te;* one may perhaps find a more synonymous word to *samanvāharanti* 'fix their mind on', i.e. *samādadhanti*: Tib. *dgoṅs-pa mdzad; samādadhanti* is more probable graphically (*v:dh*) and phonologically (cf. Pāli *daha-ti/-te;* cf. PTSD II p. 152b; also Edgerton 43 p. 216b, *dhā-* 2, s.v., and p. 217a, *dhā-* 3, s.v.); moreover, *samādadhanti* satisfies the metre perfectly; but cf. XXXI 13b *samanāharitvā* (w.n.); Tib. XI 1d seems more seriously corrupt: *yum gyur* (X *'gyur* = O) *śes-rab dam-pa* (!) *'di-la dgoṅs-pa mdzad.*

2a MSS. *ye tīta ye pi* (for *ye 'tīta ye 'pi* = OV; cf. III 5c, fn.); Tc *caṃ* (for *ca*, KXTa = OV); K *ddaśaddiśi*, Tc *daśadiśi* (= O!)(for *daśaddiśi*, XTa = V; cf. Edg.Rgs. 7): Tib. *gaṅ-dag 'das daṅ phyogs bcu'i 'jig-rten mgon gaṅ daṅ.*

2b Tc *prasūta* (for *°sūta*, KXTa = OV); Tc *bhaviṣyaṃty* (= V *°anty*!)(for *°anti*, KXTa = O; *bhaviṣyanti* may have been pronounced as *°iṣanti*, m.c. (cf. Edg.Rgs. 38).

2c Tc *loka⟨sya⟩*; XTc *janeti*, Ta *jana iti* (for *janetri*, K = OV wt.n.: Tib.A *skyed-pa*, B *skyed byed*).

2d XTac *-caritāna* (= OV)(for *-caritāni*, K); Tc *nidarśitā* (for *°ikā*, KXTa = O; V *nidarśitā(kā)*, wt.n.): cf. Tib. *sems-kyi spyod-pa ston-par byed.*

3a K *tathatārhāṇāṃ*, XTa *tathatārhatānāṃ* (= OV), Tc *tathatorhatānāṃ* (for *tathatārahāṇāṃ*, so in XVI 2b; less poss. *tathatā rahāṇāṃ*: Tib. *dgra-bcom de-bźin-ñid*).

3b V *jinānām* (w. *-m*); cf. Tib.A *rgyal-ba'i*, but B *rgyal sras*!

ekaiva bhāva-vigatā tathatā an-anyā

prajñāya pāramita buddha tathāgatena // 3 //

tiṣṭhanta loka vidunāṃ parinirvṛtānāṃ

sthita eṣa dharmata niyāmata śū(X40B)nya dharmāḥ /

tāṃ bodhisattva tathatām anubuddhayantī

tasmā hu buddha kṛtu nāma tathāgatebhiḥ // 4 //

ayu gocaro (K12B) [daśa-balāna] vināyakānāṃ

prajñāya pāramita-ramya-udyāna-ṣaṇḍo /

phala-puṣpa-saṃkusumito bala-indriyebhiḥ

dvija-saṃgha-sa<ṃ>parivṛto jina-śrāvakebhiḥ // 5 //

---

3c XTac *ekaika* (= O; but O *ekaika-*, cpd.)(for *ekaiva*, K, so r. Conze ad O p. 127 = V: Tib. *gcig-pa-ñid-de*); XTac *bhāvi-tathatā* (= O)(for *bhāva-vigatā*, K, so r. Conze ad O p. 127 = V: Tib. *dṅos bral*; Baroda MS. is reported to read *ekaika-bhāva-vigatā*, cf. V p. 168 n. 1).

4 Cf. Tib. / *mkhas-pa 'jig-rten gnas-sam mya-ṅan 'das-kyaṅ-ruṅ* /
/ *chos-ñid skyon med chos-rnams stoṅ-pa 'di gnas-te* /
/ *byaṅ-chub-sems-dpas de-bźin-ñid 'di rjes-su rtogs* /
/ *de phyir de-bźin-gśegs śes* (v.l. *źes*) *saṅs-rgyas mtshan gsol-to* //

Chin. 過現大智諸菩薩　各各住此法空行
彼諸菩薩如実已*　是故如来名作仏
[* Taki (p. 11/357 n. 2) suggests em. to 如実知 .]

4a XTac *tiṣṭhantu* (= OV)(for °*anta*, K); V *loka-*, cpd.!; O em. *vidu vā parinirvṛta vā* (for *vidunāṃ parinirvṛtānāṃ*, MSS. [Tc om. *parinirvṛtānāṃ*]).

4b Tc XII 4b-d, 6a are found after XII 8a *sūrya*; this confusion is similar to Baroda MS. (cf. V p. 368 n. 3); Tc *sthitaiṣa* (for *sthita eṣa*, KXTa = OV); XTac *niyāma* (=OV!)[OV *dharmata-*°, cpd.!](for *niyāmata*, K, 'certainly, without fail': Tib. *skyon med*; cf. Conze Rgs. 46, Index p. 143b = Dict. p. 225; also BHSD p. 298b); X *dharmā* (= OV; OV *śūnya-*°, cpd.!), Ta *dharmāṃ*, Tc *dharma* (for *dharmāḥ*, K).

4c XTac *anubuddhayanti* (= OV)(for °*antī*, K).

4d Tc *tasyāhu*, KXTa *tasmāhu* (so prints O)(for *tasmā hu* = V); O *kṛta-nāma* cpd.(wt.n.), V *kṛta nāma*(wt.n.)(for *kṛtu nāma*, MSS.); Tc *tathāgatehiḥ* (for °*ebhiḥ*, KXTa = OV; Conze Rgs. 46 suggests em. to *tathāgateti* w.Tib., but Chin. agrees exactly w.Skt.); cf. Haribhadra ad Rgs. XII 4d (Peking JA 48A7) *de-lta-bas-na de-yaṅ thams-cad-kyi de-bźin-ñid-du thugs-su chud-pas de'i phyir de-bźin-gśegs źes saṅs-rgyas daṅ rgyal-ba'i sras źes bya-ba-la sogs-par mtshan gsol-to.*

5 Only K (folio 12A6-B1) reads this verse, which makes this chapter consist of ten verses, as is clearly stated in the colophon; Conze Rgs. 57 wrongly reports that there are nine verses. This verse is supported neither by the two Tibetan recensions nor by Haribhadra's commentary; the only corresponding phrase in AsP is *prajñā-pāramitā tathāgatānāṃ gocaraḥ* (AsP 136.2); the Chin. version, however, supports MS. K, though not verbatim as usual, and reads ten verses in chapter XII:
般若園林華菓盛　仏依止故甚適悦
十力諸根等浄衆　乃至声聞衆囲繞

Translation of XII 5 (Skt. Rec. A):
'To the Guides (endowed) with ten powers this is the sphere,
A delightful garden-grove of the perfection of wisdom,
Furnished with fruits and blossoms: powers and sense-faculties,
Encompassed by flocks of birds: disciples of the Victor'.

5a K [*daśa-balāna*]; cf. XII 6a *daśa-balāna*.

5c K -*indriyebhiḥ* (w. daṇḍa) could be °*ebhi* or °*ebhir*.

ayu gocaro daśa-balāna vināyakānāṃ
    prajñaya pāramita-ramya-giriṃ śritānāṃ /
dukhitaṃ ca sattva tri-apāyi samuddharanti
    na ca sattva-saṃjña api teṣu kadā ci bhoti // 6 //

(X41A) siṃho yathaiva giri-kandari niśrayitvā
    nadate a-chambhi mṛga kṣudraka trāsayanto /
tatha prajña-pāramitu niśrya narāṇa siṃho
    (Tc16A) nadate a-chambhi pṛthu tīrthika trāsayanto // 7 //

ākāśa niśrya yatha sūrya-sahasra-raśmis
    tāpet' imā dharaṇi darśayate ca (X41B) rūpaṃ /
tatha prajña-pāramita-niśritu dharma-rājo
    tāpeti tṛṣṇa-nadi dharma nidarśayāti // 8 //

---

6 K XII 6 = XTac XII 5, Tib. XII 5 (cf. XII 5, fn.).
Cf. Chin. XII 6: 般若波羅蜜高山 十力諸仏而依止
三塗衆生悉救度 度已不起衆生相

6a Ta *-balānapināmakānāṃ*, Tc *-balāmapināyakānāṃ* (for *-balāna vināyak°*, KX = OV: Tib. *stobs bcu rnam 'dren-rnams-kyi)*.

6b XTa *-ramya-vanāśritānāṃ* (= OV: Tib.A *ñams-dgar* [!] *rab brten-pa*, B *dga' tshal-la brten-pa)*, Tc *°āśritānāṃ*(for *-ramya-giriṃ śritānaṃ*, K: Chin. 般若波羅蜜高山 ); V sep. *pāramita ramya-°*; V *°āśritānām* (w. *-m*).

6c XTac *duḥkhitāṃś* (= O), V *dukhitāṃś* (wt.n.)(for *dukhitaṃ*, K; cf. Edg. Rgs. 35); XTac *-apāya* (= OV)(for *-apāyi*, K: Tib. *ṅan-soṅ gsum-las)*; *-apāyi*, loc. for abl. (cf. Edgerton 7.82); cf. XXII 11a-b *triy-apāyi* (v.l. *tri-apāyi) sattvān parimocituṃ ... icchati;* MSS. *samuddvaranti* (for *samuddharanti*, so em. O = V: Tib. *yoṅs 'don-kyaṅ*, Chin. 悉救度 ).

6d Before starting *d*, Ta repeats: *tasmā hu kṛta nāma tathāgatebhiḥ* (XII 4d!), *ayu gocaro daśa-balāna pi nāyakānāṃ* (r. prob. *vināyak°;* XII 6a); XTac *na pi* (= OV)(for *na ca*, K, w. which r. Edg.Rgs. 40); Tc *bhoṃti* (for *bhoti*, KXTa = OV).

7 K XII 7 = XTac XII 6, Tib. XII 6 (cf. XII 5, fn.).

7a K *-kandare* (for *°ri*, XTac = OV); K *niśrayatvā* (for *°itvā*, XTac = OV).

7b Tc *aṃcchambhi* (for *a-chambhi*, KXTa = OV: Tib. *'jigs med-par*); O *mṛrga* (? mispr.)(for *mṛga*, MSS. = V); K *trā⟨sa⟩yanto(*: Tib.A *skrag-par byed-ciṅ*, B *skrag byed-ciṅ)*.

7c XTac *-pāramita* (= OV; but V *°ta-*, cpd.!)(for *°tu*, K); K *niśriṇya* (conze Rgs. 46 misr. K as *niśritya*), Ta *niśyra* (r. *niśrya*), Tc *nigpra*, V *-niśraya*, hypermetr. (wt.n.)(for *niśrya*, X = O: Tib. *brten-nas;* cf. Edg.Rgs. 20); Ta *narāna* (for *°āṇa*, KXTc = OV).

7d Tc *⟨tī⟩rthika;* O *pṛthu-tīrthika-trāsayanto* (!), V *°-tīrthika trās°*.

8 K XII 8 = XTac XII 7, Tib. XII 7 (cf. XII 5, fn.).

8a XTa *ākāśa-niśrita yathaiva hi sūrya-raśmi* (= OV; Ta *°-raśmī*), Tc *ākāśa-niśrita yathaiva hi suryya⟨-raśmi⟩*(= Baroda MS.; cf. XII 4b, fn.): Tib. *dper-na nam-mkhar gnas-pa'i ñi-ma'i 'od-zer-ni;* K agrees w. Chin. 如日千光住虚空; poss. separate *sūrya sahasra-raśmis*.

8b KXTa *tāpetimā*, O sep. *tāpeti mā*, V *tāpetimāṃ* (wt.n.), Tc *to//yetimā* (for *tāpet' imā*, so r. Edg.Rgs. 40: Tib. *'di skems-par* [v.l. *skem-par* = O] *byed-ciṅ*); Ta *rūpaṃ* (for *rūpaṃ*, KXTc = OV; but V w. *-m*).

8c Tc *prajñā-* (for *prajñā-*, KXTa = OV); XTa *-niśrita* (= OV; but O *niśrita-*, cpd.!; sep. by Edg.Rgs. 40 = V), Tc *-niśita* (for *-niśritu*, K).

8d XTac *tṛṣṭa-nadi* (for *tṛṣṇa-°*, K, so em. O = V: Tib. *sred-pa'i chu-kluṅ*, Chin. 愛河

rūpasy' a-darśanu a-darśanu vedanā(X41B)ye
    saṃ(Ta12B)jñāy' a-darśanu a-darśanu cetanāye /
vijñāna-citta-manu-darśanu yatra nāsti
    ayu dharma-darśanu nidiṣṭu tathāgatena // 9 //

ākā(X42A)śa-dṛṣṭu iti sattva pravyāharanti
    kha-nidarśanaṃ kutu vimṛṣyata etam arthaṃ /
tatha dharma-darśanu nidiṣṭu tathāgatena
    na hi darśanaṃ bhaṇitu śakya nidarśanena // 10 //

(K13A) bhagavatyāṃ ratna-guṇa-saṃcaya-gāthāyāṃ (Tc16B) loka-saṃdarśana-parivarto nāma dvādaśa(X42B)maḥ // 12 //

---

9 K XII 9 = XTac XII 8, Tib. XII 8 (cf. XII 5, fn.).

9a MSS. *rūpasyadarśanu* (Ta *rūp°*), OV sep. *rūpasya darśanu*! (but cf. O p. 50 n. 2)(for *rūpasy' a-darśanu*: Tib. *gzugs-rnams mi mthoṅ*); cf. Edg. Rgs. 40 for pādas *a-c*.

9b K *saṃjñā-adarśanu*, XTac *saṃjñāyadarśanu* (= O), V sep. *saṃjñāya dar°*! (for *saṃjñāy' a-dar°*: Tib. *'du-śes mthoṅ-ba med-la)*.

9c XTa *nāstī* (= O)(for *nāsti*, KTc = V).

9d X(Tib.trslit.)Tac *aya* (= V)(for *ayu*, KX = O); K *-darśan[u]*; K *nirdiṣṭ[u]*, Tc *nidiṣṭa* (for *nidiṣṭu*, XTa = OV; cf. Edg.Rgs. 10).

10 K XII 10 = XTac XII 9, Tib. XII 9 (cf. XII 5, fn.).

10a Tc *-dṛṣṭa* (for *-dṛṣṭu*, KXTa = OV; but OV sep. *ākāśa dṛṣṭu;* cf. Conze Index p. 135a = Dict. p. 99 *ākāśa-dṛṣṭu*: Tib. *nam-mkha' mthoṅ)*.

10b XTa *nabha-darśanaṃ* (= OV), Tc *nabha-darśa⟨naṃ⟩* (for *kha-nidarśanaṃ*, K): Tib.A *nam-mkha'* ... *mthoṅ-ba*, B ... *mthoṅ źes* (= O; v.l. *mthoṅ-ste;* XTa *vimṛṣyatha* (= OV), Tc *vimṛṣya* (for *vimṛṣyata*, K: Tib.A *rtogs-śig*, B *brtag-par gyis;* cf. Edgerton 26.13); V *artham* (w. *-m*).

10c Ta *tada*, Tc *ta* (for *tatha*, KX = OV: Tib. *de-ltar*); K *nirdiṣṭu*, XTac *nidiṣṭa* (= OV)(for *nidiṣṭu*: Tib. *bstan*; cf. Edg.Rgs. 10).

10d Tac *darśa⟨naṃ⟩* (for *darśanaṃ*, KX = OV).

XII col. Ta *bhagavatyā* (for *°tyāṃ*, KXTc = OV); K reads at the end of the colophon: *gathā 10*, which clearly attests the number of verses in this chapter; this agrees with the Chinese version; but the other recensions have nine verses; Conze Rgs. 57 wrongly reports that MS. K has only nine verses (cf. XII 5, fn.); Tc adds num. 12 at the end of the colophon.

## ⟨XIII. ACINTYA⟩

yo eva paśyati sa paśyati sarva-dharmān
    sarvaṃ amātya kariyāti upekṣi rājā /
yāvanti buddha-kriya dharmata śrāvakāṇāṃ
    prajñāya pāramita sarva karoti tāni // 1 //

na ca rāja grāma vrajate na ca rājya-rāṣṭraṃ
    sarvaṃ ca ādadati so viṣa(X43A)yātu āyaṃ /
na ca bodhisattva calate kva ci dharmatāyāṃ
    sarvāṃś ca ādadati ye guṇa buddha-dharme // 2 //

bhagavatyāṃ ratna-guṇa-saṃcaya-gāthāyām acintya-parivarto nāma trayodaśamaḥ // 13 //

---

1a XTac *-dharmā* (for *-dharmān*, K, so em. O = V).

1b K *sarvaṃm*, XTac *sarvām*, O em. *sarvān* (= V)(for *sarvaṃ*); V *amātya-kiriyā ti*(wt.n.)(for *amātya kariyāti*, MSS. = O; cf. Edg.Rgs. 29); XTc *upetya*, Ta *upebhya*, O em. *upekṣya* (= V)(for *upekṣi*, K, 3 sg.opt.; cf. Edgerton 29.14; Conze Rgs. 46 misr. K as *upekṣya*); cf. Tib. *rgyal-po btaṅ-sñoms 'dug-ciṅ blon-po kun byed ltar.*

1c Emend MSS. *dharmata* (= OV) possibly to *dharma ca*; X *śrāvakānāṃ* (for °*ṇāṃ*, KTac = OV wt.n.): Tib. *saṅs-rgyas mdzad daṅ ñan-thos chos-rnams ji-sñed-pa.*

1d Tc *prajña* (for *prajñāya*, KXTa = OV).

2a XTac *śrāma*, O *grāmaṃ* (wt.n.)(for *grāma*, K, so r. Edg.Rgs. 34 = V: Tib. *groṅ-du*); K *rāja-rāṣṭraṃ*, XTac *rājya-rāṣṭrāṃ*, V *rājya-rāṣṭrān* (wt. n)(for *rājya-rāṣṭraṃ*, so r. O wt.n.: Tib. *yul-'khor).*

2b Tc *sā* (for *so*, KXTa = OV); V *āyam* (w. *-m*).

2c Tc *bodhisattvaṃ* (for °*sattva*, KXTa = OV); Ta *carate* (for *calate*, KXTc = OV: Tib.A *gYo-la*, B *'gro-la* ); Tc *jya ci* (for *kva ci*, KXTa = OV: Tib. *gaṅ-du'aṅ).*

2d XTac *sarvāś* (= O)(for *sarvāṃś*, K, so r. Conze Rgs. 46 = V).

XIII col. Tc *aviṃtya-* (for *acintya-*, KXTa = OV: Tib. *bsam-gyis mi khyab-pa); X trāyādaśamaḥ* (for *trayod°*, KTac, so em. O = V); at the end of the colophon K reads *gāthā 2;* Tc adds num. 13.

## ⟨XIV. AUPAMYA⟩

yady asti śraddha sugate dṛḍha bodhisattvo
    (X43B) vara-prajña-pāramita-āśraya-saṃprayogo /
atikramya bhūmi-dvaya śrāvaka-pratyayānāṃ
    laghu prāpsyate an-abhibhūtu jināna bodhiṃ // 1 //

sāmudriyāya yatha nāvi praluptiyāye
    mṛtaka(Tc17A)ṃ manuṣya tṛṇa-kāṣṭham a-gṛhṇamāno /
vilayaṃ prayāti jala-madhya a-(X44A)prāpta-tīro
    yo gṛhṇate vrajati pāra-sthalaṃ prayāti // 2 //

em eva śraddh'-upagato ya prasāda-prāpto
    prajñāya pāramita mātu vivarjayanti /

---

1a XTac *yasyāsti* (= OV)(for *yady asti*, K); Tc *śuddha* (for *śraddha*, KXTa = OV: Tib. *dad*); Tc *sūgate* (for *sug°*, KXTa = OV: Tib. *bde-gśegs*); cf. Tib. *gaṅ-žig* (B *°-la*) *bde-gśegs byaṅ-chub-sems-dpa' dad brtan-žiṅ* (B *brtan yod)*, Chin. 若菩薩発堅固心.

1b X *-pāramita-āśaya-saṃprayogo* (= OV: Tib. *śes-rab pha-rol phyin-pa mchog-la bsam sbyor-ba)*, Ta *°-⟨sa⟩ṃprayogo*, Tc *-pāramitāśaya-⟨sa⟩ṃpray°* (for *-pāramita-āśraya-°*, K).

1c Tc *atikrampa* (for *°mya*, KXTa = OV: Tib. *śin-tu 'das byas-nas*); Tc *-pratyakayānāṃ* (for *-pratyayānāṃ*, KXTa = OV: Tib. *raṅ-rgyal)*.

1d XTa *prāpsate* (for *prāpsyate*, KTc, so em. O = V: Tib. *'thob*); K *anavibhūtu*, Tc *anabhibhūrbhū* (for *anabhibhūtu*, XTa = OV [V *anabhi-bhū(tu)*]: Tib. *zil-gyis mi non)*.

2a Tac *samudriyā⟨ya⟩*(cf. Edg.Rgs. 29); K *lugbhiyāye* (Conze Rgs. 46 misr. K as *praluptiyāye*), XTa *pralugbhikāye*, Tc *pralūgbhikāye*, O em. *praluptikāye* (= V; cf. Edg.Rgs. 29)(for *praluptiyāye*); this can be restored because of the presence of *sāmudriyāya*, w. fem. suffix *-iyā-*, in the same pāda; cf. Tib. *dper-na rgya-mtshor 'jug-pa'i gru-ni chag gyur-la;* also AsP 143.7, 9 *mahā-samudra-gatāyāṃ nāvi bhinnāyāṃ*: Tib. (Peking MI 171B3, 4) *rgya-mtsho chen-por žugs-pa'i gru chag-pa-na*.

2b Tac *mṛtakamanuṣya*, V *bhṛtakaṃ manuṣya* (wt.n.)(for *mṛtakaṃ manuṣya*, KX = O: Tib. *mi gaṅ ro*); cf. AsP 143.7, 10 *mṛta-śarīraṃ*: Tib.(Peking MI 171B3, 4-5 *śi-ba'i ro*.

2d Tc *ya 'gṛhṇate* (for *yo gṛhṇate*, KXTa = OV: Tib. *gaṅ-žig 'dzin-pa*); Tc *pāpāra-* (for *pāra-*, KXTa = OV: Tib. *pha-rol*); cf. Tib. *gaṅ-žig 'dzin-pa rgya-mtsho'i* (? Skt. *udadhi-* for *vrajati*) *pha-rol phyin-par 'gyur*.

3a Ta *evame* (r. *em eva* w. the scribe's inversion mark: Tib. *de-ltar*); K *śraddhupagato*, X *śraddhapadagato*, Tac *śraddhapagato*, O em. *śraddha-saṃgato*(= V)(for *śraddh'-upagato*, m.c. for *śraddhop°*: Tib. *dad ldan*; Conze Rgs. 46 misr. K as *śraddhayagato*, w. which Edg.Rgs. 40 suggests em. to *śraddhaya*, m.c. for *°yā*, plus *gato*!); Tc *praśāda-* (for *prasāda-*, KXTa = OV: Tib. *daṅ-ba)*.

3b K adds *ya* before *prajñāya* (⏑⏑ — ⏑ !); K is supported by Conze Rgs. 46; is *ya* for *iya* 'this'?; cf. *imu prajña-pāramita mātu* XII 1d, *imu prajña-pāramita māta* XXVII 4b, also *imu prajña-pāramita* XXVIII 1d; Ta *pāramite* (for *°ta*, KXTc = OV); XTa *mātra* (= OV; cf. Edgerton 13.15), Tc *mā ca* (for *mātu*, K); cf. Tib.A *śes-rab pha-rol phyin-pa rnam-par soṅ mi byed*, B ... *phyin yum rjes-su mi 'jug min*!

(K13B) saṃsāra-sāgari tadā sada saṃsaranti
    jātī-jarā-maraṇa-śoka-taraṅga-bhaṅge // 3 //

ye te bhavanti vara-prajña-(X44B)pariggṛhītā
    bhāva-sva-bhāva-kuśalāḥ paramārtha-darśī /
te puṇya-jñāna-dhana-saṃvṛta-yāna-pātrāḥ
    paramādbhutāṃ sugata-bodhi spṛśanti śīghraṃ // 4 //

ghaṭake a-pakvi yatha vāri vaheya ko cit
    jñātavyu kṣipru ayu bhetsyati durbalatvāt /
paripakvi vāri ghaṭake vaha(X45A)mānu mārge
    na ca bhedanād bhayam upeti ca svasti gehaṃ // 5 //

kiṃ cāpi śraddha-bahulo siya bodhisattvo
    prajñā-vihīnu vilayaṃ laghu prāpuṇātī /

---

3c XTac *-sāgara* (= OV)(for *°ri*, K); K *saṃsa⟨ra⟩nti* (Conze Rgs. 46 misr. K as *saṃmanti*)(for *saṃsaranti*, XTac = OV: Tib. *'khor 'gyur-ba)*.

3d Tc *-bha⟨ṅ⟩ge;* only X (folio 44A-) has a Tibetan text corresponding to Sanskrit *c-d* (cf. also XIV 4a, fn.):
    */ skye rga 'chi daṅ mya-ṅan rba-rlabs 'khrugs-pa-yis /*
        */ 'khor-ba'i rgya-mtsho der-ni rtag-tu 'khor 'gyur-ba /*
Cf. Chin. 若人不発堅信心 依於般若求解脱
    溺輪廻海無出期 処生老死常苦悩

4a Tc *bhavaṃtivaṃti* (for *bhavanti*, KXTa = OV); only X (folio 44A6-B3) has a Tibetan text corresponding to Sanskrit *a-b* (cf. also XIV 3d, fn.):
    */ gaṅ de śes-rab mchog-gis yoṅs-su zin-pa-na /*
        */ dṅos-po'i raṅ-bźin mkhas-śiṅ don dam ston-par byed /*

4b XTac *-kuśalo* (= O), V *-kuśalā* (wt.n.)(for *-kuśalāḥ*, K).

4c Tac *tena* (Ta has erased *na* later)(for *te*, KX = OV); XTa *-saṃbhṛte-*, Tc *-sbhṛte-* (!), O em. *-saṃbhata-* (r. *-saṃbhṛta-*?), V *-saṃbhṛta-* (for *-saṃvṛta-*, K): 'vessels (*yāna-pātra*) filled (*saṃvṛta-*) with wealths of merits and cognition; cf. Tib.A *de-dag thabs-kyi yon-tan śes-rab yoṅs bzuṅ-ste*, B ... *yoṅs zin-na* (!), also Chin. 是人獲福智有財.

4d K *paramādbhuta*, Ta *°dbhūtām* (for *°dbhutāṃ*, XTc = OV); Tc *suga⟨ta⟩;* O *spaśanti* (? mispr. for *spṛśanti*, MSS. = V: Tib. *reg*; but cf. Edg.Rgs. 1); V *śīghram* (w. *-m*).

5a XTa *apakṣi* (= O), Tc *apakṣī* (for *apakvi*, K, so em. Edg.Rgs. 40 = V: Tib. *ma btaṅ;* Chin. 不堅牢 ); Tc *yathā* (for *yatha*, KXTa = OV); O *pari-vaheya* (wt.n.!)(for *vari vaheya*, MSS., so Conze ad O p. 127 = V: Tib. *chu skyed-na*, Chin. 担水 ); cf. AsP 143.22, 32 *udakaṃ parivahet;* K *ko vita*, XTa *kā cit* (= OV), Tc *kā cita* (for *ko cit*: Tib. *la-las*); cf. AsP 143.22, 30 *strī vā puruṣo vā* ...; cf. also *vahamānu*, masc., in *c*.

5b Tc *kṣitapra*, V *kṣipra*(wt.n.)(for *kṣipru*, KXTa = O: Tib. *myur-du*); XTac *bheṣyati* (for *bhetsyati*, K, so em. O = V: Tib. *'jig-par*); Tc *dur-labhatvāt*(= O wt.n.!)(for *durbalatvāt*, KXTa = V: Tib. *ñam-chuṅ phyir-ni)*.

5c XTac *paripakṣi* (= O)(for *°pakvi*, K, so em. Edg.Rgs. 40 = V: Tib. *btaṅ bum-par*); K *vahamātra*, Tc *vahamānumānu* (for *vahamānu*, XTa = OV).

5d Tc *ṇa* (for *na*, KXTa = OV: Tib. *med-ciṅ*); Tc *bhedanā* (for *°nād*, KXTa = OV); Tc *hayam* (for *bhayam*, KXTa = OV: Tib. *'jigs-pa*); XTac *upaiti*(= OV)(for *upeti*, K: Tib. *phyin-par 'gyur;* cf. XXII 13d *abhyupeti*, v.l. *°upaiti* = OV; cf. Edgerton 3.67, also 43 p. 205b, *i-* 1, s.v.); O *svasti-gehaṃ*!; *svasti*, Skt. acc./adv., 'safely, successfully': Tib. *bde-bar*, V *geham* (w. *-m*).

6a Tc *si⟨ya⟩*.

6b XTac *-vihīna* (= OV)(for *°nu*, K); X *prāpuṇāti* (= OV), Tac *prāpaṇāti* (for *prāpuṇātī*, K).

taṃ caiva śraddha pari(Tc17B)gṛhṇayamānu prajñā
    atikramya bhūmi-dvaya prāpsyati agra-bodhiṃ // 6 //

nāvā yathā a-(X45B)parikarma-kṛtā samudre
    vilayaṃ prayāti sa-dhanā saha vāṇijebhiḥ /
sā caiva nāva parikarma-kṛtā su-yuktā
    na ca bhidyate (Ta13B) dhana-samaṅgi upaiti tīraṃ // 7 //

em eva śraddha-paribhāvitu bodhisattvo
    prajñā-vihīnu laghu bodhi upaiti hāniṃ /
so caiva prajña-vara-(X46A)pāramitā-su-yukto
    a-kṣato 'n-upāhatu spṛśāti jināna bodhiṃ // 8 //

puruṣo hi jīrṇu dukhito śata-viṃśa-varṣo
    (K14A) kiṃ cāpi utthitu svayaṃ na prabhoti gantuṃ /
so vāma-dakṣiṇu-dvaye puruṣair gṛhīto
    patanād bhayaṃ na bhavate vrajate sukhena // 9 //

---

6c Tc *ta⟨ṃ⟩*; XTac *parigṛhṇayamāna* (= OV)(for *°mānu*, K); X(Tib.trslit.) *prajña* (for *prajñā*, KXTac = OV).

6d Tc *atikrampa* (for *°mya*, KXTa = OV: Tib. *śin-tu 'das-te)*; V em. *bodhi-*(!)(for *bhūmi-*, MSS. = O: Tib. *sa*, Chin. 地); XTa *prāpsati* (for *°psyati*, KTc, so em. O = V: Tib. *thob 'gyur)*; V *-bodhim* (w. *-m*).

7a Tc *yathā 'parikarma-* (for *yathā a-parikarma-*, KXTa = OV).

7b XTac *vilayam upaiti* (= OV)(for *vilayaṃ prayāti*, K, so Edg.Rgs. 40; cf. XIV 2c *vilayaṃ prayāti*, XTc *vālijobhiḥ*, Ta *vārijobhiḥ*, O *vāṇijobhiḥ*(wt. n.)(for *vāṇijebhiḥ*, K, so em. Edg.Rgs. 40 = V: Tib. *tshoṅ-par bcas-te)*.

7c Tc *raiva* (for *caiva*, KXTa = OV); K *nāpi* (Conze Rgs. 46 misr. K as *nāyi*), Tc *nā* (for *nāva*, XTa = OV: Tib. *gru;* K may have intended **nāvi*, nom.sg.fem.); Tc *sūyuktā* (for *suy°*, KXTa = OV).

7d Tc *⟨dha⟩na-;* XTac *-samagram* (= OV), nom.sg.nt. (for *-samaṅgi*, K, w. *nāva*, nom.sg.f., in *c*: 'ship with all kinds of riches'; Conze Rgs. 46 misr. K as *-samagri⟨ṃ⟩*!; cf. Tib. *nor daṅ bcas-par*); Tc *upaitī tiraṃ* (for *upaiti tīraṃ*, KXTa = OV; but V *tīram* w. *-m*).

8a Tc *śuddha-* (for *śraddha-*, KXTa = OV: Tib. *dad-pas)*.

8b Tac *bodhim* (= V!; r. w. a hiatus-bridger *-m-*?)(for *bodhi*, KX = O: Tib. *byaṅ-chub-las-ni*, cf. Chin. 遠菩提 ); V *hānim* (w. *-m*).

8c KTc *sā* (for *so*, XTa = OV); Ta *-vala-* (for *-vara-*, KXTc = OV: Tib. *mchog*); Tc *-sayukto* (for *-suyukto*, KXTa = OV).

8d K *akṣato 'nupăhatu*, XTa *akṣato nupāhatu*, Tc *'kṣatānupāhati*, V *'kṣato 'nupāhatu*! (for *akṣato 'nupāhatu*, so r. O: Tib. *ma rmas ma ñams*); K *spṛśyati* (for *spṛśāti*, XTac = OV); V *bodhim* (w. *-m*).

9a XTac *jīrṇa* (= OV)(for *jīrṇu*, K); XTac *duḥkhito* (= O)(for *dukhito*, K = V wt.n.; cf. Edg.Rgs. 35).

9b XTa *uttitu*, Tc *utitu* (for *utthitu*, K, so em. O = V: Tib. *laṅs-kyaṅ*); Ta *ga⟨n⟩tuṃ;* V *gantum* (w. *-m*).

9c XTac *-dakṣiṇa-* (= OV)(for *-dakṣiṇu-*, K); K *puruṣair gṛhītvo* (Conze Rgs. 46 misr. K as *puruṣai gṛhītvau*), XTac *puruṣe gṛhīte* (= OV)(for *puruṣair gṛhīto*: Tib. *mi-yis brten byas-na*); cf. AsP 145.20-23 *tam enaṃ dvau balavantau puruṣau vāma-dakṣiṇābhyāṃ pārśvābhyāṃ sv-adhyālambitam adhyālambya su-parigṛhītaṃ parigṛhya evaṃ vadetām — gaccha tvaṃ bhoḥ puruṣa ... na ... patana-bhayaṃ bhaviṣyati ...*

9d Tc *yatanā hayan* (for *patanād bhayaṃ*, KXTa = OV: Tib. *'gyel-ba'i 'jigs-pa)*; XTa *sukhina*, Tc *sūkhinaḥ* (for *sukhena*, K, so r. OV wt.n.: Tib. *bde-blag)*.

em e(X46B)va prajña iha durbalu bodhisattvo
kiṃ cāpi prasthihati bhajyati antareṇa /
so vā upāya-vara-prajña-pariggṛhīto
na ca bhajyate spṛśati bodhi nara-ṛṣabhāṇāṃ // 10 //

(Tc18A) bhagavatyāṃ ratna-guṇa-saṃcaya-gāthāyām aupamya-parivarto nāma caturdaśamaḥ // 14 //

---

10a O *durbala-* (wt.n.)(for *durbalu*, MSS. = V).

10b Tc *prasthihaṃti*(for *°ati*, KXTa = OV); X *bhajjati*, Tac *bharjjati*, O *bhañjati* (wt.n.)(for *bhajyati*, K = V wt.n.: Tib.A *'jig-par 'gyur*, B *ñams-par 'gyur*; cf. *bhajyate* in *d*: Tib.A *'jig*, B *ñams*).

10c XTac *-bala-* (= OV)(for *-vara-*, K, so r. Conze ad O p. 127; cf. also V p. 370 n. 3); MSS. *-parigṛhīto* (= OV), unmetr. (for *-pariggṛhīto*; cf. Edg.Rgs. 37).

10d V *-ṛṣabhāṇām* (w. *-m*).

XIV col. XTa *-gāthāyāṃ* (= O)(for *°āyām*, KTc = V); Tc *aupagamya-* (for *aupamya-*, KXTa = OV: Tib. *dpe'i*); at the end of the colophon only K (folio 14A3) reads *gāthā // 10 //*; and Tc adds num. 14.

## ⟨XV. DEVA-PUTRA⟩

(X47A) ye ādi-karmi-sthita-bhūmiya bodhisattvā
adhyāśayena vara prasthita buddha-bodhiṃ /
tehī su-śiṣya-guru-gaurava-saṃprayuktaiḥ
kalyāṇa-mitra sada sevayitavya vijñaiḥ // 1 //

kiṃ kāraṇaṃ tatu guṇāgamu paṇḍitānāṃ
prajñāya pāramita te anuśāsa(X47B)yanti /
evaṃ jino bhaṇati sarva-guṇāgra-dhārī
kalyāṇa-mitram upaniśrita buddha-dharmāḥ // 2 //

dānaṃ ca śīlam api kṣānti tathaiva vīryaṃ
dhyānāni prajña (Ta14A) pariṇāmayitavya bodhau /
na ca bodhi skandha vimṛśitva parāmṛśeyā
ye ādi-karmika na deśayitavya evaṃ // 3 //

e(X48A)vaṃ carantu guṇa-sāgara vādi-candrās
trāṇā bhavanti jagatī śaraṇāś ca lenāḥ /

---

1a Ta *ya*, OV *yo* (wt.n.)(for *ye*,KXTc, so r. Edg.Rgs. 40); K *-karmita-sthita-*, XTac *-karma-sthitu-* (= OV; but V sep. *karma sthitu*!)(for *-karmi-sthita-*; cf. BHSD p. 93b, *ādi-karmika-*, *°-karmin-*, ss.vv.: Tib. *daṅ-po'i las-kyi sar gnas gaṅ*); XTac *bodhisattvo* (= OV!)(for *°sattvā*, K, so r. Edg.Rgs. 40).

1b K *⟨a⟩dhyāśayena*, Tc *adhyā⟨śa⟩yena* (for *adhyāśayena*, XTa = OV: Tib. *lhag-pa'i bsam-pas*);Ta *vala*(w. a doubting sign on *la*)(for *vara*, KXTc = OV: Tib. *mchog*); V *-bodhim* (w. *-m*).

1c Tc *te⟨hī⟩*, O sep. *te hī* (for *tehī*, KXTa, so r. Edg.Rgs. 40 = V: Tib. *de-dag-gis*); O sep. *suśiṣya guru-°*; XTac *-saṃprayukto* (= OV)(for *°ktaiḥ*, K, so r. Edg.Rgs. 40); cf. Tib. *slob-ma bzaṅ-po bla-ma gus daṅ rab ldan-pa* (B *gus ldan de-dag-gis*).

1d Tc *sata* (for *sada*, KXTa = OV: Tib.B *rtag-tu*); cf. Tib.A *mkhas-pa de-dag-gis dge-ba'i bśes-gñen-pa bsten-par bya*, B *bla-ma mkhas-pa-rnams-la rtag-tu bsten-par bya*.

2a XTac *tanu* (for *tatu*, K, so em. O = V: Tib. *de-las*).

2b Tc *prajñāpa* (for *°āya*, KXTa = OV; but O *prajñāya-*, cpd.!).

2c Ta adds *ti* after *jino*; Tc *-guṇāgu-* (for *-guṇāgra-*, KXTa = OV: Tib. *yon-tan kun-gyi mchog*).

2d Ta *upa⟨ni⟩śrita*.

3c OV *bodhi-*, cpd.! (cf. Edg.Rgs. 40); Tc *ska⟨ndha⟩*; Tc *vimaśṛtva* (for *vimṛśitva*, KXTa = OV); K *parāmṛṣeyā*, Tc *°mṛṇeyā* (for *°mṛśeyā*, XTa = OV); cf. Tib.A *phuṅ-por źen-nas mchog-tu 'dzin-par ma byed ces*, B *byaṅ-chub phuṅ-por źen-nas mchog 'dzin ma byed ces*.

3d XTac *-karmaka* (= O)(for *-karmika*, K = V wt.n.; cf. Edg.Rgs. 40 for *ādi-karmaka-*); K *deśa⟨yi⟩tavya*, O *deśayitavyaṃ* (wt.n.)(for *deśayitavya*, XTac, so r. Edg.Rgs. 40 = V); V *evam* (w. *-m*); cf. Tib. *daṅ-po'i las-can-dag-la* (B *de-la*) *de-skad bstan-par bya* (= Conze Trsl.!), but Chin. 勿為初地如是說.

4a X *caranta* (= OV)(for *carantu*, KTac); XTac *-candrāḥ* (= OV)(for *-candrās*, K; Conze Rgs. 57 misr. K as *-candrā*).

4b Tc *bhavati* (for *°anti*, KXTa = OV); XTac *śaraṇā* (= OV)(for *śaraṇāś*, K; Conze Rgs. 47 misr. K as *śaraṇāñś*); XTc *leyanā*, Ta *reyanā*, O em. *lenā* (= V)(for *lenāḥ*, K: Tib. *gnas*; cf. BHSD p. 463b, *lena-*, s.v.); cf. XXII 3b-d *mārgu* ... *obhāsa ulka* ... *āloka śāstra* ...

gati-buddhi-dīpa-pariṇāyaka artha-kāmāḥ
(K14B) pradyo(Tc18B)ta-ulka-vara-dharma-kathī a-kṣobhyāḥ // 4 //

saṃnāhu duṣkaru mahāśaya saṃnahantī
na ca skandha-dhātu na ca āyatanaiḥ sanaddhāḥ /
(X48B) tribhi yāna-saṃjña-vigatā a-pariggṛhītā
a-vivartiyā a-calitāś ca a-kopya-dharmāḥ // 5 //

te eva-dharma-samudāgata niṣprapañcāḥ
kāṅkṣā-vilekha-vimatī-vigatārtha-yuktāḥ /
prajñāya pāramita śrutva na sīdayanti
a-para-praṇeya a-vivartiya veditavyāḥ // 6 //

gambhīra-(X49A)dharma ayu durdṛśu nāyakānāṃ
na ca kena cīd adhigato na ca prāpuṇāti /
etārtha bodhim adhigamya hitānukampī
alpotsuko ka imu jñāsyati sattva-kāyo // 7 //

---

4c XTac *-dvīpa-* (= O)(for *-dīpa-*, K: Tib. *gliṅ;* cf. Edg.Rgs. 8); XTa *-pariṇāyakārtha-*, Tc *-parināyakārtha-* (for *-pariṇāyaka artha-*, K, so em. O; but O *-pariṇāyaka-°*, cpd.!); Tc *-kāmā* (for *-kāmāḥ*, KXTa = O); V *gati buddhi dvīpa pariṇayaka artha-kāmāḥ.*

4d Tc *<-u>lka;* OV sep. *pradyota ulka vara-°.*

5a Tc *sannāha* (for *°hu*, KXTa = OV); X *mahā-yaśu* (= OV: Tib. *grags chen ldan-rnams*), Tac *mahā-yaśa* (for *mahāśaya*, K, which Conze Rgs. 40 thinks better); Ta *saṃgahantī*, Tc *mantahantī* (for *saṃnahantī*, KX = OV: Tib. *gyon byed-de).*

5b X *ca āyatanais* (= O), Ta *ya āyatanais*, Tc *ca āyatatais* (for *ca āyatanaiḥ*, K = V); Tc *saraddhāḥ* (for *san°*, KXTa = OV: Tib. *go-cha*).

5c K *-saṃjñā-* (for *-saṃjña-*, XTac = OV); K *'parigṛhītā*, XTac *aparigṛhītā* (= OV)(for *apariggṛhītā;* cf. Edg.Rgs. 37).

5d XTa *avivartikā* (= OV), Tc *'vivartikā* (for *avivartiyā*, K; cf. BHSD p. 78b, *avivartya-*, s.v.; Edgerton 3.103); Ta *acaritāś* (for *acalitāś*, KXTc = OV: Tib. *gYo-ba med-ciṅ).*

6a K *-samanvāgata* (so r. Conze ad O p. 127; cf. V p. 371 n. 1), Ta *samudāgati* (for *-samudāgata*, XTc = OV): Tib. *'di-'dra'i* (v.l. *de-'dra'i*) *chos daṅ ldan-źiṅ*; *-samudāgata*, synonymous to *-samanvāgata* (cf. BHSD p. 564a, *samanvāgata-*, p. 572a, *samudāgata-*,2, ss.vv.), is metrically better (cf. Edg.Rgs. 40); OV sep. *eva dharma-°!*; XTac *niṣprapañcā* (= OV)(for *°pañcāḥ*, K; Conze Rgs. 47 misr. K as *°pañcagaḥ*); cf. XXXI 9a *eva-śīlu-samudāgatu* (K *-samanvāgatu*, XTa *-samandhāgatu*, Tc *-samaṃdhāgatu) śuddha-sattvo* (XTac *niṣprapañco).*

6c O *prajñāya-pāramita*, cpd.!

6d Ta *-praneya*, Tc *-puṇeya* (for *-praṇeya*, KX = OV); em. *a-para-°* perh.to *a-parā-°* or *a-paro-°* (cf. I 15c and VII 1b, fn.): Tib. *gźan-gyi driṅ mi 'jog-ciṅ* (no v.l.), but Chin. 化他 (? Skt. *apara-°).*

7a OV sep. *gambhīra dharma;* Ta *durdṛśū* (for *°śu*, KXTc = OV).

7b K *kena ci*, Tc *kena cid* (for *kena cīd*, XTa = OV); XTac *prāpuṇanti* (= OV)(for *°āti*, K).

7c X *etārthu* (= OV), Ta *ekārthu* (for *etārtha*, KTc); Ta *adhigemya* (for *°gamya*, KXTc = OV); cf. Tib.A *de-na gcig-ñid-du* (!) *rtogs-nas phan-byed sñiṅ-brtser 'gyur*, B *de-phyir phan-mdzad brtser ldan byaṅ-chub brñes-nas-ni* (v.l. *°-nas 'di* = O).

7d Tc *alpotsūko* (for *alpotsuko*, KXTa = OV: Tib.A *spro chuṅ*, B *thugs-khral chuṅ-bar mdzad*); Tc *-kāyaḥ* (for *-kāyo*, KXTa = OV).

sattvāś ca ālaya-ratā viṣayābhilāṣī
sthita āgrahe a-budhayo muha-andha-bhūtāḥ /
dharmo an-ā(X49B)layu an-āgrahu prāpitavyo
lokena sārdha ayu vigraha prādu-bhūto // 8 //

(Tc19A) bhagavatyāṃ ratna-guṇa-saṃcaya-gāthāyāṃ deva-putra-(Ta14B) parivarto nāma pañcadaśamaḥ // 15 //

---

8a XTac *sattvaś* (= OV)(for °*vāś*, K: Tib. *sems-can-rnams-ni*); Ta ⟨*ā*⟩*laya-*; O em. *-rato* (= V)(for *-ratā*, MSS.; Conze Rgs. 47 mispr. *ālayratā* for KX *ālayaratā*); K *viṣayābhilāsī* (for °*āṣī*, XTac = OV: Tib. *yul-rnams 'dod*).

8b KXTa *sthita agrahe* (= V; Conze Rgs. 47 misr. K as *sthitayu grahe*!), O em. *sthito grahe*(w. Tib.), Tc *sthita* ⟨*agrahe*⟩ (for *sthita āgrahe*: Tib. *'dzin-la gnas-śiṅ*); Edg.Rgs. 40 suggests em. either to *sthita agrahe* (cf. Edgerton 3.32-36) or to Skt. *āgrahe*; *āgrahe*seems to be better (cf. *an-āgrahu* in *c*); V sep. *a-budha yo* (!)(for *a-budhayo* = O, m.c. for *a-buddhayo*, nom.pl.m., Bhvr.-cpd.: Tib. *mi mkhas*; cf. Edgerton 2.89); MSS. *maha-* (= OV)(for *muha-*: Tib. *blun-rmoṅs*; cf. XXXI 11b *momuhānām*: Tib. *blun-po-rnams-la*); XTac *-bhūto* (= OV)(for *-bhūtāḥ*, K).

8c Tac *anālaya* (for °*yu*, KX = OV); Tc *anāgraha* (for °*hu*, KXTa = OV); XTa *prāpitavyoḥ*, Tc *pāpitavyoḥ* (for *prāpitavyo*, K, so em. O = V).

8d XTa *vigrahu* (= OV)(for °*ha*, KTc); K *prādurbhūto* (so em. O), XTac *prādurbhūtoḥ* (for *prādu-bhūto* = V).

XV col. XTac *deva-* (= OV: Chin. 天 , also AsP XV *deva-*)(for *deva-putra-*, K: Tib. *lha'i bu*; cf. O p. 59 n. 1, but O mispr. *deva-patra-* for °*-putra-*); at the end of the colophon K reads *gāthā 8*, and Tc adds num. 15.

## ⟨XVI. TATHATĀ⟩

ākāśa-dhātu purimā-diśi dakṣiṇāye
     tatha paścimottara-diśāya an-anta-pāro /
(X50A) ūrdhādharāya ca daśa-d-diśi yāvad asti
     nānātvatā na bhavate na viśeṣa-prāptāḥ // 1 //

atikrānta yā tathata yā tathatā (K15A) a-prāptā
     pratyutpanna yā tathata yā tathatārahāṇāṃ /
yā sarva-dharma-tathatā tathatā jinānāṃ
     sarv' eṣa dharma-tathatā na viśeṣa-(X50B)prāptā // 2 //

yo bodhisattva iṣu icchati prāpuṇetuṃ
     nānātva-dharma-vigatāṃ sugatāna bodhiṃ /
prajñāya pāramita yujyat' upāya-yukto
     vina prajña nāsty adhigamo nara-nāyakānāṃ // 3 //

---

1a *ăkāśa-* (for *ākāśa-*, XTac = OV: Tib. *nam-mkha'i*); O sep. *purimā diśi;* XTac *dakṣiṇāyāṃ* (= OV)(for *°āye*, K).

1b Tc *-diśāyāṃ* (for *-diśāya*, KXTa = OV); XTa *anantapārā* (= OV), Tc *<a>nantapāra* (for *anantapāro*, K: Tib. *pha mtha'-yas)*.

1c K *ūrdhāndharoya* (Conze Rgs. 47 r. K as *ūrddh(v)ānvaroya)*, XTa *uparādharāya* (= OV), Tc *uparāya* (for *ūrdhâdharāya*: Tib. *steṅ daṅ 'og daṅ*, Chin. 上下 ); *ūrdha-* (cf. BHSD p. 150a, q.v.) plus *adhara-* must have been intended; *ūrdha-* plus *avara-* could be intended, if Conze's r. is correct (*v* and *dh* are palaeographically similar); MSS. om. *ca* (so om. OV, unmetr. !); Tc *daśa-diśi* (for *daśaddiśi*, KXTa = OV); Tc *pāṃvad* (for *yāvad*, KXTa = OV: Tib. *ji-sñed-rnams-na'aṅ*, v.l. *'jig-rten-°*!).

1d K *labhate* (? m.c. for MInd. *labbhate/-ti*, Skt. *labhyate;* cf. Edgerton 37.27)(for *bhavate*, XTac = OV: Tib. *gyur-pa*); XTac *-prāptā* (= OV)(for *-prāptāḥ*, K).

2a XTa *tathatāprāptā*, Tc *tathatāprākā* (for *tathatā a-prāptā*, K, so em. O = V: Tib. *ma phyin* (v.l. *byon* = O) *de-bźin-ñid*).

2b MSS. *pratyutpanna* may have been pronounced as *pacupanna*, m.c. (cf. Edg.Rgs. 31); Tc *yājā* (for the first *yā*, KXTa = OV); XTa *tāthata* (= O!) (for *tathata*, KTc = V); K *tathatārhāṇaṃ*, XTac *tathatārhatānaṃ* (= OV; but V w. *-m*)(for *tathatārahāṇaṃ*, so in XII 3a).

2c K *tathā* (for the first *tathatā*, XTac = OV: Tib. *de-bźin-ñid*); X *tathatārhatāṇāṃ*, Tac *°tārhatānaṃ* (= OV)(for *°tā jinānaṃ*, K: Tib. *rgyal-ba'i de-bźin-ñid*, but v.l. *dgra-bcom de-bźin-ñid;* cf. O p. 59 n. 3, Conze ad O p. 127).

2d MSS. *sarveṣa* (so print OV; Conze Rgs. 47 misr. O as *sarveṣu*)(for *sarv' eṣa = sarvā* plus *eṣā*); Conze Rgs. 47 misr. K as *-tathatānaṃ* for *-tathatā na* (so MSS. = OV).

3a XTac *imi* (= OV)(for *iṣu*, K, which Conze Rgs. 47 doubtfully em. to *imu*); *iṣu* (Tib. *'di-ni*) must have been intended, m.c. for *eṣāṃ* (cf. Edgerton 21.9 end) by analogy w. *imu*, m.c. for *imāṃ* (cf. Edgerton 21.54, 9.23), although *m* and *ṣ* are easily confused graphically (cf. XVI 4c K *imu*: XTac *iṣu* = OV); anyhow *imi* is not found elsewhere as acc.sg.fem.; K *prāpaṇetuṃ* (for *prāpuṇ°*, XTac = OV).

3b Tc *-dharmaṃ* (for *-dharma-*, KXTa = OV); K *-vigatān* (for *°tāṃ*, XTac = OV); Tc *sūgatāna* (for *sug°*, KXTa = OV); V *bodhim* (w. *-m*).

3c O *prajāya-*(? mispr. for *prajñāya-*)*pāramita*, cpd.!; Tc *yujyata pāpa-yukto*, KXTa *yujyatupāya-yukto*, O *yujyatu pāya-yukto* (wt.n.), V em. *°atu yāya yukto*! (for *yujyat' upāya-yukto*: Tib. *thabs daṅ ldan-pas;* cf. Edg. Rgs. 40); cf. Chin. 応行方便般若行！

pakṣisya yojana-śatā maha ātma-bhāvo
    pañcā-śatāpi a-balā bhuyu kṣī(X51A)ṇa-pakṣo /
so trāya-triṃśa-bhavanād imu jambudvīpaṃ
    (Tc19B) ātmānam osariyi tad vilayaṃ vrajeyā // 4 //

yady āpi pañca ima pāramitā jinānāṃ
    bahu-kalpa-koṭi-niyutān samudānayeyā /
praṇidhīn an-anta-vipulān sada sevya loke
    an-upāya prajña-vikalo pa(X51B)ti śrāvakatve // 5 //

niryāyaṇāya iha icchati buddha-jñāne
    sama-citta sarva-jagatī pitu-mātu-saṃjñā /

---

[3d] XTac *avigamo* (for *adhi°*, K, so em. O = V: Tib. *thob-par 'gyur*); V *-nāyakānām* (w. *-m*).

[4a] XTac *-śatam* (= OV)(for *-śatā*, K); X *mahatātmabhāvo*(= OV), Tac *mahatāmabhāvo* (for *maha ātma-bhāvo*, K); cf. Tib.A *bya źig lus che dpag-tshad brgya-pa yod gyur-tam dpag-tshad lṅa-brgyar* (v.l. *lṅa-bcur*!) *gyur-pa gśog zad stobs med-pa*, B *bya źig lus che dpag-tshad brgya-rtsa-lṅa-bcu-par gyur-la 'dab-gśog zad-de ñam-rtsal yod min-na* (!).

[4b] XTa *pañcaśatāpi* (= O), Tc *pañcaśatābhi* (for *pañcā-śatāpi*, K; cf. Edg. Rgs. 32; V sep. *pañcāśata pi*); *pañcā-śatāpi* is used for *pañca-śatāpi* '500' and not for *pañcāśat-* '50': Tib.A [only MS. Tb] *dpag-tshad lṅa-brgyar gyur-pa*); XTac *avalobhaya* (= O;?r. *abalobahaya*)(for *a-balā bhuyu*, K, w. which Edg.Rgs. 40 suggests em. *abalo* [or *abalā*, but nom.sg.] plus *bhuyu* [= *bhūyāt*, m.c.]; cf. Tib.A *stobs med-pa*, B *ñams-rtsal yod min-na*); *bhuyu*, m.c. for *bhūyo*, *bhūyaḥ*, must have been intended (cf. X 2d *bhuyu*: Tib. *phyir-źiṅ*); V *abalobhayakṣīṇapakṣo*, cpd. (!).

[4c] X *trāyastriṃśa-*(= O), Ta *trāyaḥtriṃśa-*, Tc *trāyaḥtriṃśam-* (for *trāya-triṃśa-*, K, so Edg.Rgs. 40 = V); XTac *iṣu* (= OV; cf. Edgerton 21.5, 9; or perh. OV *-bhavanâdiṣu*?)(for *imu*, K; Conze Rgs. 47 misr. K as *bhavanādigra*; cf. XVI 3a, fn.); K *°dvīpam*, XTac *°dvīpe* (= OV)(for *°dvīpaṃ*); cf. Tib. *de-yis sum-cu-rtsa-gsum gnas-nas 'dzam-gliṅ 'dir*.

[4d] MSS. *osariyi*, opt. (= OV: Tib. *mchoṅs-na*) seems to be the true reading: it is a blend of **-sarayi* (cf. V 9b *osarayanti*) and **-sari* (to *-sarati*; cf. Edgerton 29.14) or **-sariya* (cf. Edgerton 29.34); Edg.Rgs. 40 however says, 'Read *°iya* (opt., or possibly gerund); "would let itself (*ātmanam*) down"'; also note that *osarati* and *osirati* are sometimes confused (cf. BHSD p. 75b, *avaśirati*, p. 76a, *avasarati*, ss.vv., also Edgerton 43 p. 233b, *śira-ti*, s.v.); V em. *taṃ* (for *tad*, MSS. = O: Tib. B *der-ni*, but A *de-ni*!); Ta *vrajeyyā*, Tc *prajaryyā* (for *vrajeyā*, K; OV *vrajeyyā* w. X, cf. Edgerton 29.23-28); cf. Tib. *bdag-ñid mchoṅs-na der-ni* (A *de-ni*!) *ñam-ñes 'gyur-ba yin*.

[5b] XTac *-niyutāṃ* (= OV)(for *°tān*, K); XTac *samudānayeyyā* (= OV)(for *°eyā*, K; cf. Edgerton 29.23); cf. XXX 2b *samudānayate* (w.n.).

[5c] Tc *praṇīdhīn*, O *prāṇadhīn* (? reprinting fault)(for *praṇidhīn*, KXTa = V: Tib. *smon-lam*); Tc *araṃta-* (for *ananta-*, KXTa = OV: Tib. *mtha'-yas*); XTac *-vipulāṃ* (= V)(for *-vipulān*, K, so em. O); O *savya* (? reprinting fault)(for *sevya*, MSS. = V: Tib. *bsten-kyaṅ*, v.l. *brten-kyaṅ*).

[5d] XTa *-vikalā* (= OV), Tc *-vikāḷā* (for *-vikalo*, K); XTac *pari* (= V)(for *pati*, K, so em. O: Tib. *ltuṅ*, Chin. 墜); cf. AsP 155.30-31 *saced ayaṃ prajñā-pāramitayā a-parigṛhīta upāya-kauśalyena ca virahito bhavet, evaṃ śrāvaka-bhūmiṃ vā pratyeka-buddha-bhūmiṃ vā patati*.

[6a] K *niryāpaṇāya*, XTac *niryāyanāya* (= OV)(for *niryāyaṇāya*; cf. Edgerton 36.15, Edg.Rgs. 29); K *ihaicchati*, Tc ⟨*iha*⟩ *i°*, V *ya i°* (wt.n.), unmetr. (w. Tib. *gaṅ*?)(for *iha i°*, XTa = O: Tib.A *'di-la ... 'dod-pas*, B ... *'dod gaṅ*); cf. Tib. *saṅs-rgyas theg-pa* (no v.l.; ? Skt. *buddha-yāne* for *°-jñāne*, MSS. = OV: Chin. 仏智!); O p. 61 n. 1 'Xyl. *buddha-yāne*' should have referred to this!

hita-citta maitra-mana eva parākrameyā
a-khilārjavo mṛdu-girāṃ ya sadālapeyā // 6 //

bhagavatyāṃ ratna-guṇa-(Ta15A)saṃcaya-gāthāyāṃ tathatā-parivarto nāma ṣoḍaśamaḥ // 16 //

---

6b K *pitur-mātu-*, XTac *pitṛ-mātṛ-* (= OV; O sep. *pitṛ mātṛ-!*; Edg.Rgs. 40 em. O to *pita-māta-*, cf. Edgerton 13.4; no MS. supports Edgerton's em.)(for *pitu-mātu-*; cf. Edgerton 13.22).

6c Tc *-cittaṃ* (for *-citta*, KXTa = OV); Ta *yeva* (cf. Edgerton 4.66, BHSD p. 448a, *yeva*, s.v.)(for *eva*, KXTc = OV); X *parākrameryā* (= O!), Tac *°eryyā*, V *°eyyā* (for *°eyā*, K; cf. Edgerton 29.23): Tib. *brtul bya-źiṅ*, cf. Chin. 当行.

6d O *madu-* (? reprinting fault for *mṛdu-*, MSS. = V: Tib. *'jam*); K *-girāṃ yaḥ*, XTac *-girāya* (= OV)(for *-girāṃ ya*: Tib. *tshig; ya-* is not supported by Tib.); X *parākrameryā*(= O!), Tac *°eryyā*, V *°eyyā* (for *sadālapeyā*, K: *sadā* plus *ālapeyā*, rather than *sadā lapeyā*: Tib. *smra-bar bya*, cf. Chin. 当 ... 常宜 ; Conze Rgs. 47 misr. K as *sadālayeyā* and suggests em. *sadā vadeyā* w. Tib.); cf. Edgerton 43 p. 228a, *lapa-ti*, s.v.; also Nobel, *Tib. Suv. Index*, p. 169, *smra-bar bgyi'o: ālapayitavya-*.

XVI col. Ta *-gāthāyā* (for *-gāthāyāṃ*, KXTc = OV); K *-parivartaḥ* (om. *nāma*) (for *-parivarto nāma*, XTac = OV); at the end of the colophon K reads *gāthā // 6 //* ; and Tc adds num. 16.

## ⟨XVII. AVINIVARTANĪYĀKĀRA-LIṄGA-NIMITTA⟩

(X52A) sthaviro subhūti paripṛcchati loka-nātham
a-raṇāya liṅga bhaṇahī guṇa-saṃcayā(K15B)nāṃ /
a-vivartiyā yatha bhavanti mahānubhāvās
taṃ vyākurū jina guṇāna pradeśa-mātraṃ // 1 //

nānātva-saṃjña-vigatā gira-yukta-bhā(Tc20A)ṇī
na ca anya te (X52B) śramaṇa-brāhmaṇa āśrayanti /
triy-apāya-varjita vidū sada-kāli bhonti
daśabhiś ca te kuśala-karma-pathebhi yuktāḥ // 2 //

dharmaṃ nirāmiṣu jagasy' anuśāsayanti
ekānta-dharma-niratā sada snigdha-vākyāḥ /
sthiti-caṅkramā-śaya-niṣadya su-saṃprajānāḥ
yu(X53A)ga-mātra-prekṣiṇa vrajanti a-bhrānta-cittāḥ // 3 //

---

[1a] Tc *sthaviraḥ subhūtiḥ* (for *sthaviro subhūti*, KXTa = OV); Ta *-nātha*, Tc *-nāthaṃm* (for *-nāthaṃ*, KX = OV).

[1b] K *-sañcayānā[ṃ]*, XTac *-sāgarāṇām* (= OV; but V *-m*: Tib. *yon-tan rgya-mtsho'i*, v.l.*-mstho*)(for *-saṃcayānāṃ*; cf. *guṇāna*: Chin. 功徳蔵 in *d*).

[1c] XTac *avivartiyo* (= O)(for *°iyā*, K = V); K *mahānubhāvāṃs*, XTac *°vā*, (= OV)(for *°vās*).

[1d] K *ta* (*-ṃ* must have been wrongly put on *°bhāvāṃs* in *c* or *vyāṃkuru* in *d*, XTac *tāṃ* (= V), O em. *tān* (O *tāna* seems to be a reprinting fault; Conze Rgs. 47 misr. O as *tānā*), Edg.Rgs. 40 em. *tān* or *tāṃ*, acc.pl.! (for *taṃ*, correl. used for *tad* w. *yatha* in *c*: Tib. *ji-ltar ... de-ltar ...*; cf. Edgerton 21.11); K *vyāṃkuru*, XTa *vyākuruṣṭa*, Tc *vyākurutha*, O em. *vyākuruṣva* (= V, hypermetr.!)(for *vyākurū*, so em. Edg.Rgs. 40); V *jina-*, cpd.!; Tc *pradeśe* (for *°śa-*, KXTa = OV); V *-mātram* (w. *-m*).

[2a] Conze Rgs. 47 misr. O as *giruyuktā-* (for *gira-yukta-*, MSS. = OV; but V sep. *gira yukta-*!: Tib.A *tshig*(v.l. *chos*!) *daṅ ldan-par smra*, B *rigs-pa ldan tshig smra*); cf. Chin. 如山谷響声相応 (? Skt. *giri-°*).

[2b] Tc *cānya* (for *ca anya*, KXTa = OV); XTac *śravaṇa-* (for *śramaṇa-*, K, so em. OV; but O mispr. *śrasaṇa-*, and V sep. *śramaṇa brāhmaṇa*!: Tib. *dge-sbyoṅ-dag*); O *-brahmaṇa* (? mispr. for *-brāh°*, MSS.: Tib. *bram-ze*); Tac *āśayanti* (for *āśray°*, KX = OV: Tib. *brten ... byed*).

[2c] K *vi[d]ū*, Tc *vidu* (for *vidū*, XTa = OV: Tib. *mkhas-pas*, v.l. *°-pa*); O *-varjita-vidū*, cpd.! (cf. Edg.Rgs. 40); Ta *-kāri* (for *-kāli*, KXTc = OV: Tib. *dus-rnams rtag-tu*, v.l. *°-par*); Tc *bhoti* (for *bhonti*, KXTa = OV).

[2d] Tc *da⟨śa⟩bhiś*; Ta *-pathe⟨bhi⟩*; X *yuktoḥ*, Tac *yukto*, V *yuktā* (for *yuktāḥ*, K); O *-pathe 'bhiyuktāḥ* (w. Tib. *lam-la mṅon-par brtson*?).

[3a] Tc *dharma* (for *dharmaṃ*, KXTa = OV); Tac *tirāmiṣu* (for *nir°*, KX = OV: Tib.A *zaṅ-ziṅ med-pas*, B *°-par*, Chin. 無礙 ; cf. BHSD p. 299b, *nirāmiṣa-*, s.v.); MSS. *jagasyanuśāsayanti* (so print OV)(for *jagasy' anu°*).

[3b] XTa *-niyatās* (= O), V *-niyatāḥ*, Tc *-nihayatā* (for *-niratā*, K: Tib. *dga'-źiṅ*; cf. V p. 373 n. 3); O *sada-*, cpd.!; K *stigu-*, X *snigva-* (for *snigdha-*, Tac, so em. O = V: Tib.A *'jam-pa'i tshig daṅ ldan*, B *tshig 'jam ldan*).

[3c] Tc *sthitaṃ* (for *sthiti-*, KXTa = OV); XTa *-caṅkramaṃ-* (= OV; but OV sep. *°maṃ śa°*!; cf. Edgerton 8.14), Tc *-cakrarma-* (for *-caṅkramā-*, K; cf. Edgerton 8.15-17); XTa *-śapa-* (= O!; and O sep. *śapa ni°*!), Tc *-sapa-* (for *-śaya-*, K = V: Tib. *ñal*); Tc *-riṣadya* (for *-ni°*, KXTa = OV; but O sep.); XTa *susatprajānā* (= O), Tc *sūsatprajānā*, V *susaṃprajānā* (for *susaṃprajānāḥ*, K); cf. Tib. *'gro 'chag ñal daṅ 'dug-par śes bźin*

śuci-caukṣa-ambara-dharās tri-viveka-śuddhāḥ
na ca lābha-kāma vṛṣabhī sada dharma-kāmāḥ /
mārasy' atīta-viṣayā a-para-praṇeyāś
catu-dhyāna-dhyāyi na ca niśrita tatra dhyāne // 4 //

na ca kīrti-(X53B)kāma na ca krodha-parīta-cittāḥ
gṛhi-bhūta nitya an-adhyoṣita sarva-vastūṃ /
na ca jīvikā-viṣama-bhoga gaveṣamāṇā
abhicāra-mantra na ca istri-prayoga-mantrāḥ // 5 //

na ca ādiśanti puruṣestriya iccha-karmāṃ
pravivikta (Tc20B) prajña-vara-pāramitābhiyuktāḥ /

---

*rab-tu ldan*, Chin. 行住坐臥四威儀 ; also XX 11c *sthiti-*(so K; v.l. *gati-*)*caṅkramaṃ-śaya-niṣadya nidarśayātī*: Tib. *'gro daṅ 'chag-pa daṅ-ni ñal daṅ 'dug-pa ston*, Chin. 行住坐臥四威儀.

3d Tc *vrajanty* (= V, unmetr.!)(for °*anti*, KXTa = O); XTa *-cittā* V *-cintā* (wt.n.)(for *-cittāḥ*, KTc, so em. O: Tib. *sems 'khrul med)*.

4a XTac *śuci-sauca-* (= O), V *śuci-śauca-* (wt.n.)(for *śuci-caukṣa-*, K: Tib. *gtaṅ byas gtaṅ-ma'i*); XTac *-dharā* (= OV)(for *-dharās*, K); XTac *-śuddhā* (= OV)(for *-śuddhāḥ*, K).

4b Ta *rāga-* (for *lābha-*, KXTc = OV: Tib.A *rñed-pa*, B *rñed*); O em.*vṛṣabhā* (= V!)(for °*bhī*, MSS., so r. Edg.Rgs. 40; cf. BHSD p. 507b, °*bhin-*,s.v.).

4c MSS. *mārasyatīta-* (so prints V), O sep. *mārasya tīta-* (for *mārasy' atīta-*); XTac *-praṇeyā* (= OV)(for °*āś*, K); em. *a-para-*° perh to *a-parā-*° or *a-paro-*°: Tib. *gźan-gyi driṅ mi 'jog* (no v.l.), but Chin. 化他 (? Skt. *apara-*°); cf. XV 6d *a-para-praṇeya;* cf. also I 15c and VII 1b, fn.

4d X *catur-* (= O)(for *catu-*, KTac, so r. Edg.Rgs. 39 = V); Tc *dhyāna*(for *dhyāne*, KXTa = OV: Tib. *bsam-gtan der)*.

5a X *-parīta-cittā* (= OV), Tac *-parita-cittā* (for *-parīta-cittāḥ*, K:Tib. *sems dkris)*.

5b Tac *gṛhī-* (for *gṛhi-*, KX = OV); Edg.Rgs. 39 r. *an-ajhoṣita*, m.c. for MSS. *an-adhyoṣita* (cf. Pāli *ajjhosita-*); XTac *-vastuṃ* (for *-vastūṃ*, K; Conze Rgs. 57 misr. K as *-vastuṃ*); O em. *anadhyoṣita-sarva-vastu* (cpd.!), V sep. *anadhyoṣita sarva vastuṃ* (wt.n.; and not *vastum*!).

5c XTac *-viṣaya-* (= OV)(for *-viṣama-*, K, so r. Conze ad O p. 127); cf. Tib.A *'tsho-ba'i loṅs-spyod mi 'thun*, B *'tsho-ba'i phyir-ni ya-ṅas loṅs-spyod* (cf. V p. 373 n. 4); XTac *gaveṣayanti* (= OV)(for *gaveṣamāṇā*, K): Tib.A *tshol-ba'i bsam-pa med*,B *tshol mi byed.*

5d Tc *isti-* (for *istri-*, KXTa = OV: Tib. *bud med)*.

6a Tc *cādiśaṃti* (for *ca ādiśanti*, KXTa = OV); XTac *puruṣaistriya* (= O; but O °*striya-*, cpd.!), V *puruṣaiḥ striya* (wt.n.)(for *puruṣestriya*, K); Edg.Rgs. 40 r. w. K *puruṣestriya-*°as a cpd. (cf. XXVI 8b *puruṣestriya-tulya*) and renders, 'and they do not report actions of desire (so Tib., *'dod-pa'i las-can;* [Conze's] Index "plausible lies"!) of men and women'; but Tib.B *'dod-pa'i las-can pho-mor 'gyur źes ston mi byed;* cf. also Tib.A *rtsva-tsam 'dod phyir mi-las* (r. °*-la*?; Skt. *puruṣe tṛṇa⟨ṃ⟩?) las-rnams len mi byed*!: Chin. 男女互相業所緣 (so r. many editions incl. Chi-sha ed.), but Taishō ed.: 更互相相業所緣 (cf. also Taki p. 14/ 360 n. 3); but AsP 166.24-25 *sa na striyaṃ na ca puruṣaṃ vyākaroti —— putro vā te bhaviṣyati, duhitā vā te bhaviṣyatīti;* AsP 166.31-167.4 *na saṃgaṇikārāma-kathā-yogānuyogam anuyuktā viharanti, ... na strī-puruṣa-napuṃsaka-kathā-yogānuyogam anuyuktā viharanti.*

6b XTa *pravivīkta*, Tc *pravivījya* (for *pravivikta*, K, so em. O; but O °*kta-*, cpd.!: Tib.B *rab-tu dben-pa'i*!, so Conze trsl.; Edg.Rgs. 40 rightly sep. *pravivikta* = V: Tib.A *rab-tu dben-pa*); but cf. XXI 4a *pravivikta*: Tib. *rab-tu dben-pa'i*!; XTac *prajñā-* (for °*jña-*,K=OV wt.n.).

(X54A) kalahā-(Ta15B)vivāda-vigatā dṛḍha-maitra-cittāḥ
    sarvajña-kāma sada śāsani nimna-cittāḥ // 6 //

pratyanta-mleccha-jana-varjita anta-deśāḥ
    svaka-bhūmi-kāṅ(K16A)kṣa-vigatāḥ sada meru-kalpāḥ /
dharmārtha jīvita tyajanti prayukta-yogāḥ
    a-vivartiyāna imi liṅga (X54B) prajānitavyāḥ // 7 //

bhagavatyāṃ ratna-guṇa-saṃcaya-gāthāyām avinivartanīyākāra-liṅga-nimitta-parivarto nāma saptadaśamaḥ // 17 //

---

6c Tac *karahā-* (for *kalahā-*, KX = OV: Tib. *'thab daṅ rtsod daṅ bral-źiṅ*); cf. AsP 167.11-12 *na ca te kalaha-bhaṇḍana-vigraha-vivāda-kathā-yogānuyogam anuyuktā viharanti*; XTac *cittā* (= OV)(for *-cittāḥ*, K).

6d K *s[a]d[a] śāsani*, Tac *sadṛśāsani* (for *sada śāsani*, X = OV: Tib. *bstan-la* (v.l. *brtan-la*!) *rtag-tu gźol sems ldan*); cf. AsP 167.14 *te tathāgata-darśanam evākāṅkṣanta(ḥ)*.

7a OV *-varjita-antadeśāḥ*, cpd.!; cf. Tib. *mtha'-'khob kla-klo* (v.l. *°-klo'i*) *skye-bo* (v.l. *°-bo'i* = O) *yul mtha' rnam-par spaṅs*!

7b Tc *khaka-* (for *svaka-*, KXTa = OV: Tib. *raṅ-gi*); V sep. *-bhūmi kāṅkṣa-*; XTa *-vigatās* (= O), Tc *-vigatā* (for *°tāḥ*, K = V wt.n.).

7c Tc *tyaṃjāti* (for *tyajanti*, KXTa = OV: Tib. *'dor-źiṅ*); Tc *-yogā* (= V) (for *-yogāḥ*, KXTa = O).

7d Tc *vivartiyāna* (for *aviv°*, KXTa = OV: Tib. *mi ldog*); K reads *jāna* after *avivartiyāna*!; Tc *itimi* (for *imi*, KXTa = OV: Tib. *'di-dag*); XTac *prajānitavyā* (= OV)(for *°itavyāḥ*, K).

XVII col. XTac *avinivartanīya-liṅgākāra-*, O *avivartanīya-liṅgākāra-* (wt.n.), V *avinivartanīya-liṅgākāra-* (wt.n.)(: Tib. *phyir mi ldog-pa'i rtags-kyi rnam-pa*)(for *avinivartanīyākāra-liṅga-nimitta-*, K, so r. AsP XVII); cf. Haribhadra ad Rgs. XVII *phyir mi ldog-pa'i rnam-pa*; Chin. 不退地祥瑞 ; K *-parivartaḥ* (omitting *nāma*)(for *-parivarto nāma*, XTac = OV); XTac *saptādaśamaḥ* (for *saptād°*, K = OV wt.n.); at the end of the colophon K reads *gātha 7* ; and Tc adds num. 17.

## <XVIII. ŚŪNYATĀ>

gambhīra rūpa api vedana cetanā ca
    vijñāna saṃjña prakṛtī a-nimitta śāntāḥ /
kāṇḍena gādhu yatha sāgari eṣamāṇo
    prajñāya (X55A) skandha vimṛśitva a-labdha-gādho // 1 //

yo bodhisattva imu budhyati sarva-dharmān
    gambhīra-yāna-paramārtha-nirūpalepān /
yasmin na skandha (Tc21A) na pi āyatanaṃ na dhātu
    kiṃ vā sa puṇya-samudāgamu kiṃ ci tasya // 2 //

yatha rāga-dharma-carito puruṣo striyāye
    saṃketa (X55B) kṛtva a-labhantu vitarkayeyā /
yāvanti citta-caritā divasena tasya
    tāvanta kalpa anubudhyati bodhisattvo // 3 //

yo bodhisattva bahu-kalpa-sahasra-koṭyo
    dānaṃ dadeyu (Ta16A) raha-pratyaya śīla rakṣe /

---

[1a] Ta *rūpi api*, Tc *rūpāpi* (for *rūpa api*, KX = OV); Tc *tetanā* (for *cet°*, KXTa = OV: Tib. *sems-pa)*.

[1b] XTac *śāntā* (= OV; but V *animitta-°*, cpd.!)(for *śāntāḥ*, K; cf. Edgerton 9.10).

[1c] Tc *kaṇḍena* (= O wt.n.)(for *kāṇḍ°*, KXTa = V: Chin. 杖 , but Tib. *mda'-yis* ); X *gādha* (= OV), Tac *mādha* (for *gādhu*, K: Tib. *gtiṅ*, Chin. 深 ); Ta *eṣamāno* (for *°māṇo*, KXTc = OV).

[1d] Tc *vimṛviṣitvālabdha-*(for *vimṛśitva alabdha-*, KXTa = OV); XTac *-gāthā*, O em. *-gādhā* (= V)(for *-gādho*, K: Tib. *gtiṅ*).

[2a] XTa *buddhyati*, Tc *buddhāti* (cf. Edgerton 28.19, 43 p. 222a, *budh-* 2, s.v.)(for *budhyati*, K, so em. O = V: Tib. *rtogs-pa*); K *budhyati/*; XTac *eva* (= OV; m.c. for *evaṃ*: Tib.A *'di-lta-bur*, B *de-ltar*)(for *sarva-*, K); K *-dharmāṃ* (= V wt.n.; cf. Edgerton 8.90), XTac *dharmāna* (for *-dharmān* = O wt.n.).

[2b] K *-nirūpalepāṃ*(cf. Edgerton 8.90), Tc *-nirūpaleyān* (for *-nirūpalepān*, XTa = OV; cf. Edg.Rgs. 33: Tib.A *gos-pa med-pa'i*, B *chags med)*.

[2c] Tc *yi* (for *pi*, KXTa = OV).

[2d] XTac *sva-* (= OV)(for *sa*,K; but cf. Chin. 有所得福 for Skt. *sa-°*?).

[3a] XTac *-caritaḥ puruṣaḥ* (= OV)(for *-carito puruṣo*, K); Tc *stripāye*(for *striyāye*, KXTa = OV: Tib. *bud-med)*.

[3b] XTac *vivartayeyā* (= OV!)(for *vitarkayeyā*, K: Tib.A *rnam rtog-pa*); cf. AsP 170.30-171.3 *kaś cid eva puruṣo rāga-carito vitarka-caritaḥ / tasya puruṣasya rāga-caritasya vitarka-caritasya striyā ... saha saṃketaḥ kṛto bhavet / sā khalu punaḥ strī para-parigṛhītā bhavet / ... tasya puruṣasya vitarkāḥ pravarteran ...*

[3c] Tc *dinasena* (? blend of *dina-* and *divasa-*)(for *divasena*, KXTa = OV: Tib. *ñin gcig*).

[3d] Ta *tāvanti* (for *tāvanta*, KXTc = OV); Tc *bodhisattvoḥ* (for *°sattvo*, KXTa = OV).

[4b] XTac *vimalaṃ tatha* (= OV: Tib.A *daṅ dri med*)(for *raha-pratyaya*, K: Tib.B *dgra-bcom raṅ-rgyal*, Chin. 羅漢縁覚 ); Tc *śīlaṃ* (for *śīla*, KXTa = OV); K *rakṣed* (followed by no daṇḍa)(for *rakṣe*, XTac = OV; cf. Edgerton 29.12).

yaś caiva prajña-vara-pāramitābhiyukto

dharmaṃ bhaṇeya kala-puṇya na bhoti dānaṃ // 4 //

(X56A) yo bodhisattva vara-prajña vibhāvayanto

tata utthito kathayi dharma nirūpalepaṃ /

taṃ cāpi nāmayi (K16B) jagārtha nidāna bodhau

nāstī tri-loki śubha tena samaṃ bhaveyā // 5 //

taṃ caiva puṇya puna khyāyati riktam eva

tatha śūnya-tuccha-vaśikaṃ ca a-sārakaṃ ca /

eva(X56B)ṃ carantu caratī sugatāna prajñāṃ

caramāṇu puṇyu parigṛhṇati a-prame(Tc21B)yaṃ // 6 //

abhilāpa-mātra imi jānati sarva-dharmā

buddhena deśita prayukta prakāśitāṃś ca /

kalpāna koṭi-niyutān bahu bhāṣyamāṇo

na ca kṣīyate na ca vivardhati dharma-dhātuḥ // 7 //

---

4c XTac *-pāramita-prayukto*, O *-pāramitā-prayukto* (wt.n.)(= V)(for *-pāramitābhiyukto*, K); cf. Tib. *gaṅ-źig śes-rab pha-rol phyin mchog ldan-pa'i chos brjod-pa'i legs-la* (v.l. *legs-pa*), but cf. AsP 171.23-25 *yaś ca bodhisattvo mahā-sattvaḥ prajñā-pāramitā-vihārī ... dharmaṃ deśayet, ayam eva ... bodhisattvo ... tataḥ pauravakād bodhisattvād bahutaraṃ puṇyaṃ prasavati.*

4d V sep. *kala puṇya;* XTac *dāna-śīle* (= OV: Tib.A *sbyin-pa'i khrims-kyis*, v.l. *sbyin daṅ tshul-khrims-kyis*, B *sbyin daṅ tshul-khrims*)(for *bhoti dānaṃ*, K); K *na bhoti dānaṃ* should mean *na* ⟨*sa kalā-puṇyo*⟩ *bhavati* ⟨*yo*⟩ *dānaṃ* ⟨*dadyāt*⟩; cf. III 4d *kala-puṇyu bhoti na sa karitva pūjāṃ.*

5a X *yau* (for *yo*, KTac, so em. O = V: Tib. *gaṅ-źig*); O *-prajña-vibh°*, cpd.

5b Tc *tatotthito* (for *tata utthito*, KXTa = OV); K *nirūpalepan* (no daṇḍa) (for *°lepaṃ*, XTac = OV; but V w. *-m*: Tib. *gos-pa med-pa'i;* cf. Edg.Rgs. 33); cf. XVIII 2b *nirūpalepān* (w. *-dharmān*); but cf. Chin. 若菩薩......... 而無相 (? Skt. *°lepan*, nom.sg.masc.pres.pple. to **lepati*).

5c Tc *nāma* (for *nāmayi*, KXTa = OV: Tib. *bsṅo-na*); X *jagartha* (= O), Tc *jagad-artha* (for *jagārtha*, KTa = V; but V *jagārtha-°*, cpd.!).

5d XTa *nāstis*, Tc *nāsti* (= OV)(for *nāstī*, m.c., so r. Edg.Rgs. 40); XTa *tri-loka* (= OV; but O *tri-loka-*, cpd.!), Tc ⟨*tri-*⟩*loka* (for *tri-loki*, K: Tib. *'jig-rten gsum-na*); XTac *sambhaveyā* (for *samaṃ bhaveyā*, K, so em. O = V: Tib. *mñam-pa ... med*).

6a O *tāṃ* (? mispr.)(for *taṃ*, MSS. = V: Tib. *bsod-nams de-yaṅ*); Tc *rijyam* (for *riktam*, KXTa = OV: Tib.A *gsob*, B *gsog*); cf. Tib. *bsod-nams de-yaṅ* (v.l. *de daṅ*) *gsob* (B *gsog*) *daṅ de-bźin stoṅ-pa daṅ, gsog* (B *gsob*) *daṅ ya-ma-brla daṅ sñiṅ-po med-par snaṅ* (B vv.ll. *med śes-par* = O) *med-par śes*).

6b V sep. *śūnya tuccha vaśikaṃ!*

6c XTac *prajñā* (for *prajñāṃ*, K, so em. O = V).

6d Tc ⟨*pu*⟩*ṇyu;* Tc *parigṛhṇaty* (for *°ati*, KXTa = OV); the neg. prefix *a-* is prosodically long; r. perh. as *a-pp(r)meyaṃ* (cf. I 15c and VII 1b, fn.); V *a-prameyam* (w. *-m*).

7a Ta *abhilāṣa-* (for *°lāpa-*, KXTc = OV: Tib. *brjod-pa*); V *ima* (for *imi*, MSS. = O); XTac *-dharmāṃ* (= V; cf. Edgerton 8.90), O em. *-dharmān* (for *-dharmā*, K; cf. Edgerton 8.92-93).

7b O *deśita-prayukta-prakāśitāṃś*, cpd.

7c K *kalyāṇa*, XTc *kalyāna* (for *kalpāna*, X[Tib.trslit.]Ta = OV: Tib. *bskal-pa*); K *-niyutām*, XTa *-nayutāṃ* (= V), Tc *-nayutā* (for *-niyutān*, so em. O); K *bhāṣyamā*⟨*ṇo*⟩, Tc *bhāṣyamāno*, O *bhāṣyamāṇu* (wt.n.)(for *°māṇo*,

ye cāpi pañca imu pā(X57A)ramitā jinānāṃ
ete 'pi dharma parikīrtita nāma-mātrā /
pa(Ta16B)riṇāmayāti na ca manyati bodhisattvo
na ca hāyate spṛśati uttama-buddha-bodhiṃ // 8 //

bhagavatyāṃ ratna-guṇa-saṃcaya-gāthāyāṃ śūnyatā-parivarto nāmāṣṭādaśamaḥ // 18 //

---

XTa = V; cf. Edgerton 43 p. 233a, *bhāṣ-* 3, s.v.); cf. XXX 8c *bhāṣyate*, 3 sg.pres.act.

7d K *na* <*ca*> *vivardhati*.

8a XTac *imi* (= OV)(for *imu*, K); Tc *pārami pāramitā* (for *pāramitā*, KXTa = OV); KTc *jinānām* (= V)(for °*āṃ*, XTa = O).

8b MSS. *ete pi* (for *ete 'pi* = OV); O em. *-mātrāḥ* (= V)(for *-mātrā*, MSS.).

8c O *bodhisattve* (? mispr.)(for °*sattvo*, MSS. = V); cf. AsP *sa bodhisattvaḥ ... anuttarāyāṃ samyak-saṃbodhau pariṇāmayati* (173.28-29, 174.1-3, 7-8, 11-13, 17-18, 22-23).

8d OV *hīyate* (wt.n.!)(for *hāyate*, MSS.; cf. Edgerton 37.38, 43 p. 238b, *hā-* 2, s.v.: Tib. *ñams-pa*); cf. AsP *iyaṃ ...* °*-pāramitā* (each of the 5 pāramitās) *vivardhate, iyaṃ ...* °*-pāramitā parihīyate* (173.26-27, 173.31-174.1, 174.5-6, 10, 15-16, 20), also AsP 174.25-26 *na ca ... tathatā vivardhate vā, parihīyate vā* (cf. Conze Trsl., p. 150 n. 27); Tc *spṛśaty* (for °*ati*, KXTa = OV); Tc *utama-* (for *uttama-*, KXTa = OV: Tib. *mchog*); V *-bodhim* (w. *-m*).

XVIII col. Tc *-guṇaṃ* (for *-guṇa-*, KXTa = OV); X *nāma aṣṭādaśamaḥ* (= O) (for *nāmāṣṭād*°, KTac = V); at the end of the colophon K reads *gāthā // 8 //* ; and Tc adds num. 18.

## ⟨XIX. GAṄGA-DEVĀ-BHAGINĪ⟩

(X57B) tailasya varti jvalitā prathame nipāte
na ca dagdha varti a-satā na vinā sa dagdhā /
na hi arci-paścima-nipāti sa varti dagdhā
a-satārci-paścima na dahyati dīpa-vartī // 1 //

prathame va citta spṛśatī na ca agra-bodhiṃ
a-satā na tasya (Tc22A) spṛśatā puna śakyu bhotī /
na (X58A) ca citta paścima śivā anuprāpuṇātī
a-satā na tasya puna (Ta17A) prāpuṇanāya śa(K17A)kyaṃ // 2 //

bījātu tamba-phala-puṣpa samāgamantī
so vā niruddha a-sato na hi tasya vṛkṣo /
em eva citta prathame tu nidāna bodhe
so vā niruddha a-sato na hi tasya bodhiḥ // 3 //

---

1a K *prathamaṃ* (for °*me*, XTac=OV = Conze Rgs. 48); Tc *nipāti* (for °*pāte*, KXTa = OV): Tib. *phrad-pa daṅ-po-yis*.

1b XTa *dagva* (for *dagdha*, KTc, so em. O = V: Tib. *tshig*); XTac *vināya* (= O!), V sep. *vinā ya* (for *vinā sa*, K; Conze Rgs. 48 r. K as *vināsa*; it should be analyzed as a pleonastic *vinā* plus *sa*, nom.sg.f.: Tib. *de*); X *dagvā* (for *dagdhā*, KTac, so em. O = V: Tib.A *tshig-pa*, B *tshig*).

1c Tac *arthi-* (for *arci-*, KX = OV; but OV sep. *arci paścima-*!); XTac *-nipāta* (= OV)(for *-nipāti*, K): Tib.A *me-lce tha-ma phrad-pas*, B *me-lce phrad-pa tha-mas*; Tc *ma* (for *sa*, KXTa = OV); X *dagvā* (for *dagdhā*, KTac, so em. O = OV: Tib. *tshig*).

1d XTac *asatāvi*, O *asatā pi* (wt.n.)(= V)(for *asatârci-*, K, so r. Conze ad O p. 127: Tib.A *me-lce tha-ma med-pas*!, B *me-lce phrad-pa tha-mas*; cf. V p. 375 n. 3); V *-varti* (wt.n.)(for *-vartī*, MSS. = O); cf. AsP 175. 9-11 *na hi ... arciṣā prathamābhinipātena sā vartir dagdhā / na ca prathamābhinipātam anāgamya arciṣā sā vartir dagdhā / na ca ... paścimābhinipātenārciṣā sā vartir dagdhā, na ca paścimābhinipātam anāgamya sā vartir dagdhā*.

2a Ta *prathamevaś*, OV *prathameva* (wt.n.)(for *prathame va*, KXTc; for *va* = *eva*, cf. Edgerton 4.2, 6, 17, BHSD p. 466a, *va*, s.v.); Tc *-bodhiṃm*, V *-bodhim* (w. *-m*)(for *-bodhiṃ*, KXTa = O).

2b K *śanyu*, XTc *śakya*(= OV), Ta *śakyo* (for *śakyu*: Tib. *nus*); X *bhyonti*, Ta *bhonti*, so em. O (= V!), Tc *bhyoti* (for *bhotī*, K; cf. Edg.Rgs. 13).

2c K [*na ca*] *citta paści*[*ma ś*]*ivā*; Tc *vanti* (for *ca citta*, XTa = OV: Tib. *sems-kyis*); XTc *śivām* (= OV)(for *śivā*, KTa); Ta *anuprāpunātī*, Tc *anuprāvuṇā⟨tī⟩*, V *anuprāpuṇāti* (for *anuprāpuṇātī*, KX = O).

2d XTa *puṇa* (for *puna*, KTc, so em. O = V; Conze Rgs. 48 wrongly reports that O om. *puna*); Ta *prāpunanāya śakyaṃ* (folio 17A1) *prāpunanāya śakyaṃ* (so repeated); XTa *prāpunanāya*, Tc *prāpunarāya*, V em. *prāpaṇanāya* (for *prāpuṇanāya*, K, so em. O); V *śakyam* (w. *-m*).

3a Tc *bījñātu* (for *bījātu*, KXTa = OV: Tib. *sa-bon-las-ni*); XTac *stamba-* (= OV; but O sep. *stamba phala-*°, V *stamba phala puṣpa*!)(for *tamba-*, K; cf. Edg.Rgs. 8; cf. Tib. *myu-gu* 'sprout', Chin. 樹 ); XTac *samāgamanti* (= OV)(for °*antī*, K; cf. Edg.Rgs. 13).

3b O *va* (? mispr.)(for *vā*, MSS.; cf. Edg.Rgs. 40); cf. XIX 3d *vā* = *eva* (cf. Edgerton 4.2, 6, 17, 3.6, BHSD p. 475b, *vā*, s.v.); V *vāniruddha*!; Ta *vṛkṣā*, Tc *vṛkṣoḥ* (for *vṛkṣo*, KX = OV).

3c XTa *prathaman*, Tc °*maṃ* (= OV)(for °*me*, K; cf. XIX 5c °*me*); K [*n*]*i*[*dāna bodhe*](K *bodhau*?); XTac *bodheḥ* (= OV)(for *bodhe*); cf. Tib. *de-bźin daṅ-po'i sems-kyaṅ byaṅ-chub rgyu yin-te*.

(X58B) bījaṃ pratītya ca bhaved yava-śālikādes
    tat tat phalaṃ na ca tad asti na cāpi nāsti /
utpattito bhavati bodhir iyaṃ jinānāṃ
    bhāva-sva-bhāva-rahitā bhavatīha māyā // 4 //

daka-bindu kumbha paripūryati stoka-stokaṃ
    prathame nipāti anupūrva sa paścimena /
(X59A) em eva citta prathame vara-bodhi-hetuḥ
    anupūrva śukla-guṇa-pūrṇa bhavanti buddhāḥ // 5 //

śūnyānimitt'-a-praṇidhīṃ caramāṇu dharmān
    na ce nirvṛtiṃ spṛśati no ca nimi(Tc22B)tta-cārī /

---

4 Only X has a Tibetan version of this verse; there is a corresponding Chinese verse.

4a Tc *pratītyaṃ* (for °*tya*, KXTa = OV: Tib. *rñed-nas*); K *bhavet* (so r. Conze ad O p. 127!)(for *bhaved*, XTac = OV); XTa *yatha* (= O), Tc *yathā* (for *yava-*, K, so r. Conze ad O p. 127 = V after having misr. O as *yava*!: Tib. *'bru*, Chin. 麦 ); XTac *śālikāde* (= O)(for *-śālikādes*, K = V; Conze Rgs. 57 misr. K as *-śālīkādes)*.

4b XTa *tat tat tat*, Tc *tatat* (for *tat tat*, K, so em. O = V: Tib. *de-yaṅ*, Chin. 彼 ); K *tadāsti*, Tc *⟨ta⟩d asti* (for *tad asti*, XTa = OV: Tib. *de-la yod)*.

4c Tc *ubhyastito bhava⟨ti⟩* (for *utpattito bhavati*, KXTa = OV; Tib. *'byuṅ-bar 'gyur)*.

4d X *bhāva-svabhāva-viditā*, Ta *bhāvaṃ vatāva-viditā*, Tc *bhāvaṃ vatā-viditā*, O em. *bhāva-svabhāva-vigatā* (= V)(for *bhāva-svabhāva-rahitā*, K; cf. Tib. *dṅos-po'i raṅ-bžin bral-bas)*; the final *-a-* of *bhāva-* is prosodically long; it could be *bhāvaṃ-*° as suggested by MSS. Tac (cf. Edgerton 8.14); Tac *bhavatīda* (*bhavati* plus *ida*, or poss. *idha*, cf. Pāli *ida*, *idha*)(for *bhavatīha*, KX = OV; but *iha* is not rendered into Tib.; Tib. *bhavatī ha*?).

5a XTac *udaka-*, unmetr. (= OV!)(for *daka-*, K: Tib. *chu-yi;* cf. Edg.Rgs. 40).

5b XTa *anupūrve* (= O), Tc °*purva* (for °*pūrva*, K; Conze Rgs. 48 misr. K as °*pūrvaṃ*, which Edg.Rgs. 34 em. to °*pūrva* = V: Tib. *rim-gyis)*.

5c MSS. *prathamaṃ* (= OV)(for °*me;* but Tib. *daṅ-po'i sems-kyaṅ;* cf. XIX 3c *citta prathame* : Tib. *daṅ-po'i sems-kyaṅ*); Tc *-hetur* (= V)(for *-hetuḥ*, KXTa = O).

5d Tac *anupurva* (for °*pūrva*, KX = OV: Tib. *rim-gyis*); O mispr. *anupūrvaśukla-*°*;* Tc *-purṇa* (for *-pūrṇa*, KXTa = OV: Tib. *rdzogs-pa*, v.l. °*-pa'i)*.

6a Tc *-cimitta-* (for *-nimitta-*, KXTa = OV: Tib. *mtshan*); XTac *-praṇidhiṃ* (= OV; cf. Edgerton 10.166)(for °*īṃ*, K; cf. Edgerton 10.165); OV print *śūnyānimittapraṇidhiṃ* (for *śūnyânimitt'-apranidhīṃ*: Tib. *stoṅ-pa mtshan med smon-pa med-par*, v.l. °*-pa'i*; Chin. 空無相無願); cf. XX 14c *śūnyânimitt'-apraṇidhīṃ ... dharmān;* also AsP 184.22 *śūnyatām ānimittam apraṇihitaṃ ca* (cf. BHSD p. 47a, *a-praṇihita-*, s.v.); Tc *caramāṇū* (for °*māṇu*, KXTa = OV); XTac *dharmā* (= OV; cf. Edgerton 8.92-93)(for *dharmān*, K).

6b Tc *na va* (for *na ca*, KXTa = OV); XTac *nivṛtti* (= O!)(for *nirvṛtiṃ*, K, so r. Conze ad O p. 127 = V wt.n.: Tib. *mya-ṅan 'das-la*, Chin. 寂静 ).

6c K *-pāram* (= V wt.n.), Tc *-pāra* (for *-pāraṃ*, XTa = O).

6d XTa *ubhayānti* (= OV), Tc *abhayāṃty* (for *ubhayānta-*, K); *-a-* of *a-sthitu* is long by position; cf. Tib. *mtha' gñis mi gnas*, Chin. 不著兩岸 ; K *arṇavesmin* (= V wt.n.; cf. Edgerton 8.70-73), XTac *ārṇavesmin*, O *ārṇave 'smin* (for *arṇave 'smin;* cf. Edg.Rgs. 40; also Bernhard, 'Gab

yatha nāviko kuśala gacchati āra-pāraṃ
    ubhayānta-a-sthitu na (X59B) tiṣṭhati arṇave 'smin // 6 //

evaṃ carantu na ca manyati bodhisattvo
    ahu vyākṛto daśa-balehi spṛśeya bodhiṃ /
na ca trāsu bodhi bhavate na ihāsti kiṃ cid
    evaṃ carantu carate sugatāna prajñāṃ // 7 //

kāntāra pāniya-dubhikṣa sa-vyādhi lokān
    paśyatva nāsti bha(X60A)ya ottari saṃnahante /
aparanta-(Ta17B)koṭi sada yukta prajānamānā
    aṇu-mātru khedu manasā na upādayanti // 8 //

---

es einen Lokativ auf *-esmiṃ* im buddhistischen Sanskrit?', 1964).

7a Tc *manya⟨ti⟩*.

7b K *-baleti* (for *-balehi*, XTac = OV: Tib. *stobs bcus*); Tc *spaya* (for *spṛśeya*, KXTa = OV: Tib.A *reg-par*, B *reg 'gyur* ); Tc *bodhi* (for *bodhiṃ*, KXTa = OV; but V w. *-m*).

7c Tc *trāsū* (for *trāsu*, KXTa = OV); XTac *ihasti* (for *ihâsti*, K, so em. O = V): XTa *cit* (= O)(for *cid*, KTc = V); cf. Tib. *'di-la ci-yaṅ med ces byaṅ-chub skrag-pa med.*

7d XTac *caratī* (= OV)(for *carate*, K); XTa *sugatān*, Tc *sugatāṃ* (for *sugatāna*, K, so em. O = V); V *prajñām* (w. *-m*).

8a XTac *kāntāra-mārgi* (= OV: Tib.A *dgon-pa'i lam-na*, B *dgon-pa'i lam*) (for *kāntāra pāniya-*, K; Conze Rgs. 40 misr. K as *kāntāra-yāniya*!); K *-durbhikṣa*, XTa *durabhikṣi* (= OV, w. epenthetic *-a-* for *durbh°*; cf. Edg. Rgs. 12, p. 4 n. 1 (for *dubhikṣa*; Edg.Rgs., *loc.cit.*, wrongly takes *dur-* of *durbhikṣa* as a long syllable for two shorts prosodically, because he has missed *pāniya-* in consequence of Conze's misreading); XTa *lokāṃ* (= V; cf. Edgerton 8.90), Tc *lokā*, O em. *lokaṃ* (for *lokān*, K: Tib.A *'jig-rten-rnams*, B *'jig-rten*); OV *kāntāra-mārgi durabhikṣi sa-vyādhi lokaṃ* (V *lokāṃ*): Tib.A *dgon-pa'i lam-na lo-ñes nad bcas 'jig-rten-rnams*, but Tib.B *'jig-rten dgon-pa'i lam daṅ mu-ge nad bcas-par* (= Conze trsl. ?); cf. AsP 178.24ff., where one finds bodhisattvas in the midst of 5 *kāntāras*: *vyāla-kāntāra-madhya-gatena bodhisattvena mahā-sattvena nottrasitavyam, na saṃtrasitavyam, na saṃtrāsam āpattavyam* (178.24-25); *cora-kāntāra-madhya-gatena ...* (178.31-32); *pānīya-kāntāra-madhya-gatena ...* (179.11-12); *bubhukṣā-kāntāra-madhya-gatena ...* (179.24-25); *vyādhi-kāntāra-madhya-gatena ...* (180.3-4).

8b Edg.Rgs. 40 wonders if O *paśyatva* (so MSS.) is a misprint and em. it to *paśyitva* (= V); *paśyatva* is a peculiar and noteworthy gerund in *-tva* added to the present stem *paśya-*, or added superfluously to *paśya* which is already a peculiar ger. (cf. Edgerton 35.16 for ger. *paś-ya*); XTac *uttari* (= OV)(for *ottari*, K), cf. Tib.A *bsgral-pa'i* (? Skt. *ud-* plus *tara-* 'crossing'), B *de-nas* (? Skt. *ud-* plus comp. suffix *tara-*, i.e. *uttara-* /*ottara-*'later'); Tc *saṃnnahaṃta* (for *saṃnahante*, KXTa = OV: T Tib. *go gyon-te*); cf. AsP 179.25 *evaṃ cānena saṃnāhah saṃnāhyaḥ*, AsP 180.15-16 *evaṃ ca ... bodhisattvena mahā-sattvena mahā-saṃnāhaḥ saṃnaddhavyaḥ*.

8c XTac *aparānta-* (= OV)(for *aparanta-*, K; cf. BHSD p. 44b, *aparanta-koṭi-*, s.v.); K *prajñānamānā*, X *prajñānumānā*, Ta *prajānumānā*, Tc *prajāvamāno*, O *prajānu māna*(wt.n.!), V *prajānamāno* (wt.n.)(for *prajānamānā*).

8d K *anumātru*, XTac *anumātra*, OV *aṇu-mātra* (wt.n.)(for *aṇu-mātru*; cf. VII 3b, fn.); XTac *kheda* (= OV)(for *khedu*, K); V *manaso* (wt.n.)(for *manasā*, MSS. = O); Tc *nopayādayati*, V em. *na upādiyanti* (? w. Tib.B *skyed ... byed*)(for *na upādayanti*, KXTa = O: Tib.A *skyed-pa*).

bhagavatyāṃ ratna-guṇa-saṃcaya-gā(K17B)thāyāṃ gaṅga-devā-bhaginī-parivarto nāmaikonaviṃśatimaḥ // 19 //

---

XIX col. K (somewhat damaged) *gaṅga-devā-bhaginyā-*, O em. *gaṅgā-devī-bhaginī-* (for *gaṅga-devā-bhaginī-*, XTac = V: Tib. *driṅ-mo gaṅga'i lha-mo*; O p. 71 n. 1 misr. X as *gaṅga-demā-°*; cf. BHSD p. 207a, *gaṅgadevī bhaginī*, s.v.); XTa *nāma ekonnaviṃśatimaḥ*, Tc *nāmaikānnaviṃśatitamaḥ*, O *nāma ekonaviṃśatimaḥ* (wt.n.), V *nāmaikānnaviṃśatimaḥ* (wt.n.)(for *nāmaikonaviṃśatimaḥ*, K); at the end of the colophon K reads *gāthā 8*; and Tc adds num. 19.

K reads cardinals in the colophons of chapters 20-31; they are most probably to be emended to ordinals ending in a suffix *-ma-*, as K itself reads in the colophons of chapters 19 and 32 (cf. Edgerton 19.36 for ordinals in Middle Indic *-ma-* instead of Sanskrit *-tama-*; cf. also Wackernagel-Debrunner III para. 206c); it is unlikely that cardinals 20-31 are used for ordinals (cf. S. Sen, *A Comparative Grammar of Middle Indo-Aryan*, 1960, para. 114).

## ⟨XX. UPĀYA-KAUŚALYA-MĪMĀṂSĀ⟩

puna bodhisattva caramāṇu jināna (X60B) prajñāṃ
    an-upāda skandha iti jānati ādi-śūnyaṃ /
a-samāhito karuṇa prekṣati sattva-dhātuṃ
    atrāntare na parihāyati (Tc23A) buddha-dharme // 1 //

puruṣo yathā kuśalu sarva-guṇair upeto
    balavān dudharṣu kṛta-yogya kalā-vidhijño /
iṣv-astra-pārami-gato pṛthu-śilpa-yu(X61A)kto
    māyā-vidhijña-paramo jagad-artha-kāmo // 2 //

mātā-pitā grahiya so svaka-putra-dārān
    kāntāra-mārgi pratipadyi bahū-a-mitre /

---

1a Tc *bodhisattvo* (for °*sattva*, KXTa = OV); Tc *cara⟨mā⟩ṇu*; Tc *jinānāṃ* (for *jināna*, KXTa = OV); K *prajñām*, O *prajāṃ* (? mispr.)(for *prajñāṃ*, XTac = V).

1b XTac *imi* (= OV)(for *iti*, K); X *ādhiśūnyāṃ*, Tac *ādhiśūnyāṃ*, O em. *ādi-śūnyān* (= V)(for *ādi-śūnyaṃ*,K);cf.Tib. *phuṅ-po 'di-dag gdod-nas stoṅ-źiṅ skye med śes*, and AsP 183.4-5 *bodhisattvena mahā-sattvena prajñā-pāramitāyāṃ caratā rūpaṃ śūnyam iti pratyavekṣitavyam / evaṃ vedanā saṃjñā saṃskārāḥ / vijñānaṃ śūnyam iti pratyavekṣitavyam.*

1c K *-dhātum* (= V), Tc *-dhātuṃm* (for *-dhātuṃ*, XTa = O).

1d KXTa *atrāntareṇa* (= O!), Tc *aṃtrāṃtareṇa* (for *atrântare na*, so em. Conze ad O p. 127 = V); Ta *-dharma*, Tc *-dharmaḥ*, V *-dharmān* (wt.n.)(for *-dharme*, KX = V); cf. Tib. *bar skabs der-yaṅ saṅs-rgyas chos-la* (1 MS. °*-las*) *yoṅs mi nams*, also AsP 183.14 *atrāntarā bodhisattvo mahā-sattvo na parihīyate bodhi-pakṣair dharmaiḥ.*

2a Ta *puruṣo hi yathā* (hypermetr.); XTac *kuśala* (= OV)(for °*lu*, K); XTa *-guṇer*, Tc *-guṇen* (for *-guṇair*, K = OV wt.n.: Tib. *yon-tan kun* (v.l. *daṅ*) *ldan-źiṅ*).

2b Tc *baravāṃn* (for *balavān*,KXTa = OV: Tib. *stobs ldan*); K *durvarṣu* (Conze Rgs. 48 misr. K as °*dharṣu*), X *dudhaṣu*, Ta *dudhuṣu*, Tc *du⟨...⟩* (for *dudharṣu* = OV wt.n.: Tib. *mi thub*); X *kalā-vidijño*, Ta *-kalā-vijño*, Tc *kalā-vijñoḥ* (for *kalā-vidhijño*, K, so em. O = V: Tib.B *sgyu-rtsal cho-ga śes*, but Tib.A *sgyu-rstal brtson byas tshul śes-la!*); cf. AsP 183.25-26 *sarvāsu ca kalāsu parama-kuśalo bhavet:* Tib. (Peking MI 218B1) *sgyur-rtsal* (r. *sgyu-rtsal*) *thams-cad-la rab-tu mkhas-par gyur-pa.*

2c XTa *iṣṭhastra-* (= O!), Tc *iṣastra-* (for *iṣv-astra-*, K, so em. Conze ad O p. 127 = V: Tib. *'phoṅ*); Tc *-pārami-⟨ga⟩to;* Tc *pṛthi-*, O *pṛṣu-* (? mispr.)(for *pṛthu-*, KXTa, so em. V: Tib. *maṅ-po'i*); Tc *-yukte* (for *-yukto*, KXTa = OV); cf. Tib. *'phoṅ daṅ bzo-gnas maṅ-po'i pha-rol phyin gyur-ciṅ!*; AsP 183.25-26 *iṣv-astre ca parama-gatiṃ gato bhavet, ... sarveṣv eva ca śilpa-sthāneṣu parama-gatiko bhavet:* Tib. (Peking MI 218A8-B1) *'phoṅ skyen-pa'i mthar phyin-par gyur-pa, ... bzo'i gnas thams-cad-kyi śin-tu mthar phyin-par gyur-pa.*

2d Tc *-kāṃmoḥ* (for *-kāmo*, KXTa = OV).

3a XTac *mātā pitā ca parigṛhya* (Tc °*gṛjya*) *sa-putra-dāraṃ* (= OV); prob. separate *sa putra-*° contextually, unless *sa-* is used for *sva-;* cf. Tib. *pha daṅ ma daṅ chuṅ-mar bcas-par* (v.l. °*-pa* = O) *yoṅs bsdus-pa!*; Conze Rgs. 48 misr. K as *grahiyo so svaja-* (for *grahiya so svaka-*); cf. AsP 184.3-4 *sa ... putras ... mātā-pitṛ-putra-dārān gṛhītvā ...*

3b K *kāntāri mārgi* (for *kāntāra-mārgi*, XTac = OV: Tib. *dgon-pa'i lam-du;* cf. X 3a *kāntāra-mārga* (B °*-mārgi*), XIX 8a *kāntāra* (B *kāntāra-mārgi*); XTac *pratiyadya*, O em. °*padya* (= V)(for °*padyi*, K: Tib. *phyin-pa;* cf.

so nirmiṇitva puruṣān bahu-śūra-vīrān

kṣemeṇa gatva puna geham upāgameyā // 3 //

em eva tasmi samaye vidu bodhisattvo

maha-maitri sa(X61B)rvi upapadyati sattva-dhātau /

caturo sa māra atikramya dvaye ca bhūmī

agre samādhi sthiti no ca spṛśāti bodhiṃ // 4 //

ākāśa niśrayi samāruta āpa-skandho

tahi niśritā ima mahā-pṛthivī jagac ca /

---

AsP 184.4-5 *mahāṭavī-kāntāraṃ pratipanno bhavet)*; XTa *bahū-amitro* (= V), O *bahū-amatro* (? mispr.), Tc *bahu-amitroḥ* (for *bahū-amitre*, K: Tib.*dgra byed maṅ-ba*); cf. AsP 184.8-9 *tatra ... aṭavī-kāntāre tasya puruṣasya ... bahavaḥ pratyamitrāḥ pratyupasthitā bhaveyuḥ*.

3c XTac *puruṣā* (= O)(for *°ān*, K = V wt.n.); V sep. *bahu śūra-*.

3d XTac *kṣemena* (for *°eṇa*, K, so em. O = V: Tib. *bde-bar*); XTac *upāgameyyā* (= V; cf. Edgerton 29.23), O *upăgameyyā* (? mispr.)(for *upāgameyā*,K).

4a K *tasmin* (Conze Rgs. 48 misr. K as *tasmi*), XTac *yasmi* (= OV)(for *tasmi*: Tib. *de-tshe;* but cf. AsP 184.26, 29 *yasmin samaye...*); O *vidu-*, cpd.

4b Tac *-maitrī* (for *-maitri*, KX = OV); XTac *upabandhati* (= OV)(for *upapadyati*, K: Tib.A *skyed*, B *bskyed-ciṅ*, v.l. *skyed-ciṅ* = O); cf. AsP 184.26-27 *sarva-sattvānam antike maitrī-cittam ārambaṇī-kṛtya tān paramayā maitryā paribadhnāti;* XTac *-dhāto* (= O)(for *-dhātau*, K, so r. Edg. Rgs. 40 = V: Tib. *sems-can khams-rnams kun-la*, B ... *kun-tu)*.

4c K *māri* (for *māra*, XTac = OV); Tc *dvaya* (for *dvaye*, KXTa = OV); XTac *bhūmim* (= O), V *bhūmim* (for *bhūmī*, K, so r. Edg.Rgs. 40 as pl.); cf. Tib. *bdud bži-dag daṅ sa gñis-las-kyaṅ rab 'das-nas;* also AsP 184.22-23 *na tv eva bhūta-koṭiṃ sākṣāt karoti, yad uta śrāvaka-bhūmau vā pratyeka-buddha-bhūmau vā*, AsP 184.27-28 *māra-pakṣaṃ cātikramya śrāvaka-bhūmiṃ pratyeka-buddha-bhūmiṃ cātikramya tatra samādhāv avatiṣṭhate ...*

4d X *asmiṃ* (= O), Tac *asmin* (= V): Tib.A *'di-la*! (for *agre*, K: Tib.B *mchog-la*!, Chin. 第一三摩地 !; so r. Conze Rgs. 48); XTa *sthitu no* (= V), Tc *ṣṭhitu no*, O *sthituno* (for *sthiti no*, K); Conze Rgs. 48 r. *sthitino* (w. K; but trsl. w. Tib.B!), which Edg.Rgs. 40 takes as a gen. of *sthiti-* 'permanent abiding'; plausible is either *sthitu* (nom.sg.m. ppp.) w. *no* (m.c. for neg. *na*) or *sthiti* (loc.sg.m.ppp.) w. *no*; K should have meant *agre samādhau sthite sati tena bodhisattvena;* Tc *va* (for *ca*, KXTa = OV); XTac *spṛśānti* (for *°āti*, K = OV wt.n.); V *bodhim* (w. *-m*); cf. Tib.A *tiṅ-'dzin 'di-la* (Skt. *asmin / asmiṃ;* but B *mchog-la*: Skt. *agre*) *gnas-śiṅ* (= *sthiti / sthitu*) *byaṅ-chub reg mi* (= *no*) *byed*: Haribhadra (Peking JA 63B8) *tiṅ-ṅe-'dzin mchog-la gnas-śiṅ / byaṅ-chub reg-par mi byed-de;* Chin. 安住第一三摩地……亦復不求 (= *no ca spṛhāti*!) 仏菩提.

5 This verse is quoted by Candrakīrti in his *Prasannapadā* (ed. L. de La Vallée Poussin, 166.11-167.2); for further details see Yuyama, '*Candrakīrti* no *Prasannapadā* ni Inyōsareta *Prajñāpāramitā-Ratnaguṇasaṃcayagāthā*' (1970).

5a X *niśritu* (= O; but O *ākāśa-niśritu*, cpd.), Ta *niśrita* (= V; but V *ākāśa-niśrita*, cpd.), Tc *niśi* (for *niśrayi*, K; Conze Rgs. 49 r. K as *-niśrayi*, cpd.!; this is not acceptable; *niśrayi* is 3 sg.opt., m.c. for *niśraye, niśrayet);* XTac *samīraṇa* (= OV)(for *samāruta*, K: Tib. *rluṅ);* cf. Tib.Rgs. = Prasannapadā (Tib.) *mkha'-la rluṅ brten de-la chu-yi phuṅ-po brten* (ed. La Vallée Poussin, p. 166 n. 8); cf. also Prasannapadā 166.11 *ākāśa-niśrita samāruta āpa-khandho* (r. *°-skandho* w. MSS.).

5b XTac *na hi* (= O)(for *tahi*, K; Conze ad O p. 128 r. *ta hi* = V!; cf. V p. 377 n. 1); *tahi*, loc.sg., is without doubt one word (cf. Edg.Rgs. 40, Edgerton 21.22, BHSD p. 250b, q.v.): Tib. *de-la;* XTac *iha* (= OV)(for

(Ta18A) sattvāna karma-upabhoga-nidānam evaṃ
    ākāśa-sthānu kutu cinta(X62A)yi etam arthaṃ // 5 //

em e(Tc23B)va śūnyata-pratiṣṭhitu bodhisattvo
    jagatī kriyā vividha darśayate vicitrā /
sattvāna jñāna-praṇidhān'-adhi(K18A)ṣṭhānam eva
    na ca nirvṛtiṃ spṛśati śūnyata nāsti sthānaṃ // 6 //

yasmiṃś ca kāli vidu-paṇḍitu bodhisattvo
    caratī imāṃ pravara-śūnya-samā(X62B)dhi śāntāṃ /
atrāntare na ca nimittu prabhāvitavyo
    na ca ānimittu-sthitu śānta-praśānta-cārī // 7 //

---

*ima*, K, so r. Edg.Rgs. 40: Tib. *'di*); XTc *jagac cha* (for *jagac ca*, KTa, so em. O = V: Tib. *'gro-ba;* Conze Rgs. 49 misr. K as *jagad ca;* one can read *jagac* although K is slightly damaged; cf. Tib. Rgs. = Tib. Prasannapadā (ed. La Vallée Poussin, p. 166 n. 8) *de-la sa chen 'di brten de-la 'gro-ba brten;* cf. also Prasannapadā 166.12 *tahi* (MSS. *bahi;* La Vallée Poussin em. *tan-*) *niśritā iya mahī* (r. most prob. *mahā-*)*pṛthivī jagac ca*.

5c Tc *-nidānaṃm* (for *-nidānam*, KXTa = OV); XTac *eva* (= OV)(for *evaṃ*, K, so r. Conze Rgs. 49: Tib. *de 'dra-ste*); cf. Tib. Rgs. (Tib. missing in the Prasannapadā) *sems-can las-la spyod-pa'i rgyu-ni de-'dra-ste;* cf. also Prasannapadā (ed. La Vallée Poussin, 167.1) *sattvāna karma-upabhoga-nidānam evaṃ* (so La Vallée Poussin; MSS. *evam*).

5d Tc *kutra* (for *kutu*, KXTa = OV: Tib.B *gaṅ-la*); Tc *artha* (for *arthaṃ*, KXTa = OV; but V w. *-m*); cf. Tib.A *don de mkha'-la gnas-pa yin-par bsam-par bya*, B *nam-mkha' gaṅ-la gnas yin don 'di bsam-par gyis* (no Tib. Prasannapadā is available); cf. also Prasannapadā (ed. La Vallée Poussin, 167.2) *ākāśa-thānu* (r. °*-sthānu* w. MSS.) *kṛta-cittama* (so La Vallée Poussin with doubt; em. MSS. *kṛta-cittama* to *kutu cintayi* as in Rgs.) *etam arthaṃ* (MSS. *artha*, et *kṛtta*, *kṛtteṣa*!).

6a V em. *eṣa sattvo* (for *bodhisattvo*, MSS. = O: Tib. *byaṅ-chub-sems-dpa'*, Chin. 菩薩 ); Vaidya's em. is absolutely unnecessary.

6b K [*jagatī kriyā*]; XTac *jagati* (= OV!)(for *jagatī*, m.c. for *jagati:* Tib. *'gro-ba;*cf. Edg.Rgs. 32); XTa *kriyāṃ* (= OV)(for *kriyā*, Tc); XTa *vicitrāṃ* (= OV; but V w. *-m*), Tc *vicitra* (for *vicitrā*, K, acc.pl.f.); but cf. XX 12c *vividhāṃ kriyāṃ jagati darśayate anantāṃ*.

6c Tc *sittvāna* (for *sat°*, KXTa = OV); K *-praṇidhānadhiṣṭhānam eva*,XTac *-praṇidhāna-balāna sevaṃ* (= O; Tc *senaṃ*)(for *-praṇidhān'-adhiṣṭhānam eva*); Conze Rgs. 57 misr. K as *seva*; Conze ad O p. 128 misr. K as °*āna-adhiṣṭhānam eva* (= V; hypermetr.!); Edg.Rgs. 40 em. *dhiṭhāna*, m.c. (cf. Pāli *adhiṭṭhāna-*); cf. Tib.A *sems-can-rnams-kyi śes daṅ smon-lam stobs-brten-te*, B *sems-can śes-pa'i smon-lam brten-can-gyis;* Chin.以衆生智及願力.

6d K *nirvṛti*, Tc *nirjñatiṃ* (for *nirvṛtiṃ*, XTa = OV); cf. *na ca nirvṛtiṃ spṛśati* I 7d, X 9d, XIX 6b, XX 8d, 14d; XTa *sthānāṃ*, Tc *sthānā* (for *sthānaṃ*, K, so em. O = V w. *-m*).

7a K *asmiṃś ca*, Tc *yaś ci* (for *yasmiṃś ca*, XTa = OV: Tib.*gaṅ-gi tshe-na);* V sep. *vidu paṇḍitu*.

7b XTa *caratīti māṃ*(= O), Tc *caratīti mā* (for *caratī imāṃ*, K, so r.Edg. Rgs. 40 = V: Tib. ... *'di spyod-pa*); K [*pravara-śū*]*nya-;* O *pravara śūnya-samādhi-śāntāṃ*, V *pravara śūnya samādhi śāntām* (for °*-śūnya-samādhi śāntāṃ*: Tib. *stoṅ-pa ži-ba'i tiṅ-'dzin dam-pa*); cf. *śānti-samādhi śreṣṭhāṃ* I 10d.

7c K *na* (for *na*, XTac = OV: Tib. *mi*); XTac *nimitta* (= OV)(for °*ttu*, K); K *prabhāvita*[*vy*]*o*.

7d XTac *ānimitta-* (= OV)(for °*ttu-*, K); K *-praśānta-* (for °*śānta-*, XTac = OV; but V sep. *śānta pra°*); cf. Tib. *mtshan-ma med-par gnas-žiṅ ži-la rab ži spyod*, but Chin. 亦復不見彼非相.

pakṣisya nāsti padu gacchati antarīkṣe

no cāpi tatra sthiti no ca patāti bhūmau /

tatha bodhisattva caramāṇu vimokṣa-dvāre

na ca nirvṛtiṃ spṛśati no ca nimitta-cārī // 8 //

(X63A) iṣv-astra-śikṣita yathā puruṣordha kāṇḍaṃ

kṣepitva anya puna kāṇḍa parampareṇa /

patanāya tasya purimasya na deya bhūmiṃ

ākāṅkṣamāṇa puruṣasya pateya kāṇḍaṃ // 9 //

em eva prajña-vara-pāramitāṃ ca(Tc24A)ranto

prajñā-upāya-bala-ṛddhi vicāramāṇo /

---

8a XTac *nasti* (for *nāsti*, K, so em. O = V); K *yadu* (for *padu*, XTac = OV: Tib. *gnas*); XTac *gacchate*, O em. *gacchata* (= V!)(for *gacchati*, K); *pakṣisya ... gacchati* is an absolute expression (cf. XXV 3c, fn., for similar constructions); cf. Tib. *bar-snaṅ 'phur-ba'i bya-la!*, but Chin. 飛鳥空而往来, AsP 185.1 *pakṣī śakunir ākāśe 'ntarīkṣe carati*.

8b Tc *cāyi* (for *cāpi*, KXTa = OV); K *sthi[ti]*, XTac *sthitu* (= OV)(for *sthiti*); *sthiti*, nom.sg.f. (and not loc.sg.ppp.), seems to be the true reading: Tib. *de-na gnas-pa ma yin;* but cf. XX 4d *agre samādhi sthiti* (loc.ppp.; Skt.B *sthitu*, nom.); K *patā⟨ti bhūmau⟩*: Tib. *sa-la ltuṅ mi 'gyur;* cf. Chin. 非住虚空非住地 ; also AsP 185.1-3 *na ca bhūmau patati, na ca kaṃ cin niśrayaṃ niśritya tiṣṭhati, ākāśa evāntarīkṣe viharati, na ca tatrāpi niśrito na pratiṣṭhitaḥ.*

8c Tc *tathai bodhisattvo caramāṇū* (for *tatha bodhisattva caramāṇu*, KXTa = OV).

9a MSS. *puruṣordha*(= O; but O may have intended *puruṣodha*, because O p. 74 n. 1 has expressly made a note on X *°ordha*), V *puruṣodha* (wt.n.!); *puruṣodha* (*puruṣo* plus *adhas* 'downwards'?) is impossible; *puruṣordha* can only be analyzed as *puruṣa(ḥ)* plus *ūrdh(v)a(ṃ)* with secondary sandhi, i.e. *puruṣordha:* Tib.A *gyen-du* 'upwards', B *gnam-du* 'into the air' (cf. BHSD p. 150a, *ūrdha-*, s.v.); cf. *ūrdha-* XVI 1c; also AsP 185.7 *sa ūrdhvaṃ kāṇḍaṃ kṣipet / ūrdhvaṃ kāṇḍaṃ kṣiptvā ...*: Tib. (Peking MI 220A2-3)*des mda' steṅ-du 'phaṅs-te mda' 'phaṅs-nas ...;* cf. Mvy 5092 *kāṇḍam ūrdhva-mukhaṃ* (Wogihara Mvy 223.20 *ūrdha-°*) *kṣiptam*: Tib. *mda' gnam-rgyaṅ-du 'phaṅs-pa / mda' rtse-mo (? kāṇḍa-mūrdhan-) (r)gyen-du (? kham) bstan-te 'phaṅs-pa.*

9b Tc *punaḥ* (for *puna*, KXTa = OV); XTac *paraspareṇa* (= V!)(for *paramp°*, K = O wt.n.: Tib.A *gcig-nas gcig-tu*, B *brgyud-mar*, Chin. 一一 ); cf. AsP 185.8 *anyaiḥ kāṇḍais tat kāṇḍaṃ bhūmau patat pratinivārayet, vārayet,...*

9c K *parimasya* (for *pur°*, XTac = OV: Tib. *sṅa-ma'i*); KTc *bhūmim* (= V) (for *°iṃ*, XTa = O); cf. AsP 185.8-9 *tasya pauravakasya kāṇḍasya kāṇḍa-paramparayā bhūmau patanaṃ na dadyāt.*

9d O *paruṣasya* (? mispr.)(for *pur°*, MSS. = V: Tib. *mi*); Tc *yateya* (for *pateya*, KXTa = OV: Tib. *ltuṅ-bar 'gyur*); cf. Tib. *mi de 'dod-na mda' de sa-la ltuṅ-bar 'gyur;* also AsP 185.9-10 *tāvat kāṇḍaṃ bhūmau na patet, yāvan nākāṅkṣet —— aho batedaṃ kāṇḍaṃ bhūmau pated iti.*

10a Tc *carato* (for *caranto*, KXTa = OV).

10b X *prajñāya*, Tac *prajñaya* (for *prajñā-*, K, so em. OV); but O *prajñā-upāya-bala-ṛddhi-°*, cpd.; V sep. *prajñā upāya bala ṛddhi vicāramāṇo!*; cf. Tib.A *śes-rab thabs stobs rdzu-'phrul-gyis-ni rnam rgyu-źiṅ* (B ... *rnam spyod-pa*, v.l. *dpyod-pa* = O), Chin. 修習智慧及方便 ); AsP 185. 11 *upāya-kauśalya-parigṛhītaḥ ...*

10c XTac *prāpuṇotī* (= OV)(for *°ātī*, K).

10d *-mula* (for *-mūla*, KXTa = OV: Tib. *rtsa-ba*).

tāvan na tāṃ parama-(X63B)śūnyata prāpuṇātī
    yāvan na te kuśala-mūla bhavanti pūrṇāḥ // 10 //

bhikṣū yathā parama-ṛddhi-balen' upeto
    gagane sthi(Ta18B)to yamaka kurvati prātihāryaṃ /
sthiti-caṅkramaṃ-śaya-niṣadya nidarśayātī
    na nivartate na pi ca khidyati yāva tatra // 11 //

em eva śūnyata-sthito vidu bodhi(X64A)sattvo
    jñānā-rddhi-pārami-gato a-niketa-cārī /
vividhāṃ kriyāṃ jagati darśayate an-antāṃ
    na ca (K18B) sajjate na pi ca khidyati kalpa-koṭīḥ // 12 //

puruṣo yathā maha-prapāti sthihitva ko ci
    duvi-pāṇi chattra-dvaya gṛhya upakṣipeyā /

---

11a XTa *bhikṣur* (= O), Tc *bhikṣu* (for *bhikṣū*, K = V); KXTa *-balenupeto* (so print OV), Tc *-balanupeto* (for *-balen' upeto*: Tib. *rdzu-'phrul stobs mchog ldan-pa źig)*.

11b Tc *gagaṇe* (for °*ne*, KXTa = OV: Tib. *nam-mkhar*); K *kurvanti*, Tac *kurthati* (for *kurvati*, X = OV); KTac *prātihāryā* (Conze Rgs. 49 misr. K as °*ryāṃ*), X °*ryāṃ* (= V)(for °*ryaṃ*, so em. O; cf. BHSD p. 392a, °*hārya-*, s.v.).

11c XTa *gatiṃ-cakramaṃ-*, Tc *gati-caṃkramaṃ-*: Tib. *'gro daṅ 'chag-pa daṅ-ni* (for *sthiti-caṃkramaṃ-*, K); Tc *-niṣadya-riṣadya* (for *-niṣadya*, KXTa); O *gatiṃ caṃkramaṃ śaya niṣadya*, V *gati-caṃkramaṃ śaya-°*; cf. XVII 3c *sthiti-caṅkramā-°*: Tib. *'gro 'chag ñal daṅ 'dug-par;* XTac *nidarśayāti*, (= OV)(for °*ātī*, K).

11d O om. *na* of *na nivartate* (so MSS.): Tib.A *ldog-pa med-ciṅ* (= Chin. 不退 ), but B *skyo-ba* (!) *med-ciṅ*.

12a O *vidu-°*, cpd.

12b K *jñāna-ṛddhi-*, unmetr., O em. *jñāna-rddhi* (= V)(for *jñānā-rddhi-*, XTac; cf. Edgerton 4.45); XTac *-pāra-gāmi-gato* (for *-pārami-gato*, K, so em O = V: Tib. *pha-rol son-la)*.

12c Tc *vividhā* (for °*āṃ*, KXTa = OV); KTc *anantān* (for °*āṃ*, XTa = OV).

12d XTa *bhajyatī* (= OV: Tib.A *ñams-pa*), Tc *bhajyati* (for *sajjate*, K, semi-MIndic for Skt. *sad-ya-te*, 'is exhausted, wearied': Tib.B *skyo-ba*); Tc *ra pi* (for *na pi*, KXTa = OV: Tib. *med*); XTac *kalpa-koṭī* (= OV)(for °*-koṭīḥ*, K).

13a XTac *puruṣā* (= OV)(for °*ṣo*, K); K *ko vi* (w. daṇḍa; Conze Rgs. 49 misr. K as *keci*), Tc *ko vid*, XTa *ke cid* (= OV: Tib. *'ga'*)(for *ko ci*).

13b K *du-pāṇi* (unmetr.!), X *ubhi-pāṇi* (= OV; but V sep. *ubhi pāṇi*!), Ta *ubhi-pāṇiṃ*, Tc *ubhi-pāṇir* (for *duvi-pāṇi*: Tib. *lag-pa gñi-gas*, v.l. *gñis-kas* = O; Chin. 二 手 ); cf. XX 14b *-duvi-*, v.l. *-dvaya-*; also XXII 2d *duvi-*(w.n.); cf. Schneider, 'Das Zahlwort im Mahāvastu' (1960) 1.2.1. 1; also Murakami, '*Samādhirājasūtra* no Goi Kenkyū' (1967), p. 90a, *duvi*, s.v.; one might perh. expect *dū-*, m.c. for *du-* (cf. Edgerton 3.44-46, 117, Schneider *ibid.*, Pischel 436, PTSD II p. 168a, *dvi-* II, s.v.); the initial *d-* can be the final *-d* of *cid* (but cf. XX 13a, fn.), and *-bhi-* of *ubhi-* is mistakenly lost, i.e. *ubhi-pāṇi*, which XTac intend; **dubhi-/ dubha-*, blend of *du- / duvi- (dvi-)* and *ubhi- / *ubha-* (cf. Geiger 114 end, PTSD II p. 162b, *dubha-*, *dubhaya-*, ss.vv.), is another possibility (cf. also Edgerton 19.2-7); K *du-* may less poss. be em. to MIndic *do-* (Skt. *dvau*; cf. Pischel 436, Tagare 106 and p. 410); cf. Girnār Aśokan *dvo* (Skt. *dvau*; cf. Mehendale 101).
Tc *-dvaye* (for *-dvaya*, KXTa = OV); XTac *gṛhṇa* (= OV; ? nom.sg.m.pres. pple. to *gṛh-ṇa-ti*, w. *puruṣo*)(for *gṛhya*, K, so r. Edg.Rgs. 40; cf.

ākāśa-vāyur atha sṛjya ma(X64B)hā-prapāte
    no ca prapāta pati yāti na yāva tatra // 13 //

em eva sthitva karuṇāṃ vidu bodhisattvo
    prajñā-upāya-duvi-(Tc24B)chattra-pariggṛhīto /
śūnyānimitt'-a-praṇidhīṃ vimṛśāti dharmān
    na ca nirvṛtiṃ spṛśati paśyayatī ca dharmān // 14 //

ratanārthiko yatha vrajitvana ratna-dvīpaṃ
    labdhāna (X65A) ratna puna geham upāgameyā /
kiṃ cāpi tatra sukha jīvayi sārtha-vāho
    api duḥkhito manasi bhoti sva-jñāti-saṃgho // 15 //

---

Edgerton 35.9, 43 p. 211a, *grah-* 4, s.v.: Tib. *'dzin-ciṅ*); XTa *upakṣayeyā* (= OV), Tc *upakṣayeryyā* (for *upakṣipeyā*, K); Conze Rgs. 49 doubtfully r. K as *upasthiyeyā* w. his conjectural r. *upakṣiyeyā* (!); Edg.Rgs. 40 rejects *upakṣiyeyā* and suggests em. to *upasthiyeyā* 'would approach'; but K *upakṣiyeyā* must be the true reading: Tib.B *mchoṅ-bar byed-ciṅ*, but A *ci mi sñam* 'would not think anything' (?? Skt. **n'upekṣiyeyā*).

13c XTac *ākāli* 'untimely' (= OV: Tib.A *dus min*)(for *ākāśa-*, K); Conze ad O p. 128 seems to r. *ākāśa* separately (acc. or loc.?) w. *upakṣipeyā* as Tib.B *nam-mkha'-la mchoṅ-bar byed-ciṅ* 'would jump off into empty space'!; K *-vāyuḥ* (for *-vāyur*, XTac = OV; but OV sep.: Tib.A *rluṅ-gis*, but B *lus*!); XTac *avasṛjya* (= OV)(for *atha sṛjya*, K; Conze Rgs. 49 r. K as *?tha sṛjya*: Tib.A *phul byas-kyaṅ* B *bor-nas*, v.l. *bor-na*).

13d MSS. *ca* should perh. be em. to *co* or *cā* as suggested by Edg.Rgs. 32 end; MSS. *patiyāti* (so prints V!) should be divided into *pati* (3 sg.opt.; cf. XVI 5d *pati*) and *yāti* (so Tib.B); but O *pariyāti* (wt.n.!), which Edg. Rgs. 40 em. to *paripāti* 'would cause to fall down'! (Conze does not report MSS. readings); render *d* as: '(he) would not fall down to the cliff, so long as he does not reach there'; cf. Tib.B *ltuṅ-bar mi 'gyur ji-srid der-ni 'gro-bar 'gyur*, but A *bdag-ñid* (?) *der-ni gYaṅ-du ltuṅ-bar 'gyur-ba med*.

14a K *karuṇān* (for *°āṃ*, XTac = OV); O *vidu-*, cpd.

14b Tc *-upāpa-* (for *-upāya-*, KXTa = OV: Tib. *thabs*); XTac *-dvaya-* (= OV) (for *-duvi-*, K: Tib. *gñis-kyi*; cf. XX 13b *duvi-* (w. fn.); MSS.*-parigṛhīto* (= OV)(for *-pariggṛhīto*; cf. Edg.Rgs. 37, Edgerton 2.7).

14c K *śūnyānimittapraṇidhīm*, XTac *śūnyānimittapraṇidhiṃ* (= V; Tc *°dhi*), O em. *°-praṇidhīn* (for *śūnyānimitt'-apraṇidhīṃ*: Tib. *stoṅ-pa mtshan med smon-pa med*, Chin. 空無相願 ); cf. XIX 6a, XX 19b *°tt'-apraṇidhīṃ*.

14d O *nā* (wt.n.)(for *na ca*, MSS. = V, so r. Edg.Rgs. 40); XTc *nirvṛti* (for *°tiṃ*, KTa = OV); cf. *na ca nirvṛtiṃ spṛśati* I 7d, X 9d, XIX 6b, XX 6d, 8d; K *paśyatayatī ca dharmān*, XTa *paśyati dharma-cārī*, Tc *paśyaṃti dharma-cārī* (for *paśyayatī ca dharmān*, so em. Edg.Rgs. 40; cf. Edgerton 38.21: Tib. *chos-kyaṅ mthoṅ*, Chin. 見法 ).

15a Tc *rathanārthiko* (for *ratan°*, KXTa = OV: Tib. *rin-chen 'dod-pa*); K *vraji[tva]na*, O sep. *vrajitva na*! (for *vrajitvana*, XTac = V, so Edg.Rgs. 40; cf. Edgerton 35.31: Tib. *rin-chen gliṅ soṅ-ste*, Chin. 往宝洲 ; cf. VII 7c, XX 16a *vrajitvana ratna-dvīpaṃ*.

15b V em. *labdhvāna* (for *labdhāna*, MSS. = O; cf. Edg.Rgs. 11, also Edgerton 35.52: Tib. *rñed-nas*; cf. XX 16b, XXIX 8b *labdhāna*); XTac *yuna* (= O!)(for *puna*, K, so em. Edg.Rgs. 40 = V: Tib. *phyir-yaṅ*).

15c XTac *jīvati* (= OV)(for *jīvayi*, K: Tib.A *'tsho*, B *'tsho byed-ciṅ*).

15d Tc *'pi* (for *api*, KXTa = OV); XTa *bhonti* (= O)(for *bhoti*, KTc = V); K *sva-jñāti-saṃghoḥ*, X *sa-jñāti-saṃgho* (= O; but O sep. *sa jñāti-°*), Ta *sa-jāti-saṃgho* (= V; but V sep. *sa jāti-°*), Tc *sa-jāti-sadyo* (for *sva-jñāti-saṃgho*, so r. Edg.Rgs. 40: Tib. [no corresp. word to *sva-*] A *gñen-bśes tshogs-kyi*, B *gñen-bśes tshogs*).

em eva śūnyata vrajitvana ratna-dvīpaṃ
    labdhāna dhyāna-bala-indriya bodhisattvo /
kiṃ cāpi nirvṛti spṛśed abhinandamāno
    api sarva-sa(X65B)ttva dukhitā manasī bhavanti // 16 //

abhyantare ya nagare ni(Ta19A)game ca grāme
    kāryārthu vāṇiju yathā gami jānanāya /
no cāpi tatra sthihatī na ca ratna-dvīpe
    saci gehi mārga-kuśalo puna bhoti vijño // 17 //

tatha jñāna śrāvaka-vimukti sa-pratyayānāṃ
    sarvatra bhoti kuśalo (X66A) vidu bodhisattvo /
no cāpi tatra sthihatī na ca buddha-jñāne
    na ca saṃskṛte (K19A) bhavati mārga-vidū vidhi-jño // 18 //

---

16a O sep. *vrajitva na* (for *vrajitvana*, KXTa = V, so r. Edg.Rgs. 40 ad XX 15a: Tib. *soṅ-ste*; cf. VII 7c, XX 15a *vrajitvana ratna-dvīpaṃ*); Tc (long lacuna from *a* to *d*) *vrajitva* ⟨.....⟩ *duḥkhitā*.

16b V em. *labdhvāna* (for *labdhāna*, KXTa = O: Tib. *thob-pa*; cf. XX 15a, fn.); O *dhyāna bala-indriya*, V *dhyāna bala indriya* (for *dhyāna-bala-indriya*: Tib. *bsam-gtan dbaṅ-po stobs*, cf. Chin. 獲得根力禅定宝).

16c XTa *spṛśadebhi-* (for *spṛśed abhi-*, K, so em. O = V: Tib.A *reg-par mṅon-par dga'*, B *reg-pa ... mṅon dga'-źiṅ*).

16d XTac *duḥkhitā* (= O!)(for *dukhitā*, K, so em. Edg.Rgs. 35 = V); Tc *manasi* (for *°asī*, KXTa = OV).

17a. Tc *atyaṃtare* (for *abhyantare*, KXTa - OV: Tib.B *bar-gyi*, but not in Tib.A); Tc *nīgame* (for *nigame*, KXTa = OV: Tib. *groṅ-rdal*).

17b XTac *kāmārtha* (= OV)(for *kāryārthu*, so r. K clearly: Tib.A *bya-ba'i phyir*, B *don gñer*, Chin. 為利 ); Conze Rgs. 49 r. K as *kā(r)yārthu*; does Conze mean to r. *kāyārthu* 'for physical exercise / purpose'?; K *vāṇij*[u], Ta *vāṇirju* (for *vāṇiju*, XTc = OV: Tib. *tshoṅ-pa*); O *yathāgami* (so Conze Index p. 150b = Dict. p. 327 'goes into ... which he comes across on his way': Tib. *gaṅ yin-par 'gro!*); *yathāgami* (so MSS.) should be divided into *yathā gami* (= V): Tib.A *'gro*, B *dper-na ... 'gro*; *yathā* is correlatively used w. *tatha* in XX 18a; *gami* (or poss. *āgami*) is 3 sg.opt. to *gamati* (cf. Edgerton 43 p. 210a, *gam-* 2, s.v.).

17c Tc *no vā cāpi* (for *no cāpi*, KXTa = OV); cf. XX 18c-d.

17d XTac *na ca* (= OV)(for *saci*, K, so r. Edg.Rgs. 40; cf. XX 18d); XTac *geha mārgi* (= OV)(for *gehi mārga-*, K); Tc *vijñaḥ* (for *vijño*, KXTa = OV); cf. Tib.A *mkhas-pas khyim-du mi gnas lam-la gnas-par* (r. perh. *mkhas-par*) *'gyur*, B *rig-pa khyim-du mi gnas lam-la mkhas-par 'gyur*, Chin. 大智善道而復還

18a V *-vimukti-sapratyayānāṃ*, cpd.!; cf. Tib.A *raṅ-rgyal bcas-pa'i ñan-thos rnam grol sems, kun-la byaṅ-chub-sems-dpa' gsal-ba mkhas-par 'gyur*; but B *byaṅ-chub-sems-dpa' gsal-te* (v.l. *gsal de* = O; Skt. *sa* sep.?) *ñan-thos daṅ, raṅ-rgyal-rnams-kyi śes rnam grol kun-la mkhas*.

18b XTac *bhonti* (= O)(for *bhoti*, K = V); K *ku*[*śa*]*lo v*[*i*]*du*; O *vidu-°*, cpd.

18c Tc *nā vāpi* (for *no cāpi*, KXTa = OV); XTac *sthihate* (= OV)(for *°atī*, K); cf. XX 17c *no ca tatra sthihatī*; Tc *na* ⟨*ca*⟩ *buddha-*.

18d XTac *saṃskṛta* (for *°te*, KX[Tib.trslit.] = OV); O sep. *mārga vidū* (cf. XX 17d *mārga-kuśalo*).

yaṃ-kāli maitri jagatī anubandhayitvā
    (Tc25A) śūnyānimitt'-a=praṇidhīṃ carate samādhīṃ /
a-sthānam eva yadi nirvṛti prāpuṇeyā
    athavāpi saṃskṛti sa prajña(X66B)panāya śakyo // 19 //

yatha nirmito puruṣa no va a-dṛśya-kāyo
    nāmena vā puna sa prajñapanāya śakyo /
tatha bodhisattva caramāṇu vimokṣa-dvāre
    nāmena vā puna sa prajñapanāya śakyaḥ // 20 //

abhipṛcchamāna cari-indriya bodhisattvo
    gambhīra-dharma-paridīpana no karoti /
(X67A) śūnyānimitta-a=vivartiya-bhūmi-dharmān
    na ca sūcayāti na sa vyākṛtu veditavyo // 21 //

---

19a OV sep. *yaṃ kāli* (for *yaṃ-kāli* = **yat-kāle* '*yasmin kāle*': Tib. *gaṅ-tshe*); cf.*yām̐ velāṃ* 'in which time' (acc.; cf. BHSD p. 509a, *velā-* 1, s.v.); KTc *maitrī* (for *maitri*, XTa = OV).

19b K *śūnyānimittapraṇidhīñ*, XTa °*praṇidhī* (so print OV), Tc °*prāni* (for *śūnyānimitt'-apraṇidhīṃ*; cf. XIX 6a, XX 14c °*ānimitt'-apraṇidhīṃ*); K *carante* (Conze Rgs. 49 misr. K as *caranti*)(for *carate*, XTac = OV); XTac *samādhiṃ* (= OV; but V w. *-m*)(for °*īṃ*, K).

19c K *asthā*[*nam eva*]; Tc *yādi* (for *yadi*, KXTa = OV); Tc *nirvṛtti* (for *nirvṛti*, KXTa = OV: Tib.A *mya-ṅan 'das-la*, B °*-pa*); XTac *prāpaṇeyā* (= O)(for *prāpuṇ*°, K = V wt.n.).

19d Tc *athāvāpi* (for *athavāpi*, KXTa = OV); Ta *saṃskṛta* (= V), Tc °*kṛṃta* (for °*kṛti*, KX = O: Tib.B *'dus byas yin-par*); K *śakyoḥ* (Conze Rgs. 49 misr. K as *śakyāḥ*), XTac *śakyaḥ* (= OV)(for *śakyo*).

20a Tc *yathā* (for *yatha*, KXTa = OV); K *nirvṛto* (for *nirmito*, XTac =OV: Tib. *sprul-pa'i*); Tc *puruṣo* (for °*ṣa*, KXTa = OV); K *māyā ca* (hyper-metric!), Tc *no* ⟨*va*⟩, O em. *naiva* (for *no va*, XTa = V; *no va* = encl. *naḥ* plus *eva*; cf. Edgerton 4.2, 6, 17, BHSD p. 466a, *va*, s.v.; but Tib. *ma yin-žiṅ*!; Conze trsl. otherwise); XTa *-kāyoḥ*, O em. *-kāyā* (for *-kāyo*, KTc, so r. Edg.Rgs. 40 = V).

20b Tc *nāmera* (for *nāmena*, KXTa = OV: Tib.A *miṅ-gis*, B *miṅ-gis-kyaṅ-ni*); Conze Trsl. seems to understand it as *nāme na*; XTac *punaḥ* (= O!)(for *puna*, K, so r. Rdg.Rgs. 39 = V); XTa *śakyaḥ* (= OV), Tc *śakyas* (no daṇḍa) (for *śakyo*, K).

20c Tc*caramāṇū*(for °*māṇu*, KXTa = OV); Tc *-dvāra*, V *-dvāraṃ* (wt.n.)(for *-dvāre*, KXTa = O: Tib. *sgor*); cf. XX 8c *tatha bodhisattva caramāṇu vimokṣa-dvāre*.

20d Conze Trsl. seems to understand *nāmena* as *nāme na*; O *va* (? mispr.) (for *vā*, MSS., so r. Edg.Rgs. 39 = V); XTac *punas sa* (= O!)(for *puna sa*, K, so r. Edg.Rgs. 39 = V); XTa *prajñayanāya*, Tc *prajñayatonāya* (for *prajñapanāya*, K, so em. O = V; cf. XX 19d, 20b *prajñapanāya*).

21a K *abhipṛcchimā*⟨*na*⟩,XTa *yadi pṛcchamāna* (= OV: Tib. *gal-te ... yoṅs dris-la*), Tc *yadi pṛcchamā*⟨*na*⟩(for *abhipṛcchamāna*); OV sep. *cari indriya* (for *cari-indriya*, dvandva-cpd., acc.sg.: Tib. *spyod-pa daṅ-ni dbaṅ-po*; cf. Edgerton 3.115, BHSD p. 225b, *carī-*, s.v.).

21b Tc *gabhīra-*, unmetr. (for *gambhīra-*, KXTa = OV); Tc *nā* (for *no*, KXTa = OV: Tib. *mi*).

21c V sep. *śūnyānimitta avivartiya-*; V *-bodhi-* (wt.n.!)(for *-bhūmi-*, MSS. = O: Tib.A *sa*, B *sa-yi*); X *-dharmāṃ* (= V), Tac *-dharmā* (for°*mān*, K, so em. O).

21d XTa *na ca sūcatī na ca sa vyākṛtu* (= OV), Tc *na ca sa vyākṛtu* (for *na ca sūcayāti na sa vyākṛtu*, K: Tib.A *mi 'chad de-ni luṅ-bstan ma yin*,

arhanta-bhūmim api pratyaya-buddha-bhūmiṃ
    trai-dhātuke na spṛhate supināntare 'pi /
buddhāṃś ca paśyati katheti jagasya dharmaṃ
    a-vivartiyo ti ayu vyākṛtu veditavyo // 22 //

(Ta19B) triy-a(X67B)pāya-prāpta supinasmi viditva sattvān
    praṇidheti tat-kṣaṇu apāya ucchoṣayeyaṃ /
satyādhiṣṭhāna praśameti ca agni-(Tc25B)skandho
    a-vivartiyo ti ayu vyākṛtu veditavyo // 23 //

bhūta-grahā vividha vyādhaya martya-loke
    satyādhiṣṭhāna praśameti hitānukampī /

---

B ... *luṅ ma bstan-pa yin).*

22a Tc *ahaṃta-* (for *arhanta-*, KXTa = OV: Tib. *dgra-bcom*); XTac *-buddha-bhūmau* (= OV)(for°*-bhūmim*, K); cf. Tib. *saṅs-rgyas ye-śes* (? Skt.*-buddha-jñānaṃ*, but Chin. 声聞緣覚地.

22b XTa *-dhātukan*, Tc *-dhātukaṃm*, OV *-dhātukaṃ* (for *-dhātuke*, K: Tib. *khams gsum-dag-la*, v.l. °*-na;* Chin. 於三界 ); XTac *spṛśate* (= OV!)(for *spṛhate*, K, so r. Conze ad O p. 128: Tib. *'dod-ciṅ*, Chin. 求 ; cf. V p. 379 n. 4); MSS. *pi* (for *'pi* = OV); cf. AsP 188.11-12 *svapnāntara-gate 'pi śrāvaka-bhūmau vā pratyeka-buddha-bhūmau vā trai-dhātukāya ca spṛhām anuśaṃsā-cittaṃ notpādayati ...*

22c V em. *janasya* (for *jagasya*, MSS. = O: Tib. *'gro-la*,Chin. 為世間 ).

22d XTac *a-vivartiyebhi*, O *āvivartiyebhi* (? mispr.), V em.*a-vivartiyeti* (for *a-vivartiyo ti*, K; Conze Rgs. 49 r. K as *avivartiyo 'ti*); cf. XX 23d, 24d *avivartiyo ti* (cf. Edgerton 4.14); XTac *veditavyoḥ*, O em.°*vyaḥ* (for °*vyo*, K = V wt.n.); cf. AsP 188.9-10, 12-13, 17, 21-22, 30-31, 189. 3-4, 11 *idam ... avinivartanīyasya bodhisattvasya mahā-sattvasya a-vinivartanīya-lakṣaṇaṃ veditavyam.*

23a XTa *tri-* (= V), Tc ⟨*tri-*⟩(for *triy-*, K = O wt.n.); XTac *-prādmu*, O em. *-prāptu* (= V)(for *-prāpta*, K); K *sattvāṃ* (so r. Conze Rgs. 49; cf. Edgerton 8.90), XTac *sattva*, O *sattva* (? mispr.)(for *sattvān* = V).

23b X *ta-kṣeṇa*, Tac *ta-kṣaṇa* (so em. O), V *tat-kṣaṇa* (wt.n.)(for *tat-kṣaṇu*, K: Tib. *skad cig de-la*, Chin. 剎那 ); Tc *apāyocchoṣayeyaṃ* (for *apāya ucch°*, KXTa = OV; but V w. *-m*).

23c V *satyādhiṣṭhāni* (wt.n.!; ? loc. for instr., cf. Edgerton 7.81: Tib. *bden-pa'i byin-gyi rlabs-kyis*)(for °*āna*, MSS. = O, Bhvr.); cf. XX 24b *satyādhiṣṭhāna ... hitānukampī*: Tib. *phan daṅ sñiṅ-brtser ldan-pa'i byin-gyis;* XXI 1b *satyādhiṣṭhāna*: Tib.A *bden-pa'i byin-gyi rlabs-kyis*, B *bden-pa'i byin rlabs* (cf. BHSD p. 554b, *satyādhiṣṭhāna-*, s.v.); Tc *cāgni-*, V em. *sa cāgni-* (for *ca agni-*, KXTa = O); K [*-s*]*ka*[*n*]*dho*, XTa *-skandhaṃ* (= OV; but V w. *-m*), Tc *-skaṃndham* (for *-skandho*, acc., cf. Edgerton 8.36); cf. Tib. *bden-pa'i byin-gyi rlabs-kyis me-yi phuṅ-po źi*, Chin. 以真実力滅火蘊 ; also AsP 189.16-18 *etena satyena satya-vacanena ayaṃ nagara-dāho vā grāma-dāho vā vartamāna upaśāmyatu, astaṃ gacchatu / sacet ... upaśāmyati, śītī-bhavati, astaṃ gacchati, veditavyam etat ... vyākṛto 'yaṃ bodhisattvo mahā-sattvas ...*

23d XTa *avivartiyeti* (= OV), Tc °*iyety* (for °*iyo ti*,K; cf. XX 22d, fn.); XTac *veditavyoḥ*, O em. °*itavyaḥ* (for °*itavyo*, K = V wt.n.).

24a MSS. *bhūta-grahā* (= OV) is the only example in our text, of which the final *-a-* of the prior member is long by position before *gr-*; it is perh. expected to be *bhūtā-°* (cf. Edgerton 8.15-17), or poss. *bhūtaṃ-°* (cf. Edgerton 8.14); cf. *prăgrahīta* VII 2a, *parīgrāhikā* IV 5c, *rāhŭ-graha-* IX 1c, also *că grāme* XX 17a, *rājă grāma*XIII 2a, *praviviktă grāma-* XXI 4a, *abhyāsă grāma-*X 3d; O *vividha-vyādhaya*, cpd.; K *ma⟨r⟩tya-loke*, Tc *-artya-loka* (for *martya-loke*, XTa = OV: Tib. *mi-yi 'jig-rten).*

24b Tc *satyadhiṣṭhāna*, V *satyādhiṣṭhāni* (wt.n.!)(for *satyādhiṣṭhāna*,

na ca tena manya(X68A)n' upapadyati nāpi mānaṃ
    a-viva(K19B)rtiyo ti ayu vyākṛtu veditavyo // 24 //

bhagavatyāṃ ratna-guṇa-saṃcaya-gāthāyām upāya-kauśalya-mīmāṃsā-parivarto nāma viṃśatimaḥ // 20 //

---

KXTa = O: Tib. *bden-pa'i byin-gyis*); cf. XX 23c, fn.; also AsP 190.10-15 *anena satyena satya-vacanena iyaṃ strī vā puruṣo vā dārako vā dārikā vā yena a-manuṣya-grahena gṛhīto vā āviṣṭo vā, so 'pakrāmatu / ...sacet ... so 'manuṣyo 'pakrāmati, veditavyam etat ... vyākṛto 'yaṃ bodhisattvo mahā-sattvas ...*

24c Tc *manyarupapadyati*, KXTa *manyanupapadyati* (so prints V), O sep. *manyanu papadyati* (for *manyan' upapadyati*); cf. XXI 1a *manyan' upap°*; Tc *nām* (for *mānaṃ*, KXTa = OV; but V w. *-m*).

24d XTac *a-vivartiyeti* (= OV)(for *°iyo ti*, K); K *vyākṛtetu* (for *vyākṛtu*, XTac = OV); XTac *veditavyoh*, O em. *°vyaḥ* (= V)(for *°vyo*, K); cf. XX 22d, 23d *a-vivartiyo ti ayu vyākṛtu veditavyo.*

XX col. K *viṃśatiḥ*, Tc *viṃśatimiḥ*, O em. *viṃśatitamaḥ* (= V)(for *viṃśatimaḥ*, XTa; cf. XIX colophon, footnote end); only K reads *gāthā 24* at the end of the colophon; Tc adds num. 20.

## 〈XXI. MĀRA-KARMAN〉

athavāsya manyan' upapadyati vyākṛto 'smi
     satyādhiṣṭhāna vividhāni samṛdhyayanti /
(X68B) yadi anya vyākṛta ku-manyati bodhisattvo
     jñātavya manyana-sthito ayu alpa-buddhiḥ // 1 //

nāmādhiṣṭhāna puna māru upāgamitvā
     evaṃ vadiṣyati idaṃ tava nāma-dheyaṃ /
mātā-pitāya ayu sapta-m-upaiti vaṃśo
     buddho yadā bhavi idaṃ tava nāma-dheyaṃ // 2 //

dhuta-vṛttu yādṛśu (X69A) sa bheṣyati yukta-(Tc26A)yogī
     pūrvaṃ pi tubhya imi āsi guṇ' eva-rūpāḥ /

---

1a Tc *manyarupapadyati,* KXTa *manyanupap°*(so prints V), O sep. *manyanu papadyati* (for *manyan' upapadyati;* cf. XX 24c *manyan' upap°);* KXTa *smi,* Tc *smiṃ* (for *'smi* = OV: Tib. *bdag luṅ-bstan,* Chin. 我得授記).

1b K *samṛddhyayanti* (= V)(for *samṛdhy°,* XTac = O: Tib.A *'grub byed,* B *'byor-pas).*

1c Tc *yady antya* (for *yadi anya,* KXTa = OV: Tib.A *gal-te pha-rol,* B *gal-te ... gźan-gyi);* OV *vyākṛtaku manyati* (for *vyākṛta ku-manyati);* *vyākṛtaku* w. a specifying suffix *-ka-* is not impossible (cf. Edgerton 22.38-39), but no other example has been reported; *anya vyākṛta* should prob. be taken as acc.pl. (*vyākṛtaku* is hardly a plural form; cf. Edgerton 8.97); contextually *ku-* is most prob. a pejorative prefix (like *ku-mati-;* cf. Wackernagel II 1 para. 34b Anm. on p. 83), which is a noteworthy verbal cpd.; render pāda *c*: 'if a bodhisattva despises ("thinks ill of") other predestined ones'; cf. AsP 191.9-14 *sa ... anyān bodhisattvān mahā-sattvān avamaṃsyate uccagghayiṣyati ullāpayiṣyati kutsayiṣyati paṃsayiṣyati —— ahaṃ vyākṛtas ... / sa ... mānam utpādayiṣyati ...;* Conze trsl. (Rgs.): 'When a Bodhisattva sets himself above other (Bodhisattvas) as one who has been predestined'! (? = Tib.B *gal-te byaṅ-chub-sems-dpa' gźan-gyi luṅ-bstan rlom;* cf. A *gal-te pha-rol luṅ-bstan yin sñam sems gyur-na*!).

2a V *māra* (wt.n.)(for *māru,* MSS. = O); Tc *drapāgamitvā* (for *upāg°,* KXTa = OV); cf. Tib. *miṅ-gi gźi-las bdud-ni ñe-bar 'oṅs gyur-nas;* also AsP 191.27 *nāmādhiṣṭhānenāpi māraḥ pāpīyān upasaṃkramiṣyati.*

2b K *vadiśyati,* XTac *vidiṣyati,* O em. *vidiśyati* (for *vadiṣyati,* so r. Conze ad O p. 128 = V: Tib. *smras-te);* K *idan,* X *iyan* (so prints O), Tac *iyaṃ* (for *idaṃ* = V; cf. *idaṃ* in *d*); Tc *noma-* (for *nāma-,* KXTa = OV); V *-dheyam* (w. *-m*); cf. AsP 191.28-29 *evaṃ vakṣyati ... tava hīdaṃ nāma-dheyam.*

2c O sep. *mātā pitā ya*! (for *mātā-pitāya* = V: Tib. *mes;* cf. Edgerton 13.11); XTa *anusaptam* (= OV), Tc *anuśaptam* (for *ayu sapta-m-,* K, w. a hiatus-bridger *-m-,* cf. Edgerton 4.59; rather than *saptam,* acc.; Conze Rgs. 50 r. K as *ayusaptam*!); Tc *udyaiti* (for *upaiti,* KXTa = OV); K *vaṃso,* Tc *vaśo,* O *vāṃśo* (? mispr.)(for *vaṃśo,* XTa, so em. Edg.Rgs. 40 = V); cf. Tib. *khyod-kyi bdun mes rgyud-kyi bar-gyi miṅ yin-źiṅ,* Chin. 或作父母七代人; AsP 191.31-32 *yāvad ā-saptaṃ mātāmaha-pitāmaha-yugasya nāma-dheyam udīrayiṣyati.*

2d KXTa *idan* (so prints O)(for *idaṃ,* Tc=V;cf. *idaṃ* in *b*); V *-dheyam*(w.*-m*).

3a XTac *-vṛtta* (= OV)(for *-vṛttu,* K); XTa *yānadṛśu,* Tc *yātadṛśu* (for *yādṛśu,* K, so em. O = V: Tib. *ci-'dra*); K *bhaviṣyati,* hypermetr. (for *bheṣyati,* XTac = OV); Tc *yuśma-yogī* (for *yukta-yogī,* KXTa = OV: Tib.A *rnal-'byor ldan,* B *... ldan-pa*); cf. AsP 192.11-12 *tathā hi te amī evaṃ-rūpā dhuta-guṇāḥ saṃvidyante, ... tvaṃ ... dhuta-guṇaiḥ samanvāgato 'bhūḥ;* AsP 192.16-17 *tathā hi tava ete evaṃ-rūpā dhuta-guṇā* (r. *°-guṇāḥ*)

yo eva śrutva abhimanyati bodhisattvo
    jñātavyu (Ta20A) māru-pariyutthitu alpa-buddhiḥ // 3 //

pravivikta grāma-nagare giri-kandarāṇi
    raṇyā-vivikta-vana-prastha niṣevamāṇo /
ātmān' ukarṣi para (X69B) paṃsayi bodhisattvo
    jñātavyu māru-pariyutthita alpa-buddhiḥ // 4 //

grāme ca rāṣṭra-nigame viharanti nityaṃ
    raha-pratya-yāni spṛhatāṃ na jananti tatra /

---

*saṃvidyante;* AsP 192.22-23*tathā hi te evaṃ-rūpā dhuta-guṇāḥ saṃvidyante.*

[3b] X *pūrve pi,* O *pūrve 'pi,* Tac *pūrva pi* (for *pūrvaṃ pi,* K, so em. V); K *guṇevarūpāḥ* (so Conze Rgs. 50), X *guṇovarūpā,* O *guṇo va rūpā!,* Ta *guṇovarūpā,* Tc *guṇevarūpā* (for *guṇ' eva-rūpāḥ,* m.c. for *guṇā evaṃ-rūpāḥ,* as correctly analyzed by Conze Rgs. 50 *'evaṃ-rūpā guṇāḥ'*: Tib.A *yon-tan tshul-yaṅ 'di,* B ... *'di-'dra).*

[3d] XTc *jñātavya* (= O)(for *°vyu,* KTa = V); Tc *mārū-* (for *māru-,*KXTa = OV; but OV sep. *māru pary°!*); K *-paryutthitu* (= V), X *-paryutthita* (= O), Ta *-paryusthita,* Tc *-payusthitâlpa-!* (for *māru-pariyutthitu*: Tib. *bdud-kyis yoṅs-su bslaṅ-źiṅ,* Chin. 魔所著 ); MSS. *pary-* (= OV!) is expected to be *pariy-* in two shorts w. epenthetic *-i-* like Pāli *pariyuṭṭhita-* (cf. Edg.Rgs. 12: p. 4 n. 1).

[4] Ta omits the whole verse.

[4a] O sep. *raṇyā vivikta-°,* V sep. *raṇyā vivikta vanaprastha* (for *raṇyā-vivikta-°,* cpd.: Tib. *dgon-pa dben-pa* (X *°-pa'i* = O) *nags-khrod,* Chin. 山林曠野寂静処; cf. AsP 194.14-15 *āraṇyakāni ... viviktāni ... vanaprastha-giri-guhā-);* XTc *niṣevamāno* (for *°māṇo,* K, so em. O = V).

[4c] K *atmānutkarsi,* XTc *ātmānukarṣi* (= OV)(for *ātmān' ukarṣi*: Tib. *bdag stod,* Chin. 自称己德 ); but Edg.Rgs. 28 analyzes it as *ātmânukarṣin-* 'exalting oneself' and makes a lexicographical note on *anukarṣin-;* this is not acceptable; *ātmān' ukarṣi* should be analyzed as *ātmānu,* m.c. for *ātmānaṃ,*the final *-u* being dropped before the initial *u-* (cf. Edgerton 4.27) plus *u(t)karṣi,* 3 sg.opt. (cf. Edgerton 29.14; also Edgerton 2.88 for *u-* = *ud-*); O *para-paṃsayi,* cpd.! (for *para paṃsayi* = V: Tib. *gźan-la smod-pa'i,* Chin. 毁他人 ); again Edg.Rgs. 28 analyzes it as *para-paṃsayin-,* which he considers to be of lexical interest; but it should be analyzed as *para* (acc.pl.) plus *paṃsayi* (3 sg.opt. to *paṃsayati* 'blames', so Dhātupāṭha X 74, WSJD p. 718a; cf. Wogihara, *Asanga's Bodhisattvabhūmi* (1907), p. 33f. (repr. 1971, p. 31f.). Cf. *Rgs* XXI 1c.

[4d] O *jñātavya* (wt.n.)(for *°vyu,* KXTc = V); Tc *mānu-* (for *māru-,* KX = OV; but OV sep. *māru pary°*); KX *-paryutthita* (= O), Tc *-paryusthita,* V *paryutthitu* (for *-pariyutthita;* cf. XXI 3d, fn.).

[5a] XTac *rāṣṭri* (= OV)(for *rāṣṭra-,* K: Tib. *yul-'khor groṅ-rdal*); K *vigame* (for *nig°,* XTac = OV: Tib. *groṅ-rdal*); Tc *⟨vi⟩haraṃti.*

[5b] MSS. *rahapratyayāni* (so print OV) should be read *raha-pratya-yāni; pratya-* is a haplological form, m.c. for *pratyaya-* (= *pratyeka-buddha-);* but Tib.A *dgra-bcom raṅ-rgyal-dag-la* (? Skt. *°-pratyayani,* pl.), B *dgra-bcom raṅ-rgyal;* cf. XXIX 9b *raha-pratya-yāni spṛha-buddhi na* (XTac *°-buddhita* = Tib.!) *saṃjaneyā*: Tib. *dgra-bcom raṅ-rgyal theg-par 'dod-pa'i blo skyed-na,* cf. Chin. 不楽羅漢及縁覚 ; XXIX 10c *raha-pratya-yāna-vigato*: Tib. *dgra-bcom raṅ-rgyal theg bral;* also XXXI 2a *pratya-yāni* (not supported by Tib.!); K *spṛhatān* (Conze Rgs. 40 mispr. K as *°tāḥ*)(for *°tāṃ,* XTac = OV); K *na janti,* unmetr. (Conze Rgs. 40 seems to support this reading), XTac *janayanti* (= OV)(for *na jananti,* so r. Edg. Rgs. 40: Tib.A *'dod med-pa,* B *'dod-pa gźar mi bskyed,* Chin. 不求声聞縁覚証).

[5c] Tc *-paripācara* (for *°ana,* KXTa = OV; but OV *°ana-,* cpd.!; cf. XXIX 6a *sattva-paripācana*); cf. IV 6d, fn. on *anyatra;* XTa *-yukta* (= OV)(for *-yukto,* KTc; cf. Edgerton 8.83; it is poss. influenced by pāda *d*).

anyatra sattva-paripācana bodhi-yukto
eṣo viveku kathito sugatātma-jānāṃ // 5 //

yo pañca-yojana-śate giri-kanda(K20A)reṣu
vyāḍā(X70A)bhikīrṇi nivased bahu-varṣa-koṭī /
no co viveku imu jānati bodhisattvo
saṃkīrṇa so viharate adhimāna-prāpto // 6 //

socej jagārthu-abhiyuktaka-bodhisattvān
bala-dhyāna-indriya-vimokṣa-samādhi-prāptān /
abhimanyate na imi raṇya-viveka-cārī
(X70B) ayu māru-gocaru-sthito ti jinena ukto // 7 //

grāmānti yo viharate athavāpy araṇye
dvaya-yāna-citta-vigato niyatāgra-bodhau /
(Tc26B) eṣo viveku jagad-arth'-abhiprasthitānāṃ
ātmā-kṣiṇo ti tulayeya sa bodhisattvo // 8 //

---

5d K [*eṣo viveku kath*]*ito*; Tc *sūgatātmajānāṃ* (for *sug°*, KXTa = O).

6b XTac *vyāḍāvakīrṇā*, O em. *vyāḍāvakīrṇa*, V *vyālāvakīrṇi* (wt.n.)(for *vyāḍābhikīrṇi*, K; Conze Rgs. 50 misr. K as *vyāḍābhikīrṇu*); Tc *-koṭi*, O em. *-koṭīḥ* (for *-koṭī*, KXTa = V).

6c XTac *nā cā* (= O), V *no cā* (wt.n.)(for *no co*, K; cf. Edgerton 3.82); Tc om. from *imu* to XXI 7c *na*.

6d Ta *sakīrṇa* (for *saṃkīrṇa*, KX = OV: Tib. *'dre-bar*); K [*adh*]*im*[*āna-*]*p*[*r*]*āp*[*t*]*o*; XTa *-prāptaḥ* (= OV)(for *-prāpto*, so intends K).

7 Tc omits from XXI 6c *imu* to 7c *na*.

7a XTa *so ca*, unmetr. (= O!)(for *socej*, K; Conze Rgs. 50 misr. K as *so ce*, w. which r. Edg.Rgs. 40!); *cet* (or *ce*) is not found in our text; only *saci* (O always sep. *sa ci*!), m.c. for *sace(t)*(cf. BHSD p. 549b, qq. vv.), is used; *socej*, m.c. for *sacej (sacet)*, in addition by analogy of *so* for *sa*, should be adopted here, although Tib. supports neither *socej* nor *so cej*; V em. *so caṃkramārtham*, which is not acceptable at all; XTa *jagārtham* (= O; w. a hiatus-bridger *-m-* ?)(for *jagārthu-*, K; Conze Rgs. 50 misr. K as *°rtha*); K *-abhiyukta-*, unmetr. (for *-abhiyuktaka-*, XTa = OV); XTa *-bodhisattvāṃ* (for *°sattvān*, K, so em. O = V): Tib. *byaṅ-chub-sems-dpa' 'gro-ba'i don brtson*.

7b XTa *-prāptāṃ* (for *°ān*, K, so em. O = V).

7d XTac *na viveka-gocaru ayaṃ hi* (= OV; em. *hi* perh. to *ti*): Tib.A *'di-ni dgon-pa'i spyod-yul* (r. perh. *dpen-pa'i spyod-yul*: Skt. *viveka-gocaru*) *min źes*; for *ayu māru-gocaru-sthito ti*, K: Tib.B *de-ni bdud-kyi spyod-yul gnas źes*, cf. Chin. 彼魔所作 ; Conze ad O p. 128 r. *ayu māru-gocaru sthito 'ti*!; V (p. 380 n. 4) suggests *ayu māru-gocaru sthito ti* w. Tib. B; Tc *uktāḥ* (for *ukto*, KXTa = OV).

8a XTac *athavā* (= OV)(for *athavāpy*, K); K *araṇyai* (for *araṇye*, XTac = OV: Tib. *dgon-par)*.

8b K *-vigatro* (for *-vigato*, XTac = OV: Tib. *bral*); XTa *niyatāgra-bodhiṃ*, Tc *niyagra-bodhiṃ*, O em. *niyato 'gra-bodhiṃ* (= V w. *-m*)(for *niyatāgra-bodhau*, K, so r. Edg.Rgs. 40: Tib. *byaṅ-chub mchog ṅes-na)*.

8c Tc <*ja*>*gad-*; MSS. *-arthabhiprasthitānāṃ* (= V; K *°nāṃ*), O *-arthyabhiprasthitānaṃ* (wt.n.!)(for *-arth'-abhiprasthitānāṃ*: Tib. *don źugs-pa-rnams-kyi)*.

8d XTa *ātma-kṣiṇo ti*, O *ātmā kṣiṇoti* (wt.n.)(= V)(for *ātmā-kṣiṇo ti*, KTc; so r. Conze Index p. 135a w. a question mark); *kṣiṇoti* is not suited to the context; *kṣīṇa-* is used for *kṣīṇa-*, m.c. (cf. Edgerton 3.37).

**bhagavatyāṃ ratna-guṇa-saṃcaya-gāthāyāṃ māra-karma-pa(X71A)rivarto nāmaikaviṃśatimaḥ // 21 //**

XXI col. Tc *māra-karmo* (for *māra-karma-parivarto*, KXTa = OV); K *nāmaikaviṃśatiḥ*, XTa *nāma ekaviṃśatimaḥ*, Tc *nāmaikaviṃśatitamaḥ* (= V), O em. *nāma ekaviṃśatitamaḥ* (for *nāmaikaviṃśatimaḥ*; cf. XIX colophon, fn. end); at the end of the colophon K reads *gātha // 8 //*; Tc adds num. 21.

## ⟨XXII. KALYĀṆA-MITRA⟩

tasmā hu māna nihanitvana paṇḍitena
guru-āśrayena vara-bodhi gaveṣamāṇo /
vaidyo va ātura-sva-roga-cikitsanārthaṃ
kalyāṇa-mitra bha(Ta20B)jitavya a-tandritena // 1 //

buddhā ya bodhi-vara-prasthita bodhisattvāḥ
kalyāṇa-mitra i(X71B)ma-pāramitā-nidiṣṭāḥ /
te cānuśāsaka imaṃ pratipatti-bhūmi
duvi-kāraṇena anubudhyati buddha-bodhiṃ // 2 //

atikrānt'-an-āgata-jinā sthita ye diśāsu
sarveṣa mārgu ayu pāramitā an-anyo /

---

1a O *tasmāhu* (cf. O *tasmāhu* for *tasmā hu* I 16d, IV 4c, VI 8a, VII 7a, XII 4d); XTac *mānu* (= OV)(for *māna*, K).

1b XTac *guru-āśayena* (= OV: Tib.A *bsam-pa drag-pos*, B *bsam-pa drag ldan*)(for *°-āśrayena*, K, w. dental *-n-*: Chin. 大智者依師学 ; cf. MWD p. 359b, *guru-padāśraya-*, s.v.); cf. XIV 1b *-āśraya-*, v.l. *-āśaya-*; also XV 1c-d *tehī su-śiṣya-guru-gaurava-saṃprayuktaiḥ kalyāṇa-mitra sada sevitavya vijñaiḥ*; X *gaveṣamāṇaḥ* (= V), O *-gaveṣamāṇaḥ* (wt.n.; cpd.), Ta *eveṣamāṇaḥ*, Tc *eveṣamāṇaḥ* (for *gaveṣamāṇo*, K).

1c K *pa* (Conze Rgs. 50 misr. K as *ya*)(for *va*, XTac = OV: Tib. *ltar*; cf. Edgerton 4.14, BHSD p. 466a, *va* 1, s.v.); XTa *ātura-svarona-*, Tc *ātura-kharona-*, O em. *ātura-svaroṇa* (?; so sep.!), V sep. *ātura svaroga-*!(for *ātura-svaroga*, K); cf. Tib.A *nad-pa śin-tu gso phyir sman-pa bsten-pa ltar*, B *nad-pa'i tshogs-kyis gso phyir ...*, Chin. 如良医除衆患 ; also Haribhadra ad Rgs. (Peking JA 68B5) ... *nad-pa'i tshogs-kyis smad-pa* (r. *sman-pa*) *bsten-par ltar / 'dod-chags-la sogs-pa raṅ-gi nad gso-ba'i phyir gYel-ba med-par dge-ba'i bśes-gñen bsten-par bya'o źes bstan-to //*

1d Cf. AsP 197.2-4, 5-7 *bodhisattvena ... anuttarāṃ samyak-saṃbodhim abhisaṃboddhu-kāmena ... kalyāṇa-mitrāṇi ... bhaktavyāni ...*

2a MSS. *buddhāya* (so prints O!; "dat. of goal"?) should be divided as *buddhā* (nom.pl.) plus *ya* (m.c. for *ye*): Tib.A *saṅs-rgyas byaṅ-chub mchog źugs byaṅ-chub-sems-dpa' daṅ*, B ... *°-dpa'-dag)*; cf. *budāhāḥ kalyāṇa-mitrāṇi* (*Sūtrālaṃkāra*, ed. S. Lévi, XIX 12/13); XTac *bodhisattvā* (= OV) (for *°sattvāḥ*, K).

2b XTac *imi* (= OV)(for *ima-*, K; cf. Edgerton 21.50); K *ca nirdiṣṭā*(hyper-metr. and unmetr.!), Tc *-nirdiṣṭāḥ* (for *-nidiṣṭāḥ*, XTa = OV; but OV sep. *imi pāramitā nidiṣṭāḥ*; cf. Edg.Rgs. 10 for *nidiṣṭa-*); cf. Tib. *pha-rol phyin daṅ mtshuṅs-* (B *bcas-*)*te dge-ba'i bśes-su bstan* (B v.l.*bsten* =O!)!

2c XTac *iyaṃ* (= OV)(for *imaṃ*, K; cf. Edgerton 9.16, 21.54); XTa *-bhūmī* (= OV)(for *-bhūmi*, KTc): Tib.A *de-dag nan-tan sa 'di rjes-su ston-pa yin*, but B *de-dag rjes-su ston byed 'di-ni sgrub-pa'i sa*!

2d K *durvikāraṇena* (unmetr. and nonsensical!; cf. Edg.Rgs. 40; but Conze Index p. 142b, 'for a double reason'!)(for *duvi-kāraṇena*, XTac (= OV; but V sep. *duvi kār°*!); *duvi-* is a stem (cf. XX 13b *duvi-*, XX 14b *-duvi-*, w. fn.): Tib.B *rgyu-rnam gñis-kyis* (cf. also Edg.Rgs. 29 and 40); Conze (Dict. p. 202) records *du-vikār°* 'for a double reason'! (cf. Tib.A *rnam-pa gñis-kyis* 'in two ways'); V *-bodhim* (w. *-m*).

3a K *atikrāntanāgata-* (so print OV wt.n.), XTa *atikrantanāgata-*, Tc *atikrantanāga-* (for *atikrānt'-anāgata-*: Tib. *'das daṅ ma byon*); Tc-*jināṃ* (for *-jinā*, KXTa = OV; but V sep. *°gata jinā*); XTac *diśāsū* (= O; cf. Edgerton 3.23, also Edg.Rgs. 13)(for *diśāsu*, K = V).

3b XTac *sarveṣu* (= OV)(for *°eṣa*, K); Tac *mārga* (for *mārgu*, KX = OV); cf. XV 4b-d *trāṇā ... śaraṇāś ca lenāḥ, gati-buddhi-dīpa-pariṇāyaka ... pradyota-ulka-vara-dharma-kathī*.

obhāsa ulka vara-bodhayi pra(K20B)sthitānāṃ
    āloka śāstra iya pā(X72A)ramitā jinānāṃ // 3 //

yatha prajña-pā(Tc27A)ramita śūnyata-lakṣaṇena
    tatha-lakṣaṇān imi prajānati sarva-dharmān /
śūnyān a-lakṣaṇa prajānayamāna dharmān
    evaṃ carantu caratī sugatānu prajñāṃ // 4 //

āhāra-kāma parikalpayamāna sattvāḥ
    saṃsāra-sakta-manasas sada saṃsaranti /
(X72B) ahu-mahya-dharma ubhi-y-eti a-bhūta-śūnyā
    ākāśa-gaṇṭhi ayu ātmana baddha bālaiḥ // 5 //

---

3c Tc *vabhāsa* (r. perh. *avabhāsa*)(for *obhāsa*, KXTa = OV); Tc *vaye bodhayi* (for *vara-bodhayi*, KXTa = OV: Tib. *byaṅ-chub mchog-la*); K *prasthitānām* (= V), Tc °*nā*, *m*- (for °*nāṃ*, XTa = O).

3d K *sāstra*, XTa *śāstri* (= OV), Tc *śāstriṃ* (for *śāstra*: Tib.A *ston-pa*, B *ston mchog*; cf. Edgerton 13.15; Conze Rgs. 40 misr. K as *lokaśāstru*, w. a question mark); XTac *imi* (= OV)(for *iya*, K); XTac *pāramitā padiṣṭāḥ*, O *pāramitopadiṣṭāḥ* (wt.n.!), V °*tā pradiṣṭāḥ*(wt.n.): Tib.A *bstan*, B *bśad*, Chin. 説 (for *jinānāṃ*, K); cf. AsP 197.14-15, 31-32 *ṣaḍ eva pāramitāḥ śāstā*, *ṣaṭ pāramitā mārgaḥ*, *ṣaṭ pāramitā ālokaḥ*, *ṣaṭ pāramitā ulkā*, *ṣaṭ pāramita avabhāsaḥ*.

4a K *prajñā*- (for *prajña*-, XTac = OV); V sep. *śūnyata lakṣaṇena*; cf. Tib. A *śes-rab pha-rol phyin-pa'i mtshan-gyis stoṅ*, B ... *phyin-pa mtshan-ñid stoṅ*, Chin. 彼般若空無相.

4b XTac *-lakṣaṇāya* (= OV; but V sep. *-lakṣaṇā ya*!)(for *-lakṣaṇān*, K, acc. pl.m., Bhvr.: Tib.B *mtshan-ñid de daṅ 'drar*, Chin. 諸法相亦如是); less. poss. *tatha lakṣaṇān'* (for °*āni*, acc.pl.nt.; cf. Edgerton 4.25): Tib.A *de-ltar mtshan daṅ chos thams-cad sus*; *yatha* is construed w. *evaṃ* in *d* (not w. *tatha* in *b*); XTac *jānati* (= OV)(for *prajānati*, K); XTac *-dharmāṃ* (for *-dharmān*, K, so em. O = V).

4c XTa *śūnyānu lakṣaṇa* (= O!), Tc *śūnyānu lakṣa⟨ṇa⟩*(for *śūnyān a-lakṣaṇa*, K = V: Tib.A *stoṅ-źiṅ mtshan-ñid med-par*, B *stoṅ-źiṅ msthan-ma med-par*); XTa *dharmāṃ*, Tc *dharmā* (for *dharmān*, K, so em. O = V; Conze Rgs. 50 misr. K as *dharmā*).

4d XTac *sugatāna* (= OV)(for °*ānu*, K); K *prajñā* (cf. Edgerton 9.20-22) (for *prajñāṃ*, XTac = OV; but V w. *-m*).

5a Cf. Tib.A *sems-can zas daṅ 'dod-la yoṅs-su rtog byed-ciṅ*, Chin. 繫著色欲及飲食; Tib.B *sems-can yoṅs-su rtog-pas* (v.l. °*-pa*) *zas-la 'dod byed-ciṅ* (so Conze Trsl.); cf. WSJD pp. 221b-222a *āhāra-gaveṣin*-, *āhārārthin*-, *āhāra-gṛddhi*- (all from AsP).

5b XTac *saṃsāri* (= OV)(for *saṃsāra*-, K); K *-khinna-*!, Tc *-mukta-*!, V em. *yukta*- (for *-sakta*-, XTa = O; but O *saṃsāri sakta*-: Tib. *chags-pa'i*); V em. *-manasaḥ* (for *-manasas*, MSS. = O; Conze Rgs. 40 msir. K as *-manasam*); Conze Rgs. 40 misr. K as *yada* (for *sada*, MSS. = OV: Tib. *rtag-tu*); V *saṃsmaranti* (wt.n.!)(for *saṃsaranti*, MSS. = O: Tib. *'khor*, Chin. 輪廻 ).

5c Tc *ahu-majya-dharmaṃ* (for *ahu-mahya-dharma*, KXTa = OV; but V sep. *ahu mahya dharma*!: Tib. *bdag daṅ bdag-gi chos*); cf. XXII 6c *ahu-mahya*, 7b *ahu-mahya-anopalabdhiḥ*; XTa *ubhi eti* (= OV), Tc *abhi ebhy* (for *ubhi-y-eti*, K, w. a hiatus-bridger *-y-*: Tib. *gñis*); V sep. *abhūta śūnyā*; cf. AsP 198.28-29 *bhagavān āha —— tat kiṃ manyase subhūte api nu ahaṃkāra-mamakārau śūnyau?* *subhūtir āha —— śūnyau bhagavan, śūnyau sugata*.

5d Tc *-dhātu gavy* (for *-gaṇṭhi*, KXTa = OV: Tib.A *mdud*, B *mdud-pa*); XTac *bāle* (= OV)(for *bālaiḥ*, K: Tib.A *byis-pa-rnams-kyis*, B *byis-pa*).

6a K *samtena* (for *śaṅkitena*, XTac = OV: Tib. *dogs-pas*, but most MSS. *dogs-pa'i*, cf. Chin. 疑 ); Tc *atyupaiti* (for *abhyup*°, KXTa = OV); cf.

yatha śaṅkitena viṣa-saṃjñata abhyupaiti
    no cāsya koṣṭha-gatu so viṣ' upadyate ca /
em eva bāl' upagato ahu-mahya eṣo
    saṃjñāya jāyi mriyate ca sadā a-bhūto // 6 //

yatha udgraho tatha pra(X73A)kāśitu saṃkileśo
    vyodāna uktu ahu-mahya-an=opalabdhiḥ /
na hi atra kaś ci (Ta21A) ya kiliśyati śudhyate vā
    prajñāya pāramita budhyati bodhisattvo // 7 //

yāvanti sattva nikhilen' iha jambudvīpe
    te (Tc27B) sarvi bodhi-vara-cittu upādayitvā /

---

Tib. *'du-śes-kyis-ni dug laṅs-pa* (= O; vv.ll. *bslaṅs-pa, bslaṅ-ba* = Conze Index-Dict.)!

6b K *viṣupadyate* (Edg.Rgs. 40 sep. *viṣu padyate!*), XTa *viṣu pātyate*(=V), Tc *viṣumātyate*, O *pi pātyate* (wt.n.!)(for *viṣ' upadyate*, 'poison is produced, is poisoned'); but cf. Tib.A *'gyed*, B *brgyal-bar 'gyur* (= Skt. *padyate* or *pātyate*); one would expect *viṣ' upadyate* contextually and syntactically; the final *-u* of *viṣu*, nom.sg.m. (cf. Edgerton 8.20), is lost before the initial *u-* (cf. Edgerton 4.27); the initial *u-* of *upadyate* (= *utpadyate*) becomes short, m.c. (cf. Edgerton 2.88, Edg.Rgs. 9); render pāda *b*: 'To him there is nothing (poisonous) gone into (his) stomach, but the poison is produced (= he is poisoned)'; cf. Tib.A *dug de* (v.l. °*-du*) *lto-bar soṅ-ba ma yin 'on-kyaṅ 'gyel*, B *dug de khoṅ-du soṅ-ba med-kyaṅ brgyal-bar 'gyur*.

6c K *bālupagato* (so prints V), XTa *vāpagato*, Tc *vāyagato*, O *bālu pagato* (wt.n.!)(for *bāl' upagato*; cf. Edgerton 4.27); *upagato* is construed w. *ahu-mahya* (= "*ahaṃ-mama-*"*saṃjñe*; cf. Speijer 236); cf. Edg.Rgs. 40 for *-saṃjñata abhyupaiti* in *a*; but freely Tib.A *khas blaṅs-pa*, B *khas len-pa*; Tc *aju-majya eṣo* (for *ahu-mahya eṣo*, KXTa = OV; but O *ahu-mahya-eṣo*, cpd.!, V sep. *ahu mahya eso!*); cf. XXII 5c *ahu-mahya-dharma*, 7b *ahu-mahya-anopalabdhiḥ*; cf. Tib.A *de-ltar byis-pa* (v.l. °*-pas*) *bdag daṅ bdag-gir* (v.l. °*-gi*) *khas blaṅs-pa*, B *de-bźin byis-pa bdag daṅ bdag-gir khas len-pa*.

6d XTac *aha-saṃjñi*(= OV: Tib.B *bdag der 'du-śes*)(for *saṃjñāya*, K: Tib.A *'du-śes*); XTa *mṛyate*, Tc *mṛgate* (for *mriyate*, K, so em. O = V: Tib.B *'chi*, v.l. *'jig* = O); cf. Tib.A *'du-śes skyes-pas rtag-tu ji-yaṅ yod ma yin!*, B *bdag der 'du-śes yaṅ-dag min* (v.l. *mi*) *rtag* (v.l. *rtog* = O!) *skye-źiṅ 'chi* (vv.ll. *mchi, 'jig* = O).

7a For *udgraha-* see Edg.Rgs. 40, also WSJD p. 254a, q.v.; XTac *katha* (for *tatha*, K, so em. O = V: Tib. *de-ltar*); K *saṃkileso* (for °*eśo*, XTac = OV: Tib. *kun-nas ñon-moṅs*).

7b XTac *ukta* (= OV)(for *uktu*, K); XTa *ahu-mahya-anopalabdhi*, Tc *aju-majyānop*°, V sep. *ahu mahya anopalabdhi* (for *ahu-mahya-anopalabdhiḥ*, K, so em. O: Tib. *bdag daṅ bdag-gir mi dmigs*; cf. XXII 5c *ahu-mahya-dharma*, 6c *ahu-mahya*); cf. Edg.Rgs. 29 and 33 for *vyodāna* (for *vyavad*°) and *opalabdhiḥ* (for *upal*°).

7c K *hy*, Tc *jy* (for *hi*, XTa = OV); K *kaś cit* (for *kaś ci*, XTac = OV); K *yaḥ*, XTac *yo* (= OV)(for *ya*, so em. Edg.Rgs. 40); MSS. *kliṣyati* (O p. 86 n. 3 misr. X as *klaṣyati*), O em. *kliśyati*, unmetr.! (= V!)(for *kiliśy*°, so em. Edg.Rgs. 40; cf. *saṃkileśa-* in *a*).

7d O *prajñāya-*, cpd.; O *badhyati* (? mispr.)(for *budhy*°, MSS. = V); Tc *bodhisattvoḥ*, O °*sattve* (wt.n.!=V!)(for °*sattvo*, KXTa, so r.Edg.Rgs.40).

8a XTac *yāvanta* (= OV)(for °*nti*, K); K *nikhileniha* (Conze Rgs. 50 misr. K as °*naha*), XTac *nikhile iha* (= OV)(for *nikhilen' iha*); *nikhilen'*, instr. (for °*lena*) is used w. loc. *iha jambudvīpe* (cf. Edgerton 7.30), the final *-a* being lost in sandhi; it may hardly be an example of a hiatus-bridger *-n-* (i.e. *nikhile-n-iha*; cf. Edgerton 4.65); cf. Tib.A *'dzam-gliṅ ma-lus-dag-na sems-can ji-sñed-pa*, but B *'dzam-gliṅ-na sems-can ji-sñed ma-lus-pa!*

dānaṃ daditva bahu-varṣa-(X73B)sahasra-koṭīḥ
    sarve ca nāmayi jagārtha nidāna bodhiṃ // 8 //

yaś caiva prajña-vara-pāramitābhiyukto
    divasasmi antamasa ek' anuvartayeyā /
kala-puṇyu so na bhavatī iha dāna-skandho
    tad a-tandritena sada osaritavya prajñā // 9 //

caramā(K21A)ṇu prajña-vara-pāramitāya yogī
    mahatīṃ ja(X74A)neti karuṇāṃ na ca sattva-saṃjñā /
tada bhoti sarva-jagatī vidu dakṣiṇīyo
    satataṃ a-mogha paribhuñjati rāṣṭra-piṇḍaṃ // 10 //

cira-baddha-deva-manu-jāṃs triy-apāyi sattvān
    parimocituṃ ya iha icchati bodhisattvo /
pṛthu-mārgu tīru upadarśayi sattva-dhātoḥ
    prajñāya (X74B) pāramita-yuktu divā ca rātrau // 11 //

---

8b K *sarve* (for *sarvi*, XTac = OV); K *-cintu upādayitvā* (Conze Rgs. 50 misr. K as *-cittu up°*), X *-citta upădayitvā*, Ta *-citta upādayitvā* (so em. O = V), Tc *-cittopădayitvā* (for *-cittu upādayitvā*: Tib. *sems bskyed-nas*); cf. AsP 199.27 *anuttarāyāṃ samyak-saṃbodhau cittam utpādya* ...

8c Tc *daditvā* (for *°tva*, KXTa =OV): XTac *-koṭī* (for *°īḥ*, K, so em. O =V).

8d OV *sarvaṃ* (wt.n.!)(for *sarve*, MSS.; cf. Edgerton 21.31); O *janārtha* (wt.n.!)(for *jagārtha*, MSS. = V; but V *jagārtha-*, cpd.!); XTac *bodhau* (= OV)(for *bodhiṃ*, K; cf. XXXI 6a, fn.); cf. AsP 199.29 *anuttarāyāṃ samyak-saṃbodhau pariṇāmayeyuḥ*.

9b XTac *divasaṃ pi* (= OV)(for *divasasmi*, K); XTac *antamaśa* (= OV)(for *°asa*, KTc; cf. Edgerton 2.63, BHSD p. 38a, *antamaśas*, s.v.); MSS. *ekanuvartayeyā* (so prints V), O *eka nuvart°* (for *ek' anuvart°*); *ek'* is a loc. w. nominal ending (i.e. *eke*, *eki*; cf. Edgerton 21.20), or poss. a loc. in *-a* (cf. Edgerton 8.11); Rec.B *divasaṃ* could be construed w. *eka* (for *ekam*) to denote the duration of time: Tib. *tha-na ñi-ma gcig-cig*, Chin. 於一日.

9c XTac *-puṇya* (= OV)(for *-puṇyu*, K).

9d Tc *atandritenaṃ* (for *°ena*, KXTa = OV); K *sa⟨da⟩*: Tib. *rtag-tu*.

10a Tc *caramānū* (w. *-n-*)(for *°māṇŭ*,KXTa = OV); Tc *yogi* (for *yogī*,KXTa=OV).

10b Tc *mahatī* (for *°tīṃ*, KXTa = OV).

10c XTa *bhonti* (= OV)(for *bhoti*, KTc); K *dakṣiṇāyo* (Conze Rgs. 50 misr. K as *°īyo*), XTac *dakṣiṇīyā* (= OV; but O *vidu-°*, cpd.!)(for *dakṣiṇīyo*); cf. AsP 200.2 *sarva-sattvānāṃ dakṣiṇīyatāṃ gacchati*; AsP 200.17-18 *sarva-lokasya dakṣiṇīyatāṃ parigṛhṇanti*.

10d K *satata⟨ṃ a⟩mogha*, XTa *satataṃ amoghu* (= OV), Tc *satatam aghoghu* (for *satataṃ amogha*: Tib. *rtag-tu* ... *don yod*); Tc *paribhaṃjati* (for *°bhuñjati*, KXTa = OV: Tib. *yoṅs-su spyod*); cf. AsP 200.21-22 *bodhi-sattvena mahā-sattvena a-moghaṃ rāṣṭraṃ piṇḍaṃ paribhoktu-kāmena* ...

11a XTac *-buddha-* (= OV!)(for *-baddha-*, K: Tib.A *'brel-ba*, B *°-ba-yi*); XTa *-manujān* (= OV), Tc *°jāṃ* (for *°jāṃs*, K); XTa *tri-apāyi* (= OV), Tc *try-°* (for *triy-°*, K); XTa *sattvāṃ*, Tc *°tvā* (for *°tvān*, K = OV wt.n.).

11b K *parimocayituṃ* (hypermetr.!), XTac *parimocitu* (for *°mocituṃ*, so em. O = V); Ta *yu* (for *ya*, KXTc = OV); Tc *⟨i⟩cchati*; Tc *bodhisattvoḥ* (for *°sattvo*, KXTa = OV); cf. AsP 200.22-23 *(bodhisattvena ...) saṃsāra-gatān sattvān saṃsārāt parimocayitu-kāmena* ...

11c Tc *pṛthva-mārga* (for *pṛthu-mārgu*, KXTa = OV; but O sep. *pṛthu mārgu*); XTa *-dhāto*, Tc *-dhātau* (= OV wt.n.: Tib.B *sems-can khams-la*)(for *-dhātoḥ*, K: Tib.A *sems-can khams-kyi*); cf. AsP 200.22 *(bodhisattvena ...) sattvānāṃ mārgam upadeṣṭu-kāmena* ...

puruṣo ya agra-ratanasya a-labdha-pūrvo
aparasmi kāli puna la(Tc28A)bdha bhaveya tuṣṭo /
saha-labdhu nāśayi puno 'pi pramāda-bhūto
nāśitva duḥkhitu sadā ratanābhikāṅkṣī // 12 //

em eva bodhi-vara-prasthita ratna-tulyo
prajñāya pārami(X75A)ta-yogu na riñcita(Ta21B)vyo /
ratanaṃ va labdha gṛhamāṇu a-bhinna-sattvaṃ
anubandhayāti tvarite śivam abhyueti // 13 //

---

11d XTac -*yukta* (for -*yuktu*, K); O *prajñāya-pāramita-°*, cpd.; V sep. *prajñāya pāramita yukta*.

12a XTa *agru-ratanasya* (= OV: but OV sep. *agru rat°*!), Tc *aśru-°* (for *agra-°*, K: Tib. *rin-chen mchog*); XTa *alabdhu-* (for *alabdha-*, KTc = OV wt.n.).

12b Ta *aparesmi*, Tc *aparaśmi* (for *aparasmi*, KX = OV); V em. *labdhva* (for *labdha*, MSS. = O); syntactically, it is better to take *labdha*, m.c. for *labdhā*, as a nom.sg.m. of *labdhṛ-* (Tib. *rñed-par 'gyur-te*); it could be a ppp., as AsP 200.28-29 *puruṣeṇa ... a-pratilabdha-pūrvaṃ mahā-maṇi-ratnaṃ pratilabdhaṃ bhavet*, AsP 201.2 *tena mahā-maṇi-ratnaṃ prati-labdhaṃ bhavet*; it is not plausible to take *labdha* as a ger., m.c. for *labdhā* (= Skt. *labdhvā*), although it would be phonologically possible (cf. Edgerton 35.52, also Edg.Rgs. 11); *labdhā*, ger., is once used in XXIX 7b; gerunds of *labh-* in our text are *labhitvā* XI 5a, *labhitva* XI 4c, 5b, *labhiyāna* XI 5a, *labdhāna* XX 15b, 16b, XXIX 8b; Tc *tuṣṭa* (for *tuṣṭo*, KXTa = OV).

12c XTac -*labdha* (for -*labdhu*, K); O sep. *saha labdha*!, V em. *sa ha labdhva*!; *saha-* is a prior member of the cpd. °-*labdhu* (nom.sg.nt.ppp.), 'as soon as it is obtained' (cf. BHSD p. 587a, 1 *saha-* 2, s.v.): Tib. *rñed ma thag-tu*; K *nāmayi*, Ta *nośayi* (for *nāśayi*, XTc = OV: Tib.A *stor-te*, B *stor-na-ni*); K *punopi* (so em. O). XTa *puṇopi*, Tc *puṇyo pi* (for *puno 'pi* = V); XTac *prasāda-* (for *pramāda-*, K = OV wt.n.: Tib.A *bag med gyur-pas-na*, B *bag med gyur-te*; Conze ad O p. 128 r. w. K, but misr. O as *pramoda-*).

12d K *nāsitva* (Conze Rgs. 51 misr. K as *nāśitva*, w. which r. Edg.Rgs. 40), Tc *nāsito*, O *nāśitva* (? mispr.)(for *nāśitva*, XTa, so em. V: Tib. *stor-bas*); XTac *duḥkhi satataṃ* (= OV)(for *duḥkhitu sadā*, K: Tib.A *sdug-bsñal rtag-tu*, B *rtag-tu sdug-bsñal-lo*; Conze Rgs. 51 r. K as *duḥkhi tu sadā*!); Tc *ra ta nābhikāṅkṣī*.

13a XTa -*para-* (for -*vara-*, KTc = OV wt.n.: Tib. *mchog*).

13b O *prajñāya-*, cpd.; V sep. *pāramita yogu*!; K *ṇa*, XTa *ṇaṃ*, Tc *ṇāṃ* (for *na*, so em. O = V: Tib. *mi*; but Chin. 功德 = Skt. *yo guṇa*?); XTa *ricitavyo*, Tc *ricitavyoḥ* (for *riñcitavyo*, K, so em. O = V: Tib. *dor ... bya*; cf. Edgerton 28.4, also 43 p. 227a, *riñca-ti*, s.v.).

13c Tac *ratana⟨ṃ⟩*; V em. *labdhva* (for *labdha*, MSS. = O; *labdha*, acc.sg. nt.ppp. (w. *ratanaṃ*), is wrongly taken by Vaidya (= Tib. *rñed-nas*!); XTac *gṛhamānu* (O p. 88 n. 3 misr. X as °*mānu*)(for *gṛhamāṇu*, K, so em. O = V: Tib.A *'dzin-par byed-ciṅ*, B *blaṅs-te*; cf. Edg.Rgs. 29, Edgerton 43 p. 211a, *grah-* 4, s.v.); K *prabhinna-sarve*, XTac °-*sattvom* (O °*sattvo*, reading -*m* w. next word!), V em. *a-bhinna-sattvo* (for *a-bhinna-sattvaṃ*: Tib.A *mi phyed-na*, B *rab-tu brtson skris-nas*!); *pra-* is a scribal error for the graphically similar *a-*; MSS. suggest °-*sattvaṃ* rather than °-*sattvo*.

13d XTac *anubuddhayāti* (= V), O *manu buddhayāti* (*m-* of *manu* should have belonged to the prec. word!)(for *anubandhayāti*, K: Tib.A *rjes-su 'brel-bar byed-ciṅ*, but B *'gro-bar byed-pa* = Skt. *yāti*?); *anubuddhayāti* is prob. a miscopying for **anubaddhayāti* (cf. XXII 1a Rec.B -*buddha-* for A -*baddha-*; also Edgerton 43 p. 221b, *bandh-* 2/3,ss.vv.); for °*bandhayāti* see Edgerton 43 p. 221b, *bandh-* 2, s.v., also Edgerton 27.1, 38.21);

bhagavatyāṃ ratna-guṇa-saṃcaya-gāthāyāṃ kalyāṇa-mitra-parivarto nāma dvāviṃśatimaḥ // 22 //

---

XTac *tvarito* (= OV)(for *°ite*, K, so r. Conze Index-Dict.: Tib. *myur-du*); XTa *abhyupaiti* (= OV), Tc *atyupaiti* (for *abhyupeti*, K; cf. XIV 5d *upeti*).

XXII col. K *dvāviṃśatiḥ*, Tc *dvāvi<ṃ>śatimaḥ*, O em. *dvāviṃśatitamaḥ* (= V) (for *dvāviṃśatimaḥ*, XTa; cf. XIX colophon, footnote end); at the end of the colophon K reads *gāthā // 13 //*; Tc adds num. 22.

## <XXIII. ŚAKRA>

udayāti sūra vigatābhra marīci-jālo
(X75B) vidhamitva sarva-tamasākulam andha-kāraṃ /
abhibhoti sarva-krimi jyotika-prāṇa-bhūtān
sarvāṃś ca tāraka-gaṇān api candra-ābhāṃ // 1 //

em eva prajña-vara-pāramitāṃ caranto
vidhamitva dṛṣṭi-gahanaṃ vidu bodhisattvo /
(K21B) abhibhoti sarva-jagatī raha pratyayāṃś ca
(Tc28B) śū(X76A)nyānimitta-carito pṛthu bodhisattvo // 2 //

yatha rāja-putra dhana-dāyaku artha-kāmo
sarveṣu śreṣṭhu bhavate abhigāminīyo /

---

1 Cf. Rgs. V 9.

1a K *śūra* (cf. VI 9d *abhibhoti ... śūro*), XTac *sūryu* (= OV)(for *sūra*: Tib.A *gñi* [= *ñi*], B *ñi-ma*); XTac *vigatâśru* (= O; but O *vigatâśru-*, cpd.!), V em. *vigatāś ca*! (for *vigatâbhra*, K, 'free from clouds': Tib. A *sprin med mkha'-la*, B *sprin daṅ bral-ba'i*); Conze Rgs. 40 misr. K as *vigatâtra*; the orig. r. must have been *vigatâbhru*, which was later mis-copied w. the graphically similar *-aśru* 'tear'; *vigatâśru* has puzzled Edg.Rgs. 29 (p. 8), but is now solved by K and w. the help of Tib.; XTa *marīci-mālā* (= OV; r. perh. °*-mālī*), Tc *marīvi-mālā* (for *marīci-jālo*, K, Bhvr.: Tib.A *'od-zer 'phro-bas*!, B *'od-zer dra-ba-can*; but Conze Rgs. 40 sep. *marīci jālo*!).

1b V sep. *sarva tam*°; Tc *-tasamākulam* (for *-tamasākulam*, KXTa = OV); XTac *-kārām* (for *-kāraṃ*, K, so em. OV; but V w. *-m*): Tib.A *mun-pas dkrigs-pa'i mun gnag (= nag) kun sel-bar byed-ciṅ*, B *mun nag thibs-po'i mun-pa 'joms*.

1c XTac *avibhonti* (= OV!)(for *abhibhoti*, K, so r. Conze Rgs. 51: Tib. *zil gyis* [*g*]*non*); cf. *abhibhoti* VI 9d, XXIII 2c, XXX 12d, XXXI 16d, 17bd; XTac *-kṛmi*, O *-kami* (? mispr. for *-kṛmi*)(for *-krimi*, K, so em. V; but V sep. *sarva krimi-*!); K *jyotika-prāṇa-bhūtāṃ*, XTac *jotika-prāṇi-bhūtāṃ* (cf. Edgerton 8.90 for acc.pl. in *-āṃ*), O *-jātika-*(? mispr.)*prāṇi-bhūtān* (wt.n.), V *-jotika-prāṇa-bhūtāṃ* (wt.n.)(for *jyotika-prāṇa-bhūtān*); °*-bhūtān*, Karmadhāraya-cpd., is used appositionally w. *sarva-krimi* (cf. Speijer 214).

1d V *-ābhām* (w. *-m*).

2a XTa *-pāramitā*, Tc *-pāramita* (for °*itāṃ*, K, so em. O = V).

2b Tc *-gaharaṃ* (for *-gahanaṃ*, KXTa = OV: Tib.A *thibs*, B *thibs-po*, v.l. *'thibs-po* = O); O *vidu-bodhisattvo*, cpd.

2c K *a*(21B1)*abhibhoti*, XTac *abhibhonti* (= OV; cf. Edgerton 25.30)(for *abhibhoti*, so suggests Edg.Rgs. 40; Conze does not report K's r.); OV *raha-*, cpd.; cf. Tib. *'gro-ba* (B *'gro*) *kun daṅ dgra-bcom raṅ-rgyal*! (note: *jagatī*, loc.; *raha*, acc.pl.m.).

2d Tc *śūnyānimitta-carito pṛthu nyānimitta caritva pṛthu* (for *śūnyāni-mitta-carito pṛthu*, KXTa = OV); but O *pṛthu-*, cpd.!; *pṛthu* is here adv.: Tib.A *yaṅs* (MSS. *yaṅ*; w. *carito*), B *maṅ* (w. *abhibhoti*).

3a Conze Rgs. 51 misr. O as *atha* (for *yatha*, MSS. = OV: Tib. *dper-na*); Tc *dāyuku* (for *dāyaku*, KXTa = OV: Tib. *gtoṅ*, v.l. *ster*).

3b XTa *śreṣṭha* (= OV), Tc *śreṣṭhā* (for *śreṣṭhu*, K), X *abhigāminīyoḥ*, Tc *abhigāminīye* (= V!)(for *abhigāminīyo*, KTa, so em. O [O *abhigābhinīyo* is certainly a misprint]: Tib. *mṅon-par 'gro bya 'os*).

ayu eva etarahi sattva pramodayātī

prāg eva rājya-sthitu bheṣyati paṭṭa-dhāro // 3 //

em eva prajña-carito vidu bodhisattvo

(X76B) a-mṛtasya dāyaku priyo maru-mānuṣāṇāṃ /

ayu eṣa etarahi sattva-sukhābhiyukto

prāg eva yāva-sthitu bheṣyati dharma-rājyo // 4 //

bhagavatyāṃ ratna-guṇa-saṃcaya-gāthāyāṃ śakra-parivarto nāma trayo-viṃśatimaḥ // 23 //

---

3c XTa *sa hi eṣa* (= O), Tc *sa jyaṣa*, V *sa hy eṣa* (for *ayu eva*, K: Tib. *'di-ni*; em. poss. to *ayu eṣa* as in XXIII 4c); K *etarhi*, Tc *etariha* (for *etarahi*, XTa = OV); XTac *pramocayāti* (= OV!), Conze ad O p. 128 *°modayāti* (cf. also V p. 383 n. 6)(for *°modayātī*, K: Tib.A *dga' byed-na*, B *maṅ dga' byed*).

3d MSS. *paṭu-* (= O, unmetr.)(for *paṭṭa-*, so em. Edg.Rgs. 40 = V; cf. BHSD p. 316a, bottom; em. poss. to *paṭṭu-*, cf. Edgerton 8.13); O *-dharo* (? mispr.), V *-dhārī* (wt.n.!)(for *-dhāro*, MSS. = Edg.Rgs. 40); cf. Tib. *thabs thob* (Conze Index p. 144b = Dict. p. 238: *paṭu-dhāro* 'resourceful' !; ? Skt. *hetu-dhāra-*, or lit. *upāya-prāpta-*); but Chin. 無疑当得嗣王位 ; also XXIII 4d *prāg eva yāva-sthitu bheṣyati dharma-rājyo*.

4a O *vidu-bodhisattvo*, cpd.

4b Tac *cāyaku* (for *dāyaku*, KX = OV: Tib. *sbyin-par byed-ciṅ*); O *'maru-!* (for *maru-*, MSS. = V: Tib. *lha*; cf. Edgerton 15.6, also BHSD p. 420a, *maru-* 2, s.v.).

4c K *etarhi*, XTac *ete hi* (= O!), V em. *eṣati hi*! (for *etarahi*: Tib. *da-lta-na-yaṅ*; cf. XXIII 3c *etarahi*: Tib. *da-lta-na-yaṅ*; cf. Edg.Rgs. 12, p. 4 n.1); Tc *-sūkhābhiyukto* (for *-sukh°*, KXTa = OV: Tib. *sems-can maṅ phan brtson)*.

4d OV sep. *yāva sthitu* (for *yāva-sthitu*, adv., 'as long as it is generally recognized'); Tc *bhe ṣyati*; Tc *-rājyoḥ*, O em. *-rājo* (for *-rājyo*, KXTa, Bhvr.); cf. Tib. *chos-kyi rgyal-por gnas-par gyur-nas* (v.l. *°-na* = O) *smos ci dgos*, Chin. 决定当証法王位.

XXIII col. K *-viṃśatiḥ*, O em. *-viṃśatitamaḥ* (for *-viṃśatimaḥ*, XTac; cf. XIX colophon, footnote end); at the end of the colophon K reads *gāthā 4*; Tc adds num. 23.

## ⟨XXIV. ABHIMĀNA⟩

(Ta22A) māro 'pi tasmi samaye bhavate sa-śalyo
    śo(X77A)kārtu duḥkhitu-manā sada alpa-sthāmo /
diśa-dāha-ulka kṣipate bhaya-darśanārthaṃ
    katham eṣa dīna-manaso bhavi bodhisattvo // 1 //

ya(Tc29A)da te bhavanti vidu āśaya-saṃprayuktā
    diva-rātri prajña-vara-pāramitārtha-darśī /
tada kāya-citta-vacanaṃ khaga-pakṣi-tu(X77B)lyaṃ
    avatāru teṣu kutu lapsyati kṛṣṇa-bandhu // 2 //

kalahā-vivād'-upagatā vidu bodhisattvā
    bhontī paraspara-viruddhaka ruṣṭa-cittāḥ /

---

1a MSS. *māro pi* (for *māro 'pi* =OV); K *tasmiṃ* (for *tasmi*, XTac = OV).

1b XTac *śokātu* (= OV!)(for *śokârtu*, K, so r. Conze Rgs. 51); XTac *duḥkhitu an-anta-mano lpa-sthāmo* (= V w. *'lpa-°*), O ... *'lpa-sthāmā* (wt.n.!; cf. Edgerton 17.4, also Wackernagel II 1 para. 50aα, or Wackernagel-Debrunner II 2 para. 602b)(for *duḥkhitu-manā sada alpa-sthāmo*, K); XTac *ananta-mano* must have been miscopied for *a-nanda-°* (Bhvr.): Tib. *yid mi bde* (v.l. *yid bde*!); Conze Rgs. 51 misr. K *-manā sada* as *manāmada*, which makes no sense (cf. Chin. 常憂悩); *duḥkhitu-manā* (cf. Edgerton 8.13, 16.29) is the true reading (cf. *dīna-manaso* in *d*; cf. Edgerton 16.3); cf. Tib.A *mya-ṅan sdug-bsṅal ñams-thag mthu chuṅ yid mi bde*, B *mya-ṅan ñams-thag* (v.l. *ñam-thag* = O) *sdug-bsṅal yid mi bde ñam chuṅ* (v.l. *yid bde ñam chuṅ-ba*!).

1c OV sep. *diśa-dāha ulka;* Tc *-darśanāyarthaṃ* (for *darśanārthaṃ*, KXTa = OV: Tib. *bstan phyir*); cf. AsP 206.11 *bhayaṃ saṃjanayanti, ulkā-pātān diśi diśy utsṛjanti, dig-dāhān upadarśayanti.*

1d Tac *eka* (for *eṣa*, KX = OV: Tib. *'di*); Tc *bodhisattvānāṃ* (for *°sattvo*, KXTa = OV).

2a Pādas *a* and *b* are missing from the Baroda MS.; Vaidya has supplied them w. O (cf. V p. 384 n. 1); XTac *yatha* (= OV)(for *yada*, K: Tib. *gaṅ-tshe*; w. *tada* in *c*); O *āśayu-* (wt.n.)(for *āśaya-*, MSS. = Vwt.n.); XTac *-saṃprayukto* (for *°tā*, K, so em. O = V).

2b O *prajñā-* (? mispr.)(for *prajña-*, MSS., so r. Edg.Rgs. 40 = V).

2c XTac *-citta khaga-pakṣi sa tulya-bhūtā*(= OV; but V prints *-citta khagapakṣisatulyabhūtā*!)(for *-citta-vacanaṃ khaga-pakṣi-tulyaṃ*, K, 'body, thought and speech like a bird flying in the air'; cf. VIII 3d *ākāśa-pakṣi-sādṛśā* ... *prajñāḥ* 'the wise like birds in the empty space'); Conze Rgs. 40 misr. O *sa* as *ca*, and sep. K as *vacanaṃ khaga-pakṣi tulyaṃ*!; Edg.Rgs. 40 misr. O *sa* as *na*, and em. *-pakṣiṇa*, gen.!; cf. Tib.A *rtag-tu* (? Skt. *sada* for *tada*) *lus daṅ sems-ni* (!) *mkha'-la 'gro bya ltar gyur*, B *de-tshe lus sems-dag-ni* (r. *sems ṅag-ni*, as suggested by Conze Rgs.40) *mkha' 'gro bya ltar gyur* (v.l. *rgyu* = O!).

2d XTac *so* (= OV)(for *teṣu*, K: Tib.A *de-la*); XTa *layiṣyati*, Tc *lāy°*, O em. *labhiṣyati* (= V)(for *lapsyati*, K: Tib. *rñed*); XTa *kṛṣṭa-bandhuḥ*, Tc *kṛṣṭa-binduḥ*, O em. *kṛṣṇa-banduḥ* (? mispr. for *°-bandhuḥ*, so V)(for *kṛṣṇa-bandhu*, K: Tib.A *nag-po'i rtsa-lag*, B *nag-po'i rtsa-lag-rnams-kyis*).

3a K *-vivādādupagatā* (Conze Rgs. 51 misr. K as *vivādā upag°*), XTac *-vivādupagatā* (so prints V), O *-vivādupagato* (wt.n.!)(for *-vivād'-upagato*: Tib. *'thab daṅ rtsod gyur-ciṅ*); XTac *yada* (= V)(correl. w. *tada* in *c*: Tib.A *gaṅ-tshe* ... *de-yi tshe-na*, B *gaṅ-tshe* ... *de-tshe;* cf. AsP 207.30-208.1 *yasmin samaye* ... *tasmin samaye*, but AsP 208.2 *sacet* ...), O *gada* (? mispr.)(for *vidu*, K, w. which r. Edg.Rgs. 40); cf. AsP 207.30-31 *bodhisattvo mahā-sattvaḥ śrāvaka-yānikena pudgalena sārdhaṃ kalahāyati vivadati ...;* AsP 208.2-3 *bodhisattva-yānikaḥ pudgalo 'nyena*

tada māra tuṣṭu (K22A) bhavatī paramaṃ udagro
ubhi eti dūri-bhaviṣyanti jināna jñāne // 3 //

ubhi eti dūri-bhaviṣyanti piśāca-(X78A)tulyā
ubhi eti ātma kariṣyanti pratijña-hāniṃ /
duṣṭāna kṣānti-vikalāna kuto 'sti bodhi
tada māru tuṣṭu bhavatī namucī a-dharme // 4 //

yo bodhisattva a-viyākṛtu vyākṛtasya
cittaṃ pradūṣayi vivāda samārabheyā /

---

*bodhisattva-yānikena pudgalena sārdhaṃ kalahāyati vivadati ...*; XTac *bodhisattvo* (= O)(for *°sattvā*, K, w. which r. Edg.Rgs. 40 = V).

3b Tac *bhonti* (= V!)(for *bhontī*, KX = O); Tc *paraspa⟨ra-⟩*; Tc *-virudhaka* (for *-viruddhaka*, KXTa = OV; but OV *°aka-*, cpd.: Tib. *mi 'thun*, v.l. *mi mthun*); Conze wrongly sep. *parasparaviruddha* and *karuṣṭa* (Index pp. 145a and 137a [*°viruddha-* and *ruṣṭa* (Dict. pp. 242 and 337)](cf. Edg.Rgs. 40); XTac *-cittā* (for *°āḥ*, K, so em. O = V: Tib. *khros-pa'i sems daṅ ldan*).

3c Tc *tuṣṭa* (for *tuṣṭu*, KXTa = OV); Tac *bhavati* (for *°atī*, KX = OV); K *paramam u⟨da⟩gro*, Tc *paramam udargo*(!)(for *paramaṃ udagro*, XTa = OV: Tib.A *mgu-bar...*, B *mchog-tu ñams bder*).

3d XTa *dūra* (= OV!), Tc *dura* (for *dūri-*, K, m.c. for *dūrī-*; cf. XXIV 4a *dūrī-°*, also XI 8c *samākuli-kṛtā*); MSS. *bhaviṣyanti* (= OV) may have been pronounced as *°iṣanti*, m.c. (cf. Edg.Rgs. 38): Tib. *de gñis rgyal-ba'i ye-śes-las-ni riṅ-du* (B *riṅ*) *'gyur*; cf. AsP 208.1-2 *dūrī-kariṣyati bayāyaṃ kula-putraḥ sarvajñatām, atidūre sthāsyati sarvajñatāyāḥ*; AsP 208.5 *ubhāv api etau bodhisattvau dūre sthāsyataḥ sarvajñatāya(ḥ)*.

4a Tc *udmeti*(for *ubhi eti*, KXTa = OV: Tib. *de gñis*); Tc *duri-* (for *dūri-*, KXTa = OV; but OV sep. *dūri bhav°*!; cf. XXIV 3d *dūri-°*; Tib. XXIV 4a *riṅ-du 'gyur-źiṅ*); MSS. *bhaviṣyanti* (= OV) may have been pronounced as *°iṣanti*, m.c.(cf. Edg.Rgs. 38); XTac *-tulyo* (for *-tulyā*, K = OV wt.n.).

4b Tc *ubhy* (for *ubhi*, KXTa = OV); MSS. *kariṣyanti* (= OV) may have been pronounced as *°iṣanti*, m.c. (cf. Edg.Rgs. 38); V *-hānim* (w. *-m*).

4c Tc *duṣṭāra* (for *°āna*, KXTa = OV); O sep. *-vikalā na*! (for *-vikalāna*, gen.pl., so em. Edg.Rgs. 40 = V); MSS. *kuto sti* (for *kuto 'sti*, OV).

4d Tc *mānu* (for *māru*, KXTa = OV: Tib. *bdud-rnams*); K *tuṣṭra*, Tc *tuṣṭa* (for *tuṣṭu*, XTa = OV: Tib.A *dga'-źiṅ*, B *dga'-bar*); cf. XXIV 3c *tada māra tuṣṭu bhavatī*; XTac *sa-pakṣo* (= OV; but OV *namucī-°*, cpd.!)(for *a-dharme*, K; Conze Rgs. 40 misr. K as *avarme*); *sa-pakṣo* 'together with the host' (Bhvr.: Tib.B *phyogs daṅ bcas-te*) seems to be better in the context, but *namucī* and *sapakṣo* should be separated (cf. BHSD p. 270b, *namuci-*; also Malalasekera, *Dict. of Pāli Proper Names*, II p. 619, *māra-*; Akanuma, *Indo Bukkyō Koyū Meishi Jiten*, p. 412a, *māra-* 2, ss.vv.); *a-dharme* is supported neither by Tib. nor by Chin.; is it merely a scribal mistake?; is the loc. form used adverbially as meaning 'wickedly'?; or, is *a-dharme*, nom.sg.m. (cf. Edgerton 8.25, also Lüders, *Beobachtungen*, para. 12-21) used for *pāpīyas-* 'wicked, evil', which is very often used together w. *māra-*? (then r. poss. *a-dharmo*); cf. Tib.A *de-ni* (r. perh. *de-na*) *bdud-rnams dga'-źiṅ bdud-la*(?) *thub mi* (? Skt. *a-śākya-*; or confused w. *thu-ba* 'wicked'?) *'gyur*, but Tib.B (= Skt. Rec. B) *de-tshe bdud-rnams phyogs daṅ bcas-te dga'-bar 'gyur*.

5a Tc *bodhisattvo* (for *°sattva*, KXTa = OV); K *avyākṛtu*, XTc *ayu vyākṛtu* (= OV!), Ta *ayu ⟨vyākṛtu⟩* (for *a-viyākṛtu*: Tib. *luṅ-bstan ma thob*); Conze ad O p. 128 em. *ayu vyākṛtu* to *a-vyākṛtu*, unmetr.!; Edg.Rgs. 40 seems to support O, rejecting Conze's unmetr. em. w. K (and Tib.); *a-viyākṛtu* w. an epenthetic *-i-* (cf. Edgerton 3.104) satisfies the metre (thus solved in other cases by Edg.Rgs. 12, p. 4 n. 1!) and the context; XTac *vyākṛtasmiṃ*(= V), O *°asmin* (wt.n.)(for *vyākṛtasya*, K, gen. w. *cittaṃ*, acc., and *pradūṣayi*; cf. BHSD p. 380a, *pradūṣayati* 1, s.v.); cf. Tib. *luṅ-bstan ma thob byaṅ-chub-sems-dpa' la-la 'zig* (B *gaṅ-źig-gis*) *luṅ-bstan thob-la sems khros ...*, Chin. 菩薩受記未受記 (T. 授 for 受)

yāvanti citta-kṣaṇi te khi(X78B)la-doṣa-yuktāḥ

tāvanti kalpa puna saṃnahitavyu potaṃ // 5 //

atha tasy' upadyati smṛtī (Tc29B) mi a-śobhanāni

kṣāntīya pāramita bodhi spṛśanti buddhāḥ /

pratideśayāti puna āyati (Ta22B) saṃvarāti

apayāti vā sa iha śikṣati buddha-dharme // 6 //

bhagavatyāṃ ratna-guṇa-saṃcaya-(X79A)gāthāyām abhimāna-parivarto nāma caturviṃśatimaḥ // 24 //

---

或起瞋怒 ; also AsP 208.6-8 *yo bodhisattvo mahā-sattvo vyākṛto 'vyākṛtena bodhisattvena mahā-sattvena sārdhaṃ ... cittaṃ cāghātayet ...*

5b Tc *citta* (= O; ? mispr.)(for *cittaṃ*, KXTa, so r. Edg.Rgs. 40 = V); Tc *pradūṣayi* (for *°dūṣayi*, KXTa = OV); XTac *vivādu* (= OV)(for *°da*, K); XTa *samārabheyyā* (= OV; cf. Edgerton 29.23), Tc *°eryyā* (for *°eyā*, K).

5c XTac *-kṣaṇikā* (so sep. Edg.Rgs. 40 = V; O *°ikā-*, cpd.)(for *-kṣaṇi te*, K, which has escaped Conze's notice); *°-kṣaṇi*, loc., 'at every moment of thought': Tib. *sems-kyi skad cig* (cf. BHSD p. 229b, *citta-kṣaṇa-* 1, s.v.) is better; XTc *-yuktās* (= OV), Ta *-yuktā,s* (for *-yuktāḥ*, K).

5d XTac *tāvanta* (= OV)(for *tāvanti*, K; cf. Edgerton 6.14); Tc *pra* (for *puna*, KXTa = OV: Tib.A *phyir-yaṅ*, B *gźi-nas*!); XTac *saṃnahitavya* (= V), O *saṃnahitatavya* (? mispr.; Edg.Rgs. 40 corrects this dittography w. K) (for *saṃnahitavyu*, K); K *peta* (Conze Rgs. 51 misr. K as *saṃnahitavyuyeta* w. prec. *°tavyu*!), XTac *bhonti* (= OV)(for *potaṃ*); cf. Tib. *go-cha bgo dgos-so*; AsP 208.8-9 *saṃnāhaḥ saṃnāhyaḥ*; *pota-*, nt. (?), 'clothes, garment', is connected w. MInd. *poa-*, *potta-* (cf. Seṭh p. 615c, *poa-* 3, p. 617c, *potta[ga]-* 1, both nt., ss.vv.; also Mayrhofer II p. 347 *potaḥ* 2, s.v.); *potaṃ* could be *pota*, *potaḥ*, or *potta*, *pottaṃ*; XTac *bhonti* (= OV) seems to be confused w. *ponti-* 'clothes' (cf. Schmidt p. 261c, BHSD p. 355a, qq.vv.; also PTSD III p. 97b, *ponti-*, s.v.).

6a KXTa *tasyupadyati* (so print OV), Tc *tasyūp°* (for *tasy' upadyati*); K *smṛtīsi* (Conze Rgs. 51 misr. K as *smṛtīmi*), XTa *matīti* (=OV), Tc *matīty* (for *smṛtī mi*); XTac *aśobhanāti* (= O), V sep. *aśobhanā ti* (wt.n.)(for *a-śobhanāni*, K); render *a*: 'Then, to him arises a reflection (*smṛti-* 'remembrance', *mati-* 'thought')[= he reflects], "To me (there were) sins [= I have committed sins]"'; *si* (of *smṛtī si*) is a scribal mistake for the graphically similar *mi* (m.c. for *me*; cf. Edgerton 20.29); *si* cannot be a gen. of the third person (cf. Edgerton 21.18-19); still less can it be a preterite form of *as-* 'to be'; OV seem to understand *matīti* as *matī* plus *iti*, but it is more likely *matī* plus *ti* (nom.pl.nt.pron.; cf. Edgerton 8.103); cf. XXX 5a *atha tasy' upadyati matī*; *a-śobhanā ti* (=V), w. *ti* (for *iti*; cf. Edgerton 4.14), is acceptable as Rec. B; *smṛtī* or *matī* is still be taken w. *tasy' upadyati*; but cf. Tib.A *de sñam sems-śiṅ ma legs sñam-pa'i blo* (Skt. *mati-*!) *skyed-de*...!, B *sems 'di bzaṅ-ba min sñam dran-pa* (Skt. *smṛti-*!) *skyed byed-ciṅ* ...!

6b K *kṣāntāya*, Tc *kṣātīya* (for *kṣāntīya*, XTa = OV); Tc *pāramitā* (for *°ita*, KXTa = OV); Tc *spṛśati* (for *°anti*, KXTa = OV); cf. XXIV 4c *duṣṭāna kṣānti-vikalāna kuto 'sti bodhi*.

6c V em. *pratidarśayāti*! (for *°deśayāti*, MSS. = O: Tib. *so-sor 'chags-par byed-ciṅ*; cf. BHSD p. 363b, *pratideśayati* 1, s.v.); XTa *saṃvarāṇi* (= OV), Tc *saścarāṇi* (for *saṃvarāti*, K, so r. Edg.Rgs. 29: Tib. *sdom byed-la*).

6d Tc *upayāti* (for *apayāti*, KXTa = OV: Tib.A *bral-bar gyur-pa*, B *dga'-bar mi byed*!); O *vāsa* (for *vā sa*, so r. Conze Rgs. 51 = V: Tib. *de-ni* B v.l. *'di-ni*); K *sikṣati* (for *śikṣati*, XTac = OV: Tib. *slob*); Tc *-dharmeḥ* (for *-dharme*, KXTa = OV).

XXIV col. K *caturviṅśatiḥ*, Tc *catuviṃśatimaḥ*, O em. *caturviṃśatitamaḥ* (= V)(for *caturviṃśatimaḥ*, XTa; cf. XIX colophon, footnote end); at the end of the colophon K reads *gāthā // 6 //*; Tc adds num. 24.

## ⟨XXV. ŚIKṢĀ⟩

yo śikṣamāṇu na upaiti kahiṃ ci śikṣāṃ
    na ca śikṣakaṃ labhati nāpi ca śikṣa-dharmān /
śikṣā-a-śikṣa ubhaye a-vikalpamāno
    yo śikṣate sa iha śikṣati buddha-dharme // 1 //

yo (X79B) bodhisattva imu jānati eva śikṣāṃ
    na ca jātu śikṣa-vikalo bhavate duśīlo /
ārādhitaiṣa iha śikṣati buddha-dharmān
    (K22B) śikṣāti śikṣa-kuśalo ti nirūpalambho // 2 //

śikṣanta eva vidu prajña prabhaṃkarāṇāṃ
    notpadyate a-kuśalaṃ api eka-cittaṃ /
sūryasya (X80A) vā ga(Tc30A)gani gacchati antarīkṣe
    raśmī-gate na purato sthihate 'ndha-kāro // 3 //

---

1a Tc *śikṣamānu* (for °*māṇu*, KXTa = OV); Tc *nopaiti* (for *na upaiti*, KXTa = OV); Tc *vi* (for *ci*, KXTa = OV); XTac *śikṣā* (= O)(for *śikṣāṃ*, K = V wt.n.; Conze Rgs. 57 misr. K as *śīkṣāṃ*).

1b K *śikṣaṃ ka* (for *śikṣakaṃ*, XTac = OV: Tib. *slob-pa-po*); K *na cāpi* (for *nāpi ca*, XTac = OV); XTac *-dharmāṃ* (cf. Edgerton 8.90)(for °*ān*, K, so em. O = V).

1c OV sep. *śikṣā aśikṣa*; Tc *-aśikṣobhayo*; XTa *ubhayo* (= OV)(for *ubhaye*, K, so r. Edg.Rgs. 40); cf. II 7d *śikṣā-aśikṣa-naya śikṣati*.

1d K *yaḥ* (for *yo*, XTac = OV; in our text *yaḥ* is found only before *c-* as *yaś*); Tc *śikṣata* (for °*ate*, KXTa = OV); Tc *śikṣaṇi* (for °*ati*, KXTa =OV); Tc *-dharmai* (for *-dharme*, KXTa = OV).

2a K *śikṣān* (for *śikṣāṃ*, XTac = OV).

2b XTac *sa* (= OV: Tib. *de-ni*)(for *ca*,K); XTac *duśīlye* (= O!)(for °*lo*, K, so em. V; Conze Rgs. 51 misr. K as °*lyo*, w. which r. Edg.Rgs. 40!).

2c XTa *ārādhiteṣu* (= V), Tc *ārādhitevu*, O *ărādhiteṣu* (? mispr.)(for *ārādhitaiṣa*, K: Tib.A *de ni* ⟨*m*⟩*ñes-par byed-ciṅ*, B *de-ni ... mñes* [v.l. *brñes* = O] *bya phyir*!); *ārādhitaiṣa* is to be analyzed as *ārādhita* (nom. sg.), or *ārādhita(ḥ)*, plus *eṣa(ḥ)* w. a secondary sandhi; Conze Rgs. 51 misr. K as *ārādhiteṣa*, w. which suggests Edg.Rgs. 40 *ārādhit'* (for °*itaḥ*, nom.sg.) *eṣa* (or *eṣu* w. O, nom.sg., or loc.pl., sc. *buddha-dharmeṣu*)!; *eṣa(ḥ)* is correl. used w. *yo* in *a* (Rec. B *sa* in *b* has been mistaken in the course of tradition); X *-dharmaṃ* (= OV), Ta *-dharmāṃ*, Tc *-dharma* (for *-dharmān*, K, so r. Edg.Rgs. 40).

2d V *śikṣâtiśikṣa-*: Tib.B *bslab lhag bslab-la mkhas-te* (= O!)(for *śikṣāti śikṣa-*, O: Tib.A *bslab-la mkhas-źiṅ ... slob*; cf. Tib.B v.l. *bslab-la mkhas-te* only); X *nirūpalambho* (= O!), Ta *nirūpalambhī* (for *nirūpalambho*, KTc, so em. Edg.Rgs. 33 = V).

3a K *śikṣānta*, XTac *śikṣantu* (= OV)(for *śikṣanta*); O *vidu-prajña-*, cpd.; XTac *prabhāṅkaraṇam* (= O)(for *prabhaṅ*°, K = V wt.n.; cf. BHSD p. 382a, *prabhaṃkara-*, s.v.); Conze Rgs. 51 misr. O as *-karānāṃ* (for °*ṇāṃ*) and K as *-kārāṇan* (for *-karāṇan*, which is to be r. *-karāṇāṃ*, XTac = OV); cf. XXV 5c, fn.

3b MSS. *akuśalam* (= OV)(for °*laṃ*, m.c.; cf. Edg.Rgs. 34); Tc *ayi* (for *api*, KXTa = OV); V *-cittam* (w. *-m*).

3c XTac *sūrya vā gati nigacchati*, O *sūrya vā gatiṃ nig*° (wt.n.), V em. *sūrye yathā gagani gacchati* (for *sūryasya vā gagani gacchati*, K); Conze ad O p. 128 misr. K as *sūryam yavā gagani gacchati*, w. which Conze r. the text!; Edg.Rgs. 40 then em. *sūryaṃ yathā gagani gacchati*, rendering

prajñāya pāramita-śikṣita-saṃskṛtānāṃ
  sarve ca pāramita bhont' iha saṃgṛhītāḥ /
sat-kāya-dṛṣṭi yatha ṣaṣṭi duve ca dṛṣṭīḥ
  antar-gatā tath' imi pāramitā bhavanti // 4 //

yatha jīvitendri(X80B)ya niruddhi ya ke cid anye
  bhontī niruddha pṛthu indriya yāvad asti /
em eva prajña ca(Ta23A)rito vidu uttamānāṃ
  sarve ti pāramita ukta 'ta saṃgṛhītāḥ // 5 //

---

pādas *c-d*, 'as, when the ray-filled atmosphere moves toward the sun, darkness does not stand (remain) before it'; the true r. is *sūryasya* (gen.) ... *gacchati* (loc., pres.pple.), which is to be taken as an absolute construction, as IV 3c *tasyāpi uddhṛta* (loc.), V 8c *jñānasya co a-sati*, XX 8a *pakṣisya* ... *gacchati*, XX 9d *ākāṅkṣamāṇa* (loc.) *puruṣasya*; *vā* is used for *iva* (cf. Edgerton 3.6, 4.2, 6., 14, BHSD p. 475b, *vā*, s. v.); pādas *c-d* would mean, 'as, when the sun in the sky (*gagani*) goes in the atmosphere (*antarīkṣe*) held in the rays, darkness does not remain before it'; Ta *antarīkṣa*, Tc *rīje* (for *antarīkṣe*, KX = OV); cf. Tib.A *ñi-ma bar-snaṅ-la-ni 'gro-bar byed-pa-na, 'od-(g)zer rnam-pas mdun-na mun-pa mi gnas bźin*, B *ñi-ma mkha'-la 'gro-ba'i (g)zer-gyis zil gnon-pa'i, mdun-gyi bar-snaṅ-la-ni mun-pa mi gnas bźin*!

3d KTa *rasmī-*, Tc *raśmi-* (for *raśmī-*, X = OV); X *sthihate purato* (= OV), Ta *sthihate parato*, Tc *sthihate paramo* (for *purato sthihate*, K); K *ndha-kāro* (Conze Rgs. 51 r. K as *'ndha-°*), XTac *ndha-kāraṃ*, OV *'ndha-kāraṃ* (V w. *-m*)(for *'ndha-kāro*, so r. Edg.Rgs. 40).

4a O *prajñāya-pāramita-*, cpd.; XTac *-śikṣata-* (for *-śikṣita-*, K = OV wt. n.); V sep. *pāramita śikṣita saṃs°*!

4b XTac *sarveṣa* (= OV!)(for *sarve ca*, K: Tib. *pha-rol phyin-pa thams-cad)*; Tc *pāramitā* (for *°ita*, KXTa = OV); MSS. *bhontiha* (so prints V), O *bhonti ha*! (for *bhont' iha*: Tib. *'dir-ni* ... *'gyur* ); XTac *saṅgrahītā* (for *saṃgṛhītāḥ*, K, so em. O = V; but OV do not report *-grah-* for *-gṛh-*; cf. Edgerton 34.13).

4c Tc *-dṛṣṭi ya dṛṣṭi yatha* (for *-dṛṣṭi yatha*, KXTa = OV); XTa *ṣasthi* (for *ṣaṣṭi*, KTc, so em. O = V; O p. 94 n. 2 mispr. X as *sasti*); XTa *dṛṣṭī* (= OV), Tc *dṛṣṭi* (for *dṛṣṭīḥ*, K; cf. Edgerton 10.167).

4d XTac *-gatās* (= OV)(for *-gatā*, K; cf. Edgerton 9.84); X *tathimi*, XTa *tathami* (so prints V!; O sep. *tatha mi*), Tc *tatha* ⟨*mi*⟩ (for *tath' imi*: Tib. *de-bźin* ... *'di-dag)*.

5a O *jīvitendriya-niruddhiya*, cpd.!, Edg.Rgs. 40 sep. *°ya niruddhiya* (ger. of *niruddhati*, cf. Edgerton 28.19)! (for *°ya niruddhi ya* = V); *jīvitendriya* (loc.) *niruddhi* is an absolute construction, meaning 'when the life-faculty is stopped': Tib. *dper-na srog-gi dbaṅ-po 'gags-na*, also AsP 213.16-17 *tad-yathāpi nāma subhūte puruṣasya jīvitendriye niruddhe* (cf. AsP 213.14-15 *jīvitendriye pravartamāne*); XTac *anyai* (= O!; Conze Rgs. 52 misr. O as *anyaiḥ*)(for *anye*, K, so r. Edg.Rgs. 40 = V); *ya* (m.c. for *ye*) *ke cid anye* 'any other (faculty; *indriya-*, masc.!) whatsoever ...': Tib. *dbaṅ-po gźan gaṅ-dag ji sñed yod-pa* (B adding *thams-cad)*.

5b XTa *bhontīti ruddha* (= O!), Tc *bhontīti rūdha* (for *bhontī niruddha*, K, so r. Conze Rgs. 52 = V); K *yāva yāvad* (for *yāvad*, XTac = OV).

5c XTac *carite* (for *°ito*, K); OV *prajña-carite*, cpd.; O *vidu-uttamānāṃ*, cpd.!; render *c*, 'when a wise one practises in the (perfection of)wisdom of the supreme ones (= Buddhas)' (nom.absolute): Tib. *de-ltar śes-rab spyod-pa mkhas-pa mchog-rnams-kyi* (literal!); cf. XXV 3a *śikṣanta eva vidu prajña prabhaṃkarāṇāṃ* 'the wise thus training himself in the (perfection of) wisdom' (nom.absol.); cf. AsP 213.13-14 *evam eva subhūte prajñā-pāramitāyāṃ śikṣamāṇasya bodhisattvasya mahā-sattvasya tasyāṃ sarvāḥ pāramitā antar-gatā bhavanti*.

yo cāpi śrāvaka-guṇā tatha pratyayānāṃ
    sarveṣu bhoti vidu śikṣitu bodhisattvo /
no cāpi tatra sthihatī na spṛheti teṣāṃ
    (X81A) ayu śikṣitavyam iti śikṣati-m-etam arthaṃ // 6 //

bhagavatyāṃ ratna-guṇa-saṃcaya-gāthāyāṃ śikṣā-parivarto nāma pañca-viṃśatimaḥ // 25 //

---

5d XTac *sarveta* (so print OV)(for *sarve ti*, K, so r. Edg.Rgs. 40); r. poss. *sarv' eti* (w. K) or *sarv' eta* (w. XTac), cf. XXV 4d *imi pāramita;* K *ukta ta* (so r. Edg.Rgs. 40 assuming *ta = ataḥ*), XTac *ukta ⟨ta⟩*, O em. *uktā tra*!, V em. *ukta ya*! (for *ukta 'ta*); contextually *'ta* seems to be used for *atra*, m.c. (cf. Seṭh p. 47c, *atta;* or BHSD p. 155b, *etta*, ss.vv.), as suggested by O: Tib. *'dir-ni;* XTa *saṃgrahīta* (cf. Edgerton 34.13), Tc *sagṛhītā*, V *saṃgṛhītā* (wt.n.)(for *saṃgṛhītāḥ*, K, so em. O); cf. XXV 4b *sarve ca pāramita bhont' iha saṃgṛhītaḥ*.

6a K *atha* (for *tatha*, XTac = OV, 'as well as'; cf. Speijer 427; but Tib. B *de-bžin*!; cf. *tatha* II 2bd, 4b, XXXI 2b).

6b X *sarveṣa* (= O)(for *sarveṣu*, KTac, so r. Edg.Rgs. 40 = V); XTac *bhonti* (= OV)(for *bhoti*, K, so r. Edg.Rgs. 40); O *bodhisattvāḥ* (wt.n.!), V em. °*sattvā*! (for °*sattvo*, MSS., so r. Edg.Rgs. 40); but cf. Tib.A *byaṅ-chub-sems-dpa' gaṅ-dag ñan-thos yon-tan daṅ, raṅ-rgyal yon-tan kun-la bslabs-par gyur-pa-rnams, de-dag ...*!, B *byaṅ-chub sems mkhas ñan-thos yon-tan gaṅ-dag daṅ, de-bžin raṅ-rgyal yon-tan kun-la slob byed-ciṅ, de-dag ...*!

6c XTac *sthihatā* (= O!)(for °*atī*, K, so r. Edg.Rgs. 40); cf. XX 17c, 18c *no cāpi tatra sthihatī*, also XX 8b *no cāpi tatra sthiti;* Tc *ra* (for *na*, KXTa = O); V *sthihatāna*! (wt.n.!); KTac *teṣām* (= V)(for °*āṃ*, X = O).

6d XTac *śikṣitavyamati* (so prints V!)(for °*itavyam iti*, K, so em. O); XTa *śikṣita etam* (= O), Tc *śikṣitaitam* (for *śikṣati-m-etam*, K, so r. Edg.Rgs. 40); Tac *artha* (for *arthaṃ*, KX = OV; but V w. *-m*); cf. Tib. *'di-ni bdag-gis bslab bya yin* (? Skt. *śikṣitavya mayi* [= *mayā;* cf. Edgerton 20.18] for XTac °*itavyamati*) *sñam* (*iti ⟨kṛtvā⟩*) *de-phyir slob*.

XXV col. K *-parivarta ⟨nāma⟩* (for *-parivarto nāma*, XTac = OV); K *pañcaviṃśatiḥ*, O em. °*viṃśatitamaḥ* (for °*viṃśatimaḥ*, XTac = V wt.n.; cf. XIX colophon, footnote end); at the end of the colophon K reads *gāthā 6;* Tc adds num. 25.

## ⟨XXVI. MĀYOPAMA⟩

a-vivartiyasya vara-bo(Tc30B)dhayi prasthitasya
    yo citt'-upādu anumodaya āśayena /
tri-sahasra meru tulayitva(X81B) siyā pramāṇo
    na tv eva tasya kuśalasy' anumodanāye // 1 //

yāvanti sattva (K23A) kuśalārthika mokṣa-kāmāḥ
    sarveṣu bhoti anumoditu puṇya-rāśiḥ /
sattvārtha te jina-guṇān anuprāpuṇitvā
    dāsyanti dharma jagatī dukha-saṃkhayāye // 2 //

yo bodhisattva a-vikalpaku sarva-(X82A)dharmān
    śūnyānimitta parijānati niṣprapañcān /
na ca prajña-bodhi parieṣati āśayena
    so yuktu prajña-vara-pāramitāya yogī // 3 //

---

1b MSS. *cittapādu* (= O), V *cittupādu* (wt.n.)(for *citt'-upādu*; cf. VI 3a, fn.); XTac *anumodatu*, gen.pres.pple. (= O), V °*itu* (wt.n.), nom.ppp. (for *anumodaya*, K); *anumodaya*, 3 sg.opt., is resulted from °*aye* as a sandhi form; but *anumodayi* can be the true r., for 3 sg.opt. ending in *-e* always becomes *-i*, m.c. (cf. Edgerton 29.12-14; cf. XX 5d *cintayi etam*; also VI 4c *anumodayi b-*): Tib. *sems bskyed-pa-la bsam-pa thag-pas yi raṅ-ba*; cf. AsP 215.21-22 *yas teṣāṃ bhagavan prathama-yāna-saṃprasthitānāṃ bodhisattvānāṃ mahā-sattvānāṃ cittopādān anumodate, avinivartanīyānāṃ apy avinivartanīya-dharmatām anumodate, ...*

1c XTac *-sahasrā maru* (O p. 95 n. 2 misr. X as °*srāsaru*)(for *-sahasra meru*, K, so em. O = V: Tib. *stoṅ gsum ri-rab*).

1d K *kuśalasya anumodanāye* (hypermetr.!), XTa *kuśalasyanum*° (so prints V), O sep. *kuśalasya num*°, Tc *kuśalasyānum*°(for *kuśalasy' anum*°).

2a XTac *yāvanta* (= OV)(for °*nti*, K); XTac *-kāmā* (= V)(for °*āḥ*, K, so em. O).

2b V *sarveṣa* (wt.n.)(for *sarveṣu*, MSS. = O); XTac *bhonti* (= OV)(for *bhoti*, K); Tc *anumodetu* (for °*itu*, KXTa = OV); K *-rāsiḥ*, XTa *-rāśi* (= V), Tc *-rāsi* (for *-rāśiḥ*, so em. O); cf. Tib. *kun-gyi bsod-nams phuṅ-po-la-yaṅ yi-raṅ 'gyur*! (? = Conze Trsl.).

2c XTa *sattvārthi* (= OV), Tc *sattvarthi* (for *sattvārtha*, K: Chin.為世間; but Tib. *de-phyir* !; Conze Rgs. 40 thinks Tib. offers a better r.); XTac *-guṇān anta* (= O!), V *-guṇa ananta* (metr. imposs.!), Edg.Rgs. 40 em. *-guṇān ata(ḥ)*(w. Tib. *de-phyir*!)(for *-guṇān anu*°, K): Tib. *de-dag rgyal-ba'i yon-tan thob gyur-nas*.

2d O *yagatī* (wt.n.!)(for *jag*°, MSS. = V: Tib. *'jig-rten*; Edg.Rgs. 40 slightly hesitates to adopt *jagatī*, referring to Edgerton 2.34); XTac *duḥkha-* (= O)(for *dukha-*, K = V wt.n.; cf. Edg.Rgs. 35, Edgerton 2.85); XTac *-saṃkṣayāye* (= OV)(for [-sa]ṃkhayāye, K; cf. Edgerton 2.25, also Pāli *saṃkhaya-*: Tib. *sdug-bsṅal zad-par bya phyir*; cf. also Edgerton 8.45); cf. VI 2d *dukha-saṃkṣayāye*: Tib. *sdug-bsṅal zad-par bya phyir*.

3a Tc *bodhisattvo* (for °*sattva*, KXTa = OV); K *-dharmāṃ* (cf. Edgerton 8.90), Tc *-dharmāna* (for *-dharmān*, XTa = OV).

3b Tc *niṣprapaṃcāra* (for °*pañcān*, KXTa = OV: Tib. *spros med*).

3c Ta *e* (for *na*, KXTc = OV: Tib. *mi*); OV sep. *prajña bodhi*; Conze Rgs. 40 em. *so dvayena* (w. Tib.B *de-ni ... gñis-kyis*)! (for *āśayena*, MSS. = OV: Tib.A *bsam-pa thag-pas)*; cf. Tib.A *śes-rab bsam-pa thag-pas byaṅ-chub mi tshol-ba*, B *de-ni śes-rab gñis-kyis byaṅ-chub tshol mi byed*!, also Chin. 内心亦不求覚智.

3d XTac *yukta* (= OV)(for *yuktu*, K).

ākāśa-dhātu-gaganasya siyā virodho
na hi tena tasya kutu kena cid eṣa prāpto /
em eva prajña-carito vi(Ta23B)du (X82B) bodhisattvo
abhyovakāśa-sadṛśo upaśānta-cārī // 4 //

yatha māya-kā(Tc31A)ra-puruṣasya na eva bhotī
toṣiṣy' imāṃ janata so ca karoti kāryaṃ /
paśyanti taṃ vividha-kārya nidarśayantaṃ
na ca tasya kāyu na pi citta na nāma-dheyaṃ // 5 //

em eva prajña-carato na kadā ci bhotī
buddhitva (X83A) bodhi jagatī parimocayiṣye /
nānopapatti vividhāṃ kriya-saṃprayogāṃ
darśeti māya-sadṛśo na vikalpa-cārī // 6 //

yatha buddha nirmita karoti ca buddha-kāryaṃ
na ca tasy' upadyati mado karamāṇa kiṃ cit /

---

4a Tac *-gamanasya* (for *-gag°*, KX = OV; but V sep. *-dhātu gag°*!); XTac *virodhe* (for *°dho*, K = OV wt.n.); cf. Tib.A *tha-dad* 'contrariety', B *'gal-ba* 'obstruction'.

4b K *cid eśa*, XTac *vid esa* (for *cid eṣa*, so em. O = V: Tib.B *de;* but Tib.A *bye-brag* = Skt. *viśeṣa*?); XTac *prāptā* (= OV!)(for *°to*, K, so r. Edg.Rgs. 40).

4c O *vidu-bodhisattvo*, cpd.

4d Tc *atyovakāśa-*, O em.*abhyāvakāśa-* (= Edg.Rgs. 40!)(for *abhyov°*, KXTa = V: Tib. *nam-mkha'*; cf. I 2c, V 7a *anovatapta-* for *anavat°*); XTa *-sadṛśā* (= O!), Tc *-sadṛśām* (for *-sadṛśo*, K, so r. Edg.Rgs. 40 = V); Tc *-cāri* (for *-cārī*, KXTa = OV).

5a Tc *va* (for *eva*, KXTa = OV, m.c. for *evaṃ*); XTac *bhontī*, O *bhonti*(wt. n.)(for *bhotī*, K, so r. Edg.Rgs. 40): Tib.A *'di sñam-du ... mi sems*, B *'di sñam-du ... sñam mi sems*.

5b K *toṣiṣyimāñ* (= Conze Rgs. 40 *toṣiṣyimāṃ*), XTa *te śiṣya māṃ* (= OV, nonsensical!), Tc *te siṣya mā* (for *toṣiṣy' imāṃ*: Tib.A *'di-dag mgu bya*, B *'di mgu bya*, Chin. 衆人……皆喜 |); XTac *ca karonti* (= O *cakaronti*!) (for *ca karoti*,K,so r.Edg.Rgs. 40 = V); V *kāryam* (w. *-m*).

5c XTac *-kāryu* (= V; but V sep. *vividha kāryu*)(for *-kārya*, K = O wt.n.); O *-kāryu-nidarśayantaṃ*, cpd.! (correctly sep. by Edg.Rgs. 40).

5d V *-dheyam* (w. *-m*).

6a K *-carito* (= Edg.Rgs. 40), XTac *-carite* (= OV)(for *-carato*); XTac *bhonti* (= O), V *bhoti* (wt.n.)(for *bhotī*, K, so r. Edg.Rgs. 40): Tib. *de-bźin śes-rab spyod-pa nams-kyaṅ* (B *nam-yaṅ*) *'di sñam-du ... mi sems* (= Conze Trsl.); cf. XXVI 5a *yatha māya-kāra-puruṣasya na eva bhotī;* AsP 218.13-14, 18-19, 23-24, 219.1-2 *evam eva bhagavan bodhisattvasya mahā-sattvasya prajñā-pāramitāyāṃ* (219.2 *°itāṃ;* ? mispr. for *°itāyāṃ*) *carato naivaṃ bhavati*.

6b XTac *parimocayitvā* (= OV)(for *°iṣye*, K, so r. Edg.Rgs. 40).

6c XTa *ātmopapatti* (= OV: Tib.A *raṅ-gi skye-ba*!), Tc *ātmoyapatti* (for *nānopapatti*, K: Tib.B *skye-ba sna-tshogs*!; Conze Rgs. 40 misr. K as *nāvop°*); XTac *vividhā*, O em. *vividhā-*! (for *vividhām*, K, so r. Edg.Rgs. 40 = V); O *ātmopapatti-vividha-°*, cpd.!; Edg.Rgs. 40 *°tti-vividhāṃ*!; O em. *-saṃprayogaṃ* (for *°yogāṃ*, MSS., so r. Edg.Rgs. 40 = V); cf. XX 6b *jagatī kriyā vividha darśayate*, XX 12c *vividhāṃ kriyāṃ jagati darśayate*.

6d Tc *darśati* (for *°eti*, KXTa = OV).

7a XTac *buddhi* (for *buddha*, K, so em. O = V); K ⟨*ca*⟩; K *-kāryan*, Tc *-kārya* (for *-kāryaṃ*, XTa = OV).

7b Tc *ra* (for *na*, KXTa = OV: Tib. *mi*); KXTa *tasyupadyati*(so print OV),

em eva prajña-carito vidu bodhi(X83B)sattvo
darśeti sarva-kriya nirmita-māyu-tulyāṃ // 7 //

(K23B) pala-gaṇḍa-dakṣa-vidunā kṛtu dāru-yantro
puruṣestri-tulya sa karot' iha sarva-kāryaṃ /
em eva prajña-carito vidu bodhisattvo
jñānena sarva-kriya kurvati nirvikalpo // 8 //

bhagavatyāṃ (Tc31B) ratna-guṇa-saṃcaya-gāthāyāṃ māyopama-(X84A)parivarto nāma ṣaḍviṃśatimaḥ // 26 //

---

Tc *tasyūpapati* (for *tasy' upadyati*); XTa *karamāṇu* (= OV), Tc °*māṇū* (for °*māṇa*, K).

7c Ŏ *vidu-bodhisattvo*, cpd.

7d V sep. *sarva kriya*; XTac *-māya-tulyaṃ* (= OV; but V w. *-m*)(for *-māyu-tulyāṃ*, K).

8a Tc *yatva-* (for *pala-*, KXTa = OV: Tib. *śiṅ-mkhan*, Chin. 木匠人 ); K *palaga[ṇḍa-dakṣa-v]i[du]nā*; V sep. *palagaṇḍa dakṣa vidunā*!

8b V sep. *puruṣe stri-*! (for *puruṣestri-*, cpd. = O; cf. Edgerton 3.113); cf. XVII 6a *puruṣestriya* (V sep. *puruṣaiḥ striya*!); KXTa *karoti* (so em. Edg.Rgs. 40 = V; Conze Rgs. 52 misr. K as *kurvate*!) *ha*, O *kāroti* (? misprint) *ha*, Tc *karotīha* (for *karot' iha*); *iha* 'here' (so trsl. Conze!) sounds better, although it is not supported by Tib.; V *-kāryam* (w. *-m*); cf. Tib.A *śiṅ-mkhan mkhas-pas rtse-phyir śiṅ-gi 'khrul-'khor byas skyes-pa bud-med 'dra de bya-ba thams-cad byed*, B *śiṅ-mkhan bzo-bo mkhas-pas skyes-pa bud-med daṅ 'dra-ba'i bzo byas de-yaṅ ...*; also AsP 219.8-9 *dakṣeṇa palagaṇḍena ... dāru-mayī strī vā puruṣo vā yantra-yuktaḥ kṛto bhavet ...*

8c O *vidu-bodhisattvaḥ*, cpd.

8d V sep. *sarva kriya* (cf. *sarva-kāryaṃ* in *b*); Tac *kurthati* (for *kurvati*, KX = OV: Tib. *byed*).

XXVI col. K *-parivarta* ⟨*nāma*⟩ (for *-parivarto nāma*, XTac = OV); KTc *ṣaḍviṃśatiḥ*, O em. °*viṃśatitamaḥ* (for °*viṃśatimaḥ*, XTa = V wt.n.; cf. XIX colophon, footnote end); at the end of the colophon K reads *gāthā 8*; Tc adds num. 26.

## ⟨XXVII. SĀRA⟩

evaṃ caranta vidunā pṛthu-deva-saṃghāḥ
    kṛta-añjalī-puṭa praṇamya namasyayanti /
buddhā pi yāvata daśa-d-diśi loka-dhātau
    guṇa-varṇa-māla-parikīrtana kurvayanti // 1 //

(Ta24A) yāvanti gaṅga-nadi-vāli-same hi kṣetre
    sattvās ti (X84B) sarvi parikalpya bhaveyu mārāḥ /
ekaika roma puna tātuka nirmiṇeyā
    sarve na śakta karaṇe vidu-antar-āyaṃ // 2 //

catu-kāraṇehi balavān vidu bodhisattvo
    bhavate dudharṣu catu-māra-a=saṃprakampyo /
śūnyā-vihāri bhavate na ca sattva-tyāgī
    yatha-vādi sattva-karuṇo sugatādhi(X85A)ṣṭhāno // 3 //

---

1a XTac *carantu* (= OV)(for °*anta*, K); Tc *vidurā*, V sep. *vidu nā*! (for *vidunā*, KXTa = O: Tib. *mkhas-rnams-la*); AsP 221.9-10, 10-12 *evaṃ carantaṃ bodhisattvaṃ mahā-sattvaṃ sendrakā devāḥ ... prāñjalī-bhūtā namasyanti*; AsP 221.14-15 *taṃ bodhisattvaṃ mahā-sattvaṃ prajñā-pāramitāyāṃ evaṃ carantaṃ namasyanti*.

1b Tc *kṛtāñjali-*, O *kṛta-añcalī-*(mispr.!)(for *kṛta-añjalī-*, KXTa = V); Tc *ramasyayaṃti* (for *nam*°, KXTa = OV); but O *-puṭa-praṇamya-namasyayanti*, cpd.! (for *-puṭa praṇamya nam*°, so correctly sep. Edg.Rgs. 40 = V): Tib. *thal-mo sbyar-ba btud-ciṅ* (B °*-nas*) *phyag-kyaṅ 'tshal-bar byed*.

1c Read poss. *buddhāpi* w. sec. sandhi (cf. Edgerton 4.12); Tac *yāva* (for *yāvata*, KX = OV); Tc *daśadiśi* (for *daśaddiśi*, KXTa = OV).

1d Separate poss. *-māla parikīrtana*; XTc *kurvayantī* (= O), Ta °*antī* (both written)(for °*anti*, K = V wt.n.).

2a Tc *gaṃgā-* (for *gaṅgā-*, KXTa = OV); O sep. *-nadi vāli-*!

2b XTac *tva*, O em. *ta*(= V)(for *ti*, K, so r. Edg.Rgs. 40); XTac *parikalpa* (= OV)(for °*lpya*, K, so r. Edg.Rgs. 40: Tib. *yoṅs-su brtag* [B *brtag-pa*] *bzuṅ-ste*; cf. III 3d *parikalpya*).

2c Tc *ecaika* (for *ekaika*, KXTa = OV: Tib.A *ñag re-re*, B *ñag re-las-kyaṅ*); K *romi*, so r. Edg.Rgs. 40! (for *roma*, XTac = OV); Tc *pura* (for *puna*,KXTa = OV); XTac *tāntaka* (= OV; Conze trsl. 'snare'!; cf. Edg.Rgs. 29, BHSD p. 447a, *yāvataka*, etc., s.v.)(for *tātuka*, K: Tib. *de-sñed*; cf. Edgerton 3.2, BHSD p. 251a, *tātaka*, etc., s.v.); cf. Rec. B III 3a *tāntaka* (= V; O em. *nāntaka-* ); XTac *nirmineyā* (O p. 98 n. 3 misr. X as °*neyā*)(for °*ṇeyā*, K, so em. O = V; but V w. °*eyyā*, cf. Edgerton 29.23): Tib.A *spu ñag* (Tc *spu-rtsa ñeg*: em. *spu-rtse ña-ga*) *re-re ji-sñed de-sñed* (Tc om. *de-sñed*) *sprul byas-kyaṅ*, B *ba-spu ñag re-las-kyaṅ de-sñed sprul byas-kyaṅ*, cf. Chin. 一一毛変.

2d K [*sa*]*rve*; K *sakta*, XTac *śakya* (= OV)(for *śakta*); XTac *karaṇa* (r.perh. °*aṇā*; cf. Edgerton 36.18)(for °*aṇe*, K, so em. O = V); XTa *-antarāyaṃ*, Tc *-jaṃtarāyaṃ* (for *-antarāyaṃ*, K, so em. O = V; but V sep. *vidu antarāyam*, w. *-m*): Tib. *de-dag kun-gyis mkhas-la bar-chad bya mi nus*.

3a O sep. *catu kāraṇehi*!; XTac *balavāṃ* (= V)(for °*vān*, K, so em. O); O *vidu-bodhisattvo*, cpd.

3b K *durdharṣu* (so Conze Index-Dict.)(for *dudharṣu*, XTac = OV); X *asaprakamyo* (= O!), Tac *asaprakarmyo* (for *asaṃprakampyo*, K, so Conze Index-Dict. = V wt.n.: Tib. *bskyod-par mi nus-te*); O sep. °*-māra asa*°!

3d O sep. *yatha vādi*!; K *-karaṇo* (Conze Rgs. 52 misr. K as *karuṇo*), XTac *karuṇa* (for *-karuṇo*: Tib.A *sñiṅ-rjes sems-can*!); XTac *sugatāvasthānaḥ* (for *sugatādhiṣṭhāno*, K: Tib.B *bde-gśegs byin brlabs-can*); O em. *sattva*

yo bodhisattva adhimucyati bhāṣyamāṇāṃ
  imu prajña-pāramita māta tathā(Tc32A)gatānāṃ /
pratipattiyā ca abhiyujyati āśayena
  sarva-jñatāya abhiprasthita veditavyo // 4 //

na ca dharma-dhātu-tathatāya upaiti sthānaṃ
  bhavatī a-sthāna-sthitu meghu va a(X85B)nta(K24A)rīkṣe /
vidyā-dharo va anilaṃ bhuvanābhiprāyo
  khagu kho su-phulla druma pattra-balādhiṣṭhāno // 5 //

---

*karuṇāsugatādhiṣṭhānaḥ!*, V em. *sattva-karuṇānugatāvasthānaḥ!*; Conze Rgs. 41 em. *tathā-kārī ca*, w. Tib.B *bžin byed* (for *sattva-karuṇo*, Bhvr.); Conze's em. is metr. impossible, but cf. AsP 222.4 *yathā-vādī tathā-kārī ca bhavati;* cf. Tib.A *ji-skad smra daṅ sñiṅ-rjes sems-can bde 'jog-pa'o*, B *ji-skad smras bžin byed daṅ bde-gśegs byin brlabs-*(v.l. *rlabs-* =O) *can.*

4a O *adhibhucyati* (mispr.!)(for °*mucyati*, MSS., so Conze ad O p. 128 = V: Tib. *mos byed-ciṅ*); K *bhāṣyamāṇe* (: Tib. *'chad tshe!*; cf. XI 3a *bhāṣyamāṇe*: Tib. *'di bśad tshe-na!*), Tc °*māṇām* (= V)(for °*māṇāṃ*, XTa = O); cf. AsP 223.30-31 *ye bodhisattvā mahā-sattvā imāṃ ... prajñā-pāramitāṃ bhāṣyamāṇāṃ śrutvā adhimokṣyanti ...*

4b XTac *ima* (= OV)(for *imu*, K); Tc *prajñā-* (for *prajñă-*, KXTa = OV); Tc *⟨ta⟩thāgatānāṃ;* V °*gatānām* (w. *-m*).

4c XTac *pratipattiya* (for °*iyā*, K, so em. O = V); O *abhiyucyati* (? misprint)(for °*yujyati*, MSS. = V: Tib.A *mṅon-du brtson byed-pa*, v.l. °*-la*, B *mṅon-par brtson byed-na*); Tc *āśanena* (for *āśayena*, KXTa = OV: Tib. *bsam-pa thag-pas*, B adding *ṅes-pa*).

4d XTac *abhiprasthitu* (= OV)(for °*ita*, K); Tc *veditavyoḥ* (for °*itavyo*, KXTa = OV).

5a Ta *-tatha⟨tā⟩*; K *u[p]aiti*: Tib.A *de-bžin-ñid-kyi gnas-su chos dbyiṅs ñer mi 'gro*, B *chos dbyiṅs de-bžin-ñid-la gnas-par* (v.l. °*-pa* = O) *mi 'gyur-žiṅ*, Chin. 法界如実不可得 ; also AsP 224.21 *na ca nāma ... kaś cid dharmas tathatāyaṃ tiṣṭhati.*

5b Tc *bhavati* (for °*atī*, KXTa = OV); XTac *athānasthita* (= V; read *a-thāna-*°), O *yathānasthita* (wt.n.!)(for *a-sthāna-sthitu*, K, so r. Conze Rgs. 41); K [*meghu va anta*]*rīkṣe*(at least *meghu* can be restored; but Conze Rgs. 41 doubtfully r. K as *so yuga!*), XTa *so laghu antarīkṣe* (so r. Edg.Rgs. 40 = OV; but O *laghu-*°, cpd.!), Tc *so lūghv ant*° (for *meghu va ant*°: Tib.A *dper-na bar-snaṅ sprin-ni gnas-med gnas-pa bžin*, B ... *sprin bžin gnas-pa med-par gnas*); *laghu* makes no sense here, and Conze (index p. 151b, Dict. p. 338, *laghu*, s.v.) suggests em. to *meghu* w.Tib. B *sprin; va* is certainly used for *iva*: Tib. *bžin* (cf. Edgerton 4.2, 6, 14, BHSD p. 466a, *va*, s.v.); but cf. AsP 224.28-29 *tad-yathāpi nāma antarīkṣe iṣuḥ kṣipto naiva kva cit sajjati.*

5c Pādas *c-d* seem to be corrupt; Ta *vu*, Tc *ca* (for *va*, KX = OV; Conze Rgs. 41 misr. O as *ca*); K *anilam* (= Edg.Rgs. 40), XTac *amilaṃ*, O *apulaṃ*? (wt.n.!)(for *anilaṃ*); X *bhuvanābhiprāyā* (= O), Tac *bhūvanābhiprāyā* (for *bhuvanābhiprāyo*, K, so r. Edg.Rgs. 40); V em. *abhilambhu vanābhiprāyā;* cf. Tib.A *rigs-sṅags 'chaṅ-ba dmigs med* (? Skt. *na abhilambhu*) *nags* (? Skt. *vana-*) *sems mkha'* (v.l. *mkhas*) *'gro* (? Skt. *khaga-*) *tshe*, B *rig-sṅags 'chaṅ-ba gnas med mkha' rgyu gnas 'dod-pa*, but Chin. 如天宮殿応念生.

5d K ⟨*khagu*⟩ ; XTa *kālu-hurṇu*, Tc *kāru-hurṇu*, O *kālu-hīna* (wt.n.), V *kāla-hīna* (wt.n.)(for *kho su-phulla*, K; Conze Rgs. 41 misr. K as *sra phulla*, adopting *phulla*); *-hurṇu*/ *-hurṇa* is undoubtedly a scribal error for the graphically similar *-phulla*; XTac *mantra-* (= OV)(for *pattra-*, K, 'feather, bird'; Conze Rgs. 41 misr. K *patra* as *yatra*); Tc *balodhiṣṭhāno* (for *balādh*°, KXTa = OV); cf. Tib.A *me-tog śiṅ-phyir sṅags-kyi* (? Skt. *mantra-*) *stobs-kyi byin rlabs byed*, B *sṅags* (? Skt. *mantra-*) *mthus dus min* (? Skt. *kāla-hīna-*) *me-tog ldan śiṅ* (= O; but MSS. °*-žiṅ*) *byin-gyis rlob*, but Chin. 亦如飛禽思菓 (Chi-sha ed. 果 ) 樹 (r. poss. 華樹 ?).

evaṃ carantu vidu-paṇḍitu bodhisattvo

    na ca budhyakaṃ labhati nāpi ca buddha-dharmān /

na ca deśakaṃ na pi ca paśyaka dharmatāyāṃ

    śāntaiṣiṇām ayu vihāra guṇe (X86A) ratānāṃ // 6 //

yāvanti śrāvaka-vihāra sa-pratyayānāṃ

    śāntā-samādhi-praśame sukha-saṃprayuktā /

arhan-vimokṣa sthapayitva tathāgatānāṃ

    sarveṣu agr' a(Ta24B)yu vihāra niruttaraś ca // 7 //

ākāśa pakṣi viharāti na co patātī

    daka-madhya matsyu viharāti (X86B) na co marātī /

em eva dhyāna-bala-pāra-gu bodhi(Tc32B)sattvo

    śūnyā-vihāri na ca nirvṛti prāpuṇātī // 8 //

yo sarva-sattva-guṇa-agratu gantu-kāmo

    agraṃ spṛśeyu paramādbhuta-buddha-jñānaṃ /

---

6a Tc *paṇḍita* (for °*itu*, KXTa = OV); V sep. *vidu paṇḍitu*.

6b Tc *nāpi va* (for *nāpi ca*, KXTa = OV); XTac *-dharmāṃ* (cf. Edgerton 8.90)(for *-dharmān*, K, so em. O = V).

6c K *deśakan*, XTac *deśikan* (= OV *deśikaṃ*), X(Tib.trslit.) *daśikan* (for *deśakaṃ*: Tib. *'chad-par byed*); *deśaka-* is to be analyzed as *deśati* plus *-aka-* (cf. BHSD p. 278b, *dharma-deśaka-*, s.v.), cf. *budhyaka-* (*budhyati* plus *-aka-*) in *b*, and *paśyaka-* (*paśyati* plus *-aka-*) in *c* (cf. BHSD p. 338b, *paśyaka-*, s.v.); cf. Tib.B *chos 'dod* (? Skt. *dharma-kāmaṃ*; cf. Conze Rgs. 41), but Tib.A *chos-ñid* = Skt. *dharmatāyāṃ*, MSS. = OV).

6d Tc *śātaiṣiṇām* (for *śānt°*, KXTa = OV: Tib. *źi 'dod*); Tc *rakānāṃ* (for *rat°*, KXTa = OV: Tib. *dga'-ba'i*).

7a XTac *yāvanta* (= OV)(for *yāvanti*, K).

7b KTc *prasame* (for °*śame*, XTa = OV); Tc *sūkha-* (for *sukha-*, KXTa = OV); V sep. *śāntā samādhi-praśame*!; Tc *-saṃprayuktāḥ* (so em. O; O p. 100 n. 2 mispr. X as *-yaktā*)(for °*yuktā*, KXTa = V): Tib. *gnas-pa źi-ba'i tiṅ-'dzin rab źi bde ldan-pa*, also Chin. 修行寂静三摩地 愛楽寂静.

7c XTa *arhā-* (= O), Tc *arhaṃ-* (for *arhan-*, K = V wt.n.; Conze Rgs. 52 misr. K as *arha-*); Tc *sthayayitva* (for *sthapayitva*, KXTa = OV: Tib. *ma gtogs-par*).

7d MSS. *agrayu* (so prints O), V *agra ayu* (wt.n.; hypermetr.!)(for *agr' ayu* [= *agro 'yam*], cf. Edgerton 4.21, 8.22-23; but poss. *agra 'yu/ yu*, cf. Edgerton 21.79); XTac *vihāru* (= OV)(for *vihāra*, K); Tc *nirutaraś* (for *niruttaraś*, KXTa = OV: Tib. *goṅ-na med-pa*).

8a V *ākāśi* (wt.n.)(for *ākāśa*, MSS. = O, loc.: Tib.A *nam-mkhar*, B *mkha'-la*); XTac *patāti* (= OV)(for *patātī*, K).

8b V *-madhyi* (wt.n.)(for *-madhya*, MSS. = O, loc.: Tib. *chu-la*, v.l. °*-na*); XTa *matsya* (= OV), Tc *yatsya* (for *matsyu*, K); MSS. *marātī* (= OV): Tib. *'tshubs-te* (MS. Tb *chu-yis 'tshubs-te*, hypermetr.) *'chi-ba* 'is not drowned and does not die' (Conze Trsl. p. 164 n. 33 wrongly reports Tib.).

8c Tc *-yāragu* (for *-pāragu*, KXTa = OV: Tib. *pha-rol son-pa*, v.l. *phyin-pa*); cf. Tib. *bsam-gtan stobs-dag-gi* (v.l. °*-gis* = O: Chin. 依禅).

8d Tc *śūnyo-* (for *śūnyā-*, KXTa = OV); Tac *prāpuṇāti* (= V)(for °*ātī*, KX = O).

9a Tc *gatu-*, O *ganta-* (? mispr.)(for *gantu-*, KXTa = V).

9b Tac *agraḥ* (for *agraṃ*, KX = OV); XTa *spṛśeya* (= OV), Tc *spṛśe* (for *spṛśeyu*, K); Tac *paramādbhūta-* (for °*dbhuta-*, KX = OV; but V sep. °*dbhuta buddha-*); V *-jñānam* (w. *-m*).

**agraṃ dadeyu vara-uttamu-dharma-dānaṃ**
**imu agru sevatu vihāru hitaṃ-ka(X87A)rāṇāṃ // 9 //**

**bhagavatyāṃ ratna-guṇa-saṃcaya-gāthāyāṃ sāra-parivarto nāma sapta-viṃśatimaḥ // 27 //**

---

9c XTa *dadeya* (= OV), Tc *dadepa* (for *dadeyu*, K); Tc *vana-* (for *vara-*, KXTa = OV); XTac *-uttama-* (= OV; but V sep. *vara uttama-*)(for *-uttamu-*, K); K *-dānam* (= V)(for *-dānaṃ*, XTac = O).

9d Tc *agra* (for *agru*, KXTa = OV); Tc *seva bhu* (for *sevatu*, KXTa = OV); K *hitaṃ-karuṇāṃ* (Conze Rgs. 53 misr. K as *°-karūṇāṃ*), Tc *hita-karāṇāṃ* (for *hitaṃ-karaṇāṃ*, XTa = OV; but V w. *-m*: Tib. *phan mdzad-rnams-kyi*; cf. BHSD p. 620a, *hitaṃkara-*, s.v.).

XXVII col. K *saptaviṃśatiḥ*, XTa *saptāviṃśatimaḥ* (O p. 101 n. 1 misr. X as *saptāviś°*), Tc *saptaviṃśatamaḥ*, O em. *saptaviṃśatitamaḥ* (for *saptaviṃśatimaḥ* = V; cf. XIX colophon, footnote end); at the end of the colophon K reads *gāthā 9;* Tc adds num. 27.

## ⟨XXVIII. AVAKĪRṆA-KUSUMA⟩

yāvanti śikṣa paridīpita nāyakena
  sarveṣu śikṣa ayu agru niruttarā ca /
yo sarva-śikṣa-vidu icchati pāra gantuṃ
  imu prajña-(X87B)pāramita śikṣatu buddha-śikṣāṃ // 1 //

agraṃ nidhānu ayu uttamu dharma-(K24B)kośo
  buddhānu gotru jagatī sukha-saukhya-gañjo /
atikrānt'-an-āgata daśa-d-diśi loka-nāthā
  itu te prasūta na ca kṣīyati dharma-dhātuḥ // 2 //

yāvanti vṛkṣa-phala-puṣpa-vanas-patīyo
  sarve ti medini-samudga(Tc33A)tu (X88A) prādu-bhūtāḥ /
na ca medinī kṣayam upaiti na cāpi vṛddhiṃ
  (Ta25A) na ca khidyatī na parihāyati nirvikalpo // 3 //

yāvanta buddha-raha-śrāvaka-pratyayāś ca
  marutaś ca sarva-jagatī sukha-saukhya-dharmāḥ /

---

1a XTa *yāvanta* (= OV)(for °*nti*, KTc); Tc *paridīpata* (for °*ita*, KXTa=OV).
1b XTac *sarveśa*, OV °*eṣa* (wt.n.)(for °*eṣu*, K).
1c XTac *yaḥ* (= OV)(for *yo*, K); O *pāra-*, cpd.; KTc *gantum* (= V), O *-gantu* (? mispr.)(for *gantuṃ*, XTa).
1d XTac *śikṣati* (= OV)(for °*atu*, K: Tib. *slobs*, v.l. *slob* = O, Chin. 当学); V *-śikṣām* (w. *-m*); cf. AsP 230.17-18 *sarva-śikṣā-parama-pāramitām anuttarāṃ samyak-saṃbodhiṃ prāptu-kāmena bodhisattvena mahā-sattvena prajñā-pāramitāyāṃ śikṣitavyam.*
2a XTac *nidhāna* (= OV)(for °*ānu*, K); XTac *uttama* (= OV; but OV *uttama-*, cpd.)(for *uttamu*, K); K [*-koś*]*o*, XTac *-kośa* (= OV)(for *-kośo*).
2b XTac *buddhāna* (= OV)(for °*ānu*, K); K *gotru* can be restored (though it is slightly damaged), XTac *gotra* (= OV; but OV *gotra-*, cpd.!); K *jagatīṃ*, X *-jananaṃ* (= OV), Ta *-jananāṃ*, Tc *-janaṃ* (for *jagatī*, loc.: Tib.A *'jig-rten-dag-na*, B *'gro-ba'i*).
2c MSS. *atikrāntanāgata* (so prints V), O sep. *atikrānta nāgata-* (here cpd.!)(for *atikrānt'-anāgata*: Tib. *'das daṅ ma byon*; cf. XXII 3a *ati-krānt'-anāgata-jinā*); Tc *daśadiśi* (= O!)(for *daśaddiśi*, KXTa = V).
2d Ta *prasuta* (for °*sūta*, KXTc = OV); XTac *-dhātuṃ* (for *-dhātuḥ*, K = OV wt.n.).
3a X *yāvanta* (= O), Ta *yāganta* (for *yāvanti*, KTc = V); V sep. *vṛkṣa phala-*!; XTac *-vanaspatīya* (= OV)(for °*patīyo*, K; cf. Edgerton 10.172).
3b XTac *ca* (= OV)(for *ti*, K: Tib. *de-dag*); XTac *-samudgata* (= OV; but O sep. *medini samud*°!)(for °*gatu*, K); KXTc *prādur-bhūtāḥ* (= O; K slightly illegible), Ta *prādur-bhūtaḥ* (for *prādu-bhūtāḥ* = V): Tib. *de-dag thams-cad sa-las yaṅ-dag 'byuṅ-źiṅ 'thon*, Chin. 皆從大地而生長.
3c XTac *vṛddhi* (= O)(for *vṛddhiṃ*, K = V wt.n.).
3d O *parihāyaki* (? mispr.)(for °*ati*, MSS., so r. Edg.Rgs. 40 = V); XTc *nirvikalpāḥ*, Ta *nirvṛkalpāḥ*, O em. *nirvikalpā* (= V)(for *nirvikalpo*, K; cf. Edgerton 6.15).
4a XTac *-sama-* (= OV; but V sep. *-sama śrāvaka-*)(for *-raha-*, K); cf. Tib. A *saṅs-rgyas ñan-thos raṅ-rgyal bcas-pa* (? = Skt. *buddha saha-śrāvaka-*°, so Chin. 仏及声聞縁覚等 ), Tib.B *saṅs-rgyas sras daṅ ñan-thos raṅ-rgyal* (? = Skt. *buddha-suta-śrāvaka-*°, cf. Conze Rgs. 41); less poss. *buddha raha śrāvaka pratyayāś* (separately).
4b K *maru*[*taś ca sarva-jaga*]*tī*; Tc *sūkha-* (for *su*°,KXTa=OV); K *-dha r maḥ*.

sarve ti prajña-vara-pāramitā-prasūtā
  na ca kṣīyate na pi ca vardhati jātu prajñā // 4 //

(X88B) yāvanta sattva mṛdu-madhyam'-ukṛṣṭa loke
  sarve a-vidya-prabhavā sugatena uktāḥ /
sāmagri-pratyaya pravartati duḥkha-yantro
  na ca yantra kṣīyati a-vidya na cāsya vṛddhiḥ // 5 //

yāvanti jñāna-naya-dvāra-upāya-mūlāḥ
  sarve ti prajña-vara-pāramitā-prasūtāḥ /
sāma(X89A)gri-pratyaya pravartati jñāna-yantro
  na ca prajña-pāramita vardhati hīyate vā // 6 //

yo tū pratītya-samupādatu a-kṣayāye
  imu prajña a-kṣayata budhyati bodhisattvo /

---

4c Separate MSS. *sarveti* (so prints O!) as *sarve ti* (so Edg.Rgs. 40 = V: Tib. *de kun*); O sep. *-pāramita prasūtā* (for °*itā-prasūtā*, cpd., so Edg. Rgs. 40 = V: Tib. *śes-rab pha-rol phyin-pa mchog-las byuṅ*, cf. Chin. 皆従般若之所生 ); cf. XXVIII 6b *sarve ti prajña-vara-pāramitā-prasūtāḥ*.

4d XTac *na ca* (= OV)(for *na pi ca*, K, so r. Edg.Rgs. 40); V *vivardhati* (wt.n.)(for *vardhati*, MSS. = O); cf. XVIII 7d *na ca kṣīyate na ca vivardhati dharma-dhātuḥ*.

5a K -[*ma*]*dhya*[*mukṛṣṭa*], X *-madhyamukṛṣṭa* (so prints O), Ta °*ukuṣṭe*, Tc °*ukṛṣṇa*, V °*utkṛṣṭa* (wt.n.)(for *-madhyam'-ukṛṣṭa*: Tib. *sems-can tha-ma 'briṅ daṅ mchog*, Chin. 上中下衆生 ); cf. Edg.Rgs. p. 9 n. 2, for *ukṛṣṭa*, m.c. for *utkṛṣṭa* (= V!).

5b K *-pra*[*bha*]*vă* (for *-prabhavā*, XTac = OV); Tc *sūgatena* (for *sug*°, KXTa = OV: Tib. *bde-bar gśegs-pas*).

5c XTac *-pratyayu* (= OV!)(for *-pratyaya*, K, abl.-adv.: Tib. *rkyen-rnams tshogs-nas*, Chin. 因緣和合 ); Tc ⟨*pra*⟩*vartatiḥ* (for *pravartati*,KXTa = OV); Ta *duḥkha-yanto*, Tc *dukha-yaṃto* (for *duḥkha-yantro*, KX = OV: Tib. *sdug-bsṅal 'khrul-'khor*); cf. XXVIII 6c *sāmagri-pratyaya pravartati jñāna-yantro*.

5d Tc *kṣīpati* (for *kṣīyati*, KXTa = OV: Tib.A *zad-pa*, B *zad*); XTac *cāpi* (= OV)(for *cāsya*, K; cf. Tib.B *de-ni*, v.l. *'di-ni*).

6a Tc *-raya-* (for *-naya-*, KXTa = OV); O sep. °*-dvāra upāya-*° (poss. right), but V wrongly sep. *jñāna naya-dvāra upāya-*°; cf. Tib. *ye-śes tshul sgo thabs-kyi* (B *thabs daṅ!*) *rtsa-ba*.

6b Separate MSS. *sarveti* (so prints O!) as *sarve ti* (so Edg.Rgs. 40 ad XXVIII 4c = V: Tib. *de kun*); cf. Tib. *las-kyi 'khrul-'khor* (? Skt.*karma-yantra-*).

6c Tc *sāmagrī-* (for °*gri-*, KXTa = OV); Tc *pravar*⟨*ta*⟩*ti*.

7a K *tu* (= V wt.n.!), Tc *tra* (for *tū*, XTa = O); K *-samutpādatu akṣayāye* (slightly vague), XTac *-samutpādu an-udbhavāye* (so r. Edg.Rgs. 40 = V; O msipr. *anuddhavāye* for *anudbh*°: Tib.A *'byuṅ med*, B *skye med*)(for *-samupādatu akṣayāye*; cf. AsP 231.31-232.2 *a-vidyākṣayatvena ..., saṃskārākṣayatvena vijñānākṣayatvena ... jarā-maraṇākṣayatvena ...*); cf. Edg.Rgs. 8-9, Edgerton 2.88, for *samup*° (m.c. for *samutp*°); cf. Edgerton 8.45, 9.39 for an ablative ending in *-āye*; cf. also Edgerton 7.47 for the predicative ablative.

7b K [*imu prajña akṣa*](24B6)*yata* [*bu*]*dhyati*; XTac *prajñaḥ* (for *prajña*, so em. O = V wt.n.); Tc *bodhisattvoḥ* (for °*sattvo*, KXTa = OV).

7c Tc *atra* (for *abhra-*, KXTa = OV: Tib.A *sprin-gyi*, B *sprin*); K *yukta-rasmī* (for *mukta-raśmī*, XTac = OV: Tib.B *'od-zer 'phro-bas*, Chin. 放光明 ).

7d MSS. *vidhamitvavidya* (so prints V), O sep. *vidhamitva vidya-*! (for

so sūrya abhra-paṭa(Tc33B)le yatha mukta-raśmī
    vidhamitv' a-vidya-paṭalaṃ bhavate sva(X89B)yaṃbhū // 7 //

bhagavatyāṃ ratna-guṇa-saṃcaya-gāthāyām avakīrṇa-kusuma-parivarto nāmāṣṭāviṃśa(K25A)timaḥ // 28 //

---

*vidhamitv' a-vidya-*: Tib.A *ma rig 'gebs-pa bsal-nas*, v.l. *bsal-nas*, B *ma rig thibs-po bcom-nas*, also Chin. 破無明障 ); XTac *-bhūḥ* (= OV) (for *-bhū*, K).

XXVIII col. Ta *-gāthāyāṃm* (for *°āyām*, KXTa = OV); Tc *-kusūma-* (for *-kusuma-*, KXTa = OV: Tib. *me-tog*); K [*nāmāṣṭāviṃśa*](25A1)*tiḥ*, O em. *nāmāṣṭāviṃśatitamaḥ* (for *°viṃśatimaḥ*, XTac = V; cf. XIX colophon, footnote end); at the end of the colophon K reads *gāthā 7;* Tc adds num. 28.

## ⟨XXIX. ANUGAMA⟩

catubhī ca dhyāni viharāti mahānubhāvo
     na ca ālayo na pi ca niśrayu kurvayātī /
api kho (Ta25B) punāśraya ime catu-dhyāna-(X90A)aṅgā
     bheṣyanti bodhi-vara-uttama prāpuṇitvā // 1 //

dhyāne sthito 'nubhavatī vara-prajña-lābhī
     ārūpya rūpi ca samādhi catasra śreṣṭhā /
upakāri-bhūta imi dhyāna varāgra-bodhau
     na punāśrava-kṣayi sa śikṣati bodhisattvo // 2 //

āścarya(X90B)m adbhutam idaṃ guṇa-saṃcayānāṃ
     dhyāne samādhi viharitva nimitta nāstī /
tatra-sthitāna yadi bhajyati cātma-bhāvo
     puna kāma-dhātu upapadya yathā(Tc34A)bhiprāyaṃ // 3 //

---

1a MSS. *caturbhī* (= OV!)(for *catubhī*, so em. Edg.Rgs. 39, cf. Edgerton 19.18; cf. *catu-dhyāna* in *c*); XTac *dhyāna* (= OV)(for *dhyāni*, K; Conze Rgs. 53 misr. K as *dhyāne*); *catubhī* (instr. for loc.; cf. Edgerton 7.30-32) is construed w. *dhyāni* (loc.sg.; cf. Edgerton 5.4-5): Tib.A *bsam-gtan bźir*, B *bsam-gtan bźis-kyaṅ*, Chin. 四禪定 ; XTac *viharanti* (= OV)(for °*āti*, K, so r. Edg.Rgs. 40); O em. *mahānubhāvā* (= V: Tib.A *mthu chen ldan-pa-dag-ni*)(for °*bhāvo*, MSS., so r. Edg.Rgs. 40: Tib.B *mthu chen ldan-pa)*.

1b V *kurvayāti* (wt.n.)(for °*ātī*, MSS. = O).

1c XTa *punāśrayu* (= V), O *panāśrayu* (wt.n.), Tc *punāścayu* (for *punāśraya*, K, so r. Edg.Rgs. 40, allowing a poss. r. *panāś*°; but O *panāś*° is simply a mispr.); MSS. *-dhyāna-saṅgā*, O °*-saṅgā* (wt.n.!), Edg.Rgs. 40 sep. *-dhyāna sāṅgā* (= V!)(for *-dhyāna-aṅgā*); no MS. supports *sāṅgā* (but cf. Tib.B *yan-lag bcas-pa*!); *-dhyāna-aṅgā* (cf. BHSD p. 287b, q.v.) must be the true r., for there is no valid reason to assume a hiatus-bridger *-s-*! (cf. XXXI 10b fn.); *saṅga-*, 'attachment', is absolutely impossible.

1d K *bodhisattvo*! (for *bodhi-*, XTac = OV); XTac *-prāpuṇāyā* (= O: Tib.B *thob-pa-yi*?), V *-prāpaṇāya* (wt.n.!)(for *prāpuṇitvā*, K, so r. Edg.Rgs. 40: Tib.A *thob-par gyur-nas)*.

2a K *sthito nubhavatī* (Conze Rgs. 53 r. K as *sthitonu* for O *sthito 'tra*), XTac *sthito tra bhavatī* (= OV w. *'tra*)(for *sthito 'nubhavatī*: Tib.A *myoṅ* ... *myoṅ*, B *ñams-su myoṅ*; *atra* is not supported by Tib.).

2b K *nāpi* (for *rūpi*, XTac = OV; but OV *ārūpya-rūpi*, cpd.)· Tib. supports *ārūpya*, but neither *nāpi* nor *rūpi*, cf. Chin. 四無色等三摩地; Tac *catasṛ-* (for *catasra*, KX = OV); Ta *śeṣṭhā* (for *śreṣṭhā*, KXTc = OV: Tib. *dam-pa*).

2d XTa *punāsrava-kṣapi* (O p. 105 n. 1 misr. X as °*vā-kṣapi*), Tc *yunāmnavakṣmapi*, O em. *punāsravā-kṣayi*, V *punāsrava-kṣayi* (for *punāśrava-kṣayi*, K; cf. VI 4b *āśrava-*); O °*vā-kṣayi* (cf. Edgerton 8.15-17) may be right, but cf. XXVIII 7a *a-kṣayāye*, 7b *a-kṣayata*, in which the negative prefix *a-* is prosodically long by position; K *se* (Conze Rgs. 53 misr. K as °*me*, w. which Edg.Rgs. 40 em. *punāśrava-kṣay' imi*!)(for *sa*, XTac = OV); Ta *bodhisavo*, Tc °*sattvaḥ* (for °*sattvo*, KX = OV).

3a Tac *adbhūtam* (for *adbhutam*, KX = OV).

3b XTac *viharanti* (= OV)(for *viharitva*, K, so r. Conze Rgs. 53: Tib. *gnas-nas*); cf. XXIX 5b *dhyāne samādhi viharitva* (no v.l.); XTa *nāsti* (= OV)(for *nāstī*, KTc).

3c OV sep. *tatra sthitāna*, Edg.Rgs. 40 em. *tatrā sthitāna* (cf. Edgerton 3.6) or *tatra-sthitāna*, cpd. (cf. Skt. *tatra-vāsin-*, °*-stha-*); the final

yatha jambudvīpaka manuṣya a-labdha-pūrvo
divi deva-uttara-kurū anuprāpuṇeyā /
(X91A) paśyitva te viṣaya tatra pariggṛhītā
puna āgameyu na ca niśrayu tatra kuryāt // 4 //

em eva te guṇa-dharā vara-bodhisattvā
dhyāne samādhi viharitva prayukta-yogāḥ
puna kāma-dhātu-sthita bhonti an-opaliptāḥ
padmeva vāriṇi a-niśrita bāla-(X91B)dharme // 5 //

anyatra sattva-paripācana kṣetra-śodhī
paripūraṇārtha ayu pāramitā mahātmā /
ārūpya-dhātu-upapatti na prārthayantī
mā syā hi (K25B) bodhi-guṇa-pāramitāna hāniḥ // 6 //

---

-*a* of *tatra-* is prosodically long by position (cf. Edgerton Meter 42), cf. XIX 6d *a-sthitu* (*a-* is long); *tatrā-sthitāna* may perh. be the true r. (cf. Edgerton 8.15-17); Tc *bhakṣati* (for *bhajyati*, KXTa = OV: Tib. *źig gyur-na*); XTac *ātma-* (= OV)(for *cātma-*, K; Conze Rgs. 53 reports K as *bhajyati ca* for O *bhajyati*!).

3d Tc *punaḥ* (for *puna*, KXTa = OV); XTa *-dhātu upapadyati*, hypermetr. (= OV!), Tc *-dhātupapadyati* (Tib. *skye-'o*)(for *-dhātu upapadya*, K, so r. Edg.Rgs. 40: Tib.A *skyes-te*); XTac *yathābhiprāyā* (= V), O em. *°āyāḥ* (for *°āyaṃ*, K, so r. Edg.Rgs. 40: Tib. *bsam-pa ji-bźin*).

4a O *-dvīpaka-manuṣya*, cpd. (cf. BHSD p. 238b, *jambudvīpaka-*, s.v.); K *manu[ṣya a]labdha-*; Tc *manūṣyālabdha-* (for *manuṣya alabdha-*, XTa = OV); XTac *-pūrvāḥ* (= O), V *-pūrvā* (wt.n.)(for *-pūrvo*, K; Conze Rgs. 57 misr. K as *-pūrvā*, but correctly reads it on p. 53).

4b K *-uttara-kurā*, XTac *-uttama-purā* (= OV: Tib.A *khaṅs-pa dam-pa*, B *groṅ-khyer mchog-tu* )(for *-uttara-kurū*: Chin. 北洲 ; Conze Rgs. 53 misr. K as *°-kṣarā*); K *-uttara-kurā* (cf. BHSD p. 123a, *Uttarakuru-*, s.v.; also MWD p. 492b, *deva-kuru-*, s.v.) could be a scribal mistake for *°-purā* (cf. BHSD p. 271a, *deva-purā-*, s.v.).

4c MSS. *parigṛhītā* (= OV)(for *pariggṛh°*, so r. Edg.Rgs. 37).

4d XTac *punar āgameya*(= OV)(for *puna āgameyu*, K).

5a O *evam ete* (? mispr.)(for *em eva ete*, MSS., so r. Edg.Rgs. 40 = V); KTc *-bodhisattvo* (for *°sattvā*, XTa = OV).

5b XTac *-yogī* (= OV)(for *-yogāḥ*, K; cf. XVII 7c *prayukta-yogāḥ*).

5c Tc *punaḥ* (for *puna*, KXTa = OV); XTac *anopaliptā* (= OV)(for *°tāḥ*, K).

5d Tc *vadyeva* (for *padmeva*, KXTa = OV: Tib. *padma bźin-du*, Chin. 如蓮華 ); Tc *vāriśi* (for *vāriṇi*, KXTa = OV: Tib.A *chu-la*, B *chu-yi*); Tc *aṇiśrita* (for *ani°*, KXTa = OV: Tib. *mi gnas*); Tac *bāṇa-* (for *bāla-*, KX = OV: Tib. *byis-pa'i*).

6a Edg.Rgs. 40 (ad IV 6d) rightly takes this *anyatra* as meaning 'on the contrary' (cf. BHSD p. 41a, *anyatra* 1, s.v.); but cf. Tib.A *ma gtogs-par* 'except', B *kho-nar zad* 'solely'; cf. IV 6d *anyatra* 'except', XXI 5a *anyatra* 'on the contrary'; Ta [*sattva-*]; K *-bodhī* (for *-śodhī*, XTac = OV: Tib. *źiṅ sbyaṅ*).

6b Tc *paripūranārtha* (for *°pūraṇārtha*,KXTa = OV: Tib.A *yoṅs rdzogs bya-ba*, B *rdzogs don byed* ); XTac *imi* (= OV)(for *ayu*, K: Tib.A *'di*, w. *pha-rol phyin*).

6c O *ărūpya-* (? mispr.)(for *ārūpya-*, MSS., so em. Edg.Rgs. 33 = V: Tib. *gzugs med*).

6d XTac *yatreha* (= V), O *yatraha* (? mispr.)(for *mā syā hi*, K; Conze Rgs. 53 misr. K as *māsyāha*, w. which Edg.Rgs. 40 r. *mā syā ha* 'lest there be'; cf. Edgerton 42.7); K *hi* (instead of *ha*) is perh. to be noted syntactically; XTa *hāni* (= OV)(for *hāniḥ*, KTc); cf. Tib.A *byaṅ-chub yon-tan pha-rol*

yatha kaś cid eva puruṣo ratanaṃ-nidhānaṃ

la(Ta26A)bdhā tu tatra spṛha-buddhi na saṃjane(X92A)yā /

ekāki so puna gṛhītv' aparasmi kāle

gṛhṇitva geha pratiśeya na bhoti lubdho // 7 //

em eva dhyāna (Tc34B) cature ca samādhi śāntāṃ

labdhāna prīti-sukha-dā vidu bodhisattvo /

avasṛjya dhyāna-sukha-prīti-samādhi-lābhaṃ

puna kāma-dhātu pravi(X92B)śanti jagānukampī // 8 //

yadi bodhisattva viharāti samādhi-dhyāne

raha-pratya-yāni spṛha-buddhi na saṃjaneyā /

---

*phyin-rnams ñams-par 'gyur, ... phyin ñams 'gyur 'oṅ (źes).*

7a Tc *yaḥ* (for *yatha,* KXTa = OV: Tib. *dper-na ... ltar,* w. XXIX 8a *em eva*); cf. Chin. 譬如天人 (? = Skt. *yatha kaś ci deva-puruṣo*); K *nidānaṃ,* XTa *nidhānāṃ* (for *nidhānaṃ,* Tc, so em. O = V; but OV sep. *ratanaṃ nidh°;* cf. Edgerton 8.14 for *ratanaṃ-°*: Tib. *rin-chen gter-rnams* [? *°-nidhānān*], Chin. 宝蔵 ).

7b V em. *labdhvā* (for *labdhā,* MSS. = O: Tib.A *rñed gyur-kyaṅ,* v.l.*°-ciṅ,* B *°-nas*); cf. XX 15b, 16b, XXIX 8b *labdhāna* (cf. Edgerton 35.52, Edg.Rgs. 11); K *saṃjaneyyā* (= OV wt.n.; cf. Edgerton 29.23), XTa *saṃyaneyyā* (cf. Edgerton 2.34), Tc *saṃyaneryyaḥ* (for *saṃjaneyā*).

7c Tc *punah* (for *puna,* KXTa = OV); KXTa *gṛhītvaparasmi,* Tc *gṛhītvaraśmiṃ,* OV sep. *gṛhītva parasmi* (for *gṛhītv' aparasmi;* OV may be right, but cf. XXII 12b *aparasmi kāli puna*).

7d Tc *gṛhṇītva* (cf. Edgerton 35.15)(for *°itva,* KXTa = OV); XTac *pra-viśitva* (= OV)(for *pratiśeya,* K; cf. Tib.A *bcug-ste,* B *soṅ-ste*); Edg.Rgs. 40 em. *praviśitvana* (cf. Edgerton 35.29-35), and assumes that Tib. has a neg. by false division; this is not acceptable;KXTa *labdho,* Tc *labdhāḥ* (cf. Chin. 不可得 !)(for *lubdho,* so r. OV wt.n.: Tib.B *chags-par mi byed;* but Edgerton's assumption is supported by Tib.A *chags-par byed-pa!*); contextually, the true r. must be *na bhoti lubdho,* as MS. K suggests; a ger. **pratiśeyana* seems very unlikely (cf. Edgerton 35.46); *pratiśeya* (cf. Skt. ger. *-śayya*) may be an opt.; cf. next verse, too.

8a XTac *catureva* (so print OV; OV intend *catur' eva?*)(for *cature ca,* K; cf. Edgerton 19.15 for *cature*); Tc *śāṃtā* (for *śāntāṃ,* KXTa = OV; but O *samādhi-śāntāṃ,* cpd.!).

8b V em. *labdhvāna* (for *labdhāna,* MSS. = O; cf. XX 15b, 16b *labdhāna,* XXIX 7b *labdhā*; cf. Edg.Rgs. 11, also Edgerton 35.52); K *prīti-sukha-do* (? w. *bodhisattvo,* so Tib.B?), Tc *prīti-sūkha-dā,* O *preti-sukha-dā*(? mispr. for *prīti-°*), V *prīti sukha-dāṃ!* (for *prīti-sukha-dā,* XTa); cf. *dhyāna-sukha-prīti-* in *c*, also Mvy 1478/1479 ...*prīti-sukhaṃ prathamaṃ/ dvitīyaṃ dhyānam upasampadya viharati;* O *vidu-°,*cpd.; XTa *bodhisattvoḥ,* Tc *°sattvaḥ,* OV *°sattvāḥ* (wt.n.)(for *°sattvo,* K); cf. Tib.A *de-bźin byaṅ-chub-sems-dpa' mkhas-pa bsam-gtan bźi, tiṅ-'dzin źi-ba dga' bde sbyin byed thob gyur-la;* B ... *mkhas-pa dga'-ba daṅ, bde sbyin bsam-gtan tiṅ-'dzin źi-ba bźi thob-nas!*

8c O *avasṛrjya* (mispr.!)(for *avasṛjya,* MSS. = V: Tib. *btaṅ-ste*); O *-lăbhaṃ* (mispr.!)(for *-lābhaṃ,* MSS. = V: Tib. *thob*).

8d Tc *punaḥ* (for *puna,* KXTa = OV).

9a Tc *viharati* (for *°āti,* KXTa = OV); O *samădhi-* (mispr. for *samādhi-,* MSS. = V, so r. Edg.Rgs. 40: Tib. *tiṅ-'dzin*).

9b MSS. *rahapratyayāni* (so print OV) is to be read *raha-pratya-yāni*: Tib. *dgra-bcom raṅ-rgyal theg-par*(cf. XXI 5b, fn.); XTac *-buddhita* (so Tib. *'dod-pa'i blo skyed-na?*)(for *-buddhi na,* K, so em. O = V: Chin. 不楽羅漢及縁覚 !); cf. XXI 5b *raha-pratya-yāni spṛhatāṃ na jananti tatra.*

a-samāhito bhavati uddhata-kṣipta-citto
     parihīṇa-buddha-guṇa nāvika bhinna-nāvo // 9 //

kiṃ cāpi rūpam api śabda tathaiva gandhān
     rasa-sparśa (X93A) kāma-guṇa pañc' abhiyukta bhotī /
raha-pratya-yāna-vigato ratu bodhi-citte
     satataṃ samāhitu prajānayitavyu śūro // 10 //

para-sattva-pudgala-nidāna viśuddha-sattvāḥ
     vicaranti vīrya-vara-pāramitābhiyuktāḥ /
yatha kumbha-dāsi a-vaśā vaśu bhartṛkasya
     tatha sarva-(X93B)sattva-vaśatām upayānti dhī(Tc35A)rāḥ // 11 //

---

9c K *'samāhito* (for *asam°*, XTac = OV: Tib. *mñam-par ma bźag*); Conze Rgs. 53 simply reports K *'samāhito*, but Edg.Rgs. 40 has misunderstood that Conze em. O *asamāhito* to *sam°*, and has rejected *samāhito* (not *'sam°*), which is wrong both in metre and sense!; Tc *-cinaḥ* (for *-citto*, KXTa = OV: Tib. *sems*).

9d XTac *parihīna-buddhi-guṇā*, O em. *°-guṇa* (= V)(for *parihīṇa-buddha-guṇa*, K: Tib. *saṅs-rgyas yon-tan yoṅs ñams*); MSS. *-bhāvo* (= O)(for *-nāvo*, so em. Edg.Rgs. 40 [= V], w. ref. to Pāli Jātaka III 159.5 *bhinna-nāvo* = III 158.26 *bhinna-plavo*: Tib. Rgs. *gru źig* 'wrecked ship').

10a Ta *rŭpam* (for *rūpam*, KXTc = OV: Tib. *gzugs*); XTac *gandho* (= OV!) (for *gandhān*, K).

10b V sep. *rasa sparśa*!; MSS. *pañcabhiyukta*, O sep. *pañca bhiyukta*, V sep. *pañcabhi yukta*! (for *pañc' abhiyukta*); cf. Tib. *'dod-pa'i yon-tan lṅa-la brtson* (? Skt. *yukta-*) *gyur-kyaṅ*, B v.l. *'dod yon lṅa-la mṅon-par brtson* (? Skt. *abhiyukta-*) *gyur-kyaṅ*; Tc *bhogī* (= V!)(for *bhotī*, KXTa = O).

10c Tc *rudra-* (for *raha-*, KXTa = OV: Tib. *dgra-bcom*); V sep. *-yāna vigato*!: cf. XXI 5b *raha-pratya-yāni* (w. footnote); K *na tu* (so r. Edg. Rgs. 40!), XTac *nanta-*, V *'nanta-*, O *nanda-* (wt.n.!)(for *ratu*: Tib.*dga'*); K *na tu* appears to be a scribal mistake for the graphically similar *ratu*; XTac *-bodhisattvo* (= OV!)(for *bodhi-citte*, K, so r. Edg.Rgs. 40: Tib. *byaṅ-chub sems*).

10d Tc *sāhitu* (for *samāhitu*, KXTa = OV: Tib. *mñam-par bźag yin-par*); K *prajānapitavyu* (Conze Rgs. 54 misr. K as *°yitavyu*), XTac *prajānayitavya* (= V), O *prajāyitavya* (undoubtedly mispr. for *prajānay°*)(for *prajānay-itavyu*: Tib. *śes-par bya*); Tc *śūroḥ* (for *śūro*, KXTa = OV).

11a XTa *-puṅgala-* (cf. I 20d MSS. *puṅgala-*, OV *pudgala-*; cf. BHSD p. 347a, *pudgala-*, s.v.), Tc *-pugala-* (for *-pudgala-*, K, so em. O = V); O *-nidāna-°*, cpd.! (cf. BHSD p. 295b, *nidāna-*, s.v. 1: Tib. *phyir*); Tc *visūddha-* (for *viśuddha-*, KXTa = OV: Tib.A *rnam dag*, B *rnam dag-pa*); XTa *-sattvā* (= OV), Tc *-sattvāṃ* (for *-sattvāḥ*, K w. daṇḍa).

11b Tc *vīrya-bala-* (= V; cf. Mvy 984)(for *°-vara-*, KXTa = O: Tib. *brtson-'grus*, Chin. 精進 ; cf. Mvy 917); XTa *°yuktā* (for *°āḥ*, KTc, so em. O = V); cf. XXX 1d *vīrya-pāramita-yuktu*, 2d *vīrya-pāramita-hīna*.

11c K *avasā*, Ta *avaśrā* (*r* erased later)(for *avaśā*, XTc: Tib. *dbaṅ med*); XTac *vaśa* (for *vaśu*, K); Tc *bhartikasya* (= V; cf. Edgerton 3.91)(for *bhartṛkasya*, KXTa = O); O *avaśāvaśabhartṛkasya*!, V *avaśāvaśa bhartik°*!; Conze trsl., 'As a maid servant is submissive to her master who is not subject to anyone else'!; render *c* as: 'As a harlot (*kumbha-dāsī-*; or poss. 'female servant'; cf. XXIX 12a *dāsī*, 13b *preṣya-*) without (free) will (falls) into (her) master's will/power': Tib. *dper-na bran-mo bum-thogs* (B *chu-chun*) *dbaṅ med rje-bo'i* (MS. Tb *°-mo'i*!) *dbaṅ*.

11d Tc *-sattve vasatām*, O om. *-sattva-* (? mispr.)(for *-sattva-vaśatām*, KXTa = V: Tib.A *sems-can-rnams-kyi dbaṅ-gis*, B *sems-can kun-gyi dbaṅ-gis*; but MS.Tc *sems-can don-kyis* [r. *°-gyis*]!: Skt. *-artha-*?, cf. Chin. 利於衆生 !

na ca svāmikasya prativākya dadāti dāsī
    ākruṣṭu cāpy atihatāpy atha tāḍitā vā /
ekānta-trasta manasā sa bhayābhibhū(K26A)tāḥ
    mām eva so (Ta26B) anu vadhiṣyati kāraṇena // 12 //

em eva bodhi-vara-prasthitu bodhisattvo
    sthātavyu sarva-jagatī yatha pre(X94A)ṣya-bhūto /
anu bodhi-āgamu guṇāna ca pāripūrī
    tṛṇa agni kāṣṭha-prabhavo dahate tam eva // 13 //

avasṛjya ātma-sukhatāṃ para-sattva-kārye
    abhiyuktu rātri-divi niṣpratikāṅkṣa-citto /
māteva eka-sutake paricaryamāṇā
    adhyāśayena a-vikhinna u(X94B)pasthihetī // 14 //

---

12a Tc *tvāmikasya* (for *svām°*, KXTa = OV: Tib. *rje-bo-*[MS.Tb *°-mo-!*]*la-ni*); XTa *prativākyu* (= OV)(for *°vākya*, KTc).

12b K *cāpi* (unmetr.!) *atihatāpy* (Conze Rgs. 41 misr. K as *abhi°*) *atha tāḍitā vā*, XTac *cāpi athavā sada tāḍitā*(Tc *tāḍi⟨tā⟩*) *vā* (= V: Tib. *spyo-ba byas-sam 'on-te rtag-tu brdegs-kyaṅ-ruṅ*), O em. *cāpi athavā sa taḍati tavā*!! (for *cāpy atihatāpy atha tāḍitā vā*, so r. Edg.Rgs. 40 w. K except *abhihatāpy*, which is so misr. by Conze Rgs. 41).

12c O *ekānta trasta-°*, V *ekānta-trasta-°*(poss. right?)(for *ekānta-trasta*, nom.sg.f., 'terribly afraid', w. *manasā*, instr.-adv., 'in the mind'); XTac *°bhūtā* (= OV)(for *°bhūtāḥ*, K; but cf. Edgerton 9.10): Tib. *śin-tu skrag-pa'i yid-kyis 'jigs-pas* (B *'jigs bcas*!: Skt. *sa-°*?)*zil-gyis gnon*.

12d K *puna anu vadhiṣyati* (hypermetr.!), XTac *anupadhiṣyati* (= O!)(for *anu vadhiṣyati*, so em. Edg.Rgs. 40 = V; Edgerton rightly says that *puna* is orig. a gloss on the adv. *anu* 'thereupon'; cf. XXIX 13c *anu*: Tib.B *'di-las*): Tib.A *gnod-pa byas-su 'oṅ*, B *bsad-par 'gyur-du 'oṅ*; Conze Index p. 132b, *anuvadhiṣyati*, Dict. p. 41 [*anu*]*vadhiṣyati* 'will kill'!; *kāraṇena*, instr., 'with torment'(??)(cf. BHSD p. 178b, *kāraṇā-*, PTSD II p. 38a, *kāraṇa-*, ss.vv.).

13b XTac *tiṣṭheya* (= OV; 3 sg.opt., cf. Edgerton 29.28)(for *sthātavyu*, K; gdve., Skt. *sthātavya-*, Epic +; cf. Whitney Roots p. 195); *tiṣṭheya* could be a peculiar and noteworthy gdve.

13c O *anubodhi āgamu*! (cf. XXIX 12d *anu*, w.n.); Tc *pāri⟨pūrī⟩*; cf. Tib.A *luṅ-gi yon-tan rtog-pa yoṅs-su rdzogs mi byed* (? Skt. ... *°-guṇā na ca* ...!), B *'di-las byaṅ-chub thob-ciṅ yon-tan rdzogs-par 'gyur*.

13d Tc *tṛṇāgni* (for *tṛṇa agni*, KXTa = OV); K *kā*[*ṣ*]*ṭha-*[*pra*](26A2)*bhavato*! (for *kāṣṭha-prabhavo*, XTac = OV); Conze Rgs. 54 reports K as *bhavato* for O *prabhavo*; XTac *dahane* (for *°ate*, K, so em. O = V); Ta *nam* (for *tam*,KXTc = OV): Tib.A *śiṅ-las me byuṅ-ba-yis śiṅ de sreg-pa bźin*,but B *rtsva daṅ śiṅ-las me byuṅ-bas-ni de-ñid (b)sreg*! (= Conze Trsl.).

14a XTa *ātma-sugatāṃ* (= OV; but V sep. *ātma sug°*!), Tc *ātme sūgatāṃ* (for *ātma-sukhatāṃ*, K, so r. Edg.Rgs. 40: Tib. *bdag-gi bde-ba*).

14b XTac *abhiyukta* (= OV)(for *°tu*, K); O *niṣpṛtikāṅkṣa-* (? mispr. for *niṣprati°*, MSS. = V, so r. Conze ad O p. 128: Tib. *re-ba med*).

14c Ta *eva-* (for *eka-*, KXTc = OV); Tc *-sūtake* (for *-sutake*, KXTa = OV): Tib. *bu gcig-pa-la*; XTac *paricāryamāṇe* (= O), V *paricāryamāṇo* (wt.n.) (for *paricaryamāṇā*, K: Tib. *mi-ni rim-gro byed-pa-na*, B ... *byed-pa*; Conze Rgs. 54 misr. K as *paricāry°*); *paricaryamāṇā*, nom.sg.fem.pres.pple. w. a new stem *-ya-* (cf. Edgerton 28.26-28), 'loving' (cf. BHSD p. 322a, *paricārayati* 2, s.v.).

14d XTac *adhyāśaye na parikhinna* (= OV)(for *adhyāśayena avikhinna*, K): Tib.A *bsam-pa thag-pas byed-de* (?; but B *rnam-par*) *skyo med*; cf. BHSD p.

bhagavatyāṃ ratna-guṇa-saṃcaya-gāthāyām anugama-parivarto nāma ekona-triṃśatimaḥ // 29 //

482, *vikhinna-*, s.v.; XTac *upasthiheti* (= V), O *avasthiheti* (wt.n.)(for *upasthihetī*, K: Tib.A *gnas-pa*, but B *gnas-par gyis*, v.l. *gnas-par bya* = O; Conze Rgs. 54 misr. K as °*hitī*, and assumes a different rec.!

XXIX col. X *-gāthāyāṃ* (= O)(for °*yām*, KTac = V); XTa *nāma ekūna-*, Tc *nāmaikuna-*, V *nāmaikūna-* (cf. Edgerton 4.24)(for *nāma ekona-*, K, so em. O); K °*triṃśatiḥ*, O em. °*triṃśatitamaḥ* (for °*triṃśatimaḥ*, XTac = V; cf. XIX colophon, footnote end); cf. XIX col. *nāmaikona*°; at the end of the colophon K reads *gāthā 14;* Tc adds num. 29.

## ⟨XXX. SADĀ-PRARUDITA⟩

yo bodhisattva cira-saṃsaraṇābhiprāyo
     sattvārtha kṣetra-pariśodhana-yukta-yogī /
na ca kheda-(Tc35B)buddhi aṇu-mātra upādayātī
     so vīrya-pāramita-yuktu (X95A) a-tandritaś ca // 1 //

saci kalpa-koṭi-gaṇa nā-vidu bodhisattvo
     cira-saṃjñi bodhi samudānayate dukhena /
cira-duḥkha bheṣyati samācaramāṇu dharmaṃ
     tatu vīrya-pāramita-hīna kusīda-rūpo // 2 //

prathamaṃ upādu vara-bodhayi citt'-upādo
     yāvann an-utta(X95B)ra-śivām anuprāpuṇeyā /

---

1a Tc *vira-* (for *cira-*, KXTa = OV: Tib.B *yun-riṅ*); cf. Tib.A *gaṅ-źig byaṅ-chub-sems-dpa'i spyad-pa spyod sems-śiṅ!*, but B *byaṅ-chub-sems-dpa' gaṅ-źig yun-riṅ 'khor 'dod-ciṅ;* Conze Rgs. 54 misr. K as *°yukto* (for *°prāyo*, MSS. = OV), assuming a different rec.!

1b K *-parisodhana-* (for *°śodhana-*, XTac = OV: Tib. *sbyoṅ*).

1c XTac *anu-* (for *aṇu-*, K, so em. O = V: Tib. *rdul;* cf. VII 3b, fn.); V *upādiyāti* (wt.n.)(for *upādayātī*, MSS. = O).

1d XTa *-yukta* (= OV; Conze Rgs. 54 misr. O as *-yukto*), Tc *yu⟨kta⟩* (for *-yuktu*, K; Conze Rgs. 54 misr. K as *-yukta*); Tc *⟨a⟩te⟨n⟩dritaś*.

2a XTac *avikalpa-* (= O!)(for *saci kalpa-*, K, so r. Conze ad O p. 128, but Conze sep. *sa ci*!; V *saci*: Tib. *gal-te*; cf. BHSD p. 549b, *saci*, s. v.); XTa *gaṇaye*, 3 sg.opt. 'would count' (= OV; but O *-koṭi-gaṇaye*, cpd.!), Tc *gaṇeya* (for *-gaṇa*, K, 'for the period of the number of koṭis of kalpas': Tib.A *bskal-pa bye 'graṅs-la*, B *bskal-pa bye-ba bgraṅ*); XTac *vidu bodhisattvo* (= V!), O *'vidu-°* (wt.n.)(for *nā-vidu bodhisattvo*, K): Tib. *byaṅ-chub-sems-dpa' mi mkhas*, but Chin. 大智菩薩!; cf. XXXI 2b *na-vidū*: Tib. *mi mkhas* (cf. Skt. *na-vidvas-*, *na-vidyā-*, but not *na-veda-*, *na-vedas-*); cf. Edgerton 3.6 for *nā* (m.c. for *na*); K offers another possibility: *-gaṇanâvidu* w. secondary sandhi (*-gaṇana*, acc., plus *a-vidu*, nom.sg.m.), or *-gaṇanâvidu-*, cpd. (*gaṇanā-* plus *a-vidu-*)?

2b XTac *-saṃjña* (= OV)(for *-saṃjñi*, K; cf. BHSD p. 522b, *saṃjñin-* 3/4, s.v.); K *bodhi* ; XTac *samudānaya* (= O; but O *cira-saṃjña-bodhi-°*, cpd.!; noted by Edg.Rgs. 40), V *samudāniya* (wt.n.!)(for *samudānayate*, K: Tib. *sgrub;* cf. BHSD p. 573a, *°nayati*, s.v.); cf. XVI 5b *samudānayeyā;* XTac *tena duḥkhe* (= OV)(for *dukhena*, K; Conze Rgs. 41 misr. K as *duḥkhena;* cf. Edgerton 2.85): Tib. *riṅ-bar 'du-śes sdug-bsṅal* (O om. *sdug-bsṅal* by mistake?) *byaṅ-chub sgrub*.

2c Tc *samācaramāṇū* (for *°māṇu*, KXTa = OV).

2d XTac *na tu*!, O *na* (? mispr. for *na tu*)(for *tatu*, K, so r. Conze ad O p. 128 = V: Tib.A *de-tshe*, B *des-na*!); XTa *cīrya-* (for *vīrya-*, KTc, so em. O = V: Tib. *brtson-'grus*); O *-pāramita-* (? mispr.)(for *-pāramita-*, MSS., so r. Edg.Rgs. 40 = V); Ta *kuśīda-* (cf. BHSD p. 189a, *kusīda-*, s. v.), Tc *kuṇīda-* (for *kusīda-*, KX); Tc *-rūpaḥ* (for *-rūpo*, KXTa = OV).

3a Tc *prathamam* (for *°maṃ*, KXTa = OV); Tc *-bodhi* (for *-bodhayi*, KXTa = OV); KXTa *cittapādo* (= O!), Tc *cittamādo*, V *cittupādo* (wt.n.)(for *citt'-upādo;* cf. VI 3a, fn.).

3b XTac *so vā* (= OV)(for *yāvann*, K: Tib.B *bar*; cf. VI 3b *yāvat*); Tc *anupāpuṇeyā* (rather a scribal mistake than a metrically required form) (for *anuprā°*, KXTa = OV).

3c K *rātrindiveka-*, XTa *rātrindivaika-* (= OV *rātriṃ-°*), Tc *rātridivaika-* (for *rātriṃ-div' eka-;* cf. XXIX 14b *rātri-diva* = Skt. *rātriṃ-divā*,

rātriṃ-div' eka-manasā tam adhiṣṭhiheyā

ārabdha-vīrya vi(Ta27A)du-paṇḍitu vedita(K26B)vyo // 3 //

saci kaś cid eva vadayeya sumeru-śailaṃ

bhinditva paśca adhigamyasi agra-bodhiṃ /

saci khedu-buddhi kurute ca pramāṇa-buddhiṃ

kauśīdya-prāptu bhavate tada bodhi(X96A)sattvo // 4 //

atha tasy' upadyati matī kim utālpa-mātraṃ

kṣaṇa-mātra bhasma nayamī vilayaṃ sumeruṃ /

ārabdha-vīrya bhavate vidu bodhisattvo

na-cireṇa bo(Tc36A)dhi-vara paśyati nāyakānāṃ // 5 //

saci kāya-citta-vacasā ca parākrameyā

pari(X96B)pācayitva jagatī kariṣyāmi arthaṃ /

---

*°-divam;* XXIV 2b *diva-rātri* = Skt. *divā-rātrau;* XXII 11d *divā ca rātrau*: Tib.Rgs. XXX 3c A *ñin daṅ mtshan-du,* B *ñin mtshan*); MSS. *adhiṣṭhiheyā* (= V; so clearly intends O, which Conze Rgs. 54 misr. as *adhiṣṭhaheyā*).

3d X *ārambha-vīryu* (= O), Tac *°-vīrya* (= V)(for *ārabdha-vīrya,* K, so r. Edg.Rgs. 40); V sep. *vidu paṇḍitu;* Tc *veditavyaḥ* (for *°vyo,* KXTa = OV): Tib. *mkhas-pa gsal-ba* (B *°-bas* = O)*brtson-'grus brtsams-par rig-par bya.*

4a O sep. *sa ci;* K *-sailaṃ* (for *-śailaṃ,* XTac = OV: Tib. *ri-rab ri*).

4b K *yaśca* (for *paśca,* XTac = OV: Tib.A *phyi-nas,* B *rjes-la*); Tc *°gaspa* (for *°gamyasi,* KXTa = OV: Tib.A *thob bya,* B *thob 'gyur*); *adhigamyasi,* 2 sg. in active force w. *-ya*-stem (cf. Edgerton 37.22-23), is contrued w. *agra-bodhiṃ,* acc.; V *-bodhim* (w. *-m*).

4c Tc *savi* (for *saci,* KXTa = OV; but O sep. *sa ci*!: Tib.A *gal-te,* B *ji-ste,* v.l. *ci-ste*); XTa *kheda-buddhi* (= OV), Tc *khyeda-buddhiḥ* (for *kheda-buddhi,* K: Tib. *skyo-ba'i blo*); XTac *pramāda-baddho* (= O!), Tc *prasāda-baddho* (for *pramāṇa-buddhiṃ,* K, so r. Conze ad O p. 128 = V): Tib.A *gal-te skyo-ba'i blo skyes tshad-du byed 'gyur-na* (v.l. *°-nas*), B *ji-ste* (v.l. *ci-ste*) *skyo-ba'i blo skyed tshad-kyaṅ sems* (v.l. *skyed* = O) *byed-na,* but Chin. 懈怠而退心.

4d XTac *kausīdya-* (= OV)(for *kauśīdya-,* K; cf. BHSD p. 196b, *kausīdya-,* s.v.); K *-prāpnu,* XTa *-prapta,* Tc *-prāpna,* O em. *-prāpta* (= V)(for *-prāptu*); Tc *bodhisattvaḥ* (for *°sattvo,* KXTa = OV).

5a KX *tasyupadyati* (so print OV), Tac *tasyap°* (for *tasy' upadyati*).

5b K *nakamī* (Conze Rgs. 54 doubtfully r. K as *nakasī*), XTac *nayatī* (=OV) (for *nayamī,* m.c. for *nayāmi*); cf. Tib. *ri-rab thal-bar klag* (B *brlag*) '(I) destroy Sumeru into ashes'; V *sumerum* (w. *-m*).

5c XTac *ārambha-* (= OV)(for *ārabdha-,* K, so r. Edg.Rgs. 40 ad XXX 3d: Tib. *brtson-'grus brtsams-pa-ste*); X *-vīryu* (for *-vīrya,* KTac = OV wt. n.); O *vidu-bodhisattvo,* cpd.

5d O sep. *na cireṇa*!; XTac *lassati* (O p. 111 n. 1 misr. X as *lapsati*), O em. *lapsyati* (= V: Tib. *thob 'gyur*)(for *paśyati,* K, lectio facil. for *prāpsyati*?; Conze Rgs. 54 misr. K as *yaśyati*); cf. X 7d *na-cireṇa bodhi-vara prāpsyati nāyakānāṃ;* V *nāyakānām* (w. *-m*).

6a O sep. *sa ci*; XTac *-vayasā,* O *-manasā* (wt.n.!)(for *-vacasā,* K, so r. Conze ad O p. 128 = V: Tib. *lus daṅ ṅag daṅ yid-kyis,* Chin. 身心語 ); KXTa *parākrameyyā* (= OV), Tc *°eryyā* (for *°eyā,* cf. Edgerton 29.23: Tib. *brtson byed-na,* Chin. 行精進 ).

6b K *paripā[ca]yitva;* MSS. *karisyāmi* (= OV) may have been pronounced as *°iṣāmi,* m.c. (cf. Edg.Rgs. 38).

6c K *kauśīdya-prāpnu,* XTa *kausīdya-prāpta* (= OV), Tc *kausīdya-prāpna* (for *kauśīdya-prāptu*); XTac *bhavatī* (= OV)(for *°ate,* K; Conze Rgs. 54 misr. K as *°ati*; cf. XXX 4d *kauśīdya-prāptu bhavate*); XTa *-saṃjñaiḥ*

kauśīdya-prāptu bhavate sthitu ātma-saṃjño
    sarva-jñatāya bhavi dūru nabho va bhūmeḥ // 6 //

yasmin na kāyu na pi cittu na sattva-saṃjñā
    saṃjñā-vivarti sthitu a-dvaya-dharma-cārī /
ayu vīrya-pāramita ukta hitaṃ-kareṇa
    ākāṅ(X97A)kṣamāṇu śivam a-cyuti prāpuṇātī // 7 //

puruṣaṃ śruṇitva vacanaṃ parato duruktaṃ
    paritoṣayāti sukhamaṃ vidu bodhisattvo /
ko bhāṣyate ka śṛṇute kutu kasya kena
    so yuktu kṣānti-vara-pāramitāya vijño // 8 //

yo bodhisattva kṣamate guṇa-dharma-(X97B)yukto
    yaś caiva ratna-bharitaṃ tri-sahasra dadyāt /
(Ta27B) buddhānu loka-vidunāṃ raha-pratyayānāṃ
    kala-puṇyu so na bhava(K27A)te iha dāna-skandho // 9 //

---

(= OV!), Tc *-sajñaiḥ* (for *-saṃjño*, K, so r. Edg.Rgs. 40).

6d XTac *nairātmṛbhāvana vidūri nabhaṃ va bhūme* (O p. 111 n. 2 misr. X as *nairātma°*), O em. *nairātya-*(r. *nairātmya-*?)*bhāvana-vidūri nabhaṃ va bhūmeḥ* (= V *nairātmya-°* ...)(for *sarvajñatāya bhavi dūru nabho va bhūmeḥ*, K, so r. Edg.Rgs. 40: Tib. *thams-cad mkhyen-pa-ñid-las riṅ 'gyur gnam sa bźin*); Conze Rgs. 41 quotes K (without giving Tib.) and neglects it; Conze Trsl. is based on O; render *d* as '(he) would be far from omniscience as the sky (is far) from the earth'; Chin. freely 而不能証仏菩提.

7a XTa *citta na* (= OV), Tc *citta* ⟨*na*⟩(for *cittu na*, K).

7b Tc om. from *-vivarti* to XXX 8b *sukhamaṃ*.

7c X *vīryu-* (for *vīrya-*, KTa = OV wt.n.); K *yukta* (for *ukta*, XTa = OV: Tib. *gsuṅs*); *yukta-* is not possible in the context, and *y-* is hardly a hiatus-bridger; Conze Rgs. 54 misr. K as *-pāramitam ukta*.

7d XTa *ākāṃkṣamāna*, O em. *°māṇa* (for *°māṇu*, K = V wt.n.; Conze Rgs. 54 mispr. K as *ākāṅṣamānu*); XTa *ayuta* (= O), V *acyutam* (for *acyuti*, K: Tib. A *ma ñams*, B *mi ñams*); XTa *agra-bodhiṃ* (= OV; but V *-m*: Tib. *byaṅ-chub ... mchog*, Chin. 無上仏菩提)(for *prāpuṇātī*, K; Conze Rgs. 41 misr. K as *°āti*).

8 Tc omits from *vivarti* XXX 7b to *sukhamaṃ* 8b.

8a Conze ad O p. 128 em. O *puruṣaṃ* (= KXTa) to *par°* (= V: Tib. *rtsub*); *puruṣaṃ*, as meaning '*paruṣam*' (cf. Edgerton 3.57), seems to be the true reading; but cf. Chin. 令人聞言悉歡喜! (? Skt. *puruṣam*[as meaning 'a man'] *śruṇetva vacanaṃ ... paritoṣayāti ...*).

8b XTa *susukhaṃ* (= OV)(for *sukhamaṃ*, K, so r. Edg.Rgs. 40; cf. Edgerton 2.25, 3.45, 101, BHSD p. 596b, *sukhama-*, s.v.); cf. Tib.A *ma-lus mgu byed byaṅ-chub-sems-dpa'* ⟨*mkhas-pa*⟩, B *bdag bde yin źes byaṅ-chub-sems-dpa' mkhas-pa dga'*; Tc *bodhisattvaḥ* (for *°sattvo*, KXTa = OV); O *vidu-bodhisattvo*, cpd.

8c XTac *bhāṣate* (= OV)(for *bhāṣyate*, K; cf. Edgerton 28.28, 43 p. 223a, *bhāṣ-* 3, s.v.); cf. XVIII 7c *bhāṣyamāṇo*, nom.sg.m.pres.pple. in active force; K *kaḥ* (for *ka*, XTac = OV); XTa *sṛṇute*, Tc *sṛṇūte* (for *śṛṇute*, K, so em. O = V: Tib. *thos*).

8d XTac *yukta* (= OV)(for *yuktu*, K); Tc *vijñoḥ* (for *vijño*, KXTa = OV).

9a XTac *so* (= OV)(for *yo*, K: Tib. *gaṅ-źig*); XTa *bodhisattvu* (= O)(for *°sattva*, KTc = V).

9b K ⟨*ratna-*⟩; KXTa *-bharitan*, Tc *-bharite* (for *-bharitaṃ*,= OV); Tac *dri-* (for *tri-*, KX = OV: Tib. *stoṅ gsum*).

9c XTac *buddhāna* (= OV)(for *°ānu*, K); XTac *-vidunārhata-* (= OV)(for

kṣāntī-sthitasya pariśudhyati ātma-bhāvo
 dvātriṃśa-lakṣaṇa-prabhāva an-anta-pāro /
sattvāna śraddha-vara-dharma niśāmayātī
 priya bho(X98A)ti sarva-jagatī kṣamamāṇu vijño // 10 //

saci kaś ci candana-puṭaṃ grahiyāṇa sattvo
 abhyokireyu guru-premata bodhisattvaṃ /
dvitiyo ca agni sakalaṃ śiri prakṣipeyā
 ubhayatra tulyu manu tena u(Tc36B)pāditavyā // 11 //

evaṃ kṣamitva (X98B) vidu-paṇḍitu bodhisattvo
 taṃ citt'-upādu pariṇāmayi agra-bodhau /
yāvanti kṣānti raha-pratyaya-sattva-dhātū
 abhibhoti sarva-jagatī kṣamamāṇu śūro // 12 //

---

*-vidunaṃ raha-*, K, so r. Edg.Rgs. 40): Tib. *'jig-rten khams* (Skt. *loka-dhātu-*!; but B correctly *'jig-rten mkhyen*) *saṅs-rgyas-rnams daṅ dgra-bcom raṅ-rgyal*, Chin. 仏縁覚及羅漢.

9d XTac *-puṇya* (= OV)(for *-puṇyu*, K); K *bha[va]te;* XTa *dānu-skandhe* (= O), Tc *dāmaru-skandhe*, V *dāna-skandhe* (for *dāna-skandho*, K).

10a KTc *kṣānti-* (for *kṣāntī-*, XTa = OV); MSS. *pariśuddhyati* (for *°śudhyati*, so em. O = V).

10b K *dvātriṃśal-* (for *°triṃśa-*, XTac = OV); Tc *⟨a⟩naṃta-pāroḥ* (for *ananta-pāro*, KXTa = OV: Tib. *pha mtha'-yas*).

10c Tc *sattvāra* (for *°āna*, KXTa = OV); XTac *śūnya-* (= OV: Tib.B *chos rab stoṅ-pa*)(for *śraddha-*, K: Tib.A *dad-pa'i chos rab*, Chin. 法信受; but Conze Rgs. 57 thinks *śraddha-* is a probable mistake!); Tc *niśāmayā⟨tī ... XXX 11c dvitiyo⟩...*; acc. to V p. 392 n. 4, Baroda MS. is damaged from XXX 10c *sattvāna* to 11c *dvitiyo pi/ca;* V supplies the portion from O; Conze Rgs. 54 misr. K as *niśyamayātī* (for *niśām°*, MSS. = OV, so r. Edg.Rgs. 40, who also rejects Conze Trsl.; Conze seems to have trsl.Tib. *sgrogs-par byed*!; *niśāmayātī* is an ordinary word meaning 'hears, listens' (cf. Skt. *niśāmayati*, Pāli *nisāmeti*), as correctly trsl. in Chin. 聞.

10d XTa *priyu* (= OV)(for *priya*, K); XTa *bhonti* (= O ≠ V)(for *bhoti*, K = V wt.n.); XTa *vijñoḥ* (for *vijño*, K, so em. O = V).

11 Tc XXX 10c *niśāmayā⟨tī ... 11c dvitiyo⟩ py agni ...*

11a O sep. *sa ci;* K *grahipāṇa* (most prob. a scribal error for *grahiyāṇa;* but cf. Tib.A *sñim bkaṅ-ste* = Skt. *grahi*, opt. or ger., plus *pāṇa* 'hand'!), XTa *grahiyāna* (= OV)(for *grahiyāṇa*: Tib.B *blaṅs;* cf. Edgerton 35.47).

11b OV *abhyokireya* (wt.n.)(for *°eyu*, KXTa); V *bodhisattvam* (w. *-m*).

11c XTa *dvitīyo pi*, Tc *⟨dvitiyo⟩ py*, OV *dvitīyo 'pi* (unmetr.!)(for *dvitiyo ca*, K, so em. Edg.Rgs. 40; K *dvitiyo* has escaped Conze's notice; cf. Edgerton 3.41); XTac *sakale śirasi kṣipeyā* (= OV)(for *sakalaṃ* [K *śak°*; Conze Rgs. 54 misr. K as *sak°;* cf. Edgerton 2.58] *śiri prakṣipeyā*, K, so r. Edg.Rgs. 40).

11d Tc *ubhayātra* (for *ubhayatra*, KXTa = OV: Tib. *gñi-ga-la*, v.l. *gñis-ka-la* = O); XTa *upāditavyo* (= OV), Tc *°vyaḥ* (for *°vyā*, K); *-ā*, nom.sg. nt. (cf. Edg.Rgs. 13); cf. XXX 13a *upāditavyā*, also XXX 12c *-dhātū*.

12a V sep. *vidu paṇḍitu*.

12b O *tām* (wt.n.!)(for *taṃ*, MSS., so r. Edg.Rgs. 40 = V); MSS. *cittapādu* (= O), V *cittupādu* (wt.n.)(for *citt'-upādu;* cf. VI 3a, fn.); Tc *pariṇāma apy* (for *°ṇāmayi*, KXTa = OV: Tib. *yoṅs bsṅos-na)*.

12c XTac *-dhātoḥ* (= OV)(for *-dhātū*, K: Tib.A *khams-kyi*, B *khams*); *-dhāto* (gen. for Skt. *dhātoḥ/dhātor;* cf. Edgerton 12.37), or poss. *-dhāto*(MInd. for Skt. *dhātau*, loc.; cf. Edgerton 3.56), is reduced to *-dhātū*(cf. Edgerton 3.24, 8.21, Edg.Rgs. 13); cf. XXX 11d, 13a *upāditavyā*(n.sg.nt.).

kṣamamāṇa eva puna cittu upāditavyā

narakeṣu tirya-yama-loki aneka-duḥkhā /

(X99A) anubhūtu kāma-guṇa-hetu a-kāma-kārā

kasyārthu adya na kṣameya nidāna bodheḥ // 13 //

kaśa-daṇḍa-śastra-vadha-bandhana-tāḍanāś ca

śira-cheda hasta-caraṇā tatha karṇa-nāsā /

yāvanti duḥkha jagatī ahu utsahāmī

kṣāntīya pāramita tiṣṭhati (X99B) bodhisattvo // 14 //

(Ta28A) bhagavatyāṃ ratna-guṇa-saṃcaya-gāthāyāṃ sadā-prarudita-parivarto nāma triṃśatimaḥ // 30 // (K27B)

---

12d XTac *avibhoti* (O p. 113 n. 3 misr. X as *āvibhoti*)(for *abhibhoti*, K, so em. O = V: Tib. *zil-gyis gnon*); XTac *śūrāḥ* (O p. 113 n. 4 misr. X as *śūrā*), O em. *śūraḥ* (= V)(for *śūro*, K).

13a XTac *kṣamamāṇu* (= OV)(for °*māṇa*, K); Tc *punaś* (for *puna*, KXTa = OV); XTac *citta* (= OV)(for *cittu*, K); XTac *upāditavyo* (= OV)(for °*vyā*, K; cf. XXX 11d, fn.: Tib.A *bskyed byas-te* is to be em. to B *bskyed bya-ste*).

13b K *nacakeṣu* (for *nar*°, XTac = OV: Tib. *sems-dmyal*); XTa *tīrya-*, Tc *tīryag-* (for *tirya-*, K, so em. O = V: Tib.A *dud-'gro'i*, B *dud-gro*); Tc *-dhama-* (for *-yama-*, KXTa = OV: Tib. *gśin-rje'i*); Tc *-duṣṭavāḥ* (for *-duḥkhā*, KXTa = O, nom.pl.m., Bhvr.; but V sep. *aneka duḥkhā*: Tib. *sdug-bsṅal maṅ*; cf. Edgerton 8.100-101).

13c XTa *anubhūya* (= OV), Tc *anabhūya* (for *anubhūtu*, K); Tc *kāma-⟨guṇa-hetu akāma-⟩*; XTac *-kārāḥ* (= O)(for *-kārā*, K = V wt.n.).

13d XTac *kasmāhu* (so prints O!), V sep. *kasmā hu* (for *kasyārthu*, K: Tib. *ci-phyir*, followed by *da* = Skt. *adya*: Conze Rgs. 55 misr. K as *kasmārthu*); V *kasmā hu* seems to be the true r. for Rec. B; Tib.X *ṅa* = O (Skt. *hu* = *aham*; cf. Edgerton 20.7) is most prob. a mistake for the graphically similar *da*; *hu* is used for *khu* (= *kho*, *khalu*), although it is not recorded by Edgerton; cf. *tasmā hu* (= V; but O *tasmāhu*) I 16d (v.l. *tasmād dhi* = V), IV 4c, VI 8a (Tib.A *bdag-gis*!), VII 7a, X 6d (Tib.B *bdag*!), XII 4d, XXII 1a; Tc *ra* (for *na*, KXTa = OV: Tib. *mi*); K *bodhiḥ*, XTac *bodhau* (= OV)(for *bodheḥ*, gen. w. *nidāna*).

14a Tc *kaśa-⟨daṇḍa-śa⟩stra-*; O *-bandhata-* (? mispr. for °*ana-*, MSS. = Conze Rgs. 55 = V).

14b XTac *śira-ccheda* (X °*-cceda*) *karṇa-caraṇā-kara-ṇāsa-*(Tc ⟨*kara-nā*⟩*sa-*) *cchedāḥ*, O em. *śiraś-cheda-karṇa-caraṇā-kara-nāsa-cchedāḥ* (O wt.n. on *ṇāsa-*), V *śira-cheda-karṇa-caraṇā-kara-nāsa-chedāḥ* (V wt.n. on *ṇāsa-*) (for *śira-cheda-*[MS. °*-ccheda*]*hasta-caraṇā tatha karṇa-nāsā*, K; Conze Rgs. 41 misr. K *hasta-* as *hanta-*): Tib. *mgo gcod-pa daṅ rna-ba rkaṅ-lag sna gcod daṅ* (= Skt.B?); cf. Edg.Rgs. 39 for *śira-cheda*.

14c XTac *tat sahāmi* (= OV)(for *utsahāmī*, K).

14d Tc *kṣāṃtiya* (for °*īya*, KXTa = OV); Tc *bodhisattvaḥ* (for °*sattvo*, KXTa = OV).

XXX col. K *triṃśatiḥ*, O *triṃśattamaḥ* (wt.n.!)(for *triṃśatimaḥ*, XTac = V; cf. XIX colophon, footnote end); at the end of the colophon K reads // *gāthā 14* //; Tc adds num. 30.

## ⟨XXXI. DHARMODGATA⟩

śīlena udgata bhavanti śamābhikāṅkṣī
    sthita gocare daśa-balāna a-khaṇḍa-śīlāḥ /
yāvanti saṃvara-kriyā anuva(Tc37A)rtayanti
    taṃ sarva-sattva-hita bodha(X100A)yi nāmayanti // 1 //

saci pratya-yāni raha-bodhi spṛhāṃ janentī
    duḥśīla bhonti na-vidū tatha chidra-cārī /
atha bodhim uttama-śivāṃ pariṇāmayantī
    sthita śīla-pāramita kāma-guṇe 'pi yuktāḥ // 2 //

yo dharma bodhi-guṇa-āgama sūratānāṃ
    so śīla-artha guṇa-(X100B)dharma-samanvitānāṃ /

---

1a Tc *ugaṃta* (for *udgata*, KXTa = OV: Tib.A *byuṅ-ba*, B *'phags-par*); MSS. *samābhikāṅkṣī*, V em. *samādhi-kāṅkṣī* (cf. Chin. 証得三摩地)(for *śamâbhi-kāṅkṣī* = O wt.n.: Tib.A *ži-ba 'dod-pa-rnams-ni*, B *ži-ba 'dod-rnams*).

1c XTac *-kriya* (=OV!)(for *-kriyā*, K, so r. Edg.Rgs. 40).

1d XTac *tāṃ* (= OV)(for *taṃ*, K, so r. Edg.Rgs. 40 ad XXX 12b); poss. sep. *sarva* (w. *taṃ*) *sattva-hita*.

2a O sep. *sa ci*; XTa *pratyayāna* (= OV; but V *pratyayāna-*, cpd.!), Tc *pratyayānaṃ* (for *pratyayāni*, K); *pratyayāni* is a haplological form (cf. Edg.Rgs. 15), although it is not supported by Tib.; XTac *janeti* (= OV) (for *janenti*, K): Tib.A *gal-te raṅ-rgyal dgra-bcom byaṅ-chub 'dod skyed-na*, B ... *byaṅ-chub reg 'dod-na* (? Skt. *spṛśaṃ spṛhenti*).

2b K *duśīla* (for *duḥśīla*, XTa = OV); Tc *duḥśīla bhonti* ; Acc. to V p. 393 n. 2, Baroda MS. omits the same part as Tc; XTa *bhoti* (= OV)(for *bhonti*, K); K *tavidū*, XTa *viduṣān*, Tc *vidupān*, O *viduṣāṃ* (= V)(for *na-vidū*: Tib. *mi mkhas*, 'un-wise', and not 'wise man'; Conze Rgs. 55 seems to suggest *a-vidū*, w. a hiatus-bridger *-t-*!; *t-* is simply a scribal mistake for *n-*; cf. XXX 2a *nā-vidu* (m.c. for *na-vidu*: Tib. *mi mkhas*) w.n.

2c XTac *bodhi* (= OV)(for *bodhim*, K); K *pariṇāmayātī*, Tc *°anti* (= V)(for *°antī*, XTa = OV); note that K *°atī* (sg.) is wrong in the plural structure of Rec.A, and XTac *°antī* is wrong in the singular structure of Rec.B.

2d XTa *sthitu* (= OV), Tc *sthirtu* (for *sthita*, K); MSS. *-guṇepi* (Conze Rgs. 55 misr. K as *-guṇeyi*), O em. *-guṇebhi* (= V wt.n.); *-guṇe* (loc.) is construed w. *yukta-* (cf. Speijer 139, also 146); XTac *yukto* (= OV) (for *yuktāḥ*, K): Tib. *'dod yon brtson-yaṅ tshul-khrims pha-rol phyin-la gnas*, cf. Chin. 足名持戒行五欲.

3a XTac *-āgamu* (= OV; but O sep. *-guṇa āgamu*!)(for *-āgama*, K); *bodhi-guṇa-āgama*, nom., Bhvr. (w. *dharma*!), 'that which has come out of the enlightenment and qualities'; Conze Trsl. seems to take *dharma* as abl. and *āgamu* as verb; Conze was rejected by Edg.Rgs. 40; but Edgerton takes *āgamu* as meaning 'authoritative doctrine'!; cf. *yo dharma bodhi-parihāṇi* in *c*; also XV 2a *guṇâgamu*, XXIX 13c *bodhi-āgamu* (Bhvr.); Tac *suratānaṃ* (for *sūr°*, KX = OV: Tib. *des-pa'i*; Conze Rgs. 57 misr. K as *sūratānā*); poss. *-āgama-sūratānāṃ*, cpd.(?).

3b X *śīlu-arthu* (= O; but O sep. *śīlu arthu*!), Ta *śīlu-artha*, V *śīla-arthu* (wt.n.)(for *śīla-artha*, KTc); Tc only *na* (for *guṇa-dharma-*, KXTa = OV); XTa *-samandhitānāṃ*, Tc *-samadh°* (for *-samanvitānāṃ*, K, so em. O = V; but V *-m*): Tib.A *de-ni yon-tan chos don ldan-pa'i tshul-khrims yin*!, B *de-ni* (vv.ll. *'di-ni*, *de-yi*!) *yon-tan chos ldan-rnams-kyi tshul-khrims don* (B is better).

3c XTac *bodhi-* (Tc *bodhiṃ*) *guṇa-hāni* (= OV)(for *bodhi-parihāṇi*, K: Tob. *byaṅ-chub yoṅs ñams-pa*); K *tataṃkarāṇāṃ*, Tc *hitaṃkarāṇaṃ* (for *hitaṃ-karāṇāṃ*, XTa = OV: Tib. *phan byed-rnams-kyi*); Conze Rgs. 41 misr. K as

yo dharma bodhi-parihāṇi hitaṃ-karāṇāṃ
     duḥśīlatā ayu prakāśitu nāyakena // 3 //

yadi pañca kāma-guṇa bhuñjayi bodhisattvo
     buddhaṃ ca dharma śaraṇaṃ gatu ārya-saṃghaṃ /
sarva-jñatā ca manasī gatu bheṣyi buddho
     sthitu śīla-pāramita vedayitavya (X101A) vijño // 4 //

yadi kalpa-koṭi daśabhī kuśalaiḥ pathebhiḥ
     caramāṇu pratyaya-rahāṇa spṛhāṃ janetī /
tada khaṇḍa-śīla bhavate api chidra-śīlo
     pārājikād gurutaro ayu (Ta28B) ci(Tc37B)tt'-upādo // 5 //

rakṣantu śīla pariṇāmayi agra-bodhau
     na ca tena manyati na (X101B) cātma ukarṣayeyā /

---

*parihāni tataṃkarānāṃ* (both w. dental *-n-*).

3d Tc *duḥśīlaṃtā* (for *°śīlatā*, KXTa = OV).

4a XTa *bhuñjati* (= OV), Tc *bhūṃjati* (for *bhuñjayi*, K).

4b Conze Rgs. 55 misr. K as *dharmā* (for *dharma*, MSS. = OV); XTac *śaraṇāgatu* (so print OV; prob. sep. *śaraṇā gatu*)(for *śaraṇaṃ gatu*, K); *śaraṇaṃ* is not poss. a cpd. as reported by Conze Rgs. 55; acc. forms sometimes remain unchanged w. *gata*-(cf. Speijer 41); cf. *buddham* (*dharmaṃ*, *saṃghaṃ*) *śaraṇaṃ gacchāmi*; K *arya-*, Tc *kārya-* (for *ārya-*, XTa = OV); K *-saṃgha⟨ṃ⟩*: Tib. *saṅs-rgyas chos daṅ 'phags-pa'i dge-'dun skyabs soṅ-ste*.

4c K *manaśī* (for *manasī*, XTac = OV); Conze Rgs. 55 reports K as *°śīgatu* (Index-Dict. *manasīgatu*) *bheṣyi* (for O *manasī bhaviṣyāmi*, XTac = V); but *manasī* (loc.) is to be separated; cf. XX 16d *manasī* (loc.); XTac *buddhā* (for *buddho*, K, so em. O = V): Tib. *saṅs-rgyas 'grub bya sñam-du kun mkhyen yid byed-pa* (B *°-na*)

4d Tc *vijñaḥ* (for *vijño*, KXTa = OV).

5a K *daśabhi*, Tc *daśabhir* (for *daśabhī*, XTa = OV); X *pathebhiḥś*, Tac *pathetiḥś*, O em. *°ebhiś* (= V)(for *°ebhiḥ*, K); Conze Rgs. 57 thinks that K *pathebhiḥ* omits *ś*!; a visarga is often kept at the ends of pādas in our text regardless of the following sounds (cf. VI 2a, 6a, XII 5c, XVII 3c, 4a, 5a, 7c, XIX 5c, XXIV 5c, XXV 4c, XXIX 11a, 12c); in this case XTac later added the palatal *ś* before *c*- without deleting the visarga; Edg.Rgs. 40 em. *kuśalaḥ-pathebhiś* (cf. Edgerton 8.12)!; this is not at all acceptable; *kuśalaiḥ* (so MSS. = OV) is a sep. word; cf. Tib. *dge-ba'i las lam* (cf. BHSD p. 170b, *karma-patha-*, s.v.) *bcu*, Chin. 十善(cf. Mvy 1685, also 1681).

5b Tc *caramāṇū* (for *°māṇu*, KXTa = OV); XTac *-rahitva*, O em. *-rahatva-*, cpd. (= V: Tib. *raṅ-rgyal dgra-bcom-ñid-la*)(for *-rahāṇa*, K, so r. Edg. Rgs. 40; Conze Rgs. 55 r. K as *-rahāṇa-*, cpd.?); XTac *janeti* (= OV)(for *°etī*, K).

5c XTa *khaṇḍa-śīlu* (= OV)(for *°-śīla*, KTc); Tc *bhavata* (for *°ate*, KXTa = OV).

5d K *pārājikāṃ*, XTac *°iko* (= OV), Edg.Rgs. 40 em. *°ikā* (abl.; cf. Edgerton 8.46-48)(for *°ikād*); *pārājikāṃ* (or *°ikān*, acc.pl.) is not possible; but it seems to have resulted from the graphical confusion of *°ikād* w. *°ikāṅ* (before gutturals); K *cintupādo* (Conze Rgs. 55 misr. K as *cittupādo*), XTa *cittapādo* (= O), Tc *cittapādaḥ*, V *cittupādo* (wt.n.)(for *citt'-upādo*; cf. VI 3a, fn.).

6a Tc *rakṣatu* (for *°antu*, KXTa = OV); X *-bodhiṃ* (= OV), Tac *-bodhi* (for *-bodhau*, K); cf. XXII 8d *nāmayi* ... *bodhiṃ* (B *bodhau*); but locatives are normally used w. *nam-*, *nāmayati*: *nāmayi bodhau* VI 4d (B *bodhi*, loc.), XVIII 5c; *pariṇāmita* ... *bodhau* VI 7b; *pariṇāmayamana bodhau* VI 9a;

aha-(K28A)saṃjñatā ca paravarjita sattva-saṃjñā
    sthitu śīla-pāramita vuccati bodhisattvo // 6 //

yadi bodhisattvu caramāṇu jinānu mārge
    imi śīlavān imi duśīla karoti sattvān /
nānātva-saṃjña-prasṛto paramaṃ duśīlo
    api chi(X102A)dra-śīla na tu so pariśuddha-śīlo // 7 //

yasyo na asti aha-saṃjña na sattva-saṃjñā
    saṃjñā-virāga kutu tasya a-saṃvaro 'sti /
yasyo na saṃvari a-saṃvari manyanāsti
    ayu śīla-saṃvaru prakāśitu nāyakena // 8 //

yo eva-śīlu-samudāgatu śuddha-sattvo
    an-a(X102B)pekṣako bhavati sarva-priyâ-priyeṣu /

---

*pariṇāmayitavya bodhau* XV 3b; *pariṇāmayi agra-bodhau* XXX 12b; *bodhayi* (loc.) *namayanti* XXXI 1d; *agra-bodhi* (loc.) *pariṇāmayate* XXXI 13d; *agra-vara-bodhayi* (loc.) *nāmayeya* XXXI 16c; cf. also *sarvajñatāya* (loc.) *pari-ṇāmayamāna* IV 7c; *pariṇāmayiṣyāmi yatra* VI 6b; *dharmi pariṇāmayate* VI 6c; *pariṇāmitaṃ ... prajānamāne* VI 6d.

6b XTac *madyati* (for *manyati*, K = OV wt.n., noted by Edg.Rgs. 29 as meaning 'is conceited': Tib. *rlom-sems*, but Chin. 作念); but cf. *manyati*XVIII 8c, XIX 7a, also *abhimanyati* XXI 3c; K *na ca atma utkarṣayeyā*, XTac *na ātmana karṣayeyā* (= OV; but V mispr. *karṣayethā*?), Edg.Rgs. 31 (p. 9 n. 2) em. *na ātma ukarṣayeyā* (Edg.Rgs. 40 deletes the unmetr. *ca*)(for *na câtma ukarṣayeyā*); Rec. B has intended *na ātman' ukarṣayeyā* (cf. Edg.Rgs. p. 9 n. 2); *na cātma-* seems to be the true r., because it is a stylistic phenomenon to repeat *na ca* in our text, although *atma-* is not unknown (cf. Edgerton 3.35).

6c XTac *ahu-* (= OV)(for *aha-*, K); Tc *-sa⟨ṃ⟩jñatā*; XTac *parivarjita* (= OV)(for *parav°*, K, m.c. for *parāv°*: Tib.A *yoṅs spaṅs-pa*, B *yoṅs-su spaṅs*; but cf. Conze Rgs. 41!).

6d Tc *sthituṃ* (for *sthitu*, KXTa = OV); XTac *ucyati* (= O), X(Tib.trslit.) *ucyaci*, V *vucyati* (wt.n.!)(for *vuccati*, K; cf. Edgerton 2.51); Tc *bodhisattvaḥ* (for *°sattvo*, KXTa = OV).

7a XTac *bodhisattva* (= OV)(for *°sattvu*, K); Tc *caramānu* (for *°māṇu*, KXTa = OV); XTac *jināna* (= OV)(for *jinānu*, K).

7b XTac *śīlavām* (for *°vān*, K, so em. O = V: Tib. *khrims ldan*); Tc *ivi* (for the second *imi*, KXTa = OV: Tib. *'di-dag*); XTac *duḥśīla* (= O)(for *duśīla*, K = V wt.n.).

7c XTa *-pasṛto* (= O), Tc *-yasṛto* (for *-prasṛto*, K, so r. Conze ad O p. 128 = V); orthographically *prasṛto* rather than a Semi-MIndic form of *pasṛto* (cf. Edg.Rgs. 40) can be adopted.

7d XTac *-śīlu* (= OV; Conze Rgs. 55 misr. O as *-śīlo*)(for *-śīla*, K); Tc *-śīla* (for *-śīlo*, KXTa = OV).

8a O omits the first *na* (by mistake?).

8b XTac *-virāgu* (= OV)(for *-virāga*, K); XTac *kṛtu* (= O!)(for *kutu*, K = V wt.n.: Tib.A *ji-phyir*, v.l. *ci-phyir*, B *ga-la*); Ta *⟨a-⟩saṃvaro*; MSS. *sti* (for *'sti* = OV).

9a XTac *-śīla-* (= OV; but O sep. *eva śīla-*!)(for *-śīlu-*, K); K *-samanv-āgatu* (so em. O = V, unmetr.!), XTa *-samandhāgatu*, Tc *-samaṃdhāgutu* (for *-samudāgatu*, so em. Edg.Rgs. 40 ad XV 6a: Tib.A *'di-lta'i khrims ldan-pa*, B *de-ltar khrims ldan-pa*); XTac *niṣprapañco* (= OV)(for *śuddha-sattvo*, K: Tib. *sems-can dag-pa*, A v.l. *dam-pa*); cf. XV 6a *eva-dharma-samudāgatu niṣprapañcā* (w.n.).

9b Tc *anapekṣoko* (for *°ako*, KXTa = OV; lexicographically noted by Edg. Rgs. 29).

śira-hasta-pāda tyajamānu a-dīna-citto
    sarvāsti-tyāgi bhavate satataṃ (Tc38A) a-līno // 9 //

jñātvā ca dharma-prakṛtī vaśikāṃ nirātmāṃ
    ātmāna mā a-tyajamānu a-dīna-citto /
prāg eva vastu tata bāhira nâ-tyajeyā
    a-sthānam a(X103A)tra yadi matsariyaṃ kareyā // 10 //

aha-saṃjña vastu-mamatā bhavate ca rāgo
    kutu tyāga-buddhi bhaviṣyāti hi momuhānāṃ /
mātsarya preta bhavate u(Ta29A)papadyayātī
    athavā manuṣyi tada bhoti daridra-bhūto // 11 //

---

9c K *-hanta-* (for *-hasta-*, XTac = OV: Tib. *lag*); XTa *tyajamāna* (= OV), Tc *bhyaj°* (for *tyajamānu*, K: Tib. *gtoṅ-źiṅ*).

10a XTac *-prakṛtīṃ* (= OV)(for *°tī*, K); XTa *vaśivā*, X (Tib.trslit.) *vaśikā* (= OV; but O *vaśikā-*, cpd.!), Tc *vaśīvā* (for *vaśikāṃ*, K, so r. Conze Rgs. 55: Tib. *ya-ma-brlar*); K *nirātmām* (Conze Rgs. 55 adopts K w. *-ṃ*), XTa *nirātmyaṃ* (= OV), Tc *nirātmya* (for *nirātmāṃ*): Tib. *bdag med.*

10b X(Tib.trslit.) *atmāna*, Tc *ātmāma* (for *ātmāna*, KXTa, 'own body' = OV: Tib. *bdag-gi śa*); XTac *māsa*, O em. *māṃsa* (= V!)(for *mā a-*, K, double neg. as *nâ-tyajeyā* in *c*!); *māṃsa* is superfluous; *māsa* is most unlikely to be analyzed as *mā-s-a-°* w. a hiatus-bridger *-s-* (cf. XXIX 1c *-dhyāna-aṅgā*, w.fn.); XTa *-tyajamāṇu* Tc *°māśv* (for *°mānu*, K, so em. O = V; but OV *tyaj°*); Tc *-cittaḥ* (for *-citto*, KXTa = OV).

10c K *tada bāhira nātyajeyā*, XTa *tada vā hiraṇā tyajeyā*, Tc *tada vā hiraṇyā tyajeyā*, O em. *yadi vā hiraṇā tyajeyâ*, V em. *tada bāhira nātyajeyā* (for *tata bāhira nātyajeyā*: Tib. *de-las* [v.l. *de-la*; B *de-tshe*!] *phyi-rol dṅos-po gtoṅ-ba*); O *yadi* (for MSS. *tada*) is not acceptable; *tada* (= Tib.B *de-tshe*!), lect.facil. for *tata*, or poss. *tatu* (m.c. for *tataḥ*/ *tato*: Tib.A *de-las*), is construed w. *bāhira* (cf. BHSD p.399b, *bāhira-*, s.v.); *hiraṇā* is wrongly divided from *bāhira* and connected w. the following double neg. *nâ-*, although it is lexicographically noted by Edg.Rgs. 29; after all V is most constructive: cf. Chin. 況外財物而不捨.

10d XTa *āsthānam*, Tc *āsthānan* (for *asthānam*, K, so em. O = V: Tib.A *gnas min-no*, B *gnas med-do*); XTa *eta* (= OV), Tc *ena* (: Tib. *de-ni*)(for *atra*, K); *eta* is poss. for *atra*; cf. *etu* II 11c (v.l. *atra*: Tib.A *de-la*, B *'di-ni*!); cf. also BHSD p. 155b, *etta*, s.v.; but XX 19c *a-sthānam eva yadi* ...!; XTa *matsari so* (= OV), Tc *matsarī so* (for *matsariyaṃ*, K, so r. Conze Rgs. 55 and Edg.Rgs. 29: Tib. *ser-sna*).

11a K *-saṃjñā vastu-mamatā*, XTa *-saṃjñatas tuṃ* (O p. 118 n. 5 misr. X as *tu*) *samatā*, Tc *-saṃjñaṃtas tu samatā*, O em. *-saṃjña-vastu-mamatā* (so cpd.!), V em. *-saṃjñatas tu mamatā* (for *-saṃjña vastu-mamatā*); O *bhavata* (? mispr. for *°ate*, MSS. = V): render *a* as, 'Through I-notion (*aha-saṃjña*, abl.) arises egotism in property and greed'; but cf. Tib.A *bdag daṅ bdag-gir* (v.l. *°-gi*) *dṅos-por 'du-śes 'dod-chags 'gyur*!, B *bdag-tu 'du-śes dṅos-la bdag-gir 'dzin-pas chags*!

11b MSS. *bhaviṣyati* (= OV, unmetr.!)(for *°āti*); *bhaviṣyāti* may have been pronounced as *°iṣāti*, m.c. (cf. Edg.Rgs. 33 end, and 38); XTa ⟨*hi*⟩ *so muhānāṃ*, Tc ⟨*hi*⟩ *so guhānāṃ*, OV *sā muhānāṃ* (wt.n.!; V *-m*)(for *hi momuhānāṃ*, K, so r. Edg.Rgs. 40: Tib. *blun-po-rmams-la*; cf. BHSD p. 440b, *momūha-*, s.v.).

11c O *upapadyayātā* (mispr. for MSS. *°ātī* = V).

11d XTac *manuṣya* (= OV)(for *°ṣyi*, K); K *bhonti* (for *bhoti*, XTac = OV); V *daridra-rūpo* (wt.n.!)(for *°-bhūto*, MSS. = O).

tada bodhisattva imi jñātva daridra-sattvān
dānādhi(X103B)muktu bhavatī sada mukta-tyāgī /
(K28B) catvāri dvīpa samalaṃkṛta kheṭa-tulyān
dattvā udagra bhavate na tu dvīpa-labdhā // 12 //

dānaṃ daditva vidu-paṇḍitu bodhisattvo
yāvanti sattva tri-bhave samanāharitvā /
sarveṣa teṣa bhavate ayu dāna-datto
taṃ cāgra-bodhi pariṇāmayate (X104A) jagārthaṃ // 13 //

na ca vastu-niśraya karoti da(Tc38B)ditva dānaṃ
vīpāku naiva pratikāṅkṣati so kadā cit /
evaṃ tyajantu bhavate vidu sarva-tyāgī
alpaṃ tyajitva bhavate bahu a-prameyaṃ // 14 //

yāvanti sattva tri-bhave nikhilena santī
te sarvi dāna dadayanti an-anta-kalpān /

---

[12a] Tc *bodhi*(38A4)*bodhisattvo* (for *bodhisattvo*, KXTa = OV).
[12b] XTac *dānādhimukta* (= OV)(for °*ktu*, K).
[12c] XTac *dvīpi* (= OV!)(for *dvīpa*, K, so r. Edg.Rgs. 40); XTac *samalaṃkṛtu* (= OV!)(for °*kṛta*, K); XTac *kheṭā-tulyāṃ*, O em. *kheṭa-tulyaṃ* (= V!)(for *kheṭa-tulyān*, K).
[12d] XTac *hi* (= OV)(for *tu*, K); XTac *-labdho* (= OV)(for *-labdhā*, K, nom. sg.masc. of *labdhṛ-*).
[13a] V sep. *vidu paṇḍitu*.
[13b] O *yāvasti* (mispr.!) is analyzed by Edg.Rgs. 29 as *yāv'(ad) asti*! (for *yāvanti*, MSS. = V); K *samanvāharitvā* (so em. O = V), XTa *samandhāharitvā*, Tc *samaṃdhīharitvā* (for *samanāharitvā*, so em. Edg.Rgs. 29: Tib.A *bsam byas-te*, B *sñam-du sems-nas*, Chin. 念 ; cf. also PTSD IV p. 142b, *samannāharati*, BHSD p. 564a, *samanvāharati*, ss.vv.; cf. Edgerton 2.89); the text seems deeply corrupt; cf. XII 1d, fn.
[13c] XTa *sarveṣu teṣu* (= OV), Tc *sarveṣu* ⟨*teṣu*⟩ (for *sarveṣa teṣa*, K); K *bhavantu*: Tib. *gyur-cig*! (for *bhavate*, XTac = OV); XTa *datta-dānaṃ* (= OV), Tc ⟨*da*⟩*tta-dānaṃ* (for *dāna-datto*, K, so r. Conze Rgs. 56).
[13d] Tc *ta* (for *taṃ*, KXTa = OV); O *jagārthe* (? mispr. for °*rthaṃ*, MSS. = V w. *-m*).
[14a] XTa *vastu-niśrayu* (= OV), Tc *vastra-riśrayu* (for *vastu-niśraya*, K: Tib. *dṅos-por* [B °*-la*] *gnas-par*).
[14b] XTac *vidu pāku* (= OV!; but O *vidu-*, cpd.!)(for *vīpāku*, K: Tib. *smin-la*); XTac *naiva* (O p. 119 n. 3 misr. X as *nava*)(for *naiva*, K, so em. O = V: Tib. *med*); Tc *putikāṃkṣati* (for *pratik*°, KXTa = OV: Tib. *re-ba*).
[14c] XTa *tyajitva* (= OV), Tc *bhyajitva* (for *tyajantu*, K): Tib. *gtoṅ-ba*, v.l. *gtoṅ-la*.
[14d] V em. *labhate*! (for *bhavate*, MSS. = O: Tib. *'gyur*); V *aprameyam* (w. *-m*); cf. XVIII 6d *aprameyaṃ*, also footnotes to I 15c and VII 1b.
[15a] XTac *yāvanta* (= OV)(for *yāvanti*, K); XTa *astī* (= O), Tc *aasti*, V *asti* (wt.n.)(for *santī*, K).
[15b] Tc *dadayaty* (for *dadayanti*, KXTa = OV; cf. Edg.Rgs. 29, Edgerton 38.21 for *dadayanti*); Tc *arnata-* (miscopying for *anaṃta-*)(for *ananta-*, KXTa = OV: Tib. *mtha'-yas*); MSS. *-kalpāṃ* (cf. Edgerton 8.90)(for *-kalpān*, so em. O = V).

(X104B) buddhāna loka-vidunāṃ raha-pratyayānāṃ
     eṣanti śrāvaka-guṇān parikalpa-sthāne // 15 //

yaś co upāya-kuśalo vidu bodhisattvo
     teṣāṃ sa puṇyu-kriya-vastv anumodayitvā /
sattvārtha agra-vara-bodhayi nāmayeyā
     abhibhoti sarva-jagatī pariṇāmayanto // 16 //

kācasya (X105A) vā maṇina rāśi siyā mahanto
     vaiḍūrya-ratna abhibhoti ta sa(Ta29B)rva eko /
em eva sarva-jagatī pṛthu dāna-skandho
     abhibhoti sarvam anumodaku bodhisattvo // 17 //

yadi bodhisattva dadamānu jagasya dānaṃ
     (Tc39A) mamatā na tatra karayen na ca vastu-premaṃ /
tatu vardhate ku(X105B)śala-mūla mahānubhā(K29A)vo
     candro v' an-abhru prabha-maṇḍala śukla-pakṣo // 18 //

---

15c XTac *buddhānu loki vidunārhati pratyayānāṃ* (Tc *pratyadyānāṃ*), O *buddhānu loka-vidunārhata-°* (wt.n.!), V *buddhānuloki vidu nārhati-°* (wt.n.!)(for *buddhāna loka-vidunāṃ raha-pratyayānāṃ*, K, so r. Edg.Rgs. 40: Tib. *'jig-rten mkhyen-pa saṅs-rgyas dgra-bcom raṅ-rgyal-la*); cf. *loka-vidunāṃ* II 10d, XXX 9c.

15d XTac *yāvanti* (= OV!)(for *eṣanti*, K, so r. Conze ad O p. 128: Tib. *tshol-ba*); K *-guṇām* (so r. Conze ad O p. 128!), XTac *-guṇat*, O *-gaṇāt* (wt.n.!)(for *-guṇān* = V: Tib. *legs*, Chin. 功徳).

16a O *vidu-bodhisattvo*, cpd.

16b XTac *puṇya-* (= OV)(for *puṇyu-*, K).

16c XTac *nāmadheyā* (= O!)(for *nāmayeyā*, K, so r. Conze ad O p. 128 = V: Tib. *yoṅs bsṅo-na*).

16d XTac *pariṇāma-yukto* (= OV!)(for *pariṇāmayanto*, K: Tib. *yoṅs-su bsṅo-bas*, B v.l. *yoṅs-su bsṅos-pas*).

17a Tc *kācesya* (for *kācasya*, KXTa = OV: Tib. *mchiṅ-bu'i*, B v.l. *'chiṅ-bu'i*); O *vāmaṇina* (? mispr. for *vā maṇina* = V); Tc *vāśi* (for *rāśi*, KXTa = OV: Tib. *phuṅ-po*); Conze Rgs. 56 misr. X as *rāśiṃ* and K as *rāśi* !; XTac *bhiyā* (= O!)(for *siyā*, K = V wt.n.: Tib. *gyur-pa-yaṅ*); XTac *mahatto* (= O!)(for *mahanto*, K = V wt.n.).

17b Tac *vaiḍuryya-* (for *vaiḍūrya-*, KX = OV); XTac *sa* (= OV)(for *ta*, K: Tib. *de kun*).

17c O *pṛthu-dāna-*, cpd.

17d X *avibhonti*, Ta *abhibhonti*, Tc *avibhoti* (for *abhibhoti*, K, so em. O = V); XTac *sarva pariṇāmaku* (= OV; but V *sarva-*, cpd.!)(for *sarvam anumodaku*, K, so r. Conze ad O p. 128: Tib. *kun rjes-su yi-raṅ*; V p. 395 n. 2 suggests Skt. *anumodaku* w. Tib.); Tc *bodhisattvah* (for *°sattvo*, KXTa = OV); but cf. Chin. 廻施世間一切衆 不及廻施無上覚!

18a Tc *pada* (for *yadi*, KXTa = OV: Tib. *gal-te*); Tc *bodhisattvo* (for *°sattva*, KXTa = OV); XTac *dadamāna* (= OV)(for *°mānu*, K).

18b Tc *mamattā*, V *mamatāṃ* (wt.n.!)(for *mamatā*, KXTa = O); Tc *ra* (for *na*, KXTa = OV: Tib. *mi*); Conze Rgs. 56 misr. O as *na* (for *na ca*, MSS. = OV); XTa *vastu-prema* (= OV), Tc *vastra-prema* (for *vastu-premaṃ*, K).

18c Tc *-mŭla* (for *-mūla*, KXTa = OV: Tib. *rtsa-ba*).

18d K *vanabhru*, XTac *vanabhra*, O *va nabhra-* (O *nabhra-*, cpd.!), V em. *va tatra*! (for *v' an-abhru*: Tib. *sprin med*); *v'* is used for *iva* (cf. Edgerton 4.14, 21): Tib.A *bźin*, B *bźin-no*; V p. 395 n. 3 misr. O as *nabhra-grabha* (? mispr. for *-prabha*); XTa *-maṇḍalu* (= OV)(for *-maṇḍala*, KTc);

bhagavatyāṃ ratna-guṇa-saṃcaya-gāthāyāṃ dharmodgata-parivarto nāmaika-triṃśatimaḥ // 31 //

XTac *-pakṣe* (= OV)(for *-pakṣo*, K); render *c-d* as, 'From that (the bodhisattva) with great might increases (his) wholesome root, just as the cloudless (*an-abhru*, Bhvr.) moon of the bright half (increases its) disk of light'.

XXXI col. X *nāma eka-* (= O)(for *nāmaika-*, KTac = V); K *-triṃśatiḥ*, O em. *-triṃśattamaḥ* (for *-triṃśatimaḥ*, XTac = V; cf. XIX colophon, footnote end); at the end of the colophon K reads *gāthā 18;* Tc adds num. 31.

## ⟨XXXII. PARĪNDANĀ⟩

dānena preta-gati chindati bodhisattvo
    dāridriyaṃ ca chinatī tatha sarva-kleśān /
bhogāṃś c' an-anta-vipulān labha(X106A)te caranto
    dānena sattva paripācayi kricchra-prāptān // 1 //

śīlena tirya-gati varjayi 'neka-rūpā
    aṣṭau ca a-kṣaṇa sa varjayi sarva-kālaṃ /
kṣāntīya rūpa labhate paramaṃ udāraṃ
    svarṇa-cchavī priyu jagasya udīkṣaṇīyo // 2 //

vīryeṇa śukla-gu(X106B)ṇa-hāni na abhyupaiti
    jñānaṃ an-antu labhate jina-kośa-gañjaṃ /
dhyānena kāma-guṇa utsṛjate jugupsyān
    vidyā abhijña (Tc39B) abhinirharate samādhiṃ // 3 //

---

1b XTac *dāridrayaṃ* (= O!), V em. *dāridrakaṃ*! (for *dāridriyaṃ*, K: Tib. *dbul-ba*, Chin. 貧乏 ); Ta *chīnatī*, Tc *chīnati* (for *chinatī*, KX = OV, m.c. for Skt. *chinatti*: Tib. *gcod*; but Edgerton derives *chinatī* from Skt. imperfect *acchinat*; cf. Edg.Rgs. 27, also Edgerton 28.12, 43 p. 212b, *chid-* 2, s.v.); XTac *-kleśāt* (for *-kleśān*, K, so em. O = V).

1c Tc *bhogāś* (for *bhogāṃś*, KXTa = OV); KXTa *cananta-* (so prints V), Tc *caraṃti-*, O sep. *ca nanta-*! (for *c' ananta-*: Tib. *mtha'-yas*); MSS. *-vipulāṃ* (= V; cf. Edgerton 8.90)(for *-vipulān*, so em. O).

1d KTc *kricchra-prāptāṃ*, XTa *kicchra-prāptāṃ* (for *kricchra-prāptān*, so em. O = V: Tib. *sdug-bsṅal gyur-pa'i)*.

2a X *tīrya-* (= OV), Tac *vīrya-* (for *tirya-*, K: Tib. *dud-'gro'i 'gro-ba*); K *naika-rūpā*, X *neka-rūpāṃ* (= OV; but V w. *-m*), Ta *neka-rūpaṃ*, Tc *neka-rūṣāṃ* (for *'n-eka-rūpā*).

2b Tc *a-kṣa⟨ṇa⟩*; XTac *kṣaṇāṃ* (Tc ⟨*kṣa*⟩*ṇāṃ*) *labhate sa nityaṃ* (= OV; but V w. *-m*: Tib.B *de-yis* [only X *de-yi* = O!] *dal-ba rtag-tu rñed*, Chin. 得正念)(for *sa varjayi sarva-kālaṃ*, K: Tib.A *dus-rnams kun-tu mi khom brgyud-kyaṅ rnam-par spoṅ* [v.l. *sbyoṅ*]; cf. AsP 260.11-12 *sarve ca anena akṣaṇā vivarjitāḥ, kṣaṇa-saṃpac cārāgitā*!).

2c Tac *rūpa* (for *rūpa*, KX = OV: Tib. *gzugs bzaṅ*); KTc *paramam*, unmetr.! (for °*maṃ*, XTa = OV).

2d XTac *suvarṇa-* (= OV, hypermetr.!)(for *svarṇa-*, K: Tib. *gser mdog*, Chin. 金 ); V *-cchavi* (wt.n.)(for *-cchavī*, MSS. = O).

3a Tc *vīryaṇa* (for °*eṇa*, KXTa = OV: Tib. *brtson-'grus-kyis-ni*); K *-hāṇi* (for *-hāni*, XTac = OV; but OV sep. *-guṇa hāni*!; OV *śukla-guṇa*, nom.sg. masc., Bhvr.?); Tc *atyupaiti* (for *abhy*°, KXTa = OV): Tib. *dkar-po'i yon-tan 'grib mi 'gyur*,

3b KTc *jñānam*, unmetr.! (for °*aṃ*, XTa = OV); XTac *ananta* (= OV)(for *anantu*, K; Conze Rgs. 57 misr. K *anaṃtu* as *anantaṃ*); XTa *-gañja* (= O), Tc *-gañjā*, V *-gañjam* (wt.n.)(for *-gañjaṃ*, K).

3c XTa *jugupsyāṃ*, Tc *juguṣṇāṃ* (for *jugupsyān*, K, so em. O = V: Tib. *smad-pa*).

3d Ta *avijña*, Tc *abhijñā* (for *abhijña*, KX = OV); read poss. *vidyā-abhijña*, cpd.: Tib. *rig daṅ mṅon-par śes daṅ tiṅ-'dzin mṅon-par sgrub* (A v.l. *bsgrub*); V *samadhim* (w. *-m*).

prajñāya dharma-prakṛtī parijānayitvā
trai-dhātukātu samatikramate apāyān /
vartitva cakra-rata(Ta30A)naṃ puru(X107A)ṣa-rṣabhāṇāṃ
deśeti dharma jagatī dukha-saṃkṣayāye // 4 //

paripūrayitva imi dharma sa bodhisattvo
api kṣetra-śuddhi parigṛhṇati sattva-śuddhiṃ /
api buddha-vaṃśu parigṛhṇati dharma-vaṃśaṃ
tatha saṃgha-vaṃśa parigṛhṇati sarva-dharmān // 5 //

vaidyotta(X107B)mo jagati (K29B) roga-cikitsa-kārī
prajñopadeśa kathito ayu bodhi-mārgo /
nāmena ratna-guṇa-saṃcayu bodhi-mārgas
taṃ sarva-sattva imu mārg' anuprāpuṇantu // 6 //

bhagavatyāṃ ratna-guṇa-saṃcaya-gāthāyāṃ parīndanā-parivarto nāma dvātriṃśatimaḥ // 32 //

(K29B2-3) śata-sāhasrikāyā bhagavatyā⟨ḥ⟩ prajñā-pāramitāyāḥ saṃcaya-gāthā-parivartaś caturaśītitamaḥ samāptaḥ // //

---

4a Tc *dharmaṃ ⟨pra⟩kṛti*(for *dharma-prakṛtī*, KXTa = OV).

4b XTac *-dhātukânta* (= OV)(for *-dhātukātu*, K: Tib.A *khams gsum-dag-las*, but B *khams gsum ma lus-pa-las*!); KXTa *apāyāṃ* (= O), Tc *ayayāṃ* (for *apāyān* = V wt.n.).

4c XTac *-ratana* (for *°naṃ*, K, so em. O = V).

4d Tc *dha⟨r⟩ma;* XTac *duḥkha-* (= O!)(for *dukha-*, K = V wt.n.).

5a Tc *yaripūrayitvā* (for *par°*, KXTa = OV: Tib. *yoṅs rdzogs byas-nas*).

5b Tc *parigṛhnati* (for *°gṛhṇati*, KXTa = OV); V *-śuddhim* (w. *-m*).

5c K *-va⟨ṃ⟩śu* (Conze Rgs. 56 misr. K as *-vaṃśu*), XTac *-vaṃśa* (= OV)(for *-vaṃśu*); Tc *parigṛ⟨hna⟩ti;* K *-vaṃśa* (most prob. a scribal mistake; but cf. Edgerton 8.31-35)(for *-vaṃśaṃ*, XTac = OV).

5d O *-vaṃśaṃ* (? mispr. for *-vaṃśa*, MSS. = V); Tc *parigṛhnati* (for *°gṛhṇati*, KXTa = OV); MSS. *-dharmāṃ* (cf. Edgerton 8.90)(for *-dharmān*, so em. O = V).

6a Tc *jagatī* (for *jagati*, KXTa = OV).

6b Tc *prajñāya darśa* (for *prajñopadeśa*, KXTa = OV: Tib.A *śes-rab bstan phyir*, B ... *bstan-pa*).

6c XTac *-saṃcaya* (= OV)(for *-saṃcayu*, K); XTac *-mārgaḥ* (= OV)(for *-mārgas*, K; Conze Rgs. 56 misr. K as *-mārgam*).

6d K *imu mārganuprāpuṇantu* (Conze Rgs. 56 misr. K as *°anta*), XTa *imu mārganupraptavanti*, Tc *imu mārganuprāptarvatiṃ*, O em. *imu mārganuprāptavanti*, V em. *itu mārgatu prāpnuvanti*! (for *imu mārg' anuprāpuṇantu*: Tib.A *lam 'di ... thob gyur-cig*, but B *lam 'di ... thob-par bya phyir* !; cf. Chin. 念……証道 ).

XXXII col. XTa *parindanā-*, Tc *parindanāma-* (for *parīndanā-*, K, so em. O = V); O em. *dvātriṃśattamaḥ* (for *°śatimaḥ*, MSS. = V; cf. XIX colophon, footnote end; at the end of the colophon K reads *gātha // 6 //*; Tc adds num. 32.

Final colophon: This statement is found only in K (cf. 'Introduction' para. 13, and 'Bibl. Notes' IA1 N.B. 9-11 above).

## INDEX TO PĀDAS

# S U P P L E M E N T

## Tibetan Text

(Recension A, or Tunhuang Recension)

CONTENTS OF THE SUPPLEMENT

PREFATORY NOTES

1. The text of the Tibetan Recension A is based on five manuscripts from Tunhuang: MSS. Tb, Tc, Th, Ti and Tj (cf. 'Bibl. Notes' IIA).

2. The critical apparatus had to be omitted. I plan to edit the text together with a critical apparatus and a detailed comparison with the text of Recension B.

3. I have used the following signs:

——— indicates that this part differs from Recension B.

~~~~~~ indicates that there are two variant readings in Recension B, and one of them is identical with that of Recension A.

====== indicates that there are two variant readings in Recension B, and both of them are entirely different from that of Recension A.

4. Adjacent words are sometimes underlined, if there is a word (or words) missing in one recension but found in the other. Minor variants are disregarded.

5. Variant readings in Recension A are listed in Appendix 5 of this supplement. Some of them are identical with the readings of Recension B. Variants which are important for the study of the text are to be found with asterisks. Minor variants are disregarded.

6. The paginations of the bilingual Chinese blockprint text X (cf. 'Bibl. Notes' IIB2a) and of the texts in the well-known Kanjur C, D, L, N, P (cf. 'Bibl. Notes' IIB1a) and C', D', L', N', P' (cf. 'Bibl. Notes' IIB4) are indicated.

7. The numbers of chapters and verses are put by the present editor.
~~~~~~

'PHAGS-PA ŚES-RAB-KYI PHA-ROL-TU PHYIN-PA YON-TAN RIN-PO-CHE

SDUD-PA TSHIGS-SU BCAD-PA

'phags-pa śes-rab-kyi pha-rol-tu phyin-pa yon-tan rin-po-che

sdud-pa tshigs-su bcad-pa

oOo

// rgya-gar-skad-du / ārya-pra-dzñā-pā-ra-mi-tā-sañtsa-ya-gā-thā / bod-skad-du / 'phags-pa śes-rab-kyi pha-rol-tu phyin-pa sdud-pa tshigs-su bcad-pa //

O

saṅs-rgyas daṅ byaṅ-chub-sems-dpa' thams-cad-la phyag-'tshal-lo //

o

de-nas bcom-ldan-'das-kyis 'khor bźi-po de-dag yaṅ-dag-par rab-tu dga'-bar mdzad-pa'i phyir-yaṅ śes-rab-kyi pha-rol-tu phyin-pa 'di ston-ciṅ / de'i tshe tshigs-su bcad-pa 'di-dag bka' stsal-to //

I.

/ dga' daṅ gus daṅ dad-pa'i mchog-la ñer gnas-te /
/ sgrib-pa ñon-moṅs dri-ma bstsal-nas rab źi-bas /
/ 'gro don mṅon źugs des-pa'i śes-rab pha-rol phyin /
/ gaṅ-la dpa'-rnams spyod-pa de-ni mñan-par gyis // 1 //

/ 'dzam-bu'i gliṅ 'dir chu-kluṅ ji-sñed 'bab-pa daṅ /
/ ma-dros gnas-pa'i klu-dbaṅ klu-bdag rab brten-nas /
/ me-tog 'bras-bu sman daṅ nags-tshal skyed byed-de /
/(Tb2A) de-ni klu bdag de-yi dpal-gyi mthu yin-no // 2 //

/(D2A) rgyal-ba'i ñan-thos-pa-dag ji-sñed chos ston-te /
/ 'chad-ciṅ rigs-pa-dag daṅ ldan-par brjod-pa daṅ /
/ bde-ba mchog daṅ byed daṅ de-yi 'bras thob-pa /
/ de-dag kun-kyaṅ de-bźin-gśegs-pa'i skyes-bu'i mthu // 3 //

/ ci-phyir źe-na rgyal-bas chos-tshul gaṅ bstan-pa /
/ de-la mi mchog slob-mar gyur-pas (C2B) mṅon bslabs-śiṅ /
/ mṅon-sum byas-nas bslabs-pa ji-bźin ston byed-de /
/ saṅs-rgyas mthus byed raṅ-gi stobs (Tb2B) daṅ mthus ma yin //4//

/ gaṅ-la śes-rab pha-rol phyin mchog mi dmigs-śiṅ /
/ byaṅ-chub-sems-dpa' mi dmigs byaṅ-chub sems mi dmigs /
/ de-skad thos-nas rmoṅs-pa med-ciṅ mi skrag-pa /
/ byaṅ-chub-sems-dpa' de-ni bde-gśegs śes-rab spyod // 5 //

/(N197B) gzugs med tshor-ba med-ciṅ 'du-śes sems-pa med /
/ de-la rnam-śes gnas-ni (Tc2A) rdul tsam mi rñed-pa /
/ de-ni chos kun mi gnas gnas med rgyu-ba-(Tb3A)ste /
/ yoṅs-su (N'148A) gzuṅ med bde-gśegs-rnams-kyi byaṅ-chub 'thob//6//

/ ji-ltar kun-tu rgyu-ba bzo-sbyaṅs phyi-rol-gyi /
/ phuṅ-po rnam-par 'jig-ciṅ śes-pa dmigs-par gyur /
/ byaṅ-chub-sems-dpa' gaṅ-źig de-ltar chos śes-śiṅ /
/ mya-ṅan 'das-la mi reg de-ni śes-rab gnas // 7 //

/ gźan-yaṅ śes-rab 'di-ni gaṅ yin gaṅ-gi phyir /
/ gaṅ-las byuṅ źes chos 'di thams-cad stoṅ-par rtog /
/ ñe-bar brtags-nas (Tb3B) źum-pa med-ciṅ skrag med-pa /
/ byaṅ-chub-sems-dpa' de-ni byaṅ-chub ñe-ba yin // 8 //

/ gal-te mi śes bźin-du gzugs daṅ 'du-śes daṅ /
/ tshor-ba sems-pa rnam śes phuṅ-por spyod byed-ciṅ /
/ phuṅ (L190A) 'di stoṅ źes yoṅs rtog byaṅ-chub-sems-(D2B)dpa'-ni /
/ mtshan-mar spyod-de skye med gnas-la reg ma yin // 9 //

/ gzugs daṅ tshor-ba daṅ-(Tc2B)ni 'du-śes sems-pa daṅ /
/ rnam-par śes-la mi spyod gnas med gaṅ rgyu-ba /
/(Tb4A) śes-rab brtan-te spyod ces khas-len mi byed-de /
/ skye med blo-yis źi-ba'i tiṅ-'dzin mchog-la reg // 10 //

/ byaṅ-chub-sems-dpa' de-ltar rab źi 'dir gnas-te /
/ sṅon-gyi de-bźin-gśegs-pa-rnams-kyis luṅ bstan yin /
/ bdag-ni mñam-(P2B)par bźag (N198A) ce'am laṅs źes rlom-sems med /
/ ci-phyir-źe-na don chos raṅ-bźin yoṅs śes phyir // 11 //

/ de-ltar spyod-na bde-gśegs-(Th565B)rnams-kyi śes-(C3A)rab (P'181A)spyod/
/ des-(Tb4B)ni spyod daṅ mi spyod rab-tu śes-pas-na /
/ chos gaṅ spyod-pa de-yaṅ dmigs-par mi 'gyur-(X6B)te /
/ 'di-ni śes-rab pha-rol phyin-pa'i spyod mchog yin // 12 //

/ gaṅ-źig yod-pa ma yin de-ni med ces bya /
/ byis-pa-rnams-kyis de brtags med-pa yod-par byed /
/ yod daṅ med-pa 'di gñis med-pa'i chos yin-te /
/ byaṅ-chub-sems-dpa' gaṅ-gis 'di śes de ṅes 'byuṅ // 13 //

/(Tc3A) gaṅ 'dir phuṅ-po lṅa-dag sgyu-ma 'drar śes-śiṅ /
/(Tb5A) sgyu-ma gźan (X7A) daṅ phuṅ-po gźan-du mi byed-la /
/ sna-tshogs 'du-śes bral-źiṅ ñe-bar źi spyod-pa /
/ 'di-ni śes-rab pha-rol phyin-pa'i spyod mchog yin // 14 //

/ dge-ba'i bśes daṅ ldan-źiṅ lhag-mthoṅ ldan gyur-(L190B)pa /
/ rgyal-ba-rnams-kyi yum (C'195A) thos skrag-par yoṅ mi 'gyur /
/ gaṅ-źig sdig-pa'i grogs ldan gźan-gyi driṅ 'jog-pa /
/(X7B) de-ni snod so-ma btaṅ chus reg źig-pa bźin // 15 //

/(L'255A) ci-phyir 'di-ni byaṅ-chub-(Tb5B)sems-dpa' bya źe-na /
/ chags-pa'i byed-pa kun-la chags-pa gcod 'dod-pas /
/(Tc3B) rgyal-ba-rnams-kyi byaṅ-chub chags med gyur-la reg /
/ des-na 'di-ni byaṅ-chub-sems-dpa'i miṅ thob-bo // 16 //

/ ci-phyir de-ni sems-dpa' (N198B) che źes bya źe-na /
/ 'di-ni sems-can phuṅ-po chen-po'i mchog 'gyur daṅ /
/ sems-can khams-kyi ltar-gyur chen-po gcod-pa-ste /
/ de-phyir 'di-ni sems-(Tb6A)dpa' che źes brjod-pa yin // 17 //

/ gtoṅ-ba che daṅ blo che-ba daṅ mthu che daṅ /
/(Tc3B)rgyal-ba-rnams-kyi (N'149A)theg chen mchog-la źugs-pa daṅ /'
/ bdud-kyi gYo-sgyu gdul phyir go-cha che bgos-pa /
/ de-yi phyir-na sems-dpa' che źes brjod-pa yin // 18 //

/ dper-na sgyu-ma mkhan-gyis bźi-mdor sprul byas-te /
/ skye-bo phal chen mgo maṅ bye-ba gcod-par byed /
/ sgyu-ma ci-'dra de-'drar sems-can de kun śes /
/ 'gro kun sprul-pa 'dra-(Tb6B)bar de-la 'jigs-pa med // 19 //

/ gzugs daṅ 'du-śes tshor-(P3A)ba daṅ-(C3B)ni (D'164B)sems-pa daṅ /
/ rnam-par śes-pa ma bciṅs ma grol yod-pa min /
/ de-ltar (P'181B)byaṅ-chub 'jug-ciṅ źum-(X9A)pa'i sems med-pa /
/ 'di-ni gaṅ-zag dam-pa-rnams-kyi go-cha mchog // 20 //

/ ci-phyir 'di-ni byaṅ-chub theg ces bya źe-na /
/ de-ni gaṅ źon sems-can thams-(L191A)cad mya-ṅan zlo /
/ theg-pa 'di-ni gźal-med khaṅ chen nam-mkha' (Tb7A) mtshuṅs /
/ dga' skyid bde-ba mṅon-par thob byed theg-pa mchog // 21 //

/ źon-nas gaṅ-źig phyogs-su 'gro-ba de mi dmigs /
/ mya-ṅan 'das-par 'gro-bar gsuṅs-na 'gro mi dmigs /
/ dper-na me śi de-yi 'gro rgyu mi dmigs bźin /
/ de-phyir de-ni mya-ṅan 'das śes brjod-pa yin // 22 //

/ sṅon-gyi mtha' daṅ phyi-ma'i mtha' daṅ da-ltar-yaṅ /
/ byaṅ-chub-sems-dpa' mi dmigs dus gsum (Tb7B) dag-pa-ste /
/ gaṅ dag de-ni 'dus byas ma yin spros med-de /
/ 'di-ni śes-rab pha-rol phyin-pa'i spyod mchog yin // 23 //

/ byaṅ-chub-sems-dpa' mkhas-pa gaṅ tshe gaṅ dus-na /
/ skye-ba med-par bsams-te de-ltar spyod byed-ciṅ /
/ sñiṅ-rje chen-po skyed-kyaṅ sems-can 'du-śes med /
/ 'di-ni śes-rab pha-rol phyin-pa'i spyod mchog yin // 24 //

/ gal-te sems-can 'du-śes sdug-bsṅal 'du-śes skyed /
/(Tb8A) sdug-bsṅal spyad-par bya-źiṅ 'gro don bya sñam de /
/ bdag daṅ sems-can yoṅs rtog byaṅ-chub-sems-dpa'-ste /
/ de-ni śes-rab pha-rol phyin-pa'i spyod mchog min // 25 //

/ bdag ci-'dra-ba de-'drar sems-can thams-cad śes /
/ sems-can thams-cad ci-'dra de-'drar chos kun śes /
/ skye-ba med daṅ skye-ba gñi-gar mi rtog-pa /
/ de-ni śes-rab pha-rol phyin-pa'i spyod mchog yin // 26 //

/ 'jig-rten-dag-na (Tb8B, L191B) chos miṅ ji-sñed yoṅs brjod-pa /
/ skye-ba kun-las yaṅ-dag 'das-śiṅ thal byas-nas /
/ 'chi med ye-śes mchog thob de-las gźan med-de /
/ de-phyir 'di-ni śes-rab pha-rol phyin ces bya // 27 //

/ byaṅ-chub-sems-dpa' gaṅ-źig dogs (P3B) med de-(L'256A)ltar spyod /
/ de-ni thabs daṅ śes-rab gnas-par śes-par bya /
/ chos-(N199B)rnams raṅ-(P'182A)bźin (X11B)med-par yoṅs-su śes gyur-pa /
/ 'di-ni śes-(D'165A)rab pha-rol phyin-pa'i (Tb9A)spyod mchog yin // 28 //

II.

/ gaṅ-źig gzugs-la mi gnas tshor-la mi gnas-śiṅ /
/ gaṅ-źig 'du-śes mi gnas sems-par mi gnas-la /
/ rnam śes (X12A) gaṅ mi gnas-pa chos-ñid (N'150A) gnas-pa-ste /
/ 'di-ni śes-rab pha-rol phyin-pa'i spyod mchog yin // 1 //

/ rtag daṅ mi rtag bde daṅ sdug-bsṅal sdug mi sdug /
/ bdag daṅ (C'196A) bdag med de-bźin-ñid daṅ stoṅ-ñid daṅ /
/ 'bras-bu thob daṅ dgra-bcom sa-la mi gnas-(Tb9B)śiṅ /
/ raṅ-rgyal sa daṅ saṅs-rgyas sa-la mi gnas-te // 2 //

/ ji-ltar ston-pa 'dus ma byas khams mi (X12B) gnas-śiṅ /
/ de-bźin 'dus byas-la-yaṅ mi gnas gnas med rgyu /
/ de-ltar byaṅ-chub-sems-dpa' gnas-la gnas med gnas /
/ gnas med gnas yin 'di-ni rgyal-bas gnas śes gsuṅs // 3 //

/ gaṅ bdag bde-gśegs ñan-thos 'gyur-bar bya sñam daṅ /
/ raṅ saṅs-rgyas daṅ chos rgyal 'gyur-bar byed (Tb10A) 'dod-pa /
/ bzod-pa 'di-la ma brten thob-par (X13A) mi nus-te /
/ dper-na pha-rol tshu-rol 'gro ṅogs mi mthoṅ bźin // 4 //

/ gaṅ-źig chos-ñid 'gro daṅ gaṅ bśad thos-pa daṅ /
/ 'bras-bu thob daṅ raṅ-rgyal de-bźin 'jig-rten mgon /
/ mkhas-pa gsal-ba mya-ṅan 'das-pa gaṅ thob-pa /
/ de-dag thams-cad de-bźin-gśegs-pas sras-su gzigs // 5 //

/ gaṅ-zag bźi-(X13B)po 'di-dag de-la mi skrag-ste /
/ rgyal sras bden-la (Tb10B) mkhas daṅ phyir mi ldog-pa-dag /
/ dgra-bcom dri-ma bstsal-źiṅ som-ñi spaṅs-pa daṅ /
/ dge-ba'i bśes-kyis yoṅs-su smin byas bźi-pa yin // 6 //

/ byaṅ-chub-sems-dpa' mkhas rig de-ltar spyod-pa-ni /
/ dgra-bcom sa-la mi slob rkyen-rtogs sar mi slob /
/ thams-cad mkhyen-(X14A)ñid ched-du saṅs-rgyas chos-la (D4A) slob /
/ bslab-pa mi slob tshul-gyis bslob-pa de bslabs yin // 7 //

/ gzugs 'phel-ba daṅ yoṅs 'bri yoṅs-(Tb11A)su gzuṅ phyir min /
/ sna-tshogs chos-rnams yoṅs-su gzuṅ phyir slob-pa min /

/ de-ltar slob-pa thams-cad-mkhyen-ñid yoṅs 'dzin-ciṅ /
/ ṅes-'byuṅ 'di-ni yon-tan dga'-ba'i bslab-pa yin // 8 //

/(X14B) gzugs-ni śes-rab ma yin gzugs-la śes-rab med /
/ tshor daṅ 'du-śes sems-pa-dag daṅ rnam-par śes /
/ 'di-dag śes-rab ma yin de-la śes-rab med /
/ de-dag nam-mkha'i khams mtshuṅs tha-dad yod ma yin // 9 //

/(Tb11B) dmigs-pa-rnams-kyi raṅ-bźin de-ni pha mtha' med /
/ sems-can raṅ-bźin gaṅ yin de-yaṅ pha (Tc6A) mtha' med /
/ nam-mkha'i khams-kyi (X15A) raṅ-bźin de-yaṅ (L192B) pha mtha' med /
/ 'jig-rten mkhas-pa'i śes-rab de-yaṅ pha mtha' (N200B) med //10//

/ 'du-śes tshu-rol yin źes 'dren-pas yoṅs-su bsgrags /
/ 'du-śes rnam-par (L'257A) bśigs-nas spoṅ-ba pha-rol 'gro /
/ gaṅ-dag de-la 'du-śes bral-ba (Tb12A) rjes thob-pa /
/ de-dag pha-rol phyin-nas ston-pa'i bka'-la gnas // 11 //

/ gal-te gaṅ-gā'i bye-ma sñed-kyi bskal bźugs-te /
/ ston-pa 'di-yis sems-can źes bya'i sgra brjod-kyaṅ /
/(N'151A) gzod-nas dag-pas sems-can skye-ba ga-la yod /
/ 'di-ni śes-rab pha-rol phyin-pa'i spyod mchog yin // 12 //

/ gaṅ-tshe ṅa-ni śes-rab pha-rol phyin 'di daṅ /
/ mthun-par smra gyur de-tshe sṅon-gyi skyes mchog-gis /
/(Tb12B) ma-'oṅs-pa-yi dus-na saṅs-rgyas (Tc6B) 'gyur-ro źes /
/ ṅa-la luṅ bstan gyur ces rgyal-bas de-skad gsuṅs // 13 //

III.

/ śes-rab pha-rol phyin-pa gaṅ mgon-rnams spyod-pa /
/ 'di-ni gaṅ-źig rtag 'dzin kun-tu chub byed-pa /
/ de-la dug daṅ me daṅ mtshon daṅ chus mi tshugs /
/ bdud daṅ (X16B)bdud-kyi phyogs-kyis glags-kyaṅ rñed mi 'gyur//1//

/ la-las bde-gśegs yoṅs-su mya-ṅan 'das-pa-yi/
/ mchod-rten rin-chen bdun-las (Tb13A)byas-śiṅ mchod byed-la /
/ bde-gśegs mchod-rten gaṅ-gā'i kluṅ-gi bye-ma sñed /
/ de-dag-rnams-kyis bye-ba-phrag stoṅ źiṅ gaṅ-ste // 2 //

/ yoṅs-su brtag bzuṅ źiṅ-rnams (C5A)bye-ba mtha'-(P'183A)yas-na /
/ sems-can (X17A) ji-sñed (D4B)'khod-pa de-dag thams-cad-kyis /
/ las gźan mi byed lha-yi me-tog (N201A) spos rab daṅ /
/(Tc7A)byugs-pas dus gsum bskal-(L193A)pa'am de-bas lhag mchod-la // 3 //

/ gaṅ-(C'197A,L'257B)źig gaṅ-las rnam 'dren stobs bcu (Tb13B)'byuṅ 'gyur-na /
/ bde-bar gśegs-(D'166A)kyi yum 'di glegs-bam bris byas-te /
/ 'chaṅ-źiṅ me-tog byug-pas sti-staṅ byed 'gyur-na /
/ mchod-(X17B)rten byas mchod bsod-nams des-ni char mi (N'151B) phod // 4 //

/ rgyal-ba'i śes-rab pha-rol phyin 'di rig-sṅags che /
/ sems-can khams maṅ mya-ṅan sdug-bsṅal chos źi byed /
/ gaṅ-dag 'das daṅ gaṅ-dag phyogs bcu'i 'jig-rten mgon /
/ rig-(Tb14A)sṅags 'di bslabs sman-pa'i rgyal-po bla med 'gyur//5//

/ gaṅ-dag phan daṅ sñiṅ-brtser bcas-par (X18A) spyad spyod-pa /
/ rig-sṅags 'di-la bslabs-nas mkhas-pa byaṅ-chub reg /
/ 'dus byas bde daṅ 'dus ma byas bde gaṅ yin-pa /
/ bde-ba de kun 'di-las 'byuṅ-bar rig-par bya // 6 //

/ sa-bon (Tc7B) btab-nas sa-la gnas-te 'byuṅ 'gyur-ba /
/ tshogs-pa rñed-nas rnam maṅ gzugs-dag rnam-par skyed /
/ pha-rol phyin lṅa (X18B)byaṅ-chub (Tb14B)yon-tan ji-sñed-pa /
/ de-dag kun-kyaṅ śes-rab pha-rol phyin-las skyed // 7 //

/ 'khor-los-sgyur rgyal lam gaṅ-nas-ni rtag 'gro-ba /
/ lam de-ñid-nas rin-chen bdun daṅ dpuṅ-tshogs kun /
/ gaṅ-nas rgyal-ba'i śes-rab pha-rol phyin 'di 'gro /
/ de-ñid-nas-ni yon-tan chos kun 'gro-bar 'gyur // 8 //

IV.

/ rgyal-bas brgya-byin dri-ba yoṅs dris-lan (N201B) gsol-ba /
/ gal-te gaṅ-gā'i bye sñed (L193B) saṅs-rgyas źiṅ gyur-la /
/(Tb15A)de kun rgyal-ba'i riṅ-bsrel byur-bur gtams gyur-kyaṅ /
/(P5A)bdag-ni śes-(X19B)rab pha-rol phyin-(L'258A)pa 'di-ñid len // 1 //

/ ci-slad ce-na sku-gduṅ mi gus bdag ma lags /
/ 'on-kyaṅ śes-rab yoṅs-su bsgoms-pas mchod-par 'gyur /
/ dper-na rgyal-po brten mi rim-(N'152A)gro thob-pa ltar /
/ saṅs-rgyas riṅ-bsrel śes-rab pha-rol phyin-la brten // 2 //

/(Tc8A)nor-bu (C5B,P'183B)rin-chen yon-tan kun ldan rin-thaṅ med /
/ gab-tshe (C'197B)gaṅ-du stsal-ba de-(X20A)ni phyag (Tb15B)bgyi-'os/
/ de phyuṅ gyur-kyaṅ gab-tshe-la-ni dga' bgyid-de /
/ yon-tan de-dag nor-bu rin-chen de-yi lags // 3 //

/ de-(D5A)bźin śes-rab pha-rol phyin mchog yon-tan-gyis /
/ rgyal-ba mya-ṅan 'das-pa'i riṅ-bsrel mchod-pa brñes /
/ de-ltar gaṅ-źig rgyal-ba'i yon-tan 'dzin 'tshal (D'166B) des /
/ śes-rab pha-rol phyin blaṅ 'di-ni thar-pa lags // 4 //

/ sbyin-pa (X20B) sbyin-pa'i sṅon-du 'gro-ba śes-rab-ste /
/ tshul-khrims bzod-pa brtson-'grus (Tb16A)bsam-gtan de-bźin-no /
/ dge chos chud mi gzan-phyir yoṅs-su 'dzin-pa yin /
/ 'di-ni chos-rnams thams-cad tshul gcig ston-par byed // 5 //

/ dper-na 'dzam-bu'i gliṅ-na śiṅ-rnams bye-ba stoṅ /
/ rnam-pa sna-tshogs rnam-pa du-ma gzugs maṅ-ba /
/(X21A)grib-mar gyur-pa'i graṅs-su brjod-pa ma gtogs-par /
/ grib-ma sna-tshogs (Tc8B) med-ciṅ bye-brag yod ma yin // 6 //

/ de-bźin rgyal-ba'i pha-(N202A)rol phyin lṅa 'di-dag-kyaṅ /
/(Tb16B) śes-rab pha-rol phyin-pas yoṅs-su bsṅos gyur-te /
/ thams-cad (L'258B) mkhyen-pa-ñid phyir yoṅs-su bsṅos byas-na /
/ byaṅ-chub bsṅos-pas drug kun 'dir-ni tshul gcig 'gyur // 7 //

V.

/ byaṅ-chub-sems-dpa' gal-te rab-tu mi śes-bźin /
/ gzugs daṅ 'du-(N'152B)śes tshor-ba sems daṅ rnam-par śes /
/ mi rtag yoṅs-su brjod-pa bcos-la spyod-pa-ste /
/ mkhas-pas nam-yaṅ chos-rnams chud-gzon mi byed-do // 1 //

/(Tb17A) gaṅ-(X22A)la gzugs daṅ tshor-ba 'du-śes mi dmigs-śiṅ /
/ rnam-par śes-pa-dag daṅ sems-pa mi dmigs-la /
/ chos kun skye med (P5B) stoṅ-pa'i tshul-du rab śes-pa /
/ 'di-ni śes-rab pha-rol phyin-pa'i spyod mchog yin // 2 //

/ gaṅgā'i kluṅ-gi bye sñed źiṅ-rnams ji-sñed-pa /
/ de-sñed sems-can la-las dgra-bcom-ñid btul-bas /
/ gaṅ-gis (X22B) śes-rab pha-rol phyin 'di yig bris-te /
/(C'198A)sems-can gźan-la glegs byin bsod-nams khyad-(C6A)par 'phags // 3 //

/(P'184A) ci-phyir źe-na smra mchog de-dag 'dir bslabs-nas /
/ chos-rnams mtha'-dag stoṅ-pa-ñid-du 'dir ston byed /
/ de thos ñan-thos myur-du rnam-par grol-la reg /
/ raṅ-rgyal byaṅ-chub daṅ-ni saṅs-rgyas byaṅ-chub reg // 4 //

/ lcug-ma med-par sdoṅ 'byuṅ 'jig-rten yoṅ med-na /
/ de-la yal 'dab me-tog 'bras-bu ga-la 'byuṅ /
/ byaṅ-chub sems med (N202B)rgyal 'byuṅ 'jig-(D5B)rten yoṅ med-na /
/(Tb18A)'bras-bu brgya-byin tshaṅs-pa ñan-thos ga-la 'byuṅ // 5 //

/(D'167A) ñi-ma'i dkyil-'khor (L194B) gaṅ-tshe 'od-kyi dra-ba 'gyed /
/ de-tshe sems-can las byed brtson-pa de-(L'259A)bźin-du /
/ mkhas-pa śes-(X23B)phyir 'jig-rten byaṅ-chub sems byuṅ-na /
/ ye-śes-kyis-ni sems-can yon-tan chos daṅ ldan // 6 //

/ dper-na ma-dros mtsho-la klu bdag med gyur-na /
/ chu-kluṅ 'dzam-bu gliṅ 'dir 'dab-par ga-la 'gyur /
/ chu-kluṅ med-na me-tog 'bras-bu 'byuṅ mi (Tb18B) 'gyur /
/ rgya-mtsho-la-yaṅ rin-chen gzugs maṅ med-par 'gyur // 7 //

/ de-bźin 'dir-yaṅ byaṅ-(X24A)chub sems med bder-gśegs-kyi /
/ ye-śes 'jig-rten 'di-dag kun-tu ga-la 'byuṅ /
/ ye-śes med-na yon-tan 'phel med byaṅ-chub med /
/ rgya-mtsho 'dra-ba'i saṅs-rgyas chos-kyaṅ med-par 'gyur // 8 //

/ 'jig-rten 'di-na srin-bu me-khyer ji-sñed-pa /
/ kun-gyis snaṅ-bar bya-phyir 'od-rnams phyuṅ-ba-bas /

/ ñi-ma'i dkyil-(X24B)'khor 'od-(Tb19A,P6A)zer gcig phyuṅ ches mchog-ste/
/ me-khyer tshogs-kyi 'od-rnams kun-gyis char mi phod // 9 //

VI.

/ ñan-thos-tshogs-rnams ji-sñed sbyin daṅ tshul-khrims daṅ /
/ sgom daṅ rab-tu ldan-pa'i bsod-(X25A)nams skyed-pa-yaṅ /
/ byaṅ-chub-sems-dpa' rjes-su yi raṅ sems gcig-la /
/ ñan-thos-(C'198B)tshogs-kyi bsod-nams phuṅ-pos char mi phod//1//

/ 'das dus sṅon-gyi saṅs-rgyas bye-(N203A)ba khrag-khrig gaṅ /
/ źiṅ maṅ mtha'-(Tb19B)yas-dag-na bye stoṅ gaṅ bźugs daṅ /
/ gaṅ yaṅ mya-ṅan 'das-pa 'jig-rten mgon-po-rnams /
/ sdug-bsṅal (P'184B)zad-par (L195A)bya-phyir rin-chen (X25B)chos
ston-to // 2 //

/ daṅ-po byaṅ-chub mchog-tu sems bskyed bskyed-pa-nas /
/ rnam-par 'dren-pa-rnams-kyi dam chos zad-kyi dus /
/ de-bar rgyal-ba de-dag (N'153B) bsod-nams gaṅ yin-pa /
/ pha-rol phyin daṅ ldan daṅ saṅs-rgyas chos gaṅ daṅ // 3 //

/ gaṅ yaṅ saṅs-rgyas sras-rnams daṅ-ni ñan-thos (Tb20A) daṅ /
/ slob daṅ mi slob dge-ba zag bcas zag med-pa /
/ bsdus-nas byaṅ-chub-(X26A)sems-dpa' rjes-su yi raṅ byed /
/ 'gro-ba'i don-du byaṅ-chub rgyu-phyir thams-cad bsṅo // 4 //

/ yoṅs bsṅo gal-te sems daṅ 'du-śes gnas byed-ciṅ /
/ byaṅ-chub 'du-śes yoṅs bsṅo sems-can 'du-śes-pa /
/ 'du-śes daṅ-ni lta-bas sems gsum ldan-par gnas /
/ dmigs-pa yod-pas yoṅs-su bsṅos-par chud ma (X26B) yin // 5 //

/(Tb20B) gal-te 'di-ltar chos-rnams 'gags-śiṅ zad-pa daṅ /
/ gaṅ-du yoṅs-su bsṅo-ba de-yaṅ zad-pa daṅ /
/ chos-kyis chos-la nam-yaṅ mi bsṅo śes gyur-na /
/ de-ltar rab-tu śes-pas yoṅs-su bsṅos-pa yin // 6 //

/ gal-te mtshan-mar byed-pa de-ni bsṅo ma yin /
/ ji-ste mtshan-ma med-na byaṅ-chub bsṅo-ba yin /
/ ji-ltar dug daṅ (X27A) 'dres-(P6B)pa'i kha-zas bzaṅ za-ba /
/(N203B)dkar-po'i chos-la dmigs-pa'aṅ de-'drar rgyal-bas gsuṅs//7//

/(Tb21A) de-ltar bdag-gis yoṅs-su bsṅo-ba bslab bya-ste /
/ ji-ltar rgyal-ba de-dag dge-ba rab mkhyen-pa'i /
/ rnam-pa gaṅ-dag (L195B)'byuṅ gaṅ mtshan-ñid gaṅ yin-la /
/ rjes-su yi raṅ de-lta de-ltar yoṅs-su bsṅo // 8 //

/ de-ltar bsod-nams (L'260A)byaṅ-chub yoṅs-(X27B)su bsṅo byed-na /
/ dug med saṅs-(C'199A)rgyas mi spoṅ (N'154A)rgyal-bas gsuṅs-pa smra/
/ de-ltar yoṅs (C7A) bsṅo dpa'-bo 'jig-rten dmigs-can-gyi /
/ byaṅ-chub-sems-dpa' ji-sñed thams-(Tb21B)cad zil-gyis non // 9 //

VII.

/(X28A) dmus-loṅ dmigs-bu med-pa bye-ba khrag-khrig-rnams /
/ lam-yaṅ mi śes groṅ-khyer 'jug-par ga-la 'gyur /
/ śes-rab med-na mig med pha-rol phyin (P'185A) lṅa 'di /
/ dmigs-bu med-pas byaṅ-chub reg-par nus ma yin // 1 //

/(Tc11A) gaṅ-tshe śes-rab-kyis-ni rab-tu zin gyur-na /
/ de-tshe mig rñed gyur-ciṅ 'di-dag miṅ 'thob-bo /
/ dper-na ri-mo'i las-ni yoṅs (X28B) zin mig med-pa /
/ mig ma byas-(Tb22A)pas de-tshe rñan-pa mi thob bźin // 2 //

/ gaṅ-tshe 'dus byas 'dus ma byas daṅ dkar nag chos /
/ śes-rab rnam-par bśigs-nas rdul tsam mi dmigs tshe /
/ 'jig-rten-dag-na śes-rab pha-rol phyin graṅs 'gro /
/ nam-mkha' gar mi gnas-pa ji-yaṅ med-pa bźin // 3 //

/ gal-te bdag-ni rgyal-ba'i śes-rab spyad bya-źiṅ /
/(X29A,D'168A)sems-can sdug-bsṅal reg-pa khrag-khrig maṅ dgrol sems/
/ sems-can 'du-śes (Tb22B)yoṅs brtags byaṅ-chub-(D6B)sems-dpa'-(N204A)ste/
/ 'di-ni śes-rab pha-rol phyin-pa'i spyod mchog min // 4 //

/ byaṅ-chub-sems-dpa' gaṅ-źig sṅon-chad spyod-pa'i tshe /
/ pha-rol phyin 'dir spyad-pa mkhas-pa som-ñi med /
/ thos ma thag-tu (L'260B)de-ni ston-(X29B)pa'i 'du-śes (L196A)bskyed/
/ de-ni byaṅ-chub źi-ba (P7A)myur-du rtogs-par (N'154B)'gyur //5//

/ sṅon spyod tshe-na saṅs-rgyas khrag-khrig bkur byas-kyaṅ /
/ rgyal-ba'i śes-rab pha-rol phyin-(Tb23A)la ma dad-na /
/(Tc11B) de-ni dper-na tshoṅ-pa rin-chen gliṅ soṅ-la /
/ zoṅ-rnams zad-par byas-nas phyir ldog byed daṅ mtshuṅs // 6 //

/ de-lta-bas-na gal-te saṅs-rgyas ye-śes mchog /
/ reg-par 'dod-na rgyal-ba'i yum (X30A) 'dir dad-par gyis /
/ thos-nas blo chuṅ gaṅ-źig 'di-ni spoṅ byed-pa /
/ de spaṅs-pas-na mnar-med 'gro-ste skyabs med 'gyur // 7 //

VIII.

/ gzugs-kyi dag-pa 'bras-bu dag-par rig-par bya /
/ 'bras-bu gzugs (X30B)dag thams-(Tb23B)cad mkhyen-ñid dag-par gsuṅs/
/ thams-cad mkhyen-ñid 'bras-bu dag-pas gzugs-kyaṅ dag /
/ nam-mkha'i khams daṅ mtshuṅs-śiṅ gcad med dbye-ba med // 1 //

/ dpa'-bo śes-rab pha-rol phyin-pa gar spyod-pa /
/ byaṅ-chub-sems-dpa' khams gsum yaṅ-dag 'das gyur-ciṅ /
/ ñon-moṅs bstsal-bar (P'185B) gyur-kyaṅ skye-ba ston-par byed /
/ rga daṅ na daṅ 'chi-ba med-kyaṅ (X31A) 'chi-'pho ston // 2 //

/ 'gro-ba 'di-dag 'dod daṅ gzugs-kyi 'dam-la (Tb24A) chags /
/ til-gyi 'khor-lo lta-bu'i 'khor-(N204B)ba'i 'khor-lo 'khyam /

/ 'gro-ba 'khral-pa ri-dvags rgyar chud 'drar śes-nas /
/ śes-rab ldan-pa mkha'-la bya bźin rnam-par rgyu // 3 //

/ spyod-pa yoṅs dag gaṅ-źig gzugs-la mi spyod-ciṅ /
/ rnam śes 'du-śes tshor-(L196B)ba sems-(L'261A)par mi spyod-na /
/(X31B) de-ltar spyod-pa chags-pa thams-(N'155A)cad yoṅs-su śpoṅ /
/ chags-las rnam-par grol-ba bde-gśegs śes-rab spyod // 4 //

IX.

/ de-ltar spyod-pa'i byaṅ-chub-sems-dpa' (Tb24B) mkhas gsal-ba /
/ chags-pa bcad-nas (D'168B) 'jig-rten chags-pa med-par 'gyur /
/(X32A) ñi-ma sgra-gcan gza' bral lhaṅ-ṅer 'dug-pa daṅ /
/ me btaṅ rtsva daṅ śiṅ daṅ nags-tshal sreg-pa bźin // 1 //

/(P7B) chos rnams thams-cad (D7A) raṅ-bźin dag-par yoṅs rtogs-śiṅ /
/ byaṅ-chub-sems-dpa' śes-rab pha-rol phyin mthoṅ-ba /
/ byed-pa-po-yaṅ mi dmigs chos kun mi dmigs-te /
/ 'di-ni śes-rab pha-rol phyin-pa'i spyod mchog yin // 2 //

X.

/ rgyal-(Tb25A)ba-la-ni lha rgyal brgya-byin-gyis źus-pa /
/(C8A) byaṅ-chub-sems-dpa' śes-rab spyod-pa ji-ltar brtson /
/ phuṅ-po khams-la rdul tsam brtson-par mi byed-ciṅ /
/ phuṅ-por mi brtson de-ni byaṅ-chub-sems-(C200A)dpa'i (X33A)brtson/1/

/ gaṅ-źig chos 'di sprul daṅ sgyu-ma 'drar thos-nas /
/ som-ñi med-ciṅ slob-la phyir-źiṅ sbyor byed-pa /
/ sems-can de-ni riṅ-nas thegs źugs rig-par bya /
/ saṅs-rgyas bye-ba khrag-khrig maṅ-la lhag byas yin // 2 //

/ dpag-tshad maṅ-por dgon-(Tb25B)pa'i lam-du źugs-pa'i mis /
/ gnas-rdzi mtshams daṅ nags-tshal phun-sum-tshogs mthoṅ-na /
/(X33B) 'di-dag groṅ daṅ groṅ-khyer ñe-ba'i rtags sñam-ste /
/(L'261B)dbugs-'phyin rñed-par gyur-ciṅ chom-(N'155B)rkun 'jigs-pa med // 3 //

/ de-bźin byaṅ-chub yoṅs-su tshol tshe rgyal-rnams-kyi /
/ śes-rab pha-rol (L197A)phyin (P'166A)'di mñan-pa gaṅ thob-pa /
/ de-ni dbugs-'phyin thob-par gyur-ciṅ 'jigs med-de /
/ dgra-bcom sa-la ma yin rkyen rtogs sa-la min // 4 //

/(Tb26A) mi źig rgya-mtsho'i chu-(X34A)ni blta-phyir 'gro-ba-yis /
/ gal-te śiṅ nags-rnams mthoṅ-na da-duṅ ruṅ /
/ ji-ste ma mthoṅ rgya-mtsho ċhe de mi riṅ-ste /
/ ñe-bar gyur-pa'i rtags yin sñam-(Tc13A)du som-ñi med // 5 //

/ de-ltar byaṅ-chub dam-par rab źugs rig bya-ste /
/ rgyal-ba'i śes-rab pha-rol phyin-pa 'di ñan-pa /

/ rnam-par 'dren-pas mṅon-sum luṅ bstan ma gyur-(X34B)kyaṅ /
/ riṅ-por mi tshogs saṅs-rgyas byaṅ-chub reg-par 'gyur // 6 //

/ dpyid dus bzaṅ 'byuṅ rtsva daṅ lo-ma yal-ga-rnams /
/(Tb26B) lo-ma 'bras-bu me-tog yaṅ-dag skyed-par byed /
/ śes-rab pha-rol phyin 'di su-yi lag thob-pa /
/ riṅ-por (D'169A)mi thogs 'dren-pa'i byaṅ-chub mchog thob 'gyur//7//

/ dper-na bud-med sbrum-ma sdug-bsṅal ñen gyur-na /
/ de-ni de-yi (X35A) btsa'-ba'i dus bab śes-par bya /
/ de-bźin byaṅ-chub-(D7B)sems-dpa' rgyal-ba'i śes-rab ñan /
/ 'dun-pa rtog-ciṅ myur-du byaṅ-chub reg-par 'gyur // 8 //

/(C8B) śes-rab pha-rol phyin mchog spyod tshe rnal-'byor-pa /
/ gzugs-kyi 'phel-ba daṅ-ni yoṅs-su 'grib (Tb27A) mi mthoṅ /
/ chos dbyiṅs chos daṅ chos min-rnams su mi mthoṅ-ste /
/ mya-ṅan (X35B)'das-la mi reg de-ni śes-rab gnas // 9 //

/ gaṅ-źig 'dir (Tc13B) spyod saṅs-rgyas chos rnams mi rtog-ste /
/stobs daṅ (L197B) rdzu-'phrul rkaṅ daṅ byaṅ-chub źi mi rtog /
/ rnam-par mi rtog rtog bral byin-gyi rlabs-kyis spyod /
/ 'di-ni śes-rab pha-rol phyin-pa'i spyod mchog yin // 10 //

XI.

/ smra-ba'i zla-ba saṅs-rgyas-la-ni rab-'byor źus /
/ ston-pas bar-du gcod-par 'gyur-ba maṅ gsuṅs-na /
/ yon-(Tb27B)tan dga'-ba-rnams-kyi bar-du gcod gaṅ lags /
/ de-la cuṅ-zad tsam źig yoṅs-su brjod-par bya // 1 //

/ rgyal-ba'i śes-rab pha-rol phyin 'di yig (X36B) 'bri tshe /
/ spobs-pa tha-dad rnam-pa du-ma (P'186B) 'byuṅ 'gyur-te /
/ 'gro-ba'i don ma byas-par glog bźin myur-du yaṅ /
/ yoṅs-su ñams-par 'gyur-ba 'di-ni bdud-kyi las // 2 //

/ 'di bśad tshe-na kha-cig som-ñi-za 'gyur-te /
/ 'dren-pas 'dir-ni bdag-gi miṅ-yaṅ yoṅs ma brjod /
/ rigs daṅ sa daṅ rus-kyaṅ yoṅs-su ma brjod (Tb28A) ces /
/ de-ni ñan-par mi 'gyur spoṅ 'gyur (X37A)bdud-kyi las // 3 //

/ de-ltar rtsa-ba thabs-ni yoṅs-su mi śes-pas /
/ blun-po de-dag yal-ga 'dab-ma tshol-bar 'gyur /
/(P8B) glaṅ-po rñed-kyaṅ glaṅ-po'i rjes-ni tshol-ba ltar /
/ śes-rab pha-rol phyin thos mdo tshol de-bźin-no // 4 //

/ dper-na la-las ro (L'262B) brgya ldan-pa'i zad rñed-la /
/ zad mchog rñed-nas drug-cu-pa-dag tshol byed ltar /
/(X37B) byaṅ-chub-sems-dpa' pha-rol phyin-pa 'di rñed-nas /
/ dgra-bcom sa-las byaṅ-chub tshol byed (Tb28B) de-bźin-no // 5 //

/ sti-stan 'dod-par 'gyur-źiṅ rñed-pa 'dod 'gyur-ba /
/ lta-ba'i sems daṅ bcas-te (N206A)khyim 'dris byed ldan-(L198A)źiṅ /
/ chos btaṅ-nas-ni chos min bya-ba spyod 'gyur-ba /
/ lam bor lam gol soṅ-ba 'di-ni bdud-(C9A)kyi las // 6 //

/ gaṅ-(X38A)dag de-yi tshe-na chos-kyi dam-pa 'di /
/ ñan-par 'dun-ciṅ dad-pa skyed-par gyur-pa-las /
/ de-dag chos smra bya-ba min daṅ ldan rig-nas /
/ dga'-ba med-par gyur-ciṅ yid-kyaṅ mi bde-ba // 7 //

/ de-yi tshe-na bdud-kyi las 'di (Tb29A) 'byuṅ-bar 'gyur /
/ gźan-yaṅ bar-chad 'gyur-ba rnam-pa du-ma-ste /
/ de-tshe gaṅ-dag-gis-ni dge-sloṅ maṅ dkrugs-nas /
/ śes-rab pha-rol phyin-pa 'di-ni 'dzin mi byed // 8 //

/ rin-chen gaṅ-dag rin-thaṅ med-ciṅ dkon gyur-pa /
/ de-dag-la-ni rtag-tu dgra-yaṅ rab-tu maṅ /
/ de-bźin rgyal-ba'i śes-rab pha-rol phyin-pa mchog /
/ dkon chos rin-chen-la-yaṅ gnod-pa byed-pa maṅ // 9 //

/ theg-par gsar-du źugs-pa'i sems-can blo chuṅ-ba /
/ gaṅ-źig dkon-pa'i rin-chen 'di-(X39A)ni (Tb29B,P'187A)ma rñed-pa /
/ de-la bar-chad bya-phyir bdud-ni spro-bar 'gyur /
/ phyogs bcu'i saṅs-rgyas de-dag yoṅs-su 'dzin-la ldan // 10 //

## XII.

/ ma źig na-bar gyur-la bu-ni (N'157A) maṅ yod-pa /
/ de kun (X39B) yid mi bde-źiṅ de-la rim-gro byed /
/ de-bźin phyogs bcu'i 'jig-rten khams-kyi saṅs-rgyas-kyaṅ /
/ yum gyur śes-rab dam-pa 'di-la dgoṅs-pa mdzad // 1 //

/ gaṅ-dag 'das daṅ phyogs (P9A) bcu'i 'jig-rten mgon gaṅ daṅ /
/ ma-'oṅs dus-na 'byuṅ 'gyur de-dag 'di-(L198B)las 'byuṅ /
/ 'jig-rten ston-pa skyed-pa rgyal-(Tb30A)ba-rnams-kyi yum /
/ sems-can gźan-gyi sems-kyi (X40A)spyod-pa ston-par byed // 2 //

/ 'jig-rten de-bźin-(N206B)ñid daṅ dgra-bcom de-bźin-ñid /
/ raṅ-rgyal de-bźin-ñid daṅ rgyal-ba'i de-bźin-ñid /
/ gcig-pa-ñid-de dṅos bral gźan min de-bźin-ñid /
/ śes-rab pha-rol phyin-pa de-bźin-gśegs-pas mkhyen // 3 //

/ mkhas-pa 'jig-(Tc15A)rten gnas-sam mya-ṅan 'das-kyaṅ-ruṅ /
/ chos-ñid skyon med chos-rnams (X40B)ston-pa 'di gnas-(D'170A)te /
/ byaṅ-chub-sems-dpas de-bźin-(C9B)ñid 'di (Tb30B) rjes-su rtogs /
/ de-phyir de-bźin-gśegs śes saṅs-rgyas mtshan gsol-(C'201B)to //4//

[*Note that no Tibetan version, but only the Chinese version, offers a verse corresponding to the Sanskrit Recension A, chapter XII, verse 5.*]

/ śes-rab pha-rol phyin-pa ñams-dgar rab brten-pa /
/ stobs bcu rnam 'dren-rnams-kyi spyod-yul 'di yin-te /
/ sems-can sdug-bsṅal ṅan-soṅ gsum-las yoṅs 'don-kyaṅ /
/ de-dag nam-yaṅ sems-can 'du-śes (D8B,X41A) 'gyur-ba med // 5 //
[= Skt. XII 6]

/ dper-na seṅge ri-sul (L'263B) brten-nas 'jigs med-par /
/ ri-dvags phra-mo (N'157B)skrag-par byed-ciṅ sgra sgrogs ltar /
/ mi-yi seṅge śes-(Tb31A)rab pha-rol phyin brten-nas /
/ mu-stegs-can maṅ skrag byed 'jigs med sgra-yaṅ sgrogs // 6 //
[= Skt. XII 7]

/ dper-na nam-mkhar gnas-pa'i ñi-ma'i 'od-zer-ni /
/ sa 'di skems-par byed-ciṅ gzugs-kyaṅ rzb-tu ston /
/ de-bźin (X41B) chos rgyal śes-rab pha-rol phyin brten-pa /
/ sred-pa'i chu-kluṅ skems-śiṅ chos-kyaṅ (Tc15B) rab-tu ston // 7 //
[= Skt. XII 8]

/ gzugs-rnams mi mthoṅ tshor-ba-dag-kyaṅ mi mthoṅ-źiṅ /
/ 'du-śes (L199A) mthoṅ-ba med-la sems-pa mi mthoṅ-źiṅ /
/ gaṅ-la rnam-par śes daṅ sems-kyaṅ mi mthoṅ-ba /
/ 'di-ni chos mthoṅ yin źes de-bźin-gśegs-pas bstan // 8 //
[= Skt. XII 9]

/(P9B)nam-mkha' mthoṅ źes sems-can (N207A,X42A)tshig-tu rab brjod-pa /
/ nam-mkha' ci-ltar mthoṅ-ba don 'di rtogs-śig ltar /
/ de-ltar chos mthoṅ-ba-yaṅ de-bźin-gśegs-pas bstan /
/ mthoṅ-ba dpes-ni brjod-par nus-pa ma yin-no // 9 //
[= Skt. XII 10]

XIII.

/ gaṅ-gis de-ltar mthoṅ-ba de-yis chos kun mthoṅ /
/ rgyal-po btaṅ-sñoms 'dug-ciṅ blon-po kun byed ltar /
/ saṅs-rgyas mdzad daṅ ñan-thos chos-rnams ji-sñed-pa /
/ de-dag (Tb32A) thams-cad śes-rab pha-rol phyin-pa byed // 1 //

/ rgyal-po groṅ-du mi 'gro yul-(Tc15B)'khor mi 'gro-la /
/ raṅ-gi yul-nas 'du-ba thams-cad sdud-pa ltar /
/ byaṅ-chub-(X43A)sems-dpa' chos-ñid gaṅ-du'aṅ mi gYo-la /
/ saṅs-rgyas sa-yi yon-tan (L'264A)gaṅ yin (N'158A)thams-cad sdud//2//

XIV.

/ gaṅ-źig bde-gśegs byaṅ-chub-sems-dpa' dad (X43B)brten-źiṅ /
/ śes-rab pha-rol phyin-pa mchog-(C'202A,D'170B)la bsam sbyor-ba /
/ ñan-thos raṅ-rgyal sa gñis śin-tu 'das byas-nas /
/ zil-gyis mi non (C10A)rgyal-ba'i (Tb32B)byaṅ-chub myur-du 'thob//1//

/ dper-na rgya-mtshor 'jug-pa'i gru-ni chag gyur-la /
/ mi gaṅ ro'am rtsva'am śiṅ-ni mi 'dzin-pa /
/ chu dbus 'jig-par 'gyur-te ṅogs-su phyin mi 'gyur /
/(X44A)gaṅ-źig 'dzin-pa rgya-mtsho'i pha-rol phyin-par 'gyur // 2 //

/(L199B) de-ltar gaṅ-dag dad ldan daṅ-ba rñed gyur-na /3a/
/ śes-rab pha-rol phyin-pa rnam-par soṅ mi byed /3b/

[*Note that only the bilingual Chinese blockprint text (= X) reads the following four pādas corresponding to the Sanskrit version (both Recensions A and B), XIV 3cd, 4ab.*]

[/(X44A6)skye rga 'chi daṅ mya-ṅan rba-rlabs 'khrugs-pa yis /3c/]
[/ 'khor-ba'i rgya-mtsho der-ni rtag-tu 'khor 'gyur-ba // 3 //]

[/ gaṅ de śes-rab mchog-gis yoṅs-su zin-pa-na /4a/]
[/ dṅos-po'i raṅ-(X44B3)bźin mkhas-śiṅ don dam ston-par byed /4b/]
/(D9A) de-dag thabs-kyi yon-tan śes-rab yoṅs bzuṅ-ste /4c/
/ mchog-tu rmad byuṅ bde-gśegs byaṅ-chub myur-du reg // 4 //

/ dper-na (Tb33A) la-las (N207B) rdza-so ma btaṅ chu skyed-na /
/ ñam-chuṅ phyir-ni myur-du 'jig-par rig-par bya /
/ so btaṅ bum-par chu skyed lam-du 'jig-pa-yi /
/ 'jigs-pa med-ciṅ bde-bar khyim-du phyin-par (X45A) 'gyur // 5 //

/ gźan-yaṅ byaṅ-chub-sems-dpa' dad-pa maṅ gyur-kyaṅ /
/ śes-rab rnam-par ñams-na myur-du 'jig-par 'gyur /
/ dad-pas śes-rab de-ni yoṅs-su (P10A) zin gyur-na /
/ sa gñis (P'188A) śin-tu 'das-te byaṅ-chub mchog thob 'gyur // 6 //

/ dper-na bcos legs ma byas (Tb33B) gru-ni rgya-mtsho'i naṅ /
/ nor daṅ bcas-(X45B)śiṅ tshoṅ-par bcas-(L'264B)te 'jig-(N'158B)par 'gyur /
/ gru de legs-par bcos legs byas daṅ ldan gyur-na /
/ mi 'jig nor daṅ bcas-par ṅogs-su phyin-par 'gyur // 7 //

/ de-ltar byaṅ-chub-sems-dpa' dad-pas yoṅs bsgos-kyaṅ /
/ śes-rab med-na byaṅ-chub-las-ni myur ñams 'gyur /
/ de-ñid śes-rab pha-rol phyin-pa mchog ldan-na /
/ ma (X46A)rmas ma ñams rgyal-ba'i byaṅ-chub reg-par 'gyur // 8 //

/(Tb34A) lo brgya-ñi-śu lon-ste rgas-śiṅ sdug-bsṅal ni /
/ laṅs-kyaṅ bdag-ñid 'gro-bar nus-pa ma yin-te /
/ de-ni gYas-gYon gñis-nas mi-yis brten byas-nas /
/ 'gyel-ba'i 'jig-(C'202B)pa med-ciṅ bde-blag 'gro-bar (L200A)'gyur/9/

/ de-bźin byaṅ-chub-sems-(X46B)dpa' śes-rab stobs chuṅ-ba /
/ rab-tu źugs-par gyur-kyaṅ bar-du 'jig-par 'gyur /
/ de-ñid thabs daṅ śes-rab mchog-gis yoṅs (C10B) zin-na /
/ mi 'jig de-bźin-(D'171A)gśegs-kyi byaṅ-(Tb34B)chub reg-par 'gyur // 10 //

XV.

/(X47A) byaṅ-chub-sems-dpa' daṅ-po'i las-kyi sar gnas gaṅ /
/ lhag-pa'i bsam-pas (N208A)saṅs-rgyas byaṅ-chub mchog źugs-pa /
/ slob-ma bzaṅ-po bla-ma gus daṅ rab ldan-pa /
/ mkhas-pa de-dag-gis dge-ba'i bśes-gñen-pa bsten-par bya // 1 //

/ ci-phyir źe-na mkhas-pa'i yon-tan de-las 'byuṅ /
/ de-dag śes-rab pha-rol phyin-pa rjes-su (X47B) ston /
/ saṅs-rgyas chos-rnams dge-ba'i bśes-la brten-to źes /
/ yon-tan kun-gyis mchog (Tb35A)mṅa' rgyal-(L'265A)ba de-skad gsuṅ/2/

/(D9B,N'159A)sbyin daṅ tshul-khrims bzod daṅ de-bźin brtson-'grus daṅ /
/ bsam-gtan śes-rab byaṅ-chub yoṅs-su bsṅo-bar gyis /
/ phuṅ-por źen-nas mchog-tu 'dzin-par ma byed ces /
/ daṅ-po'i las-can-dag-la de-skad bstan-(P10B)par (X48A) bya // 3 //

/ de-ltar spyod-pa legs mtsho smra-ba'i zla-ba-rnams /
/ 'gro-ba'i skyabs daṅ dpuṅ-gñen daṅ-ni (P'188B) gnas yin-te /
/ rten daṅ blo daṅ gliṅ daṅ yoṅs 'dren don 'dod daṅ /
/ gsal-byed sgron-ma chos mchog (Tb35B)smra-ba mi 'khrugs yin //4//

/ grags chen ldan-rnams bya-dka' go-cha gyon byed-de /
/ phuṅ-po khams daṅ skye-mched-rnams-kyi go-cha min /
/ theg gsum (L200B,X48B) 'du-śes bral-źiṅ yoṅs-su bzuṅ-ba med /
/ mi ldog gYo-ba med-ciṅ chos-rnams 'khrugs-pa med // 5 //

/ de-dag 'di-'dra'i chos daṅ ldan-źiṅ spros-pa med /
/ som-ñi yid-gñis 'gyod daṅ bral-źiṅ don daṅ ldan /
/ śes-rab pha-rol phyin-pa thos-nas mi nur-ba /
/ gźan-gyi driṅ mi 'jog-ciṅ mi ldog rig-par (Tb36A) bya // 6 //

/ 'dren-pa-rnams-kyi chos 'di zab-ste (X49A) mthoṅ-bar dka' /
/ sus-kyaṅ (N208B)rtogs-pa med-ciṅ thob-(C'203A)par 'gyur med-pa /
/ de-na gcig-ñid-du rtogs-nas phan-byed sñiṅ-brtser 'gyur /
/ spro-chuṅ sems-can tshogs sus 'di-ni śes-par 'gyur // 7 //

/ sems-can-rnams-ni gnas-la dga'-źiṅ yul-rnams 'dod /
/(L'265B)'dzin-la gnas-(N'159B)śiṅ mi mkhas (Tc18A)blun-rmoṅs mun-pa bźin /
/ thob-par bya-ba'i (X49B)chos-ni gnas med (C11A)'dzin med-de /
/ 'di-ni 'jig-rten-dag daṅ rtsod-(D'171B)pa 'byuṅ-ba yin // 8 //

XVI.

/ nam-mkha(Tb36B)'i khams-ni śar-gyi phyogs daṅ lho phyogs daṅ /
/ de-bźin nub-kyi phyogs daṅ byaṅ phyogs pha mtha'-yas /
/(X50A) steṅ daṅ 'og daṅ phyogs bcu'i ji-sñed-rnams-na'aṅ yod /
/ tha-dad gyur-pa med-ciṅ bye-brag gyur-pa med // 1 //

/ 'das-pa'i de-bźin-ñid gaṅ ma phyin de-bźin-ñid /
/ da-ltar de-bźin-ñid gaṅ dgra-bcom de-bźin-ñid /
/ chos kun de-bźin-ñid gaṅ rgyal-ba'i de-bźin-ñid /
/ de-ni chos-kyi de-bźin-ñid de bya-brag med // 2 //

/(P11A)bde-gśegs byaṅ-chub (X50B)tha-dad chos daṅ bral gyur-pa /
/(Tb37A)'di-ni byaṅ-chub-sems-dpa' gaṅ-źig thob (L201A)'dod-pa /
/ thabs daṅ ldan-pas śes-rab pha-(D10A)rol phyin-la sbyor /
/ 'dren-pa'i śes-rab med-na thob-par 'gyur ma yin // 3 //

/ bya źig lus che dpag-tshad brgya-pa yod gyur-tam /
/ dpag-tshad lṅa-brgyar gyur-pa gśog zad stobs med-pa /
/(Tc18B) de-yis sum-cu-rtsa-gsum gnas-nas 'dzam-(X51A)gliṅ 'dir /
/ bdag-ñid mchiṅs-na der-ni ñam-ñes 'gyur-ba yin // 4 //

/ rgyal-ba-rnams-kyi pha-rol phyin-pa lṅa 'di-yaṅ /
/ bskal-pa bye-ba khrag-khrig maṅ-por bsgrubs (Tb37B) byas-śiṅ /
/ smon-lam mtha'-yas rgya-chen (N209A) 'jig-rten rtag bsten-kyaṅ /
/ thabs med śes-(L'266A)rab bral-ba (N'160A)ñan-thos-ñid-du ltuṅ/5/

/ saṅs-rgyas theg-(X51B)pa 'di-la ṅes-par 'byuṅ 'dod-pas /
/ 'gro-ba kun-la sems sñoms pha-ma'i 'du-śes daṅ /
/ phan-pa'i sems daṅ byams-(C'203B)pa'i yid daṅ brtul bya-źiṅ /
/ tha-ba med-ciṅ draṅ-la tshig 'jam smra-bar bya // 6 //

XVII.

/(X52A) 'jig-rten mgon-la gnas-brtan rab-'byor yoṅs źus-pa /
/ yon-tan rgya-mtsho'i ñon-moṅs (Tb38A)ma mchis rtags bstan gsol /
/ mthu che-ba-dag ji-ltar slar ldog mi 'gyur-ba /
/ de-ltar yon-tan phyogs tsam rgyal-bas luṅ bstan gsol // 1 //

/ tha-dad 'du-śes bral-źiṅ tshig daṅ ldan-par smra /
/ dge-sbyoṅ-dag daṅ bram-ze gźan-la (C11B)bsten (X52B) mi byed /
/ mkhas-pas dus-rnams rtag-tu ṅan-soṅ gsum-po spaṅs /
/ de-dag dge-ba bcu'i las lam-la mṅon-par brtson // 2 //

/ zaṅ-ziṅ med-pas 'gro-la chos-ni rjes-su (D'172A) ston /
/ chos-la gcig-tu dga'-źiṅ (Tb38B) 'jam-pa'i tshig daṅ ldan /
/ 'gro 'chag ñal daṅ 'dug-par śes bźin rab-tu ldan /
/ gña'-śiṅ gaṅ-tsam lta-źiṅ 'gro-la sems 'khrul med // 3 //

/(P11B,X53A) gtsaṅ byas gtsaṅ-ma'i gos 'chaṅ gsum-po dben-źiṅ dag /
/ khyu-mchog rtag-tu chos 'dod rñed-pa 'dod ma yin /
/ bdud-kyi yul-las 'das-śiṅ gźan-gyi driṅ mi 'jog /
/ bsam-gtan bźi-la bsam byed bsam-gtan der mi gnas // 4 //

/ grags-(N'160B)pa 'dod-pa ma yin khro-bas sems dkris (Tb39A) med /
/ khyim-par (X53B) gyur-na rtag-tu dṅos-po (P'189B) kun (N209B) ma chags /

/ 'tsho-ba'i loṅs-spyod mi 'thun tshol-ba'i bsam-pa med /
/ drag-śul (D10B)spyod sṅags bud-med sbyor-ba'i sṅags mi byed // 5 //

/ rtsva-tsam 'dod phyir mi-las las-rnams len mi byed /
/ rab-tu dben-pa śes-rab pha-rol phyin mchog brtson /
/ 'thab daṅ rtsod daṅ bral-źiṅ byams-pa'i sems-kyaṅ (X54A) brtan /
/ kun-mkhyen 'dod-ciṅ bstan-la rtag-tu gźol sems ldan // 6 //

/ mtha'-'khob kla-klo (Tb39B) skye-bo yul mtha' rnam-par spaṅs /
/ raṅ-gi sa-la dogs med rtag-tu ri-rab 'dra /
/ chos phyir srog-kyaṅ 'dor-źiṅ rnal-'byor rab-tu (C'204A) brtson /
/ mi ldog rtags-ni 'di-dag yin-par śes-par bya // 7 //

XVIII.

/ gzugs daṅ tshor daṅ 'du-śes sems-pa rnam śes-rnams /
/ zab-ciṅ raṅ-bźin mtshan-ma med-de rab źi-ba /
/ śes-rab-kyis-ni phuṅ-po brtags-pas gtiṅ mi rtogs /
/ dper-na mda'-yis rgya-mtsho'i gtiṅ thug tshol daṅ mtshuṅs // 1 //

/ byaṅ-chub-(Tb40A)sems-dpa' gaṅ-źig zab-mo 'di-lta-bur /
/ don dam gos-pa med-pa'i chos-rnams rtogs-pa de /
/ gaṅ-na phuṅ-po med-ciṅ khams daṅ skye-mched med /
/ de-la bsod-nams stsogs (Tc20A) lta ci-ga ga-la byed // 2 //

/ dper-na 'dod-chags chos-la spyod-pa'i skyes-pa źig /
/ bud-(X55B)med dus (C12A,L'267A,N'161A) btab de daṅ ma phrad rnam rtog-pa /
/ de-yi ñin gcig sems-kyi spyod-pa ji-sñed-pa /
/ de-sñed bskal-par byaṅ-chub-sems-dpa' rjes-su rtog // 3 //

/ byaṅ-chub-sems-(Tb40B)dpa' (P12A)gaṅ-źig bskal (D'172B)maṅ bye stoṅ-du/
/ sbyin-pa sbyin daṅ tshul-khrims dri-med sruṅ byed-kyaṅ /
/ gaṅ-źig śes-rab pha-rol phyin mchog ldan-pa'i chos /
/ brjod-pa'i (X56A)legs-la sbyin daṅ khrims-kyis char mi phod// 4 //

/ byaṅ-chub-sems-dpa' gaṅ-źig śes-rab mchog bsgoms-te /
/ de-las laṅs-nas gos-pa med-pa'i chos brjod-ciṅ /
/ de-yaṅ 'gro-ba'i don-du byaṅ-chub rgyur bsṅo-na /
/ dge-ba de daṅ mñam-pa 'jig-rten (P'190A)gsum-na med // 5 //

/(Tb41A) bsod-nams de-yaṅ gsob daṅ de-bźin stoṅ-pa daṅ /
/(X56B) gsog daṅ ya-ma-brla daṅ sñiṅ-po med-par snaṅ /
/ de-ltar spyad-pa spyod-pa bde-gśegs śes-rab (Tc20B) spyod /
/ de-ltar spyod-pa bsod-nams dpag med yoṅs-su 'dzin // 6 //

/ saṅs-rgyas rab-tu bśad-pa mdzad-ciṅ gzuṅ mdzad-ciṅ /
/ chos de thams-cad (L202B) brjod-pa tsam-du zad-par śes /
/ bskal-pa bye-ba khrag-khrig maṅ-por brjod byas-kyaṅ /
/ chos-kyi dbyiṅs-la zad-pa med-ciṅ 'phel-ba med // 7 //

/ gaṅ-źig rgyal-ba'i (Tb41B) śes-rab pha-rol phyin 'di daṅ /
/ miṅ tsam zad-par yoṅs-su brjod-pa'i chos de-dag /
/ yoṅs bsṅo rlom (N'161B)sems (L'267B)med-pa'i byaṅ-chub-sems-dpa'-ni /
/ ñams-pa med-ciṅ saṅs-rgyas byaṅ-chub mchog reg 'gyur // 8 //

XIX.

/(X57B) 'bru-mar sñiṅ-po 'bar-ba phrad-pa daṅ-po-yis /
/ sñiṅ-po tshig min de med-pas-kyaṅ de mi tshig /
/ me-lce tha-ma phrad-pas sñiṅ-po tshig min-la /
/ me-lce tha-ma med-pas sñiṅ-po tshig min ltar // 1 //

/ daṅ-po'i sems-kyis byaṅ-chub mchog reg ma yin-la /
/(Tb42A,N210B) de med-pas-kyaṅ de-la reg-par nus ma yin /
/ tha-ma'i sems-kyis byaṅ-chub źi-ba thob min-la /
/ de med-pas-kyaṅ (Tc21A,X58A) de thob nus-pa ma yin-no // 2 //

/ sa-bon-las-ni myu-gu me-tog 'bras-bu 'byuṅ /
/ de-yaṅ 'gags-la de med-par-yaṅ śiṅ de med /
/ de-bźin daṅ-po'i sems-kyaṅ byaṅ-chub rgyu yin-te /
/ de-yaṅ 'gags-la de med-par-yaṅ byaṅ-chub med // 3 //

[*Note that only the bilingual Chinese blockprint text (= X) reads a verse corresponding to the Sanskrit version, XIX 4.*]

/ chu-yi tshig-pa daṅ-po chu-ṅu chu-ṅu-yaṅ /
/ rim-gyis tha-mas rdza-ma yoṅs-su gaṅ-bar byed /
/ de-bźin (Tb42B) daṅ-po'i sems-kyaṅ byaṅ-chub mchog rgyu-ste /
/ rim-gyis (D'173A)dkar-po'i yon-tan (X59A)rdzogs-pa saṅs-rgyas 'gyur // 4 // [= Skt. XIX 5]

/ stoṅ-pa mtshan med smon-pa med-par chos spyod-ciṅ /
/ mya-ṅan 'das-la mi reg mtshan-mar mi spyod-pa /
/(P'190B)dper-na mñan-pa (L203A)mkhas-pa phar 'gro tshur 'gro-yaṅ /
/ mtha' gñis mi gnas rgya-mtshor gnas-pa med-pa bźin // 5 // [= Skt. XIX 6]

/ de-ltar spyod-(X59B)pa'i byaṅ-chub-sems-dpa' 'di sñam bdag /
/ stobs bcus byaṅ-chub reg-par luṅ-bstan sñam mi sems /
/(Tb43A) 'di-la ci-yaṅ med xes byaṅ-chub skrag-pa med /
/ de-ltar spyod-pa bde-(Tc21B)gśegs śes-rab spyod-pa yin // 6 // [= Skt. XIX 7]

/ dgon-pa'i lam-na lo-ñes nad bcas 'jig-rten-rnams /
/ mthoṅ-(D11B)nas skrag-pa med-ciṅ bskal-pa'i go gyon-te /
/ phyi-ma'i mu mthar (C'205A) rtag-tu brtson-źiṅ rab śes-nas /
/ yoṅs-su skyo-ba'i yid-ni rdul tsam skyed-pa med // 7 // [= Skt. XIX 8]

XX.

/ byaṅ-chub-sems-dpa' rgyal-ba'i śes-rab spyod (X60B) byed-ciṅ /
/ phuṅ-po 'di-dag gdod-nas stoṅ-źiṅ skye med śes /
/(Tb43B) mñam-par ma bźag sems-can (N211A) khams-la sñiṅ-rje 'jug /
/ bar-skabs der-yaṅ saṅs-rgyas chos-la yoṅs mi ñams // 1 //

/ dper-na skyes-bu mkhas-pa yon-tan kun ldan-źiṅ /
/ stobs ldan mi thub sgyu-rtsal brtson byas tshul śes-la /
/ phoṅ daṅ bzo-gnas maṅ-po'i pha-rol phyin gyur-(X61A)ciṅ /
/ sgyu-ma bsgrub śes 'gro don rab-tu 'dod-pa źig // 2 //

/ pha daṅ ma daṅ chuṅ-mar bcas-par yoṅs bsdus-nas /
/ dgra byed maṅ-ba dgon-(Tb44A)pa'i (P13A) lam-du phyin-pa daṅ /
/ de-yis dpa'-źiṅ rtul-phod (Tc22A) skyes-bu maṅ sprul-nas /
/ bde-bar soṅ-źiṅ phyir-yaṅ khyim-du 'oṅ-ba ltar // 3 //

/ de-bźin de-tshe byaṅ-chub-sems-dpa' mkhas-pa-yaṅ /
/(L203B)sems-(X61B)can khams-rnams kun-la sñiṅ-rje chen-po skyed /
/ bdud bźi-dag daṅ sa gñis-las-(N'162B)kyaṅ rab 'das-nas /
/(L'268B)tiṅ-(C13A)'dzin 'di-la gnas-śiṅ byaṅ-chub reg mi byed//4//

/ mkha'-la rluṅ brten de-la chu-yi phuṅ-po brten /
/ de-la sa chen 'di brten de-la 'gro-ba brten /
/ sems-can (Tb44B) las-la spyod-pa'i rgyu-ni de-'dra-ste /
/ don de mkha'-la gnas-pa yin-par bsam-par bya // 5 //

/ de-(D'173B)bźin byaṅ-chub-sems-dpa' stoṅ-pa-ñid gnas-pa /
/ bya-ba rnam-pa sna-tshogs 'gro-la rab ston-ciṅ /
/ sems-can-rnams-kyi śes daṅ smon-lam stobs-brten-te /
/ mya-ṅan 'das-la mi reg stoṅ-par gnas-pa med // 6 //

/ gaṅ-gi tshe-na byaṅ-chub-sems-dpa' mkhas gsal-ba /
/ stoṅ-pa źi-ba'i tiṅ-'dzin (X62B) dam-pa 'di spyod-pa /
/ bar-(C'205B)skabs der-(Tc22B)ni mtshan-ma bsgom-par (Tb45A)mi bya-ste /
/ mtshan-ma med-par gnas-śiṅ źi-la rab źi spyod // 7 //

/ bar-snaṅ 'phur-ba'i bya-la gnas yod ma yin-te /
/ de-na gnas-pa ma yin sa-la ltuṅ mi 'gyur /
/ de-ltar byaṅ-chub-sems-dpa' rnam thar sgor spyod /
/ mya-ṅan 'das-la mi reg (D12A) mtshan-mar spyod ma yin // 8 //

/ dper-na 'phoṅ (X63A) bslabs skyes-bus gyen-du mda' 'phaṅs-te /
/ mda' gźan-dag-ni gcig-nas gcig-tu loṅ btags-nas /
/ sṅa-ma'i mda' de sa-la ltuṅ-ba'i skabs mi 'byed /
/(Tb45B) mi de 'dod-na mda' de sa-la ltuṅ-bar 'gyur // 9 //

/ de-ltar śes-rab pha-rol phyin-pa mchog (N'163A) spyod-pa /
/ śes-rab thabs stobs rdzu-(L'269A)'phrul-gyis-(L204A)ni rnam rgyu źiṅ/

/ de-dag dge-(X63B)ba'i rtsa-ba ji-srid ma rdzogs-pa /
/ de-(P13B)srid stoṅ-ñid dam-pa de-ni thob mi byed // 10 //

/ dper-na dge-sloṅ rdzu-'phrul stobs mchog ldan-pa źig /
/ nam-mkhar gnas-te cho-'phrul zuṅ-dag rnam-par 'phrul /
/ 'gro daṅ 'chag-pa daṅ-ni ñal daṅ 'dug-pa ston /
/ de-ni ldog-pa med-ciṅ de-la skyo-ba (Tb46A) med // 11 //

/ de-bźin byaṅ-chub-sems-dpa' mkhas-pa stoṅ gnas-śiṅ /
/ ye-śes (X64A) rdzu-'phrul pha-rol son-la gnas med rgyu /
/ 'gro-ba-dag-la bya-ba rnam-pa mtha'-yas ston /
/ bskal-pa bye-bar ñams-pa med-ciṅ skyo-ba med // 12 //

/ dper-na mi 'ga' gYaṅ-sa chen-por (C13B) 'dug byed-ciṅ /
/ lag-pa gñi-gas gdugs gñis 'dzin-ciṅ ci mi sñam /
/ dus min rluṅ-gis gYaṅ-sa chen-por phul byas-kyaṅ /
/ bdag-ñid der-ni gYaṅ-du ltuṅ-bar 'gyur-ba med // 13 //

/(Tb46B)de-bźin byaṅ-chub-sems-dpa' (P'191B)mkhas-pa sñiṅ-(N212A)rje gnas/
/ thabs daṅ śes-rab gñis-kyi gdugs-ni yoṅs bzuṅ-ste /
/ chos-rnams stoṅ-pa mtshan med smon-(D'174A)pa med rtog-ciṅ /
/ mya-ṅan 'das-la reg-pa med-la (C'206A)chos-kyaṅ mthoṅ // 14 //

/ dper-na rin-chen 'dod-pa rin-chen gliṅ soṅ-ste /
/ rin-chen rñed-nas phyir-yaṅ khyim-(X65A)du 'oṅ-bar byed /
/ ded-dpon de-ni de-na bde-bar 'tsho mod-kyi /
/ 'on-kyaṅ gñen-bśes tshogs-kyi sdug-bsṅal yid-(Tb47A)la 'byuṅ//15//

/ de-ltar stoṅ-pa-ñid-kyi rin-chen gliṅ soṅ-ste /
/ byaṅ-chub-sems-dpa' bsam-gtan dbaṅ-po stobs thob-pa /
/ mya-ṅan 'das-la reg-par mṅon-par dga' mod-kyi /
/ 'on-kyaṅ sdug-bsṅal sems-can sdug-bsṅal yid-la 'byuṅ // 16 //

/ tshoṅ-pa gaṅ-źig groṅ-khyer gaṅ-nas groṅ-rdal daṅ /
/ groṅ-du bya-ba'i phyir daṅ śes-par bya phyir 'gro /
/ der-yaṅ mi gnas rin-(P14A)chen gliṅ-du'aṅ mi gnas-la /
/ mkhas-pas khyim-du mi gnas lam-la gnas-(Tb47B)par 'gyur // 17 //

/ de-bźin raṅ-rgyal bcas-pa'i ñan-thos rnam grol sems /
/ kun-la byaṅ-chub-sems-dpa' gsal-ba mkhas-par 'gyur /
/ de-la mi gnas saṅs-rgyas ye-śes gnas ma yin /
/ lam mkhas cho-ga śes-pa 'dus byas gnas mi 'gyur // 18 //

/ gaṅ-tshe 'gro-la byams-pa rjes-su 'brel byas-nas /
/ stoṅ-pa msthan med smon-pa med-pa'i tiṅ-'dzin spyod /
/ gal-te mya-ṅan 'das-la reg byed de-la med /
/ de-ltar mod-kyi de-ni (Tb48A) 'thob-par byed-kyaṅ nus // 19 //

/(Tc24A) dper-na sprul-pa'i mi lus mi snaṅ ma yin-źiṅ /
/ de-ni miṅ-gis gdags-par bya-bar nus-pa-ste /
/ de-bźin (N212B) byaṅ-chub-sems-dpa' rnam thar sgor spyod-pa /
/ de-ni miṅ-gis gdags nus rnam-pa gźan-du min // 20 //

/ gal-te spyod-pa daṅ-ni dbaṅ-po yoṅs dris-la /
/ byaṅ-chub-sems-dpa' zab chos yoṅs-su mi ston-te /
/ stoṅ-pa mtshan-ma med daṅ mi ldog sa chos-rnams /
/(P'192A)mi 'chad de-ni luṅ-bstan ma yin (Tb48B)rig-par bya// 21 //

/ dgra-bcom sa daṅ rkyen-gyi saṅs-rgyas ye-ŝes daṅ /
/ khams (L205A) gsum-dag-la rmi-lam-na-yaṅ mi 'dod-ciṅ /
/ 'gro-la chos ston mdzad-pa'i saṅs-rgyas-rnams mthoṅ-ba /
/ de-ni mi ldog luṅ-bstan yin-par rig-par bya // 22 //

/ rmi-lam-na-ni sems-can (D'174B) ṅan-soṅ (X67B) gsum gnas mthoṅ /
/ skad cig de-la ṅan-soṅ rgyun bcad smon-lam btab /
/ bden-pa'i byin-gyi rlabs-kyis me-yi phuṅ-po ži /
/ de-ni mi ldog luṅ-bstan yin-par (Tb49A)rig-par (Tc24B)bya // 23 //

/ mi-yi 'jig-rten 'byuṅ-po'i gdon daṅ nad maṅ-ba /
/ phan daṅ sñiṅ-brtser ldan-pa'i bden-pa'i byin-gyis ži /
/ 'on-kyaṅ (P14B) rlom-sems med-ciṅ ṅa-rgyal skye med-pa /
/ de-ni (X68A) mi ldog luṅ-bstan yin-par rig-par bya // 24 //

## XXI.

/ byaṅ-chub-sems-dpa' bdag luṅ-bstan sñam rlom-sems-sam /
/ bden-pa'i byin-gyi rlabs-kyis rnam-par 'grub byed-dam /
/ gal-te pha-rol luṅ-bstan yin sñam sems gyur-na /
/ rlom-sems gnas-pa (Tb49B) de-ni blo chuṅ rig-par bya // 1 //

/ miṅ-gi gži-las bdud-ni ñe-bar 'oṅs gyur-nas /
/ 'di-skad smras-te 'di-ni khyod daṅ pha ma daṅ /
/ khyod-kyi bdun mes rgyud-kyi bar-gyi miṅ yin-(L'270B)žiṅ /
/ 'di-ni saṅs-rgyas 'gyur-ba'i khyod-kyi miṅ yin že'am // 2 //

/(N'164B) sbyaṅs sdom ci-'dra brtson-pa rnal-'byor ldan de-la /
/(N213A) khyod sṅon yon-tan tshul-yaṅ 'di žes brjod byed-de /
/ de-skad gaṅ thos rlom-sems byaṅ-chub-sems-dpa'-ni /
/ bdud-kyis yoṅs-su bslaṅ-žiṅ blo chuṅ (L205B) rig-par bya // 3 //

/ rab-tu (Tb50A) dben-pa'i groṅ daṅ-khyer ri sul daṅ /
/ dgon-pa dben-pa nags-khrod rab-tu sten byed-ciṅ /
/ bdag stod gžan-la smod-(X69B)pa'i byaṅ-chub-sems-dpa'-ni /
/ bdud-kyis yoṅs-su bslaṅ-žiṅ blo chuṅ rig-par bya // 4 //

/ rtag-tu groṅ daṅ yul-'khor groṅ-rdal gnas byed-ciṅ /
/ byaṅ-chub ldan-pa sems-can smin byed ma (P'192B) gtogs-par /
/ de-na dgra-bcom raṅ-rgyal-dag-la 'dod med-pa /
/ 'di-ni bde-bar gŝegs-kyi sras-kyi dben-par gsuṅs // 5 //

/(Tb50B) gaṅ-žig dpag-tshad lṅa brgya yod-pa'i ri-yi sul /
/(X70A) sbrul-gyis gaṅ-bar lo maṅ bye-bar gnas byed-kyaṅ /
/ dben-pa 'di mi ŝes-pa'i byaṅ-chub-sems-dpa' de /
/ lhag-pa'i ṅa-rgyal rñed-nas 'dre-bar gnas-pa yin // 6 //

/ byaṅ-chub-sems-dpa' 'gro-ba'i don brtson bsam-gtan daṅ /
/(P15A) stobs daṅ dbaṅ-po rnam thar tiṅ-'dzin thob-rnams-la /
/ 'di-ni dgon dben spyod-pa min (D'175A) sñam sems skyed-pa /
/ 'di-ni dgon-pa'i spyod-yul min źes (Tb51A) rgyal-bas gsuṅs // 7 //

/ gaṅ-źig groṅ-ṅam 'on-te dgon-par (L'271A) gnas-kyaṅ-ruṅ /
/ theg-pa gñis-kyi sems bral (N'165A) byaṅ-chub mchog ṅes-na /
/ 'di-ni 'gro don źugs-pa-rnams-kyi dben-pa-ste /
/ byaṅ-chub-sems-dpa' de-ni bdag ñams gźan ma yin // 8 //

XXII.

/ de-lta-bas-na mkhas-pas ṅa-rgyal bcom byas-te /
/ bsam-pa drag-pos byaṅ-chub dam-pa tshol-ba-na /
/(D13B) nad-pa śin-tu gso phyir sman-pa bsten-(L206A)pa ltar /
/ gYel-ba med-par dge-ba'i bśes-gñen bsten-par bya // 1 //

/(Tb51B) saṅs-rgyas byaṅ-chub mchog źugs byaṅ-chub-sems-dpa' daṅ /
/(X71B) pha-rol phyin daṅ mtshuṅs-pa dge-ba'i bśes-su bstan /
/ de-dag nan-tan sa 'di rjes-su ston-pa yin /
/ rnam-pa gñis-kyis saṅs-rgyas byaṅ-chub rjes-su rtogs // 2 //

/(Tc26A) rgyal-ba 'das daṅ ma byon phyogs bcu gaṅ bźugs-pa /
/ kun lam pha-rol phyin-pa 'di yin gźan ma yin /
/ pha-rol phyin 'di byaṅ-chub mchog-la źugs-rnams-kyi /
/ gsal daṅ sgron daṅ snaṅ (X72A) daṅ ston-pa yin źes (Tb52A)bstan/3/

/ ji-ltar śes-rab pha-rol phyin-pa'i mtshan-gyis (C'207B) stoṅ /
/ de-ltar mtshan daṅ chos 'di thams-cad-sus śes-śiṅ /
/ chos-rnams stoṅ-źiṅ mtshan-ñid med-par rab śes-na /
/ de-ltar spyod-pa bde-gśegs śes-rab spyod-pa yin // 4 //

/(P'193A) sems-can zas daṅ 'dod-la yoṅs-su rtog byed-(C15A)ciṅ /
/ 'khor-bar chags-pa'i yid (X72B) daṅ (L'271B) ldan-(N'165B)rnams rtag-tu 'khor /
/ bdag daṅ bdag-gi chos gñis yod min stoṅ-pa-ste /
/ byis-pa-rnams-kyis bdag-la nam-mkha'i mdud (Tb52B)'di bciṅs//5 //

/(P15B) dper-na dogs-pas 'du-śes-kyis-ni dug laṅs-pa /
/ dug de lto-bar soṅ-ba ma yin 'on-kyaṅ 'gyel /
/ de-ltar byis-pa bdag daṅ bdag-gir khas blaṅs-pa /
/ 'du-śes skyes-pas rtag-tu ji-yaṅ yod ma yin // 6 //

/ ji-(X73A)ltar 'dzin-pa de-ltar kun-nas ñon-moṅs (L206B) bstan /
/ bdag daṅ bdag-gir (Tc26B) mi dmigs rnam-par dag-par gsuṅs /
/ 'di-la ñon-moṅs rnam dag gaṅ-yaṅ yod min-par /
/ byaṅ-chub-(D'175B)sems-dpa' śes-rab pha-rol phyin-pa rtogs // 7 //

/(Tb53A,C15A) 'dzam gliṅ ma-lus-dag-na sems-can ji-sñed-pa /
/ de-dag thams-cad byaṅ-chub mchog-tu sems (X73B) bskyed-nas /

/ lo stoń bye-ba mań-por sbyin-pa byin byas-la /
/ kun-kyań 'gro-ba'i don-phyir byań-chub rgyur sṅo-yań // 8 //

/ gań-źig śes-rab pha-rol phyin mchog mṅon brtson-pa /
/ tha-na ñi-ma gcig-cig rjes-su 'thun byed-pa /
/ bsod-nams de-la sbyin-pa'i phuń-pos char mi phod /
/ de-phyir gYel med rtag-tu śes-rab 'jug-par bya // 9 //

/ śes-rab pha-rol phyin mchog (Tb53B) spyod-pa'i rnal-(X74A)'byor-pa /
/ sñiń-rje chen-po skyed-ciń sems-can 'du-śes med /
/ de-tshe mkhas-pa 'gro-ba kun-gyi sbyin gnas 'gyur /
/ rtag-tu yul-'khor bsod-(N'166A)sñoms don yod yońs-su spyod // 10 //

/ lha mi sems-can riń-nas ṅan-soń gsum 'brel-ba /
/ yońs-su dgrol-bar 'dod-pa'i byań-chub-sems-dpa' de /
/ śes-rab pha-rol phyin-la ñin mtsnan brtson byed-pa /
/(Tc27A) lam yańs 'di-ni sems-can khams-kyi 'bab-stebs (Tb54A)ston/11/

/ mi źig sṅon-chad ma rñed-pa-yi rin-chen mchog /
/ dus gźan źig-na rñed-par gyur-te dga'-ba-las /
/ rñed ma thag-tu stor-te bag-med gyur-pas-na /
/(P16A) stor-nas sdug-bsṅal rtag-tu rin-chen mṅon-du 'dod // 12 //

/(C15B) de-ltar byań-chub mchog (P'193B) źugs rin-chen mtshuńs-pa-yi /
/ śes-rab pha-rol phyin-(L207A)la rnal-'byor dor mi bya /
/ rin-chen (N214B) rñed-nas 'dzin-par byed-ciń mi phyed-na /
/ rjes-su 'brel-bar byed-ciń myur-du dbań-du 'gyur // 13 //

XXIII.

/ 'od-zer 'phro-(Tb54B)bas mun-pas dkrigs-pa'i mun snag kun /
/ sel-bar byed-ciń sprin med mkha'-la gñi śar-na /
/ srog-chags 'byuń-po srin-bu me-khyer thams-cad dań /
/ skar-ma'i tshogs dań zla-ba'i 'od kun zil-gyis non // 1 //

/ de-ltar śes-rab pha-rol phyin-pa mchog spyod-pa'i /
/ byań-chub-sems-dpa' mkhas-pa lta thibs sel byed-ciń /
/ 'gro-ba kun dań dgra-bcom (Tc27B) rań-rgyal zil-gyis non /
/ byań-chub-sems-dpa' stoń-pa mtshan med yańs spyad-phyir // 2 //

/(Tb55A) dper-na (N'166B) rgyal-po'i bu źig nor gtoń don 'dod-pa /
/ kun-gyi gtso-bor (L'272B)gyur-te mṅon-par 'gro bya (D'176A)'os /
/ 'di-ni da-lta-na-yań sems-can dga' byed-na /
/ thabs thob rgyal-srid gnas-par gyur-nas smos ci dgos // 3 //

/ de-ltar śes-rab spyod mkhas byań-chub-sems-dpa'-yań /
/ bdud-rtsi sbyin-par byed-ciń (X76B) lha dań mi-rnams dga' /
/ 'di-ni da-lta-na-yań sems-can mań phan brtson /
/ chos-kyi rgyal-por gnas-(D14B)par gyur-nas smos ci dgos // 4 //

## XXIV.

/ de-yi tshe-na bdud-(Tb55B)ni zug-rṅu ldan-par 'gyur /
/ mya-ṅan sdug-bsṅal ñams-thag mthu chuṅ yid mi bde /
/ ci-ltar byaṅ-chub-sems-(C'208B)dpa' 'di yid nur 'gyur źes /
/ 'jigs-pa bstan phyir phyogs-rnams sreg-ciṅ skar-mda' gtoṅ // 1 //

/(L207B) gaṅ-tshe mkhas-pa de-dag bsam-pa rab ldan-źiṅ /
/(N215A,P16B) ñin mtshan śes-rab pha-rol phyin-pa mchog don lta /
/(Tc28A) rtag-tu lus daṅ sems-ni mtha' 'gro bya ltar (X77B) gyur /
/ de-la nag-po'i rtsa-lag glags rñed ga-la 'gyur // 2 //

/(Tb56A) gaṅ-tshe byaṅ-chub-sems-dpa' 'thab daṅ rtsod gyur-ciṅ /
/ phan-tshun mi 'thun khros-pa'i sems daṅ ldan gyur-pa /
/ de-yi tshe-na bdud-kyi dga'-źiṅ mgu-bar 'gyur /
/ de gñis (C16A) rgyal-ba'i ye-śes-las-ni riṅ-du 'gyur // 3 //

/ de gñis riṅ-(P'194A)du 'gyur-źiṅ śa-za 'dra-bar 'gyur /
/ de gñis raṅ-gi dam-bcas ñams-par byed-par (N'167A) 'gyur /
/ sdaṅ-źiṅ bzod daṅ bral-la byaṅ-chub ga-la yod /
/ de-na bdud-rnams dga'-źiṅ bdud-la thub mi 'gyur // 4 //

/(L'273A)luṅ-bstan ma (Tb56B)thob byaṅ-chub-sems-dpa' la-la-źig /
/ luṅ-bstan thob-la sems khros rtsod-pa rtsom byed-na /
/ tha-ba skyom ldan sems-kyi skad cig ji-sñed-pa /
/ de-sñed bskal-par phyir-yaṅ go-cha bgo dgos-so // 5 //

/ saṅs-rgyas bzod-pa'i pha-rol phyin-pas byaṅ-chub reg /
/ de sñam sems-śiṅ ma legs sñam-pa'i (Tc28B) blo skyed-de /
/ so-sor 'chags-par byed-ciṅ phyir-yaṅ sdom byed-la /
/ bral-bar gyur-pa de-ni saṅs-rgyas chos 'dir slob // 6 //

## XXV.

/ gaṅ-(Tb57A)źig slob-la bslab-pa gaṅ-du'aṅ spros med-ciṅ /
/ slob-pa-po daṅ bslab-pa'i chos-rnams mi dmigs-la /
/ bslab (D'176B) daṅ bslab-pa ma yin 'di gñis mi rtog-pa /
/ de-ltar gaṅ slob de-ni saṅs-rgyas chos 'dir (L208A) slob // 1 //

/ byaṅ-chub-(N215B)sems-(X79B)dpa' gaṅ-źig bslab 'di de-ltar śes /
/ de-ni bslab ñams tshul-khrims 'chal-bar gźar mi 'gyur /
/ de-ni mñes-par byed-ciṅ saṅs-rgyas chos 'dir slob /
/ bslab-la mkhas-śiṅ dmigs-pa med-par gyur-(Tb57B)pas slob // 2 //

/ mkhas-pa 'od-byed-rnams-kyi (D15A) śes-rab de-ltar slob /
/ dge-ba ma yin (P17A) sems gcig-tsam-yaṅ skyed mi byed /
/(X80A) ñi-ma bar-snaṅ-la-ni 'gro-bar byed-pa-na /
/ 'od-zer rnam-pas mdun-na mun-pa mi gnas bźin // 3 //

/ śes-rab pha-rol phyin-la bslab-pa byas-rnams-kyi /
/ pha-rol phyin-(Tc29A)pa thams-cad 'dir-ni 'dus-par 'gyur /

/(L'273B) 'jig-tshogs lta-bar lta-ba drug-cu-gñis 'dus ltar /
/ de-bźin pha-rol phyin-pa 'di-dag 'dus-par gsuṅs // 4 //

/(Tb58A) dper-na srog-gi (X80B) dbaṅ-po 'gags-na dbaṅ-po gźan /
/ gaṅ-dag ji-sñed yod-pa zad-par 'gags-par 'gyur /
/ de-ltar śes-rab spyod-pa mkhas-pa mchog-rnams-kyi /
/ pha-rol phyin-pa thams-cad 'dir-ni 'dus-par gsuṅs // 5 //

/ byaṅ-(P'194B)chub-sems-dpa' gaṅ-dag ñan-thos yon-tan daṅ /
/ raṅ-rgyal yon-tan kun-la bslabs-par gyur-pa-rnams /
/ de-dag de-la mi gnas 'dod-pa mi skyed-de /
/ 'di-ni bdag-(X81A)gis bslab bya yin sñam de-phyir slob // 6 //

XXVI.

/ mi ldog byaṅ-chub (Tb58B) mchog-la rab-tu źugs-pa-yi /
/ sems bskyed-pa-la bsam-pa thag-pas yi-(L208B)raṅ-ba /
/ stoṅ gsum ri-rab sraṅ-la gcal-na tshad gzuṅ ruṅ /
/(X81B) rjes-su yi-raṅ dge-ba de-ni de-lta min // 1 //

/ dge-ba (Tc29B) don gñer thar 'dod sems-can ji-sñed-pa /
/ kun-gyi bsod-nams phuṅ-po-la-yaṅ yi-raṅ 'gyur /
/(N216A) de-phyir de-dag rgyal-ba'i yon-tan thob gyur-nas /
/ sdug-bsṅal zad-par bya phyir 'jig-rten chos sbyin byed // 2 //

/ byaṅ-chub-sems-dpa' (N'168A)gaṅ-źig mi (Tb59A)rtog chos-rnams kun /
/ stoṅ daṅ mtshan-ma med daṅ spros med yoṅs (C'209B) śes-pa /
/ śes-rab bsam-pa thag-pas byaṅ-chub mi tshol-ba /
/ rnal-'byor-pa de śes-rab pha-rol phyin mchog (D'177A)brtson//3//

/ nam-mkha'i khams daṅ mkha' gñis tha-dad gyur-du-ni /
/ de daṅ de-la gaṅ-phyir cis-kyaṅ bye-brag med /
/ de-bźin śes-rab (P17B) spyod mkhas byaṅ-chub-sems-dpa'-yaṅ /
/ nam-mkha' mtshuṅs-śiṅ 'dra-bar ñe-bar źi-bar spyod // 4 //

/(Tb59B) skye-bo'i dbus-na sgyu-(X82B)ma'i skyes-bu 'di sñam-du /
/ skye-bo 'di-dag mgu bya mi sems bya-ba byed /
/ gYo-sgyu sna-tshogs rab-(Tc30A)tu ston-pa de-yaṅ mthoṅ /
/ 'on-kyaṅ de-la lus med sems med miṅ-yaṅ med // 5 //

/ de-bźin śes-rab spyod-pa nams-kyaṅ 'di sñam-du /
/ byaṅ-chub rtogs-nas 'gro-ba yoṅs-su dgrol mi sems /
/ raṅ-gi skye-ba bya-ba sna-tshogs ldan-pa'aṅ ston /
/ sgyu-ma lta-bur rnam-par rtog-pa med-par spyod // 6 //

/ dper-na saṅs-rgyas sprul-pa saṅs-rgyas (Tb60A) mdzad-pa byed /
/ de-ni ci-źig bya sñam-du-yaṅ sems mi byed /
/ de-bźin śes-(L209A)rab (C17A)spyod mkhas byaṅ-chub-sems-dpa'-yaṅ /
/ sprul-pa sgyu-ma bźin-du bya-ba thams-cad ston // 7 //

/ śiṅ-(X83B)mkhan mkhas-pas rtse-phyir śiṅ-gi 'khrul-'khor byas /
/ skyes-pa bud-med 'dra de bya-ba (P'195A)thams-cad (N'168B)byed /
/ de-bźin śes-rab spyod mkhas byaṅ-chub-sems-dpa'-yaṅ /
/ rnam-par mi rtog ye-śes bya-ba thams-cad byed // 8 //

XXVII.

/ de-ltar spyod (N216B) mkhas-rnams-la lha tshogs maṅ-po-dag /
/(Tb60B) thal-mo sbyar-ba btud-ciṅ phyag-kyaṅ 'tshal-bar byed /
/ phyogs bcu'i 'jig-(Tc30B)rten khams-kyi saṅs-rgyas ji-sñed-kyaṅ /
/ yon-tan bsṅags-pa'i 'phreṅ-ba yoṅs-su brjod-(L'274B)pa mdzad //1//

/ gaṅgā'i kluṅ-gi bye sñed źiṅ-na sems-can-rnams /
/ de kun bdud-du gyur-pas yoṅs-su brtag bzuṅ-ste /
/ spu ñag re-re ji-sñed de-sñed sprul byas-kyaṅ /
/ de-dag kun-gyis mkhas-la bar-(C'210A)chad bya mi nus // 2 //

/ rnam bźis byaṅ-chub-sems-dpa' mkhas-pa stobs ldan-pa /
/ thub-par (Tb61A) dka'-źiṅ bdud bźis bskyod-par mi nus-te /
/ stoṅ-par gnas daṅ sems-can yoṅs-su mi gtoṅ daṅ /
/ ji-skad smra daṅ sñiṅ-rjes sems-can bde 'jog-pa'o // 3 //

/ de-bźin-gśegs yum śes-rab pha-rol phyin-pa 'di /
/(P18A) 'chad tshe byaṅ-chub-sems-dpa' gaṅ-źig mos byed-ciṅ /
/(D'177B) bsam-pa thag-pas bsgrub-par mṅon-du brtson byed-la /
/ thams-cad mkhyen-pa-ñid-phyir mṅon źugs rig-par bya // 4 //

/ de-bźin-ñid-kyi gnas-su chos dbyiṅs ñer (Tb61B) mi 'gro /
/ dper-na bar-snaṅ sprin-ni gnas med (Tc31A) gnas-pa bźin /
/ rigs-sṅags 'chaṅ-ba dmigs med nags sems mkha' 'gro tshe /
/ me-tog śiṅ-phyir sṅags-kyi stobs-kyi byin rlabs byed // 5 //

/ de-ltar spyod-pa byaṅ-chub-sems-dpa' mkhas gsal-ba /
/ rtogs-par byed daṅ saṅs-rgyas chos-rnams dmigs mi 'gyur /
/(C17B) 'chad-par byed daṅ chos-ñid mthoṅ-ba mi dmigs-pa /
/ 'di-ni źi 'dod yon-tan dga'-ba'i gnas-pa yin // 6 //

/(Tb62A)de-bźin-gśegs-kyi dgra-bcom rnam thar ma gtogs-(N217A)par /
/ gnas-pa (L'275A) 'di-ni ñan-thos raṅ-rgyal bcas-pa-yi /
/ gnas-pa źi-ba'i tiṅ-'dzin rab źi bde ldan-pa /
/ ji-sñed kun-gyi mchog daṅ goṅ-na med-pa yin // 7 //

/ 'dab-chags nam-mkhar gnas-kyaṅ ltuṅ-bar 'gyur ma yin /
/ ña-ni chu-la gnas-kyaṅ 'tshubs-te 'chi-ba med /
/ de-ltar byaṅ-(X86B)chub-sems-dpa' bsam-gtan stobs-dag-gi /
/ pha-rol son-pa stoṅ gnas mya-ṅan 'da' mi 'gyur // 8 //

/ sems-(Tb62B)can (Tc31B) kun-gyi yon-tan mchog 'gro gaṅ 'dod-pas /
/ chos-kyi sbyin-pa rab mchog dam-pa sbyin bya-źiṅ /
/ phan mdzad-rnams-kyi gnas-pa mchog 'dir sten cig daṅ /
/ saṅs-rgyas ye-śes mchog-tu rmad-byuṅ mchog reg 'gyur // 9 //

XXVIII.

/ bslab-pa 'di-ni 'dren-pas bslab-pa yoṅs brjod-pa /
/ bslab-pa ji-sñed kun-gyi mchog daṅ goṅ-na med /
/ mkhas-pa gaṅ-źig bslab kun pha-rol 'gro 'dod-pas /
/(L210A) saṅs-rgyas (N'169B) bslab-pa śes-rab (X87B) pha-rol phyin 'di slobs // 1 //

/ chos mdzod (Tb63A) dam-pa 'di-ni gter-gyi phul-tu byuṅ /
/ 'jig-rten-dag-na saṅs-rgyas rigs-kyi bde skyid mdzod /
/ 'das daṅ ma byon phyogs bcu'i 'jig-rten mgon-po-rnams /
/ de-dag 'di-las byuṅ-ste chos dbyiṅs zad mi 'gyur // 2 //

/ śiṅ daṅ 'bras-bu me-tog nags-tshal ji-sñed-pa /
/ de-dag thams-cad sa-las yaṅ-dag 'byuṅ-źiṅ 'thon /
/(X88A) 'on-kyaṅ sa-la zad-pa (D'178A,L'275B)med-(Tc32A)ciṅ 'phel-ba med /
/ skyo-ba med-ciṅ yoṅs-su mi ñams rnam rtog med // 3 //

/ saṅs-rgyas ñan-thos raṅ-rgyal (Tb63B) bcas-pa ji-sñed daṅ /
/ 'jig-rten-dag-na lha daṅ bde skyid chos yod-pa /
/ de kun śes-rab pha-rol phyin-pa mchog-las byuṅ /
/ śes-rab nams-kyaṅ zad-pa med-ciṅ 'phel-ba med // 4 //

/ sems-(C18A)can tha-(D16B)ma 'briṅ daṅ mchog gyur ji-sñed-pa /
/ de kun ma (X88B) rig-las byuṅ bde-bar gśegs-pas gsuṅs /
/ rkyen-rnams tshogs-nas sdug-bsṅal 'khrul-'khor rab-tu 'byuṅ /
/ 'khrul-'khor zad-pa med-ciṅ ma rig 'phel-ba med // 5 //

/ ye-śes tshul sgo thabs-(Tb64A)kyi rtsa-ba ji-sñed-pa /
/ de kun śes-rab pha-rol phyin-pa mchog-las byuṅ /
/ rkyen-rnams tshogs-nas las-kyi 'khrul-'khor rab-tu 'byuṅ /
/ śes-rab pha-rol (X89A) phyin-la zad-pa'am 'phel-ba med // 6 //

/ byaṅ-chub-sems-dpa' (N'170A) gaṅ-źig rten-ciṅ 'brel 'byuṅ 'di /
/ śes-rab-kyis-ni 'byuṅ med zad med rtogs-pa de /
/ dper-na sprin-gyi sgrib med ñi-ma'i 'od-zer ltar /
/ ma rig 'gebs-pa bstsal-nas (C'211A) raṅ-byuṅ 'thob-par 'gyur//7//

XXIX.

/ mthu chen ldan-pa-(Tb64B)dag-ni bsam-gtan (Tc32B) bźir gnas-kyaṅ /
/ rten-par byed-pa ma yin gnas-par byed-pa med /
/ 'on-kyaṅ bsam-gtan bźi-po 'di-dag rten yin-źiṅ /
/ thob-par gyur-nas byaṅ-chub dam-pa mchog-kyaṅ thob // 1 //

/ śes-rab mchog thob-pa-dag bsam-gtan gnas-pa myoṅ /
/ gzugs (L'276A)med tiṅ-'dzin dam-pa bźi-po-rnams-kyaṅ myoṅ /
/ bsam-gtan 'di-dag byaṅ-chub mchog-la phan byed 'gyur /
/ byaṅ-chub-sems-dpa' zag-pa zad (Tb65A)phyir slob-pa min // 2 //

/ bsam-pa ji-bźin 'dod-pa'i khams-su yaṅ skyes-te /
/ 'di-ni (N218A) yon-tan stobs-pa'i ṅo-mtshar rmad-byuṅ yin /

/(X90B) bsam-gtan tiṅ-'dzin-la gnas-nas mtshan-ma med /
/ de-la gnas-rnams gal-te lus-ni źig gyur-na // 3 //

/ dper-na 'dzam-gliṅ mi źig sṅon-chad ma rñed-pa'i /
/ lha-yul lha-yi khaṅ-pa dam rñed gyur-ciṅ /
/ mthoṅ-nas de-yis der-ni yul-rnams yoṅs bzuṅ-la /
/ de-na gnas-par mi byed phyir-(Tb65B)yaṅ 'oṅ-ba ltar // 4 //

/(D'178B)de-bźin byaṅ-chub-sems-dpa' yon-tan mchog (N'170B)'chaṅ-ba /
/ rnal-'byor brtson-pa bsam-gtan tiṅ-ṅe-'dzin gnas-kyaṅ /
/ phyir-(Tc33A)yaṅ 'dod-pa'i khams-su gnas-te gos-pa med /
/ chu-la padma bźin-du byas-pa'i chos mi gnas // 5 //

/ sems-can yoṅs-su smin-par bya daṅ źiṅ sbyaṅ daṅ /
/ pha-rol phyin 'di yoṅs rdzogs bya-ba ma gtogs-par /
/ bdag-ñid chen-po gzugs med khams-su skye mi byed /
/(Tb66A)byaṅ-chub yon-tan pha-rol phyin-rnams ñams-par 'gyur //6//

/ dper-na mi źig rin-chen gter-rnams rñed gyur-kyaṅ /
/ de-la 'dod-pa'i blo-ni bskyed-par ma byas-la /
/ des-kyaṅ dus gźan źig-na de-dag yoṅs (L'276B) blaṅs-śiṅ /
/(X92A)blaṅs-nas (C'211B)khyim-du bcug-ste chags-par byed-pa ltar/7/

/ de-bźin byaṅ-chub-sems-dpa' mkhas-pa bsam-gtan bźi /
/ tiṅ-'dzin źi-ba dga' bde sbyin byed thob gyur-la /
/ bsam-gtan bde daṅ bsam-(Tb66B)gtan (P'196B)tiṅ-'dzin thob (N218B)btaṅ-ste/
/ 'gro-la sñiṅ-brtser ldan-pa phyir-yaṅ 'dod khams 'jug // 8 //

/ gal-te byaṅ-chub-sems-(X92B)dpa' tiṅ-'dzin bsam-gtan gnas /
/ dgra-bcom raṅ-rgyal theg-par 'dod-(Tc33B)pa'i blo skyed-na /
/ mñam-par ma bźag rgod-ciṅ sems gYeṅs gyur-pa-ste /
/ saṅs-rgyas yon-tan yoṅs ñams-(P19B)pa gru źig bźin // 9 //

/ gźan-yaṅ gzugs daṅ sgra daṅ de-bźin dri daṅ ro /
/ reg daṅ (Tb67A,N'171A)'dod-pa'i yon-tan lṅa-la brtson gyur-kyaṅ /
/ dgra-(X93A)bcom raṅ-rgyal theg bral byaṅ-chub sems dga'-na /
/ dpa'-bo rtag-tu mñam bźag yin-par śes-par bya // 10 //

/ sems-can rnam dag sems-can gaṅ-zad gźan-gyi phyir /
/ brtson-'grus pha-rol phyin-la brtson-źiṅ rnam-par rgyu /
/(L211B) dper-na bran-mo bum-thogs dbaṅ med rje-bo'i dbaṅ /
/ de-bźin dpa'-rnams sems-can-rnams-kyi dbaṅ-gis (X93B) 'gro// 11 //

/ spyo-ba byas-sam 'on-te (Tb67B)rtag-tu brdebs-kyaṅ-ruṅ /
/ bran-mo rje-bo-la-ni 'khyal-ba'i tshig mi smra /
/ bdag-la des-ni gnod-pa byas-su 'oṅ sñam-nas /
/ śin-tu skrag-pa'i yid-kyis 'jigs-pas zil-gyis gnon // 12 //

/ de-bźin byaṅ-(L'277A)chub ched-du (D'179A)byaṅ-chub mchog źugs-(C19A)pa/
/ 'gro-ba kun-la bran gyur bźin-(Tc34A)du gnas-par bya /
/ luṅ-gi yon-tan rtogs-pa yoṅs-su rdzogs mi byed /
/ śiṅ-las me byuṅ-ba-yis śiṅ de sreg-pa bźin // 13 //

/ bdag-gi bde-ba btaṅ-nas (Tb68A) re-ba med sems-kyis /
/ sems-can gźan-gyi dgos-la ñin mtshan mṅon-par (N219A) brtson /
/ bu gcig-pa-la ma-ni (D17B) rim-gro byed-pa-na /
/ bsam-pa thag-pas byed-de skyo med gnas-pa bźin // 14 //

XXX.

/(C'212A)sems-can don (N'171B)daṅ źiṅ sbyoṅ brtson-pa'i rnal-'byor-pa /
/ gaṅ-źig byaṅ-chub-sems-dpa'i spyad-pa spyod sems-śiṅ /
/ skyo-ba'i blo-ni rdul tsam skye-bar mi 'gyur-ba /
/ de-ni gYel med brtson-'grus pha-rol phyin-pa brtson // 1 //

/(Tb68B) byaṅ-chub-sems-dpa' mi mkhas bskal-pa bye 'graṅs-la /
/ gal-te riṅ-bar 'du-śes sdug-bsṅal byaṅ-chub sgrub /
/ chos sgrub byed-pa'i tshe-na riṅ-du sdug-bsṅal 'gyur /
/ de-tshe brtson-'grus (P'197A)pha-rol phyin ñams le-lo-can // 2 //

/ źi-ba bla-na med-pa thob-par bya sñam-ste /
/ byaṅ-chub mchog-tu (Tc34B) sems bskyed thog-mar bskyed byas-nas /
/ ñin daṅ mtshan-du de-la yid gcig gnas byed-pa /
/ mkhas-pa gsal-ba brtson-'grus (Tb69A)brtsams-par rig-par bya //3//

/ gal-te la-la 'di-skad ri-rab ri bśig-la /
/ phyi-nas byaṅ-chub mchog (L'277B) thob bya źes smras-pa-las /
/ gal-te skyo-ba'i blo skyes tshad-du byed 'gyur-na /
/ de-tshe byaṅ-chub-sems-dpa' le-lo rñed-par 'gyur // 4 //

/ ci-ste cuṅ-zad 'di-lta ci smos blo skyes-te /
/ skad cig tsam-la ri-rab thal-bar klag sñam-pa /
/ byaṅ-chub-sems-dpa' mkhas-pa brtson-'grus brtsams-pa-ste /
/ riṅ-por mi thogs 'dren-pa'i byaṅ-chub mchog (Tb69B)thob 'gyur/5/

/ yoṅs-su smin-par byas-la 'gro-ba'i don bya źes /
/(N219B) gal-te lus daṅ ṅag daṅ yid-kyis brtson byed-na /
/ bdag-tu 'du-śes gnas-pa (C19B) le-lo rñed 'gyur-te /
/ thams-cad mkhyen-pa-ñid-las riṅ 'gyur gnam sa bźin // 6 //

/ gaṅ-tshe lus daṅ sems daṅ sems-can 'du-śes med /
/ 'du-śes rnam-par log-nas chos gñis mi spyod-pa /
/ 'di-ni byaṅ-chub ma ñams mchog źi tshol-ba-yi /
/ brtson-(Tb70A)'grus pha-rol phyin ces phan-pa mdzad-pas gsuṅs/7/

/ gźan-las ṅan-du rjod-pa'i tshig rtsub thos gyur-na /
/ sus smra sus thos ga-la su-yi gaṅ-taṅ źes /
/ ma-lus mgu byed byaṅ-chub-sems-(C'212B)dpa' mkhas-pa de /
/ bzod-pa'i pha-rol phyin (L212B)daṅ ldan-pa mdzaṅs-pa yin // 8 //

/ byaṅ-chub-sems-dpa' gaṅ-źig bzod-pa'i legs chos ldan /
/ gaṅ-źig stoṅ gsum rin-(X97B)chen bkaṅ-ste 'jig-rten khams /
/ saṅs-rgyas-rnams daṅ dgra-bcom raṅ-rgyal (Tb70B) phul byas-pa /
/ sbyin-pa'i (L'278A)phuṅ-pos de-yi bsod-nams char mi phod // 9 //

/ bzod-la gnas-pa'i lus-ni yoṅs-su dag 'gyur-te /
/ sum-cu-rtsa-gñis mtshan daṅ mthu-stobs pha mtha'-yas /
/(P20B) sems-can-rnams-la dad-pa'i chos rab sgrogs-par byed /
/ bzod-pa mkhas-la 'jig-rten 'di-na dga'-bar 'gyur // 10 //

/ gal-te sems-can la-las tsandan sñim bkaṅ-ste /
/ bla-ma phaṅs-pas byaṅ-chub-sems-dpa' 'thor-ba daṅ /
/ gźan źig (Tb71A,N'172B) me-mdag mgo-la 'thor byed gñi-ga-la /
/ de-yis mñam-źiṅ sñoms-pa'i yid-ni bskyed-par bya // 11 //

/ byaṅ-chub-sems-dpa' mkhas-pas de-ltar (X98B) bzod byas-(N220A)nas /
/ sems bskyed de-ni byaṅ-chub mchog-tu yoṅs bsṅos-na /
/ dpa'-bo bzod-pas 'jig-rten kun-na dgra-bcom daṅ /
/ raṅ-rgyal sems-can khams-kyi bzod kun zil-gyis non // 12 //

/ bzod byed 'di sñam-du yaṅ sems-ni bskyed bya-ste /
/ sems-dmyal dud-'gro'i gśin-rje'i 'jig-rten (Tb71B)sdug-bsṅal maṅ/
/ 'dod-pa'i yon-(X99A)tan rgyu-yis mi 'dod gnod myoṅ-na /
/ byaṅ-chub ched-du ci-phyir da bzod mi bya sñam // 13 //

/ lcag (C20A) dbyig mtshon daṅ gsad daṅ bciṅ daṅ brdeg-pa daṅ /
/ mgo gcod-pa daṅ rna-ba rkaṅ-lag sna gcod daṅ /
/ 'jig-rten sdug-(L213A)bsṅal ji-sñed bdag-gis bzod sñam-pa /
/ byaṅ-chub-sems-dpa' bzod-pa'i pha-rol phyin-la (X99B) gnas //14//

## XXXI.

/ źi-ba 'dod-pa-rnams-ni khrims-kyis byuṅ-ba yin /
/ stobs (D'180A)bcu'i spyod-(Tb72A)yul gnas-śiṅ tshul-khrims ñams-pa med /
/(C'213A) sdom-pa'i bya-ba ji-sñed kun-gyi rjes-su 'jug /
/ sems-can kun-la (X100A)phan phyir de-yaṅ byaṅ-chub sṅo // 1 //

/ gal-te raṅ-rgyal dgra-bcom byaṅ-chub 'dod skyed-na /
/ tshul-khrims 'chal-ciṅ mi mkhas de-yi spyod-pa ñams /
/ ji-ste byaṅ-chub źi-ba mchog-tu yoṅs (D18B) sṅo-na /
/ 'dod (N'173A)yon brtson-yaṅ tshul-khrims pha-rol phyin-la gnas/2/

/ chos gaṅ des-pa'i byaṅ-chub yon-tan 'byuṅ byed-pa /
/ de-ni yon-tan chos don ldan-pa'i (Tb72B) tshul-khrims yin /
/(P21A) chos gaṅ phan byed-rnams-kyi byaṅ-chub yoṅs ñams-pa /
/ 'di-ni tshul-khrims (N220B)'chal ces rnam-par 'dren-pas gsuṅs/3/

/ gal-te byaṅ-chub-sems-dpa' 'dod yon lṅa spyod-la /
/ saṅs-rgyas chos daṅ 'phags-pa'i dge-'dun skyabs soṅ-ste /
/ saṅs-rgyas 'grub bya sñam-du kun mkhyen yid byed-pa /
/ mkhas-pa tshul-khrims pha-rol (X101A)phyin gnas rig-par bya //4//

/(P'198A) gal-te bskal-pa bya-bar dge-ba'i las (Tb73A) lam bcu /
/ spyod-ciṅ raṅ-rgyal dgra-bcom-ñid-la 'dod skyed-na /

/ de-tshe tshul-khrims skyon byuṅ tshul-khrims ñam-pa yin /
/ sems bskyed de-ni phas pham-pas-kyaṅ śin-tu lci // 5 //

/ tshul-(L213B)khrims sruṅ-źiṅ byaṅ-chub mchog-tu yoṅs sṅo-la /
/ de-yis rlom-sems med-(X101B)de bdag stod mi byed-ciṅ /
/ ṅa-yi 'du-śes sems-can 'du-śes yoṅs spaṅs-pa /
/ tshul-khrims pha-rol phyin gnas byaṅ-chub-sems-dpar brjod // 6 //

/ gal-te byaṅ-chub-(Tb73B)sems-dpa' rgyal-ba'i lam spyod-pa /
/ sems-can 'di-dag khrims ldan 'di-dag (C20B)khrims 'chal (N'173B)ces/
/ sna-tshogs 'du-śes źugs-pa śin-tu tshul-khrims 'chal /
/ tshul-(X102A)khrims ñams-śiṅ de-la yoṅs dag tshul-khrims med //7//

/ gaṅ-la bdag-gi 'du-śes sems-can 'du-śes (C'213B) med /
/ 'du-śes 'dod-chags (Tc37A) bral-la sdom-pa ji-phyir med /
/ gaṅ-la sdom daṅ sdom-pa ma yin rlom-sems med /
/ 'di-ni tshul-khrims sdom-par (Tb74A)rnam-par 'dren-pas gsuṅs //8//

/ sems-can dag-pa gaṅ-źig 'di-lta'i khrims ldan-pa /
/(X102B) sdug daṅ mi sdug kun-la lta-ba med-pa yin /
/ mgo daṅ (D'180B)rkaṅ-lag gtoṅ-(N221A)źiṅ źum-pa'i sems-kyaṅ med /
/ bdog-pa thams-cad gtoṅ-źiṅ rtag-tu źan-pa med // 9 //

/ chos-rnams raṅ-bźin bdag med ya-ma-brlar śes-nas /
/ bdag-gi śa-yaṅ gtoṅ-źiṅ źan-pa'i (P21B) sems med-na /
/ de-las phyi-rol dṅos-po gtoṅ-ba smos ci (Tb74B) dgos /
/(D19A)gal-te ser-sna byed-pa de-ni (X103A)gnas min-no // 10 //

/ bdag daṅ bdag-gir dṅos-por 'du-śes 'dod-chags 'gyur /
/ blun-po-rnams-la gtoṅ-ba'i blo-lta ga-la yod /
/ ser-snas yi-(Ti-A)dvags gnas-su skye-bar byed-pa-ste /
/ ci-ste (L'279B)mir skyes-na-yaṅ de-tshe dbul-por 'gyur // 11 //

/ de-tshe (L214A) byaṅ-chub-sems-dpa' sems-can dbul śes-nas /
/ gtoṅ-la (Tc37B)mos-par 'gyur-źiṅ rtag-tu lhug-(X103B)par gtoṅ /
/ gliṅ bźi legs-par brgyan-pa mchil-ma'i (Tb75A)thal-(N'174A)ba 'dra /
/ byin-nas dga'-bar 'gyur-gyi gliṅ thob de-lta min // 12 //

/ byaṅ-chub-sems-dpa' mkhas gsal sbyin-pa byin byas-nas /
/ srid-pa gsum-gyi sems-can ji-sñed bsam byas-te /
/ de-dag kun-la sbyin-pa 'di byin gyur-cig sems /
/ de-yaṅ 'gro-ba'i don-phyir byaṅ-chub mchog-tu bsṅo // 13 //

/(X104A) sbyin-pa byin-nas dṅos-por gnas-par byed-pa med /
/ de-ni nam-du'aṅ rnam-par smin-la re-ba med /
/ de-ltar gtoṅ-ba mkhas-pa (Tb75B) thams-cad gtoṅ-ba-ste /
/ chuṅ-du btaṅ-la dpag-tu med-pa maṅ-por 'gyur // 14 //

/ srid-pa gsum-na (C21A) sems-can ma-lus ji-sñed-pa /
/ yoṅs-su brtag-pa bzuṅ-ste de-dag thams-cad-kyis /

/ 'jig-rten mkhyen-pa saṅs-(N221B)rgyas (X104B) dgra-bcom raṅ-(C'214A) rgyal-la /
/ bskal-pa mtha'-yas sbyin ñan-thos legs tshol-na // 15 //

/ byaṅ-chub-sems-dpa' mkhas-pa thabs mkhas gaṅ-ẑig-gis /
/(Tc38A) de-dag bsod-nams bya-ba'i dṅos-(Tb76A)la yi-raṅ-nas /
/ sems-can don-du byaṅ-chub mchog rab yoṅs bsṅo-na /
/ yoṅs-su bsṅo-bas 'gro-ba thams-cad zil-gyis non // 16 //

/ nor-bu mchiṅ-(X105A)bu'i phuṅ-po chen-por gyur-pa-yaṅ /
/ rin-chen vaidūrya gcig de kun (L'280A) zil-gyis gnon /
/ de-bẑin 'gro kun sbyin-pa'i (L214B) phuṅ-po rgya-chen kun /
/ rjes-su yi-raṅ byaṅ-chub-sems-dpas zil-gyis gnon // 17 //

/(D'181A) gal-(N'174B)te byaṅ-chub-sems-dpa' 'gro-la sbyin byin-nas /
/(P22A) de-la bdag-gir (Tb76B) mi byed dṅos-po phaṅs med-na /
/ de-las dge-ba'i rtsa-ba mthu chen (X105B) 'phel 'gyur-te /
/ sprin med zla-ba yar ṅo'i 'od-kyi dkyil-'khor bẑin // 18 //

XXXII.

/ byaṅ-chub-sems-dpa'i sbyin-pas yi-dvags 'gro-ba gcod /
/ dbul-ba daṅ-ni de-bẑin ñon-moṅs thams-cad gcod /
/ rnam-par rgyu-tshe loṅs-spyod mtha'-yas yaṅs-pa thob /
/ sdug-bsṅal gyur-pa'i sems-can sbyin-pas yoṅs smin byed // 1 //

/(Tc38B) khrims-kyis dud-(Tb77A)'gro'i 'gro-ba du-ma'i ṅo-bo spoṅ /
/ dus-rnams kun-tu mi khom brgyad-kyaṅ rnam-par spoṅ /
/ bzod-pas gzugs bzaṅ dam-pa rgya-chen thob 'gyur-te /
/ gser mdog sdug-ciṅ 'gro-bas blta-ba'i 'os-su 'gyur // 2 //

/ brtson-(X106B)'grus-kyis-ni dkar-po'i yon-tan 'grib mi 'gyur /
/ rgyal-ba'i baṅ-mdzod ye-ŝes mtha'-yas thob-par (N222A) 'gyur /
/ bsam-gtan-gyis-ni 'dod-pa'i yon-tan smad-pa 'dor /
/(Tb77B) rig daṅ mṅon-par ŝes daṅ tiṅ-'dzin mṅon-par sgrub // 3 //

/ ŝes-rab-kyis-ni chos-kyi raṅ-bẑin yoṅs (C21B) ŝes-nas /
/ ṅan-soṅ gsum-po'i khams gsum-dag-las ŝin-tu 'da' /
/ mi-yi 'dren-pa 'khor-lo rin-chen bskor byas-nas /
/ sdug-bsṅal (L'280B) zad-par bya phyir 'gro-la chos-kyaṅ ston /4/

/ chos 'di yoṅs rdzogs byas-nas byaṅ-chub-sems-dpa' de /
/(N'175A) yoṅs dag ẑiṅ daṅ sems-can (Tb78A) dag-pa (Tc39A) yoṅs-su (L215A) 'dzin /
/ saṅs-rgyas rgyud daṅ chos-kyi rgyud-kyaṅ yoṅs-su 'dzin /
/ de-bẑin dge-'dun rgyud daṅ chos (X107B) kun yoṅs-su 'dzin // 5 //

/ byaṅ-chub lam 'di ŝes-rab bstan phyir brjod-pa-ste /
/ 'jig-rten-dag-na nad gso byed-pa sman-pa'i mchog /

/ miṅ-ni yon-tan <u>thams-cad</u> sdud-pa byaṅ-chub lam /
/ lam 'di sems-(Ti-B)can <u>thams-cad-kyis-ni thob gyur-cig</u> // 6 //

(Tb78B) /:/ 'phags-pa śes-rab-kyi pha-rol-tu phyin-pa sdud-pa tshigs-su bcad-pa rdzogs-so //

## APPENDIX 1.
## TITLES (RECENSION A)

* (Tb1A1) // rgya-gar-skad-du / arya-prad-ña-pa-ra-myi-tā-san-tsa-yā-ga-ta // bod-skad-du 'phags-pa śes-rab-kyi (1A2) pha-rol-tu phyin-pa' sdud-pa'i tshigs-su bcad-pa' //

* (Th565A1) / rgya-gar-skad-du / śa-ta-sā-hā-sri-kā-yā bha-ga-va-tya prad-ña-pa-ra-mi-ta-ta sa-na-tsa-yā-ga-ta-pa-ri-va-rta // // bod-skad-du 'phcom-[*read* 'phags-pa bcom-]ldan-'das-ma śes-rab-kyi pha-rol-tu phyin-pa stoṅ-phrag-brgya'-pa-las sdud-pa'i tshigsu [*r.* tshigs-su] bcad-(A2)pa'i le'u /

* (Tj-B1) / rgya-gar-skad-du / śa-ta-sā-hva-sri-kā-yā ḅha-ga-va-tya phrad-ña-pa-ra-mi-ta-ya sa-na-tsa-yā-ga[.....(B2) .....]'i le'u //

## APPENDIX 2.
## FINAL COLOPHONS (RECENSION A)

* (Tb78B1) /:/ 'phags-pa śes-rab-kyi pha-rol-tu phyin-pa' // sdud-pa'i tshigs-su bcad-pa rdzogsho [*r.* rdzogs-so] //

* (Tc39A4) // 'phags-pa śes-rab-kyi pha-rol-tu phyin-pa stoṅ-phrag-brgya-pa-las sdud-pa tshigs-su bcad-pa'i le'u źes bya-ste // brgyad-cu-rsta-bźi-pa // rdzogs-so //

* (Ti-B1) [.....] phrag-brgya'-pa-las sdud-pa'i tshigs-su bcad-pa rdzogs-so //::// (B2) / bcom-ldan-'das-ma śes-rab-kyi pha-rol-tu phyin-pa stoṅ-phrag-brgya'-pa-las sdud-pa'i tshigs-su bcad-pa'i [.....]

## APPENDIX 3.
## TABLE OF INTERCHANGES OF PĀDAS BETWEEN THE TWO RECENSIONS

| Recension A | | Recension B | |
|---|---|---|---|
| I | 2bc | I | 2cb |
| VII | 6cd | VII | 7cd [= Skt.] |
| | 7cd | | 6cd [= Skt.] |
| XI | 1bc | XI | 1cb |
| | 8bcd | | 8dbc |
| XVIII | 1cd | XVIII | 1dc |
| XX | 6bc | XX | 6cb |
| XXVII | 9bcd | XXVII | 9cdb |
| XXIX | 3abcd | XXIX | 3dabc |
| | 6cd | | 6ac |
| XXX | 1ab | XXX | 1ba |
| | 8bc | | 8cb |
| XXXII | 6ab | XXXII | 6ba |

N.B. In some cases the whole pāda offers a reading which is different from the other recension.

## APPENDIX 4.

## APPARENT MISPRINTS IN OBERMILLER'S EDITION

XII 6b (end): Obermiller *-par* (for *-ltar*)

XXV 6c: Obermiller *skyed-das* (for *skyed-de*)

N.B. 1) Naturally no MS. supports the above readings by Obermiller.
2) In some cases Obermiller has emended the text (i.e. the readings in X) without any reference.

## APPENDIX 5.

## VARIANT READINGS IN RECENSION A

Note that minor variants and apparent mistakes are omitted from this list. Variants which appear to be important for the study of the text are to be found with asterisks.

I 6c: Tc *gnas med mi gnas* (for *mi gnas gnas med)*
7d: Tc *'das-pa* (for *'das-la)*
8c: Tc *skrag-pa med* (for *skrag med-pa)*
11a: Tc *bźin 'dir gnas-ste* (for *źi 'dir gnas-te)*
11d: Tb *chos don* (for *don chos)*
13b: Tc *bya* (for *byed)*
14d: Tb *de-ni* (for *'di-ni)*
16b: Tb *kun-las* (for *kun-la)*
17c: Tc *lta-'gyur* (for *ltar-gyur)*
20d: Tc omits *dam-pa* (9 syll.).
21a: Tc *cen* [r. *chen*, so B](for *ces)*
21b: Tc *'di-ni* (for *de-ni)*
*21c: Tc *theg* (for *khaṅ)*

II 4a: I have emended Tb *gaṅ-dag* (so r. most texts of Rec. B) to *gaṅ bdag* (so C', L', N', P'; cf. Skt. *haṃ* 'I').
9b: I have emended Tb *sems-dpa'-dag* to *sems-pa-dag* (B *sems-pa:* Skt. *cetanā)*.
10a: Tb *de'i* [r. *de-yi*](for *de-ni)*

III 1a: Tc *mgon-po rnams* (12 syll.)(for *mgon-rnams)*
2a: Tb *bder-gśegs* (for *bde-gśegs)*
2c: I have emended Tbc *bder-gśegs* to *bde-gśegs* as in *a*; but cf. B *bde-bar gśegs-pa'i.*
4b: Tc *gśegs-pa'i* (for *gśegs-kyi)*
4b: Tc *bris* [*bya*]*s-nas* (for *bris byas-te)*
4d: Tc *de-ni* (for *des-ni)*
6c: Tc *bde-ba* (12 syll.)(for *bde)*
7d: Tb *skye*(for *skyed)*
8a: I have emended Tbc *'khor-lo-* to *'khor-los* (so most texts of Rec. B).

IV 2c: I have emended Tbc *thob ltar* (10 syll.) to *thob-pa ltar* (so B).
3b: I have emended Tbc *bgyir-'os* to *bgyi-'os* (so B).
3c: Tc *de phyir phyuṅ-yaṅ* (for *de phyuṅ gyur-kyaṅ)*
7b: Tc *gyur-kyaṅ* (for *gyur-te)*

V 6c: I have emended Tb *mkhas-pa'i* (so a few texts of Rec. B) to *mkhas-pa* (so most texts of Rec. B).

VI 8a: I have emended Tb *byas-te* to *bya-ste* (so B).

VII 1c: I have emended Tb *dmigs med* to *mig med* (so B: Skt. *a-cakṣū)*.
3c: Tc *'jig-rten pha-rol dag-na* (13 syll.)(for *'jig-rten-dag-na)*
5a: Tc *byaṅ-chub-sems-pa* (for *°-dpa')*
5b: Tc *spyad-pa'i* (for *spyad-pa)*

VIII 1ab: Tc *'bras-bu'i* (for *'bras-bu)*
2a: Tb *'dir gar* (12 syll.)(for *gar)*

2a: Tc *'dir* (for *gar)*
2c: Tc *brtsar-bar* (?)(for *btsal-bar;* B *bsal-bar)*; cf. I 1b, XXVIII 7d A *btsal-nas,* B *bsal-nas*; cf. KTRS p. 574 *stsol,* pf., fut. *btsal;* however, acc. to Jäschke p. 442a, *stsol-ba* 3, s.v., *stsol-ba* is sometimes incorrectly used for *bsal-ba (sel-ba).*
3b: Tc omits *'khor-ba'i* (9 syll.).
3b: Tbc *til-gyi* is a result of the apparent misreading of Skt. MSS. *'nila-* or *nila- (= anila-* 'wind'; so Rec. B *rluṅ-gi)* as *tila-* 'sesame'.

IX 1c: I have emended Tb *lha-ṅer* (so some texts of Rec. B) to *lhaṅ-ṅer* (so most texts of Rec. B).

X 6a: Tb *byas-te* (for *bya-ste)*
7a: Tc *yal-ga lo-ma-rnams* (for *lo-ma yal-ga-rnams)*
8a: Tb *sbrum-ba* (r. *-pa)*(for *sbrum-ma)*
8b: Tb omits *de-yi* (9 syll.).
10a: Tb *rtogs-ste* (for *rtog-ste)*
10b: Tb *rtogs* (for *rtog)*

XI 1c: Tc *dga'-bar* (for *dga'-ba)*
*1c: Tc *rab-tu* (for *bar-du)*
*1d: Tc *rab-tu gcod-par* (for *yoṅs-su brjod-par)*
2a: I have emended Tbc *'dri* (so some texts of Rec. B) to *'bri* (so em O, too).
3c: Tc *dus-*(for *rus-)*
4b: Tc *btsal-bar*(for *tshol-bar)*
9d: I have emended Tb *dkon-mchog rin-chen-*(MS. *-cen-)la-yaṅ* to *dkon chos ...:* Skt. *durlābhu dharma-ratanaṃ* ...
10a: Tb *źugs-pa* (for *źugs-pa'i)*

XII 4a: Tc *'jig* (15A1) *'jig* (for *'jig-rten)*
4b: Tb *'dir* (for *'di)*
4c: Tc *byaṅ-chub-sems-dpa'* (for °*-dpas)*
5d: I have emended Tbc *nams-kyaṅ* (so Ta, Te, Tg) to *nam-yaṅ*(so most texts of Rec. B, but NX *-rnams-kyaṅ* = O).
6d: Tc *skrag-par byed-pa'i* (13 syll.)
8b: Tc *sems-dpa'* (for *sems-pa)*

XIII 1a: Tc *mthoṅ-bas* (for *mthoṅ-ba)*
1c: Tc *ñan-thos-rnams-ni* (for *ñan-thos chos-rnams)*

XIV 5a: I have emended Tb *la-la* (so some texts of Rec. B) to *la-las* (so most texts of Rec. B).
5c: I have emended Tb *bum-pa* to *bum-par* (so B).
5d: Tb *'jig-pa'i 'jigs-pa* (13 syll.)
7a: Tb *bcos legs ma byas* (33B1) *bcos legs ma byas*
9d: I have emended Tb *gYos* (so one Tunhuang MS. of Rec. B) to *gYon* (so the rest of Rec. B).

XV 8d: Tc has later erased *na* of *'jig-rten-dag-na* (so two Tunhuang MSS. of Rec. B in 12 syll.).

XVI 1c: Tc *bcu* (for *bcu'i)*
1c: Tb *'jig-rten-* (for Tc *ci-sñed,* which I have emended to *ji-sñed* w.B).
2abc: I have emended Tbc *daṅ* to *gaṅ* (so B: Skt. *yā).*
*4b: Tc *-bcur* (for *-brgyar*; cf. Skt. text XVI 4b, fn.)
4d: I have emended Tb *de-ni* and Tc *de* to *der-ni* w. B).
5b: Tb *maṅ-pos* (for *maṅ-por)*

XVII *2a: Tc *chos* (for *tshig)*
2d: I have emended Tb *lam* (10 syll.) to *lam-la* w. B.

XVIII 2d: Tb *stsogs-par ji-ga* (for *stsogs lta ci-ga)*
4b: Tb *dri med tshul-khrims* (for *tshul-khrims dri-med)*
4d: Tc *daṅ tshul-khrims-kyis char mi* (for *daṅ khrims-kyis char mi phod)*
6a: Tc *gsog* (so B)(for *gsob;* cf. Jäschke p. 580a, *sob*, s.v.)
6b: Tb *gsog* (for *gsob*, so B)

*6b: Tc *de-bźin stoṅ-par sna* (for *sñiṅ-po med-par snaṅ)*
7a: Tbc *gzuṅ* is poss. a mistake for *gsuṅ* (cf. Skt. *prakāśita-)*

XIX 1c: Tc omits this pāda.
1d: Tc *med-par* (for *med-pas)*
5a: Tc *mtshan-ma med-ciṅ* (13 syll.)
5b: Tc *mtshan-ma* (for *mtshan-mar)*
5d: Tc *mi gnas bźin* (9 syll.)(for *gnas-pa med-pa bźin)*
6a: Tc *'di-ltar* (for *de-ltar)*
6b: Tc *bcu* (for *bcus)*

XX 1d: Tb *chos-las* (for *chos-la)*
3a: Tc *bcas-pa* (for *bcas-par)*
*6c: Tb *sems-can khams-kyi* (for *sems-can-rnams-kyi)*
6c: Tc *śes-rab* (for *śes daṅ)*
7b: Tc *tiṅ-ṅe-'dzin* (12 syll.)
8c: Tc *rnam-par* (for *rnam thar)*
8d: Tc *mtshan-ma* (for *mtshan-mar)*
9a: Tc *phoṅs* (for *'phoṅ)*
9a: Tc *skyes-bu* (for *skyes-bus)*
9b: Tb *gźan-dag-gis* (for *gźan-dag-ni)*
10c: Tc *ci-sñed* (for *ji-srid)*
10d: Tc *stoṅ-pa'i ñid* (12 syll.)(for *stoṅ-ñid)*
(16b: Note that there are two variant readings in Rec. B.)
21a: Tc *gal-te daṅ-po spyod-pa* (13 syll.)(for *gal-te spyod-pa)*
21a: Tc *daṅ-po* (for *dbaṅ-po)*
21d: Tc omits *mi 'chad* (9 syll.).
21d: Tc *luṅ bstan de-ni* (for *de-ni luṅ bstan)*
23b: Tb *rgyud* (for *rgyun)*

XXI 1c: Tc omits *pha-rol.*
1d: Tc *yin-par rig-par bya* (13 syll.)(for *rig-par bya)*
2c: Tc *yin śes* (for *yin-źiṅ)*
3a: Tb *sbyaṅ* (for *sbyaṅs)*
8b: I have emended Tb *gñis-gyis* to *gñis-kyi* (so B).

XXII 3b: Tc *kun-la* (for *kun lam)*
4d: Tc *bder-gśegs* (for *bde-gśegs)*
6a: Tc *dogs-pa'i* (for *dogs-pas)*
6b: Tc *dug-du* (for *dug de)*
6c: Tb *byis-pas* (for *byis-pa)*
6d: Tb *bdag-gi* (for *bdag-gir)*
7b: Tc omits *dag-par.*
*7c: Tc *dmig-gi* (for *ñon-moṅs)*
7c: Tc *gaṅ-[ ] yod*; There is a blank.
12d: Tc omits *rtag-tu.*

XXIII 2a: Tc *phyin* (10 syll.)(for *phyin-pa)*
2d: I have emended Tbc *yaṅ* to *yaṅs*: Skt. *pṛthu.*
3c: Tc *da-lta-yaṅ-na*(for *da-lta-na-yaṅ)*
3d: Tc *gnas-nas* (9 syll.)(for *gnas-par gyur-nas)*
4b: Tc *sbyin-pa* (for *sbyin-par)*
4c: Tc *da-lta-yaṅ-na* (for *da-lta-na-yaṅ)*

XXIV 3d: Tc omits *ye-śes.*
4b: Tb *ñams-pa* (for *ñams-par)*
4d: I have emended Tbc *de-ni* to *de-na* (cf. B *de-tshe*:Skt. *tada)*.
6c: Tc *phyis-kyaṅ* (for *phyir-yaṅ)*

XXV 3d: Tc *rnam-pa du-mas mdun-du* (13 syll.)(for *rnam-pas mdun-na)*
4c: Tc *drug-cu-rtsa-gñis 'dus-pa ltar* (13 syll.)
4d: Tc omits *'di-dag.*
6d: Tb *bdag-gi* (for *bdag-gis)*

XXVI 1b: Tc *btags-pas* (for *thag-pas)*
1b: Tb *yid raṅ-ba* (for *yi-raṅ-ba)*
1c: Tc *gcal-nas* (for *gcal-na)*
1c: Tc *gzuṅ-du* (12 syll.)
2c: Tc *'gyur-nas* (for *gyur-nas)*
2d: Tc *mchod* (for *chos)*
3a: Tc *rtogs* (for *rtog)*

3b: Tb *ṡes-la* (for *ṡes-pa)*
4a: Tc *mkhas* (for *mkha')*
5b: I have emended Tbc *myed* [r. *med*] to *byed.*
5d: Tc omits *sems med.*
*5d: Tb *spyod* (for *med)*
*6a: Tb *spyod mkhas* (for *spyod-pa)*
6c: Tc *ldan-pa-yaṅ* (12 syll.)(for *ldan-pa'aṅ)*
7d: Tb *lta-bur* (for *bżin-du)*
8a: Tc omits *rtse-phyir.*

XXVII *1d: Tc *ṡes-rab* (for *'phreṅ-ba)*
*1d: Tc *rdzogs-par* (for *brjod-pa)*
2a: Tc *gaṅ-'ga'* (for Tb *gaṅga'i*, which I have emended to *gaṅgā'i*, so most texts of Rec. B).
2b: Tb *gyur-par* (for *gyur-pas)*
2c: Tc *spu-rtsa ñeg* [r. *spu-rtse ña-ga*](for *spu ñag)*
2c: Tc omits *de-sñed.*
3d: Tc omits *sñiṅ-rjes.*
4c: Tc *bsgrub-pa* (for *bsgrub-par)*
4c: Tc *brtsom* (for *brtson)*
4c: Tb *byed-pa* (for *byed-la)*
4d: Tc *żugs-par* (for *mṅon żugs)*
5c: Tc *mkhas* (for *mkha')*
5d: Tc *men-tog* (for *me-tog)*
6c: Tc *mthoṅ-ba-yaṅ* (12 syll.)
6d: Tc omits *żi 'dod.*
6d: Tc *gnas ma yin* (for *gnas-pa yin)*
7a: Tb *de-bżin* (62A1) *de-bżin-gṡegs-kyi*
7a: Tc *rnam-par* (for *rnam thar)*
8b: Tc *chu-ba* (for *chu-la)*
8b: Tb *gnas-kyaṅ chu-yis 'tshubs-te* (13 syll.)
8d: Tc *phyin-pa* (for *son-pa)*
8d: Tc *'das* (for *'da')*
9c: Tc *gnas-pa'i* (for *gnas-pa)*

XXVIII 3a: Tc omits *me-tog.*
3d: Tc *skye(?)-ba* (for *skyo-bo)*
3d: Tb omits *yoṅs-su.*
5b: Tc *de-dag* (for *de kun)*
6: Tc omits the whole verse.
7a: Tc omits *-ciṅ* of *rten-ciṅ.*
7a: Tc *'di-la* (for *'di)*
7c: Tc *sprin-gis* (for *sprin-gyi)*
*7c: Tb *dkyil-'khor* (for *'od-zer)*
*7d: Tb *bsal-nas* (for *bstsal-nas;* cf. I 1b A *bstsal-nas,* B *bsal-nas;* VIII 2c A *bstsal-bar,* B *bsal-bar)*

XXIX 1a: Tb *bżi* (for *bżir)*
1d: Tc *dam dpa'* (for *dam-pa)*
5d: Tc omits *-du* of *bżin-du.*
7a: Tc *'gyur-ciṅ* (for *gyur-kyaṅ)*
7c: Tc *de-yaṅ* (for *des-kyaṅ)*
8a: Tc *de-ltar* (for *de-bżin)*
8c: Tc *de* (for *bde)*
8d: Tc *sñiṅ-rjer* (for *sñiṅ-brtser)*
8d: Tb *ldan-pa'i* (for *ldan-pa)*
9c: Tc *gYeṅ* (for *gYeṅs)*
11a: Tb *zag-pa* (for *gaṅ-zag)*
11b: Tc omits *phyin-la.*
11c: Tc *rje-mo'i* (for *rje-bo'i)*
*11d: Tc *sems-can dbn-kyis* (for *sems-can-rnams-kyi)*
12b: I have emended Tb *rjo-mo-*,Tc *rjo-bo-* tc *rje-bo-.*

XXX 2b: Tb *riṅ-rab* (for *riṅ-bar)*
3c: Tc inserts *ñin* after *de-la* (12 syll.).
4c: Tc *byes 'gyur-nas* (for *byed 'gyur-na)*
7a: Tc *gal-te* (for *gaṅ-tshe)*
8c: Tb omits *mkhas-pa.*

11a: Tb *candan* (for *tsandan)*
13a: I have emended Tb *byas-te* to *bya-ste.*
14b: I have emended Tb *rka-lag* to *rkaṅ-lag.*

XXXI 7c: I have emended Tbc *sna-tshog* to *sna-tshogs.*
8d: Tc *'dren-par* (for *'dren-pas)*
*9a: Tc *dam-pa* (for *dag-pa)*
10c: Tc *de-la* (for *de-las)*
10d: Tc *min-na* (for *min-no)*
11a: Tb *bdag-gi* (for *bdag-gir)*
11c: Tc *ser-sna* (for *ser-snas)*
12a: Tc omits *sems-can.*
12b: Tc omits *'gyur-źiṅ.*
12c: Tb *brgyan-pa'i* (for *brgyan-pa)*
12d: Tb *de-ltar* (for *de-lta)*
13a: Ti omits *mkhas.*
13a: Tci omit *-pa* of *sbyin-pa*
13a: Tci omit *byas-* of *byas-nas.*
13b: Tc *bya-ste* (for *byas-te)*
13c: Tc *sbyin 'di byin-par* (for *sbyin-pa 'di byin)*
14b: Tci *nam-du-yaṅ* (for *nam-du'aṅ)*
15b: Tc *bzuṅs-te* (for *bzuṅ-ste)*
17b: I have emended Tbc *ve-dū̆-rya* to *vaiḍūrya* (so most texts of Rec. B).
17d: Tci *byaṅ-chub-sems-dpa'* (for °*-dpas)*
18d: Tc *yar-gi* (12 syll.)(for *yar)*

XXXII 1a: Tc *byaṅ-chub-sems-pa,* Ti °*-dpa'* (for °*-dpa'i*; Tb °*-dpa'-'i)*
2a: Tc *dud-'gro* (for *dud-'gro'i)*
2ab: Tb *sbyoṅ* (for *spoṅ)*
3a: Ti *'gri-pas*[r. perh. *'gribs* ](for *'grib)*
4b: Ti *'das*(for *'da')*
4c: Tc *'drenpa'i* (for *'dren-pa)*
4d: Tc omits *zad-* of *zad-par.*
5d: Tc *rgyu* (for *rgyud)*
6b: Ti *na* (for *nad)*
6c: Tb *sdud-pa thams-cad*(for *thams-cad sdud-pa)*

# B I B L I O G R A P H Y

List of works quoted in this book

N.B. For manuscripts, blockprints and editions see further 'Bibliographical Notes', pp. xxiii-liii, above.


AALTO, P., 'Notes on the Collection of Mongolian Books in the Ethnographical Museum in Sweden, Stockholm', *Ethnos*, XV, 1-2 (Stockholm, 1950), pp. 1-14, 3 figs.

- - , 'Le Mdo-maṅ conservé à la Bibliothèque Universitaire de Helsinki', *Miscellanea Bibliographica*, VI *(= Helsingfors Universitetsbiblioteks Skrifter*, XXIII)(Helsinki, 1952), pp. 27-47.

- - , 'A Catalogue of the Hedin Collection of Mongolian Literature', *Reports of the Sino-Swedish Expedition*, Publication No. 38 (Stockholm, 1953), pp. 69-108.

AKANUMA, Chizen 赤沼智善, *Indo Bukkyō Koyū Meishi Jiten: Genshiki-hen* 印度仏教固有名詞辞典: 原始期篇 (Nagoya: Hajinkaku, 1931; reprinted with additions and corrections by Hōzōkan, Kyōto, 1967, and 1975).

- - , *Bukkyō Kyōtenshiron* 仏教経典史論 (Nagoya: Hajinkaku, 1939).

AOKI, Bunkyō [ 青木文教 ], *Study on Early Tibetan Chronicles regarding Discrepancies of Dates and their Adjustments* (Tōkyō: The Japan Society for the Promotion of Science, 1955).

AOYAMA, Sadao 青山定雄 (ed.), *Sōdai Kenkyū Bunken Teiyō* 宋代研究文献提要 (Tōkyō: Tōyō Bunko, 1961).

BACOT, J., 'La collection tibétaine Schilling von Canstadt à la Bibliothèque de l'Institut', *Journal Asiatique*, CCV (1924), pp. 321-348.

- - , *Grammaire du tibêtain littêraire*, 2 tomes (Paris: Adrien-Maisonneuve, 1946-1949).

BAGCHI, Prabodh Chandra, *Le canon bouddhique en Chine: Les traducteurs et les traductions*, 2 tomes *(= Sino-Indica: Publications de l'Université de Calcutta*, tomes I et IV)(Paris: Paul Geuthner, 1927-1938).

BARUCH, W., 'Compte rendu de E. Lamotte, *Le traité de la Grande Vertu de Sagesse de Nāgārjuna*, I-II (Louvain, 1944-1949)', *Asia Major*, New Series, III, 1 (London, 1953), pp. 109-112.

BECKH, H., *Verzeichnis der tibetischen Handschriften der Königlichen Bibliothek zu Berlin*, I: Kanjur (Bkah-hgyur) *(= Die Handschriften-Verzeichnisse der Königlichen Bibliothek zu Berlin*, XXIV)(Berlin: Behrend & Co., 1914).

BENDALL, C., *Catalogue of the Buddhist Sanskrit Manuscripts in the University Library, Cambridge, with introductory notices and illustrations of the palaeography and chronology of Nepal and Bengal* (Cambridge: Cambridge University Press, 1883).

BERNHARD, F., 'Gab es einen Lokativ auf *-esmiṃ* im buddhistischen Sanskrit?', *Nachrichten der Akademie der Wissenschaften in Göttingen*, I: *Philologisch-historische Klasse*, Jahrgang 1964, Nr. 4 (1964), pp. 199-209.

BISCHOFF, F. A., *Der Kanjur und seine Kolophone*, 2 Bände (Bloomington: The Selbstverlag Press, 1968).

BÖHTLINGK, O., 'Über einige Sanskrit-Werke in der Bibliothek des Asiatischen Departements', *Bulletin de la Classe des Sciences hitoriques, philologiques et politiques de l'Académie Impériale des Sciences de Saint-Pétersbourg*, II, 22 (1845), Sp. 339-349.

- - , 'Verzeichniss der auf Indien bezüglichen Handschriften und Holzdrucke im Asiatischen Museum der Kaiserlichen Akademie der Wissenschaften', *Das Asiatische Museum der Kaiserlichen Akademie der*

*Wissenschaften zu St.-Petersburg*, von B. Dorn (St. Petersburg: Buchdruckerei der Kaiserlichen Akademie der Wissenschaften, 1846), Beilage Nr. 153, pp. 720-736.

BUDDHAŚRĪJÑĀNA —— see 'Bibl. Notes' VIII 2.

BU-STON —— see OBERMILLER.

CHAKRAVARTI, Chintaharan, 'Sanskrit Manuscripts in the Asiatic Society', *Indian Studies Past and Present*, I (1959-1960), pp. 663-672.

CHATTOPADHYAYA, Alaka, *Catalogue of Indian (Buddhist) Texts in Tibetan Translation: Kanjur & Tanjur (Alphabetically Rearranged)*, I: Texts (Indian titles) in Tanjur. In collaboration with M. Gangopadhyaya & D. Chattopadhyaya (Calcutta: Indo-Tibetan Studies, 1972).

CHIH-P'AN 志磐, *Fo-tsu-t'ung-chi* 仏祖統記 (1258-1269) —— *Taishō Shinshū Daizōkyō*, No. 2035 (Vol. XLIX).

CHIMPA, Lama, and CHATTOPADHYAYA, Alaka (trsl.), *Tāranātha's History of Buddhism in India*, edited by D. Chattopadhyaya (Simla: Indian Institute of Advanced Study, 1970).

CH'ING Chi-hsiang 慶吉祥, etc., *Ta-yüan Chih-yüan fa-pao k'an-t'ung tsung-lu* 大元至元法宝勘同総録 (1287 A.D.) —— *ıōwa Hōbō Sōmokuroku*, II (1929), No. 25.

CHOS-GRAGS, *Dge-bśes Chos-kyi grags-pas brtsams pa'i brda-dag miṅ tshig gsal-ba* / 格西曲札蔵文辞典 (Peking: Min-tsu Ch'u-pan-shê, 1957) —— Abbr.: Chos-grags.

*Chung-hua Ta-tsang-ching* 中華大蔵経, First Series [Chi-sha edition] (Taipei: Hsiu-ting Chung-hua Ta-tsang-ching-hui, 1965).
*Shou-pien* 首編 (Taipei, 1968).
—— cf. *Ying-yin Sung Chi-sha tsang-ching*.

CONZE, E., 'Hymn to Perfect Wisdom', *The Middle Way*, XXV, 1 (1951), pp. 24-25.
= Conze, E. (ed.), *Buddhist Texts through the Ages*, newly translated from the original Pali, Sanskrit, Chinese, Tibetan, Japanese and Apabhramsa, in collaboration with I. B. Horner, D. Snellgrove, A. Waley (Oxford: Bruno Cassirer, 1954), pp. 147-149 (Text No. 142).
[= German edition: *Im Zeichen Buddhas: Buddhistische Texte*, herausgegeben und eingeleitet von E. Conze unter Mitarbeit von I. B. Horner, D. Snellgrove, A. Waley (= *Bücher des Wissens*, Nr. 144)(Frankfurt am Main-Hamburg: Fischer Bücherei, 1957), pp. 123-125 (Text Nr. 137: 'Hymnen an die Vollkommene Weisheit')].
= Conze, E., *Buddhist Scriptures* (= *The Penguin Classics*, L-88)(Harmondsworth: Penguin Books Ltd., 1959), pp. 168-171.

- - , 'The Composition of the Aṣṭasāhasrikā Prajñāpāramitā', *Bulletin of the School of Oriental and African Studies*, XIV (1952), pp. 251-262.
= Conze, E., *Thirty Years of Buddhist Studies* (Oxford: Cassirer, 1967), pp. 168-184.

- - , *A Collection of Prajñā-pāramitā Texts* [Typescript, 1952]: 1. 'Ratnaguṇasaṃcayagāthā in Sanskrit and Tibetan'; 7. 'An English translation of the Ratnaguṇasaṃcayagāthā'. —— Unseen.
Reference: *Library Catalogue* (School of Oriental and African Studies, University of London), Vol. XXII, p. 57c: No. 96341.

- - , *Dictionary to the Prajñāpāramitā Texts* [Typescript, 1954]. —— Unseen.
Reference: *Library Catalogue* (School of Oriental and African Studies, University of London), Vol. XXII, p. 55c: No. 96340.

- - , *Selected Sayings from the Perfection of Wisdom*, chosen, arranged and translated by E.C. (London: The Buddhist Society, 1955; 2nd. ed. 1968).

- - , 'The Oldest *Prajñāpāramitā*', *The Middle Way*, XXXII, 4 (1958), pp. 136-141.

- - , *Aṣṭasāhasrikā Prajñāpāramitā*, translated into English by E.C. (= *Bibliotheca Indica*, Work No. 284, Issue No. 1578)(Calcutta: The Asiatic Society, 1958). —— cf. CONZE (1973), below.

- - , 'Review of R. Hikata, *Suvikrāntavikrāmi-Paripṛcchā Prajñāpāramitā-Sūtra* (Fukuoka, 1958)', *Indo-Iranian Journal*, III, 3 (1958), pp. 232-234.

- - , 'A Sanskrit-Tibetan-English Index' to Obermiller's edition of the *Rgs* (1960), pp. 129-157. —— Abbr.: Conze Index.

- - , 'The Calcutta Manuscript of the *Ratnaguṇasaṃcayagāthā*', *Indo-Iranian Journal*, IV, 1 (1960), pp. 37-58. —— Abbr.: Conze Rgs.

- - , *The Prajñāpāramitā Literature (= Indo-Iranian Monographs*, VI) ('s-Gravenhage: Mouton & Co., 1960).

- - , 'The Development of the Prajñāpāramitā Thought', *Suzuki Daisetsu Hakushi Shōju Kinen Ronbunshū: Bukkyō to Bunka* 鈴木大拙博士頌寿記念論文集・仏教と文化 (Kyōto: Ōtani University / Tōkyō: Suzuki Research Foundation, 1960), pp. 24-45.
= Conze, E., *Thirty Years of Buddhist Studies* (Oxford: Cassirer, 1967), pp. 123-147.

- - , 'Verses on the Accumulation of Precious Qualities (*Ratnaguṇasaṃcayagāthā*)', *Indo-Asian Studies*, Part I *(= Śatapiṭaka Series*, XXXI)(New Delhi: International Academy of Indian Culture, 1962), pp. 126-178. —— Abbr.: Conze Trsl. —— cf. CONZE (1973), below.

- - , *Materials for a Dictionary of the Prajñāpāramitā Literature* (Tōkyō: Suzuki Research Foundation, 1967). —— Abbr.: Conze Dict.

- - , *The Perfection of Wisdom in Eight Thousand Lines & its Verse Summary (= Wheel Series*, 1)(Bolinas: Four Seasons Foundation, 1973). —— cf. CONZE (1958 and 1962), above.

CORDIER, P., *Catalogue du fonds tibétain de la Bibliothèque Nationale*, Troisième partie: Index du Bstan-ḥgyur 180-332 (Paris: Imprimerie Nationale / Ernest Leroux, 1915).

CSOMA, A., 'Analysis of the Sher-Chin__P'hal-Ch'hen__Dkon-Séks__Do-Dé__Nyáng-Dás__and Gyut; Being the 2nd, 3rd, 4th, 5th, 6th, and 7th Divisions of the Tibetan Work, entitled the Kah-gyur', *Asiatic Researches*, XX, 1 (Calcutta, 1836), Article XI, pp. 393-552. —— cf. FEER, below.

*Dainippon Kōtei (Shukusatsu) Daizōkyō* —— see FUKUDA-SHIMADA-SHIKIGAWA.

DAS, Sarat Chandra, *Pag Sam Jon Zang* [Dpag-bsam ljon-bzaṅ] *by Sumpa Khan-po Yeçe Pal Jor, the great historiographer and chronologist of Tibet*, edited with a list of contents and analytical index by S.C.D. 2 parts (Calcutta: Presidency Jail Press, 1908).

DEMIÉVILLE, P., *L'Inde classique: Manuel des études indiennes*, par L. Renou et J. Filliozat, tome II (Paris: Imprimerie Nationale / Hanoi: École Française d'Extrême-Orient, 1953): chapitre XI. Le bouddhisme, 1.4 'Les sources chinoises', pp. 398-463.

- - , *Hôbôgirin* 法宝義林 *: Dictionnaire encyclopédique du bouddhisme d'après les sources chinoises et japonaises*, publié sous la direction de S. Lévi et J. Takakusu [Rédacteur en chef: P. Demiéville], fascicule annexe: *Table du Taishô Issaikyô* (Tôkyô: Maison Franco-japonaise, 1931).

DEVI, Sushama, *Samantabhadracaryāpraṇidhānarāja (= Śatapiṭaka Series*, IV) (New Delhi: International Academy of Indian Culture, 1958).

DHARMAPĀLABHADRA —— see 'Bibl. Notes' IIB5a.

DHARMAŚRĪ —— see 'Bibl. Notes' VIII 3.

DPAL-BRTSEGS —— see 'Bibl. Notes' IIB N.B. 1.

DURT, H., 'Chōmyōtō', *Hôbôgirin* [see DEMIÉVILLE above], fasc. IV (Paris: Adrien-Maisonneuve / Tōkyō: Maison Franco-japonaise, 1967), pp. 360-365.

EDGERTON, F., 'Meter, Phonology, and Orthography in Buddhist Hybrid Sanskrit', *Journal of the American Oriental Society*, LXVI (1946), pp. 197-206. —— Abbr.: Edgerton Meter.

- - , *Buddhist Hybrid Sanskrit Grammar and Dictionary*, 2 vols. *(= William Dwight Whitney Linguistic Series)*(New Haven: Yale University Press, 1953). —— Abbr.: Edgerton & BHSD.
Photomechanical reprint (Delhi-Patna-Varanasi: Motilal Banarsidass, 1969).

- - , 'The Prajñā-Pāramitā-Ratna-Guṇa-Saṃcaya-Gāthā', *Indo-Iranian Journal*, V, 1 (1961), pp. 1-18. —— Abbr.: Edg.Rgs.

*Eiin Pekin-ban Chibetto Daizōkyō Sōmokuroku / Sakuin* 影印北京版西蔵大蔵経総目録・索引 : *Catalogue and Index of the Tibetan Tripiṭaka, Peking Edition, kept in the Library of the Otani University, Kyoto, reprinted under the supervision of the Otani University, edited by D. T. Suzuki* (Tōkyō-Kyōto: Tibetan Tripiṭaka Research Institute, 1961).

FA-HSIEN —— see 'Bibl. Notes' III N.B. 6-9.

FEER, L., 'Analyse du Kandjour (et du Tandjour). Recueil des livres sacrés du Tibet par Alexandre Csoma, de Körös. Traduite de l'anglais et augmentée de diverses additions et remarques par L.F.', *Annales du Musée Guimet, Grande Bibliothèque*, II (Lyons: Imprimerie Pitrat Ainé, 1881), pp. 131-577.

FARQUHAR, D., 'A Description of the Mongolian Manuscripts and Xylographs in Washington D.C.', *Central Asiatic Journal*, I, 3 (1955), pp. 161-218.

FILLIOZAT, J., *L'Inde classique: Manuel des études indiennes*, par L. Renou et J. Filliozat, tome II (Paris: Imprimerie Nationale/Hanoi: École Française d'Extrême-Orient, 1953): chapitre XI. Le bouddhisme, 1: 'Les sources', pp. 313-397.

FONAHN, A., 'Notes on the Tanjur in Oslo', *Oslo Etnografiske Museums Skrifter*, III, 4 (Oslo, 1936), pp. 161-208.

*Fo-tsang tzu-mu yin-te* —— see HSÜ.

FRAUWALLNER, E., *Die Philosophie des Buddhismus (= Philosophische Studientexte, Texte der indischen Philosophie*, II)(Berlin: Akademie-Verlag, 1956; 3. durchgesehene Auflage, 1969).

FUJITA, Kōtatsu 藤田宏達, *Genshi Jōdo Shisō no Kenkyū* 原始浄土思想の研究 (Tōkyō: Iwanami Shoten, 1970).

FUKUDA, Gyōkai 福田行誡, SHIMADA, Bankon 島田蕃根, and SHIKIGAWA, Seiichi 色川誠一 (eds.), *Dainippon Kōtei (Shukusatsu) Daizōkyō* 大日本校訂(縮刷)大蔵経 (Tōkyō: Kōkyō Shoin, 1880-1885). —— For the Chinese *Rgs* see 'Bibl. Notes' IIIb. —— Abbr.: Shuku.
*Dainippon Kōtei Daizōkyō Mokuroku* (Dec. 1885).

GEIGER, W., *Pāli Literatur und Sprache (= Grundriss der indo-arischen Philologie und Altertumskunde*, I, 7)(Strassburg: K. J. Trübner, 1916). —— Abbr.: Geiger.
English edition: *Pāli Literature and Language*, translated by B. Ghosh (Calcutta: University of Calcutta, 1943; photomechanically reprinted by the Oriental Books Reprint Corp., Delhi, 1968).

GORBAČEVA, Z.I., i KYČANOV, E.I., *Tangutskie rukopisi i ksilografy* (Moskva: Izdatel'stvo vostočnoj literatury, 1963).

GRINSTEAD, E. D., 'The Manuscript Kanjur in the British Museum', *Asia Major*, New Series, XIII, 1-2 (London, 1967), pp. 48-70.

- - , *Tangut Studies: Working notes on texts from Kharakhoto, .....; Index to Buddhist and Taoist literature*, 10 vols. (Leiden, 1967; also in microfiche form - Zug: Inter Documentation Co.). —— Unseen.

- - , *The Tangut Tripiṭaka*, edited by E. Grinstead from the collections of Raghu Vira, 9 parts *(= Śatapiṭaka Series*, LXXXIII-XCI)(New Delhi: International Academy of Indian Culture, 1971).

HAARH, E., 'A Comparative List of the Derge and Lhasa Editions of the Kanjur', *Asia Major,* New Seris, IX, 2 (1963), pp. 179-205.

HADANO, Hakuyū 羽田野伯猷, 'Himitsushū Tantora ni okeru Jinyānapāda-ryū ni tsuite 秘密集タントラにおけるヂニャーナパーダ流について'. *Bunka* 文化, New Series, No. 5 [= Vol. II, No. 1](Sendai, March 1950), pp. 13(152)-25(165).

- - , 'Chibetto Daizōkyō Engi (Sono Ichi) —— Narutan Daigakumonji no Senkuteki Jigyō o megutte —チベット大蔵経縁起（その一）ナルタン大学問寺の先駆的事業をめぐって—', *Suzuki Gakujutsu Zaidan Kenkyū Nenpō* 鈴木学術財団研究年報, No. 3 (Tōkyō, 1966), pp. 35-83.

HANAYAMA, Shōyū [花山勝友], 'A Summary of Various Research on the Prajñāpāramitā Literature by Japanese Scholars', *Acta Asiatica: Bulletin of the Institute of Eastern Culture,* No. 10 (Tōkyō, 1966), pp. 16-93.

HARIBHADRA —— see 'Bibl. Notes' VIII 1.

HASHIMOTO, Kōhō 橋本光宝, *Mōko no Ramakyō* 蒙古の喇嘛教 (Tōkyō: Bukkyō Kōronsha, 1942).

HEISSIG, W., 'Die Libri Mongolici der westdeutschen Bibliothek Marburg', *Zeitschrift der deutschen morgenländischen Gesellschaft,* CIII, 2 (1953), pp. 394-424.

- - , *Die Pekinger lamaistischen Blockdrucke in mongolischer Sprache. Materialien zur mongolischen Literaturgeschichte (= Göttinger Asiatische Forschungen,* II)(Wiesbaden: Otto Harrassowitz, 1954).

- - , *Mongolische Handschriften - Blockdrucke - Landkarten.* Herausgegeben unter Mitarbeit von K. Sagaster *(= Verzeichnis der orientalischen Handschriften in Deutschland,* I)(Wiesbaden: Franz Steiner, 1961).

HIKATA, Ryūshō [干潟龍祥], *Suvikrāntavikrāmi-Paripṛcchā Prajñāpāramitā-Sūtra,* edited with an introductory essay (Fukuoka: Committee of Commemoration Program for Dr. Hikata's Retirement from Professorship, Kyūshū University, 1958).

HIRAKAWA, Akira 平川彰, 'Yōroppa no Chūō Ajiya Bukkyō Shahon ヨーロッパの中央アジヤ仏教写本', *Indogaku Bukkyōgaku Kenkyū* 印度学仏教学研究, X, 1 (Tōkyō, Jan. 1962), pp. 314-323.

- - , *Shoki Daijō Bukkyō no Kenkyū* 初期大乗仏教の研究 (Tōkyō: Shunjū-sha, 1968).

- - , and CEADEL, E. B., 'Japanese Research on Buddhism Since the Meiji Period', *Monumenta Nipponica,* XI, 3 (Tōkyō, 1955), pp. 221-246; XI, 4 (1956), pp. 398-424.

HOFFMANN, H., *Die Religionen Tibets: Bon und Lamaismus in ihrer geschichtlichen Entwicklung* (Freiburg-München: Karl Alber, 1956). English edition (unseen): *The Religions of Tibet,* Translated by E. Fitzgerald (London: Allen & Unwin, 1961).

[HSÜ Ti-shan 許地山], *Fo-tsang tzu-mu yin-te* 仏蔵子目引得 / *Combined Indices to the Authors and Titles of Books and Chapters in Four Collections of Buddhistic Literature,* 3 vols. *(= Harvard-Yenching Institute Sinological Index Series,* XI)(Peking: Yenching University Library, 1933).

IKEMOTO, Jūshin 池本重臣, 'Muryōjukyō Shohon no Seiritsu Katei —— tokuni Sōyaku Shōgongyō ni tsuite —— 無量寿経諸本の成立過程 —— 特に宋訳荘厳経について ——', *Ryūkoku Daigaku Ronshū* 龍谷大学論集, No. 367 (Kyōto, March 1961), pp. 21-42. —— Unseen.

INABA, Shōju 稲葉正就, *Chibettogo Koten Bunpōgaku* チベット語古典文法学 (Kyōto: Hōzōkan, 1954).
[Revised edition, 1966 (unseen)].

- - , 'Chibetto Chūsei Shoki ni okeru Hannya-Chūgan Ronjo no Yakushutsu チベット中世初期における般若中観論書の訳出', *Bukkyōgaku Seminā* 仏教学セミナー, No. 4 (Kyōto, Oct. 1966), pp. 15-33; No. 5 (May 1967), pp. 13-25.

JAN Yün-hua [冉雲華], 'Buddhist Relations between India and Sung China', *History of Religions*, VI, 1 (Chicago, Aug. 1966), pp. 24-42; VI, 2 (Nov. 1966), pp. 135-168.

JÄSCHKE, H. A., *A Tibetan-English Dictionary with special reference to the prevailing dialects, to which is added an English-Tibetan vocabulary* (London: Routledge & Kegan Paul, 1881; reprinted 1934, 1949, 1958, 1965). —— Abbr.: Jäschke.

JONG, J. W. de, 'Compte rendu de R. Yamada, "Hannyakyōtenrui no Keisei-sareta Jidai no Haikei" (1951)', *T'oung Pao*, XLII (1954), pp. 345-347.

- - , 'Compte rendu de J. May, *Candrakīrti: Prasannapadā Madhyamaka-vṛtti* (Paris, 1959)', *Indo-Iranian Journal*, V, 2 (1961), pp. 161-165.

- - , *Buddha's Word in China (= 28th George Ernest Morrison Lecture in Ethnology 1967)* (Canberra: The Australian National University, 1968).

- - , 'Korea's Edition of the Chinese Buddhist Canon', *Hemisphere: An Asian-Australian Magazine*, XIII, 4 (Canberra, April 1969), pp. 26-29.

JOSHI, Lalmani, *Studies in the Buddhistic Culture of India (during the 7th and 8th centuries A.D.)* (Delhi-Patna-Varanasi: Motilal Banarsidass, 1967).

KAGAWA, Takao 香川孝雄, '*Mahāvyutpatti* no Hensan Nendai ni tsuite —— G. *Tucci* Kyōju no Saikin no Gyōseki yori —— Mahāvyutpatti の編纂年代について —— G. Tucci教授の最近の業績より—', *Bukkyō Ronsō* 仏教論叢, No. 4 (Kyōto, March 1956), pp. 68-71. —— Unseen.

- - , '*Mahāvyutpatti* no Hensan Nendaikō / Mahāvyutpatti の編纂年代考', *Indogaku Bukkyōgaku Kenkyū*, VII, 1 (Dec. 1958), pp. 160-161.

KAJIYOSHI, Kōun 梶芳光運, 'Butsumo Hōtokuzō Hannya Haramitsukyō 仏母宝徳蔵般若波羅蜜経', *Bussho Kaisetsu Daijiten* 仏書解説大辞典, edited by Genmyō Ono 小野玄妙, Vol. IX (Tōkyō: Daitō Shuppansha, 1933, reprinted 1964, and 1972), p. 344a-b.

- - , *Genshi Hannyagyō no Kenkyū* 原始般若経の研究 (Tōkyō: Sankibō Busshorin, 1944).

KANAKURA, Yenshō 金倉円照, YAMADA, Ryūjō 山田龍城, TADA, Tōkan 多田等観, and HADANO, Hakuyū 羽田野伯猷 (eds.), *Chibetto Senjutsu Butten Mokuroku* 西蔵撰述仏典目録 / *A Catalogue of the Tohoku University Collection of Tibetan Works on Buddhism* (Sendai: Seminar of Indology, Tōhoku University, 1953). —— 'Tōhoku' Catalogue (cf. also UI-SUZUKI-KANAKURA-TADA).

*Katalog' knigam', rukopisjam' i kartam', na kitajskom', man'žurskom', mongol'skom', tibetskom' i sanskritskom' jazykax', naxodjaščimsja v' Biblioteke Aziatskago Departamenta* (Sanktspeterburg' v' Tipografii Eduarda Praca, 1843).

KRUEGER, J. R., 'Catalogue of the Laufer Mongolian Collections in Chicago', *Journal of the American Oriental Society*, LXXXVI (1966), pp. 156-183.

LALOU, Marcelle, *Catalogue du fonds tibétain de la Bibliothèque Nationale*, Quatrième partie, I: Les Mdo-maṅ (= *Buddhica*, Deuxième série: Documents IV)(Paris: Paul Geuthner, 1930).

- - , *Répertoire du Tanjur d'après le Catalogue de P. Cordier* (Paris: Département des manuscrits, Bibliothèque Nationale, 1933).

- - , *Inventaire des manuscrits tibétains de Touen-houang conservés à la Bibliothèque Nationale (Fonds Pelliot tibétain)*, 3 tomes (Paris: Adrien-Maisonneuve, 1939-1950-1961).

- - , 'Les textes bouddhiques au temps du Roi Khri-sroṅ-lde-bcan. Contribution à la bibliographie du Kanǰur et du Tanǰur', *Journal Asiatique*, CCXLI (1953), pp. 313-353.

LAMOTTE, É., *Le traité de la Grande Vertu de Sagesse de Nāgārjuna (Mahāprajñāpāramitāśāstra)*, tomes I et II *(= Bibliothèque du* Muséon, XVIII) (Louvain: Institut Orientaliste / Publications Universitaires, 1944-1949, réimpression 1966-1967); tome III *(= Publications de l'Institut Orientaliste de Louvain,* II)(Louvain, 1970).

- - , *Histoire du bouddhisme indien des origines à l'ère Śaka (= Bibliothèque du* Muséon, XLIII)(Louvain: Institut Orientaliste / Publications Universitaires, 1958).

LAUFER, B., 'Verzeichnis der tibetischen Handschriften der Königlichen Bibliothek zu Dresden', *Zeitschrift der deutschen morgenländischen Gesellschaft,* LV (1901), pp. 99-128.

LA VALLÉE POUSSIN, L. de, *Mūlamadhyamakakārikās (Mādhyamikasūtra) de Nāgārjuna avec la Prasannapadā, commentaire de Candrakīrti (= Bibliotheca Buddhica,* IV)(St.-Pétersbourg: L'Académie Impériale des Sciences, 1903-1913).
Photomechanical reprint (Tōkyō, 1960?; Osnabrück: Biblio Verlag, 1970).

- - , *Catalogue of the Tibetan Manuscripts from Tun-Huang in the India Office Library.* With an appendix on the Chinese manuscripts by Kazuo Enoki (London: Oxford University Press, 1962).

LÉVI, S., *Asaṅga, Mahāyāna-Sūtrālaṃkāra, exposé de la doctrine du grand véhicule selon le système Yogācāra,* édité et traduit d'après un manuscrit rapporté du Népal, tome I: Texte *(= Bibliothèque de l'École des Hautes Études, Sciences historiques et philologiques,* CLIX)(Paris: Librairie Honoré Champion, 1907). —— Abbr.: Sūtrāl.

LIGETI, L., 'La collection mongole Schilling von Canstadt à la Bibliothèque de l'Institut', *T'oung Pao,* XXVII (1930), pp. 119-178.

- - , *Catalogue du Kanǰur mongol imprimé,* Vol. I: Catalogue *(= Bibliotheca Hungarica,* III)(Budapest: Société Körösi Csoma, 1944).

LOKESH CHANDRA, 'A Newly Discovered Urga Edition of the Tibetan Kanjur', *Indo-Iranian Journal,* III, 3 (1959), pp. 175-191.

LÜDERS, H., *Beobachtungen über die Sprache des buddhistischen Urkanons.* Aus dem Nachlass herausgegeben von E. Waldschmidt *(= Abhandlungen der deutschen Akademie der Wissenschaften zu Berlin, Klasse für Sprache, Literatur und Kunst,* Jahrgang 1952, Nr. 10)(Berlin: Akademie-Verlag, 1954).

MALALASEKERA, G. P., *Dictionary of Pāli Proper Names,* 2 vols. *(= Indian Texts Series)*(London: J. Murray, 1937-1938; reprinted for the Pāli Text Society by Luzac & Co., London, 1960).

MATSUNAMI, Seiren [松濤誠廉], *Catalogue of the Kawaguchi-Takakusu Collection of Sanskrit Manuscripts* [Handwritten catalogue kept in the University of Tōkyō Library). —— Unseen.

- - , *A Catalogue of the Sanskrit Manuscripts in the Tokyo University Library* (Tōkyō: Suzuki Research Foundation, 1965).

MATSUMOTO, Tokumyō [松本徳明], *Die Prajñāpāramitā-Literatur nebst einem Specimen der Suvikrāntavikrāmi-Prajñāpāramitā (= Bonner Orientalistische Studien,* I)(Stuttgart: W. Kohlhammer, 1932).

MAY, J., *Candrakīrti: Prasannapadā Madhyamakavṛtti.* Douze chapitres traduits du sanscrit et du tibétain, accompagnés d'une introduction, de notes et d'une édition critique de la version tibétaine *(= Collection Jean Przyluski,* II)(Paris: Adrien-Maisonneuve, 1959).

MAYRHOFER, M., *Kurzgefasstes etymologisches Wörterbuch des Altindischen (= Indogermanische Bibliothek,* II: Wörterbücher)(Heidelberg: Carl Winter, 1952-1974), 3 Bände (in 25 Lieferungen). —— Abbr.: Mayrhofer.

MEHENDALE, M. A., *Historical Grammar of Inscriptional Prakrits (= Deccan College Dissertation Series,* III)(Poona: Deccan College Post-graduate and Research Institute, 1948). —— Abbr.: Mehendale.

MEISEZAHL, R. O., 'Die tibetischen Handschriften und Drucke des Linden-Museums in Stuttgart', *Tribus: Veröffentlichungen des Linden-Museums*, Nr. 7 (Stuttgart: Museum für Länder- und Völkerkunde, 1957), pp. 1-166.

- -, 'Besprechung - E. Obermiller, *Prajñā-Pāramitā-Ratna-Guṇa-Saṃcaya-Gāthā* (Reprint 1960)', *Oriens*, XVII (Leiden, 1964), pp. 289-301.

- - , 'Zwei alttibetische Ratnaguṇasaṃcayagāthā-Handschriften und andere Prajñāpāramitā-Texte im Victoria and Albert Museum, London', *Serta Tibeto-Mongolica: Festschrift für Walther Heissig zum 60.Geburtstag am 5.12.1973* (Wiesbaden: Otto Harrassowitz, 1973), pp. 205-236.

MIBU, Taishun [壬生台舜], 'A Comparative List of the Bkaḥ-ḥgyur Division in the Co-ne, Peking, Sde-dge and Snar-thaṅ Editions with an Introduction to the Bkaḥ-ḥgyur Division of the Co-ne Edition', *Taishō Daigaku Kenkyū Kiyō* 大正大学研究紀要 / *Memoirs of Taishō University*, No. 44 (Tōkyō, March 1959), pp. 1-69.

MITRA, Rājendralāl, *Ashṭasāhasrikā, a collection of discourses on the metaphysics of Mahāyāna school of Buddhists*, now first edited from Nepalese Sanskrit MSS. by R.M. (= *Bibliotheca Indica*, Work No. 110, Issue Nos. 603, 620, 629, 645, 671, 690)(Calcutta: The Asiatic Society of Bengal, 1888).

MITSUKAWA, Toyoki 光川豊芸 , 'Shōben - Gesshō no Chūronshaku ni Mirareru Hannyagyō —— *Prajñāpradīpa* to *Prasannapadā* o Chūshin ni —— 清辨月称の中論釈にみられる般若経 —— Prajñāpradīpa と Prasannapadā を中心に —— ', *Bukkyōgaku Kenkyū* 仏教学研究, No. 24 (Kyōto, Dec. 1967), pp. 1-24.

MOCHIZUKI, Shinkō 望月信亨 , *Bukkyō Daijiten* 仏教大辞典 , 10 vols. Begun by S. Mochizuki and continued in collaboration with many other scholars [Revised edition](Tōkyō: Suzuki Research Foundation, 1956-1963)[First edition: Vols. I-II (1932), III-V (1933), VI 'Chronological tables' (1909), VII (1936); Supplementary vols. VIII (1958), IX-X (1963)].

- - , *Bukkyō Kyōten Seiritsushiron* 仏教経典成立史論 (Kyōto: Hōzōkan, 1946).

MONIER-WILLIAMS, M., *A Sanskṛit-English Dictionary, etymologically and philologically arranged with special reference to cognate Ind-European languages*. New edition with the collaboration of E. Leumann and C. Cappeller and other scholars (Oxford: Clarendon Press, 1889). —— Abbr.: MWD.

MURAKAMI, Shinkan 村上真完 , '*Samādhirājasūtra* no Goi Kenkyū / Samādhirājasūtra の語彙研究 ', *Hachinohe Kōgyō Kōtō Senmon Gakkō Kiyō* 八戸工業高等専門学校紀要 , No. 2 (Dec. 1967), pp. 72-109.

NAGAO, Gadjin M. [ 長尾雅人 ], *Index to the Mahāyāna-Sūtrālaṃkāra (Sylvain Lévi edition)*, 2 parts (Tōkyō: Japan Society for the Promotion of Science, 1958-1961).

NAKAMURA, Hajime [ 中村元 ], 'A Critical Survey of Mahāyāna and Esoteric Buddhism chiefly based upon Japanese studies', *Acta Asiatica: Bulletin of the Institute of Eastern Culture*, No. 6 (Tōkyō, 1964), pp. 57-88.

NAMBIYAR, Raghavan, *An Alphabetical List of Manuscripts in the Oriental Institute, Baroda*, Vol. II (= *Gaekwad's Oriental Series*, CXIV)(Baroda: Oriental Institute, 1950).

NANJIO, Bunyiu [南条文雄], *A Catalogue of the Chinese Translation of the Buddhist Tripitaka, the Sacred Canon of the Buddhists in China and Japan* (Oxford: Clarendon Press, 1883). —— Abbr.: Nanjio Catalogue.
Reprinted together with a *Japanese Alphabetical Index of Nanjio's Catalogue of the Buddhist Tripiṭaka with supplement and corrections*, by Daijō Tokiwa and Unrai Wogihara, assisted by Kōjun Mino (Tōkyō: Maruzen, 1929-1930).

- - (ed.), *The Laṅkāvatāra Sūtra (= Bibliotheca Otaniensis*, I)(Kyōto: Ōtani University Press, 1923, reprinted 1956). —— Abbr.: Laṅk.

NISHIDA, Tatsuo 西田龍雄, *Seikago no Kenkyū* 西夏語の研究, 2 vols. (Tōkyō: Zauhō Kankōkai, 1966).

NOBEL, J., *Suvarṇaprabhāsottamasūtra: Das Goldglanz-Sūtra. Ein Sanskrittext des Mahāyāna-Buddhismus. Die tibetischen Übersetzungen mit einem Wörterbuch,* II: Wörterbuch Tibetisch-Deutsch-Sanskrit (Leiden: E. J. Brill, 1950). —— Abbr.: Nobel Suv. Index.

OBERMILLER, E., *History of Buddhism (Chos-ḥbyung) by Bu-ston,* 2 parts (= *Materialien zur Kunde des Buddhismus,* XVIII-XIX)(Heidelberg: In Kommission bei O. Harrassowitz, Leipzig, 1931-1932).
Photomechanical reprint (= *Suzuki Research Foundation Reprint Series,* V)(Tōkyō: Suzuki Research Foundation, 1964).

- - , 'The Doctrine of Prajñā-pāramitā as exposed in the Abhisamayālaṃkāra of Maitreya', *Acta Orientalia,* XI (1933), pp. 1-133.

- - (ed.), *Prajñā-Pāramitā-Ratna-Guṇa-Saṃcaya-Gāthā: Sanscrit and Tibetan Text* (= *Bibliotheca Buddhica,* XXIX)(Moscow-Leningrad: U.S.S.R. Academy of Sciences, 1937). —— Abbr.: O.
Photomechanical reprint with a Sanskrit-Tibetan-English Index (pp. 129-157) and Corrections of Obermiller's Text (pp. 127-128) by E. Conze (= *Indo-Iranian Reprints,* V)('s-Gravenhage: Mouton & Co., 1960).
Photomechanischer Neudruck der Ausgabe 1937 (Osnabrück: Biblio Verlag, 1970).

ONO, Genmyō 小野玄妙, 'Bukkyō Kyōten Sōron 仏教経典総論': *Bussho Kaisetsu Daijiten* 仏書解説大辞典, XII (Tōkyō: Daitō Shuppansha, 1936).

ŌNO, Hōdō 大野法道, *Daijō Kaikyō no Kenkyū* 大乗戒経の研究 (Tōkyō: Sankibō Busshorin, 1954, reprinted 1963).

[Ōtani University Library], *Chibetto Daizōkyō Kanjūru Kandō Mokuroku* 西蔵大蔵経甘殊爾勘同目録 / *A Comparative Analytical Catalogue of the Kanjur Division of the Tibetan Tripiṭaka, edited in Peking during the K'ang-hsi Era, and at present kept in the Library of the Otani Daigaku, Kyoto, in which the Contents of Each Sutra are Collated with their Corresponding Parts in the Existing Sanskrit, Pali and Chinese Texts, and in which Page-references of the Narthang and the Derge Editions of the Tripiṭakas are also entered* (Kyōto: Ōtani University Library, 1930-1932).

PETECH, L., *Mediaeval History of Nepal (c. 750-1480)* (= *Materials for the Study of Nepalese History and Culture,* 3)(= *Serie Orientale Roma,* X)(Roma: Istituto Italiano per il Medio ed Estremo Oriente, 1958).

*P'ing-chiang-fu Chi-sha-pan Yen-shêng-yüan hsin-tiao-tsang ching-lü-lun-têng mu-lu* 平江府磧砂版延聖院新雕蔵経律論等目録 (1234 A.D.). —— *Shōwa Hōbō Sōmokuroku,* I (1929): No. 12.

PISCHEL, R., *Grammatik der Prākrit-Sprachen* (= *Grundriss der indo-arischen Philologie und Altertumskunde,* I, 8)(Strassburg: K. J. Trübner, 1900). —— Abbr.: Pischel.
Photomechanischer verkleinerter Neudruck (Hildesheim-New York: Georg Olms Verlag, 1973).
English edition: *Comparative Grammar of the Prākṛit Languages,* translated by S. Jhā (Delhi-Patna-Varanasi: Motilal Banarsidass, 1957; reprinted with M. de Zilva Wickremasinghe, 'Index of All the Prākrit Words Occurring in Pischel's "Grammatik der Prākrit-Sprachen"' [originally: *Indian Antiquary,* XXXIV-XXXVIII (1905-1909), Appendixes, 204 pp.], 1965).
Hindī edition (unseen): *Prākṛt-bhāṣāõ kā vyākaraṇ,* translated by H. C. Hoshi (Paṭnā: Bihār Rāṣṭra Bhāṣā Pariṣad, 1958).

POPPE, N., HURVITZ, L., and OKADA, H., *Catalogue of the Manchu-Mongol Section of the Toyo Bunko* (Tōkyō: Tōyō Bunko / Seattle: University of Washington Press, 1964).

REGAMEY, C., *Buddhistische Philosophie* (= *Bibliographische Einführungen in das Studium der Philosophie,* 20/21)(Bern: A. Francke AG, 1950).

REGMI, D. R., *Medieval Nepal*, Part I (Early Medieval Period 750-1530 A.D.)(Calcutta: K. L. Mukhopadhyay, 1965).

RENOU, L., *Grammaire sanscrite*, 2 tomes (Paris: Adrien-Maisonneuve, 1930; deuxième édition revue, corrigée et augmentée, 2 tomes réunis, 1961).

- - , 'Les divisions dans les textes sanskrits', *Indo-Iranian Journal*, I, 1 (1957), pp. 1-32.

RHYS DAVIDS, T. W., and STEDE, W., *The Pāli Text Society's Pāli-English Dictionary* (London: The Pāli Text Society, 1921-1925). —— Abbr.: PTSD.

ROBINSON, R. H., *Early Mādhyamika in India and China* (Madison-Milwaukee-London: The University of Wisconsin Press, 1967).

ROERICH, G. N., *The Blue Annals*, 2 parts (= *Monographs Series*, VII) (Calcutta: The Asiatic Society, 1949-1953).
Photomechanical reprint (Introduction, Books I, X, XIII): Rerix, Ju. N., *Izbrannye Trudy* (Akademija Nauk SSSR - Institut Narodov Azii) (Moskva: Izdatel'stvo "Nauka", 1967), pp. 255-451.

SAKAI, Shirō (Shinten) 酒井紫朗(真典), *Ramakyō no Tenseki* 喇嘛教の典籍 (= *Ramakyō Jijō* 喇嘛教事情, II)(Kōyasan: Shingonshū Ramakyō Kenkyūjo, 1944).

- - , 'Honyaku Myōgi Taishū no Nangoshaku *Pañjikā-Madhyavyutpatti* ni tsuite 翻訳名義大集の難語釈 Pañjikā-Madhyavyutpattiについて', *Mikkyō Bunka* 密教文化, No. 29/30 (Kōyasan, May 1955), pp. 66-57.

SAKAKI, Ryōzaburō 榊亮三郎, *Honyaku Myōgi Taishū* 翻訳名義大集 / *Mahāvyutpatti* (with a Sanskrit index), 2 parts (= *Kyōto Teikoku Daigaku Bunka Daigaku Sōsho* 京都帝国大学文科大学叢書, III)(Kyōto, 1916).
Tibetan Index: NISHIO, Kyōo 西尾京雄, *Zō-Bon Taishō Honyaku Myōgi Taishū Chibettogo Sakuin* 蔵梵対照翻訳名義大集・西蔵語索引 (= *Butten Kenkyū* 仏典研究, I)(Kyōto: Butten Kenkyūkai, 1936).
Photomechanical reprint with Nishio's Index, 2 vols. (= *Suzuki Research Foundation Reprint Series*, I)(Tōkyō: Suzuki Research Foundation, 1962). —— Abbr.: Mvy.

SĀṄKṚTYĀYANA, Rāhula, 'Sanskrit Palm-leaf MSS. in Tibet', *Journal of the Bihar and Orissa Research Society*, XXI, 1 (Patna, March 1935), pp. 21-43.

SANSKRIT SEMINAR OF TAISHO UNIVERSITY, 'Buddhist Manuscripts of the Bir Library', *Taishō Daigaku Kenkyū Kiyō*, XL (Jan. 1955), pp. 55-84.

ŚĀSTRĪ, Haraprasād, *A Catalogue of Palm-leaf and Selected Paper MSS., belonging to the Durbar Library, Nepal*, Vol. II (Calcutta, printed at the Baptist Mission Press, 1915).

- - , *A Descriptive Catalogue of Sanskrit Manuscripts in the Government Collection under the Care of the Asiatic Society of Bengal*, Vol. I: Buddhist Manuscripts (Calcutta, printed at the Baptist Mission Press, 1917).

SATŌ, Hisashi 佐藤長, *Kodai Chibettoshi Kenkyū* 古代チベット史研究, 2 vols. (= *Tōyōshi Kenkyū Sōkan* 東洋史研究叢刊, V, 1-2)(Kyōto: Tōyōshi Kenkyūkai/Société pour l'Étude de l'Histoire d'Extrême-Orient, Universitá de Kyoto, 1959).

- - , 'Rendaruma-ō no Zaii Nenji ni tsuite レンダルマ王の在位年次について', *Shirin* 史林, XLVII, 5 (Kyōto, Sept. 1963), pp. 32-57.

SCHIEFNER, A., 'Bericht über die neueste Büchersendung aus Peking', *Bulletin de la Classe des Sciences historiques, philologiques et politiques de l'Académie Impériale des Sciences de Saint-Pétersbourg*, IX (1852), Sp. 10-14, 17-32.
= *Mélanges Asiatiques*, I, 4 (1851), pp. 405-429 [Offprint pp. 1-25].

- - , *Târanâthae de doctrinae buddhicae in India propagatione narratio. Contextum tibeticum e codicibus petropolitanis*, edidit A. Schiefner (St.Petersburg, 1868).
Photomechanical reprint (= *Suzuki Research Foundatation Reprint Series*, II)(Tōkyō: Suzuki Research Foundation, 1963).

- - , *Târanâtha's Geschichte des Buddhismus in Indien*. Aus dem Tibetischen übersetzt von A. Schiefner (St. Petersburg, 1869).
Photomechanical reprint *(= Suzuki Research Foundation Reprint Series*, III)(Tōkyō: Suzuki Research Foundation, 1963).

SCHMIDT, R., *Nachträge zum Sanskrit-Wörterbuch in kürzerer Fassung von Otto Böhtlingk* ([Hannover: Heinz Lafaire, 1924-1926]/Leipzig: Otto Harrassowitz, 1928). —— Abbr.: Schmidt.

SCHNEIDER, U., 'Das Zahlwort im Mahāvastu', *Zeitschrift für vergleichende Sprachforschung auf dem Gebiete der indogermanischen Sprachen*, Neue Folge, LXXVI (1960), pp. 249-272.

SCHOOL OF ORIENTAL AND AFRICAN STUDIES (University of London), *Library Catalogue*, Vol. XXII: Catalogue of Manuscripts and Microfilms (Boston: G. K. Hall & Co., 1963). —— see CONZE (1952 and 1954).

SEMIČOV, B. V., PARFIONOVIČ, Ju. M., i DANDARON, B. D., *Kratkij tibetsko-russkij slovar'* (Moskva: Gosudarstvennoe izdatel'stvo inostrannyx i nacional'nyx slovarej, 1963). —— Abbr.: KTRS.

SEN, Sukumar, *A Comparative Grammar of Middle Indo-Aryan (= Special Publications of the Linguistic Society of India*, I)(Poona: Linguistic Society of India, 1960).
Originally published in the *Indian Linguistics*, XII (1952-1953)[reprint edition, Vol. III (1965), pp. 211-354].

SEṬH, Haragovinddās Trikamachaṃd, *Pāia-sadda-mahaṇṇavo (= Prakrit Text Society Series*, VII)(Varanasi: Prakrit Text Society, 1963)[first published 1928]. —— Abbr.: Seṭh.

SHIBATA, Tōru 柴田泰, 'Muryōju Shōgongyō Honganbun ni tsuite 無量寿荘厳経本願文について', *Indogaku Bukkyōgaku Kenkyū*, XI, 1 (Jan. 1963), pp. 199-202.

- - , 'Muryōju Shōgongyō ni tsuite 無量寿荘厳経について', *Indogaku Bukkyōgaku Kenkyū*, XII, 1 (Jan. 1964), pp. 178-181.

- - , 'Hōken Yakushutsu Kyōten ni tsuite —— Muryōju Shōgongyō o Chūshin to shite —— 法賢訳出経典について —— 無量寿荘厳経を中心として ——', *Indogaku Bukkyōgaku Kenkyū*, XIV, 2 (March 1966), pp. 166(620)-170(624).

- - , 'Hōten Kaimei Hōken-setsu ni tsuite 法天改名法賢説について', *Shūkyō Kenkyū* 宗教研究, No. 186 [= Vol. XXXIX, No. 3](Tōkyō, Oct. 1965), pp. 80-81.

SHIIO, Benkyō —— see TAKI.

*Shōwa Hōbō Sōmokuroku* 昭和法宝総目録 *(= Taishō Shinshū Daizōkyō Bekkan* 大正新修大蔵経別巻, Vols. I & II (Tōkyō: Taishō Issaikyō Kankōkai, 1929), Vol. III (Tōkyō: Daitō Shuppan K.K., 1934).

SIMON, W., 'Tibetan Lexicography and Etymological Research', *Transactions of the Philological Society, 1964* (Hertford, 1965), pp. 85-107.

SIMONSSON, N., *Indo-tibetische Studien: Die Methoden der tibetischen Übersetzer, untersucht im Hinblick auf die Bedetung ihrer Übersetzungen für die Sanskritphilologie*, I (Uppsala: Almqvist Wiksells Boktryckeri, 1957).

SNELLGROVE, D. L., *A Catalogue of the Tibetan Collection* (and C. R. Bawden, *A Catalogue of the Mongolian Collection*)[of the Chester Beatty Library, Dublin](Dublin: Hodges, Figgis & Co., 1969).

SPEIJER, J. S., *Sanskrit Syntax* (Leiden: E. J. Brill, 1886). —— Abbr.: Speijer.
Photomechanical reprint (Kyōto: Rinsen Shoten, 1968).

- - [Speyer], *Vedische und Sanskrit-Syntax (= Grundriss der indo-arischen Philologie und Altertumskunde*, I, 6)(Strassburg: K. J. Trübner, 1896). —— Abbr.: Speyer.
Photomechanischer Nachdruck (Graz: Akademische Druck- und Verlagsanstalt, 1974).

SUM-PA MKHAN-PO (1704-1788 A.D.) —— see DAS.

SUZUKI, Daisetsu Teitarō [ 鈴木大拙貞太郎 ], *An Index to the Laṅkavatara Sutra (Nanjio Edition)*. Second, revised and enlarged edition (Kyōto: The Sanskrit Buddhist Texts Publishing Society, 1934). —— Abbr.: Suzuki Index Laṅk.
Photomechanical reprint (= *Suzuki Research Foundation Reprint Series*, VI)(Tōkyō: Suzuki Research Foundation, 1965).

TACHIBANA, Shūkō 立花秀孝, 'Chibetto Bukkyōshi Josetsu 西藏仏教史序説', *Gendai Bukkyō* 現代仏教 (Tōkyō, Sept. 1934). —— Unseen.

TAGARE, G. V., *Historical Grammar of Apabhraṃśa* (= *Deccan College Dissertation Series*, V)(Poona: Deccan College Post-Graduate and Research Institute, 1948). —— Abbr.: Tagare.

*Taishō Shinshū Daizōkyō* —— see TAKAKUSU-WATANABE.

TAKAHASHI, Moritaka 高橋盛孝, 'Kengugyō to Zan-run 賢愚経とザン・ルン', *Tōhōgaku* 東方学, No. 26 (Tōkyō, July 1963), pp. 47-55.

TAKAKUSU, Junjirō 高楠順次郎, and WATANABE, Kaikyoku 渡辺海旭 (eds.), *Taishō Shinshū Daizōkyō* 大正新修大蔵経 (Tōkyō: Taishō Issaikyō Kankōkai, 1924-1934). —— For the Chinese *Rgs* see 'Bibl. Notes' III Text a).

- - & - - (eds.), *Taishō Shinshū Daizōkyō Mokuroku* (Tōkyō: Taishō Issaikyō Kankōkai, 1930).
New revised edition (Tōkyō: Taishō Shinshū Daizōkyō Kankōkai, 1969).

TAKASAKI, Jikidō 高崎直道 *Tōkyō Daigaku Shozō Rasaban Chibetto Daizōkyō Mokuroku* 東京大学所蔵ラサ版チベット大蔵経目録 / *A Catalogue of the Lhasa Edition of the Tibetan Tripiṭaka in comparison with other editions* (Tōkyō: The Institute of Tibetan Studies, Faculty of Letters, University of Tōkyō, 1965).

TAKI, Shōdō 滝照道, and SHIIO, Benkyō 椎尾辨匡 (trsl.), 'Bussetsu Butsumo Hōtokuzō Hannya Haramitsukyō 仏説仏母宝徳蔵般若波羅蜜経', *Kokuyaku Issaikyō* 国訳一切経 : *Shaku-kyōron-bu* 釈経論部 Vb (Tōkyō: Daitō Shuppansha, 1936), pp. 339-374. —— Abbr.: Taki.
Photomechanical reprint with a new introduction by Gadjin M. Nagao (1974?). —— Unseen. —— cf. 'Bibl. Notes' VI 2, above.

TĀRANĀTHA —— see SCHIEFNER.

TAUBE, M., *Tibetische Handschriften und Blockdrucke*, I-IV (= *Verzeichnis der orientalischen Handschriften in Deutschland*, XI, 1-4)(Wiesbaden: Franz Steiner, 1966).

TERAMOTO, Enga 寺本婉雅 (trsl.), *Tāranātha Indo Bukkyōshi* ターラナータ印度仏教史 (= *Chibetto-den Butten Yakuchū - Bukkyō Kenkyū* 西藏伝仏典訳註・仏教研究, No. 1)(Tōkyō: Heigo Shuppansha, 1928).
Photomechanical reprint (Tōkyō: Kokusho Kankōkai, 1974).

THUMB, A., *Handbuch des Sanskrit mit Texten und Glossar. Eine Einführung in das sprachwissenschaftliche Studium des Altindischen*. Dritte, stark umgearbeitete Auflage von R. Hauschild (= *Indogermanische Bibliothek*, I. Reihe: Lehr- und Handbücher)(Heidelberg: Carl Winter, 1958). —— Abbr.: Thumb-Hauschild.

T'IEN-HSI-TSAI —— see 'Bibl. Notes' III N.B. 6-9.

TRENCKNER, V., *A Critical Pāli Dictionary*, begun by V. Trenckner, published by the Royal Danish Academy of Sciences and Letters (Copenhagen: Commissioner E. Munksgaard, 1924- ). —— Abbr.: CPD.

TSUKAMOTO, Zenryū 塚本善隆, 'Bukkyō Shiryō to shite no Kinkoku Daizōkyō —— tokuni Hokusō Shakkyō Mokuroku to Tō-Ryō no Hossōshū Kankei Shōso ni tsuite ——仏教史料としての金刻大蔵経 — 特に北宋釈教目録と唐遼の法相宗関係章疏に就いて—', *Tōhō Gakuhō (Kyōto)* 東方学報(京都), VI (1934), pp. 26-100. —— Unseen.

TUCCI, G., *The Tombs of the Tibetan Kings* (= *Serie Orientale Roma*, I) (Roma: Istituto Italiano per il Medio ed Estremo Oriente, 1950).

- - , *Minor Buddhist Texts*, Part II (= *Serie Orientale Roma*, IX, 2) (Roma: Istituto Italiano per il Medio ed Estremo Oriente, 1958).

UI, Hakuju 宇井伯寿, SUZUKI, Munetada 鈴木宗忠, KANAKURA, Yenshō 金倉円照, and TADA, Tōkan 多田等観 (eds.), *Chibetto Daizōkyō Sōmokuroku* 西蔵大蔵経総目録 / *A Complete Catalogue of the Tibetan Buddhist Canon*, 2 vols. (Sendai: Tōhoku Imperial University, 1934). —— 'Tōhoku' Catalogue (cf. also KANAKURA-YAMADA-TADA-HADANO). Photomechanical reprint: 2 vols. in one (Tōkyō: Meicho Shuppan, 1970).

VAIDYA, P. L. (ed.), *Aṣṭasāhasrikā Prajñāpāramitā with Haribhadra's Commentary called* Āloka (= *Buddhist Sanskrit Texts*, No. 4)(Darbhanga: The Mithila Institute of Post-Graduate Studies and Research in Sanskrit Learning, 1960). —— Abbr.: AsP.

- - , *Mahāyāna-Sūtra-Saṃgraha*, Part I (= *Buddhist Sanskrit Texts*, No. 17)(Darbhanga: The Mithila Institute of Post-Graduate Studies and Research in Sanskrit Learning, 1961): Text No. 22: 'Ratna-guṇa-saṃcaya-gāthā', pp. 352-397, with bibliographical notes, pp. X-XI (English) and XX-XXI (Hindī), and 'Critical notes', pp. 399-404. —— Abbr.: V.

VEKERDI, J., 'Some Remarks on Tibetan Prosody', *Acta Orientalia Hungarica*, II, 2/3 (1952), pp. 221-234.

VIDYĀKARASIṂHA —— see 'Bibl. Notes' IIB N.B. 1-3.

VOSTRIKOV, A. I., *Tibetan Historical Literature*, translated by H. C. Gupta (= *Soviet Indology Series*, IV)(Calcutta: Indian Studies Past & Present, 1970).

WACKERNAGEL, J., *Altindische Grammatik* (Göttingen: Vandenhoeck & Ruprecht, 1896- ):
Band I: L. Renou, *Introduction générale* (1957)[Nouvelle édition du texte paru en 1896]; J. Wackernagel, *Lautlehre* (1957)[Unveränderter Nachdruck der 1896 Auflage]; A. Debrunner, *Nachträge zu Band I* (1957).
Band II 1: J.Wackernagel, *Einleitung zur Wortlehre. Nominalkomposition* (1905; 2. unveränderte Aufl. 1957); A. Debrunner, *Nachträge zu Band II 1* (1957).
Band II 2: A. Debrunner, *Die Nominalsuffixe* (1954).
Band III: A. Debrunner und J. Wackernagel, *Nominalflexion - Zahlwort - Pronomen* (1930).
—— Abbr.: Wackernagel(-Debrunner).

WESTERGAARD, N. L.: - *Pāṇini's Grammatik*, herausgegeben, übersetzt, erläutert und mit verschiedenen Indices versehen von O. Böhtlingk (Leipzig: H. Haessel, 1887; reprografischer Nachdruck - Hildesheim: Georg Olms Verlag, 1964): 'Der Dhâtupâṭha nach N. L. Westergaard', pp. 61*-84*; 'Alphabetisches Verzeichniss der Wurzeln', pp. 84*-94*.

WHITNEY, W. D., *A Sanskrit Grammar, including both the classical Language, and the Older Dialects, of the Veda and Brahmana* (= *Bibliothek indogermanischer Grammatiken*, II)(Leipzig: Breitkopf & Härtel, 1879); - Second edition (Cambridge, Mass.: Harvard University Press, 1889; reprinted many times; Indian reprint - Delhi 1969). —— Abbr.: Whitney.

- - , *The Roots, Verb-Forms, and Primary Derivatives of the Sanskrit Language. A Supplement to his Grammar* (= *Bibliothek indogermanischer Grammatiken*, Band II, Anhang 2)(Leipzig: Breitkopf & Härtel, 1885). Photomechanical reprint (= *American Oriental Series*, XXX)(New Haven: The American Oriental Society, 1945; Indian reprint - Delhi 1963). —— Abbr.: Whitney Roots.

WINTERNITZ, M., *Geschichte der indischen Litteratur*, II: *Die buddhistische Litteratur und die heiligen Texte der Jainas* (= *Die Litteraturen des Ostens*, IX, 2)(Leipzig: C. F. Amelangs Verlag, 1920). Unveränderter Nachdruck der 1920 Auflage (Stuttgart: K. F. Koehler, 1968).
Japanese edition: *Indo Bukkyō Bungakushi* 印度仏教文学史, translated by Gishō Nakano 中野義照 and Mamoru Osaragi 大仏衛 under the supervision of J. Takakusu (Tōkyō: Heigo Shuppansha, 1923).
English edition: *A History of Indian Literature*, II: *Buddhist Literature and Jaina Literature*, translated by S. Ketkar and H. Kohn and revised by the author (Calcutta: University of Calcutta, 1933; reprinted by the Oriental Books Reprint Corporation, New Delhi, 1972).

- - : *Literary History of Sanskrit Buddhism (From Winternitz, S. Lévi, Huber)*, translated by G. K. Nariman (Bombay: D. B. Taraporevala Sons & Co., 1920; second impression - Bombay: Indian Book Depot, 1923).
Indian reprint of the first edition (unseen): - (Delhi, 1972?).

WOGIHARA, Unrai [荻原雲来], *Asanga's Bodhisattvabhūmi: Ein dogmatischer Text der Nordbuddhisten nach dem Unikum von Cambridge im allgemienen und lexikalisch untersucht (= Indica*, Heft VI)(Leipzig: Otto Harrassowitz, 1905), pp. 1-45 [Dissertation Strassburg 1905] —— Unseen.
- - (Leipzig: Druck von G. Kreysing, 1908), pp. 1-46.
- - : Wogihara, U., *Bodhisattvabhūmi: A Statement of Whole Course of the Bodhisattva (Being Fifteenth Section of Yogācārabhūmi)*(Tōkyō: Seigo Kenkyūkai, Taishō University, 1930-1936; photomechanically reprinted by Sankibō Busshorin, Tōkyō, 1971), 43 pp. [photomechanical reprint of the 1908 edition, pp. 3-45].

- - , 'Yo ni Shiraretaru Bongo Butten 世に知られたる梵語仏典', *Tōa no Hikari* 東亜の光 , IX, 6 (Tōkyō, June 1914).
= *Wogihara Unrai Bunshū* 荻原雲来文集 (Tōkyō: Dr. Wogihara Felicitation Committee, Taishō University, 1937; photomechanically reprinted by Sankibō Busshorin, 1972), pp. 445-460.

- - , *Bon-Kan Taiyaku Bukkyō Jiten* 梵漢対訳仏教辞典 / *The Sanskrit-Chinese Dictionary of Buddhist Technical Terms based on the* Mahāvyutpatti (Tōkyō: Heigo Shuppansha, 1915; 2nd ed. 1926, reprinted by Sankibō Busshorin, Tōkyō, 1959). —— Abbr.: Wogihara Mvy.

- - , *Abhisamayālaṃkār'āloka Prajñāpāramitāvyākhyā*. Together with the text commented on (Tōkyō: The Tōyō Bunko, 1932-1935; photomechanically reprinted by Sankibō Busshorin, Tōkyō, 1973, in 1 vol.). —— Reference to this edition has been made according to Vaidya's notes in his edition of the AsP; the reprint of Wogihara's edition appeared, to my regret, too late to be used.

- - , *Kanyaku Taishō Bon-Wa Daijiten* 漢訳対照梵和大辞典 , begun by U. Wogihara, continued and edited by Jun Ohrui in collaboration with other scholars under the supervision of Naoshirō Tsuji (Tōkyō: Suzuki Research Foundation, 1964-1974, in 16 fascicles)[Fasc. 1-6, first published 1940-1943]. —— Abbr.: WSJD.

YAMADA, Ryūjō 山田龍城 , 'Genson Bonbun Butten Mokuroku 現存梵文仏典目録', *Ryūkoku Daigaku Ronsō* 龍谷大学論叢, No. 287 (Kyōto, Oct. 1929), pp. *1-*30 [a supplement to his article 'Bonbun Butten Kenkyū no Ni-hōmen 梵文仏典研究の二方面', *ibid.*, pp. 26-100].

- - , 'Hannya Kyōtenrui no Keiseisareta Jidai no Haikei 般若経典類の形成された時代の背景', *Tōhoku Daigaku Bungakubu Kenkyū Nenpō* 東北大学文学部研究年報 II (1951), pp. 1-41.
= *Daijō Bukkyō Seiritsuron Josetsu* 大乗仏教成立論序説 (Kyōto: Heirakuji Shoten, 1959, reprinted 1965), pp. 523-532.

- - , *Bongo Butten no Shobunken* 梵語仏典の諸文献 *(= Daijō Bukkyō Seiritsuron Josetsu*, Shiryō-hen 資料篇 )(Kyōto: Heirakuji Shoten, 1959).

YAMAGUCHI, Susumu 山口益 , *"Jōmyōkuron" to Nazukuru Gesshō-zō Chūron-shaku* 浄明句論と名づくる月称造・中論釈, 2 vols. (Tōkyō: Kōbundō Shobō, 1947-1949, reprinted 1968).

YANG I 楊億 , etc., *Ta-chung Hsiang-fu fa-pao-lu* 大中祥符法宝録 (1011-1015 A.D.) —— *Sung-tsang i-chen*, Text No. 41 (cf. *Ying-yin Sung Chi-sha tsang-ching*, below) —— *Chung-hua Ta-tsang-ching*, First Series, Vol. X, fasc. 80.

YAZAKI, Shōken 矢崎正見 , 'Hokekyō Denyaku to sono Keitai 法華経伝訳とその形態', *Hokekyō no Shisō to Bunka* 法華経の思想と文化, edited by Yukio Sakamoto (Kyōto: Heirakuji Shoten, 1965), pp. 228-248.

*Ying-yin Sung Chi-sha tsang-ching* 影印宋磧砂蔵経 (Shanghai: Ying-yin Sung-pan tsang-ching-hui, 1935). —— cf. 'Bibl. Notes' IIIc.
*Sung-tsang i-chen* 宋蔵遺珍 (Shanghai-Peking, 1934-1935).
*Shou-t'sê* 首冊 (Shanghai, 1936).
--- For the Taipei reprint see *Chung-hua Ta-tsang-ching*, above.

YOSHIMURA, Shyuki (Shūki)〔芳村修基〕, *The Denkar-Ma, an Oldest Catalogue of the Tibetan Buddhist Canons* (Kyōto: Ryūkoku University, 1950), (xviii), 72, 11 pp.
Photomechanically reprinted in his *Indo Daijō Bukkyō Shisō Kenkyū* インド大乗仏教思想研究 (Kyōto: Hyakkaen, 1974), pp. *99*-*199*.

– – , 'Tibetan Translators of the Tri-Pitaka —— in the Derge edition ——', *Ryūkoku Daigaku Ronshū* 龍谷大学論集」, No. 350 (Kyōto, Oct. 1955), pp. *1*-*36*.
Photomechanically reprinted in his *Indo Daijō Bukkyō Shisō Kenkyū* (1974), pp. *63*-*98*.

– – , 'Shoki Chibetto Bukkyō ni okeru Honyaku Keisei 初期チベット仏教における翻訳形成', *Indogaku Bukkyōgaku Kenkyū*, VI, 2 (March 1958), pp. 194 (505)-197 (508).

YUYAMA, Akira〔湯山明〕, *Indic Manuscripts and Chinese Blockprints (Non-Chinese Texts) of the Oriental Collection of the Australian National University Library, Canberra (= Occasional Paper Series,* No. 6)(Canberra: Centre of Oriental Studies, Australian National University, 1967).

– – , 'The *Bodhi* Tree in the *Mahāvastu-Avadāna*', *Pratidānam: Indian, Iranian and Indo-European Studies presented to F. B. J. Kuiper on his sixtieth birthday (= Janua Linguarum,* Series Maior, XXXIV)(The Hague-Paris: Mouton & Co., 1968), pp. 488-492.

– – , '*Candrakīrti* no *Prasannapadā* ni Inyōsareta *Prajñāpāramitā-Ratnaguṇasaṃcayagāthā* / Candrakīrti の Prasannapadā に引用された Prajñāpāramitā Ratnaguṇasaṃcayagāthā', *Shūkyō Kenkyū* 宗教研究, No. 201 (= Vol. XLIII, No. 2)(Tōkyō, Feb. 1970), pp. 75(237)-92(254), English summary on pp. 124(286)-123(285).

– – , *A Bibliography of the Sanskrit Texts of the Saddharmapuṇḍarīkasūtra (= Oriental Monograph Series,* V)(Canberra: Centre of Oriental Studies/Faculty of Asian Studies in association with Australian National University Press, 1970).

– – , 'Some Glossarial Notes on the *Prajñā-pāramitā-ratna-guṇa-saṃcaya-gāthā*', *Proceedings and Papers of the XIVth Congress of the Australasian Universities Language and Literature Association held 19-26 January 1972 at the University of Otago, Dunedin, New Zealand* (Dunedin, 1972), pp. 30-37.

– – , 'Remarks on the Metre of the *Prajñā-pāramitā-ratna-guṇa-saṃcaya-gāthā*', *Studies in Indo-Asian Art and Culture,* Vol. II: *Commemoration Volume on the 70th Birthday of Acharya Raghu Vira (= Śatapiṭaka Series,* XCVI)(New Delhi: International Academy of Indian Culture, 1973), pp. 243-253.

– – , *A Grammar of the Prajñā-pāramitā-ratna-guṇa-saṃcaya-gāthā (Sanskrit Recension A) (= Oriental Monograph Series,* XIV)(Canberra: Faculty of Asian Studies in association with Australian National University Press, 1973).

## Addenda

BEAUTRIX, P., *Bibliographie de la littérature Prajñāpāramitā (= Publications de l'Institut Belge des Hautes Études Bouddhiques: Série "Bibliographies", N° 3)*(Bruxelles: Institut Belge des Hautes Études Bouddhiques, 1971), p. 25 (item Nos. 155-159: *Rgs*). --- The *Rgs* is classified under the *AsP*; cf. my 'Introduction' para. 8-17 esp. 8-9 (pp. xiv-xv).

SCHUBERT, J., 'Besprechung - E. Obermiller (ed.), *Rgs* (repr.: The Hague, 1960)', *Orientalistische Literaturzeitung*, LVII. Jahrgang (1962), Nr. 9/10, Sp. 524. --- Add to my 'Bibl. Notes' IC1 N.B. 3 (p. xxviii).

TSUKAMOTO, Z., 'Bukkyō Shiryō to shite no Kinkoku Daizōkyō': reprinted in his collected works *Tsukamoto Zenryū Chosakushū*, Vol. V: *Chūgoku Kinsei Bukkyōshi no Shomondai* (Tokyo: Daitō Shuppansha, July 1975), pp. 93-164. --- On Fa-hsien see pp. 126-128; cf. my 'Bibl. Notes' III N.B. 6 (p. xli).

YUYAMA, A., '*Svalpākṣarā Prajñāpāramitā*', *Commemoration Volume to H. V. Guenther* (Saskatoon-Berkeley, in press). --- Sanskrit and Tibetan texts critically edited with a straightforward translation of the Chinese version (Taishō No. 258); another example of Fa-hsien's free translation (982 A.D.); cf. my 'Bibl. Notes' III N.B. 3 (p. xl).

- - , 'The First Two Chapters of the *Rgs*', *Festschrift for Edward Conze* (Berkeley, in press). --- Recension B, of both Sanskrit and Tibetan versions, edited critically; cf. my 'Bibl. Notes' IC (p. xxviii).

Lightning Source UK Ltd.
Milton Keynes UK
UKHW012054120820
368157UK00001B/15

9 780521 143202